DO NOT REMOVE
CARDS FROM POCKET

S0-BRI-348

The English Bible From KJV to NIV

A History and Evaluation

Second Edition

Jack P. Lewis

BAKER BOOK HOUSE

Grand Rapids, Michigan 49516

Copyright 1981, 1991 by
Baker Book House Company

ISBN: 0-8010-5666-7

Second printing, May 1992

Printed in the United States of America

Library of Congress Cataloging–in–Publication Data

Lewis, Jack Pearl, 1919–
        The English Bible, from KJV to NIV / Jack P. Lewis—2nd ed.
            p.   cm.
        Includes bibliographical references and indexes.
        ISBN 0-8010-5666-7
        1. Bible.   English—Versions.   I. Title.
    BS455.L38   1991
    220.5'2—dc20   91-258
                                                                            CIP

Contents

List of Abbreviations

ASV	*American Standard Version*
CBQ	*Catholic Biblical Quarterly*
DNB	*Dictionary of National Biography*
GNB	*Good News Bible*
IDB	*Interpreter's Dictionary of the Bible*
JB	*Jerusalem Bible*
JBL	*Journal of Biblical Literature*
KJV	*King James Version*
LB	*Living Bible*
NAB	*New American Bible*
NASB	*New American Standard Bible*
NEB	*New English Bible*
NIV	*New International Version*
NJKB	*New King James Bible*
NPNF	*The Nicene and Post-Nicene Fathers*
NT	*New Testament*
NTS	*New Testament Studies*
NWT	*New World Translation*
OT	*Old Testament*
RSV	*Revised Standard Version*
RV	*Revised Version*
TEV	*Today's English Version*
TR	*Textus Receptus*
UBS	*United Bible Societies*
WThJ	*Westminster Theological Journal*

Preface to the Second Edition

The author is grateful for the positive reviews given the first edition of this work. He is also grateful to a negative reviewer who considered it worthy of an article of forty pages.[1]

The process of translation has moved on with revisions made in some of the translations studied in the previous edition and numerous new translations issued. All cannot be dealt with; hence, three have been chosen for detailed analysis. Except for the chapter dealing with the NKJV, the chapters of the first edition have been left unmodified in this second edition. The NKJV, available only in the N.T. when the first edition of this work was published, was completed in 1982. Since that date it has undergone editorial changes equaling about 1 percent of the text. Most of these changes, which affect vocabulary, footnotes, italicized words, and technical terms, have appeared in printings since 1985, but there are others since that time.[2]

In addition, a history of and defense of the revision has been issued by the editor, Arthur L. Farstad.[3] As of 1990, the NJKV is consistently running third in Bible sales following the NIV and the KJV in the list of the *Bookstore Journal* but fourth following the Living Bible in the list of Spring Arbor Distributors.

---

[1]Theodore P. Letis, "Hugh Broughton Redivivus": A Review of Jack P. Lewis's 'The Doctrinal Problems with the King James Version,'" pp. 69-109 in *The Majority Text: Essays and Reviews in the Continuing Debate* (Grand Rapids: Institute for Biblical Textual Studies, 1987).

[2]Private letter from Arthur L. Farstad.

[3]Arthur L. Farstad, *The New King James Version in the Great Tradition* (Nashville: Thomas Nelson Publishers, 1989.

Two studies and a video circulated by Zondervan have told the story of the making of the NIV.[4] Within ten years of its being issued the NIV has come to be the leading English translation in sales with 31 percent of the market, followed by the KJV and the NKJV in that order or by the KJV, Living Bible, and NKJV in another listing. By 1990 more than sixty million copies had been sold. Meanwhile, the Committee on Bible Translation, which has charge of the text, had approved four hundred changes in 1983. The committee meets once a year and is now projecting further a revision to be issued possibly in the year 2000. The editor insists that the statements made in the first edition of this work (pp. 302 and 304) concerning instances of the NIV's not following the Hebrew text are erroneous. He insists that the difference from the RSV is due to different philosophies of translation rather than to the following of different texts.

The Living Bible is currently undergoing a revision made by eighty scholars in cooperation with Tyndale House Publishers. At this time the extent of the revision has not been made public.

The NASV was issued in its latest official edition in 1977 with minor changes made since that time up to the 1988 printing.

The Good News Bible (Today's English Version) by 1989 had 26.8 million copies in worldwide circulation. More than 77 million copies of the Good News Bible New Testament have been distributed since its publication in 1966.

The New Testament of the New American Bible was issued in a revised edition in 1988. The revision represents work done in eighty sessions between December 1980 and September 1986. The preface describes this work as moving in the direction of formal-equivalence approach to translation as contrasted with dynamic-equivalence. The level of language aimed at is that of "liturgical proclamation." Consistency of vocabulary has been sought. Sensitivity to feelings of minorities and of women has been considered.

By its very nature, any work treating translations is out of date before it appears from the press. Translation must continue as language, translation philosophy, and information change. As translation is done by the making of thousands of judgments on which not all members of the committee participating in any effort are in agreement, so evaluation of translations is a matter of thousands of judgments. Each translation has more virtues than it has faults. The public is indebted to those who have labored to open God's Word to the masses.

[4]Kenneth L. Barker, ed., *The NIV: The Making of a Contemporary Translation* (Grand Rapids: Zondervan, 1986); Burton L. Goddard, *The NIV Story* (New York/Los Angeles/Chicago: Vantage Press, 1989).

Introduction

When William Tyndale was discussing a theological point with a cleric who argued that men would be better off without God's law than without the Pope's law, Tyndale retorted that if God spared his life, before long he would make the boy that drives the plough know more Bible than the cleric did.

Just as the driving force of Tyndale's life was the effort to accomplish that goal, so the entire history of the translation of the Bible into English should be seen as a movement in that direction. Its goal is to make the Bible plain to the common man. The modern speech movement in particular is aiming at this goal.

It has been argued that we should not translate the Bible down to the people but that we should educate the people up to the Bible. This logic, carried to its ultimate conclusion, would leave the Bible in Hebrew, Aramaic, and Greek and impose upon us the obligation of teaching all people those languages. Only those who learned the original languages could read the Bible. It would remain a closed book to all except the learned few. Only a small percentage of preachers could read it fluently.

9

The story of the making of the English Bible has been told many times; and for general use perhaps the best handbook is Ira M. Price's *The Ancestry of our English Bible*, third revised edition by William A. Irwin and Allen P. Wikgren, New York: Harper and Brothers, 1956. A brief but very usable treatment is Margaret T. Hills's *A Ready-Reference History of the English Bible*, revised edition, New York: American Bible Society, 1971. These may be supplemented by F. F. Bruce's *History of the Bible in English*, third edition, New York: Oxford University Press, 1978. More comprehensive still is *The Cambridge History of the Bible*, Cambridge: Cambridge University Press, 1963-1970, 3 vols. It is not the purpose of this study to compete with or to attempt to displace those studies.

Introductory chapters of this work discuss the story of the Bible prior to the English versions and the English versions prior to the King James Version. The remaining part of the book is devoted to the strengths and weaknesses of the major translations and revisions that are available today. Most of the ideas dealt with are not in any sense new. An indebtedness to all those who have written on these topics before is hereby gratefully acknowledged. Some of the sections have previously appeared in periodicals. I express my gratitude to the editors of those journals for permission to revise and use them.

My purpose is not to discourage the reading and study of the Bible in any English version in which men are willing to read it. Neither is it my purpose to destroy confidence in the Bible. It is my conviction that the basic duties to man and God can be learned from any translation that men read prayerfully. However, in some versions the Word of God may be more easily grasped than in others.

These evaluations are not in any sense an attack upon the message of the Bible. English phraseology is merely the clothing in which God's Word is dressed for communication purposes. Translation is a human—not a divinely inspired—process. It is thereby subject to all the faults man is heir to. The perfect translation does not exist. I hope that the reader will not confuse my calling attention to some of these "flyspecks" on the masterpiece of the English Bible with an attack upon the Bible and its message. Nothing could be further from my intention. I work under the admonition: "Prove all things, hold fast to that which is good."

The careful student of the Bible will not rely completely upon one version of the Bible, but he will seek to recognize the strengths and weaknesses of the versions he uses. *The New Testament Octapla, The*

New Testament in 26 Translations, and *The New Testament in Four Versions* will enable him to see the form a New Testament verse has had in the various English versions. He should compare these with the original language. True faith can only be strengthened by a fair and complete examination of the truth. The main lines of the message of the Bible are readily understandable in the English versions that are on the market. The items pointed out in this study comprise the minor part rather than the major portion of the content of the Bible.

1

The Bible in History

The Bible was originally written in Hebrew, Aramaic, and Greek for the people to whom these languages were native languages used in everyday speech. Though tradition has supplied names for the writers of all the books, many of them are actually anonymous. Some books are named for the topics they treat—like Kings and Chronicles. Others are named for a chief character—like Samuel; still others—like Psalms and Proverbs—are named for their literary form.

Jeremiah 36 gives the best description we have of the writing of a book in the Old Testament period. Jeremiah dictated to his secretary Baruch what he had been preaching. Paul dictated his letters and then added a personal greeting in his own hand (I Cor. 16:21; Gal. 6:11; Col. 4:18; II Thess. 3:17; Philem. 19). It seems to be a sound opinion that all the books, except for the writings of Luke, were written by Jews to whom Paul says were entrusted the oracles of God (Rom. 3:2).

Though starting out as individual compositions, the books of the Bible were collected by persons unknown to us, upon bases unknown to us, and at a time not specifically known. However, by the New Testament period there were these collections: the Law, the Prophets, and the Writings. Josephus speaks of the Bible as containing twenty-two books written between the time of Moses and Artaxerxes. Artaxerxes ruled Persia when Ezra and Nehemiah carried out their work. About the three-quarter mark of the second Christian century, Melito, Bishop of Sardis, gave the earliest surviving list of books of the Old Testament.

From its beginning the church had the Old Testament and the oral teaching of the apostles for its guidance, but soon the message was written down in order to preserve it. The books of the New Testament were completed before the end of the first Christian century. Many of these books are of the occasional sort written to specific churches to help where problems had arisen. Paul's letter to the Colossians gives an insight into how churches came to have more letters than their own (Col. 4:16). The church in Colossae was to see that its letter from Paul was also read to the church in Laodicea; and in turn it was to read the letter sent to Laodicea. Thus we can envision a church having many of Paul's letters; and indeed, at the end of the first century, Clement of Rome, our earliest nonbiblical Christian writer, knew of a number of letters of Paul and made use of them. As the second-century church emerged from the conflict with Marcion and with the Gnostics, evidence from Justin Martyr reveals that in its worship it was reading the "memoirs of the apostles" along with the writing of the prophets as though these were regarded as of equal authority. It is at this period that the Muratorian Fragment gives the first list of books of the New Testament that is extant.

Taken together, the sixty-six books form the Bible. The name "Bible" comes from the town of Byblos, which was located on the Lebanese coast north of Beirut and today is called Jebail. The name *Byblos* comes from the Greek word for papyrus, the writing material of the first century, for which the town was an import center. The diminutive form *biblion* means "the book." Chrysostom in the fourth century seems the first to apply the term to the whole collection of books. In English, Chaucer had used "Bible" to describe any book, but John Purvey used it for Scripture, speaking of "the Bible late translated."[1]

In the Dead Sea Scrolls, copies of some Old Testament books antedate the Christian period. For example, the copy of Isaiah dates within five

[1]John Stoughton, *Our English Bible, Its Translations and Translators* (London: The Religious Tract Society, 1878), p. 46.

hundred years of the time when the book itself must have been written. A complete copy of the Old Testament is available from the tenth Christian century. Within the last twenty years a complete copy of the Gospel of John, dating about the year A.D. 200 and now in the possession of the Bodmer Library of Geneva, Switzerland, has been published. The letters of Paul from a papyrus codex of the third century are available in the Chester Beatty Papyri. Almost complete New Testaments survive from the fourth century in the vellum codices Vaticanus and Sinaiticus. All of these finds indicate that the gap between the original writing of the Bible and the point at which a text can be established is a relatively narrow one; this fact is particularly impressive when one compares this time span with that separating the earliest manuscripts of other ancient writings from their date of composition.

The Bible in Translation

Through most of its history the Bible has been read by more people in translation than in its original languages. This process began at least as early as the third century B.C. when, at the suggestion of Demetrius of Phaleron, Ptolemy Philadelphus invited Jewish scholars to Alexandria to prepare a Greek translation for the library there. Because the story told in the *Letter of Aristeas* relates that seventy-two scholars worked on it, it came to be known as the Septuagint, the Latin word for seventy. Though the initial account attributes no miraculous power to the translators, legend soon made it an inspired translation and spoke of seventy separate cells in which the translators worked independently. The legend claimed that at the end of the work the independent translations were in perfect agreement. Philo, in the first century, and Augustine, in the fourth century, made the claim for inspiration of the Septuagint.

Most of the sixty-eight direct quotations from the Old Testament in the New Testament are from the Greek Bible rather than from the original Hebrew. The Greek Bible was the Bible of the early church. However, as the Christian community made use of the Septuagint in polemics, the Greek-speaking Jewish community abandoned it and prepared for itself other translations. The result is that the Septuagint of today has come through Christian channels.

In time, large segments of the church no longer read Greek, and translations were made into Syriac, Ethiopic, and other vernaculars of the areas

15

to which Christianity spread. Latin became the language of Western Christendom. Defective, on-the-spot Latin translations had already been made by unknown persons and were being used. The Old and New Testaments were both translated from Greek into Latin; Jerome said that no two manuscripts agreed with each other. The need for an accurate Bible was apparent. Damasus, Bishop of Rome, commissioned Jerome to prepare such a Latin Bible. In several stages which finally culminated in his work at Bethlehem (ca. A.D. 404), Jerome translated the Old Testament from Hebrew and Aramaic and the New Testament from Greek.

Jerome's work was unwelcome to a large segment of the church of his day. Men said he was Judaizing the church by going back to Hebrew. A North African congregation rioted when their bishop read the new version in the service, and peace was restored only when the familiar version was reinstated. However, with the passage of time the merits of Jerome's work, later called the Vulgate, were recognized. For more than a thousand years, men in the western world who studied the Bible studied the Vulgate. Many came to speak accommodatingly of Jerome as an "inspired translator." Our own English Bible is molded in form and vocabulary by the Vulgate.

Later still, common men in the British Isles came to speak English, though the scholars still studied in Latin. John Wyclif, who lived in Chaucer's time, and his associates prepared a manuscript English Bible for the common man. After another hundred years, printing was invented. The Protestant Reformation had dawned. William Tyndale set himself to prepare an English Bible so that "the boy who drives the plough" could know more Scripture than the clerics did, but he paid with his life for his trouble. Nevertheless, in the next eighty-six years after 1525, English Bibles appeared in rapid succession. First was Coverdale's, then Matthew's, Taverner's, the Great Bible, the Geneva Bible, the Bishops' Bible, the Rheims-Douay, and finally the King James in 1611. To this story we now turn our attention.

2

The Early English Versions

In the early period, the Scripture read in the British Isles was in Latin. The common people heard the gospel proclaimed by word of mouth and saw its scenes depicted in the art adorning church buildings. The earliest efforts at translation into Anglo-Saxon (the ancestor of English) were designed for the use of the inhabitants of monasteries rather than for the common people. The age of vernacular translations had not dawned; authorities were suspicious of the effect vernacular translations might have upon the masses. The Anglo-Saxon period saw the preparation of paraphrases on Scripture like those of Caedmon,[1] of interlinear word-for-word glosses on the Latin text like those of the Lindesfarne Gospels and the Rushworth Gospels,[2] and of some elementary translations like the

---

[1]The definitive study of early English materials is Minnie Cate Morrell, *A Manual of Old English Biblical Materials* (Knoxville: University of Tennessee Press, 1965); see also Geoffrey Shepherd, "English Versions of the Scriptures before Wyclif," in *The Cambridge History of the Bible*, ed. P. . Ackroyd, C. F. Evans, G. W. H. Lampe, and S. L. Greenslade (Cambridge: University Press, 1963-70), 2:362ff.

[2]Morrell, *A Manual*, pp. 166f.; Shepherd, "English Versions," 2:371.

work of Bede. Also belonging to this period are some of the sections of the glosses on the Rushworth Gospels and the work of Aelfric (ca. 1000), who, going against the widespread opposition to vernacular Scripture, said, "Happy is he, then, who reads the Scriptures, if he convert the words into actions."[3]

The movement for a vernacular Bible had three basic hurdles to overcome. The first was the traditional feeling that Latin was the proper medium of religious expression. The second was the uneasiness of the clergy over offering Scripture to the laity lest unorthodox teachings should result. The third was the conviction that English was unsuitable for use in religious expression. As some today would feel that American slang is inappropriate for English Bible translation, so in the Middle Ages the English vernacular was thought to lack the cultural standing needed. As late as the time of Tyndale this feeling had to be combated. Tyndale said:

> ...the Greek tongue agreeth more with the English than with the Latin. And the properties of the Hebrew tongue agreeth a thousand times more with the English than with the Latin. The manner of speaking is both one; so that in a thousand places thou needest not but to translate it into the English, word for word; when thou must seek a compass in the Latin.[4]

English translators had a church tradition that was heavily dependent upon Latin with its fixed mode of religious expression, but there was no well-beaten path to guide them in proper procedures and inerrant choices as they weighed alternate ways of expressing an idea. The specific phraseology of the English Bible is the result of trial and error, progression and regression, out of which the student can see phrases taking the turn which commended them to the readers and to the translators who came after.

It is now thought that John Wyclif was the first man to give the English public the Bible in its entirety, though it is uncertain how much is the work of Wyclif and how much that of his associates.[5] Nicholas of Hereford translated a part of the Old Testament, and the whole was completed about A.D. 1382. After Wyclif's death in 1384, a revision was carried through

---

[3]Cited in J. I. Mombert, *English Versions of the Bible* (London: Samuel Bagster and Sons, 1907), p. 17; see also *DNB* 1:166.

[4]William Tyndale, "Obedience of the Christian Man," reprinted in *Doctrinal Treatises*, ed. Henry Walter (Cambridge: University Press, 1848), pp. 148-49.

[5]The definitive study of Wyclif is Margaret Deanesly, *The Lollard Bible* (Cambridge: University Press, 1920; reprint ed., 1966).

which is conjecturally attributed to John Purvey. As a manuscript Bible, the Wyclif Bible was expensive. There are about two hundred copies extant. All but thirty are of the Purvey revision rather than of the earlier edition.[6]

Wyclif insisted that "no man is so rude a scholar but that he might learn the words of the Gospel according to his simplicity"; but his involvement in the ecclesiastical quarrels of his day assured opposition to his Bible. Wyclif had so successfully trained his lay preachers, nicknamed "the Lollards," to go about two-by-two preaching that one opponent said that should one meet two men in England, one would be a Lollard.[7] Opposition did come. A bill before the House of Lords in 1390 to suppress the translation was opposed and defeated by John of Gaunt.[8] Nevertheless, Bishop Arundel influenced a provincial council meeting at Oxford in July, 1408, to decree:

> that no one henceforth on his own authority translate any text of Holy Scripture into the English or any other language...until the translation itself shall have been approved by the diocesan of the place.[9]

Arundel himself, about 1411, wrote:

> This pestilent and wretched John Wyclif ... that son of the old serpent ... endeavoured ... to fill up the measure of his malice ... [by] the expedient of a new translation of the Scriptures into the mother tongue.[10]

Somewhat later, the continuator of Henry Knighton's *Chronicle* complained of the work that "the pearl of the Gospel is scattered abroad and trodden underfoot by swine."[11] The Council of Constance in 1415 ordered

---

[6]Margaret T. Hills, *A Ready-Reference History of the English Bible* (revisions by Elizabeth Eisenhart; New York: American Bible Society, 1971), p. 4; see also Henry Hargreaves, "The Wycliffite Versions," in *The Cambridge History of the Bible* (Cambridge University Press, 1969), 2:387-415.

[7]George M. Trevelyan, *England in the Age of Wycliffe* (London: Longmans Green, and Co., new ed. 1909; reprint, 1948), p. 319.

[8]Deanesly, *The Lollard Bible*, p. 282.

[9]Text and translation in A. W. Pollard, ed., *Records of the English Bible* (Oxford: Henry Frowde, 1911), pp. 79-81.

[10]Quoted in Henry Hargreaves, "The Wycliffite Versions," 2:388.

[11]Ibid.

19

that Wyclif's body be disinterred and burned, and the ashes thrown into the river Swift.[12]

The style of the Wyclif Bible was stilted. It often was a word-for-word rendering of the Latin and in some places was not very intelligible to the person with no knowledge of Latin. It is not likely that the Wyclif Bible was widely known by Tyndale's time — Lollardism was no longer popular — but there are interesting coincidences of expression between the two without any evidence that Tyndale borrowed from Wyclif. Some phrases may have become a common heritage. Some recent versions revert in isolated cases to Wycliffite phrases rather than using those chosen by his successors.

Reformation and Post-Reformation Period

The Renaissance with its stress on returning to the sources of truth, the invention of printing by Johannes Gutenberg in 1453 which reduced the price of books, and the Reformation with its appeal to the authority of Scripture all played a part in the demand for a vernacular Bible. England was late among European nations in having a printed Bible — not because of the backwardness of the English people, and not because of the lack of skill of the English printers, but because of the prohibition of translations by the Oxford Council of 1408.[13] It was not until the time of Henry VIII that church officials authorized a translation to be made. Meanwhile, William Caxton in his *Golden Legend* (1483) had printed some Scripture passages in English.[14] Also, the *English Primers*, which were printed in 1529 and the years following, had Scripture passages.[15] Each of these made some contribution to English Bible phraseology.

It is with William Tyndale that English Bible printing really begins. Tyndale, retorting to a cleric who argued that men would be better off without God's laws than the Pope's laws, said that if God spared his life, before long he would make the boy who drove the plough to know more

[12]Joseph H. Dahmus, *The Prosecution of John Wyclif* (New Haven: Yale University Press, 1952), pp. 153-54.

[13]Text in Pollard, *Records*, pp. 79-81. Bibles were printed in Germany in 1645, Italy in 1471, France in 1474, the Low Countries in 1477, and Bohemia in 1488. See H. A. Guppy, "Miles Coverdale and the English Bible 1488-1568," *Bulletin of the John Rylands Library* 19 (July 1935): 2.

[14]Charles C. Butterworth, *The Literary Lineage of the King James Bible* (Philadelphia: University of Pennsylvania Press, 1941), pp. 51-55.

[15]Charles C. Butterworth, *The English Primers (1529-1545)* (Philadelphia: University of Pennsylvania Press, 1953).

Scripture than the cleric did.[16] Tyndale devoted the remainder of his life to the task but found it necessary to leave England to complete his work. His New Testament was first printed at Cologne[17] and at Worms[18] in 1525. It was then smuggled in bales of cloth back into England for sale. In the following years there were pirated editions, some issued in Holland. A coworker, George Joye,[19] in 1534 issued an edition in which he modified some of Tyndale's words in favor of those suitable to his own ideas. A heated exchange between the two resulted.[20] Tyndale published his translation of the Pentateuch at Marburg in 1530[21] and that of the Book of Jonah at Antwerp in 1531.[22] His translations were accompanied by bitter anti-Catholic notes, but the notes were softened in later editions of his New Testament, and the last edition had no notes. He revised the New Testament in 1534[23] and said, "I ... have weded oute of it many fautes which lacke of helpe at the begynninge and oversyght dyd sowe therin."[24] His last New Testament edition was printed in 1535.[25] After being betrayed by a friend, Tyndale was imprisoned and was executed on October 6, 1536.[26] He left unpublished in manuscript form a translation of the books of the Old Testament from Joshua to Chronicles.

Church officials identified Tyndale's writings with Lutheranism and vigorously opposed the circulation of his translations. Tunstall, Bishop of London, claimed to find 3,000 errors in Tyndale's New Testament.[27] Copies were bought and burned. Thomas More asserted that to study to find errors

---

[16]The definitive study of William Tyndale is J. F. Mozley, *William Tyndale* (London: S.P.C.K., 1937). The source of the quotation is John Foxe, *The Acts and Monuments of John Foxe*, ed. George Townsend (London: Seeley, Burnside and Seeley, 1843-49; reprint ed., New York: AMS Press, Inc., 1965), 5:117.

[17]T. H. Darlow and H. F. Moule, *Historical Catalogue of Printed Editions of the English Bible, 1525-1961* (London: John Day, 1903), revised and expanded by A. S. Herbert (London: The British and Foreign Bible Society, 1968), Number 1.

[18]*Historical Catalogue*, Number 2.

[19]See Charles C. Butterworth and Allan G. Chester, *George Joye* (Philadelphia: University of Pennsylvania Press, 1962), p. 293.

[20]See Pollard, *Records*, pp. 178-94.

[21]*Historical Catalogue*, Number 4.

[22]Ibid., Number 5.

[23]Ibid., Number 13.

[24]Quoted from J. R. Dore, *Old Bibles*, 2nd ed. (London: Eyre and Spottiswoode, 1888), p. 34.

[25]*Historical Catalogue*, Number 15.

[26]Foxe, *Acts and Monuments*, 5:127; Mozley, *William Tyndale*, pp. 294-342.

[27]James Gairdner, *Lollardy and the Reformation in England* (London: Macmillan, 1908-13; reprint ed., New York: Burt Franklin, n.d.), 2:227.

in Tyndale's work was like studying to find water in the sea.[28] More found fault particularly with Tyndale's choice of "congregation," "senior," "love," and "repent" in place of the ecclesiastically established words "church," "priest," "charity," and "do penance." Tyndale published a reply to More in which he defended his choices.[29] In 1529 and again in 1530, Henry VIII prohibited Tyndale's writings, insisting in the last case that the common people had no need for all the Scripture in English, but promising that a translation would be made.[30] Tyndale in 1531 declared that if Henry would "graunte only a bare text of the scriptures to be put forthe emonge h[is] people ... be it of the translation of what perso[n] soever shall please his majestie, I shall ... promyse, never to wryte more."[31]

It has been estimated that 50,000 copies of the New Testament circulated before Tyndale's death and that many other copies were made available shortly thereafter. Between 1525 and 1566, forty editions are recorded. The English Bible is indebted in some sections of the Old Testament and in all of the New Testament to Tyndale more than to any other single individual. It has been estimated that 92 percent of the New Testament as left by Tyndale is carried over into the KJV. From our vantage point it is easy to pick out faults in Tyndale's work. He gave current Christian names to biblical holidays; there are oddities as when the serpent in Genesis 3:4 says to Eve, "Tush, ye shall not dye"; and Tyndale used a variety of renderings for the same Greek or Hebrew word, creating confusion in some passages. But a great host of his phrases have become the language of our religious life.

The religious atmosphere in England changed rapidly through Tyndale's last years. The fortunes of the Reformation and the story of the English Bible go hand-in-hand. In 1530 Hugh Latimer reminded the king of his earlier promise to see that the New Testament was faithfully translated,[32] but Henry delayed. In 1533 Henry married Anne Boleyn and broke with the church of Rome. In 1534 a Convocation petitioned the king to decree that the Scriptures should be translated.[33] Archbishop Thomas Cranmer

[28]From More's *Dialogue*, reprinted in Pollard, *Records*, pp. 126-31.
[29]William Tyndale, *An Answer to Sir Thomas More's Dialogue*, ed. Henry Walter (Cambridge: University Press, 1850).
[30]Text reprinted in Pollard, *Records*, pp. 163-69.
[31]Ibid., pp. 169-72.
[32]Robert Demaus, *Hugh Latimer* (new ed., London: The Religious Tract Society, n.d.), p. 110.
[33]Text and translation in Pollard, *Records*, pp. 175-77.

divided portions of the Bible to fellow bishops for review, but when one bishop sharply declined, Cranmer's project became fruitless.[34]

On October 5, 1535, a year before the death of Tyndale, Miles Coverdale issued a Bible, possibly from Marburg or Zürich, based on Tyndale's work and on that of Zwingli, Leo Judah, Pagninus, the Vulgate, and Luther.[35] Coverdale, though no Greek or Hebrew scholar, thus gained for himself the distinction of being the first man to issue a complete printed English Bible. The prologue to the reader carried his name. Two-thirds of the Old Testament (the poetical and prophetical books) and all the Apocrypha were his own. Coverdale put the collection of Apocrypha at the end of the Old Testament and thereby set a pattern for subsequent English Bibles.

Coverdale claimed in his prologue that he had not wrested one word for the maintenance of any sect. He dedicated his work to Henry VIII whom he flattered as "Our Moses"; nevertheless, he failed to get the royal approval he sought for this edition. It circulated without hindrance, but with "permitted" rather than "authorized" status. The dedications of the successive editions reflect the marriage-life of the king and the changing religious atmosphere in England. The title page of the edition of 1537 carried the phrase "Set forth with the Kynges moost gracious license."[36] Coverdale brought back into the Bible the established ecclesiastical terms that Tyndale had banished, and thereby avoided controversy; but he also made his own contribution to the wording of the English Bible.

Once the door was opened, Bibles appeared in rapid succession in the third decade of the sixteenth century. The Matthew's Bible was issued in 1537 at Antwerp, only one year after the death of Tyndale, and was the second complete Bible in English.[37] It is thought to be the work of John Rogers and is dedicated to King Henry and Queen Jane. Rogers, who was martyred in 1555, made use of Tyndale's Pentateuch, already published. For Joshua to Chronicles he used material left unpublished by Tyndale at his death, for Ezra to the end of the Apocrypha he used Coverdale, and for the New Testament he used Tyndale's revision of 1535. Cranmer commended the translation as "better than any other translacion heretofore

[34]Ibid., pp. 196-98.

[35]*Historical Catalogue*, Number 18. The definitive study of Coverdale is J. F. Mozley, *Miles Coverdale* (London: Lutterworth Press, 1953).

[36]*Historical Catalogue*, Number 33.

[37]Ibid., Number 34.

made" and requested a license for it.[38] The license was granted,[39] and so it was the first English Bible to hold this status. But the same year (1537) a license was also granted for the third edition of the Coverdale Bible.

Another step toward the free circulation of the Bible was taken in 1538 when the Royal Injunctions ordered that by a certain date Bibles were to be set up in all churches.[40] In 1539 Richard Taverner issued his Bible from London.[41] He had made slight changes in the text of the Matthew's Bible and had corrected some of its notes. His is the first Bible to be completely printed in England. To Taverner we owe the use of "parable" and "passover," but his contribution to the ongoing history of the English Bible was not a major one.

To offset the offensive notes in the Matthew's Bible and to supply the need for Bibles in the churches, Cromwell set in operation machinery to create a satisfactory Bible. Coverdale was chosen to oversee the project. In April, 1539, 111 years after the burning of the bones of Wyclif, this Bible, called "The Great Bible" because of its size, was issued.[42] The king was assured that no heresies were maintained in it, and he approved its circulation. An edition of it appearing in 1540 had a preface by Cranmer and for the first time had the words, "This is the Byble apoynted to the vse of the churches."[43] For this reason it may be thought of as the first "Authorized Version." Notes were intended, but these never received the sanction of the Privy Council and were never printed. In keeping with the practice of the times, copies were chained to the stand in the churches. The Great Bible was read with joy by the English people.[44] Seven editions were issued in two years' time (1539-1541).[45] It was last printed in 1569, after which it was displaced by the Geneva and the Bishops' Bibles. However, its influence continues through its Psalms which were attached to the Prayer Book (1549, 1662) and which with modified spelling remained

[38]Pollard, *Records*, pp. 214-15.

[39]Ibid., p. 216.

[40]Henry Gee and William John Hardy, comps., *Documents Illustrative of English Church History* (London: Macmillan, 1910), pp. 275-76.

[41]*Historical Catalogue*, Number 45.

[42]Ibid., Number 46.

[43]Ibid., Number 53.

[44]John Strype, *Memorials of Thomas Cranmer* (London: George Routledge, 1853), 1:92-94, 117-24.

[45]See Francis Fry, *A Description of the Great Bible* (London and Bristol: Willis and Sotheran, 1865).

in use until a recent (1963) revision. Though some of its changes were for the worse rather than for the better, the Great Bible also made its contribution to the lasting phraseology of the English Bible.

A second effort by Cranmer on February 16, 1542, to get the bishops to do a translation was frustrated when Bishop Gardiner produced a long list of Latin words that must be retained in an English translation.[46] Then in his last years Henry VIII had second thoughts about free circulation of the Bible, and new regulations restricting the circulating and reading of the Bible were made in 1543 and 1546.[47] However, Henry VIII died in January, 1547.

At the accession of Edward VI, the regulations restricting the circulation of the Bible were removed, and churches were again ordered to have Bibles. During his brief reign (1547-1553), thirty-five editions of various New Testaments and thirteen of various Bibles — Tyndale's, Coverdale's, Matthew's, Taverner's, and Cranmer's — were printed. However, with the accession of Mary a complete eclipse came. Public reading of Scripture was prohibited on August 18, 1553, by a proclamation. No Bibles were published in England during Mary's reign (1553-1558). Church Bibles were confiscated, martyrs abounded, and Reformers fled to the Continent.

Those exiles at Geneva, the center of the Calvinistic reform, prepared a translation and presented it to Elizabeth in 1560, a year and a half after her accession, in the name of "Your humble subiects of the English Churche at Geneva."[48] William Whittingham, Anthony Gilby, and Thomas Sampson claim that they had spent "two yeres and more day and night" in its preparation. The Geneva Bible was accompanied by copious notes which were both anti-Catholic and pro-Calvinistic in nature. Matthew Parker later spoke of them as "diverse preiudicall notis which might have ben also well spared."[49] While earlier Bibles had indicated sections by A, B, C, and D on the margins of pages but had no verses, each verse in the Geneva Bible was a separate paragraph. Roman type was used, and words supplied to complete the sense in English were in italics. It was not until 1576, after

[46]Pollard, *Records*, pp. 272-75.

[47]J. D. Mackie, *The Earlier Tudors, 1485-1558* (Oxford: Clarendon Press, 1952), pp. 429, 432. A translation of the 1546 decree is in P. L. Hughes and J. L. Larkin, eds., *Tudor Royal Proclamations* (New Haven: Yale University Press, 1964), 1:373-76.

[48]*Historical Catalogue*, Number 107. A recent extensive study of the influence of the Geneva Bible has been done by Lewis Lupton, *History of the Geneva Bible* (London: Fauconberg Press, 1966-81), 13 vols.

[49]In a letter to Queen Elizabeth; reprinted in Pollard, *Records*, p. 295.

the death of Parker, that it was printed in England. The Geneva Bible was favored by the Puritans and enjoyed a remarkable popularity as is evidenced by its 180 editions.

Both large and small sizes of Geneva Bibles were printed so it was owned and used in homes and to some extent in churches. In his later plays Shakespeare reflects a knowledge of the wording of the Geneva Bible. The Mayflower Compact was signed on the Geneva Bible, and the Geneva played an important role in the history of early America. Also, it was formally authorized for use in the churches in Scotland.

There are three types of Geneva Bibles. In addition to the early form, a revision was done in 1576 by Laurence Tomson; later Geneva Bibles are therefore known as the Tomson revision. In 1595 Junius' extensive anti-Catholic comments on Revelation were added to make a third form. Though the phrase was not original with the Geneva Bible, the use of "breeches" for Adam's and Eve's clothing in Genesis 3:7 gave it the nickname of the "Breeches Bible."[50]

Church officials found more fault with the notes of the Geneva Bible than with its translation. To offset its popularity, Matthew Parker carried through a revision in which most of the work was done by bishops, and it came to be known as the Bishops' Bible. Sections of the Great Bible were parceled out to eighteen or nineteen men for revision; there was no face-to-face consultation of the participants, but Parker put the finishing touches on the whole. A copy was ready for presentation to Queen Elizabeth on October 5, 1568, which, by coincidence, was the year of Coverdale's death[51] and was only thirty-two years after the burning of Tyndale.

From the viewpoint of art, the first edition of the Bishops' Bible was the most imposing of the English Bibles. As a translation it had its shortcomings and was plagued with printing errors, but it served as the "church Bible" of the Elizabethan Age. A Convocation in 1571 ordered that copies be in the house of every bishop and in every cathedral.[52] It thereby became the second authorized English Bible. The entire Bible was printed over a period of thirty-four years, with the last edition appearing in 1602; the New Testament was printed over a period of sixty-five years, and its last edition was in 1633. There were about nineteen editions of the whole

---

[50]The term is used by Wyclif, Caxton's *Golden Legend* (1483), and Coverdale.

[51]*Historical Catalogue*, Number 123.

[52]B. F. Westcott, *A General View of the History of the English Bible*, 3rd ed., revised by W. A. Wright (New York: Macmillan, 1927), p. 101, citing E. Cardwell, *Synodalia*, 1:152.

Bible and about the same number of New Testaments. Meanwhile, the Geneva Bible was outstripping it in popularity with 120 editions before 1611. The Bishops' Bible has been less thoroughly studied than the other English Bibles. About 4 percent of the form of the KJV came from it.[53]

During Elizabeth's reign, Catholics also felt the need of preparing a Bible. Exiles led by Gregory Martin, William Allen, and Richard Bristow issued the New Testament at Rheims in 1582,[54] but because of financial problems did not issue the Old Testament until twenty-seven years later in 1609-1610.[55] Copious notes accompanying the text, chiefly written by Allen, carry on a running debate with the Protestants. No opportunity is spared to press the teachings of Rome. The translation was based on the Vulgate text and shows heavy influence of Latin. A translation which had renderings like "every knee bowe of the celestials, terrestrials, and infernals" (Phil. 2:10) could not be calculated to be popular. There were only four editions of the New Testament (1582, 1600, 1621, 1633) up to 1633, and then the next was in 1750. There were only two editions of the Old Testament (1610, 1635) before 1750. Its Latinisms caused Thomas Fuller to call it a "translation which needed to be translated."[56]

While the use of the Rheims-Douay version was limited to Catholic circles, its significance lies in the enrichment of the Protestant Bible that it was designed to offset. Carleton has demonstrated that the Rheims New Testament heavily influenced the King James translators.[57] This influence may well have come through the work of William Fulke who printed it alongside the Bishops' New Testament (1589, 1601, 1617, and 1633) in order to refute its notes. Numerous instances can now be cited where the Latin words the Rheims-Douay found necessary to explain in the glossary have become accepted English words.

The King James Version

The King James Bible was born out of a need to still the voices of critics who had agitated against the Bishops' Bible in the later years of

---

[53]Charles Butterworth, *The Literary Lineage of the King James Bible* (Philadelphia: University of Pennsylvania Press, 1941), p. 231.

[54]*Historical Catalogue*, Number 177.

[55]Ibid., Number 300.

[56]Thomas Fuller, *The Church History of Britain*, ed. J. S. Brewer (Oxford: University Press, 1845), 5:76.

[57]James Carleton, *The Part of Rheims in the Making of the English Bible* (Oxford: University Press, 1902).

27

Elizabeth's reign and also out of a need to bring uniformity into a confused situation. Geneva Bibles were commonly used in homes, Bishops' Bibles in churches. Some Great Bibles were still around, and perhaps even Tyndale and Coverdale Bibles could be found, though none of these three had been reprinted for a generation.[58] Miles Smith in the "Translators to the Reader" of the KJV spoke of making one translation out of many good ones, to which men could not justly take exception.[59] Though one can hardly envision King James doing a lasting service to Christendom,[60] fate has its odd turns. John Reynolds' proposal of a new translation made at the Hampton Court Conference in 1604[61] caught King James's fancy, and he set in order the machinery to bring about the translation.

The qualifications of the King's translators[62] and the guide rules set up assured the best revision possible at the time. Though information is not abundant, scattered records reveal that the various committees were at their tasks during the years following 1604. Some workers died before the work was completed, and some new appointments were made. A letter speaks of fifty-four translators; however, only forty-seven names have been preserved.[63] Some of the translators advanced in church offices as a reward for their services. How meticulously the guide rules were followed is not known. John Selden spoke of a procedure in which one person read the text while others followed in Bibles of various languages and made suggestions they felt appropriate.[64] It is thought that the notes John Bois made during the sessions have now been identified and published.[65] Notes

---

[58]The last printing of the Tyndale Testament was 1566, of the Coverdale Bible, 1553, and of the Great Bible, 1569.

[59]Reprinted in Pollard, *Records*, p. 369; E. J. Goodspeed, ed., *The Translators to the Reader* (Chicago: University of Chicago Press, 1911, 1935), p. 33.

[60]See J. D. Douglas, "The King Behind the Version," *Christianity Today* 19 (March 28, 1975): 632-34.

[61]William Barlow, *The Summe and Substance of the Conference Which It Pleased His Excellent Majestie to Have with the Lords, Bishops, and Other of His Clergie at Hampton Court, January 14, 1603 (1604)* (Gainesville, Florida: Scholars' Facsimiles and Reprints, 1965), pp. 45-48.

[62]Alexander W. McClure, *The Translators Revived* (New York: Board of Publication of the Reformed Dutch Church, 1855); Gustavus S. Paine, *The Learned Men* (New York: Thomas Y. Crowell Co., 1959).

[63]Fuller, *The Church History of Britain*, 5:370-80.

[64]John Selden, *Table Talk*, ed. E. Arber (Wing #2437; London: Foy E. Smith, Alex. Murray & Son, 1868), p. 20.

[65]Ward Allen, *Translating for King James* (Nashville: Vanderbilt University Press, 1969).

in a Bishops' Bible in the Bodleian Library are thought by some scholars to have been placed there in the course of the 1611 revision.[66] A final committee of twelve reviewed what the lower committees had prepared, and then Bishop Thomas Bilson and Dr. Miles Smith added the finishing touches, including the preparation of introductory material. By 1611 the whole revision was ready for the public. Though the king contributed no money to its production, and though no record of an official authorization of the finished product survives (if such were ever given), the Bible came to be known as the King James Bible. King James died in 1625. He did not see it attain the goal he had stated at the Hampton Court Conference of its being a new translation of such acceptable excellence that "this whole Church ... be bound vnto it, and none other."[67]

The translators of the KJV anticipated that their effort would be criticized, and they must not have been disappointed.[68] Thomas Fuller remarked, "Some of the brethren were not well pleased with this translation."[69] Published without notes, it seemed lacking in comparison with its rival, the Geneva Bible.[70] In fact, Bibles with the KJV text but with Geneva notes were printed in Holland in 1642, 1672, 1679, 1683, 1708, 1715, and in England in 1649.[71] Among the most vocal of the critics was Hugh Broughton who, after examining the translation, declared that it was so poorly done that it would grieve him as long as he lived. He insisted that he would rather be tied between wild horses and torn apart than to let it go forth among the people. He contended that the translators had put the errors in the text and the correct readings in the margins.[72]

Anticipating that their work would not please the Puritans, the translators speak scornfully of them in their preface.[73] They also foresaw that the Catholics would say:

---

[66]E. C. Jacobs, "A Bodleian Bishops' Bible, 1602" (Ph.D. dissertation, University of Alabama, 1972).

[67]Barlow, *The Summe and Substance*, p. 46.

[68]Luther A. Weigle, "English Versions since 1611," in *The Cambridge History of the Bible*, 3:361.

[69]Fuller, *The Church History of Britain*, 5:409.

[70]Ibid., 5:409-10.

[71]*Historical Catalogue*, Numbers 564, 620, 708, 742, 782, 897, 936.

[72]Hugh Broughton, *A Censure of the Late Translation for Our Churches*, c. 1612 (S.T.C. 3847).

[73]Reprinted in Pollard, *Records*, p. 375; and Goodspeed, *The Translators to the Reader*, p. 37.

> Was their Translation good before? Why doe they now mend it? Was it
> not good? Why then was it obtruded to the people? ... Nay, if it must be
> translated into English, Catholicks are fittest to doe it.[74]

Catholics said that by the alternate readings in the margin the translators
were shaking the certainty of the Scripture.[75]

Agitation for additional revision may be noted in the following sequence
of events. John Lightfoot in 1629 objected to the Apocrypha's being included between the two Testaments. When preaching before the House of
Parliament on August 26, 1645, he urged a "review and survey of the
translation of the Bible" so that people "might come to understand the
proper and genuine reading of the Scriptures by an exact, vigorous, and
lively translation."[76] John Selden commented on the KJV's style, noting
that "the Bible is rather translated into *English* Words, than into *English*
Phrase. The Hebraisms are kept and the Phrase of that Language is kept."[77]
Printing errors plagued all of the early editions. A tract written by William
Kilburne in 1659 pointed out the errors in certain printings.[78] As a result
of the agitation for revision, a bill was introduced into the Long Parliament
on January 11, 1653, for "a new English translation of the Bible out of the
original tongues," and a committee was appointed to consider the question.[79] In 1655 John Row in Scotland, pointing out certain deficiencies in
the KJV, proposed a revision.[80] In 1657 a further committee of Parliament
was appointed to look into the question;[81] however, Parliament was dis-
solved before the committee could render a report. Had the British church

---

[74]Reprinted in Pollard, *Records*, p. 358; and Goodspeed, *The Translators to the Reader*, p. 26.

[75]John Lewis, *A Complete History of the Several Translations of the Hebrew Bible and
New Testament into English* (London: W. Baynes, 1818), p. 329.

[76]John Lightfoot, *The Whole Works of the Rev. John Lightfoot*, ed. J. R. Pitman (London: J. F.
Dove, 1823), 6:194; S. Newth, *Lectures on Bible Revision* (London: Hodder and Stoughton, 1881),
p. 92; Christopher Anderson, *The Annals of The English Bible*, abridged by S. I. Prime (New York:
Robert Carter and Bros., 1849), pp. 473-74.

[77]Selden, *Table Talk*, p. 20.

[78]William Kilburne, *Dangerous Errors in Several Late Printed Bibles to the Great Scandal
and Corruption of Sound and True Religion* (Wing #435; London: R. Norton for Andrew Crook,
1659), pp. 38-39.

[79]Anderson, *The Annals of the English Bible*, p. 413; Lewis, *A Complete History*, p. 354;
J. Collier, *An Ecclesiastical History of Great Britain* (London: Straker, 1840-41; new ed. by
F. Barham), 8:395; Mombert, *English Versions of the Bible*, p. 443.

[80]See John Eadie, *The English Bible* (London: Macmillan, 1876), 2:322-23.

[81]Lewis, *A Complete History*, p. 355; Anderson, *The Annals of the English Bible*, pp. 415-16;
text in Mombert, *English Versions of the Bible* p. 444.

been less tied to the state, the history of the King James Bible would likely have been different. In 1659 Robert Gell, also urging revision, said:

The further we proceed in survey of the Scripture, the translation is the more faulty, as the *Hagiographa* more than the *Historical Scripture*, and the *Prophets* more than the *Hagiographa*, and the *Apocrypha* most of all; generally the *New* more then the Old Testament.[82]

Gell, in agreement with the charge earlier brought by Broughton that the translators had put errors in the text and the better readings in the margin, said: "The Translators ... have placed some different significations in the *Margent*; but those mostwhat the *better*; because when *truth* is tryed by *most voyces*, it is commonly out-voted."[83] John Eadie in the nineteenth century compiled a list of places in which such a judgment was justified in his opinion.[84] The Presbyterian ministers at a meeting held on May 4, 1661, presented their "Exceptions against the Book of Common Prayer" to the bishops. The seventh of eighteen exceptions was "A new Royal translation of the Scriptures is to be uniformly introduced."[85] All of these criticisms demonstrate that the feeling toward the KJV when it was new was no different from that shown toward new versions in the twentieth century. Only the passage of time has afforded the KJV a privileged status.

The criticisms, however, are only one side of the coin. Others were pleased with what the translators had done. Thomas Fuller said, "Wheresoever the Bible shall be preached or read in the whole world, there shall also this that they have done be told in memorial of them."[86] The success of the KJV was almost certain from the beginning, though that was not immediately evident. The title page phrase "Appointed to be read in Churches" taken over from the Bishops' Bible, the use of illustrations from that Bible, and the maintaining of a similar general appearance suggest that it was intended to supersede the Bishops' Bible. The entire Bishops' Bible was never printed after 1602. The King James Bible went through

---

[82]Robert Gell, *An Essay Toward the Amendment of the Last English Translation of the Bible* (Wing #470; London: R. Norton for Andrew Crook, 1659), Preface, pp. 38-39.

[83]Ibid., Preface, p. 34.

[84]Eadie, *The English Bible*, 2:218.

[85]Cited in Horton Davies, *The Worship of the English Puritans* (Westminster: Dacre Press, 1948), p. 147.

[86]Fuller, *The Church History of Britain*, 5:410.

fifteen printings in the first three years;[87] however, Robert Barker, its printer, also continued to print Geneva Bibles until 1616,[88] and other printers issued them until 1644. Even during those years the KJV was moving ahead, for there were 182 printings of the KJV and only 15 for the Geneva.[89] Church authorities showed open hostility to the Geneva. It could not be printed in England after 1618. Bishop Laud ordered copies burned and actively hindered importation of Geneva Bibles from abroad.[90] Without the force of the Puritan movement, the editions of the Geneva Bible would likely have been even fewer.

As might be expected, older bishops like Dillingham, Overall, and Laud continued to use the Geneva Bible in their sermons.[91] As late as 1650 the Bishops' Bible was used in the pulpit of the First Church of Hartford, Connecticut.[92] Others also continued using the Bishops' Bible. Lancelot Andrewes took his text from it in preaching before the King in 1621.[93] However, by 1622 some bishops urged the use of the KJV in churches by inquiring in their visitation articles if the church had a Bible "of the last translation."[94] The Scottish canons of 1636 say, "The Bible shall be of the translation of King James."[95] That the Prayer Book in its revision of 1662, fifty-one years after the publication of the KJV, used passages of the Gospels and Epistles from the KJV in the liturgy attests that by then the KJV had gained ecclesiastical recognition.

In time the attacks on the KJV lessened, but throughout its history there has been some agitation for additional revision. The statement often encountered that the Pilgrims would not allow a KJV on the Mayflower is likely in error, for John Alden's Bible, preserved in Pilgrim Hall at

[87]Lupton, *A History of the Geneva Bible*, 7:104.

[88]Ibid., 7:185-86.

[89]F. G. Kenyon, *Our Bible and the Ancient Manuscripts*, rev. A. W. Adams (New York: Harper & Brothers, 1958), p. 305.

[90]Lupton, *A History of the Geneva Bible*, 2:203, 211.

[91]W. J. Heaton, *The Puritan Bible* (London: Francis Griffiths, 1913), p. 287; Anderson, *The Annals of the English Bible*, p. 407.

[92]Matthew Brown Riddle, *The Story of the Revised New Testament* (Philadelphia: The Sunday School Times Company, 1908), p. 71.

[93]Paine, *The Learned Men*, pp. 136-37.

[94]Westcott, *A General View*, p. 119.

[95]Andrew Edgar, *The Bibles of England* (London: Alexander Gardner, 1889), p. 295; also cited in John Stoughton, *Our English Bible* (London: The Religious Tract Society, n.d.), p. 249.

Plymouth, Massachusetts, is a KJV.[96] Printing outside of England was not permitted until after America had broken away from British rule. The first English Bible printed in America (1782) was of the King James text.[97]

The translators had delivered "Gods booke unto Gods people in a tongue which they understand."[98] It was "vnderstood euen of the very vulgar."[99] In the seventeenth century a "hand labouring man" of Northhamptonshire said that "the last translation of the Bible which no doubt was done by those learned men in the best English, agreeth perfectly with the common speech of our country."[100] The KJV came to be loved by the English-speaking people. For more than two centuries it accomplished what a Bible translation should. It spoke directly to the heart of the common man; that he forgot it was a translation and came to think that it was the original Bible does not negate its worth. Well-turned tributes concerning the KJV would fill a book.[101] Perhaps none is more eloquent than that of Frederick W. Faber, who in 1845 left the Church of England for that of Rome:

It lives on the ear like a music that can never be forgotten, like the sound of church bells which the convert hardly knows how he can forgo. Its felicities seem often to be almost things rather than mere words. It is part of the national mind, and the anchor of national seriousness, nay, it is worshipped with a positive idolatry in extenuation of whose grotesque fanaticism its intrinsic beauty pleads unavailingly with the man of letters and the scholar. The memory of the dead passes into it. The potent traditions of childhood are stereotyped in its verses. The power of all the griefs and trials of a man is hidden beneath its words. It is the represen-

[96]The assertion is made by Eugene Nida, *Toward a Science of Translation* (Leiden: E. J. Brill, 1964), p. 17, who is dependent on P. Marion Simms, *The Bible in America* (New York: Wilson-Erickson, 1936), p. 93n. Simms cites *Massachusetts Historical Society Proceedings* I, 227n., 54. 1. See, however, now C. C. Forman, "Four Early Bibles in Pilgrim Hall," *Pilgrim Society Notes*, Plymouth, Massachusetts 9 (April 1959): 3. The Bible is No. 90 in the Pilgrim Hall catalogue.

[97]Anderson, *The Annals of the English Bible*, p. 486.

[98]Reprinted in Pollard, *Records*, p. 359; and in Goodspeed, *The Translators to the Reader*, p. 27.

[99]Reprinted in Pollard, *Records*, p. 376; and in Goodspeed, *The Translators to the Reader*, p. 37.

[100]Thomas Fuller, *The Worthies of England*, edited with an Introduction and Notes by John Freeman (London: George Allen, 1952), p. 423.

[101]See Mombert, *English Versions of the Bible*, pp. 384-86.

tative of his best moments, and all that there has been about him of soft, and gentle, and pure, and penitent, and good, speaks to him for ever out of his English Bible. It is this sacred thing which doubt never dimmed and controversy never soiled. It has been to him all along as the silent, but oh, how intelligible voice of his guardian angel, and in the length and breadth of the land there is not a Protestant, with one spark of religiousness about him, whose spiritual biography is not in his Saxon Bible.[102]

[102]F. W. Faber, *St. Francis of Assisi, Oratorian Lives of the Saints*, pp. 116f. Quoted in Hugh Pope, *English Versions of the Bible* (St. Louis: B. Herder, 1952), p. 322.

3

Doctrinal Problems in the King James Version

M̲ost of the problems raised by biblical revision stem from people's misconceptions about the KJV. Many people believe that the KJV is *the* Bible against which all new translations are to be measured. Some assume that the KJV, if not inspired, is at least free of doctrinal problems and thus becomes a refuge from questions raised by the novelties in new translations. These assumptions need critical evaluation.

The Authorized Version?

The tradition that the King James Bible was authorized seems to rest merely upon a printer's claim on the title page which continued the phrase from earlier Bibles "Appointed to be read in Churches." There are extant proclamations and canons about Matthew's, Cranmer's, and the Bishops' Bibles in 1537, 1541, and 1571, respectively;[1] but history has no record of an official authorization of the KJV. The claim of its title page likely meant that it was intended to supersede the Bishops' Bible, which had

[1]A.W. Pollard, ed., *Records of the English Bible* (London: Henry Frowde, 1911), pp. 214ff., 257-65, 38.

held an authorized status by order of the *Constitutions and Canons Ecclesiastical* of 1571.[2] The phrase simply meant that it was appointed (or permitted) to be read in British churches. It did not imply compulsion; for despite the aim of having one version, which King James stated at the Hampton Court conference,[3] other versions continued to be used.[4] In no sense does "authorized" denote divine authorization. Without dispute, the KJV was superior to both the Bishops' and the Geneva Bibles which it was designed to displace. It obtained its standing in English life because it was better.

Current KJV printings unfortunately do not print the preface which the translators prepared and in which they explain in part what their aims were. Recognizing that they were by no means the first translators, they commended the earlier work of the Septuagint translators, of Jerome, of those who translated into the European languages, and of their own English predecessors. "We are so farre off from condemning any of their labours that traueiled before us in this . . .," they said. But they also recognized that "nothing is begun and perfited at the same time." They saw their effort not that of trying to make a new translation, but out of the several good ones then existing to make one principal one to which exception could not be taken. They were an academic group composed of university professors, churchmen, and scholars of the Church of England, who made no claim to verbal inspiration for their finished work. They had not hesitated to consult whatever sources were available and had not hesitated to revise what they had previously done. While seeking "to deliver Gods booke vnto Gods people in a tongue which they vnderstand," they granted that perplexities remained about the meanings of some words. They aimed to translate so that Scripture could speak like itself and so that it could be understood by "the very vulgar" (the unlearned). Asking, "But how shall men meditate in that which they cannot vnderstand?" they said, "Indeede without translation into the vulgar tongue, the vnlearned are but like children at Iacobs well (which was deepe) without a bucket or some thing to draw with."

---

[2]E. Cardwell, ed., *Synodalia*, 2 vols. (Oxford: University Press, 1842), 1:123.

[3]The King's words were: ". . . and so this whole Church to be bound unto it, and none other." See William Barlow, *The Hampton Court Conference* (London: John Windet for Matthew Law, 1604), p. 46.

[4]D. Beaton, "Notes on the History of the Authorized Version of the Bible in Scotland," *The Princeton Theological Review* 9 (1911): 414-37.

The translators were aware that their translation would encounter strong opposition from Catholics and from non-conformists—that they themselves would be "tossed upon tongues." To the anticipated critics they said, "the very meanest translation of the Bible in English, set foorth by men of our profession ... containeth the word of God, nay, is the word of God."

They stated that the fear of weakening the authority of Scripture did not deter them from setting variant meanings in the margin. They said, "Doth not a margine do well to admonish the Reader to seeke further, and not to conclude or dogmatize vpon this or that peremptorily?" Unfortunately, these variant readings are often omitted in current printings of the KJV. The translators felt that "varietie of Translation is profitable for the finding out of the sense of the Scriptures." They recognized the necessity of some paraphrase. Uniformity in translation of phrases appeared to them "to sauour more of curiositie than of wisedome"; therefore, they used a variety in renderings which in current opinion creates confusion for the reader. They claimed to steer a middle course between the practices of the Puritans who abandoned the old ecclesiastical words and those of the Catholics who held to Latin phraseology.[5]

Which King James Version?

Few people seem conscious of the fact that a currently circulating King James Bible differs in significant details (though not in general content) from the one issued in 1611; they assume that the King James is a fixed phenomenon like "the faith which was once for all delivered unto the saints" (Jude 3; ASV). However, a current KJV differs from the 1611 edition in numerous details. According to modern standards, books produced in the seventeenth century were carelessly printed. The 1611 editions of the KJV had "Then cometh Judas" in Matthew 26:36, which should have been "Then cometh Jesus." The second edition by dittography repeated twenty words of Exodus 14:10.[6] The two editions of the KJV issued in 1611 differ from each other in several other respects.[7] Printers' errors in

[5]E. J. Goodspeed, ed., *The Translators to the Reader: Preface to the King James Version 1611* (Chicago: University of Chicago Press, 1935).

[6]Walter E. Smith, "The Great 'She' Bible," *The Library*, Ser. I, 2 (1890): 1-11, 96-102, 141-53.

[7]T.H. Darlow and H.F. Moule, *Historical Catalogue of Printed Editions of the English Bible, 1525-1961*, ed. A.S. Herbert (London: The British and Foreign Bible Society, 1968), Number 309.

various later printings created oddities like the "Wicked Bible" (which omitted "not" from the seventh of the ten comandments),[8] the "Unrighteous Bible" (in which the unrighteous inherit the Kingdom),[9] the "Vinegar Bible" (with its "Parable of the Vinegar"),[10] the "Ears to Ear Bible,"[11] and many others. Though quite humorous, these examples show that the printing of the Bible is a process subject to human error. The running together of "headstone" (Zech. 4:7) is a printer's error of 1611 which remains uncorrected. Another printing error continued in modern printings and defying explanation is "strain at a gnat" (Matt. 23:24) where the 1611 version correctly had "strain out a gnat."

But there have also been intentional changes since 1611. Some improvements were made as early as 1612;[12] in a 1613 edition another 413 changes were made.[13] In 1616 an edition improved the reading "approved to death" (I Cor. 4:9) to "appointed to death."[14] Omission of the Apocrypha, which had been printed between the Testaments in all English Bibles since Coverdale's, is one of the marked ways in which a current King James Bible differs from that of 1611. A 1629 edition was the first to omit the Apocrypha,[15] but the omission did not become general until the nineteenth century.

Additional revisions of the KJV were made in a Cambridge edition which appeared in 1629.[16] In 1638 an edition of the King James Bible prepared by Goad, Ward, Boyse, and Mead (two of whom had served on committees preparing the 1611 KJV) contained other revisions. The most controversial of these revisions was the reading "ye may appoint" for "we may appoint" in Acts 6:3, which some have thought to be a deliberate change under nonconformist influence.[17] William Kilburne, in 1659,[18]

[8]*Historical Catalogue*, Number 444.

[9]Ibid., Number 635.

[10]Ibid., Numbers 942, 943.

[11]Ibid., Number 1498.

[12]Ibid., Numbers 313, 314, 315, 316, 318.

[13]Ibid., Numbers 319-26.

[14]Ibid., Number 349; F. H. A. Scrivener, *The Authorized Edition of the English Bible (1611)* (Cambridge: University Press, 1910), p. 17.

[15]Scrivener, *The Authorized Edition*, p. 19, n.1.

[16]*Historical Catalogue*, Number 424.

[17]Ibid., Number 520.

[18]William Kilburne, *Dangerous Errors in Several Late Printed Bibles to the Great Scandal and Corruption of Sound and True Religion* (Finsbury: n.p., 1659).

claimed to find 20,000 errors that had crept into six different editions printed in the 1650s. New marginal references were introduced into printings in 1660, and still other changes came as Dr. Anthony Scattergood in 1683 added 7,250 references in an edition no longer extant.[19] In 1727 the King's printer at Edinburgh issued an edition in which several thousand errors in the marginal materials on the Old Testament were amended and corrected.[20]

In a quite revolutionary step, Bishop Lloyd, in an edition of 1701, inserted a biblical chronology—taken from Bishop Ussher—at the head of the reference column at the beginning of numerous Old Testament books.[21] Up to this point, in keeping with rule two of the King's instructions to the translators, the KJV had ordinarily been printed with references and marginal readings but without notes. Though Ussher's dates are no longer thought to be correct, they are still being printed. F. S. Paris and H. Therold in 1762 extended the use of italics, modernized the language, and added 360 marginal references.[22] Benjamin Blayney in 1769 did extensive revision, added 76 notes—including many on weights, measures, and coins[23]—and added 30,495 new marginal references.[24] At this time the spelling and punctuation were modernized.[25] "Hierusalem," "Marie," "assone," "foorth," "shalbe," "fet," "creeple," "fift," "sixt," "ioy," "middes," "charet," and the like were no longer used.[26] Blayney's edition became the standard edition until the publication of the Cambridge Paragraph Bible, edited by Scrivener in 1873.[27] The American Bible Society in the nineteenth century, after examining six editions of the KJV then circulating and finding 24,000 variants in the text and punctuation, claimed that "of the great number, there is not one which mars the integrity of the text or affects any doctrine or precept of the Bible"; but the Society did a revision

---

[19]*DNB* 17:896.

[20]*Historical Catalogue*, Number 987.

[21]Ibid., Numbers 867, 868.

[22]Ibid., Number 1142.

[23]Ibid., Number 1194; Scrivener, *The Authorized Edition*, pp. 28-34; and *The Gentleman's Magazine* 39 (1769): 517.

[24]A. C. Partridge, *English Biblical Translation* (London: André Deutsch, Ltd., 1973), p. 163.

[25]John Eadie, *The English Bible* (London: Macmillan, 1876), 2:303-7.

[26]Goodspeed, ed., *The Translators to the Reader*, p. 2.

[27]F. H. A. Scrivener, ed., *The Cambridge Paragraph Bible* (Cambridge: University Press, 1870-1873), 3 vols.

in 1860 which was later abandoned because of protests from its supporters.[28] A study of all these matters was made by F. H. A. Scrivener in *The Authorized Edition of the English Bible (1611)*.[29] Additional revision in punctuation, spelling, and running heads was done by the Bible Society in 1932. In 1962 it was decided to omit the short explanatory statements following certain epistles in the New Testament, to change some spelling, to omit hyphens in some words, and to omit some capitals.[30] Even after all these revision efforts, careful comparison of various current printings of the KJV will show that there are still minor variations in spelling. For example, the Oxford, Cambridge, and some Nelson printings have "an hungred" (Matt. 4:2); other Nelson and Zondervan printings have "an hungered"; and the American Bible Society printing has "ahungered." The marginal readings and chapter headings of the 1611 edition are often not printed in current printings.

The King James Bible, then, as a currently circulating book, becomes a phantom, a figment of an imagination clinging to the past. Which of all these revisions is to be considered the real King James? If we are to use only the KJV and read the other versions for comparison, which King James shall we use? If revision has been tolerated and even encouraged in the past, why should it be terminated now?

Is the King James Sacrosanct?

Admirable as the KJV was when it was launched, valuable as has been its contribution to the religious and literary life of the English-speaking public, and loved as it is by those who have studied it in detail from their childhood, time has done to the KJV what it does to all works of men. The message of the Bible should not be the peculiar possession either of scholars or of those initiated into and trained in the church; it should be open (as the King James scholars themselves said) "to the very vulgar," that is, to the uneducated and to children. However, the KJV is no longer completely intelligible to all readers. It is no longer the most accurate and the most readable English rendering of the Word of God. Who wishes to affirm that the KJV in all its aspects accurately represents what the in-

---

[28]Scrivener, *The Authorized Edition*, pp. 36-38; W. Canton, *The Bible and the Anglo-Saxon People* (London: J. M. Dent & Sons, Ltd., 1914), pp. 259-60.

[29]Scrivener, *The Authorized Edition*.

[30]*Historical Catalogue*, p. 399.

spired writers originally gave us? It is a sad commentary on the attitudes of those who claim to love the Bible that they, with oratory about its literary merits, are zealous to bind men to that which has demonstrated inaccuracies and is not completely intelligible in all its parts.

The Need for Revision

Though they recognized the merits of the KJV and praised them, Trench, Ellicott, Lightfoot, Plumptre, Schaff, Eadie, and others in the nineteenth century set forth the need for a revision of the English Bible as a preparation for and a justification for issuing the Revised Version.[31] It is dishonest to use their phrases of praise for the KJV to imply that there is no need for revision today. It is also less than honest to quote without qualification the praises of other men who lived before there was any viable option to the KJV.

That the English Revised Version (American Standard Version) did not displace the King James in popular use does not diminish the cogency of the revisers' arguments. Although their books are no longer in print or readily available, the revisers' arguments remain valid and unrefuted. Furthermore, the discovery of additional manuscripts, the rise of the study of biblical archaeology, the developments in comparative Semitics, the changes in the English language, and the other changes brought by the passage of another hundred years have, beyond dispute, made the need only more urgent.

The Text

The place to begin in considering the Bible's accuracy is its original text—the Hebrew and the Greek. When men first printed the Hebrew and Greek Testaments, rather than doing extensive textual criticism they printed from available (and almost contemporary) manuscripts. It is unfortunate in Bible transmission that the KJV was based on a late text rather than upon an early one.

To state that the text now available is superior to that of 1611 is to repeat a truism. Of the five primary uncial manuscripts now received as authority for the purity of the text of the New Testament, only Codex

---

[31]A list of works proposing revision prior to 1907 was published by J. I. Mombert, *The English Versions of the Bible* (London: Samuel Bagster and Sons, Ltd., 1907), p. 445.

Bezae was then available, and there is no evidence that it was used. Papyrus discoveries came three hundred years later. The King James scholars could have known fewer than twenty-five late manuscripts of the New Testament, and these were carelessly used. Today there are 5,358 known New Testament manuscripts and fragments.[32] The King James scholars had the text of Erasmus as it had been further revised in its third edition by Stephanus in 1551 (the first to have the text in separate verses) and the text issued by Beza in 1589 and in 1598. The 1611 situation for the Old Testament was even poorer. The Complutensian Polyglot (1517) and the Antwerp Polyglot (1572) would have been the sources from which they would have known the Old Testament. Where these two differ, the KJV agrees with one or the other except in about a half-dozen places where it agrees with neither. Modern discovery has supplied earlier Masoretic manuscripts dating to the tenth century in the Leningrad manuscript, the Aleppo Codex, and the British Museum manuscript (Or 4445). For portions of the Old Testament, discovery has supplied pre-Masoretic manuscripts dating to the second century B.C. in the Qumran scrolls. About 800 Hebrew manuscripts have now been studied.[33] The KJV scholars had only a single text for the Septuagint. Now there are many manuscripts, plus fragments of Aquila, Theodotion, and Symmachus. They had only the ordinary edition of the Latin, disfigured by corruptions. Now Codex Amiatinus (A.D. 541) presents Jerome's final work and mature judgment.[34]

The text followed by the KJV in II Kings 7:13 had an erroneous repetition of several words. The one followed in the New Testament included phrases that the best Greek manuscripts will not support. Critical texts drop the following sixteen whole verses to the footnotes: Matthew 17:21; 18:11; 23:14; Mark 7:16; 9:44, 46; 11:26; 15:28; Luke 17:36; 23:17; John 5:4; Acts 8:37; 15:34; 24:7; 28:29; and Romans 16:24. Additions of less than a whole verse include the words "openly" in "Your Father will reward you openly" (Matt. 6:4, 6, 18) and "without a cause" in "angry without a cause" (Matt. 5:22). The phrase "Him that liveth for ever and ever" (Rev.

---

[32]C. M. Martini, "Text, N.T.," in *IDB*, Supplementary volume, p. 884; Kurt Aland, "The Greek New Testament: Its Present and Future Editions," *Journal of Biblical Literature* 87 (June 1968): 184.

[33]H. M. Orlinsky, "The Hebrew Text and the Ancient Versions of the Old Testament," in *An Introduction to the Revised Standard Version of the Old Testament*, by Members of the Revision Committee (New York: Thomas Nelson and Sons, 1953), p. 26.

[34]T. W. Chambers, *A Companion to the Revised Old Testament* (New York: Funk and Wagnalls, 1885), p. 25.

5:14) has no known Greek manuscript support. Neither the phrase "of our Lord Jesus Christ" (Eph. 3:14) nor the phrase "who walk not after the flesh, but after the spirit" (Rom. 8:1) is in the better Greek text. In Luke 17:9 an answer, "I trow not," is supplied. In Matthew 6:13 "For thine is the kingdom, and the power, and the glory, for ever" is added. The words "and he trembling and astonished said, Lord, what wilt thou have me to do? And the Lord said unto him ..." (Acts 9:6) occur in no known Greek manuscript. It came into the *Textus Receptus* when Erasmus translated it from the Vulgate in 1516. The added "if" of II Corinthians 5:14 makes doubt of that which has no doubt for Paul. In Hebrews 11:13 "and were persuaded of them" is an addition. The word "not" (Rom. 4:19; Col. 2:18), missing in the better texts, makes in the KJV a negative of a positive statement. "We love him, because he first loved us" (I John 4:19) adds "him," and the addition changes the meaning of the statement. The so-called *Comma Johanneum* (I John 5:7), included in the third edition of the text by Erasmus on a wager, is now dropped from almost all texts without the courtesy of a footnote. No known Greek manuscript reads "book of life" in Revelation 22:19; the manuscripts have "tree of life." Colossians 1:14 carried the phrase "through his blood" which is not supported by the manuscripts. The 1611 text had a liturgical "amen" at the end of Matthew and had a postscript at the end of I Corinthians. Still other cases of scribal additions are found in Acts 9:5; Romans 7:6; 8:1; II Corinthians 1:6; Revelation 1:8, 11; 2:3, 20; 5:10; 15:3; 16:5; 17:16; 18:2; etc.

The opposite side of the problem is that the text followed by the KJV revisers had lost certain phrases which the discovery of earlier manuscripts has enabled scholars to restore to their rightful place. Matthew 24:36 had dropped "nor the son." Acts 4:25 had lost the words "by the Holy Spirit." Acts 16:7 had lost "the spirit of Jesus" and merely had "the Spirit." Romans 8:28 had lost "God" as the subject; hence the KJV has "And know that all things work together for good to them that love God." In I Peter 2:2 in the phrase "grow up into salvation," "unto salvation" was dropped. The phrase "and judge" in I John 2:23 was lost. Still other examples of dropped phrases are found in Genesis 4:8; 44:4-5; Judges 16:13; I Samuel 10:1; 14:41; John 19:3; I Thessalonians 4:1; I Peter 5:2; I John 3:1.[35]

There are cases of divergent readings where the KJV follows the poorer text. The phrase "which is broken for you" (I Cor. 11:24; dropped in ASV;

---

[35]Mombert, *The English Versions of the Bible*, p. 389.

RSV; etc.) creates tension with John 19:36 which affirms that the Lord's bones were not broken. Matthew 16:13 (cf. Mark 8:27 and Luke 9:18) has "I the Son of man am," making Jesus anticipate the answer to his question. The pronoun, not in the better manuscripts, is omitted in the ASV and later versions.[36] The KJV, except for the marginal citation of thirteen variants in the New Testament, did not indicate to the reader that textual problems existed; hence it does not indicate that there are textual disputes over such passages as Mark 16:9-20 and John 7:53—8:11.

Loyalty to the Text

A second area of concern in measuring the accuracy of a translation is that of its loyalty to the text from which it is translated. Though the KJV is rated good in overall accuracy, there are some matters to be considered. Though it is widely assumed by those who object to examples of paraphrase in twentieth-century translations that the KJV is literal and is free of paraphrase, the assumption is false. The structure and grammar of the Hebrew and Greek languages differ so markedly from that of English that an absolutely literal translation would not be intelligible to the English reader. In some cases the KJV does paraphrase, as all other translations do. An example of paraphrase can be seen where David's sons are said to be "rulers" (II Sam. 8:18), though the relevant term *Kohen* is otherwise rendered "priest" as is recognized in the ASV margin to this verse. Other cases of paraphrase include "God save the King" (I Sam. 10:24; II Sam. 16:16; I Kings 1:25; II Kings 11:12), a phrase very natural to the British; however, the text says, "Let the King live" (cf. I Kings 1:31). The phrases "God forbid" (I Sam. 14:45; etc.) and "would God" (Num. 11:29) add the word "God" to the text. "Give up the ghost" (Gen. 25:8; Jer. 15:9; etc.) paraphrases a verb which simply means "to expire." "Tithes after three years" (Amos 4:4) paraphrases a text that has "three days." "Every cow at that which is before her" (Amos 4:3) paraphrases an obscure sentence, but in doing so fails to give a clear meaning. In Psalm 8:5 *'elohim* is paraphrased "angels" in the interest of monotheism, but in Psalm 138 (137):1 *'elohim* is correctly rendered "gods." "They covenanted with him (Judas) for thirty pieces of silver" (Matt. 26:15) would more literally be "they paid him." They "cast the same in his teeth" (Matt. 27:44) is a paraphrase

---

[36]B. M. Metzger, *A Textual Commentary on the Greek New Testament* (London, New York: United Bible Societies, 1971), p. 42.

meaning they "reviled him." The phrase "exceeding fair" (Acts 7:20) in 1611 carried a literal marginal reading "fair to God." The repetitions of "Rabbi" (Matt. 23:7), "Master" (Mark 14:45), and "Lord" (Luke 13:25), though in the *Textus Receptus*, appear to be either paraphrases or ditto-graphies (that is, erroneous repetitions). It would be possible to accumulate many more examples of paraphrase.[37]

No translator would argue for a completely literal translation, but the degree of paraphrase permitted is always under dispute. Smith, in his concordance to the Greek New Testament, lists about 100 different Greek words and particles that are not rendered by any English word in the KJV in some of their occurrences. Some are untranslated more than once; hence the total number of instances is about 1,000.[38] No translation can corre-spond word-for-word to the language from which it has been translated; one need not suppose that the KJV is in error in each case where a Greek word has no corresponding word in the English translation. However, the paraphrase within the KJV should be remembered when one evaluates paraphrase in other versions.

In the matter of accuracy, we should also remember that there is a lengthy list of cases where it is agreed that the King's revisers missed the meaning of the text. They rendered Genesis 12:19 as "I might have taken her to me to wife" when the text really says "I took her." They used a mixed figure when having men take "a graving tool and make a molten image" (Exod. 32:4; KJV; ASV; RSV). They used "scapegoat" (Lev. 16:8, 10) where the Masoretic text has "for 'aza'zel" and "described" where the text has "wrote" (Judg. 8:14). The comparison between the former and latter temples (Hag. 2:9) would be better as a comparison between two stages of the latter temple—the former and latter stages. The elders are said to prophesy in the wilderness "and did not cease" (Num. 11:25; ASV: "did so no more"). The geographical orientation of the story of the spies is obscure. The spies are told to go "southward" from Kadesh to Palestine (Num. 13:17); however, the orientation is made clearer in verse 22 in the phrase "by the south." This obscurity is partly clarified by the ASV: "Get you up this way by the south," but is made even more clear by the RSV in the light of current terminology: "Go up into the Negeb." "The Son of

---

[37]The 1611 edition gave 112 literal renderings in the margin; see Scrivener, *The Authorized Edition*, p. 56.

[38]J. B. Smith, *Greek-English Concordance to the New Testament* (Scottsdale, Pennsylvania: Herald Press, 1955).

God" (Dan. 3:25) can only be taken by the reader as implying that Jesus was in the furnace, but Nebuchadnezzar says he saw an "angel" (Dan. 3:28); hence "a son of god" or "of the gods"—that is, an angelic being—must be understood. "My sore ran in the night" (Ps. 77:2) should be "my hand was stretched out." T. W. Chambers published an extended list of other inaccurate renderings in the Old Testament.[39]

Longer lists of incorrect renderings are available for the New Testament. Herod "observed him" (Mark 6:20) should be "preserved him." "Pineth away" (Mark 9:18) should be "becomes rigid." Luke 18:12 has "I give tithes of all that I possess," but the tithing law applies to increase only, and not to capital holdings; hence the passage should read "all I acquire." Instead of "bare what was put therein" (John 12:6), Judas "took away" what was put in it. To say "supper being ended" (John 13:2) conflicts with verses 12 and 26. The "Brook Cedron (Kidron)" should be the "Valley of the Kidron" (John 18:1). "Touch me not" (John 20:17) raises the perplexity of why Mary is prohibited from doing what the women elsewhere are permitted (Matt. 28:9), but the Greek present tense here used should be "Do not keep on holding me." Acts 2:6 reads, "Now when this was noised abroad," but the Greek noun involved never signifies a report or rumor; it refers to sound made—"And at this sound." "Slew and hanged on a tree" (Acts 5:30; 10:39) should be "slew by hanging on a tree" lest one think one act is successive to the other. "Have ye received the Holy Ghost since ye believed?" (Acts 19:2) ought to be "Did you receive the Holy Ghost when you believed?" "Baptized in" should be "baptized into" (Matt. 28:19; Acts 8:16; 19:5). In Acts 28:1 a "we" passage—one of the characteristics of the book—is rendered as "they." The rendering "for the remission" (Rom. 3:25) confuses the words *paresis* ("passing over") and *aphesis* ("remission"). "God be thanked, that ye were the servants of sin, but ye have obeyed" (Rom. 6:17) leaves the impression that Paul is thanking God that people were servants of sin. "For he hath made him *to be* sin for us, who knew no sin" (II Cor. 5:21) gives an idea of sinlessness on our part. "I knew a man" (II Cor. 12:2) should be "I know a man." "Corrupt the word of God" (II Cor. 2:17) should be "trade" or "peddle" the Word of God. The use of either "schoolmaster" (Gal. 3:24) or "instructor" (I Cor. 4:15) as renderings for *paidagōgus* is refuted by a papyrus letter which shows that *paidagōgus* was a male slave who had charge of the boy to take him to school.

[39]Chambers, *A Companion to the Revised Old Testament*, p. 982.

The added words "to bring us" of Galatians 3:24 turn the reader from the more likely interpretation "until Christ came" suggested by the context. "How large a letter" (Gal. 6:11) should be "how large letters"; that is, the size of the script, not the length of the letter, is spoken of. "The sabbath *days*" (Col. 2:16) should be "a sabbath." "Abstain from all appearance of evil" (I Thess. 5:22) should be "every form of evil." "For in many things we offend all" (James 3:2) should be "in many things we all offend." "Euodia" is taken as a masculine name, "Euodias," despite the feminine plural pronoun which in Greek follows the two names included in the context (Phil. 4:2). "Embraced" the promise (Heb. 11:13) is specifically what the patriarchs did not do. "Kings and priests" (Rev. 1:6) should be "a kingdom, priests," and "kingdoms" (Rev. 11:15) should be a singular — "kingdom."

Besides the above mentioned passages — the list of which could be greatly extended — there are also problems in the KJV with the policy concerning specific words. The word *doulos*, always softened to "servant," should be rendered "slave," for there is great difference in the social position of a servant and a slave; furthermore, there are other Greek words which mean "servant." There is no logical justification for the translators choosing a limited number of verses (such as those of I Cor. 13) and rendering *agapē* in these as "charity" (borrowed from the Latin Bible) when in all except 26 (all found after I Cor. 8:1) of its 312 occurrences *agapē* is rendered "love."

The accuracy of the KJV as a translation for current use has been affected by archaeological study which has clarified the meaning of some words that were unclear in 1611. The cities of Palestine stood on "their tells," not "in their strength" (KJV: Josh. 11:13). "Que" (I Kings 10:28) is a place in Cilicia where Solomon got his horses rather than being "linen yarn" (KJV). The symbol of the Canaanite goddess was an "asherah" and not a "grove" as it is uniformly rendered (I Kings 16:33; II Kings 13:6; etc.). "Pul" and "Tiglath-pilneser" (I Chron. 5:26) are names for the same Assyrian king; and the conjunction in the verse should be taken as explanatory, not as coordinate. Pharaoh Necho went "to aid" the king of Assyria, not "against" him (II Kings 23:29). It seemed normal in seventeenth-century England to translate "light a candle" (Matt. 5:15; Luke 15:8) and to set the candle on a "candlestick," but the oil lamp — not the candle — was the light source in ancient Palestine. Men "reclined" at the table rather than "sitting" at it, they used "wineskins" rather than "bottles," wore "sandals" rather than "shoes," and had ointment in "flasks" instead

47

of in "boxes." "All the world" (Luke 2:1) was the Roman world, not "the whole earth."

Communication

A third area of concern in the accuracy of translation is that of communication. The unskilled reader must be able to understand clearly what he is reading. In this area the KJV has definite shortcomings. Confusion is created by variety in the spellings of names of persons and places. Sometimes a Hebrew form is used, sometimes a Greek form, and sometimes a Latin form. Hence we have Sheth and Seth; Pua and Puah; Cis and Kish; Agar and Hagar; Jeremiah, Jeremias, and Jeremie; Enos and Enosh; Henoch and Enoch; Jered and Jared; Noe and Noah; Jonah, Jona, and Jonas; Jephthae and Jephthah; Balak and Balac; Sara and Sarah; Gidion and Gideon; Elijah and Elias; Kora and Core; Elisha and Eliseus; Hosea and Osee; Isaiah, Esaias, and Esay; Hezekiah and Ezekiah; Zechariah and Zecharias; Judas, Judah, Juda, and Jude; Zera, Zara, and Zarah; Marcus and Mark; Lucas and Luke; Timothy and Timotheus; and Jesus and Joshua — both for the Old Testament character (Acts 7:45 and Heb. 4:8). Variety in geographical names occurs in Tyrus and Tyre, Azza and Gaza, Sina and Sinai, Canaan and Chanaan, Midian and Madian, Sodom and Sodoma, Phoenicia and Phenice, Areopagus and Mars' Hill, Saron and Sharon, Raamses and Rameses, Jewry (Luke 23:5; John 7:1) and Judea, Kidron and Cedron. This lack of uniformity in names of persons and places only creates perplexities. Current versions of the Bible simplify the matter by adopting one form of a name throughout.

The coinage of the KJV is British where it is not merely transliterated from Hebrew. Pounds, pence, penny (the British coin), mites, shekels, shillings, and talents are as foreign to the American reader as though they were not translated or transliterated. On the other hand, certain coins may be referred to in vague terms when they are definite in Greek. Examples are "a piece of silver" (Luke 15:8) and "a piece of money" (Matt. 17:27). The true significance of weights and measures presents still another problem. Some are transliterated; but other measures, like "deal" (Num. 29:3; etc.), are even less known in America.

Uniformity of rendering has a significant bearing on communication. The KJV translators insisted that to render the same Hebrew or Greek word always by the same English equivalent would "sauour more of curiositie then wisedome." While none would contend that the policy is entirely wrong, it is universally agreed that by their variety the translators confuse the reader. The word "sign" is a stylistic feature of the Gospel of John necessary to understand the argument of the Gospel (2:11, 23; 6:26, 30; 20:30-31), but in the KJV "miracles" is used more often than "signs."[40] Consideration of the varied use of "comfort" and "consolation"; "creation" and "creature"; "apostleship" and "mission"; "teaching" and "doctrine"; "soul" and "life"; "blessed" and "happy"; "serve" and "worship"; "castaway" and "reprobate"; "righteous" and "just"; "reckon," "impute," and "account"; "covenant" and "testament"; "coming," "appearing," and "manifestation"; "dispensation" and "stewardship"; "sanctification" and "holiness" will make one conscious of the variety used.[41]

Other evidence of variety in rendering is seen in the fact that *dabhar* (a "word" or "thing") is rendered by eighty-four separate English words: *panim* ("face") by thirty-four, *sim* ("to set" or "place") by fifty-nine, *shubh* in the *hiph'il* ("to turn back") by sixty, *nasah* ("to lift up") by forty-six, *ᶜabhar* ("to pass over") by forty-eight, *rabh* ("much" or "many") by forty-four, and *tobh* ("good") by forty-one. Similar variety is seen in the New Testament, where *katargein* ("to make void") appears twenty-seven times and is rendered seventeen different ways; or where *logizesthai*, dealing with God's treatment of Abraham's faith, is "counted" (Rom. 4:3), "reckoned" (Rom. 4:9), or "imputed" (Rom. 4:22, 23) "for righteousness"—all in the same context.

The variety in rendering is more crucial in some instances than in others. In some cases distinctions are created where there is no difference. Genesis 2:7 has "living soul" for a term that is "living creature" in all other instances (Gen. 1:24; etc.), inviting the reader to conclude that something unique to man is being said. "Ye thought evil . . . God meant it unto good" renders one Hebrew word in two ways (Gen. 50:20). Matthew 25:46 (cf. Matt. 19:16; Mark 10:17) has "everlasting punishment" and "life eternal" for the rendering of the same adjective; Matthew 21:23 and 28:18 have "authority" and "power" for the same word. Numbers 35:11 has "slayer," verse 12 has "manslayer," and verse 16 has "murderer"—all for one word. In Romans 5:2, 3, 11 we read "rejoice," "glory," and "joy" for one word. James 2:2, 3 has "apparel," "raiment," and "clothing"; Matthew 20:20 has

[40]B. F. Westcott, *Some Lessons of the Revised Version of the New Testament* (London: Hodder and Stoughton, 1897), p. 37.

[41]R. B. Girdlestone, *Suggestions for Translators, Editors, and Revisers of the Bible* (London: Richards, 1877), p. 27.

49

"children" and "sons"; Matthew 18:33 has "compassion" and "pity"; and I Corinthians 12:4, 5 have "diversities" and "differences." In I Corinthians 13:8, 10 we have "fail," "vanish away," and "done away" for one word. In I Corinthians 16:1, 2 *logia* is rendered both as "collection" and as "gatherings" in one context. Other cases where the point of the passage is obscured by variety in translation are found in Acts 24:5, 14; Romans 10:15, 16; Hebrews 12:27, 28.[42] There are cases where verses of identical wording (Isa. 35:10 and 51:11) are cast in different moods—one musical and the other not. Other instances of differences are found with I Kings 22:28 and II Chronicles 18:27, and with I Peter 1:7 ("the appearing of Christ") and 1:13 ("the revelation of Christ"). There are instances where Old Testament verses are quoted in the New Testament in different wording though the verses are identical in Greek (e.g., Rom. 12:19 and Heb. 10:30; or Rom. 4:3; 4:22; and Gal. 3:6; or James 5:20 and I Peter 4:8).

The opposite situation also creates problems when distinctions that should be maintained are wiped out by the use of one English word to translate several Greek words. *Douloi* and *diakonoi* are both rendered "servants" in the parable of the wedding feast (Matt. 22:1ff.), obliterating the fact that they are two classes of beings, one men and the other angels. No distinction is made in the two sorts of baskets, *kophinos* and *spuris*, in the miracles of the four thousand and the five thousand (Matt. 16:9, 10; Mark 8:19, 20). "He came to his own and his own received him not" (John 1:11) should be something like "his own home . . . his own people." "Before Abraham was, I am" (John 8:58) is more properly rendered "Before Abraham was born, I am." *Pais theou* ("servant" or "son of God"; KJV: Matt. 12:18; Acts 3:13, 26; 4:27, 30) should consistently be "servant of God" in each case, perhaps reflecting Isa. 53:11; etc., and to be distinguished from *huios theou* ("Son of" or "Child of God"). Two different words are translated "children" (I Cor. 14:20) but should be "children" and "babes." A distinction between "repentance" and "regret" (II Cor. 7:10) is not made, though the Greek has two separate words. In II Corinthians 11:4 and Galatians 1:6 "another" which appears twice might be clarified by using "different" and "another." Two words, *morphē* and *schēma*, are rendered "form" (Phil. 2:6, 7) but should preferably be "form" and "fashion." In the Book of Revelation both *zōon* and *thērion* are rendered "beast," whereas the first (Rev. 4:8; 5:6, 8; 6:1; etc.) designates the creatures of heaven, and

---

[42]Ibid., p. 26.

the second, the beasts of earth (Rev. 6:8) and the monsters of the abyss (Rev. 11:7; 13:1; 17:8).[43]

In a translation the reader's understanding is affected by several aspects of its typographical makeup. The use of italics (a practice begun in the Geneva Bible) in the KJV was intended to alert the reader to textual uncertainties and to those phrases not in the original languages which had been supplied by the translator to complete the sense. The use of italics has to some degree been fluid from printing to printing of the KJV, but there are those cases where the italics have become a hindrance to understanding instead of a help. The fact that in current use italics signifies emphasis invites the reader to place an emphasis on that which is not in the original text at all. In I Kings 13:13 "saddled *him*" becomes an improper emphasis. In Psalm 19:3, "*where* their voice is not heard," the addition changes the meaning of the statement. In John 3:34 "*unto him*" improperly limits the sense. Perhaps the most striking case is "*unknown* tongue" of I Corinthians 14, which surely is partly responsible for the glossolalia movement. "This *man*" (Heb. 7:24) is in error, also.

The use of italics also involves another problem: the KJV made unnecessary additions without italicizing the added word. An example is "thine" in the phrase "thine alms" (Matt. 6:2). In the phrase, "But the rest of the dead lived not again *(ezēsan)* until the thousand years were finished" (Rev. 20:5), there is no reason to supply the word "again."

The verse divisions, and especially the practice of printing each verse as a separate paragraph (borrowed in the KJV from the Geneva Bible), broke the Bible into small units that encouraged memorizing of Scripture; but this printing practice is actually a misfortune, leading people to suppose that the Bible is composed of disconnected maxims. The verse division often interrupts the thought. For example, I Corinthians 13 is broken off from "a more excellent way" (I Cor. 12:31) by which it is introduced. The thought of harvest and workers begins at Matthew 9:36, and the selection of the twelve apostles of chapter ten is a continuation of that theme. It is not a separate section. The verse divisions contribute to prooftexting in Bible exegesis. A prominent case is seen in Colossians 2:21 where "Touch not, taste not" can be taken as a rule of life, when Paul was actually insisting that one should not submit to such rules. While printing

[43]Other examples of this problem are collected by R. C. Trench, *On the Authorized Version of the New Testament* (London: John Parker and Son, 1859), pp. 102-12; and by J. B. Lightfoot, *On a Fresh Revision of the English New Testament,* 2nd ed. (London: Macmillan, 1872), pp. 60-80.

each verse as a separate paragraph, the KJV also attempted to indicate beginnings of sense paragraphs; however, for an unexplained reason its paragraph indicators stop at Acts 21. Yet another printing handicap is the fact that the KJV is printed as prose throughout, making no clear distinction between the prose and poetry in the Bible. The nature of Hebrew poetry had not been discovered in 1611.

Another matter which creates confusion for the reader of the KJV as it is printed today is the chapter summary printed at the beginning of the chapters. While not a part of the original text from the manuscripts, most of these summaries go back to the 1611 edition; Scrivener found only twelve variations from the original ones in the printings of his day. While many of the summaries are factual and unobjectionable, others suggest an interpretation that is of doubtful veracity, if not positively misleading.

In particular, a group of headings expounds the christological interpretation of the Old Testament. For example, every chapter of the Song of Solomon is interpreted as descriptive of the church. Seventeen of the Psalms in the Book of Psalms are so interpreted. The heading to Psalm 93 reads, "The Majesty, Power, and Holiness of Christ's Kingdom." Thirty chapters of Isaiah have christological headings. The fortieth chapter, "Comfort ye, comfort ye, my people," is headed "The promulgation of the Gospel"; verse 3, "the voice of him that crieth," is headed "The preaching of John the Baptist"; and verse 9, "O Zion, that bringest good tidings," is headed "The preaching of the Apostles." Isaiah 60, "Arise, shine; for thy light is come," is headed "The glory of the Church in the abundant success of the Gentiles"; Psalm 72, "Give the king thy judgments, O God," is headed "David, praying for Solomon, sheweth the goodness and glory of his kingdom in type, and of Christ's in truth." Then there is that heading which anyone is challenged to defend—Isaiah 22, "He prophesieth Shebna's deprivation, and Eliakim, prefiguring the Kingdom of Christ, his substitution." Still other examples of the christological interpretation are to be seen in the headings used in Jeremiah, Ezekiel, and in many of the Minor Prophets. These headings are objectionable; the mind of the reader should not be prejudiced toward the christological interpretation they expound.

Other headings might raise an eyebrow. Nimrod is called "the first monarch" (Gen. 10), Abraham entertains three "angels" when the text says three "men" (Gen. 18), and Daniel 11 is said to deal with the "tyranny of the Romans."

The book headings, "The Gospel According to St. Matthew," "St. Mark," etc., used in the Gospels have no basis in Greek. The Greek merely has "According to Matthew," "According to Mark," etc. "The Revelation of St. John the Divine" adds both "Saint" and "Divine" to that title. The first edition KJV has "Saint" in only five New Testament titles, but its use reflects and perpetuates the Catholic doctrine of sainthood. The Epistle to the Hebrews is declared to be "The Epistle of Paul the Apostle" when the Greek has only "To the Hebrews." Furthermore, the title "General," used of the Epistles of James, Peter, John, and Jude, is of late date and certainly is not suitable for III John, which is a letter to an individual. The subscripts at the end of New Testament books which state the place of writing, the amanuensis, and the messenger are late and not entirely reliable.

It has already been pointed out that the marginal references have been greatly modified since 1611, but one could hardly defend that now carried at Revelation 13:14. The passage speaks of deceitful "miracles," but the reference is to II Kings 20:7 which records the fact that the prophet laid figs on the boil, and Hezekiah recovered.

Finally, the practice of printing Ussher's chronology at the top of the reference column, begun in 1701, cannot be blamed upon the translators. Yet it is one of the most obvious causes for the acute tension between many Bible students and the claims of geology, since the student assumes that these figures accurately represent the teaching of the Bible on the age of the earth. No informed student today would champion the accuracy of Ussher's chronology. The Bible does not claim to inform us how old the earth is.

Understandest Thou What Thou Readest?

While a major portion of the KJV is understandable to any person who reads English, because of the choice of words and/or the change of the English speech since 1611, some sentences in the King James will not be understood without the help of a commentary. Champions of the use of the KJV forget that they have been conditioned to its oddities by a lifetime of study. The new reader and the uneducated reader have not had that conditioning. The following are examples of expressions which require explanation to be made clear:

And Jacob sod pottage; and Esau came from the field, and he was faint (Gen. 25:29).

And Mt. Sinai was altogether on a smoke (Exod. 19:18).

And all to brake his skull (Judg. 9:53).

For who can eat, or who else can hasten *hereunto*, more than I? (Eccles. 2:25).

Thou shalt destroy them that speak leasing (Ps. 5:6).

Nevertheless even him [Solomon] did outlandish women cause to sin (Neh. 13:26).

Solomon loved many strange women (I Kings 11:1).[44]

Dead *things* are formed from under the waters, and the inhabitants thereof (Job 26:5).

The noise thereof sheweth concerning it, the cattle also concerning the vapour (Job 36:33).[45]

Woe to them that ... stay on horses (Isa. 31:1; cf. 10:20; 30:12; 50:10).

The ships of Tarshish did sing of thee in thy market (Ezek. 27:25).

I trow not (Luke 17:9).

He purgeth it, that it may bring forth more fruit (John 15:2).

We do you to wit of the grace of God (II Cor. 8:1).

I know nothing by myself; yet am I not hereby justified (I Cor. 4:4).

Ye are not straitened in us, but ye are straitened in your own bowels (II Cor. 6:12).[46]

Not to boast in another man's line of things made ready to our hand (II Cor. 10:16).

The words of the wise *are* as goads, and as nails fastened *by* the masters of assemblies, *which* are given from one shepherd (Eccles. 12:11).

For some with conscience of the idol unto this hour eat *it* as a thing offered unto an idol (I Cor. 8:7).[47]

---

[44]One may compare to this usage the phrases "the names of those who married strange wives" (Ezra 10:18, 44; Neh. 13:23, 27) and "strange children" (Hos. 5:7).

[45]This verse has no clear meaning at all.

[46]There are thirty-seven uses of "bowels"; nineteen refer to the internal organs and the rest imply, often metaphorically, one or another of the emotions.

[47]Does an idol have a conscience?

54

Not only are there difficult sentences, but there are words used in the KJV which have passed completely out of use, so that they convey no meaning to the modern reader:

almug, algum, chode, charashim, chapt, earing, gat, habergeon, hosen, kab, knob, ligure, leasing, maranatha, nard, neesed, pate, pilled, rabboni, raca, ring-straked, stacte, strake, sycamyne, thyme wood, trode, wimples, ouches, tatches, brigandine, ambassage, occurrent, purtenance, bruit, fray, cracknels, nusings, mufflers, anathema, corban, talitha cumi, ephrata, aceldama, centurion, quaternion, delectable, sanctum sanctorum, carriage, let, pityful (for full of pity), wot, trow, sod, and swaddling clothes.[48]

Do most people recognize "ouches of gold" (Exod. 28:11), meteyard" (Lev. 19:35), "rereward" (Josh. 6:9, 13), "collops of fat" (Job 15:27), "mallows" (Job 30:4), and "wist" (Josh. 8:14)? "Wimples" (Isa. 3:22) were "shawls." But what about "nitre" (Jer. 2:22), "lien with" (Jer. 3:2), "sottish" (Jer. 4:22), "rentest thy face" (Jer. 4:30), "noise of the bruit" (Jer. 10:22), "skirts discovered" (Jer. 13:22), "the ground is chapt" (Jer. 14:4), "a brasen wall" (Jer. 15:20), "naughty figs" (Jer. 24:2), "subscribe evidences" (Jer. 32:44), "cast clouts" (Jer. 38:12), "hole's mouth" (Jer. 48:28), "dwell deep" (Jer. 49:8), and "they shall dote" (Jer. 50:36)? One encounters "Woe worth the day" (Ezek. 30:2), "sith" (Ezek. 35:6), and "tabering" (Nah. 2:7). He must be reminded that "vain jangling" (I Tim. 1:6) is "vain talking." Surely anyone can remember being perplexed as a child about the plague called "murrain of the cattle" (Exod. 9:3) which could simply have been called "death of the cattle."

More subtle, however, is the problem created by those words that are still in use but which now have a different meaning from what they had in 1611. These are hidden rocks on which the ship of understanding runs aground. What child would know without aid that the "mean *man*" (Prov. 22:29; Isa. 2:9; 5:15; 31:8) meant "common man"; now it means "cruel man." Then "meat" meant "food," but now it means "flesh"—a meaning it never has in the KJV. The "meat offering" was a cereal grain offering (Lev. 14:10). "Flesh" is used in the KJV where "meat" is intended (I Cor. 15:39), but "flesh" in the KJV also means "human nature" in other contexts. "Peculiar" (Ps. 135:4; Titus 2:14; I Peter 2:9) meant that which

[48]Partridge, *English Biblical Translation*, p. 211; James Edmonds and T. S. Bell, *Discussion on Revision of the Holy Oracles* (Louisville, Kentucky: Morton & Griswold, 1856), p. 148.

belongs to one person; now it means "strange." "To ear his ground" (I Sam. 8:12) then meant "to till it" (cf. Gen. 45:6; Exod. 34:21; Deut. 21:4). Did Goliath really carry a "target" of brass between his shoulders (I Sam. 17:6), or was it a "javelin"? Did David make a "road today" (I Sam. 27:10)—as though he were a civil engineer? Would we not say that he made a "raid"? "Cherish" (I Kings 1:2, 4) merely meant "to keep warm." "Passengers" is used to mean "passers by" (Prov. 9:15; Ezek. 39:11, 14, 15).

Trench pointed out that "its," the neuter possessive pronoun, is rarely used by Shakespeare and that it was not in common use in 1611.[49] The result is that "its" did not occur in the version of 1611 and is in the modern KJV only at Leviticus 25:5 where the 1611 printing had "it." "His" in the KJV is not used as we would use it today. That each produces after "his" kind (Gen. 1:11) should be "its kind." That "God giveth it a body ... and to every seed his own body" (I Cor. 15:38) means "its own body," and not that God gives the seed "His own body." Exodus 35:11 has "The tabernacle, his tent and his covering, his taches, his boards, his bars, his pillars, and his sockets." Each of these should be "its." Other cases of the strange use of "his" are in Leviticus 1:6; II Samuel 6:17; Daniel 4:14; 7:9; Matthew 5:13; 24:32; 26:52.

"Prevent" now means "hinder," but in the KJV it means "come before." Examples are seen in: "In the morning shall my prayer prevent thee" (Ps. 88:13), "I prevented the dawning of the morning" (Ps. 119:147, 148), and "The evil shall not overtake nor prevent us" (Amos 9:10). "Prevent" occurs fifteen times (II Sam. 22:6, 19; Job 3:12; 41:11; Pss. 18:5; 21:3; 59:10; 79:8; 88:13; Isa. 21:14; Amos 9:10; Matt. 17:25; I Thess. 4:15).

"Let" in certain cases in the KJV means "prevent," which is exactly the opposite of its present meaning. "But was let hitherto" (Rom. 1:13) and "he who now letteth *will let*" (II Thess. 2:7; cf. Exod. 5:4; Isa. 43:13) are examples. "Wealth" means "welfare": "Let no man seek his own, but every man another's *wealth*" (I Cor. 10:24; cf. Ezra 9:12; Esther 10:3). "Wealthy" means "happy" rather than "rich" (Ps. 66:12; Jer. 49:31). "Forward" now means "self-assertive" but then meant "ready" or "willing" (II Cor. 8:8, 10, 17; 9:2; Gal. 2:10). "Wound him up" (Acts 5:6) should be "wrapped him up." Was not the sheet Peter saw "let down" by the four corners (Acts 10:11) rather than "knit" at them?

[49]R. C. Trench, *On the Authorized Version of the New Testament* (New York: Redfield, 1858), p. 41; Stella Brook, *The Language of the Book of Common Prayer* (London: André Deutsch, 1965), pp. 108-9.

"Conversation" is now "talk," but in 1611 it meant behavior in general (Gal. 1:13; Eph. 2:3; 4:22; I Tim. 4:12; James 3:13; I Peter 3:1; II Peter 2:7) or living with others (Phil. 3:20). "The husband may be won by the conversation of the wife," that is, by her behavior, not by her talk. "Filthy conversation" (II Peter 2:7) meant "immoral conduct." "Advertise" meant "advise" (Num. 24:14; Ruth 4:4). "Apparently" (Num. 12:8) meant "clearly." "Evidently" (Acts 10:3), rather than suggesting uncertainty, meant "clearly." "Comprehended" meant "overcome" (John 1:5). "Shamefacedness" (I Tim. 2:9), a printer's correction, should be "shamefastness," as it was in the 1611 edition; but even that word is not now current. "Modesty" could clarify the meaning.

"Carriage" was then that which was carried, and nowhere in the Bible is it a vehicle (I Sam. 17:22; Judg. 18:21; Isa. 10:28; 46:1; Acts 21:15; the Geneva Bible had in this last verse, "trussed up our fardeles"). "Fetching a compass" means "making a circuit" (Num. 34:5; Josh. 15:3; II Sam. 5:23; II Kings 3:9; Acts 28:13). The compass was brought from China about A.D. 1260 and was not available in Bible times at all. "Debate" now means "discussion," but is used in the KJV of violent actions and is condemned (Isa. 58:4; Rom. 1:29; II Cor. 12:20). "Carefulness" (I Cor. 7:32; Luke 10:41) and "Be careful" in "Be careful for nothing" (Phil. 4:6) meant "worry." "Take no thought" meant "do not be anxious" (Matt. 6:34; 10:19). "Pitiful" meant "full of pity," but to us it means arousing or deserving pity (Lam. 4:10; James 5:11; I Peter 3:8).

"Virtue" was a broad word in 1611 that could include healing power (Luke 8:46; Mark 5:30; Luke 6:19), but elsewhere the word is probably narrower in meaning. Today it is most often used in connection with sex morals. "Who can find a virtuous woman?" (Prov. 31:10) is not primarily asking about her sex behavior. "Communicate" meant to "share" (Heb. 13:16). "Evil communications corrupt good manners" (I Cor. 15:33) refers to the whole group of influences. "Feeble minded" meant "faint hearted" I Thess. 5:14—not those of low intelligence. "Unspeakable gift" (II Cor. 9:15) meant "inexpressible gift" not "contemptible gift." "Room" now means a part of a house; it then meant a "place" where one sat (Matt. 23:6; Mark 12:39; Luke 14:7-9; 20:46). "Chief *estates*" (Mark 6:21) meant the leading men, not land holdings. "Liking" meant "appearance": "For why should he see your faces worse liking than the children which are of your sort?" (Dan. 1:10).

"Nephew" was then a word for grandchildren and other lineal descendants (Judg. 12:14; I Tim. 5:4); now it is a brother's or a sister's son. "Quick" now means "rapid," but in nine cases it then meant "alive" (Num. 16:30; Ps. 119:25; John 5:21; Heb. 4:12; I Peter 3:18; 4:5). It is not used once in the KJV in its present meaning. What child would know that "Then they had swallowed us up quick, when their wrath was kindled against us" (Ps. 124:3) has nothing to do with speed but only means "they would have swallowed us up alive"? To us "coast" means the border of the sea, but then meant "district": "Coasts of Bethlehem" (Matt. 2:16), "Coast of Og" (Josh. 12:4), and "Coasts of Caesarea Philippi" (Matt. 16:13). "Artillery" meant "small armor" (I Sam. 20:40); "charger" was a large dish (Num. 7:13; Matt. 14:8), not a horse. "Usury" was interest of all sorts (Matt. 25:27), not just excessive interest.

"Sometimes" in the KJV meant "formerly" and never "occasionally" (Eph. 2:13, 5:8; Titus 3:3). "By and by" meant "at once" (Matt. 13:21; Mark 6:25; Luke 17:7; 21:9). "Presently" meant "at once" (I Sam. 2:16; Prov. 12:16; Matt. 21:19; 26:53), and "instantly" meant "earnestly" (Luke 7:4; Acts 26:7)—an adverb of manner and not of time. "Anon" meant "immediately," not "after a time" (Mark 1:30); that is, they immediately tell Jesus that Peter's mother-in-law is sick. "There should be time no longer" (Rev. 10:6) means "there shall no longer be delay."

"Suffer" meant "to permit" (Gen. 20:6; Matt. 19:14; 23:13; Mark 11:16; Luke 4:41; I Cor. 10:13; I Tim. 2:12). The misconception arising from this word has been reflected in "Suffer the Little Children," a caption used recently in magazines and on television to refer to the suffering of children in war zones. "Purchase a good degree" in the KJV means "gain a good standing" (I Tim. 3:13). Outside of religious circles, "ghost" now carries an entirely different idea from that intended by *pneuma*, "spirit."[50]

The KJV uses expressions which are strange to the modern reader but are not necessarily misunderstood by him. The ox "pushes" where we would say "gores" (Exod. 21:29, 32, 36; Deut. 33:17; I Kings 22:11; II Chron. 18:10). Judged by current usage, the KJV has slips of grammar. "Which" rather than "who" is used for persons (Acts 22:3).[51] Singular and plural elements are mixed (Phil. 2:5). "Unseemly," an adjective, is used as an

[50]The type of material which has been included in this section has been collected by Ronald Bridges and Luther A. Weigle, *The Bible Word Book* (New York: Thomas Nelson & Sons, 1960).

[51]Other examples are collected by Trench, *On the Authorized Version of the New Testament*, pp. 46-47.

adverb (I Cor. 13:5). "Let each esteem the other better than themselves" (Phil. 2:3) should be "himself." "If any man have ears" (Mark 7:16) should be "has ears."

"Cherubim" and other words of Hebrew origin ending in "im" are already plural in form; but we have "cherubims" (Heb. 9:5), "seraphims," "nethinims," and "Anakims." The pleonasm such as "And Abel, he" (Gen. 4:4, 26) is used. There is inverted syntax: "and there was taken up of fragments that remained to them twelve baskets" (Luke 9:17). Word order is reversed: "Cakes unleavened . . . and wafers unleavened" (Exod. 29:2). Awkward sentences are encountered: "For thou knowest that there is not among us any that can skill to hew timber like unto the Sidonians" (I Kings 5:6; cf. II Chron. 2:7-8; 34:12). Other examples are: "I told you before, and foretell you, as if I were present, the second time; and being absent now I write to them which heretofore have sinned, and to all other, that, if I come again, I will not spare" (II Cor. 13:2); "Take *that* thine is" (Matt. 20:14); and "I am verily a man *which am* a Jew" (Acts 22:3). "Moses . . . gat him up into the mount" (Exod. 24:18) and "David gat *him* a name" (II Sam. 8:13) are awkward constructions. There are many cases of the superfluous use of "did" for the past tense in phrases like "did eat" (Matt. 14:20). There are double superlatives like "the most straitest sect" (Acts 26:5). The added "ye" to designate a plural subject creates an emphasis not intended — "Go ye"; "know ye."

The punctuation needs improvement. The KJV created five titles in Isaiah 9:6 which were popularized in Handel's *Messiah* but the Hebrew really has only four pairs; the comma in the KJV between "wonderful" and "counselor" should be deleted. Even such a small detail as capitalization influences interpretation. "Sun of righteousness" (Mal. 4:2) will naturally be taken erroneously by the reader to be messianic in import. "Spirit," when capitalized, can be understood only as the Holy Spirit, but *ruach* and *pneuma* in some cases may be "wind" (Gen. 8:1; John 3:8) and in others the human "spirit."

The reader of the KJV has to deal with "thees" and "thous" and their corresponding old English verbal endings *th* and *est* in words such as "sayeth," "doeth," "heareth," and "goest." He encounters strange spellings like "minish" (Exod. 5:19), "astonied," and "throughly." He sees "discovered" (Ps. 29:9; Prov. 25:9) for "uncovered." He finds "clift" (Exod. 33:22; Isa. 57:5) for "cleft," "champaign" (Deut. 11:30) for "campaign," "pranse" (Judg. 5:22; Nah. 3:2) for "prance," "glistering" for "glittering" (I Chron.

29:2; Luke 9:29), and "specially" for "especially." He reads "dureth" (Matt. 13:21) for "endureth," "intreat" for "entreat," "ware" (Acts 14:6) or "beware" (II Tim. 4:15) for "aware," "adventure" (Acts 19:31) for "venture," "hoised" (Acts 27:40) for "hoisted," "musick" (Dan. 3:5; Amos 6:5), "vail" (Ruth 3:15; II Cor. 3:13), "holpen" (Luke 1:54), and "bewrayeth" (Matt. 26:73). He also finds "graff" (Rom. 11:23) for "graft," "ensue" (I Peter 3:11) for "pursue," and "stablish" for "establish" (I Peter 5:10). Herod "observed" John (Mark 6:20); the word should be "preserved." These spellings make the KJV seem to speak in malapropisms.

The reader of the KJV comes across Semitisms that should have been converted into English phrases; for example, "she called his name Joseph" should be "she named him Joseph." "Die the death" (Matt. 15:4) should be "surely die," "son of peace" should be "peaceable man," and "man of sin" should be "sinful man." There are genitives which in Hebrew are used for the superlative degree: "Song of Songs," "king of kings," "Lord of Lords," and others.[52] Though many of these Semitisms, under the influence of the KJV, have been naturalized into English religious usage, they are still Semitisms and would be clearer if they were rendered into idioms native to English.

Confusion is created by the wrong use of prepositions. "Friends of the mammon of unrighteousness" (Luke 16:9) should be "by the mammon." "I know nothing by myself" should be "against myself" (I Cor. 4:4). "Nothing worthy of death is done unto him" (Luke 23:15) should be "by him." "Took to wife" should be "as wife" (Exod. 2:1), and "Abraham to our father" should be "as our father" (Matt. 3:9).

The KJV is deficient in its use and omission of the definite article. "The man," "a man," and "man" are all different ideas in current English, but the use of the article in Hebrew and Greek (neither of which has an indefinite article) differs from that of English, and Latin has no definite article at all. The King James scholars were unduly influenced by their knowledge of Latin and seem to have had no fixed rule about whether to insert or omit the article. The erroneous insertion of the definite article is encountered in "the Son of God" (Dan. 3:25), "the woman" (John 4:27), "the sin" (Heb. 12:1ff.), and "the everlasting gospel" (Rev. 14:6). "The love of money is the root of all evil" (I Tim. 6:10) should be "a root." "The unknown god" (Acts 17:23) should be "an unknown god." "The hope of

---

[52]Eadie, *The English Bible,* 2:228.

the promise" (Acts 26:6) is "hope of the promise," "the Gentiles" (Rom. 2:14) is "Gentiles," "the temple of God" (I Cor. 3:16) is "a temple," "the members of Christ" (I Cor. 6:15) are "members of Christ," and "the Son of man" (Rev. 1:13; 14:14) is "a Son of man." The opposite situation occurs when the definite article has been omitted in error. For an example, see the contrast between "the one" and "the many" in Romans 5:12, 15, 17. Matthew 2:4 should have "the Christ," and Hebrews 11:10 should have "the city." "Great tribulation" (Rev. 7:14) is "the great tribulation" in Greek. Erroneous insertion of the indefinite article gives us "God *is* a spirit" (John 4:24) where there should be "God is spirit."

Because of the policy followed in rendering terms for the bodily functions, there are sections in the KJV that are embarrassing for public or family reading (I Sam. 25:22, 34; I Kings 14:10; II Kings 9:8; 18:27; Isa. 36:12).

Reflecting on all these tedious examples (and more could be cited in each category),[53] we are confronted with four simple questions: Do we understand what we read because we are familiar with the wording, or because someone told us the words should mean something different from what they say? Are we acting in obedience to what the words say or what they mean? Would it not be simpler and better to have a translation which would at the first reading, without comment, suggest the meaning the writer intended? Is it not time to do what the King James scholars said they were attempting to do: "To deliver God's book unto God's people in a tongue they understand"?

But Is This Doctrine?

The theological issues of one generation are not those of another, and the issues felt in one religious community are not those felt in another. Consequently, some may object to a rendering passed over in silence by others. To take a Bible version, check it by a limited number of shibboleths, and then declare that it is free of doctrinal problems is to act arbitrarily. "Doctrine" means "teaching," and any failure to present the Word of God accurately, completely, and clearly in a translation is a doctrinal problem. The matters that we have surveyed in this chapter all affect the

---

[53]See the lists in Philip Schaff, Introduction, *The Revision of the English Version of the New Testament* (New York: Harper and Brothers, 1873), pp. xxiv-xliv.

61

teaching the reader is to receive from his Bible. It is naive to declare that they have no doctrinal significance. It would be miraculous if the early seventeenth-century struggle between Catholics and Anglicans, the Prelate party and the Puritans, and the Calvinists and non-Calvinists did not influence the way scholars at that time chose between options.

Throughout its entire history, the KJV has been charged with reflecting doctrinal bias; and there have also been replies by its defenders. Quite early, some insisted that the translators favored the king's notions of predestination, election, perseverance, witch-craft, and familiar spirits. Robert Gell insisted that both the views of Calvinism and those of the Prelate party in England were reflected in the translation.[54] John Lewis,[55] however, while not denying that these teachings were in the translation, felt that in some instances the views of the translators and those of the king may have been identical. Attention has been focused on certain renderings as leaning toward Calvinism. These include the phrases "such as should be saved" (Acts 2:47), "ye cannot do the things that ye would" (Gal. 5:17), and "If they shall fall away" (Heb. 6:6). The last phrase is continued from Tyndale and is thought to lend encouragement to the doctrine of the perseverance of the saints. In Greek it is not a contingent statement and should be rendered "and have fallen away." Perseverance is also thought to be supported by the insertion of "any man" in Hebrews 10:38. In 1611, Romans 5:12 carried a marginal reading *"in whom* all have sinned" which is clearly reflective of the doctrine of original sin. Some have seen the influence of belief in predestination in Matthew 19:23, "a rich man shall hardly enter into the kingdom of heaven." Others have felt that "be converted" (in seven passages for *metanoein* and *strephein*; Matt. 18:3; Acts 3:19; etc.) can be interpreted to say that man is passive in conversion. "Repent" or "turn" would have removed the problem. However, to be completely fair to the translators, one should observe that these are isolated verses and that in many other passages which could have been crucial to these same doctrines no such leanings can be detected.

Undue Prelate influence has been seen in the phrase "robbers of churches" (Acts 19:37) said to have been inserted under the influence of Bancroft;[56]

---

[54]Robert Gell, *An Essay Toward the Amendment of the Last English Translation of the Bible* (London: R. Norton for Andrew Crook, 1659), Preface and pp. 607, 750.

[55]John Lewis, *A Complete History of the Several Translations of the Holy Bible and New Testament into English* (London: Baynes, 1818), p. 330.

[56]W. J. Heaton, *The Puritan Bible* (London: Francis Griffiths, 1913), p. 321.

but Lightfoot demonstrated that in seventeenth-century English "church" was used for pagan and Jewish temples as well as for Christian church buildings.[57] It has been thought that the varied use of "bishoprick" (Acts 1:20), "overseers" (Acts 20:28), "oversight" (I Peter 5:2), and "bishop" (I Tim. 3:1) was an effort to avoid identification of bishops and elders. That "presbyter" occurs only once was believed due to translator Bilson's readiness to squelch Presbyterian nonsense.[58] How are we to explain that out of thirty occurrences of *diakonos* in the New Testament, only those that clearly refer to church organization (Phil. 1:1; I Tim. 3:8, 10, 12, 13) are rendered "deacon"? Whether to use "congregation" or "church" had been an issue, and the translators used "congregation" only once (Acts 13:43), and that time for the assembly of a Jewish synagogue. The translators, in their "Preface to the Reader," confess that there is a polemic interest in retaining certain ecclesiastical words like "baptism" and "church"; but one should then ask if there are not also other words retained for theological motives.

Though it is not possible to settle the question of the motivation of the translators, one can evaluate doctrinal problems raised by their product. How often is the question raised, Was God tired when Scripture says he "rested" on the seventh day (Gen. 2:2)? The original word only meant cessation of activity. To name mythical animals — the unicorn (Deut. 33:17; Ps. 22:21; Isa. 34:7; etc.),[59] the satyr (Isa. 13:21; 34:14), the dragon (Deut. 32:33; Job 30:29; Ps. 44:19; etc.), and the cockatrice (Isa. 11:8; 14:29; 59:5; Jer. 8:17) — did not bother men in 1611. They probably thought the creatures existed. They did encounter trouble in Deuteronomy 33:17 where the unicorn has horns, but the translators solved the problem by reading "unicorns." The arrowsnake (Gen. 49:11, margin) is also a creature unknown to zoology. In a more enlightened day these renderings have a bearing on what the English Bible is teaching.

Even when translators are not consciously selecting words that reflect their religious bias, the words they select do influence the reader's thinking. A different wording would create a different pattern of thought. There would have been less persecution of strange women (as in Salem, Massachusetts) had the translation used "sorceress" instead of "witches" (Exod. 22:18; Deut. 18:10), less emphasis on the need of being different and of

[57]Trench, *On the Authorized Version of the New Testament*, pp. 27-28.
[58]G. S. Paine, *The Learned Men* (New York: Thomas Y. Crowell, Co., 1959), p. 97.
[59]Ibid., p. 61.

dressing strangely had the people read "God's own people" instead of "peculiar people" (Titus 2:14; cf. Exod. 19:5; Deut. 14:2; 26:18; Ps. 135:4; Eccles. 2:8; I Peter 2:9), and less sport by unbelievers over the inaccuracy of the Bible had they read "fish" instead of "whale" (Matt. 12:40). Although "the voice of the turtle" (Song of Sol. 2:12) has stimulated several efforts to prove that this creature makes sounds, that passage is speaking of a "turtledove" and not of a reptile.

The KJV properly renders *qebher* as "the grave" thirty-four times, but also, without justification, translates *Sheol* as "the grave" thirty-one times and as "hell" thirty-one times. In all ten uses of *Hades*, it is translated "hell." The distinction between the intermediate state of the dead in "Sheol" or "Hades" and the final state of the wicked in *gehenna*, "hell," (used eleven times) was introduced into English religious language through the RV(ASV). These changes have doctrinal implications. The reader of the KJV has no knowledge of what "Hades" really is unless he knows Greek or is acquainted with later English versions. He thinks of the final place of punishment when he reads "hell" (Matt. 11:23; 16:18; Luke 10:15; 16:23; Acts 2:27; Rev. 1:18; 6:8; 20:13, 14) when he should think of the intermediate state of the dead.

The ethics of the Bible would have been less questioned if "borrow" (Exod. 3:22; 11:2), which suggests returning goods, had been "ask," which is the literal meaning of the verb involved. "Thou shalt not kill" (Exod. 20:13) can be interpreted to be a blanket prohibition against taking life. The prohibition is actually against murder. Judicial execution is provided for in more cases in the Old Testament than in our own law.

People would have been less likely to misunderstand Jesus' teaching about his people had they read "of this fold ... one flock, one shepherd" (John 10:16), which reflects the variety of Greek words used, instead of "fold ... one fold, and one shepherd."[60] People would have been less perplexed over the age of the earth had they not accepted the dates from Ussher's chronology printed at the head of the reference column of King James Bibles. One can trap any unsuspecting student on what the tithing obligation was if he has been influenced by the phrase "tithes of all that I possess" (Luke 18:12). The tithing law applied to increase and not to capital holdings; the passage should read "all I acquire." Most people have

---

[60]C. J. Ellicott, *Considerations on the Revision of the English Version of the New Testament* (New York: Harper & Brothers, 1873), p. 81.

not been greatly disturbed by the possibility that total consumption is commanded in "Drink ye all of it" (Matt. 26:27), though some have taken it that way. They have not assumed that we should be offensive to everyone from "For in many things we offend all" (James 3:2); nor have they greatly exercised themselves over "he that giveth, let him do it with simplicity" (Rom. 12:8), which should be "with liberality."

Under the influence of the KJV, "Lucifer" remains a name of the devil; however, Isaiah 14:12 really speaks of the King of Babylon and has nothing to say about the devil. The failure to distinguish between *daimonios* and *diabalos*, translating both "devil," obscures the fact that in the Greek text of the Gospels there is one devil but many demons. The sufferers of the New Testament were possessed by "demons," according to the original, not by "devils." They are never said to be possessed by the devil. This item has relevance to present-day beliefs about exorcism.

The KJV added "unto him" in John 3:34. On this phrase men built an elaborate doctrine of measures of the Spirit in which Jesus alone had the Spirit "without measure." The addition makes the passage say something quite different from what it says in the Greek. They built a doctrine of the second blessing on "Have ye received the Holy Ghost since ye believed?" (Acts 19:2), which should have read "when ye believed."[61] People made a rule of ascetic behavior out of "Touch not; taste not; handle not" (Col. 2:21), which they could not have done had the context been made clear. A great deal is made of the command "from such withdraw thyself" (I Tim. 6:5), but readers of the KJV are oblivious to the fact that the command rests on the poorer text of a textual variant. The same is true of "We love him, because he first loved us" (I John 4:19), but how different that statement is from "We love because he loved us." "He that is begotten of God keepeth himself" (I John 5:18) is quite different in teaching from "the One who was born of God keeps him safe," but the readings rest on a textual variant.

At the Lord's Table one frequently hears the expression "the broken body of the Lord" (reflecting I Cor. 11:24 KJV). This is a textually disputed phrase which in reality creates a contradiction with John 19:36— "a bone of him shall not be broken." The implications of "gain is godliness"

[61] J. H. Moulton, *Grammar of the New Testament Greek*, 3rd ed. (Edinburgh, 1908), 1:131n.

(I Tim. 6:5) are quite different from those of the correct phrase, "godliness is gain."

The textually-disputed reading "churches" (Acts 9:31), rather than "church," suggests individual congregations (cf. Acts 8:1; 15:41; 16:5). But all these form one church (cf. Acts 20:28; Eph. 3:10, 21), and it is this idea of unity which is suggested when the preferable reading is followed in Acts 9:31.[62] *Diathēkē*, which should be "covenant," is incorrectly rendered "testament" in numerous New Testament passages. The concepts "covenant" and "testament " are entirely different concepts. God deals in covenants.[63] The omission of the article "the" in Romans 5:15, 17 has obscured the sense, weakened the antithesis intended, and left an opening for inferences on redemption and reprobation which are not substantiated by the passage.[64] The rendering "lived not again" for *ezēsan* (Rev. 20:5), which varies from the rendering in the preceding verse, "they lived," lends encouragement to the millennial understanding of the chapter. The ASV more correctly has "lived not" in this verse.

"I certify to you ... the gospel" (Gal. 1:11; cf. II Sam. 15:28; Ezra 4:14, 16; 5:10; 7:24; Esther 2:22) is taken by many to mean that the gospel is guaranteed, but the original word merely means "to make known" and carries no implication of guarantee at all. The passage "the wayfaring men, though fools, shall not err therein" (Isa. 35:8) is still taken by most people to mean that the way is so plain that a fool cannot miss it; but the Hebrew is likely saying that no fools—just as no unclean and no ravenous beast— will be found there. The fool is the irreligious man, not the mentally deficient man. We have preached sermons on "the sin which doth so easily beset us" (Heb. 12:1), oblivious to the fact that the definite article was supplied by the translators.

Faulty translations and interpretations have been carried over into religious songs, to which people have become emotionally attached. The song phrase, "Gates of hell can never against that church prevail" is based on the rendering "hell" for *Hades* (Matt. 16:18). "When the trumpet of the Lord shall sound and time shall be no more" is based on the wording of Revelation 10:6 in the KJV, which passage is really saying "there shall be no more delay." "He is the lily of the valley" and "He is mine and I am

<hr>

[62]Metzger, *A Textual Commentary on the Greek New Testament*, p. 367.

[63]Westcott, *Some Lessons of the Revised Version of the New Testament*, p. 143.

[64]Ellicott, *Considerations on the Revision of the English Version of the New Testament*, p. 101.

66

his" ultimately rest on the allegorical interpretation of the Song of Songs. In the KJV, "by and by" means "immediately" (Matt. 13:21; Mark 6:25; Luke 17:7; 21:9). This phrase is used in the song "In the Sweet By and By," but it has a different meaning. "Are you washed in the blood?" was suggested by Revelation 1:5—a passage which in the earlier manuscripts reads "loosed" *(lusanti)* rather than "washed" *(lousanti)*. In Revelation 7:14 people wash their robes and make them white "in the blood of the Lamb"; but no biblical verse, other than the variant in Revelation 1:5 in the *Textus Receptus*, speaks of persons being washed in the blood. The songwriters have arrived at these ideas we hold dear because they misunderstood the wording of the KJV. It is not altogether out of order to remember that songs need to be measured by the biblical text properly interpreted and understood and not the converse.

In short, the truth is that the reader of the KJV reads into it the meaning he has been taught to receive. Its expounders read its words and then say, "Now the real meaning is. ..." Its readers take great pleasure in debating despite the fact that their Bible lists debates as a sign of depravity (Rom. 1:29; II Cor. 12:20). They make elaborate plans for the future while reading. "Take no thought for your life" (Matt. 6:25). They exercise great care while reading "Be careful for nothing" (Phil. 4:6). They look after their neighbor's welfare although their Bible tells them to look after his "wealth" (I Cor. 10:24: cf. Ezra 9:12; Esther 10:3). They care for widows and orphans when their version says merely to "visit [them] in their affliction" (James 1:27). Though told to "enter into thy closet" (Matt. 6:6) to pray, they do otherwise.

Conclusion

Our survey has shown that those who feel they can escape the problem of translations by retreating into the citadel of the KJV have a zeal for God that is not in accord with knowledge. The same sort of attacks that are now made on new translations were made on the KJV when it was new. If the same kind of fine-tooth combing that is expended on the new translations is used on the KJV, we see that the problems of the KJV are as numerous and as serious as those of the new translations. The need for new translations lies in the inadequacies of the KJV. Though shortcomings of the KJV complicate the task of learning, they have not kept the person who is willing to expend the effort from learning what God would have him do. At the same time, there are no valid reasons for one to insist fanatically that everyone should read only the KJV; to declare that it is a mark of orthodoxy to use the KJV as a standard, consulting other translations only for comparisons; and to look with suspicion on the person who calls attention to the shortcomings of the KJV or who has other preferences in his reading.

Were the KJV the form in which God first gave the Bible there would be justification for the insistence that everyone must learn its brand of English in order to learn the will of God. But it is not the original Bible. The translators worked neither by inspiration nor with special divine approval. There is no valid reason why God's Word should be frozen in seventeenth-century English by those who have educated themselves to understand it while men perish for want of understanding. The King James Preface asks, "How shall men meditate on that which they do not understand?" Progress has been made since 1611. It is now possible to have a more accurate and a more readable translation than the KJV.

4

The American Standard Version

T he American Standard Version, the outgrowth of American participation in the revision project which produced the Revised Version (1881-85), may be thought of as an American edition of that version rather than as an independent one. The agitation for an English Bible revision had continued across the 250 years of the circulation of the KJV and finally resulted in the introduction of a motion for revision in the Upper House of the Convocation of Canterbury on February 20, 1870.[1] The appropriate committees, with Anglicans in the lead but with Baptists, Congregationalists, Methodists, Presbyterians, and Unitarians also represented, were set up and instructed. Openly acknowledging the charm and the merits of the KJV, the revisers envisioned a minimal revision in order to bring the English Bible into harmony with the original texts; but the project ended with 5,788 changes in the underlying Greek text of the New

[1]Preface to *Revised Version*, *The New Testament*, p. x; F. F. Bruce, *History of the Bible in English*, 3rd ed. (Oxford: University Press, 1978), p. 135.

Testament which was followed. About one-fourth of these are said to alter the subject matter.[2]

The RV was also an effort to put the Bible into English that could be understood, but staid British loyalty to that which is traditional changed only archaisms where they were likely to be misunderstood by the reader; and even in those cases another archaism of the King James period which was still understood was chosen over a current phrase.[3] The instructions stated that the style and language of the KJV were to be maintained; nevertheless, in the end more than 36,191 corrections of various sorts were made in the New Testament.[4] These included changes resulting from alteration in the Greek text itself, changes where the KJV appears to have chosen the poorer of two readings, changes where the KJV is ambiguous or obscure, changes where the KJV is not consistent with itself in rendering phrases or passages that are alike or parallel, and changes that are required because of the other changes made.[5]

After the British revision project was already well under way, it was decided on July 7, 1870, to invite American scholars to participate. Dr. Joseph Angus carried on negotiations for the British. On the American side, Dr. Philip Schaff, after preparing a list of rules to be followed and a list of possible participants, issued invitations to selected people. Schaff claims to have considered first the participant's ability and reputation in biblical learning. The second consideration was denominational connection and standing, in order to have a fair representation of the leading churches and theological institutions. He also took into account a person's place of residence, to insure regular attendance at the committee meetings. The result was that the group chosen represented nine denominations: Baptist, Congregationalist, Dutch Reformed, Friends, Methodist, Episcopal, Presbyterian, Protestant Episcopal, and Unitarian. The group was organized December 7, 1871, and began work at the Bible House in New York on October 4, 1872. Copies of the preliminary revision already completed by the British were distributed at the first meeting.[6]

---

[2]F. G. Kenyon, *Our Bible and the Ancient Manuscripts*, revised by A. W. Adams (New York: Harper & Brothers, 1958), p. 313.

[3]Preface to *Revised Version, The New Testament*, p. xx.

[4]Correspondent to *The Guardian* (August 10, 1881), pp. 1136, 1675, cited in P. Schaff, *Companion to the Greek and English Version* (New York: Harper & Brothers, 1883), p. 419 n.

[5]Preface to *Revised Version, The New Testament*, p. xv.

[6]Philip Schaff, *The Revision of the English Version of the Holy Scriptures* (New York: Harper & Brothers, 1877), pp. xvi-xvii.

The group conceived its object to be "to make a good translation still better, more accurate and self-consistent, and to bring it up to the present standard of Biblical scholarship."[7] During the early period of its work, the group met on the last Friday and Saturday of each month, and then met for longer sessions in the summer. Of the nineteen members listed as the New Testament committee, only fifteen actually engaged in the work, and two of these worked only briefly. H. B. Smith, G. R. Crooks, W. P. Warren, Charles Hodge, James Hadley, and H. B. Hackett dropped out. Timothy Dwight was chosen to replace Hadley. No compensation was given to any of the committee for their work of twenty-nine years (from 1872 to 1901). Contributions by friends, totaling about $50,000, were used for travel and incidental expenses. Each member of the committee received ten copies of a memorial edition to present to friends in exchange for their contributions to the project.

In the ten and one-half years the British revision required, the British and American companies did not meet together to discuss their results. The British work was sent to America and then returned with suggestions from the American committee. A second revision was sent for the same treatment; then a third revision was made in England. Suggestions made by the American group had to gain approval of two-thirds of the British committee in order to be accepted. It was agreed that an appendix would be published containing the more important preferences of the American company which were not adopted by the British. Bishop Alfred Lee estimated that about one thousand suggestions offered by the Americans were incorporated either in the text or the margin of the revision.[8]

No one edition of the Greek text was accepted by the preparers of the New Testament of the RV. Each variant reading was discussed, first in England and then in America. The discussion in Britain put Scrivener opposite Westcott and Hort. A preliminary copy of the Westcott-Hort text was furnished the British, and a copy was sent to America; however, the British followed Tregelles as often as they did Westcott-Hort. According to Riddle, no member of the American committee personally endorsed the "Westcott-Hort" theory of textual criticism. The British views in textual

<hr />

[7]Ibid., p. xxii.

[8]Alfred Lee, cited in Matthew Brown Riddle, *The Story of the Revision of the New Testament* (Philadelphia: The Sunday School Times, 1908), p. 24: see Alfred Lee, "List of Changes Proposed by the American Committee and Adopted by the British Committee," in P. Schaff, *Companion*, pp. 579-606.

matters were often approved by the Americans. Ezra Abbott was the foremost American text critic, and where there were problems his opinions prevailed in America. When, after the passing of some years, textual problems were reconsidered by Dwight, Riddle, and Thayer in preparation for the American edition, it was not found necessary to modify the textual judgments rendered by the whole American company.[9]

According to a note preserved in a memorandum of Dr. Schaff published by his son,[10] the committee members disagreed over the extent of the projected American appendix to the British work. The group had decided to reduce the size of the appendix at a meeting on July 7, 1880, but were surprised when the 1881 edition of the New Testament reached this country to find a different appendix used with the heading, "List of Readings and Renderings Preferred by the American Committee Recorded at their Desire." The heading suggested that the only points of difference between the two companies were those included in the appendix. This erroneous heading, as well as the use of certain British phraseology within the text itself, had the effect of strengthening the desire for an American Revised Bible. With its publication completed, the British committee disbanded, and the publishers showed no inclination toward further revision that would adopt the American suggestions. The Americans made no public protest against the appendix lest it affect adversely the sale of the British revision. They had agreed that they would not publish a rival edition for fourteen years after the appearance of the Revised Version. The American committee, however, continued its work, and with the expiration of the time agreed upon, issued in 1901 the ASV, which incorporates its suggestions in the text and lists points of difference with the British in an appendix— exactly the opposite of what the British had done. However, the number of changes made is considerably greater than the number of items that had been in the appendix of the previous RV editions.[11]

Philip Schaff, leader of the American revision, died October 20, 1893, leaving three members of the New Testament committee: Drs. T. Dwight, J. H. Thayer, and M. B. Riddle to do the editing of the American edition and to secure a publishing firm. Of the Old Testament committee, G. E. Day, J. DeWitt, C. M. Mead, and H. Osgood were left; however, most of

[9]Riddle, *The Story of the Revision*, pp. 27-33.
[10]David S. Schaff, *Life of Philip Schaff* (New York: Scribner's, 1897), pp. 381-82.
[11]Preface to *American Standard Version, The New Testament*, pp. v ff.

the work, including the editing, was done by Mead.[12] In April, 1897, an agreement on publication was reached with Thomas Nelson and Sons who were to hold the copyright.

Although action for future publication had been taken in 1885, with annual meetings in succeeding years, the beginning date of the final American revision of the New Testament was June 24, 1897. Thayer had kept full records of earlier meetings and suggestions of earlier members of the New Testament committee so that the three committee members could review work previously done and could represent the desires of their colaborers. Thayer had done additional work on the word "which" as applied to persons, and while on a sabbatical in Germany in 1898-1899 he had selected references and headings for the edition. The last meeting of the committee was held April 19, 1900, and the book was placed on sale August 26, 1901. It was copyrighted by Thomas Nelson and Sons to protect the purity of the text.[13]

The American Revision and the English Revision

Some of the noticeable differences between the British and the American revisions are the American use of "who" and "that" for "which" when it refers to a person, "know" and "knew" for "wot" and "wist," and "Jehovah" instead of "the Lord" or "God" for the God of Israel (the KJV had used "Jehovah" only six times). "Holy Spirit" is preferred to "Holy Ghost." "Sheol" is used instead of "grave," "pit," and "hell" in the Old Testament and "Hades" instead of "hell" in the New Testament to express the idea of the unseen world. The KJV had neglected this distinction by rendering two Greek words as "hell." The British version has used "Sheol" in only twenty-nine out of sixty-four occurrences.[14] The use of "love" instead of "charity" as the rendering for *agapē* returns to the practice of Tyndale, Coverdale, and the Geneva Bible. In seventeen passages "try," "trial," or "make trial of" are used (instead of "tempt" or "temptation") where no direct reference is made to wrongdoing. "Are" is substituted for "be" in using the indicative mood. Such archaisms as "bewray," "grisled," "holpen," "hough," "marish," "pourtray," "sith," and "strawed" are eliminated. The

---

[12]John W. Lea, *The Book of Books* (Philadelphia: John C. Winston, 1922), p. 325.
[13]Riddle, *The Story of the Revision*, pp. 59-62; J. W. Lea, *The Book of Books*, p. 325.
[14]Preface to *American Standard Version*, p. iv.

Americans used "astonished" where the British used "astonied" (Isa. 52:14); "frighten" for "fray" (Deut. 28:26); "boil" for "seethe" and "sod," and "boiled" for "sodden" (Gen. 25:29; Exod. 12:9; 16:23); "number" or "count" for "tell" (Gen. 15:5; Ps. 22:17); and "number" for "tale" (Exod. 5:18). "Despoil," "plunder," or "ravage" is used where the British had "spoil." British spellings using the letter u (labour, favour, behaviour, etc.) are dropped.

The American edition eliminated certain expressions of the RV not likely to be understood in America. "Corn" in Britain refers to all grain, but means Indian maize in America. Except in I Corinthians 9:9 and I Timothy 5:18, "grain" was used by the ASV. "Chargers" are not "platters" in America, "chapmen" are not "traders," "occupiers" are not "merchants," a "chapiter" is not the "capital" of a column, a soldier does not wear a "harness," and Americans do not have shoes "clouted." The ASV dropped "the caperberry shall fail" (Eccles. 12:5) in favor of "desire shall fail" (as KJV), since the purpose of the berry is unknown in America. "The way of the transgressor is rugged" (Prov. 13:15) is dropped for "the way of the transgressor is hard." "Heart" is used instead of "reins." The translators said of reins, "Most readers attach to it no meaning whatsoever."[15] "Its" is used for "his" or "hers" two hundred more times than in the British version,[16] and one may see the gain in clarity made by this change, especially in Psalm 1 where "his fruit" and "his leaf" are awkward. The "dragon" (Deut. 32:33) and the "arrowsnake" (Isa. 34:15), both mythical, are dropped. Many other differences can be found listed in the appendix which is printed in some (but not all) of the Nelson editions of the ASV.

In the American edition the text was reparagraphed, verse numbers were carried within the text, and the use of punctuation and italics was improved. Changes in interpretation reflected in punctuation are encountered at Genesis 2:5; 14:24; and Ezekiel 29:9, 21. The ASV carried carefully selected references in a center column. Titles of the Gospels (left unchanged from the KJV in the RV) do not use "Saint," "The Acts" stands in place of "The Acts of the Apostles," "Apostle" is dropped from the title of the Pauline letters, and Paul's name is removed from the title of the Epistle to the Hebrews. The word "General" is dropped from the titles of the epistles of James, I and II Peter, I John, and Jude. The title "The Revelation of St. John the Divine" is modified in favor of "The Revelation

---

[15]Ibid., p. vi.
[16]H. M. Whitney, "The Latest Translation of the Bible," *Bibliotheca Sacra* 59 (July 1902): 456.

of John." By reducing the number of marginal readings in the Old Testament cited from the Septuagint, the Vulgate, and other versions from 240 in the RV to about 42, the Americans retained only one-sixth of the total.[17] Furthermore, unlike the British who had published a revision of the Apocrypha in 1894, the Americans did not include the Apocrypha in their revision.

A notable difference in interpretation from both the KJV and the RV is seen in the ASV when Paul compliments the Athenians on being "very religious" (Acts 17:22), whereas all predecessors, influenced by the Vulgate, had some form of "superstitious." Another difference is seen in Acts 26:28: "With but little persuasion thou wouldest fain make me a Christian." The British version has retained the wording of the KJV, which does not take Agrippa's words ironically. The two phrases in John 14:1 are paralleled as imperatives: "Believe in God, believe also in me." One adds a cubit "to the measure of his life" (Matt. 6:27), not to "his stature." Weightier matters of the law are "justice, and mercy, and faith," not "judgment, mercy, and faith" (Matt. 23:23). A complete list would reveal other changes.

There are cases where the American revisers rejected the revision of the British and went back to the wording of the KJV. Examples may be seen in Exodus 20:4, 13; Leviticus 19:22; Psalms 48:1; 104:26; 114:4; 116:11; Proverbs 13:15; Amos 6:5; Zechariah 4:14.[18] One unfortunate case of reversion is the use by the ASV of "Thou shalt not kill" for the commandment where the RV more correctly had "Thou shalt do no murder" (Exod. 20:13; Deut. 5:17). However, both the KJV and RV use "kill" in New Testament citations of the commandment (Matt. 5:21; 19:18; Luke 18:20; Rom. 13:9; James 2:11). The ASV rendering leaves the impression that all killing is prohibited, but the Pentateuch provides for capital punishment for many offenses. More fortunate is the reversion to "perfect gift" (James 1:17) where the British had chosen "perfect boon."

The Reception of the Revision

In the light of their relationship, the reception of the RV is of importance in the picture of the reception of the ASV. While received at first with

---

[17]B. B. Warfield, review of *The American Standard Bible* in *Presbyterian and Reformed Review* 13 (1902): 647.

[18]Preface to *American Standard Version*, p. v.

unprecedented enthusiasm and sales on both sides of the Atlantic, the RV, like all new versions, also stimulated a furor of criticism. Chief among its opponents in England was Dean John W. Burgon, whose essays were eventually collected in a volume entitled *The Revision Revised*.[19] Burgon took exception to the text chosen by the revisers and to many translation choices. He also objected to calling the readers' attention to so many variant readings in the marginal material. He saw the version as "the most astonishing, as well as the most calamitous literary blunder of the Age." He declared that the revisers ought to receive from the church "nothing short of stern and well-merited rebuke." He insisted that the Westcott-Hort text, "the systematic depravation of underlying Greek, ... is nothing else but a poisoning of the River of Life as its sacred source. Our Revisers (with the best and purest intentions, no doubt) stand convicted of having deliberately rejected the words of Inspiration in every page." Other scholars replied to Burgon, and it is doubtful that his censures had any great effect on the impact of the revision. Burgon's line of argument has been applied to the ASV in recent years by D. O. Fuller.[20]

Many critics found the style of the British version to be distinctly inferior to that of the KJV. This type of criticism is aptly summarized in Spurgeon's evaluation so often quoted, "Strong in Greek, but weak in English."[21] The Bishop of Durham said of it, "While it is beyond all praise as an aid to study, it seriously lacks that ENGLISH FELICITY ... which should entitle it to take the place of the authorized version in our national heart."[22] Still more harshly, one said of the literalness of the revision, "The revisers were not appointed to prepare an interlinear translation for incompetent school boys."[23] To put the problem in the bluntest way, the RV did not maintain its initial popularity. However, F. F. Bruce, more recently speaking from the British viewpoint, says of it, "The RV with these marginal references is still the most useful edition of the Bible for the careful

[19]J. W. Burgon, *The Revision Revised* (London: John Murray, 1883); some other critics are E. Beckett, *Shall the RV Be Authorized?* and E. B. Wilkinson, *Our Authorized Bible Vindicated*. Wilkinson takes exception to the doctrinal beliefs of the American revisers.

[20]D. O. Fuller, *Which Bible?* 3rd ed. (Grand Rapids: Grand Rapids International Publications, 1972).

[21]Cited in *An Introduction to the Revised Standard Version of the New Testament* (n.p., 1947), p. 12.

[22]Handley C. G. Moule (Bishop of Durham), "Preface" to Samuel Lloyd, *The Corrected English New Testament* (New York: G. P. Putnam's Sons, 1905), p. xii.

[23]An anonymous reviewer in *The Edinburgh Review* 154 (American edition; July, 1881): 96.

student who knows no language but English."[24] Bruce's comment is also valid for the American revision. Its superiority to the British effort was early recognized by Americans,[25] and that superiority determined that the RV would not be the successor of the KJV in popular use.[26] More recently, E. C. Colwell, after a sampling investigation of sixty-five passages in seventeen New Testaments, ranked both of the revisions as textually more accurate than the KJV, but found the ASV to be slightly more accurate than the RV.[27]

In America, the Presbyterian Church (North), which had previously used the KJV without formally authorizing its use, now authorized the use of the ASV. David G. Wylie, former moderator of the Presbyterian Synod of the state of New York, found the ASV free from the sort of infelicitous renderings and typographical errors that had marred some earlier translations. He stated that its spelling and punctuation were better than the British version, and its grammar more in keeping with current usage. Its chapter headings were clear enough to indicate the meanings of the chapters, yet were free of dogmatic implications. The titles of its books were in harmony with most ancient manuscripts. It sought to make the Bible intelligible for both learned and unlearned people. Many archaisms were dropped, and misunderstood words were replaced by better words. Euphemisms were used to express matters that might offend good taste (I Sam. 25:22; II Kings 18:27; Isa. 36:12). It made the Bible a living book by translating it into the living language of the hour.[28] All in all, Wylie found that the ASV gives the meaning of the original better than any other version. Clyde W. Votaw, in *The Biblical World*, though listing some defects, claimed:

The American Standard edition is by far, and in every respect, the best English translation of the Bible in existence, both for scholars and for the

[24]Bruce, *History*, p. 147.

[25]Warfield, review of *The American Standard Bible*, p. 646; cf. also Thomas F. Lockyer, "The Bible in English: Some Recent Versions and Editions," *London Quarterly Review* 98 (July 1902): 139.

[26]H. M. Whitney, "The Latest Translation," 59 (October 1902): 653; cf. G. N. Luccock, "The New Translations," *Biblical Review* 11 (January 1926): 28.

[27]E. C. Colwell, *What Is the Best New Testament?* (Chicago: University of Chicago Press, 1947), pp. 85-97.

[28]David G. Wylie, *The American Standard Edition of the Revised Bible in Pulpit and Pew* (New York: n.p., 1903).

people. It is the privilege, but also the duty, of every man, woman, and child in America ... to use the best English translation of the Bible which is available to them, namely, the edition of 1901.[29]

Others were not so well pleased. The General Convention of the Protestant Episcopal Church in 1904 rejected a petition requesting permission to use the ASV.[30] E. W. Alderson, a Methodist, in an open letter to the secretary of the American Bible Society, took exception to the uniform use by the ASV of "baptize" as the rendering of *baptizō*. He felt that the four immersionist members of the committee (the Presbyterian Schaff and the three Baptists: Conant, Kendrick, and Hackett) had exercised an undue partisan influence on the committee. Some of these men had participated earlier in the preparation of the Bible Union Translation which Alderson considered to be "the most intensely partisan translation of the New Testament the world has ever seen." He also took exception to the retaining of "saved through water" from the RV (I Peter 3:20), for which he preferred "brought safely through the water" as is in the margin; and he objected to the marginal reading of Mark 1:9 where the text has "baptized ... in the Jordan" and the margin reads "into." He particularly protested the rendering "in water" in Matthew 3:11 where he preferred "with water," and the supplying of "with" before "fire" in the same verse where the Greek has no preposition. He thought that this passage alone would render the ASV unacceptable. He felt that the final revisers should have sought aid from committees representing various churches. He asserted that the work as executed and published was a "fake, pure and simple."[31]

Another critic objected to the use of "it" for the Holy Spirit (Acts 8:16), while elsewhere "himself" (Rom. 8:16, 26), "he," and "him" (John 16:7-14) are used. He argued that although *pneuma* is neuter, the rendering "it" is not justified, since John 16:14 has the masculine *ekeinos* where the antecedent is *pneuma*.[32]

Though a number of the above criticisms of the ASV are tendentious and invalid, it has become obvious with the passing of seventy-nine years

[29]Clyde W. Votaw, "The American Standard Edition of the Revised Bible," *The Biblical World* 17 (October 1901): 267.

[30]Whitney, "The Latest Translation," 61 (January 1905): 89.

[31]A copy of the letter is preserved in the library at Southwestern Baptist Seminary, Fort Worth, Texas.

[32]C. E. W. Dobbs, "The Preferences of the American Revisers," *Homiletical Review* 25 (February 1893): 182.

that the revision, either in its British or in its American form, can never gain the popularity of the KJV. The British version was seldom used in the churches. The ASV appeared just at the dawn of the age of great advance in biblical archaeology and in comparative Semitics. It also appeared just at the time when the age of modern speech versions began to dawn — and it was far from modern speech. When its copyright had nearly expired in 1928, the ownership of the copyright was obtained by the International Council of Religious Education. That organization's committee — the Standard Bible Committee — decided, though not unanimously, that a new revision was needed. The outcome of this revision project was the Revised Standard Version; the New Testament was issued in 1946 and the Old Testament was completed in 1952. No longer protected by a copyright, the ASV can be printed by any printer, but because the major printers of Bibles are promoting other versions, it seems likely that its influence will decrease rather than increase.

The American Standard Version and The King James Version

As compared with the KJV, the ASV represents definite improvement in text, in interpretation, in wording, and in typographical form. While it is not entirely certain what text the King James translators had for the New Testament, it is agreed that it could only have been a medieval form of text known from few manuscripts. Of the versions, only the Vulgate was known in 1611, and that from late and corrupt manuscripts. Quotations from the Scripture in the writings of the church fathers could have helped the translators establish the text, but their value was not appreciated. In the years between the KJV and the ASV, the vellum codices (Vaticanus, Sinaiticus, Alexandrinus, Ephraem, and Beza), dating from the fourth and fifth centuries, had become available. This enabled the text critics to reconstruct the text as it appeared in about the fourth century, whereas earlier they only had sources from the Middle Ages.

The RV (1881), out of which the ASV developed, had the great textual critics Scrivener, Westcott, and Hort on its New Testament translation committee. The textual work of Westcott and Hort and their predecessors with their textual theory (favoring codices Vaticanus and Sinaiticus) was to dominate the textual scene for several generations. The Westcott-Hort Greek text was published five days before the RV of the New Testament, but their materials had been made available to the translators in advance of publication. The revision did not adopt their suggestions in an estimated 200 cases; but many of the suggestions, not adopted in the text, are supplied in the marginal readings. The Greek text of the New Testament of the RV (and therefore of the ASV) is estimated to differ from the KJV text in 5,788 cases. Sixteen complete verses carried in the KJV, thought on textual evidence to be spurious, are absent from the text of the ASV and are relegated to the margin.[33] One count suggests that there are 122 sentences or parts of sentences omitted.[34] Other verses, though carried in the text, have a note to the effect that they are absent in some manuscripts. Numerous phrases of less than a whole verse receive the same type of treatment. Among them would be the doxology at the end of the Model Prayer (Matt. 6:13), prayer phrases (Luke 11:2-4), the troubling of the water at the pool of Bethesda (John 5:3ff.), and the phrase "of the dead" (Acts 24:15). Still others, such as the *Comma Johanneum* (the "heavenly witnesses" of John 5:7), are dropped completely without a note. Another category of passages is that regarded as textual problems (such as that of the ending of Mark 16:9-10 and that of the woman taken in adultery in John 7:53—8:11) which are set off from the rest of the text by space. The latter passage is also bracketed. In only ten passages, phrases not in the KJV are added in the text of the ASV.[35] These additions include the phrases "this he said" (Mark 7:19), "and they came to him" (John 19:3), "by the Holy Spirit" (Acts 4:25), "even so do ye walk" (I Thess. 4:1), "unto salvation" (I Peter 2:2), "according to the will of God" (I Peter 5:2), and "such we are" (I John 3:1).

There is a sizable list of passages in which a different textual reading is chosen in the ASV from that chosen in the KJV. Included would be the reading "He who was manifested" (I Tim. 3:16) where the KJV had "God was manifest," "they ... they" (Acts 13:42) where there was "Jews ... Gentiles," "Spirit of Jesus" (Acts 16:7) where there was "Spirit," "eagle" (Rev. 8:13) where there was "angel," "wash their robes" (Rev. 22:14) where the KJV had "do his commandments," and "tree of life" where there was "book of life" (Rev. 22:19). Other lesser changes are too numerous to list.

---

[33]F. G. Kenyon, *Our Bible*, p. 313. The verses are Matt. 17:21; 18:11; 23:14; Mark 7:16; 9:44, 46; 11:26; 15:28; Luke 17:36; 23:17; John 5:4; Acts 8:37; 15:34; 24:7; 28:29; Rom. 16:24.

[34]S. Cox, "Doctrinal Effect of the Revised Version," *The Expositor*, 2nd ser. 3 (1882): 434-35.

[35]Ibid.

While Hebrew was doubtlessly better known in 1885-1901 than it was in 1611, the progress in Old Testament manuscript discovery and textual criticism — even with the benefit of the manuscript studies of B. Kennicott, G. de Rossi, and C. D. Ginsberg — is not comparable to that in the New Testament. The Hebrew text of the ASV is substantially the same as that of the KJV. However, in I Samuel 13:1 a numeral which seems by conjecture to be a necessary addition is placed in brackets. In Isaiah 9:3 what seems a superfluous negative is dropped.[36] The Masoretic text was not followed at Deuteronomy 32:14; I Samuel 6:18; II Samuel 16:13; II Chronicles 3:1; 22:6; Job 37:9; Isaiah 30:32; 35:8; Ezekiel 46:9; Hosea 11:3; Amos 5:21; Micah 3:5; and Haggai 1:5.

With some reservations, it can be said that the typographical makeup of the ASV is good. However, though it has a title page for the New Testament, there is no separate title page for the Old Testament. It begins with a general introduction to the whole revision. "New Covenant" is used on a title page, but "Old Covenant" is not. Though one might question the heading "The Millennial Reign" for Revelation 20, the chapter headings in general do not suggest a particular theological interpretation. Also on the credit side, the dates from the chronology of Bishop Ussher, printed at the top of the column of KJV reference Bibles since 1701 and no longer thought to be accurate, were dropped altogether. Poetical sections such as the Psalms are printed in verse form instead of prose form. The essential nature of Hebrew poetry had first been made clear by Robert Lowth in 1753. However, the practice of printing poetry as poetry is not followed adequately in the prophetic books which, to a large degree, are poetical.

The ASV reverts to the pre-Geneva practice of paragraphing material. Its more modern paragraphing is a marked improvement over the KJV where each verse is a separate paragraph, and over the RV's long paragraphs. The ASV did not hesitate to carry the last phrase of a chapter into the first paragraph of the next chapter (II Kings 24:20) and to start a paragraph in the middle of a verse (Isa. 59:15); but even with its improvements, the ASV needs additional attention to paragraphing. It would be still more readable if its paragraphs were shorter. There are yet isolated cases where material should be carried from one paragraph to the other. "I show you a more excellent way" (I Cor. 12:31) should begin the chapter on love, the practice now followed in critical Greek texts.

[36]Kenyon, *Our Bible*, p. 314, n. 1.

One distinguishing feature of the translation is that it aimed to be as nearly literal as possible. Unlike the KJV, which sought to use English synonyms where possible to express the same Greek and Hebrew words in their various occurrences (one Hebrew word is rendered ninety different ways), The American Standard sought, not always with success, to render a word uniformly by the same English word. It is therefore good for the concordance type of study where the occurrences of a word are traced, but it ignores the fact that a word may have many shades of meaning. An attempt is made to express the shade of meaning conveyed in the Greek aorist tense.

The ASV is also careful to reproduce exactly the similarities or divergencies found in the original Greek in related passages in the Gospels. The above-mentioned variety in the KJV often obscured the similarity. For example, an expression characteristic of Matthew is variously rendered by the KJV and RV as "had ended," "had made an end," and "had finished" though the Greek uses the same word throughout. The ASV used "had finished" in each (Matt. 7:28; 11:1; 13:53; 19:1; 26:1). For the person who wants to work back from the English wording to the Greek and Hebrew original, the ASV affords the best opportunity of the choices now available.

That the ASV differs significantly in details from the KJV may be seen in the 2,000 changes made in the Psalms, 1,300 in Jeremiah, 1,400 in Job, and a total of 36,191 in the New Testament.[37] The translators of the ASV attempted in many places to turn the reader from interpretations they wished him to avoid.[38] Unfortunately, the care they gave is often wasted on the common reader because he is not searching his Bible as carefully as the translators themselves did. Where the KJV had said of the prophesying of the elders "and did not cease," the ASV has "but they did so no more" (Num. 11:25). Passages which men cited for having a Calvinistic bias in the KJV (Matt. 19:23; Acts 2:47; Heb. 6:6; 10:38) were modified in the ASV. The marginal option "in whom all sinned" is absent from Romans 5:12. The teaching of depravity is no longer suggested by Gala-

---

[37]J. H. Lupton, "Versions (English)," in *Hastings Dictionary of the Bible*, Extra Volume, p. 264.

[38]A. Roberts, "Renderings and Readings in the Revised New Testament," *The Expository Times* 3 (1891-2): 129-30; George Milligan, "The Doctrinal Significance of the Revision," *The Expository Times* 7 (1895-96): 377-79, 435-54; 8 (1896-97); 171-75; Llewelyn J. Evans, "Doctrinal Significance of the Revision," *Presbyterian Review* 4 (1883): 275-307; William Caven, "The Revision of the Bible as a Whole," *Presbyterian Review* 7 (1886): 85-86.

tians 5:17.[39] The word for "conversion" is rendered actively—"except ye turn"—instead of passively, "be converted" (Matt. 18:3; cf. 13:15; Mark 4:12; Luke 22:32; John 12:40; Acts 3:19; 28:27). "Foreordained" (Rom. 8:29; Eph. 1:5) is favored over "predestinated." Shifts relevant to other questions can be seen. The rendering "and" (I Cor. 11:27), sometimes alleged to be anti-Catholic, is modified to "or." The ethical problem raised by the word "borrow" in the KJV is avoided by using "ask" (Exod. 3:22; 12:35). The implication that God "deceived" the prophet is avoided by using "persuaded" (Jer. 20:7). In the substitution of "Servant" for "Child" (Acts 3:13, 26; 4:27, 30), the Christ is identified with the Servant of Jehovah in the Book of Isaiah.

The ASV distinguishes between "demons" and the "devil"—which distinction the KJV had neglected—but also gives emphasis to the personality of the devil in the shift from "evil" to "evil *one*" (Matt. 5:37; 6:13; John 17:15; Eph. 6:16; II Thess. 3:3; I John 5:18), though giving a marginal reading "evil." "Evil" could be evil men, impersonal evil, or both; "the evil one" can only be the devil. For the phrase *ho poneros* the KJV had "wicked one" at I John 5:18 but had "wickedness" at I John 5:19. The choices of both the ASV and KJV are of doubtful validity since there is no objective way by which one can know whether *ho poneros* is "the evil" or "the evil one." The use of a masculine pronoun in the ASV in Mark 13:14 suggests that the "abomination of desolation" is a person, but there is no certainty. "Abomination of desolation" might require a neuter pronoun.

Besides the shift in translation from "Holy Ghost" to "Holy Spirit" in all occurrences, the ASV dropped the restricting addition *"unto him"* in John 3:34. The masculine pronoun is used for the Holy Spirit where the KJV had a neuter (Rom. 8:16, 26; Eph. 4:30), and the present tense is used in I Thessalonians 4:8 for the giving of the Spirit. The omission of a supplied "of," resulting in a reading "of water and the Spirit" (John 3:5), removes the possibility of a baptism of two actions.[40] "Through" replacing "by" suggests Christ as the mediator rather than as the source of creation (John 1:3; I Cor. 8:6). Modification in the insertion or omission of the definite article suggests changes of meaning, e.g., "a temple" (I Cor. 3:16). We also have "the outer darkness ... the weeping" (Matt. 8:12; cf. 13:42, 50; 22:13; 24:51; 25:30; Luke 13:28), "the wrath" (Rom. 5:9), "the white

[39]C. J. Ellicott, *Considerations on the Revision of the English Version of the New Testament* (New York: Harper & Brothers, 1873), p. 25, n. 1.

[40]Roberts, "Renderings and Readings," pp. 129-30, 549-50.

robes ... the great tribulation" (Rev. 7:13-14), "the city ... the foundations" (Heb. 11:10), and "the sin" (Heb. 12:1). This policy of using the article because it was in the Greek sometimes gives a non-English use of "the"; e.g., "the life" (Matt. 6:25).

The RV and ASV dropped the words "damn," "damnation," "damnable," and "damned," insisting that because of current usage they carried false ideas. They were replaced by "judge," "judgment," "condemn," "condemned," and "condemnation." The shift from "hell" to "Hades" in ten passages while retaining "hell" in only fourteen has theological implications in its eschatalogical teaching. Some have also seen such implications in the shift from "everlasting" to "eternal" in describing life and punishment.[41] In the KJV, II Timothy 3:16 affirms two things—that Scripture is inspired and is profitable; but in the ASV it affirms only one—that inspired Scripture is profitable. The other translation is carried in the margin.

The ASV corrects those passages where it has been recognized that the KJV missed the proper translation. For example, "Easter" is deleted from Acts 12:4.

Other improvements include a more uniform spelling of personal and place names. The ASV also reckons with the difference between Hebrew and English psychology. The "heart" is used for the psychological and emotional functions ascribed in the KJV to "bowels" and "reins." God tries "the minds and hearts" (Ps. 7:9; Jer. 17:10; 20:12). Jeremiah no longer complains that God "is in their mouth, and far from their reins" (Jer. 12:2); and one no longer reads "receive him, that is, my own bowels" (Philem. 12). One reads "my heart instructeth me" (Ps. 16:7) where the KJV had "my reins." Nevertheless, "reins" (the kidneys) is unfortunately retained in the ASV at Job 16:13; Lamentations 3:13; and Revelation 2:23. "Bowels" is retained when used for the physical organ (II Sam. 20:10)—even though it may convey a distasteful picture to the modern reader (cf. II Sam. 7:12)—but is replaced by "anguish" (Jer. 4:19) or "heart" (cf. Gen. 43:30) when used in a psychological sense. Another correction is seen when "sincere milk" becomes "spiritual milk" (I Peter 2:2). Many animals that are named in the KJV of the Old Testament are given a different identification in the ASV.[42]

---

[41]Evans, "Doctrinal Significance," p. 306; Milligan, "The Doctrinal Significance," p. 174.
[42]H. M. Whitney, "The Latest Translation," 61 (April 1904): 257-58.

Great gain is made in intelligibility in the ASV by dropping some archaisms and modernizing English speech and spelling. "Prevent" gives way to "precede" (I Thess. 4:15; etc.) and "peculiar people" to "a people for his own possession" (Titus 2:14; etc.). The ASV substituted "a" for "an" before nouns beginning with an aspirated *h* and before the letter *o*, so that one no longer has to read "an one" (I Cor. 5:5), "an hungered" (Matt. 4:2), "an high priest" (Heb. 5:5), and the like. Nevertheless, a word-by-word check reveals that the revision was not consistent in the elimination of archaic words. For example, the verb "espy" occurs six times in the KJV and is retained once (Gen. 42:27) in the ASV. "Study," eliminated in II Timothy 2:15, is retained in I Thessalonians 4:11. Other cases can be found where archaic words, such as "certify" (II Sam. 15:28; Ezra 4:14, 16; 5:10; 7:24), have been removed from the New Testament but are retained in the Old Testament.

It is not to be concluded that the ASV renderings were in every case superior to those of the KJV. For example, Jonah 1:13 has "rowed hard to get them back to the land," which does not improve "to bring *it* back to land." Luke 10:18 speaks of "Satan fallen as lightning from heaven." One cannot see lightning "fallen"; hence the KJV rendering "fall" is preferable. The ASV correctly used the same verb, but in another tense, as "fallen" in Revelation 9:1. Another case is "horses' bridles into their mouths" (James 3:3). The KJV correctly has "bits." "Our redemption" (Eph. 1:7) does not improve "redemption." "His child" (Matt. 10:21) supplies a pronoun not in the Greek. "Hats" in Daniel 3:21 (KJV) is superior to "mantles" (ASV).

In some cases the ASV continues the obscurities of the KJV. Examples in point are the twenty-eight occurrences (Exod. 16:23; Lev. 23:36; Num. 29:35; etc.) of "solemn rest" or "solemn assembly" derived from the Latin *solumnis* meaning a "fixed" or "stated" meeting. "Swellings" (II Cor. 12:20) is unintelligible. "Now we see in a mirror, darkly" (I Cor. 13:12) would be clearer if it were "indistinctly." Matthew 5:48 would be better stated as an imperative paralleling in structure Luke 6:36.

Since 1901

The most serious matter for consideration in evaluating the ASV is what has happened in the world since 1901. Those eighty years were one of the most productive periods of exploration and discovery in Palestine, and of the diligent study of linguistics, communications, and comparative Semitics. It would be a sad commentary on human mentality if those years had cast no light on the problem of Bible translating. No translation is perfect; none is final; all are subject to improvement; and the ASV is no exception.

The ASV had the fate of being made just before significant manuscripts were discovered of both Old and New Testament material. This rendered it out of date before it had a fair chance to displace the KJV in popular esteem. In the Old Testament area these manuscripts include the Cairo Geniza find, the Dead Sea Scrolls, and the Aleppo Codex, which moved knowledge of the state of the text from the twelfth to fourteenth centuries back to the tenth century, and in the case of sections, back to the second century B.C. Philip Schaff stated in 1877 that there were about 1,500 manuscripts of the Greek New Testament that had been compared.[43] Now there are 5,358 manuscripts and fragments known. The Washington Gospels give us a significant new uncial. Though some papyri had come to light before the twentieth century, it is the age of papyrus discoveries. There are now eighty-six known papyrus portions of the New Testament. Of these, the Chester Beatty and the Bodmer Papyri are the most significant. Knowledge of the ancient versions of Scripture has also materially increased.[44] The Sinaitic Syriac found by Mrs. Lewis and Mrs. Gibson in 1892 is a witness to the state of the text about A.D. 150. As a result of these discoveries, scholars can talk about the state of the text of portions of the New Testament in the third century whereas previously they were restricted to materials from the fourth century—the date of the great uncials, Vaticanus and Sinaiticus.

The Westcott-Hort theory of textual criticism, though still very influential, has largely been replaced in textual study by the Eclectic Principle in which each variant reading is judged on its own merits in the effort to determine what the scribe would likely have written.

These discoveries and textual studies would suggest that in rare cases the text of the Old Testament followed by the ASV had lost phrases that can be restored by consulting the ancient versions, such phrases as "Let us go out to the field" (Gen. 4:8); "Why have you stolen my silver cup?" (Gen. 44:4-5); "I shall become weak, and be like any other man" (Judg.

[43]Schaff, On the Revision, p. xxv.
[44]Kenyon, Our Bible, p. 319; B. M. Metzger, The Early Versions of the New Testament (Oxford: Clarendon Press, 1977).

16:13); and the alternative, "but if the guilt is in thy people Israel, give Thummin" for the lot casting (I Sam. 14:41). The ancient versions seem correct in having "she" rather than "he" in Ruth 3:15 and "So be it, O Lord" in place of "Jehovah said" (Jer. 15:11). The reading "coals" from Symmachus seems preferable to that of "snares" (Ps. 11:6). Manuscript discoveries suggest needed changes; for example, where the ASV reads "he cried as a lion" (Isa. 21:8), the Qumran scroll reads "a watchman cried out."

In numerous cases the new materials add support to the textual judgments made in the New Testament by the ASV. For example, the variant "in whom he is well pleased" (Luke 2:14), as against "peace, good will to men," has support from Qumran hymns. The Bodmer manuscripts, P 66 and P 75, omit the troubling of the waters passage (John 5:3b-4) which was dropped to the margin in the ASV. They omit the adulteress passage (John 7:53– 8:11) which the ASV set off from the text as a problem. They omit the giving of the bread to the disciples (John 6:11) and the adjective "Holy" (John 7:39) which the ASV omitted. In certain cases specific variants chosen by the ASV have gained support; for example, the inclusion of the second cup at the last supper (Luke 22:19b-20). The second cup is in P 75.

In some cases, new evaluation of the evidence supports moving a marginal reading given by the ASV into the text while moving the reading of its text into the margin (Matt. 4:23; 5:25; 11:9; 14:24, 29; 17:22; 19:4; 21:12; 22:23; 24:31; 26:20; 27:24; 28:6; etc.). Finally, there are those cases where it would seem that the text followed by the ASV is in need of correction. The variant "and he who marrieth her when she is put away committeth adultery" (Matt. 19:9) is rejected in modern textual study. "Only God" (John 1:18) is supported as against "only begotten Son"; but "his" (John 6:52), which is bracketed in the UBS text, may be spurious. "Not yet *given*" (John 7:39; cf. Acts 19:2), perhaps a scribal addition, is not in P 66, P 75, and other weighty witnesses. "He who is born of God keeps him" improves on "keepeth himself" (I John 5:18). There are other cases, as I Corinthians 13:3 which has the variants "burned" and "boast" (UBS and Nestle Greek texts), where the weight of the evidence is still under debate.

There are some cases where the new evidence supports the reading followed in the KJV against that followed in the ASV. For example, "church of God" (Acts 20:28) has gained support against "church of the

Lord." "Tempt Christ" in the KJV (I Cor. 10:9), found in P 45, is now better supported than "make trial of the Lord" of the ASV. These illustrative cases in the various categories are in no sense exhaustive of the new light cast on the New Testament text since 1901. The interested student should go through the examples cited in a textual commentary.

The ASV appeared just as significant changes in ideas about the nature of New Testament Greek developed. Under the impact of nonbiblical papyrus discoveries and of the thesis of A. Deissmann, the idea was advanced that the New Testament was written in Koine Greek, the language of ordinary people of the Roman world, rather than in either a special language of the Holy Spirit or a "biblical Greek." The appearances of the Twentieth-Century New Testament, The Bible—An American Translation, the translation of Ferrar Fenton, and that of Weymouth (though these translations had their limitations and were not destined to displace the KJV) showed that new winds were beginning to blow in translation philosophy. Archaism could not permanently maintain itself.

The meaning of some obscure words in the Old Testament has been clarified by the discovery of many new languages in the Semitic world, the study of comparative Semitics, and the discovery of specific objects. These discoveries have broadened the base for defining a biblical word. New linguistic tools have appeared in the Old Testament area in the form of the Brown, Driver, Briggs *Lexicon*, the Köhler-Baumgartner *Lexicon*, and now Botterweck's *Theological Dictionary of the Old Testament* that is slowly being issued. With the fourth edition of the Kittel Bible, called *Biblia Hebraica Stuttgartensia* to distinguish it from the third edition, an improved critical text of the Old Testament is available.

In the New Testament area, information from the classical Greek sources has been made available in the Liddell-Scott-Jones *Greek-English Lexicon*; that from the papyri and other Koine sources in the Moulton-Milligan *Lexicon*, the Bauer *Lexicon of New Testament Greek* revised and augmented by Gingrich and Danker, and the Kittel *Theological Dictionary of the New Testament*. Light from patristic sources is available in the Lampe *Lexicon of Patristic Greek*. Grammars include those of Moulton-Howard-Turner and of Blass-Debrunner-Funk. New critical Greek texts for students include those of the United Bible Societies, third edition, and the twenty-sixth edition of the Nestle. The International New Testament Manuscript Project promises an even better tool for establishing the text.

It is not at all suggested that these tools radically change the biblical message, but each new insight is a welcome one for the English reader.

Illustrations of vocabulary changes needed in the Old Testament as a result of discovery would include "brooding over" for "moved" (Gen. 1:2), "Reed Sea" for "Red Sea" (Exod. 15:4; etc.), "lapis lazuli" for "sapphire" (Exod. 24:10; etc.), "glaze" for "silver dross" (Prov. 26:23), "upsurgings of the deep" for "fields of offering" (II Sam. 1:21), "sandals" for "shoes" (Exod. 3:5; etc), "incense altars" for "sun images" (Lev. 26:30; etc.), "Beth-haggan" (II Kings 9:27) for "the garden house," "Beth-eked" for "shearing-house" (II Kings 10:12), and "pim" for "file" (I Sam. 13:21). Necho goes "to" rather than "against" Assyria (II Kings 23:29), and "Que" is a place instead of "in droves" (I Kings 10:28). "Beyond the river" (Ezra 6:6, 13; etc.) is a title of a province rather than merely a directional indication; "a thing of nought" and "horns" are better as the place names "Lodebar" and "Karnaim" (Amos 6:13). "Tartan," "Rabshakeh," "Rabsaris," and "Rabmag" are now known to be titles (as the ASV margin suggests) rather than proper names (II Kings 18:17; Jer. 39:13; etc.). "Syrian" (II Kings 18:26; Ezra 4:7; Isa. 36:11; Dan. 2:4) is now "Aramaic."

Assyriology revealed that the word rendered "glory" should be "liver," thought at that time to be the seat of the emotions (Ps. 16:9). "Negeb" (Num. 13:17) would be an improvement over what may suggest confused geography in the KJV and ASV. The conjunction of I Chronicles 5:26 should be explicative, "namely," since Pul is an alternative name for Tilgath-pileser. "Inkhorn" (Ezek. 9:2, 3, 11) should be "writing kit."

Greek finds have made an equal contribution to New Testament vocabulary. "Beelzebul" (Matt. 10:25; 12:24) is preferred to "Beelzebub," "I have received full payment" to "I have all things" (Phil. 4:18), "scroll" to "book" (Luke 4:17, 20; Rev. 5:1; etc.), and "letter" to "epistle" (II Cor. 3:1; Col. 4:16; etc.). Other improved readings would favor "pure" rather than "without guile" (*adolon*; I Peter 2:2), "impossible" rather than "void of power" (Luke 1:37), "generous" rather than "single" (Matt. 6:22; Luke 11:34), "idle" rather than "disorderly" (I Thess. 5:14; II Thess. 3:6, 7, 11), and "delight in riches" rather than "deceitfulness of riches" (Matt. 13:22; Mark 4:19). The Greek word *opse* (Matt. 28:1) is almost certainly "after" rather than "late on." "Serjeants" (Acts 16:35, 38) should be something like "magistrates." A papyrus letter demonstrates that *paidagōgus* is not "tutor" (I Cor. 4:15; Gal. 3:24, 25), but is "guardian" or "custodian." "Diana" (Acts 19:24ff.) is more correctly "Artemis." These word changes are only a few of the examples that could be given. Only a word-for-word examination of the vocabulary of the Bible using modern lexicons could reveal the full contribution of discovery to vocabulary.

Revision Needed

Despite the unquestioned motives and the quality of scholarship of the men who produced it, despite the long, careful attention given to details, the ASV, like all works produced by men, has from the beginning had its problematic renderings. Some arise through failure to carry through on the policies set up. Though an effort was made to render a Greek word in each of its occurrences by the same English word, complete consistency was not achieved. Out of seventeen occurrences of *charisma*, only three (Rom. 5:15, 16 [as KJV and RV]; 6:23) are rendered by the redundant "free gift"; there is also one case (Rom. 5:18) where the term "free gift" is supplied by the translators, but the other instances are rightly "gift." *Teleios* is "fullgrown man" (Eph. 4:13; I Cor. 2:6) or "man" (I Cor. 14:20), but elsewhere (Phil. 3:15; Col. 1:28; 4:12; Heb. 5:14^m; James 3:2) is "perfect," a word which may convey a misconception to the reader. There is also little reason to render the verb *katartizein* as "perfect" (Heb. 13:21; I Peter 5:10; etc.). In the parable of the virgins (Matt. 25:1-13), in the midst of twenty-one uses of the past tense, the ASV has two cases of the present — "is" (v. 6) and "come" (v. 11). "Come" has become "came" in current printings, but the "is" remains. The KJV consistently used the past tense throughout.[45] *Apaggellein* is "to bring ... word" (Matt. 28:8), but is also "told" (Luke 24:9).

Differing Greek phrases are rendered alike — "knowing their thoughts" — in Matthew 12:25 and Luke 11:17. Also, confusion is created by the rendering of two different Greek words in the same context by one English word: "Bear ye one another's burdens" (*barē*; Gal. 6:2) and "For every man shall bear his own burden" (*phortion*; Gal. 6:5; margin, "load"). The prodigal did not eat the "husks" (Luke 15:16; cf. Num. 6:4), but the "pods" of the carob tree. A rendering "the preaching of foolishness" (I Cor. 1:21), instead of "the foolishness of the preaching," could have avoided the possible misconception that preaching is foolishness.

[45]Whitney, "The Latest Translation," 59 (1902): 220ff.

Other problems arise through a failure to give a proper sense to the passage. Surely the translators did not ask what their sentence said when they rendered *ki* as "for" in II Chronicles 26:23. Where would they have buried Uzziah if he had not been a leper? It would seem that *ki* should in this case be "although." Though a literal rendering, what is a "bow of brass" (II Sam. 22:35; Job 20:24; Ps. 18:34)? Do men make bows out of brass? Another case is "some of them they will kill and persecute" (Luke 11:49; ASV and RSV). Can a man be persecuted after he is killed? Though one alternative is to have some "killed" and some "persecuted" (NIV), the construction likely should be taken as a hendiadys for "persecuted to the death." Luke 12:49 reads, "What do I desire, if it is already kindled?" which seems to say, "What do I care?"; however, "How I wish" (NIV) would clarify the statement.

Surely the translators did not examine what they were saying in I Corinthians 15:19: "If we have only hoped in Christ in this life, we are of all men most pitiable." The verse should read something like, "If only for this life we have hoped in Christ" (NIV). "For" as the rendering of *gar* gives trouble in Mark 16:4: "They see that the stone is rolled back: for it was exceeding great." By its rendering of the particle *de*, the ASV makes every member of the Corinthian church to be a member of each of the four parties into which the Corinthian church was split: "Each one of you saith, I am of Paul; and I of Apollos; and I of Cephas; and I of Christ" (I Cor. 1:12). The problem could have been avoided by rendering *de* as "or." What does "shadow ... cast by turning" (James 1:17) mean? Who are "widows indeed" (I Tim. 5:3)? What does "our heart is enlarged" or "be ye also enlarged" (II Cor. 6:11, 13) mean to the reader? What is the meaning of "It shall turn out unto you for a testimony" (Luke 21:13)? Finally, the expression "He will give it you" (John 16:23) in ordinary English would have "it" receive "you."

The adversative use of *kai*, most frequently rendered "and," is not adequately recognized. In the following cases "but" would be better than "and": "but they likewise received" (Matt. 20:10), "but they feared the multitude" (Mark 12:12), "but they were all afraid of him" (Acts 9:26), "but yet unto me" (Acts 10:28), "but the same Lord" (I Cor. 12:5), "but Satan hindered" (I Thess. 2:18), "but the whole world" (I John 5:19), "but there shall not enter" (Rev. 21:27), "but the throne of God" (Rev. 22:3), and "but he said" (Rev. 22:9).

91

Though the ASV was a marked improvement over the KJV in consistent use of proper names, particularly those of well-known major characters, improvement is still needed for names of minor characters. The transliteration of Hebrew letters is not consistent. The *dagheshed* letter *kaph* in a name is transliterated "Kittim" (Gen. 10:4; etc.); but it is also "Chidon" (I Chron. 13:9), "Chilmad" (Ezek. 27:23), and "Chesed" (Gen. 22:22). The *undagheshed kaph* is "Cozeba" (I Chron. 4:22), and "Cub" (Ezek. 30:5), but elsewhere it is "Chelub" (I Chron. 4:11), "Chezib" (Gen. 38:5), and "Chileab" (II Sam. 3:3). The spellings "Mica" (II Sam. 9:12; etc.) and "Micaiah" (I Kings 22:8; etc.) occur for *kaph*, but "Michael" (Num. 13:13; etc.) and "Michal" (I Sam. 14:49) also occur.

One encounters "Elasah" (Ezra 10:22; Jer. 29:3) and "Eleasah" (I Chron. 2:39, 40; 8:37; 9:43) for the same name, though applied to different characters. There is "Imla" (II Chron. 18:7, 8) and "Imlah" (I Kings 22:8, 9). "Eladah" is changed to "Eleadah" (I Chron. 7:20), but "Dilean" is changed to "Dilan" (Josh. 15:38). The second vowel of these names is the same in Hebrew in the two cases. If one can dispense with "Timotheus" in favor of "Timothy," then why not "Silvanus" in favor of "Silas" (II Cor. 1:19; I Thess. 1:1; II Thess. 1:1; cf. Acts 15:22, 32, 40)? Why have both "Stephen" and "Stephanus"?[46]

Other inconsistencies can be seen. Though removing "candle" and "candlestick" from Matthew 5:15, the ASV retained "candlestick" frequently in the Old Testament and in Hebrews 9:2 for a piece of tabernacle and temple furniture but also for other sources of light (II Kings 4:10; Dan. 5:5). It also used "candlestick" in the Book of Revelation in numerous places as a symbol of the churches (1:12, 13, 20; 2:1, 5; 11:4). The oil lamp (not the candle) was the source of light in the Old and New Testament periods. Though dropping "Holy Ghost," the ASV retained "gave up the ghost" fifteen times. There is the inconsistency that Jesus gives up the "ghost" in Mark 15:37, 39, but in Luke 23:46 he has commended his "spirit" to God (Matt. 27:50; Luke 23:46). Stephen also commits his "spirit" to the Lord (Acts 7:59); but when the dead revive, it is their "spirit," not their "ghost," which returns to them (Luke 8:55). One encounters "Sabaoth" (Rom. 9:29; James 5:4) for the divine name which was "hosts" in the Old Testament (Ps. 80:14), with no hint that they are related; there is

---

[46]J. Shillidy, "Transliteration of Proper Names in the Revised Version of the Bible," *Expository Times* 9 (1897-1898): 238-39.

"leathern girdle" (Matt. 3:4; Mark 1:6) but also "girdle of leather" (II Kings 1:8), "forbare" (I Sam. 23:13; II Chron. 25:16; Jer. 41:8) but also "forbear" (Exod. 23:5; Deut. 23:22; I Kings 22:6; etc.), and "fishermen" (Luke 5:2) but also "fishers" (Isa. 19:8; Jer. 16:16; Ezek. 47:10; Matt. 4:18, 19; Mark 1:16, 17). Though dropping "corn" and "cornfields" in favor of "grain" and "grainfields," the ASV retained "ears" (cf. Matt. 12:1) in nineteen cases where "heads" would be what Americans would say. Furthermore, the troublesome "whale" remains (Matt. 12:40) for what is "fish" elsewhere, to give the same sort of problem noted about the KJV.

There are other examples of the breakdown of consistency. *Elohim* is rendered "God" (Ps. 8:5; KJV: "angels"), but when the Psalm is quoted in Hebrews 2:7 with *angeloi*, the ASV uses "angels." The ASV uses "Comforter" (as KJV), with "Advocate" in the margin, as the rendering of *paracletos* (John 14:16, 26; 15:26; 16:7), but does just the reverse in I John 2:1 (KJV has "advocate"). To translate the same word "transfigure" (Matt. 17:2) and "transform" (Rom. 12:2; II Cor. 3:18) may obscure a connection. "Living soul" (Gen. 2:7) is used for man, but "living creature" (Gen. 1:24; etc.) is used when rendering the same term for beasts. Both "privately" (Matt. 24:3; etc.) and "privily" (I Sam. 24:4; Acts 16:37; etc.) are used.

The ASV has areas that need improvement. Consider that there is a better way of describing the sound the lion makes than "yell" (Jer. 2:15), that the term "wise men" would be better rendered "magi" (Matt. 2:1), and that "pant" (Ps. 42:1) is not the action suggested in the relevant Hebrew verb. "Drink ye all of it" (Matt. 26:27, ASV and KJV) has "all" in the wrong place, leading the unlearned to a doctrine of total consumption. "Thou shalt not forswear yourself" (Matt. 5:33) is not as clear as "you shall not swear falsely" (RSV) or "do not break your oath" (NIV); "against the day of my burying" is clearer when rendered "for the day" (John 12:7). "Unto God" (II Cor. 5:13, 15) should be "for God." Revelation 22:5 needs a "shall"— "shall need no light of lamp"—to match the tense of the other two words of the sentence.

Though in general the ASV is one of the most literal of the English translations, there are cases where it has not been literal. There is no Hebrew word for "frame" in Judges 12:6. "Believer" (margin, "sister"; I Cor. 9:5) is not a literal rendering; neither is "All hail" (Matt. 28:9) nor "God of truth" (Isa. 65:16; margin "Amen"; cf. Rev. 3:14). The rendering of I Kings 20:23 is not literal. In that verse, rather than a singular, the Masoretic Text has a plural "gods"; but the Septuagint made a substitution to avoid phraseology offensive to monotheism. There are cases of unnecessary supplying of possessive pronouns: "his philosophy" (Col. 2:8), and "his child" (Matt. 10:21). The phrase "God forbid," retained in fifteen instances (Luke 20:16; I Cor. 6:15; etc.), is not literal. However, not all of the ASV additions are bad. "Godliness is a way of gain" (I Tim. 6:5) enlarges "gain is godliness." "Joshua" (for Greek "Jesus") clarifies Acts 7:45 and Hebrews 4:8.

The translators of the ASV readily made additions in italics which affect its literalness. Some of these additions seem necessary: "*How is it* that we could not cast it out?" (Mark 9:28) and "the more *the prophets* called them, the more they went from them" (Hos. 11:2). However, there are numerous cases where words supplied to complete the meaning are not italicized; for example, "may" (Ruth 1:11), "aught" (Ruth 1:17), "fast" (Ruth 2:8), " 'his' child" (Matt. 10:21), and " 'our' redemption" (Eph. 1:7; Col. 1:14). The ASV followed the KJV in rendering *pneumatikos* as "spiritual gift" in Romans 1:11 but as "spiritual *gift*" in I Corinthians 12:1. "Could" is inserted by both versions (Judg. 1:19) without italics to supply what seems a defect in the Masoretic Text. The ASV also retains italics from the KJV which unduly change the meaning of a passage. Both the KJV and the ASV were reluctant to have Stephen pray to Jesus. The KJV had "calling upon *God* and saying, Lord Jesus"; the ASV had "calling upon *the Lord* and saying, Lord Jesus"; but the RSV and NIV correctly drop the unjustified addition and read, "He prayed, 'Lord Jesus, receive my spirit' " (Acts 7:59). Another case is the addition of "our" in the phrase "finisher of *our* faith" (KJV) and "perfecter of *our* faith" (Heb. 12:2, ASV). The addition goes back to Tyndale. Without the addition, it is Jesus' own faith that is perfected; with the addition it is the believer's faith. "The perfecter of faith" (NASB) would be literal.[47] Another case is the insertion of "daughter" after "virgin" in three instances in I Corinthians 7:36ff. to give a certain interpretation of an obscure passage—an interpretation that is at least open to question. Since italics in current usage signifies emphasis, it is not surprising that though the margin suggests uncertainty, the addition of "words" to give "spiritual *words*" (I Cor. 2:13) often invites an emphasis upon the phrase that is not in the original at all.

[47]Principal Brown, "Some Minor Gains of the Revised Version of the New Testament and Some of the Reverse," *Expository Times* 3 (1891-92): 260.

The aim at literalness of the ASV caused it to duplicate Semitic constructions that are not native to English. The most common examples are "And it came to pass," "Behold," and "and" used too frequently. There are other Semitisms even more strange, such as the genitive absolute construction, "in blessing, I will bless" (Gen. 22:17) which should be "I will surely bless." Still others are "die the death" (Mark 7:10) and "with desire I have desired" (Luke 22:15). There is the use of the verb "add" meaning "to continue": "he added and spake a parable" (Luke 19:11). There is the genitival construction which uses the word "God": "fire of God" (Job 1:16), "terror of God" (Gen. 35:5), and "the mount of God" (Exod. 4:27; 18:5; I Kings 19:8). These should be "mighty fire," "mighty terror," and "mighty mountain." There is the use of the genitive with adjectival force: "spirit of infirmity" (Luke 13:11), "the gospel of the glory" (meaning "the glorious gospel," I Tim. 1:11), and "the liberty of the glory" (meaning "the glorious liberty"; Rom. 8:21). Though many of the cases of the construction "son of" or "children of," giving characteristics of a person rather than his descent, were translated into corresponding English phrases, many others are noted in the margin. For example, "sons of the bride-chamber" (Mark 2:19; Luke 5:34) are "companions of the bridegroom." In these cases the margin would be better in the text; but other cases are left unexplained: "sons of this world" (Luke 16:8), "sons of light" (John 12:36), "sons of disobedience" (Eph. 2:2), "son of peace" (Luke 10:6), "children of wrath" (Eph. 2:3), "son of the devil" (Acts 13:10), "children of light" (Eph. 5:8), and others. Other Semitic idioms which are continued but which need translation are "horn of my salvation (II Sam. 22:3, "seed" for "descendants" (Mark 12:19, 20; Rom. 4:13; etc.), and "old and full of days" (I Chron. 23:1).

Numerous cases may be cited where the ASV has the preferable rendering in the margin rather than in the text. The margins are excellent sources for exegesis. Later translations have followed them. Though in some cases (e.g., John 8:34) the ASV comes nearer the idea of *doulos* by its rendering "bond-servant" than did the KJV which had "servant." In others "servant" is retained in the text and "bond-servant" only makes the margin (Luke 17:7; Titus 1:1). Preferable to either of these renderings is "slave," the current English equivalent of *doulos*. Isaiah 9:6 continues in the ASV with the punctuation "Wonderful, Counselor" but the margin drops the comma. Another case of a better margin is at II Peter 2:4 where "hell" is in the text, but "Tartarus" is in the margin. Religious teachers have made use of this marginal note. Colossians 4:15 has "Nymphas and the church that is in their (margin: "her") house." John 12:2 has "sat at meat" (margin: "reclined"). The marginal reading "pasture lands" is preferable to the text's "fields of the suburbs" (Lev. 25:34; Num. 35:2, 3, 4). In the margin, words are recognized as titles of Assyrian officials (Jer. 39:3; Isa. 20:1; 36:2ff.; II Kings 18:17), but they are proper names in the text. "Oracle" (Isa. 14:28; 15:1; etc.) is preferable to "burden," and "stewardship" (I Tim. 1:4; cf. I Cor. 9:17) to "dispensation." "Buildeth up" (I Cor. 8:1) is better than "edifieth," and "sons of tumult" (Num. 24:17) would be better as "sons of Sheth," as in the margin. "Gazelle" is more meaningful than "Dorcas" (Acts 9:36). There are other cases far too numerous to list (cf. Prov. 6:13; John 1:5).

The American Standard Version and Current English

Many constructions in the KJV, judged by modern standards to present grammatical problems, are continued in the ASV, though not with the same prevalence. Adverbs like "sore" (Acts 4:2; etc.) and "exceeding" (Mark 16:4; Luke 23:8) need an *ly* to complete them, but would preferably be modified to "greatly," "very," or "very much." One encounters "sore troubled," "sore afraid," "sore displeased," "sore distressed," and "wept sore" (Acts 20:37); but one also encounters "sore" describing the severity of a famine (Gen. 47:13). In the ASV in a few instances the wrong case is used: we read, "save we two" (I Kings 3:18) and "save he that is from God" (John 6:46).[48] "Yourselves" is used as a subject (I Thess. 2:1; 3:3; 5:2; II Thess. 3:7). There is "but myself" (Esther 5:12; cf. 6:6), "as myself" (Philem. 17), "having under myself soldiers" (Matt. 8:9), "hear from himself" (John 7:51), and "turned herself back" (John 20:14) where "turned back" is adequate. "Less," a comparative (Heb. 7:7; etc.), is used awkwardly in the phrase "less than all seeds" (Matt. 13:32; Mark 4:31). In the epithet "James the Less" (Mark 15:40), no comparison is stated. "Both" is used for more than two (Acts 19:16; 23:8) where, in keeping with Koine usage, "all" would be preferable.

In striving for literalness, the ASV sometimes imitates Hebrew and Greek word order and puts the speaker first where current use demands a reversal lest the speaker appear ill-mannered: "I and the Father" (John

---

[48]"Save" with the nominative is used by Shakespeare, but should now be abandoned.

10:30), "Jehovah watch between me and thee" (Gen. 31:49), "concerning me and concerning thee" (Josh. 14:6), "me and thee" (Matt. 17:27), and "to me and Barnabas" (Gal. 2:9). There are cases of the hanging clause which is natural to Hebrew but considered illiterate usage in English: "Jehovah, he is God" (I Kings 18:39); "Now Hannah, she spake" (I Sam. 1:13); "Whosoever . . . , he is debtor" (Matt. 23:18); and "John, whom I beheaded, he is risen" (Mark 6:16).

There are instances in which the wrong preposition is used. "Of" (e.g., Matt. 1:18; Acts 23:27) and "against" (Exod. 19:15) are used where "by" is needed; "of" where "in" is needed, as in "lame of his feet" (II Sam. 9:3); and "to" where "with" is needed (Acts 15:15). The phrase "Abraham to our father" (Matt. 3:9; Luke 3:8) should be "as our father," "to him they agreed" (Acts 5:40) should be "with him," and "in him" should be "at him" (Mark 6:3). Furthermore, the ASV continued using "a" unnecessarily in verbal constructions: "the ark was a preparing" (I Peter 3:20) and "I go a fishing" (John 21:3). The expressions "fat-fleshed" (Gen. 41:2, 18), "return back" (Matt. 24:18), "close sealed" (Rev. 5:1), "from whence" (Job 2:2), and "the which" (Heb. 10:11) are redundant.

Coleridge said, "A truth couched in archaic diction is, largely or wholly, to some or to many, out of view."[49] The language of the ASV is translation English, not the native idiom. It is a language that was never spoken or written in any country at any time. The Old Testament examples of English words in Hebrew word order can be multiplied: "He that . . . taketh it, to him will I give Achsah" (Judg. 1:12); "and if we drink of thy water, I and my cattle, then will I give the price thereof" (Num. 20:19); "gat him up upon his mule" (II Sam. 13:29); "the king, and all the people that were with him, came weary" (II Sam. 16:14); "Now the name of the man of Israel that was slain, who was slain with the Midianitish woman, was Zimri" (Num. 25:14); and "Now Boaz went up to the gate, and sat him down there" (Ruth 4:1). "Reproach her not" (Ruth 2:15) is improper word order for both Hebrew and English. At times Hebrew structure is carried through Greek into English in the New Testament, as in "Male and female made he them" (Mark 10:6).

A major cause of the quaintness and awkwardness of the language of the ASV is the frequent use of reversed word order: "wash not" (Matt. 15:2), "defileth not" (Matt. 15:20), "charged he" (Matt. 16:20), "they under-

---

[49]Cited in H. M. Whitney, "The Latest Translation," *Bibliotheca Sacra* 60 (July 1902): 453.

stood not the saying" (Mark 9:32), "they marveled all" (Luke 1:63), "weep not" (Luke 7:13), "clean every whit" (John 13:10), "faith unfeigned" (I Tim. 1:5), and "brother beloved" (Philem. 16). Another cause is the use of the auxiliary verb "did" in past-tense constructions like "did grind" (Judg. 16:21), "did eat" (Gen. 3:6, 12, 13; Matt. 15:38; Mark 1:6; Luke 6:1), "did ... spit" (Matt. 26:67), "didst hide" (Matt. 11:25), "didst suck" (Luke 11:27), "didst teach" (Luke 13:26), "didst send" (John 17:8), and "didst put" (Heb. 2:8). The expression "shut to the door" (Gen. 19:10; Luke 13:25) is likely a Briticism.

The New Testament also has English words in Greek structure: "And they ate, and were all filled: and there was taken up that which remained over to them of broken pieces, twelve baskets" (Luke 9:17); "my brother had not died" (John 11:21); "What do we? for this man doeth many signs" (John 11:47); and "finding nothing how they might punish them" (Acts 4:21). In II Cor. 3:10 one encounters only English words, all of which can be understood, but the sentence is a Greek construction, not an English one, and is hardly intelligible: "For verily that which hath been made glorious hath not been made glorious in this respect, by reason of the glory that surpasseth." The RSV clarifies the idea: "Indeed, in this case, what once had splendor has come to have no splendor at all, because of the splendor that surpasses it." The ASV maintains Ephesians 1:3-14 and Colossians 1:9-17 each as one long complicated sentence because they are one sentence in Greek.

Because the ASV tried to use the vocabulary of Tudor and Jacobean authors (sixteenth—seventeenth century), it was an artificially created antique when it appeared, and eighty years have only made its language more outdated. Of the list of archaic words in the KJV compiled by the makers of the RSV, the ASV retains sixty-five;[50] however, this list does not exhaust the archaisms in it.

While the ASV was making an effort to update the language of the KJV by the use of modern spellings and the elimination of archaisms that would be misunderstood, some new archaisms, not in the KJV, were created, such as "howbeit," "peradventure," "holden," "aforetime," "sojourn," "must needs" (Luke 14:18; 21:9), "would fain" (Luke 13:31; 15:16), "behoove" (Luke 24:26), and "egress" (Ezek. 43:11; 44:5). In seventeen cases

---

[50]George Dahl, "The Authorized Revisions of the King James Version," in *An Introduction to the Revised Standard Version of the Old Testament* by members of the Revision Committee (New York: Thomas Nelson & Sons, 1952), p. 22.

the word "haply" is joined to the word "lest" (cf. Matt. 4:6; 7:6; Luke 4:11) where the KJV did not have it. The ASV also increases the number of times the word "ward" is used in such phrases as "thee-ward" (I Sam. 19:4), "to us-ward" (Rom. 8:18), "to you-ward" (Gal. 5:10; Col. 1:25; I Thess. 5:18), and "Godward" (II Cor. 3:4). It uses "thitherward" (Jer. 50:5; Rom. 15:24) and "thereunto" (Exod. 36:36; Deut. 1:7; Isa. 13:15, margin; Eph. 6:18). Where the KJV had "your treasure ... your heart" the ASV has "thy treasure ... thy heart" (Matt. 6:21). Where the KJV had "in the evening" the ASV has "at eventide" (Gen. 8:11), and where there was "had sworn" (Acts 7:17) there is "vouchsafed."

The ASV is replete with other archaisms that make the communication of God's Word to the uninitiated more difficult. There are the old English pronouns: "ye," "thy," "thine," "thee," and "thou"—all used for addressing man, God, and beast. Unlike some have contended, these forms do not show special reverence for God since they are also used in derogatory statements like "thou son of the devil" (Acts 13:10) and "Get thee behind me, Satan" (Matt. 16:23). If this usage creates a binding, or even an admirable example, then everyone should be talking like the early Quakers. In the ASV these pronouns are accompanied by the old English forms of verbs that end in "th": "doth" (Luke 22:26), "hath," "believeth," "sweareth," "saith," "bringeth," "crieth," "goeth," "runneth," "longeth," and the like. Out-of-date tenses are used: "forgat" (Gen. 40:23), "sware," "brake," "tare" (II Kings 2:24; Mark 9:20; Luke 9:42), "bare," "spake," "clave" (Gen. 34:3), "chode" (Gen. 31:36), "baken" (Lev. 6:21), "wreathen" (Exod. 28:14), "espied" (Gen. 42:27), "laded" (Gen. 44:13), "crew" (Luke 22:60), "wetted" (Luke 7:44), "durst" (Mark 12:34; Luke 20:40), "hungered" (Luke 4:2), and "digged" (Mark 12:1).

There are archaic numbers: "sixscore thousand," "fourscore," "threescore and ten," "ninety and nine," "thrice," and others. While Abraham Lincoln may have created an English classic with such phrases, they are archaic and are no more sacred than "a hundred and twenty thousand," "eighty," "seventy," "ninety-nine," and "three."

The accurate communication of God's Word is seriously hampered by the use in the ASV of those archaisms which now have acquired a different meaning. Few would know that "mean man" (Isa. 2:9; 5:15; Prov. 22:29; cf. Acts 21:39) is only the "common man," and that "replenish" means only "fill" (Gen. 1:28). God's "unspeakable gift" (II Cor. 9:15; cf. I Peter 1:8) is his "indescribable gift." "Pitiful" (Lam. 4:10) is "compassionate," and "apart" (Matt. 17:1) means "by themselves" rather than that the mountain is "apart." "Denounce" (Deut. 30:18) merely means "to tell," "perfected" (Gal. 3:3) means "ended," "parts" (Matt. 2:22; 15:21; 16:13) means "borders" or "regions," "bread" often means "food" in general (Matt. 15:26; 16:5; Luke 7:33; etc.), and "meat" means food of any sort rather than solely "flesh." "Sat at meat" (Mark 6:22; Luke 5:29; 11:37; 22:27) designates a meal. "Garnished" (Matt. 12:44; Luke 11:25) means "cleansed" rather than "decorated." "Room" may mean "place" rather than a room in a house (Matt. 2:22). "Soul" may mean "the individual" (Rom. 13:1), "communicate" (Gal. 6:6) means "to share," "science" (Dan. 1:4) means "knowledge," a "stalled ox" (Prov. 15:17) is one fed in a stall, an "angle" (Hab. 1:15) is a "hook," "patience" means "steadfastness" (Luke 21:19; Heb. 10:36; 12:1; James 5:11; Rev. 1:9; 2:2, 3, 19; 3:10; 13:10; 14:12), "band" (Acts 10:1) is an army unit, "lord" (Amos 4:1) means "husband," "quit" (I Cor. 16:13) means "act," but "be quit of him" (Luke 12:58) means "be rid of." "Defraud" (I Cor. 7:5) means "deny" or "deprive," "libertines" (Acts 6:9) are men freed from slavery, and "gnashed on him" (Acts 7:54) means "ground their teeth at him." "The striker" (Titus 1:7) is not a participant in a labor dispute but is a quarrelsome person, "certify" merely means "inform" (II Sam. 15:28; Ezra 4:14, 16; 5:10; 7:24), "usury" means any interest (Neh. 5:7, 10; Hab. 2:7[m], "tender" (Gen. 29:17) means "weak," "simplicity" (II Cor. 11:3) means "singlemindedness," "slime" (Gen. 11:3; 14:10; Exod. 2:3) is "tar," "still" means "continually" (Ps. 84:4), "outwent" means "outran" (Mark 6:33), and "overcharge" means "overload" (Luke 21:34). "Translate" means "transfer" (Col. 1:13; Heb. 11:5), and "suddenly" means "quickly" (Isa. 29:5; 30:13).

A wrong impression may be gained from Acts 17:3 where Paul is "opening and alleging that it behooved the Christ to suffer." "Alleging" in current English suggests affirming that which is of doubtful truth, and that is not what Paul was doing. The twenty-two cases of "commune" meaning "to talk" (cf. Luke 6:11; etc.) may also confuse the reader. The queen of Sheba "communes" with Solomon (I Kings 10:2), and Felix "communes" with Paul (Acts 24:26). "Communications" (Luke 24:17) are "conversations." "City" is used for a small village like "Nain" (Luke 7:11). The serpent is called a "beast" (Gen. 3:1), though not now so classified. The admonition "See that ye fall not out by the way" (Gen. 45:24) is likely to be understood as a caution against falling out of the wagons Joseph was supplying or against dropping out of the party, as soldiers "fall out." Actually it was a warning not to quarrel. Joseph had not completely forgotten his brothers' past.

"Questionings" (Acts 15:2; I Tim. 6:4) would be better as "discussion." James "answers" (Acts 15:13) when no one asks; "spoke up" would be better. "Slumbered and slept" (Ps. 121:3, 4; Matt. 25:5) now means "slept and slept"; that the disciples "became drowsy and slept" is preferable. "Poll" now is a voting place, but in the ASV it means "a head" (Num. 1:2; etc.). "Palsied" (Matt. 8:6; Acts 8:7) is now a disease characterized by trembling; "paralyzed" would be suitable for the disorder spoken of. "Saluted" (Luke 1:40; etc.) calls to mind a military situation, but the word merely means "greeted." "Strolling Jews" (Acts 19:13) suggests that they are walking; "itinerant" is preferable. "Mad" (Acts 12:15; 26:24, 25) now means "angry" but should be understood in the ASV as "insane." "Sell," now a commercial transaction, then meant "deliver" (Judg. 2:14; 4:9); "lusty" (Judg. 3:29) is now "lustful," but then meant "strong" or "vigorous." "Estate" (Acts 13:50; 17:12) is now a land holding—not a station in life. "Privy" is an "outhouse," not a state of being aware (I Kings 2:44; Acts 5:2). "Mark" in the ASV means "notice" (Ruth 3:4). "Suffer" means "permit" (Matt. 3:15; 8:21; 19:8, 14; Luke 4:41; 9:59; 18:16; Acts 28:16). "Dispensation" then meant "stewardship" (Eph. 3:2, 9; Col. 1:25; I Tim. 1:4). "Advertise" meant "to inform" (Num. 24:14). "Swellings" (II Cor. 12:20) meant "conceit," "providence" (Acts 24:2) meant "provision," "provided" (Heb. 11:40) meant "foreseen," "report" (Matt. 4:24) meant "news of him," "knew" (Matt. 1:25; etc.) was used for sexual intercourse, and "mocked" (Matt. 2:16) meant "deceived." "With observation" meant "to be visible" (Luke 17:20), "couch" meant "mat" (Luke 5:24), "save" meant "except" (Luke 18:19), and "staves" (Matt. 26:47; Luke 22:52) meant "clubs." "Worship" (Matt. 9:18) meant "do homage," but now worship is offered exclusively to divine beings. "Visit" (James 1:27) meant "look after the needs of." The "evil eye" (Matt. 20:15; Mark 7:22) meant "envy," not "witchcraft."

The coins named in the ASV may have been familiar to nineteenth-century Englishmen who used "penny" (Matt. 10:29), "farthing" (Matt. 5:26; Mark 12:42), "mites" (Mark 12:42), "shilling" (Matt. 18:28; 20:2, 9, 10; John 12:5), and "pound" (Luke 19:16); but such coins are completely foreign to twentieth-century Americans. So also are the weights and measures: "firkins" (John 2:6), "flagons" (Exod. 25:29; 37:16; Isa. 22:24), "homer" (Num. 11:32), "cor" (Ezek. 45:14), "ephah" (Zech. 5:6-10), "cubit" (Matt. 6:27), and "furlongs" (Luke 24:13). They create a problem for the reader beyond that caused by the transliterated terms. Ordinarily the reader passes over them with no clear concept of the quantities involved.

In some cases the vocabulary of the ASV is so archaic that it conveys no meaning at all to the reader unless he is aided. "Murrain" (Exod. 9:3), "blains" (Exod. 9:10), "withes" (Judg. 16:7-9), "besom" (Isa. 14:23), "emerods" (Deut. 28:27; I Sam. 5:6, 9, 12, margin), "avouched" (Deut 26:17), "scall" (Lev. 13:30-37), "pulse" (Dan. 1:12, 16), "hosen" (Dan. 3:21; margin, "turbans") "gin" (Pss. 140:5; 141:9; Amos 3:5), "covert" (Ps. 27:5), "quarternions" (Acts 12:4), "concision" (Phil. 3:2), "caul" (Lev. 3:4; Isa. 3:18; Hos. 13:8), "maw" (Deut. 18:3; Jer. 51:34), "churl" (Isa. 32:5, 7), "ravin" (Nah. 2:12), "rapine" (Nah. 3:1), "shambles" (I Cor. 10:25), "sottish" (Jer. 4:22), "drag" (Hab. 1:15), "draught" (Matt. 15:17; Luke 5:4, 9), "draughthouse" (II Kings 10:27), and "shamefastness" (I Tim. 2:9)—all fall in this category. To these may be added the transliterated words like "Raca" (Matt. 5:22), "mammon" (Matt. 6:24; Luke 16:9, 11), and "anathema, Maranatha" (I Cor. 16:22) which must be interpreted.

In some cases the reader may guess a meaning from the context, but he really has no clear concept of what is meant by the word, or he may understand it but seldom use it. "Kine" (Gen. 41:2), "clean passed over" (Josh. 4:1), "surfeiting" (Luke 21:34), "travail" (Gen. 38:27; etc.), "upbraid" (Matt. 11:20), "constrain" (Matt. 14:22), "straitened the way" (Matt. 7:14), "hunger-bitten" (Job 18:12), and "effulgence" (Heb. 1:3)—all fall into this group. Other examples are the words "fuller" (Mark 9:3), "contemn" (Ps. 10:13), "garner" (Ps. 144:13; Matt. 3:12; Luke 3:17), "bier" (Luke 7:14), "mete" (Ps. 60:6; Matt. 7:2; Luke 6:38), "meet" (meaning "suitable"; Luke 15:32), "sop" (John 13:26), "swaddling clothes" (Luke 2:7, 12), "apparelled" (Luke 7:25), "cruse" (Luke 7:37), "bands" (Col. 2:19), "froward" (Ps. 18:26; etc.), "discomfited" (Ps. 18:14), "reins" meaning "kidneys" (Rev. 2:23), "forswear" (Matt. 5:33), "undressed" cloth (Matt. 9:16), "assayed to join" (Acts 9:26), "lucre" (I Tim. 3:8), "vainglory" (Phil. 2:3), and "perdition" (Phil. 1:28; Heb. 10:39). There is "laded" (Gen. 44:13), "unlade" (Acts 21:3), and "lading" (Acts 27:10). There is "determinate counsel" (Acts 2:23), "suborned" (Acts 6:11), "ward" (Acts 4:3), "adventure himself" (Acts 19:31), and "consort with" (Acts 17:4).

The reader can guess the meaning of some words because of familiar elements, but the words are still strange: "Cumber" (Luke 10:40; 13:7), "gratulation" (Gal. 4:15), "ensample" (Phil. 3:17; I Thess. 1:7; II Thess. 3:9; I Tim. 1:16; 4:12; I Peter 5:3), "oft" (Matt. 9:14), "oft-times," "abode," "was wont," "her hap" (Ruth 2:3), "betimes" (Gen. 26:31; Prov. 13:24) meaning "seasonably," and "mess" (Heb. 12:16). There is "broidered" (Ps. 45:14; etc.), "undersetter" for "support" (I Kings 7:30, 34), "gender" (Lev. 19:19; Job 21:10; 38:29), and "headtire" (Ezek. 24:17). There are adverbs like "grievously," "haply," "privily," "exceedingly," "hither and thither," "provoked her sore" (I Sam. 1:6), and "sore troubled" (Acts 16:18). There are adjectives like "gross" (Isa. 60:2; Jer. 13:16; Matt. 13:15), "uttermost parts" (Deut 30:4; Acts 1:8), "brutish" (Ps. 49:10), "divers" (Heb. 13:9), and "evil affected against" (Acts 14:2). There are nouns like "malefactor" (Luke 23:33, 39; II Tim. 2:9) and participles like "purloining" (Titus 2:10) and "situate" (Nah. 3:8).

The largest category of all is that group of archaisms which the educated reader likely will understand but which are not the vocabulary of twentieth-century speech: "say thee nay" (I Kings 2:17), "bestir" (Joel 3:12), "rent" (II Sam. 1:2), "yesternight" (Gen. 19:34; etc.), "yon" (Judg. 5:5), "trafficker" (Hos. 12:7), "crossway" (Obad. 14), "sojourn" (Ps. 15:1), "tidings" (Gen. 29:13), "vesture" (Pss. 102:26; 104:6), "extolled" (Ps. 66:17), "man child" (Rev. 12:5, 13), "woman child" (Num. 31:18), "woman-servant" (Gen. 20:14), "woman-singer" (Eccles. 2:8), "womankind" (Lev. 18:22; 20:13), "whole" meaning "well" (Matt. 9:12, 22; Mark 5:34), "saving" meaning "except" (Matt. 5:32; 11:27; Mark 9:29), "nether" (Judg. 1:15), "well stricken in years" (Josh. 13:1), "morsel" (I Sam. 2:36), "lachet" (Mark 1:7; Luke 3:16), "aught" meaning "anything" (Matt. 5:23; Luke 19:8), "manifold" (Luke 18:30), "host" meaning "army" (II Sam. 17:25; etc), "dung it" (Luke 13:8), "feign" (Luke 20:20), "magnify" (Luke 1:46; Acts 10:46), "nothing bettered" (Mark 5:26), "damsel" (Ruth 2:5; etc.), "fast by" (Ruth 2:8, 21, 23), "fall" meaning "turn out" (Ruth 3:18), "sheepcote" (I Chron. 17:7), "to wit" meaning "namely" (I Chron. 27:1), "hard" meaning "closely" (I Chron. 10:2), "waxed" meaning "became" (II Chron. 13:21), "far spent" (Luke 24:29), "over against" (Luke 24:50), "over against you" (Matt. 21:2), "abide" (Luke 24:29), "fetch" (Gen. 18:5; etc.), "drew on" (Luke 23:54), "thereabout" (Luke 24:4), "compass" (Matt. 23:15; Luke 19:43; 21:20), "gotten this injury and loss" (Acts 27:21), "howbeit" (Gen. 48:19; etc.), "aforepromised" (II Cor. 9:5), "scrabbled" (I Sam. 21:13), "must needs" (Luke 21:9), "lodge" (Luke 19:7), "straightway" (Luke 17:7; Matt. 3:16), "silverlings" (Isa. 7:23), "press upon *him* vehemently" (Luke 11:53), "straitened" (Luke 12:50), "would fain" (Luke 15:16), "heavy with sleep" (Luke 9:32; cf. Matt. 26:43), "no wise" (Mark 16:18), "rend" (Luke 5:36), "in health" (Luke 5:31), "smite"

(Luke 6:29), "beseech" (Mark 8:22), "would not" meaning "did not wish to" (Mark 9:30), "moved with indignation" (Mark 10:41), "how hardly" (Mark 10:23), "sorrowful" (Mark 10:22), "accounted to rule" (Mark 10:42), "thereon" (Mark 11:13), "rid you of care" (Matt. 28:14), "noteable" meaning "notorious" (Matt. 27:16), "make it as sure" for "secured" (Matt. 27:65), "raiment" (Matt. 3:4; 28:3), "give suck" (Matt. 24:19; Mark 13:17), "was wroth" (Matt. 22:7), "husbandmen" (Matt. 21:38) meaning "tenants," "stand without" (Matt. 12:47), "leaven" (Matt. 13:33), "do iniquity" (Matt. 13:41), "in no wise" (Matt. 16:28), "whithersoever" (Matt. 8:19), "befallen" (Matt. 8:33), "besought" (Matt. 8:34), "fishers" (Matt. 4:18, 19), "thence" (Matt. 4:21; 5:26), "savor" meaning "saltiness" (Matt. 5:13), "on this wise" (Matt. 1:18), "parts" meaning "borders" (Matt. 2:22), "privily" (Matt. 1:19), "alms" (Matt. 6:2), "assayed" meaning "tried" (Acts 26:21), "no wise" (I Thess. 4:15), "any wise" (II Thess. 2:3), "menstealers" (I Tim. 1:10), "verily, verily" (John 3:5), "vaunt" meaning "boast" (James 4:16), "aforetime" (I Peter 3:5), "separations" meaning "divisions" (Jude 19), "sup" meaning "to eat" (Rev. 3:20), "hindermost" (Gen. 33:2; Jer. 50:12), "hindmost" (Deut. 25:18; Josh. 10:19), "hinder part" (Joel 2:20; etc.), and "strange children" (Hos. 5:7).

Other strange expressions are "clean passed over" (Josh. 4:1), "clean bare" (Joel 1:7), "stanched" (Luke 8:44), and "was like to be" (Jonah 1:4). We read that Aaron "cast down his rod" (Exod. 7:10: etc.), but we would say "He threw down his rod"; for "Ye have made our savor to be abhorred" (Exod. 5:21), we say "You made us to stink"; for "he took to wife" (Exod. 2:1), we say "He married." Instead of "When there falleth out any war" (Exod. 1:10), we say "If war breaks out." We would replace "Draw not nigh hither" (Exod. 3:5) with "Come no nearer," "Put off thy shoes from off thy feet" (Exod. 3:5) with "Take off your shoes," "Put forth thy hand" (Exod. 4:4) with "Put your hand out." We say "brothers," not "brethren." One does not see a doctor because one is "holden with divers diseases" (Matt. 4:24). We do not say that one army has "discomfited" another (cf. Exod. 17:13; I Sam. 7:10), nor that it "smote the hindmost" of them (Deut. 25:18; Josh. 10:19).

Conclusion

The purpose of this study is not to suggest that the ASV is a poor version of Scripture, but merely to demonstrate that improvements are needed. The major message of the Bible is clear; the examples of deficiencies, numerous as they are, deal with secondary matters.

Even as late as 1901, homes were lighted by gas and kerosene lamps. Electricity was not generally available. Though the telephone had been invented, it was not yet widely used. Few people had radios, and no one had watched a television program. Trains were available, but the basic means of transportation was horse and buggy. Very few people had cars and no one had flown an airplane, not even the Wright brothers. The ocean could be crossed only by ship, and the trip took almost thirty days. Each winter many people died of pneumonia, for no one had dreamed of miracle drugs. Each summer some were crippled with dreaded polio; Salk vaccine was yet a half-century away. The ASV represented the best scholarship and biblical learning of its time. It is not, however, the final word in Bible translation. Scholarship has advanced with the passing of years, and the ASV now lags behind.

5

The Revised Standard Version after Twenty-five Years

T he copyright of the American Standard Version (originally held by Thomas Nelson and Sons) was acquired and renewed in 1928 by the International Council of Religious Education. This council is now the Department of Christian Education of the National Council of Churches of Christ in the United States, representing forty member churches of the United States and Canada. The Council appointed a committee of fifteen scholars to consider whether further Bible revision was desirable. Though the committee was divided over the urgency of revision, they recommended, after two years of work, that a revision be made. It was stipulated that the revisers stay as close as possible to the Tyndale-King James tradition while utilizing modern knowledge of the Hebrew and Greek texts and their meaning and employing current English. However, the Depression years brought an interruption in the work. With the passing of those lean years, in 1937, upon the committee's recommendation, the International Council voted to authorize a revision designed "for use in public and private worship" which also would preserve "those qualities which have given to the King James Version a supreme place in English literature."[1] This purpose set the project apart from modern speech translations and paraphrases, which are designed primarily for easy reading and as aids to study. At the same time, the revisers were not restricted to the use of Elizabethan English as their predecessors of 1885 and 1901 had been.[2]

Thirty-two scholars, whose names are carried in the booklet *An Introduction to the Revised Standard Version of the New Testament*, served on the committee making the revision. They represented the faculties of twenty universities and theological schools. One Jewish scholar, an expert in Septuagint studies, participated. Luther A. Weigle served as chairman of the committee. Some committee members were chosen for their knowledge of English literature, others for their experience in conducting public worship, and still others for their expertise in biblical scholarship. In addition, an advisory board of fifty representatives of various churches was selected to review the work. The thirty-two scholars were formed into New and Old Testament groups, each of which submitted its work for the review of the other. Apart from the secretary, who devoted a major portion of his time to the project, the revisers received no remuneration other than travel and incidental expenses for fifteen years of work. The New Testament was published in 1946, the complete Bible (Old Testament and New Testament) in 1952, and the Apocrypha (which had not been included in the initial plans for revision) in 1956.

The first printing of the completed Bible produced a million copies; if stacked they would have made a pile twenty-four miles high. More than three thousand religious services, which were attended by an estimated two million people, were held simultaneously across the nation to celebrate the publication.[3]

However, despite the massive publicity campaign, like all things new in religion, the RSV was both praised and faulted. Some critics objected to the National Council and its work; some charged that the theology of the revisers had intruded into their work. While some thought the revision too radical, others found it too conservative. Some read it avidly; others

---

[1] Preface to RSV.

[2] Luther A. Weigle, "Revision of the English Bible," in *An Introduction to the Revised Standard Version of the New Testament* (n.p., The International Council of Religious Education, 1946).

[3] H. G. May, "The RSV Bible and the RSV Bible Committee," *Perspective* 12 (Fall 1971): 218.

publicly burned it.[4] Although Moffatt (1913), Smith-Goodspeed (1923), Phillips (1947), and others had offered translations, the appearance of the RSV was for many people the first major challenge to the KJV/ASV domination of the English Bible field. It therefore has borne the brunt of the criticism of new versions.

Now that the RSV has been on the market for more than twenty-eight years, perhaps we have gained perspective enough to evaluate it. With the passing of these years, the heat generated by some of the prejudicial charges first levied has somewhat subsided, as the charges have been found to be without validity. Its promoters have categorically denied that the translators had any connection with the Communist party, and fair-minded people have accepted that.[5] Other personal charges against the translators also are heard less frequently now. The trend is to recognize that a version must be evaluated upon the merit of its renderings and not upon the background out of which it came. We sing songs composed by men with whom we disagree because the songs have merit, and in the same way we read translations made by men with whom we disagree because they also have merit. We reject both the songs and the translations when the problems outweigh the merits.

Editions of the RSV printed on India paper and bound in black leather have become available to those who objected to the red-covered modern-book appearance of the first edition. Those who objected to its being copyrighted should know that all English Bibles, including the KJV and ASV, were copyrighted when first issued. The King James still enjoys copyright protection in Britain. It is only right that the purity of the text be protected and that the investment made by the publisher be safeguarded. The RSV will not become public domain until A.D. 2008, but ten years after its initial publication by Thomas Nelson and Sons, the right to publish it was granted to five other firms. Use of the royalties from the sale of the version has been restricted to further work on the actual text of the Bible.[6]

---

[4]R. L. Roy, *Apostles of Discord* (Boston: The Beacon Press, 1953), pp. 203-11; S. M. Gilmour, "New 'Textus Receptus'?" *Christianity Today* 4 (September 26, 1960): 6-10.

[5]"An Open Letter Concerning the *Revised Standard Version of the Bible*" (New York: Division of Christian Education, National Council of Churches of Christ in the USA, n.d.).

[6]Luther A. Weigle, "The Standard Bible Committee," in *Translating and Understanding the Old Testament*, ed. H. T. Frank and W. L. Reed (Nashville/New York: Abingdon, 1970), pp. 29-41; "The Scriptures: *The Revised Standard Version of the Bible*," in *Yearbook of American Churches 1959*, ed. Benson Y. Landis (New York: National Council of Churches of Christ in the USA, 1959),

The Text

In the revision, changes from the ASV had to be agreed upon by a two-thirds vote of the total committee. The revisers of the Old Testament claim to have followed the consonantal Masoretic text except in those places (e.g., Judg. 16:13; Isa. 1:29; etc.) in which it is assumed that other vowels give a better reading; where errors in copying can be corrected by recourse to the Greek, Aramaic, Syriac, and Latin versions (e.g., Gen. 4:8; Deut. 32:8; I Sam. 14:41; I Kings 10:28-29; etc.); or where conjectural emendation seemed necessary to correct the text (cf. Ps. 2:11; Amos 6:12; etc.). Qumran material was followed in thirteen cases in the Book of Isaiah. Seven of these cases also had the support of the ancient versions (Isa. 14:30; 15:9; 45:2; 49:24; 51:19; 56:12; 60:19). Although second thoughts concerning some of the thirteen cases were expressed later, readings from Qumran in Isaiah 21:8 and 53:11 are judged by scholars to be well established. In the RSV, verse rearrangement was done at Exodus 22:1-4 to give the sequence of verses 1, 3a, 4, 2, 3b to produce a more logical order of thought. Footnotes ordinarily indicate cases of departure from the Masoretic text, but no note accompanies the reading "Edom" for "Syria" (II Sam. 8:12) or that of "sea" created by a new division of the Hebrew letters (Amos 6:12). Departures from the Masoretic text are more numerous (as many as six hundred instances) in the RSV than in either the KJV or the ASV.[7]

Although the Westcott-Hort type of Greek text for the New Testament was dominant when the RSV committee began its work, the committee came to realize that "no one type of text is infallible" and that "each reading must be examined on its own merits."[8] Their textual work is therefore a representative of the so-called Eclectic Principle. Two hundred and forty-three textual variants are cited in the footnotes of the New Testament.[9] In general, the readings chosen are to be found either in the

pp. 304-8; H. G. May, "*The Revised Standard Version* After Twenty Years," *McCormick Quarterly* 19 (May 1966): 305.

[7]Millar Burrows, "The Revised Standard Version of the Old Testament," *Supplements to Vetus Testamentum* (Leiden: E. J. Brill, 1960), 7:214; O. T. Allis, "R.S.V. Appraisal: Old Testament," *Christianity Today* 1 (July 1947): 21.

[8]F. C. Grant, "The Greek Text of the New Testament," in *An Introduction to the Revised Standard Version of the New Testament*, p. 41.

[9]Robert G. Bratcher, *Why So Many Bibles?* (n.p., The Evangelical Foundation, Inc., 1961), p. 38.

text or margin of the seventeenth edition of the Nestle *Novum Testamentum Graece* (1941).[10] Discovery of the Washington Gospels, papyrus fragments, and especially the Chester Beatty Papyri—the oldest known copy of the letters of Paul—disclosed an earlier state of the text than was previously known.

Vocabulary

In the Old Testament revision, use was made of the increased knowledge of the Semitic languages, sometimes giving a meaning quite different from the traditional interpretation. The note system at times calls attention to such cases, but the instances are more numerous than the use of the abbreviation "Cn" in the notes (cf. Judg. 16:13, Isa. 1:29) suggests. The minority opinion in the committee is sometimes reported in the notes introduced by "Or" (e.g., Gen. 1:1, 2; I Kings 10:22).[11]

The revisers also benefited from the study of the vocabulary, grammar, and idiom of the New Testament which resulted from the Egyptian papyrus finds. A. Deissmann's theory of Koine Greek as the language in which the New Testament was written sheds new light upon the meaning of Greek words.

Of equal significance were the changes made because the English language itself is continuously changing, so that once accurate translations no longer say what they did when the translation was made. Some words are no longer in use. The reader is even more confused by words which are still in use but which have taken on a different meaning. The RSV revisers did not attempt a new translation. Their work was considered a revision; changes were made only for good reason, but the end product is a more thorough revision than was the ASV. Rather than printing each verse as a separate paragraph (as in the KJV), the RSV paragraphed thought units (as in the ASV) with verse numbers printed throughout the paragraphs in smaller type at the top of the line.

Disputed Features

In the matter of specific verses, the rendering "young woman" for 'al-mah in Isaiah 7:14 has without doubt created more discussion than any

---

[10]Grant, "The Greek Text," p. 41.

[11]Millar Burrows, "The Revised Standard Version of the Old Testament," pp. 208-9.

other single point. *'Almah* is a feminine form whose masculine counterpart *'elem* is rendered "stripling" or "youth" in its two occurrences (I Sam. 17:56; 20:22). Both masculine and feminine forms come from *'alam*, a root meaning "to be mature." *'Almah* is found seven times in the Hebrew Bible, and in no case does it indisputably refer to a married woman. While some occurrences of the word are very clear, others are ambiguous. Outside the Bible, its use for a woman no longer a virgin can be cited from the Aramaic Targum of Judges 19:1 and from the Palmyrene language where it is used for harlots. In Ugaritic it is used for the goddess Nikkal and for Lady Hurriya. In one text it is parallel to the word for woman. *Bethulah* (rather than *'almah*) is the term used in the Old Testament when technical virginity is under discussion. It is striking that none of the Greek, Latin, or English Bibles prior to the RSV have consistently rendered *'almah* as "virgin" in all of its occurrences. The Septuagint used *parthenos* (virgin) in some cases and *neanis* (maiden) in others. The Latin Vulgate used *virgo* (virgin), *puella* (girl), and *adolescentulae* (female adolescents). The KJV uses "maid" in Exodus 2:8 and Proverbs 30:19, and "damsel" in Psalm 68:26 (25). The ASV uses "maiden," "damsel," and "virgin," with "maiden" also given in the margin at Isaiah 7:14 where "virgin" is in the text. All of these show that "young woman" is a possible rendering for *'almah*. The RSV has "virgin" as a marginal reading of Isaiah 7:14, a reversal of what the ASV did.

The sign of which Isaiah speaks is likely not the child but the time it takes a child to be born and to grow up to the age of choice. The statement of Isaiah 7:16 about the coming of age of the child is parallel in meaning to another statement made in Isaiah 8:4. The claim that a "sign" *must* be a miracle, a contention at least as old as the time of Tertullian, will not stand up under linguistic investigation (cf. Exod. 3:12; Isa. 8:18; 20:3). Still another sign involving a span of time is encountered at Isaiah 37:30.

There was no virgin birth, of course, in Isaiah's day, but this episode of which the prophet speaks prefigures the virgin birth of our Lord. Matthew, in citing the passage, is likely using a typological form of fulfillment of prophecy in chapter 1:23 just as he does in the cases of Rachel's weeping for her children (2:18) and of "Out of Egypt have I called my Son" (2:15). The RSV rendering of Isaiah 7:14 would permit such a typical fulfillment. The New English Bible, The Jerusalem Bible, Phillips' Four Prophets, and Today's English Version all render *'almah* in Isaiah 7:14 by "young woman." The New American Bible, issued by Catholics in 1970, because of special episcopal intervention in the matter has "virgin" in the text but carries a note explaining that the word really means "maiden." With its clear teaching concerning the virgin birth of Jesus in Matthew 1:18-23 and in Luke 1:26-28, the RSV cannot justly be charged with denying the virgin birth. The Isaiah passage has been the subject of debate since the beginning of the Christian era, and the RSV merely stimulated a reexamination of the passage.[12]

An initial criticism involved the dropping in the RSV of "begotten" from the KJV phrase "only begotten son" (John 3:16) as a rendering for *monogenēs*. However, additional examination reveals that the KJV itself rendered *monogenēs* as "only" in Luke 7:12; 8:42; and 9:38. *Monogenēs* occurs ten times in the New Testament. In view of its use to describe such figures as Jairus' daughter, the widow's son, and the epileptic child (as well as Jesus), the claim that "only begotten" in a unique way expresses Jesus' sonship better than "only" does is without validity. Since women do not beget sons, *monogenēs* could not be rendered "only begotten" in Luke 7:12, and the child must be the "only son" of his mother. *Monogenēs* derives from *genos* ("sort" or "kind") rather than from *gennaō* ("to beget"). While the Old Latin Version used *unicus* ("only") for *monogenēs*, Jerome inconsistently introduced *unigenitus* ("only begotten") as the rendering for some of the occurrences of *monogenēs*. Though Tyndale had used "only son," the KJV (as well as other English Bibles, beginning with the Great Bible) seems erroneously to have followed Jerome's lead in its rendering "only begotten." A considerable number of current evangelical scholars believe that the RSV is not at fault in its rendering. The NIV, when issued in completed form, used "one and only" (with "only begotten" as a footnote) for this expression.[13]

[12]Robert G. Bratcher. "A Study of Isaiah 7:14," *Bible Translator* 9 (1958): 97-126; John Scullion, "An Approach to the Understanding of Isaiah 7:10-17," *JBL* 87 (1968): 288ff.; J. Massingberd Ford, "The Meaning of Virgin," *NTS* 12 (1965-66): 1293-99, E. Hammershaimb, "The Immanuel Sign," *Studia Theologica* 3 (1949): 124-42; J. A. Motyer, "Context and Content in the Interpretation of Isa. 7:14," *Tyndale Bulletin* 21 (1970): 118-25; Stefan Porubcan, "The Word 'Ot in Isaiah 7:14," *CBQ* 22 (April 1960): 144-59; Raymond F. Surburg, "The Interpretation of Isaiah 7:14," *Springfielder* 38 (September 1974): 110-18; H.M. Wolf, "Solution to the Immanuel Prophecy in Isaiah 4:14-8:22," *JBL* 91 (December 1972): 449-56; Dale Moody, "Isa. 7:14 in the *Revised Standard Version*," *The Review and Expositor* 50 (January 1953): 57; John J. Owens, "The Meaning of '*Almah* in the Old Testament," *The Review and Expositor* 50 (January 1953): 60.

[13]Dale Moody, "God's Only Son: The Translation of John 3:16 in the R.S.V.," *JBL* 72 (1953): 213-19; F. C. Grant, " 'Only-begotten'—A Footnote to the R.S.V.," *Bible Translator* 17 (1966): 11-14; R. L. Roberts, "The Rendering 'only begotten' in John 3:16," *Restoration Quarterly* 16 (1972): 2-22.

Sometimes the RSV was criticized for concurring with decisions that had already been made in the ASV. The dropping, on textual ground, of the phrase "through his blood" (Col. 1:14) is an example. The phrase is well attested as authentic in Ephesians 1:7 but is a harmonization not supported by any ancient Greek manuscript in Colossians 1:14. The RSV, along with all other accurate translations, clearly teaches redemption through the blood of Jesus (Matt. 26:27-28; Mark 14:24; John 6:53-56; Acts 20:28; Rom. 3:23-25; 5:8-10; I Cor. 10:16; 11:25-27; Eph. 2:13; Heb. 9:12-14, 22; 13:12, 20; I Peter 1:2, 19; I John 1:7; 5:6; Rev. 1:5; 5:9; 7:14; 12:11).

Yet another criticism of the RSV has been its handling of passages in which there are textual problems. For example, Mark 16:9-16 was printed in the first edition as a footnote, but in the latest printing is included in the regular type of the text and is accompanied by a note. However, all texts and Bibles since the time of Westcott-Hort (1881) have in some way indicated that this passage offers textual problems. Westcott-Hort set off the passage in their text in double brackets. The ASV set it off from the text by a space. The NEB prints both the so-called short and the long endings, each separated from the text by a space and accompanied by an explanatory footnote. The GNB heads the section "An Old Ending to the Gospel."

The RSV gives a similar treatment to the story of the woman taken in adultery (John 7:53 — 8:11), at first printing it in the notes, but since 1971, setting it off in the text by a wide space and a note. All Greek texts and English versions since the time of Westcott-Hort have also used one means or another to indicate a textual problem in this section. The NEB prints it at the end of the Gospel. It seems that the manner of indicating textual problems is solely a matter of judgment, and one cannot really claim that one method is better than another. The ASV's use of space to indicate this textual problem makes the problem less obvious to the unlearned reader, but the obscuring of information does not prove to be an advantage.

The RSV attempts to indicate direct address by the use of quotation marks. Since neither Hebrew nor Greek identifies direct address in this way, an element of judgment is involved, particularly in the Gospel of John where the ending point of an address is not always clear. Such a passage is seen in John 3 where the RSV ends the quotation at verse 3:15, making John 3:16 a statement of the author rather than of Jesus. The point at which Jesus' speech ends has been a matter of debate in recent years, and the RSV indicates the difference of opinion in a footnote. A like ambiguity over the end of a quotation is found in Revelation 19:10. The red-letter Bibles (not a part of the 1611 edition of the KJV) make the same type of judgment. Older versions (KJV and ASV) that use no quotation marks or other indications of direct speech did not have to commit themselves on the matter.

Reception of the RSV

While enjoying the phenomenal sale of more than twenty-five million copies of the New Testament and of the complete Bible in its first twenty-five years,[14] and thirty million up to 1974,[15] the RSV has by no means displaced the KJV in popular use. The American Bible Society estimated that in 1969 the KJV still outsold its nearest competitor three-to-one.

Nor has the RSV stemmed the spate of English translations, unparalleled since the days of the Reformation, that our generation has seen. The New English Bible, which was begun before the RSV and was not intended as a rival to it, appeared in 1970 with tremendous publicity. Also, in 1970 Catholics carried through to completion the New American Bible. The Lockman Foundation published the New American Standard Bible in 1971. The American Bible Society issued the Good News Bible, edited by R. Bratcher, which sold the phenomenal number of fifty-two million copies of the New Testament (under the name Today's English Version) before the completed Bible appeared in 1976.[16] Evangelicals prepared the New International Bible and, after issuing the New Testament in 1973, released some books of the Old Testament between 1973 and 1977. The completed Bible was published in 1978. The past generation has seen translations of the New Testament by individuals such as J. B. Phillips and, more recently, William Barclay.

These Bibles all differ from the RSV. The RSV attempts to revise the wording and style of the ASV while retaining the flavor of the KJV. Except

[14]Personal letter to the author from Howard N. Woodland, Executive Secretary, Division of Christian Education, National Council of Churches of Christ in the USA, dated October 29, 1970.

[15]H. G. May, "Revised Standard Version," in *Which Bible Can You Trust?* (Nashville: Broadman Press, 1974), p. 49.

[16]G. E. Jones, "Another 'Readable' Bible, But Is It Any Better?" *U.S. News & World Report* 81 (December 20, 1976): 54; Eugene A. Nida, *Good News for Every One* (Waco, Texas: Word Books, 1977), p. 115.

for the New American Standard Bible, the recent translations strive to be independent of earlier versions and are modern speech translations. What their ultimate success will be remains to be seen. The paraphrasing tendencies in the NEB, in the TEV, and in the New Testament of Phillips make them inadequate for detailed study of the Bible. The TEV's use of language intelligible to people without much formal education limits its ability to express many shades of meaning found in the original. Those who are not concerned about details of the biblical message may find these versions edifying reading, for they are quite readable. From them one can learn the general trend of the biblical message, but for detailed study, the RSV is one of the best versions now available. It uses reasonably current English, the results of archaeological discovery, and current linguistic knowledge. Compared with the treatment of the text of the NEB (where there are many rearrangements), the RSV is a conservative revision.

A concordance to the RSV produced by electronic methods was prepared in 1957. An analytical concordance to the New Testament was issued in 1979. *Gospel Parallels*, edited by B. H. Throckmorton, using the RSV text, appeared in a third edition in 1967. The version has also been the basis of such commentaries as *The Interpreter's Bible, Torch Bible Commentaries, Peake's Commentary, New Bible Commentary, Broadman Bible Commentary*, and *The Living Word Bible Commentary*. It has been used in dictionaries like the *Interpreter's Bible Dictionary*, has been adopted by many churches as the Bible to be used in both church worship and in Bible school, and has been used in a host of Bible study materials. It has been recorded as a talking book for the use of the blind.

A Catholic edition of the RSV, issued in 1966 by the Catholic Biblical Association of Great Britain, contained sixty-seven changes in the New Testament text and certain changes in the note material, all congenial to Catholic thought. The notes laid more stress on tradition than did the original edition of the RSV. The Deutero-canonical books were placed among the Old Testament books. Sixteen passages of the New Testament which the RSV carried in the footnotes were restored to the text. It seems that the more poorly attested reading was chosen at Mark 13:33 when the variant "and prayer" was inserted. Translation changes were made at Matthew 1:19; 12:41-42; Mark 3:31ff.; Luke 1:28 (with no Greek textual support); Luke 8:19ff.; John 7:34; Romans 5:5; 8:11; 9:5; and Ephesians 1:14. The change from "brothers" to "brethren" (Matt. 12:46), accompanied by a note, allowed room for the contention that Jesus had no brothers. Protestants would take exception to the note accompanying Matthew 16:18-19. The appendix of the edition carried a complete list of the changes.[17]

In May, 1966, shortly after the issuing of the RSV-Catholic Edition, the Oxford Annotated Bible, which has the regular RSV text (including the Apocrypha), was approved for use by the Catholic Church when it received the imprimatur of Richard Cardinal Cushing, Archbishop of Boston.[18] This step marked the first time in four hundred years that Catholics and non-Catholics read from the same Bible with official approval. The KJV (definitely a Protestant production) was never a common Bible. In 1973 the RSV Common Bible was issued with a special arrangement of the Apocrypha in recognition of its usage by Catholic, Orthodox, and Protestant groups.[19] While Catholics may now also read the JB (1966) and the NAB (1970), Protestants are not likely to make any great use of these; thus the RSV is the leading contender to become the Bible used by some readers in all the divisions of Christendom.

Among evangelicals there continues to be a divided mind on the usability of the RSV. While some outstanding leaders, though recognizing its defects, have found it usable,[20] others continue to be quite vocal in denouncing it.[21] This controversy led to the launching of a new translation project (the NIV) under the auspices of the Evangelical Theological Society and the New York Bible Society. *Christianity Today* of September 27,

[17]Adam Fox, "RSV CE (NT)," *Theology* 69 (1966): 164-70; B. M. Metzger, "RSV Modified for Catholics," *Christianity Today* 11 (1966): 44, 46; Luther A. Weigle, "The Scriptures: *The Revised Standard Version*," in *Yearbook of American Churches for 1965*, ed. Benson Y. Landis (New York: National Council of Churches of Christ in the USA, 1965), pp. 291-94; "The Scriptures: *The Revised Standard Version*," in *Yearbook of American Churches for 1966*, ed. Benson Y. Landis (New York: National Council of Churches of Christ in the USA, 1966), pp. 229-31; "The Scriptures: *The Revised Standard Version of the Bible*," in *Yearbook of American Churches for 1967*, ed. Benson Y. Landis (New York: National Council of Churches of Christ in the USA, 1967), pp. 230-33.

[18]James Daniel, "At Last: One Bible for All Christians," *Reader's Digest* 90 (May 1967): 112-16; R. A. Kraft, review of *Oxford Annotated Bible with Apocrypha*, ed. H. G. May and B. M. Metzger, in *JBL* 85 (1966): 486-89; James M. Ward, review of *The Oxford Annotated Bible with the Apocrypha (Revised Standard Version)*, ed. H. G. May and B. M. Metzger, in *Perkins Journal* 27 (Summer 1973): 46.

[19]H. G. May, "The Revised Standard Version Bible," *Vetus Testamentum* 24 (1974): 239-40; R. Swanton, "Common Bible," *The Reformed Theological Review* 32 (1973): 99-100.

[20]D. G. Barnhouse, "I Have Read the RSV," *Eternity* 24 (April 1970): 4; George E. Todd, "RSV Appraisal: New Testament," *Christianity Today* 1 (July 1957): 7-11; Edwin M. Good, "With All Its Faults," *Christianity Today* 5 (January 16, 1961): 306-7.

[21]O. T. Allis, *Revision or New Translation?* (Philadelphia: The Presbyterian and Reformed Publishing Company, 1948).

1968, carried a lively exchange between R. Laird Harris[22] and Stanley E. Hardwick[23] over whether or not the project was necessary and desirable. Harris denounced the RSV, but Hardwick argued that it is adequate.

Changing Editions

Unlike most previous translation committees which disbanded when their product was published, the Standard Bible Committee which produced the RSV has continued in active existence. Additional members were appointed to replace deceased members and to enlarge the ecumenical aspect of the committee. It is composed of thirty-four members, including five Roman Catholics, one Greek Orthodox, and one Jewish person. The committee's purpose is to have charge of the text of the Revised Standard Version of the Bible, to recommend when revision should be made, and to make revisions or new translations as the sponsoring body authorizes.[24] Meetings of the committee were held in 1954, 1959, 1965, 1968, and 1970, and more recently, annually.

Over the past years some church committees, like those of the Missouri Synod Lutheran and the Christian Reformed churches, as well as some individuals, have made evaluations of the RSV and submitted them to the Standard Bible Committee.[25] Such a procedure will likely prove to be the only effective means of producing changes in future editions. Millar Burrows, one of the translators, made a minute comparison of the differences between the Old Testament of the RSV and that of the KJV and published it under the title *Diligently Compared and Revised*, New York: Nelson, 1964.

As a result of the various evaluations and criticisms of the 1946 edition, the New Testament issued in the completed Bible of the RSV in 1952 was emended in eighty places. Some changes were made in the interest of consistency. Since "sanctify" was used in the Old Testament, the words

[22]R. Laird Harris, "Do Evangelicals Need a New Bible Translation? Yes," *Christianity Today* 12 (September 1968): 1242, 1244-46.

[23]Stanley E. Hardwick, "Do Evangelicals Need a New Bible Translation? No," *Christianity Today* 12 (September 1968): 1243, 1246-47.

[24]H. G. May, "The RSV Bible and the RSV Bible Committee," *Perspective* 12 (Fall 1971): 217-34; B. M. Metzger, "Trials of the Translator," *Theology Today* 33 (April 1976): 99.

[25]Harold S. Bender, Chester K. Lehman, and Millard C. Lind, *The Revised Standard Version: An Examination and Evaluation* (Scottdale, Pennsylvania: Herald Press, 1953), pp. 145-46.

"sanctify" and "sanctification" were restored in some passages where "consecrate" and "consecration" had been used in 1946 and had provoked criticism.[26] Other changes are in Luke 24:28; John 8:53; 11:50; 17:2; Acts 17:28; I Corinthians 4:5; Philippians 1:7; II Timothy 3:8; I John 3:10.

In 1959 the committee considered about two thousand other criticisms and suggestions that had been made between 1952 and 1959, recommending about two hundred changes. These have appeared in all printings since October 1, 1962. Some changes concerned capitalization, punctuation, and footnotes, but others dealt with wording in the interest of clarity and accuracy. "A son of God" becomes "the Son of God" in Matthew 27:54 and Mark 15:39; "married only once" becomes "husband of one wife" in I Timothy 3:2, 12 and Titus 1:6 or "wife of one husband" in I Timothy 5:9. Examples of other changes are "from" ("then from my flesh I shall see God") for "without" (Job 19:26), "bread" for "loaf" (Matt. 7:9; I Cor. 10:17), "is he" for "be he" in Matthew 21:9 and parallels, "ask nothing of me" for "asked me no questions" (John 16:23), and "for this life only" for "If in this life we who are in Christ have only hope" in I Corinthians 15:19. "Come to life again" and "did not come to life again" (Rev. 20:4, 5) are now "came to life" and "did not come to life."[27]

At a meeting held in 1968 the matter of "You/Your" forms for divinity was considered, but it was decided that though these forms are becoming more popular, the time was not then right for this change.[28] Of particular note is the fact that the committee considered this usage to be solely a matter of tradition and expediency. Such distinctions do not exist in Hebrew, Greek, or Latin. The second edition of the RSV Old Testament projected for issue in the mid-80s will drop "thee," "thou," and "thine" and the accompanying *th* endings for verbs in the prayers and psalms.[29]

In a second edition of the New Testament issued in 1971, in keeping with the third edition of the United Bible Societies' Greek New Testament, the ending of Mark (16:9-20) and the *Pericope Adulterae* (John 7:53—

---

[26]E. H. Robertson, *The New Translations of the Bible* (London: SCM Press, 1959), pp. 145-46.

[27]R. G. Bratcher, "Changes in the New Testament of the *Revised Standard Version*," *Bible Translator* 12 (1961): 61-68; Luther A. Weigle, "The Scriptures: *The Revised Standard Version of the Bible*," in *Yearbook of American Churches for 1961*, ed. Benson Y. Landis (New York: National Council of Churches of Christ in the USA, 1961), pp. 289-92.

[28]Luther A. Weigle, "The Scriptures: *The Revised Standard Version of the Bible*," in *Yearbook of American Churches for 1969*, ed. Benson Y. Landis (New York: National Council of Churches of Christ in the USA, 1969), p. 216.

[29]B. M. Metzger, "The Trials of the Translator," *Theology Today* 33 (April 1976): 100.

8:12) are moved from the footnotes to the text, with a space separating them from the rest of the text. Luke 22:19b-20 and Luke 24:47a are restored, the latter on the evidence of the Bodmer manuscript. In the contrary direction, a phrase of Luke 12:39 and the whole of Luke 22:43-44 are dropped to the footnotes. "Men" (italicized in the KJV) is dropped in Luke 17:34. Pre-1611 translations did not have the word, and the situation described in the passage is not limited to males. Other changes in wording are at I Corinthians 3:9 and II Corinthians 5:19.[30] It is projected that under the impact of the women's liberation movement, masculine usage which can be removed without changing the intent of the original writers will be eliminated in the forthcoming edition. Fuller use will be made of Qumran materials than has been done in past editions.[31]

The RSV and the ASV

The publicity thrust with which the RSV was issued, designed to show its superiority to the KJV, laid the RSV open to the charge that its alleged improvements had already been made in the ASV. In actuality, the very trends that had made the ASV superior to the KJV continued to make the RSV superior in many respects to the ASV. Improvement was made in all areas, overcoming many of the weaknesses that have been cited earlier for both the KJV and the ASV. In many cases the ASV margin had anticipated the choices the RSV moved into the text. The RSV was based on superior textual study, additional knowledge of the culture and languages of the biblical world, further interpretation of the biblical text, a new concept of the translator's task, and recognition of changes in the English language itself.

Textual studies were advanced by the discovery of the Dead Sea Scrolls (1947ff.) for the Old Testament, and the Washington Gospels (1906) and the Chester Beatty papyri (1933) for the New Testament. The Bodmer group, which only came to light in 1955-1956, was not available for use. Some of the text of the New Testament could be studied in its state at the beginning of the third century rather than only from the fourth. Rather

---

[30]G. H. Jones, review of *The Holy Bible. Revised Standard Version*, 2nd ed., in *Religious Studies* 9 (1973): 366-77.

[31]Metzger, "Trials of a Translator," p. 100; Bratcher, "Change in the New Testament of the *Revised Standard Version*," pp. 61-68; Jones, "*The Holy Bible. Revised Standard Version*," pp. 366-67.

than follow a particular type of text, the scholars followed the Eclectic Principle in which variant readings for each passage were evaluated on their own merits. A striking difference in interpretation dependent upon a different reading of the text is found in Romans 8:28. The RSV can claim support of the Chester Beatty papyrus for its reading, "in everything God works for good"; the ASV had a different subject: "all things work together for good." Another case is in I John 5:18 where only one Greek letter differs between the KJV/ASV reading "keepeth himself" (ASV margin: "some ancient authorities read *him*") and the RSV "He who was born of God keeps him." Other RSV passages based on improved textual readings derived from the ancient versions are Genesis 4:8; 21:9; 44:4-5; Judges 16:13; I Samuel 10:1; 14:41-42; and Jeremiah 15:12. A superior text is followed in Matthew 6:4, 6, 18; Luke 17:9; Mark 6:20; I Corinthians 7:2; Ephesians 5:20; Revelation 17:8; etc.[32]

In the second category (additional knowledge of the culture and languages of the biblical world), the great advance in the knowledge of the cognate Semitic languages has given new meanings for some Old Testament words. Translators felt the influence of the papyrus discoveries that gave rise to A. Deissmann's theory which contended that the language of the New Testament was the Koine (common) language of the first century. Numerous examples of vocabulary improvement (giving more exact meaning for words) can be cited. Tilgath-pilneser and Pul (I Chron. 5:26) are identified with each other, and Pharaoh Necho goes "up to" rather than "against" the king of Assyria (II Kings 23:29)—they were allies, not opponents. The "Rabsaris" and "Rabmag" (Jer. 39:3), "Tartan" (Isa. 20:1), and "Rabshakeh" (Isa. 36:2, 4, 11, 13; 37:8; II Kings 18:17ff.) are recognized to be titles (not proper names), as the ASV margin also acknowledged them to be. Solomon got his horses in a place called "Kue" rather than "in droves" (I Kings 10:28; II Chron. 1:16), and Balaam came from Amaw (a place-name created by transliteration; Num. 22:5) rather than from "the land of the children of his people." The "file" of the Philistines (I Sam. 13:21) was really the "pim" charged by them—weight stones with the word on them have been found. The "slime" used for building (Gen. 11:3) or for daubing the ark of bulrushes (Exod. 2:3) is "bitumen." The "candle" and "candlestick" retained at times in the ASV should be the "lamp" and "lampstand," while "torch" is proper in some places (Rev. 4:5) where

[32]Grant, "The Greek Text," p. 41.

"lamp" occurs in the ASV. "Sandals" are more accurate for footgear than "shoes," and a "pallet" than a "bed" (John 5:8). "Custodian" (Gal. 3:24) is more accurate than "tutor," and the "idle" man than the "disorderly" man (II Thess. 3:6, 7, 11; I Thess. 5:14). "Swaddling clothes" (Luke 2:7, 12) became "swaddling cloths." "Money box" (John 13:29) is more accurate than "bag," and "crops" (Luke 12:17) than "fruits." "Plan," "stewardship," or "divine office" is preferable to "dispensation" (Eph. 1:10; 3:2; Col. 1:25), since the Greek word does not mean a "span of time." Paul's letters are correctly called "letters" rather than "epistles." Paraphrastic renderings like "God forbid" (Rom. 6:2; etc., for *mē genoito*) have given way to "by no means," which is an emphatic negative but does not needlessly supply the name of God. "Those who mutilate the flesh" (Phil. 3:2) is an improvement over "concision," which was a failure of the KJV/ASV to reproduce successfully a play on words in Greek. "Thomas, called the Twin" (as "Jesus who is called Justus"; Col. 4:11) is better than "Thomas Didymus" (John 11:16; 20:24; 21:2).

The RSV did not hesitate to abandon revisions made in the ASV and revert to KJV usage where it seemed expedient. A striking case is its use of "Lord" as the divine name where the ASV had used "Jehovah."[33] Second Timothy 3:16 is translated in a manner to affirm the inspiration of Scripture as was true in the KJV. The alternative reading is given in a note.

Those cases in which it is recognized that the ASV missed the interpretation of the verse are corrected. Rather than Paul's "opening and alleging" that the Christ should suffer (Acts 17:3), he is "explaining and proving." "If we have only hoped in Christ" (I Cor. 15:19) becomes "If for this life only." (The 1946 edition reads "we who are in Christ have only hope.") "He will give it you in my name" (John 16:23) becomes "He will give it to you in my name." It shall turn out unto you for a testimony" (Luke 21:13) becomes "This will be a time for you to bear testimony." Other clarifications can be seen if one will compare II Corinthians 3:10 and 10:13 in the ASV with their form in the RSV.

The RSV represents a different concept of the translator's task from that followed in the ASV. Variety (as in the KJV) is used in rendering Hebrew and Greek words rather than striving for consistency. For example, the Greek word *splanchnizomai* is rendered both "pity" (Matt. 18:27; 20:34) and "compassion" (Matt. 9:36; 15:32). The idea of a mechanically

---

[33]See the explanation in the preface of the RSV.

exact, literal word-for-word translation which attempts to follow the order of Hebrew or Greek words is abandoned in favor of an idiom and word order more natural to English. While the ASV was more accurate than the KJV, it had lost some of its beauty and power as English literature.

Though usually retaining the Semitism "Behold" to introduce statements, the RSV reduced the use of expressions from Semitic speech not native to English which the ASV had preserved. Other ways of beginning sentences are used rather than "And it came to pass." For example, "When men began to multiply" (Gen. 6:1) is used instead of "And it came to pass, when men began to multiply." "Answered and said" becomes "answered" (Gen. 18:27; etc.) or "replied." The monotonous use of "and," linking sentences together in imitation of Hebrew style, is varied by the use of "when," "so," or "then," or is omitted altogether. "People of Israel" is preferred to the time-honored rendering "children of Israel" for the phrase which literally is "sons of Israel." "Wedding guests" (Mark 2:19) replaces "sons of the bridechamber." "With desire I have desired" (Luke 22:15) becomes "I have earnestly desired," and "He added and spake" (Luke 19:11) becomes "he proceeded to tell." Some have criticized this loss of Semitic flavor in the material,[34] but the RSV's gain as literature cannot be denied.

The RSV does not use italics to indicate words supplied to clarify meanings, as its predecessors (KJV; ASV) had done. By adopting such a policy it does not invite the unlearned to suppose that the italicized ideas should be given special emphasis in such expressions as "*unknown* tongue." While there is room for debate on whether supplied words should be indicated, all people who are skilled in translating from one language to another know that it is futile to attempt to use the same number of words in translated language that there are in the original language. In the RSV a noun may be supplied for a pronoun (e.g., "Eli"; I Sam. 4:18) when it is needed for clarity. The KJV had done so in some cases but had put the noun in italics. A subject of a clause is at times supplied (e.g., "the slave"; Exod. 21:21) to avoid ambiguity. The RSV sometimes indicates in the notes that a word was supplied (e.g., Lev. 18:17; I Sam. 20:12).

While theories of translation will always remain a topic of debate among scholars, one cannot deny that in the area of current English usage, the RSV is a marked improvement over the ASV. Some of the awkwardness in language which had from the beginning been considered one of the

[34]H. F. D. Sparks, *On Translations of the Bible* (London: Athlone Press, 1973), p. 14.

major handicaps of the ASV has been removed. The readability of the RSV comes in part from the recognition of the nature of Hebrew poetry and from the printing of poetic sections as poetry. The RSV has made an effort to exhibit the parallelism characteristic of Hebrew poetry and has printed poetical sections in poetic form. Only 15 percent of the Old Testament in the ASV was printed as poetry, whereas in the RSV 45 percent of the Old Testament appears as poetry.[35]

Simple improvement in English in the RSV can be seen in many examples where reversal of normal word order in the ASV resulted in awkwardness. Scattered examples include: "wash not" (Matt. 15:2), "defileth not" (Matt. 15:20), "charged he" (Matt. 16:20), "believed him not" (Matt. 21:32), "all their works they do" (Matt. 23:5), "other five talents" (Matt. 25:16), and "know not" (Matt. 26:70, 72, 74). There is improvement where the ASV used "did" to express the past tense; for example, "did eat" for "ate" (Matt. 14:21; 15:38). There are cases where "be" was used for "is and has"; for example, "be risen" (Matt. 17:9) and "be gone" (Matt. 18:12). Numerals are given in their current form in the RSV so that "twenty and four" (Num. 7:88; I Kings 15:33; Rev. 11:16) becomes "twenty-four" and "ninety and nine" (Luke 15:4, 7) becomes "ninety-nine."

Another improvement is the reduction of the number of dangling clauses (*casus pendens*): "Abel, he also brought" (Gen. 4:4); "Now Hannah, she spake in her heart" (I Sam. 1:13); "The ancient and honorable, he is the head; and the prophet that teaches lies, he is the tail" (Isa. 9:15). However, despite the trend, a dangling clause is retained at John 14:26. The use of the accusative pronoun where a nominative would be expected is corrected: "Himself took our infirmities" (Matt. 8:17; cf. Acts 8:9). "James the less" (Mark 15:40) becomes "James the younger."

The archaic expressions that have been removed in favor of more current words would fill a book if all were listed. "Murrain of cattle" (Exod. 9:3; also chapter heading) is replaced by "Plague on Cattle." "Besom of destruction" (Isa. 14:23) becomes "the broom of destruction." "Cumber" (Luke 13:7), not now in common use, has given way to "use up the ground"; "mansions" (John 14:2; with "abiding places" in the margin) to "rooms"; "pressed on every side, yet not straitened" (II Cor. 4:8) to "afflicted in every way, but not crushed"; "Defraud ye not one the other" (I Cor. 7:5) to "Do

---

[35]James Muilenberg, "The Poetry of the Old Testament," in *An Introduction to the Revised Standard Version of the Old Testament* (New York: Thomas Nelson and Sons, 1952), pp. 62-63.

not refuse one another." American coinage is used instead of British when "farthing" gives way to "penny" (Matt. 5:26) and "mite" to "copper" (Luke 12:59). "Mote" and "beam" become "speck" and "log." "Forswear" becomes "swear falsely." "Garnished" (Luke 11:25), which may suggest "decorated," becomes "put in order." "Cruse" becomes "jar" (Matt. 26:7). "Kine" (Gen. 41:3ff.; I Sam. 6:7, 10) becomes "cows." "Cut down" conforms more to current use than "hewn down" (Matt. 7:19). The "froward" master (I Peter 2:18) becomes "overbearing." The "mean man" (Isa. 2:9; 5:15; Prov. 22:29) is "man" or "obscure man." The "husks" (Luke 15:16) are "the pods," not the shells, of the carob bean.

The ASV had attempted to remove many of the archaisms found in the KJV but had been quite inconsistent in its effort. Some forms removed in the New Testament are retained in the Old Testament. Every page contains archaisms. In the RSV, "thee," "thou," "thy," and "thine" (used in the KJV and ASV for all persons) are retained only in direct address to divinity. Except in liturgical passages, old English "saith" becomes "says"; "sendeth" becomes "send"; and other present-tense verbs ending in *th* like "doeth" and "heareth" are no longer used. Past-tense forms such as "spake," "bare," and the like are eliminated. Indefinite pronouns ending in "soever," and words like "fain," "howbeit," and "peradventure" are abandoned. The RSV, in correcting these various sorts of problems, represents a definite step forward in the communication of God's Word.

Criticisms of the RSV

The preparers of the RSV would have been the last to claim any sort of infallibility or finality for their work. If three men of identical theological views translated any chapter of the Bible, they would have three different opinions on some points. It is inevitable that the RSV should be criticized in areas other than those already noted.

Some would challenge the instances where the RSV differs from the ASV in interpretation of a passage. For example, the using of "betrothed" (I Cor. 7:36-38) instead of "virgin" is an interpretative rendering in which one possibility is preferred to others. "Those who come from Italy" (Heb. 13:24), in preference to "they of Italy," excludes the possibility that the letter was written in Italy. "He is able to guard until that Day what has been entrusted to me" (II Tim. 1:12) is a different concept from "that which I have committed unto him." The RSV scholars decided not to read Christian theology into their translation of Old Testament passages that have been traditionally interpreted messianically, and they have been taken to task for it.[36] The issue is of long standing and likely will never be resolved to everyone's satisfaction.

Certain elements of inconsistency are to be found in the RSV. Passages which are often used in church liturgies (such as the Model Prayer) are left unrevised. It is perhaps this inconsistency, in part, that caused one critic to call it a "philological anachronism and tribute to tradition."[37] While the retaining of the liturgical passages may please the liturgically-oriented churches, a revision of the Bible should be across the board. One section should not be considered more sacred than another.

Another inconsistency is in the retention, after long debate, of the old English pronouns and verb forms when divinity is addressed—in the language of prayer. This practice put the translators in the awkward position of shifting from current English to Old English in the same verse (e.g., Matt. 26:39). They were also forced to make value judgments upon whether the intent of a speaker was to address Jesus in his preexistent state, his exalted state, or in his human nature. The version has been justly criticized for this inconsistency. It gives us the anomaly of "You are my son" (Ps. 2:7), but "Thou art my Son" (Heb. 1:5) when the same Psalm is quoted in the New Testament. Psalm 45:6 has "your divine throne" (with "Your throne, O God" as an alternative in the footnote), but Hebrews 1:8 quotes the same Psalm as "Thy Throne, O God." The assumption of the revisers is that the Psalm in the Old Testament is addressed to an Israelite king. The traditional rendering of this passage is to be preferred as more straightforward than that of the RSV. In another case, Saul says, "Who are you, Lord?" (Acts 9:5; 22:8; 26:15) on the road to Damascus since it is assumed that he did not know whom he was addressing, but later in a prayer he says, "I imprisoned and beat those who believed in thee" (Acts 22:19). Other cases where "you" is used for Christ—cases that some would debate—are found in Matthew 16:16; John 6:69; and John 21; then the old pronouns are used in Hebrews 1:5-13; 5:5, 6; 7:17, 21; and Revelation 5:9. A version should use either modern pronouns or Old English pronouns in

[36]Harris, "Do Evangelicals Need a New Bible Translation? Yes," p. 1244; *Inspiration and Canonicity of the Bible* (Grand Rapids: Zondervan Publishing House, 1957), p. 58.

[37]F. W. Danker, review of *New American Bible; Translated from the Original Language with Critical Use of All the Ancient Sources by Members of the Catholic Biblical Association of America*, in *Catholic Biblical Quarterly* 33 (1971): 405.

all occurrences. The former choice seems preferable even though it involves abandoning the indication of singular and plural which both Hebrew and Greek indicate.

Paraphrastic renderings in II Samuel 8:12 ("Edom" for "Syria"), Amos 6:12 ("sea" for "there"), I Corinthians 7:36-38 ("betrothed" for "virgin"), Hebrews 13:24 ("those who come from Italy" for "they of Italy") and Luke 22:15 ("I have earnestly desired" for "with desire I have desired") have drawn the critic's fire.[38] Some cases can be found where it would appear that words have been supplied unnecessarily, such as "of God" in the phrase "oracle of God" (Hab. 1:1).

Still further movement away from "Bible English" would seem desirable. The RSV retains such phrases as "raiment," "brethren," "such an one" (for "a certain one"), "begone," "smote," "made a feast," "took his journey," and "made haste." "Ears of grain" (Gen. 41:5ff.; Exod. 9:31; Ruth 2:2; etc.) is retained, whereas an American would say "heads of grain," as does the second edition of the RSV New Testament (Matt. 12:1). The commandment "You shall not kill" (Exod. 20:13; etc.) would be more accurate if rendered "You shall not murder." "The love of money is the root of all evils" (I Tim. 6:10) is an erroneous reversion from the revision made by the ASV.

Other specific renderings in the RSV that create problems include "Noah was the first tiller of the soil" (Gen. 9:20), whereas earlier we are informed that Cain was "a tiller of the ground" (Gen. 4:2). Jonah is swallowed by "a great fish" (Jonah 1:17), but is in the belly of a "whale" (as in the KJV and ASV) in the New Testament (Matt. 12:40). The reading "only through faith" (Rom. 11:20) adds "only" to the text to give an unbiblical doctrine. The use of "immorality" (I Cor. 5:1; 6:13, 18; 7:2; II Cor. 12:21; Gal. 5:19; Eph. 5:3) as a synonym for fornication is misleading, since murder, bribery, theft, and all other types of unethical conduct are also immoral.

The preceding examples of the various peculiarities of the RSV are by no means exhaustive; they are only illustrative.

Conclusion

The publication of the RSV marked both the end of one era and the opening of another in the effort to communicate God's Word to the English

---

[38]Sparks, *On Translations of the Bible*, pp. 14-15.

reader. For many its publication marked the end of the age in which "The Bible" meant the KJV. The RSV opened the era of the multiple translations flooding today's market, all competing with each other. Though the RSV was regarded by some as representing the avant-garde at the time of its publication, more recent developments show it to be quite traditional in its method of translation and in its retention of archaisms.

Those trends that made the RSV superior in some aspects to the ASV now leave the RSV to some extent in the backwater of Bible translations. Textual study has moved on, language study has made progress, the English language has continued changing. Equally significant is the fact that the Bible-reading public is less insistent on the perpetuation of archaisms than it was a generation ago. The demand for a Bible in the speech of the current day is persistent, and the RSV in its original form cannot claim to be that. The future of the RSV depends as much on its continuous revision to meet these changes as upon its original revision of the Tyndale, King James, and American Standard versions.

6

The New English Bible

The New English Bible (accompanied by an introductory booklet, *The Story of the New English Bible*), was published on March 16, 1970 (with a print run of a million copies), by the Oxford and Cambridge University Presses, which had underwritten the translation project and which hold the copyright. It is the product of a cooperative effort of the Protestant churches in the British Isles. These churches (Church of England, Church of Scotland, the Churches of Wales and Ireland, the Methodist, Baptist, and Congregational churches, and the Society of Friends) previously favored the KJV, which had been produced solely by scholars of the Church of England for use by the Church of England in 1611. The New Testament of the NEB, the preparation of which required thirteen years, has been available to the public since 1961 (350 years after the KJV and 80 after the RV New Testament). Seven million copies were sold — about a third of these (2.8 million) in the United States — in the nine years before the whole Bible was issued.[1] The completed Bible of the NEB

---

[1]"*New English Bible*: On Its Way to Best-Seller Lists," *U.S. News & World Report* 68 (April 6, 1970): 34.

contains a second edition of the New Testament incorporating some needed changes.

Taking twenty-four years to complete, the entire translation project began with a proposal from the General Assembly of the Church of Scotland in 1946 (long before the RSV was completed). Invitations to participate were then issued to various denominations and to the British and Scottish Bible Societies. Later Roman Catholic scholars were invited as observers. A joint committee was set up in 1947 and translating panels, made up chiefly of men from the colleges and universities, were appointed to deal with the Old Testament, the New Testament, and the Apocrypha. A panel of literary advisers with A. T. P. Williams at its head was appointed to ensure good style. Participants in the project were chosen without regard to denominational affiliation. Their names, found in G. Hunt's *About the New English Bible*,[2] read like a British Hall of Fame for biblical scholarship. C. H. Dodd was general director; participants included W. D. McHardy, T. H. Robinson, G. R. Driver, G. D. Kilpatrick, and a host of others, some of whom died before the translation was finished.

Chosen scholars prepared draft translations of individual books, each of which was submitted to a panel of translators who went over it verse by verse. Each draft was then given to the stylists, and then returned to the translating panel to check that the meaning had not been distorted. It was finally submitted to the joint committee which, like an earlier group of translators (the RV, 1881), met in the Jerusalem Chamber of the Westminster Abbey.[3]

The NEB translators set for themselves the ambitious goal of preparing a completely new translation "of the best available Greek text into the current speech of our time, and a rendering that should harvest the gains of recent biblical scholarship."[4] Since the aim differed from that of the RSV, the two were not intended to be rivals. The RSV claimed to be a revision of the Tyndale– King James– American Standard line of Bibles; the NEB was to be independent of earlier translations and was to break with the tradition of "Bible English." It aimed at taking advantage of the best current scholarship in manuscripts, lexicography, and translation skill. It aimed at expressing biblical thought in "the language of the present day"

---

[2]G. Hunt, *About the New English Bible* (Cambridge: Oxford and Cambridge University Presses, 1970), pp. 80-82.

[3]Preface to *The New English Bible*, p. vi.

[4]Ibid., p. v.

while avoiding transient modernisms. Dodd spoke of the use of "timeless English" and voiced the hope that the New Testament would be "as intelligible to contemporary readers as the original version was to its first readers — or as nearly as possible."[5] A statement affixed to the Old Testament declared: "They have made every effort not only to make sense but also to offer renderings that will meet the needs of readers with no special knowledge of the background of the Old Testament."[6] Not primarily planned for reading in the churches, the NEB was prepared for the unchurched, young people, and the intelligent churchman who, because of familiarity with the traditional wording of the Bible, is unmoved by its message. The translators hoped that "this translation may open the truth of the Scriptures to many who have been hindered in their approach by the barriers of language."[7] Not entirely consistent with the statement of purpose of the translators is the claim by the publishers on the dust jacket and in advertising materials: "It is offered as a new and authoritative version of the Bible for use in worship, for teaching, or for private reading."

Tremendous sums had been spent for publicity. Supported by the officials of the British and Scottish churches, the Bible Societies, and the prestigious Oxford and Cambridge University Presses, the NEB was destined to enjoy wide circulation. Though it was not designed to displace the KJV, it could become in time a serious rival to it, at least in Britain, and could largely displace it in the use of the churches.

Though the limp leather editions came later, the NEB, like all recent translations, when first issued had the appearance of a contemporary book, with one column of text to the page. The text appeared in paragraphs rather than in single verses. Traditional verse numbers were placed in the margin rather than within the lines of text, creating some problems of citation, since it is not always clear exactly where one verse ends and the next starts. Poetic sections were printed in verse form, and some effort was made to indicate poetic meter; however, the system may escape the uninitiated reader. Traditional chapters were retained, but section headings and page headings were supplied for the guidance of the reader. In the New Testament all cross references to other Scripture were omitted. Foot-

[5]C. H. Dodd, as quoted by T. H. Robinson, "A New Translation of the English Bible," *Bible Translator* 2 (1951): 197-98; and by J. K. S. Reid, "Concerning the New Translation," *Expository Times* 53 (September-October 1952): 174.

[6]Introduction to the Old Testament, *The New English Bible*, p. xviii.

[7]Ibid., pp. vi-vii.

notes indicated transposition of phrases or verses, gave the meaning of Hebrew proper names, noted alternative interpretations where the Hebrew or Greek is capable of other interpretation (introduced by "Or" in the footnotes), and called attention to emendations in the text if the translators thought it was necessary. Brackets indicate sections the translators think are late additions to the text (e.g., Isa. 6:13; Job 11:6; 26:14c). Quotation marks are used. The NEB continues the first quotation in John 3 through verse 21 (the RSV ended it at v. 15), but notes the other possibility. The second quotation ends at verse 30 as in the RSV. Old Testament quotations in the New Testament are ordinarily in quotation marks, but the quotation of Deuteronomy 19:15 at II Corinthians 13:1 is an exception. Also, the NEB does not treat the words from Genesis 2:24 as a quotation in Matthew 19:5. In keeping with its policy of transliteration where exactness is wanted, the NEB merely transliterates measures of length, weight, and content, as well as sums of money — leaving the reader uninformed as to what is really meant. A helpful table giving relationships between measures, between weights, and between coins was supplied between the Old Testament and the New Testament; however, the relationship between these measures and currently-known values was not given.

Earlier translators felt that fidelity demanded that they reproduce, as far as possible, characteristic features of the original languages such as the order of words, the structure and division of sentences, and even the irregularities of grammar. In contrast, the translators of the NEB were enjoined to replace Hebrew and Greek constructions and idioms with those of contemporary English. Rather than a "word-for-word" translation, their work rendered "meaning for meaning." Their task was first to decide what the text meant and then to express the meaning in good English form. Thought units rather than individual words were considered. Substitution of the noun antecedent for a pronoun was considered legitimate where English style requires it for clarity. Thus "Jesus" is inserted in Luke 17:16; 22:8; Acts 9:22; etc. and "God" in Matthew 27:43; Acts 7:4; etc. This procedure allows the omission of words that are thought to create redundancy in English; for example, "gospel" in I Corinthians 9:18 and the second occurrence of "woe" in Revelation 9:12; 11:14.

Not aiming at a paraphrase, the translators saw their work as a free but faithful translation. They claim to have used great caution in deliberate paraphrase; nevertheless, a fair analysis of their product must deny their claim. The NEB is frequently paraphrastic. A difficulty inherent in paraphrase is that when more than one interpretation is possible, the paraphraser chooses one and eliminates the others.[8] The reader who knows only English is at the mercy of the interpretation of the paraphraser.

The Text

The value of the NEB as a translation is to be judged (as are other translations) by the text chosen, the use of the best linguistic tools, the fidelity with which the text is rendered, and the quality of the English style into which it is translated. It is beside the point to ask, "Why have they changed this?" The questions should be, "Why have they chosen this text?" and "Why have they translated it this way?" In this study, when phrases from the KJV, ASV, or RSV are cited, they are noted for identification purposes or for contrast; I am not suggesting that they are the "authentic" renderings of the phrases.

The approach to the text is one of the distinctive features of the NEB. The third edition of R. Kittel's *Biblia Hebraica* (which, with reservations, was used by all modern students) has been used as the basic text from which the Old Testament is translated. The reader should be aware, however, that numerous conjectural emendations from the apparatus of Kittel (one of the areas in which the Kittel Bible has been most heavily criticized) have been accepted into the text. The dependence upon the Dead Sea Scrolls is significantly greater than was true of the RSV. About fifty scroll readings have been accepted in the text of Isaiah in the NEB, resulting, for example, in the reading "advocate" in Isaiah 41:27, "we despised him" in Isaiah 53:3, and "light" in Isaiah 53:11.[9] Versional evidence has been more heavily depended upon for correction of the Masoretic text than has been true of any previous English Bible.[10] For example, a line in I Kings 8:12 has been inserted from the Septuagint, accompanied by a note in the Library edition only. Though the notes of the Library edition are considerably more extensive than are those of the Standard edition, which most

---

[8]Some cases where the Greek would permit another translation are given by B. H. Throckmorton, Jr., "The New English Bible," *Journal of Bible and Religion* 29 (July 1971): 202; reprinted in Dennis Nineham, ed., *The New English Bible Reviewed* (London: Epworth Press, 1965), p. 90.

[9]D. F. Payne, review of *The New English Bible, Old Testament* in *Biblical Theology* 20 (May 1970): 30; review of *The New English Bible, Old Testament* in *The Churchman* 84 (Summer 1970): 111.

[10]Keith Crim, "The New English Bible," *Bible Translator* 21 (1970): 149.

people will read, even in the Library edition these corrections are not always indicated (e.g., Gen. 2:2). The public waited eagerly for the explanation of the textual innovations, but when L. H. Brockington's list of readings adopted by the translators appeared, it contained no explanations at all.[11] Explanation or defense of the choices remains yet to be made.

The NEB represents the freest handling of the text of the Old Testament of any major English version yet to appear. The passages judged by the translators to need conjectural emendations are usually, but not always, cited in the footnotes and are considerably more numerous than those in the RSV. The notation "Probable reading" is missing in the notes to Genesis 4:8; 10:10; I Kings 13:12; II Kings 18:20; Isaiah 3:1; 7:1; etc. The choices made do not in all cases represent the consensus of scholarship. Some phrases, well-attested in the Hebrew text, are dropped to the footnotes (e.g., in Isa. 3:1; 7:17, 20). The phrases "milk and wine" (Isa. 55:1) and "evil" (I Sam. 16:23) are dropped to the footnotes. Ten words found in Hebrew are omitted in Judges 12:4; a whole verse is relegated to the footnotes at Isaiah 9:15; and at Hosea 1:7, the relegation is on critical ground and not on textual ground. A case of special interest is that of Psalm 40:7 (8) where a phrase found in Hebrew is relegated to the margin as an addition. This phrase is quoted as Scripture in the New Testament in Hebrews 10:7.

The substitution "invaded the ploughlands" for the Hebrew text "ripped up the pregnant women" (Amos 1:13) has no note. The person of pronouns is changed without an accompanying note in Psalms 22:26 (25); 32:5; and 77:14. No note calls attention to the fact that "my guilt" and "my suffering" have displaced "thy guilt" and "thy suffering" of the Hebrew text. "Who will go for me?" in Isaiah 6:8 is a change from the first person plural, but the plural pronoun for a like construction is retained at Genesis 1:26 and 11:7. There are cases of addition in accord with the translators' interpretation of the passage, for example, "my people" (Isa. 52:14), which interprets the second person pronoun.

At numerous places (affecting 136 verses according to one count)[12] the texts of books, especially those of Job, Psalms, Isaiah, and Zechariah, have been rearranged by the transposing of phrases, verses, and series of verses

[11]L. H. Brockington, *The Hebrew Text of the Old Testament* (Oxford: Oxford and Cambridge University Presses, 1973).

[12]T. H. Brown, "The New English Bible—1970," *Bible League Quarterly* 281 (April-June 1970): 294.

to give what the translators judged to be a better sense than does the Masoretic text. Attention is called to these cases in the footnotes as well as in the versification which preserves the traditional verse numbers even when the verses are out of traditional order. Job 31:1 is transposed to follow 31:5, a section of Job 14:14 is transposed into verse 12 and the order of verses 21 and 22 is reversed, and six verses of Job 41 are transposed to precede Job 40. Verses 24 and 25 of Isaiah 5 are transposed to Isaiah 10 between verses 4 and 5. Rearrangements are found in Isaiah 49:3ff. and in Isaiah 52:14—53:2. Amos 5:7 follows verse 9. Major transpositions are seen in Zechariah, resulting in a book of vastly different order from that of the Masoretic text. Chapter 3:1-10 is transposed to follow 4:14, and 4:1ff. follows 2:13. Zechariah 4:4-10 follows 3:10, while 13:7-9 is transposed to follow 11:17.

The fivefold division of the Psalms is retained, but the headings which are a part of the manuscript tradition of the Psalms have been omitted; e.g., the heading of Psalm 51, connecting that Psalm with David's sin, is omitted. "Selah," which occurs seventy-one times in thirty-nine Psalms, is everywhere omitted. In contrast, speaker identifications (not in Hebrew manuscripts) have been introduced into the Song of Songs on the evidence of two Septuagint manuscripts,[13] though the introduction ties the reader to only one (and not the most accepted) of the possible interpretations of the book. It is to be noted that in the headings to the Song of Songs the poems are not interpreted as references to Christ and the church, as was unjustifiably done in the headings in the KJV.

In addition to the transpositions, additions, and omissions, one also encounters the substitution of an English proverb which is not used in America for a Hebrew one: "The lame must not think himself a match for the nimble." The Hebrew proverb is difficult but understandable when freely rendered: "Let not him that girds on his armor boast himself as he that puts it off" (I Kings 20:11; RSV).

In the New Testament the preparers of the NEB neither depended solely upon a previously existing critical text nor attempted to construct one themselves. They voiced the opinion that the fluid state of New Testament textual studies made it inexpedient to construct a critical text at this time. Their work represents an eclectic text in which the reading for each passage is selected from evidence in the manuscripts, the versions, and the

---

[13]Introduction to the New Testament, *The New English Bible*, p. xviii.

church fathers which, in the judgment of the textual scholars, most likely represents what the author originally wrote. Other readings which deserve serious consideration have in 275 cases been recorded in the footnotes.[14] The reconstructed Greek text upon which the New Testament translation rests has been published by R. V. G. Tasker in *The Greek New Testament* (Oxford and Cambridge University Press, 1964), an innovation in itself. This procedure by the translators of publishing the chosen text contrasts with that of Souter, who in 1910 published the text Edwin Palmer inferred was back of the RV (1881);[15] but publication of a Greek text had not been followed by other groups of translators. Tasker furnished thirty-four pages of brief notes on variant readings and the reasons for the committee's choices. With its use of the Chester Beatty Papyri, the Freer Gospels, the Koridithi Gospels, and P 52 (a fragment of the Fourth Gospel from the second century), the NEB represents a state of certain sections of the text a century older than that known to the revisers of 1881 and 1901. Tasker notes that the Bodmer materials were not available when the translators were discussing the parts of the New Testament where those materials would have been relevant.

Scholarly analysis of the underlying text shows that the distinctive readings in the NEB have a heavier dependence on the versional evidence than has been true of earlier English Bibles. In such cases the traditional reading is usually listed in the margin. Most of the verses dropped to the margin by Westcott-Hort are also found only in the margin of the NEB. The verse enumeration skips the relevant number. Though differing on some individual points, the over-all text of the NEB is similar to that followed by the RSV. Both exclude those phrases and verses that the RV/ASV excluded.[16] The real textual divergence is between that followed by the KJV (the *Textus Receptus*) and the text followed by the ASV and all translations since.

The doxology of the Model Prayer (Matt. 6:13), "without a cause" (Matt. 5:22), "openly" (Matt. 6:4, 6), and "fasting" (Mark 9:29) are dropped to the footnotes, as also is I John 5:7b-8a. The so-called "Western noninterpolations" in the last chapters of Luke are put into the footnotes; however,

---

[14]Ibid., pp. v-vi; Robert G. Bratcher, "The New English Bible," *Bible Translator* 12 (July 1961): 101.

[15]Alexander Souter, *Novum Testamentum Graece* (Oxford: Clarendon Press, 1910).

[16]For a sample list of readings where the NEB differs from the RSV, see B. H. Throckmorton, Jr., "The New English Bible," pp. 103ff.; reprinted in Dennis Nineham, *The New English Bible Reviewed*, pp. 78-79.

Luke 22:43-44 and 23:34 remain in the text. Strangely enough, the section called "the short ending of Mark" (found in a few manuscripts, but not seriously thought by any textual scholar to be the original ending of Mark) is printed as an unnumbered section between verses 8 and 9 of chapter 16. Mark 16:9-20 is printed in the text separated from the other text by a space. A note on the textual problem involved is given. John 7:53 — 8:11 is printed at the end of the Gospel of John under the heading, "An incident in the temple." John 7:37-38 is split into two parallel members: "If any is thirsty let him come to me; whoever believes in me, let him drink." Another alternative is given in the note. "Isaiah" is favored over "the prophets" at Mark 1:2; "Son of Man" is chosen at John 9:35 over "Son of God." "At Ephesus" is retained (Eph. 1:1). "Through the shedding of his blood" is absent from Colossians 1:14, but the phrase is thought genuine at Ephesians 1:7. "We love because he loved us first" (I John 4:19) is chosen where the KJV has "We love him." "Seventy-two" (Luke 10:1) is favored over "seventy."

The NEB translators recognize that their textual decisions are provisional, and the reviewers have compiled their lists of instances in which they feel the poorer text was followed.[17] One such case is the acceptance of "Jesus Bar-Abbas" (Matt. 27:17), in preference to "Bar-Abbas," for the thief's name. The accompanying note, "Some witnesses omit 'Jesus',", is misleading about the evidence. Most witnesses omit it; only nine include it, and only one of them is early; nevertheless, some scholars do favor its inclusion.[18] Matthew 9:34 is relegated to the footnotes. The UBS text includes that verse in the text on a "C" rating of probability as necessary to prepare the reader for the accusation in 10:25. The omission of "my words" (Mark 8:38) seems to favor the weaker evidence, as also does the choice of "the Chosen One" over "Son of God" (RSV; John 1:34). The translation given in the note to I John 2:13 seems unjustified from the Greek. Other cases that seem to be poor choices include the preference for "twelve" rather than "the eleven" (Acts 1:26), the omission of "making no distinction" (Acts 11:12), and "in the Lord" (Eph. 6:1). In John 19:29 the translators chose "javelin," the reading of one manuscript, against all other authorities, and rendered the alternate reading as "marjoram" in the note. The NEB still rejects the longer reading at Luke 22:19-20, though

[17]F. W. Danker, "The New English Bible," *Concordia Theological Monthly* 31 (1962): 324.

[18]See B. M. Metzger, ed., *A Textual Commentary on the Greek New Testament* (New York: United Bible Societies, 1971), pp. 67-68.

scholarly opinion now favors that reading. At Acts 13:33 "the children" has no textual support to displace "[their] our children." The reading "the new way" (Acts 18:26) is unsupported by any manuscript evidence. The word "ambassador" (Philem. 9) is based on an emendation in spelling and should have a note to that effect.

The Second Edition of the New Testament

The first edition of the New Testament of the NEB was extensively reviewed by many scholars over the nine years which elapsed before the appearance of the second edition. Some of the representative reviews from many viewpoints have been collected and published by Dennis Nineham in *The New English Bible Reviewed* (London: Epworth Press, 1965). A file was kept of the suggestions made, and the second edition benefits from them. The numerous changes in the new edition (estimated by one reviewer to total over 400)[19] do not change the basic character of the NEB but do include both textual and translation changes. "He casts out devils by the prince of devils" (Matt. 9:34) is dropped and a note inserted to cover the omission. "Blessings on him who comes in the name of the Lord" is included at Matthew 21:9. The footnote at Matthew 1:16 drops the erroneous adjective "early." A note to Mark 15:39 calls attention to the variant "the Son of God" and a modified note at I Peter 3:18 gives a second alternative to the text.

In the second edition of the New Testament, some Old Testament quotations have been harmonized with the Old Testament translation (e.g., Mark 4:29; Gal. 3:13).[20] Obvious translation errors are corrected in the second edition when "Bethany" is made "Bethphage" (Matt. 21:1), "church" is "church of God" (I Cor. 15:9), and "free woman's sons" gives way to "free woman's son" (Gal. 4:30). "Do not feed your pearls to pigs" becomes "Do not throw your pearls to the pigs" (Matt. 7:6). "I am still a virgin" (Luke 1:34) replaces "I have no husband," "sycamore" becomes "mulberry-tree" (Luke 17:6), "eclipse of the sun" (Luke 23:45) is replaced by "the sun's light failed" (an eclipse is impossible at the time of full moon), "quenched the light" (John 1:5) becomes "mastered it," and "Peter" be-

---

[19]A. A. MacIntosh, G. Stanton, and D. L. Frost, "The New English Bible Reviewed," *Theology* 79 (April 1971): 154-66.

[20]Introduction to the New Testament, *The New English Bible*, p. vii.

comes "Simon Peter" (John 18:25). A note is added (Matt. 6:13) that "the evil one" could be "evil." A note to Matthew 8:2 explains "leprosy"; however, other occurrences of the word have no explanation.

Some of the unnecessary explanatory glosses of the first edition are dropped; for example, "general" (Luke 2:1), "the apostles" (Acts 2:6), and "in the world" (Rev. 3:17) are gone. There is some return to the traditional: "Where your wealth is" becomes "where your treasure is" (Matt. 6:21), and "wrapped him round" becomes "swaddling clothes" (Luke 2:7, 12). Whereas Mary was called "pregnant" in the first edition, she is "expecting a child" (Luke 2:5) in the second; nevertheless, "pregnant" is still used for the woman of Revelation 12:2.

Improvements are made in style. The Old Testament quotations in Matthew all use the phrase "to fulfill" to bring out their "formula" character. Matthew 5:3 is now "know their need of God" where it was "know that they are poor"; Mark 15:1 is "the full Council" instead of "all the Council." That people "rounded on them" (Matt. 20:31; cf. Mark 10:48) becomes "the people told them sharply"; nevertheless, "rounding" is retained in Acts 16:18. "Never overpower it" (Matt. 16:18) has become "never conquer it." The awkwardness of the rendering of Matthew 5:48 is gone. "Aim was to frame" gives way to "They wanted to frame" (Matthew 12:10), "grown gross" is "become gross" (Matthew 13:15), and "perceived its drift" becomes "grasp its meaning" (Luke 9:45). "God speaks true" is "God speaks the truth" (John 3:33), and "that we may not have to hurt you" becomes "that you may do no wrong" (II Cor. 13:7; no note in the NEB shows that the Greek is ambiguous here).

Other changes move toward more contemporary English. "Defiant" takes the place of "recalcitrant" (Rom. 10:21); "you swindler, you rascal" (Acts 13:10) replaces "You utter impostor and charlatan." "Cloister" (John 10:23) becomes "portico." Instead of "bailiff" there is a reversion to the traditional "steward" (Luke 16:1). "Paralysed man" replaces "paralytic" (Matt. 9:2, 6). The colt that was "tethered to the door" is "tethered at a door" (Mark 11:4). "Charge ... solemnly" (II Tim. 2:14) is used instead of "adjure," and "be straightforward" (II Tim. 2:15) is used instead of "driving a straight furrow." Perhaps some changes were made for consistency. The one occurrence of "gallows" (I Peter 2:24) has become "gibbet" as *xulon* is rendered in its other occurrences (Acts 5:30; 10:39; 13:29). "He has risen" (Mark 16:6) is changed to "He has been raised again" to agree with the wording of Matthew 28:6.

Archaeological Discovery

The British scholars have made use of some of the results of archaeological discovery. Of the list of RSV changes cited earlier, the NEB also identifies Tiglath-pileser and Pul (I Chron. 5:26), states that Necho went "to help" the King of Assyria (II Kings 23:29), uses the "chief eunuch" for "Rabsaris," "commander of the frontier troops" for "Rabmag" (Jer. 39:3), "commander in chief" for "Tartan" (Isa. 20:1), and "chief officer" for "Rabshakeh" (Isa. 36:2, 4, 11, 12; 37:8; II Kings 18:17ff.). Solomon's horses are from "Coa" ("Kue"; RSV; I Kings 10:28; II Chron. 1:16), Balaam is from the "land of the Amavites" (Num. 22:5), "two-thirds of a shekel" ("pim"; RSV; I Sam. 13:21) is what the Philistines charged, and "bitumen" was used at Babel and "tar" in the ark of Moses (Gen. 11:3; Exod. 2:3). The NEB accepted the reading "like glaze" (Prov. 26:23; as RSV) on evidence from Ugarit where before the reading was "silver dross" (KJV; ASV). It has "turtle-dove" (as ASV and RSV; Song of Sol. 2:12) where the KJV had "turtle." Where the KJV had "dragon," the NEB has "wolf" (Job 30:29), "serpent" (Ps. 91:13), and "water-spout" (Ps. 148:7). The "unicorn" is the "wild ox" (Ps. 22:21).

However, one is sometimes puzzled why the translators were not more diligent in their use of archaeological material. After ordinarily using "sandals" and "thongs of sandals" (Isa. 5:27), "shoes" (Pss. 60:8; 108:9; Amos 2:6; Matt. 3:11; John 1:27; etc.) and "shoe-string" (Gen. 14:23) are also used. In one instance the Old Testament has "sandals" (Exod. 3:5) and the New Testament has "shoes" (Acts 7:33) for the same statement. There is ample proof of the cutting off of the hands of enemies in war; the Hebrew, Greek, and Latin texts read: "Are the hands of Zeba and Zalmunna in your hands?" Yet the NEB reads, "Are Zebah and Zalmunna . . . already in your hands . . .?" (Judg. 8:15). Why have the translators rejected the possibility, "rider of the clouds" (Ps. 68:5 [4]), which is widely accepted by scholars from Ugaritic parallels?[21] *Nesher* is rendered "vulture" (with a note, "eagle") when occurring in a list of unclean creatures (Deut. 14:12) or when suggesting a hostile image (Jer. 48:40; 49:16, 22). Where the image is favorable, *nesher* is an "eagle" (Isa. 40:31; Ps. 103:5), leaving the reader wondering how certain the translators are that *nesher* was a "vulture."

[21]James Barr, "After Five Years: A Retrospect on Two Major Translations of the Bible," *Heythrop Journal* 15 (1974): 401-2.

New Vocabulary

The most significant innovation of the NEB is in the area of vocabulary. James Barr points out that there are hundreds of new meanings for Hebrew words — meanings not found in the standard lexicons but derived from the study of the cognate Semitic languages. While some of the new meanings had been proposed in the writings of the members of the translating panels, others had not appeared in print before. Consequently, some of the vocabulary of the NEB does not represent the consensus of scholarship, only untried proposals. No explanation for the semantic reorientation has yet been given. The reader has no way of knowing in what cases new meanings have been introduced.[22]

The method of drawing meanings from cognate languages is here to stay, but its limitations have not yet been set by scholars. One may legitimately question the validity of giving the word *keseph* (Isa. 55:1) the meaning of "food," which is derived from Akkadian,[23] especially when in the same verse its normal Hebrew meaning of "money" is used. *Barar* is rendered "savage" in Psalm 18:27 (26) and II Samuel 22:27 because of its analogy with Arabic and Syriac words, though other occurrences in the Old Testament mean "pure" (Dan. 11:35; 12:10), the traditional rendering in Psalm 18. Not only is the rendering "picking lice" (Song of Sol. 1:7) a departure from the traditional text, but in its context it is unlikely.[24] "Poor louse" (Isa. 41:14) is from a Kittel conjecture. There are cases where common meanings for words like "covenant" (Isa. 42:6) and "acquainted" (Isa. 5:23) have been set aside for the new conjectures. *Yada'* ("know") is at times (Isa. 53:3) given the meaning "humbled" because of its analogy with Arabic. What were "dogs" have become "huntsmen" (Ps. 22:16) or "the axe" (Ps. 22:20). The verb which was previously thought to mean "he took" is now taken to mean "challenge the authority" (Num. 16:2), that which was "to choose" is "venting your spite" (Zech. 3:2) and "to burn down" (II Chron. 34:6); yet these novelties have not been explained or justified to the public.

Among the animals making their first appearance in the English Bible, the reader will find the "buffalo" and the "bison" (Isa. 34:7), which before were "mighty bulls." He will read of the "cobra" (Isa. 11:8), raising the

---

[22]Ibid., pp. 385-87.
[23]Crim, "The New English Bible," p. 150.
[24]Ibid., p. 151.

question whether or not the cobra was known in Palestine. There are "porpoise hides" (Exod. 35:23) which were "rams' skins" (RSV). Among plants he will read of "the citrus-tree" (Lev. 23:40) where the RSV has "goodly trees," "mulberry-wood" (Isa. 40:20) where the species was previously unspecified, and the "asphodel" (Song of Sol. 2:1) where the RSV had "rose." New geographical names include "the gorge of the Kidron" ("valley of Kidron"; RSV), "Lebo-Hamath" ("Entrance of Hamath"), and "Perath" (Jer. 13:5-6; RSV: "Euphrates"). Joseph is imprisoned in the "Round Tower" (Gen. 39:20; RSV: "prison").

New names for the types of offerings under the law are "shared-offering" (Num. 7:17; RSV: "peace offering"), "food offering" (Num. 28:8; "offering by fire"), "grain offering" (Num. 28:8; Lev. 6:14; "cereal offering"), and "holy gift" (Lev. 22:10; "holy thing"). The priest "flings" the blood around the altar (II Chron. 30:16; "sprinkles"). There is the "bread of the presence" ("shew bread"), "Tent of the Presence" ("Tent of Meeting"), and "expiation" ("atonement").

Various Hebrew names for God are rendered "Ancient in Years" (Dan. 7:21), "the Eternal" (Gen. 49:24), and even on occasion (but not at Gen. 4:26) "Jehovah," though this last term is usually "the Lord" as in the KJV. "Jehovah" is retained where the name is explained (Exod. 3:15f.; 6:3) and in four cases where it forms a constituent element of a name (Gen. 22:4; Exod. 17:15; Judg. 6:24; Ezek. 48:35).

In the New Testament new meanings from Koine Greek usage have been employed for some words; in other cases finer shades have been found in old meanings, thereby clarifying some passages. One reads that the prodigal "turned the whole of his share into cash" (Luke 15:13) and that the Thessalonians were "idling their time away" (II Thess. 3:11; cf. 3:6-7; I Thess. 5:14). What previously were "epistles" are "letters." Recognition of an idiom gives "at home" (Mark 2:1) instead of "in the house." Barabbas is a "bandit" (John 18:40; Matt. 26:55; etc.). "Advocate" for *paracletos* is preferred to "comforter" (John 14:16; etc.).

Fidelity in Translation

Improvements

The merits of the NEB are in part to be seen in those places where it has a more accurate rendering than the KJV, the ASV, or the RSV. "Great fish" (Jonah 1:17), "fish" (Jonah 2:1, 10), and "sea-monster" (Matt. 12:40) leave the species unidentified; in the Gospel the KJV, ASV, and RSV had "whale." "The festival" (John 7:8) rather than "this feast" (KJV; ASV) reflects that the Greek has no demonstrative adjective in this phrase. "All of you" (Luke 22:31) reflects the plural in Greek where KJV and ASV merely had "you." In I Timothy 5:23 the KJV's "drink no longer water" or the ASV's "Be no longer a drinker of water" could suggest total abstinence from water. The NEB renders it, "Stop drinking nothing but water." There are cases of more exact rendering of verb tenses, such as "used to be carried" (Acts 3:2; "was being carried," RSV) as opposed to "was carried" (KJV; ASV). In some cases the NEB follows the improvements in the RV and ASV: "Remained unknown" (Gal. 1:22) follows "was still unknown" (ASV) and "was still not known" (RSV), as opposed to "was unknown" (KJV); and "no more delay" (Rev. 10:6; ASV; RSV) where the KJV had "time no longer." In other cases the NEB is more accurate, than the RSV; for example, in the use of the plural possessive "masters' " (Matt. 15:27) where the RSV had the singular.

The new translation is very readable, and in numerous cases ambiguities are clarified. Attention is given to the fact that poetry is poetry. The sixth commandment is clarified by the rendering, "You shall not commit murder" (Exod. 20:13). The Old Testament clearly distinguishes between manslaughter, judicial execution, and murder. It does not prohibit slaughtering animals; it provides for judicial execution. "Thou shalt not kill" conveys an idea in English that is not in the original text. The rendering "living creature" (Gen. 2:7) removes the problem created by the rendering "living soul" (KJV). "Hill-shrines," where previously there were "high places," is a clarification. In the NEB the special seasons are "pilgrim feasts" and uncleanness is "ritual uncleanness." The plague formerly called "leprosy" in houses is a "fungus infection" (Lev. 14:33, 34), and in clothes it is "mould" (Lev. 13:47). Nadab and Abihu offer "illicit fire" where before it was "strange fire" (Lev. 10:1; 16:1; Num. 3:4). There are "cracked cisterns" where before there were "broken cisterns" (Jer. 2:13). The way where "no fool shall trespass on it" is better than "no fool shall err therein" (Isa. 35:8). "Ring in the ears" (Jer. 19:3) is clearer than "his ears shall tingle." "Tattoo" (Lev. 19:28) is preferred to "you shall not print marks on you." "Autumn and spring rain" (Deut. 11:14) is a more communicative phrase than "early and latter rain" when one considers Palestinian climate. Other improvements are: "Start a boy on the right road, and even in old age he will not leave it" (Prov. 22:6), "May all that I say and think be acceptable to thee" (Ps. 19:14), and "Egypt is a splintered cane that will run into a man's hand and pierce it if he leans on it" (II Kings 18:21). Another fine translation is: "My father used the whip on you; but I will use the lash" (I Kings 12:14).

In many cases the NEB has created fine sayings at the expense of literalness — "A wise man who speaks his mind calmly is more to be heeded than a commander shouting orders among fools" (Eccles. 9:17). The RSV has the more literal, "The words of the wise heard in quiet are better than the shouting of a ruler among fools." "Chastise your son while there is hope for him, but be careful not to flog him to death" (Prov. 19:18) is clearer though less literal than "do not set your heart on his destruction." These are only a few of the many excellencies.

The translators felt obliged to offer an apology for the obvious difference between renderings of the same passage in the Old Testament and the citation of it in the New Testament. In one case they are translating Hebrew and in the other case they are translating Greek;[25] where there are genuine differences in the two texts, these discrepancies are accepted. But we discover that Rachel weeps for her "sons" in the Old Testament (Jer. 31:15), but for her "children" (Matt. 2:18) in the New. Deuteronomy 8:3 has "every word that comes from the mouth of the Lord," but Matthew 4:4 has "every word that God utters." It seems that some additional harmonization is in order.

Biblical Interpretation

Marked changes in interpretation are reflected in many Old Testament passages. Some of these represent positions advocated by some scholars but rejected by others. Only a few can be cited. Rendering Psalm 121:1 as a contingent statement, "If I lift up my eyes to the hills, where shall I find help?" is based on the view that worship on the hills in Palestine was idolatry. Another example is "Prepare a road for the Lord through the wilderness" (Isa. 40:3), but a different interpretation is suggested in the New Testament (Mark 1:3). The possibility of any element of hope is rejected in the rendering of Isaiah 6:13.

The addition "which tribe" (Judg. 1:1) turns the reader's thought in the wrong direction and makes the task of exegesis more difficult. The question in Hebrew is "who?" "To walk wisely" (Mic. 6:8) will hardly do for the

[25]Introduction to the New Testament, *The New English Bible*, p. vii.

phrase that previously was rendered "humble." The Daniel alluded to in Ezekiel (Ezek. 14:14, 20) is identified in the NEB with the Ugaritic hero, Danel, rather than with the biblical character. The traditional identification is relegated to the footnotes. Supporting this interpretation are Ugaritic discoveries and acceptance of the Maccabean date of the Book of Daniel. In another example, Amos declares, "I am no prophet" (Amos 7:14). The alternate "was" is given in the footnote. The nominal sentence of this sort has no verb in Hebrew. Earlier versions supplied the past tense, interpreting the allusion to be to Amos' background. The NEB follows those scholars (also reflected in the RSV) who wish to separate the early prophets from the literary prophets and who insist that Amos is distinguishing himself from the professional prophetic movement. According to this view, he is saying, "I am not a prophet (now); I am only prophesying." Those on the opposite side of this quarrel ask, "What is a prophet except one who prophesies?" A third case of interpretation concerns the age of Mordecai (Esther 2:5). In lieu of the Hebrew relative pronoun 'asher, the NEB supplies "he," whose antecedent can only be "Mordecai," and thus makes clear that Mordecai was carried off into exile by Nebuchadnezzar. If so, Mordecai must have been more than one hundred years old at the time referred to. It is very unlikely that a man of that age could play the role that Mordecai did. Other scholars have insisted that the antecedent of 'asher is Kish, who precedes Mordecai by three generations. The interpretation "Passion [is] cruel as the grave" (Song of Sol. 8:6) misses the parallelism which suggests that love pursues its object as Sheol pursues human beings. "The use of books is endless" (Eccles. 12:12) misses the point of the context. "For you alone have I cared" (Amos 3:1) overlooks the theological point of the statement.

Thus far the British translators have not furnished a companion volume which would supply the evidence that underlies the many new interpretations which their version includes. One is somewhat shocked when he reads in parallel passages of Achsah, "As she sat on the ass, she broke wind, and Caleb asked her, What do you mean by that?" (Josh. 15:18; Judg. 1:14). The same verb, when used of Sisera, reads, "his brains oozed out" (Judg. 4:21).[26] Of Og, the NEB says "His sarcophagus of basalt" (Deut. 3:11); previous English versions had a "bedstead of iron." Issachar, formerly

---

[26]Support for the rendering is given by G. R. Driver in *Mélanges bibliques rédigée en l'honneur de André Robert* (Paris: n.p., 1957), pp. 72-76; and by Robert B. Coote, "Aksah, Sisera, and Hebrew *tsnh*," in George MacRae, ed., *Abstracts of the Society of Biblical Literature* (Missoula, Montana: Scholars' Press, 1976), p. 23.

compared to a "strong ass," is compared to a "gelded ass" (Gen. 49:14), and what was formerly "doves' dung" is "locust-bean" (II Kings 6:25). Why introduce a figure of undoubted pagan mythological background: "As he came from the womb of mother earth" (Eccles. 5:15) when "as he came from the womb of his mother" would be literal and understandable? Why introduce the mythological creature "the Dragon" (note: "or Bashan") in Psalm 68:22? Why "the goddesses of the field" (Song of Sol. 2:7) when biblical Hebrew has no word for "goddess"?

The NEB's handling of certain traditional messianic passages is interesting. In the fifth century, Jerome announced his translation principle by which such Old Testament passages would be rendered in the light of their New Testament fulfillment.[27] This principle is not generally followed today, and in the NEB some instances of the opposite tendency can be seen. Note a few cases: "I will put enmity between you and the woman, between your brood and hers. They shall strike at your head, and you shall strike at their heel" (Gen. 3:15). The traditional virgin birth interpretation cannot be seen here, nor does it suggest Paul's allusion to the passage: "The God of peace will soon crush Satan beneath your feet" (Rom. 16:20). The promise to Abraham (Gen. 12:3) is: "All the families on earth will pray to be blessed as you are blessed." While granting the possibility of a reflexive rendering of the Hebrew verb form (also seen in the RSV) as one of two alternatives, it is impossible to see how Paul could have arrived at his interpretation of the passage in Galatians had he understood the verse in this way. It is difficult to see the rationale for an alternative which creates instead of alleviates problems. Consider yet another passage: "The sceptre shall not pass from Judah, nor the staff from his descendants, so long as the tribute is brought to him" (Gen. 49:10). This interpretation, also adopted by E. A. Speiser in the *Anchor Bible*, represents considerable juggling of the Hebrew letters of the text. Still another passage is Psalm 45:6: "Your throne is like God's throne, eternal." There is no linguistic reason why 'elohim ("God") cannot be vocative in this passage, as it was understood to be by the Greek translators and as the Greek is rendered in the NEB

---

[27]Jerome in his "Preface" to his translation of the Pentateuch; also cited in *Apology* II.25 (NPNF, 2nd ser., III.516): "They translated before the Advent of Christ, and expressed in ambiguous terms that which they knew not. We after His Passion and Resurrection write not prophecy so much as history. For one style is suitable to what we hear, another to what we see. The better we understand a subject, the better we describe it."

when this verse is cited in Hebrews 1:8. The NEB introduces an element of comparison that is not suggested in the Hebrew text.

At times, such as in "Jesus and Resurrection" (Acts 17:18) and "water and spirit" (John 3:5), the definite article which is present in Greek is omitted. Some cases reflect an ecclesiastical approach; e.g., "to synagogue" (Mark 1:21; Luke 4:16; Acts 13:14), "keeping a fast" (Mark 2:18), and "in synagogue" (John 5:59; 18:29). In other cases the definite article was kept: "Here begins the Gospel" (Mark 1:1), "The day of Pentecost was running its course" (Acts 2:1), and "said the blessing" (Matt. 26:26; Mark 14:22).

In some cases the validity of the comments made by the NEB translators has been questioned. The rendering of Jude 7 seems to reflect pseudepigraphical legends in which the angels were guilty of unnatural lusts, whereas the text seems to ascribe this fault to Sodom and Gomorrah and surrounding cities. Angels are cited only as examples of those bound, not as examples of unnatural lust.

The insertion of "only" gives "only laughed" (Mark 5:40), "only done our duty" (Luke 17:10), and "only in hope" (Rom. 8:24). In the phrase "only through faith in Christ Jesus" (Gal. 2:16), some may see support for "faith only" teaching.

"The kingdom of God already come in power" (Mark 9:1) reflects C. H. Dodd's doctrine of "Realized Eschatology." "Is upon you" is favored in Matthew 3:2; 4:17; 10:8 for *ēggiken*. The choice "among you" (Luke 17:21) is only one of several possibilities. Three others are cited in the notes.

The supplying of both a name and its interpretation is responsible for the reading, "You are Peter, the Rock" (Matt. 16:18; John 1:42) which invites the conclusion that the church is built on Peter. "Language of ecstasy," "ecstatic utterance" (I Cor. 14:26; cf. 12:10), "tongues of ecstasy" (Acts 10:46; 19:6), "ecstatic speech," "ecstatic language," and "strange tongues of ecstasy"—all are used to translate the Greek word *glōssais*; but *glōssais* is "tongues" in Acts 2:4. The reader must conclude that the phenomenon in the Book of Acts is different from that in Corinthians. With the NEB, "guardian angels" (Matt. 18:10) make their appearance in the English Bible for the first time. Phoebe "holds office in the congregation at Cenchreae" (Rom. 16:1). To find one's "true self" and to find "one's life" (Matt. 16:25b) are not the same idea. The term "final rebellion" and the capitalization of "Restrainer" (II Thess. 2:3, 7) reflect a particular eschatological view. The rendering of *pascha* (John 18:28) as "Passover meal" (though everywhere else in the Gospel it means "the week") probably reflects the translators' view of a direct conflict between John and the Synoptics about the question of the day on which Jesus observed the "Passover."

The translators reverted unjustifiably to the earlier practice of giving names of Christian festivals to Jewish feasts; therefore, we encounter "Whitsuntide" (I Cor. 16:8), though the same phrase is elsewhere correctly rendered "Pentecost" (Acts 2:1; 20:16). The gathering at Troas is "on Saturday night" (Acts 20:7) despite the fact that the same phrase in other occurrences (Matt. 28:1; Mark 16:2; Luke 24:1; John 20:1, 19; I Cor. 16:2) is rendered "Sunday." The adverb of manner, *houtōs* (Rom. 11:26), is rendered as an adverb of time: "when that has happened, the whole of Israel...."

Variety in Rendering

The effort to preserve stylistic features of Hebrew or Aramaic has been abandoned in the NEB in favor of idiomatic English. No effort has been made to indicate by italics those words that had to be added to complete the English meaning or to indicate that some Hebrew words need not be rendered into English. No effort is made to consistently render a Hebrew or Aramaic word in each of its occurrences by the same English word. Both good and bad result from this practice.

On the credit side, the policy of variety in rendering allows room for the variety of meanings a word may have in different contexts. For example, *torah* can be both "law" (Neh. 8:2) and "teaching" (Isa. 42:4). However, this variety can create some acute problems. Word study—the tracing of the occurrences of a particular word or expression—becomes impossible. When we use "Vale of Achor" (Josh. 7:26; Isa. 65:10) and "Vale of Trouble" (Hos. 2:15) for the same expression, the allusion is lost, for no ordinary English reader could be aware that the phrase is actually the same. The NEB's treatment of the Hebrew *ben 'adam* and the Aramaic *bar 'enosh* is worth noting. This Semitic expression is translated "man" in Ezekiel (Ezek. 5:1; etc.), Daniel 7:13, and Psalm 107:8; but in Psalm 8:4 it is translated "mortal man" to furnish needed variety from "man" of the preceding line of poetry. The equivalent term in the New Testament— in Greek, *huios tou anthrōpou*—when spoken by Jesus is maintained in its Semitic form: "son of man." It is also maintained in this form when Psalm 8:4 is cited in Hebrews 2:6, and is in Revelation 1:13. If the phrase is a Semitism in the Old Testament (and it is) which needs transposing to its nearest English equivalent, the phrase also needs transposing in the New Testament.

Within the same chapter, Naaman is a leper (II Kings 5:1; with a footnote that his skin was diseased), but Gehazi contracts a "skin disease" (II Kings 5:27). Who would realize that Gehazi, by poetic justice, acquired the disease Naaman previously had? Elsewhere the malady is also called "a malignant skin-disease" (Deut. 24:8; Lev. 13:2).

Abner asks, "Am I a baboon?" where the text has "dog's head" (II Sam. 3:8); however, Mephibosheth and others do compare themselves to dogs in expressions such as "a dead dog" (II Sam. 9:8; 16:9; cf. II Kings 8:13). The ark of Noah, the tabernacle, and the temple are measured in cubits; but Goliath is "over nine feet in height" (I Sam. 17:4). Zechariah 3:1-3 alternates between use of "Satan" and "Adversary," but Job 1 and I Chronicles 21:1 have "Satan." "Sheol" is sometimes transliterated (e.g., Ps. 139:8), but at other times is translated as "grave" (e.g., Gen. 37:35).

The Semitic phrase formerly rendered "and it came to pass" is one of the most frequent features of Semitic style and one which certainly does not need perpetuation in English. It is varied in the NEB to read: "After the death of Moses (or Joshua)" (Josh. 1:1; Judg. 1:1), "Long ago" (Ruth 1:1), "There was a man" (I Sam. 1:1), "When David returned" (II Sam. 1:1), "Now in the first year" (Ezra 1:1), "The events here related" (Esther 1:1), and "The Word of the LORD came to Jonah" (Jonah 1:1). In Genesis 11:1, the idiom is rendered "Once upon a time." While this rendering may be suitable for a fable (Judg. 9:8), its use for the tower of Babel story has drawn particular criticism because of the English use of the phrase as the beginning of a legend or a fairy tale. Its use for the Babel episode may suggest to the reader that the biblical story is mythical.

The Hebrew word 'almah, which created much discussion when the RSV translated it "young woman" in Isaiah 7:14, caused the NEB translators some trouble, as it did their predecessors. They vacillated between "young woman" (Gen. 24:43; Song of Sol. 6:8; Isa. 7:14), "girl" (Exod. 2:8; Ps. 68:26 [25]; Prov. 30:19), and "maiden" (Song of Sol. 1:3). In Isaiah 7:14 they dropped the definite article (which is in Hebrew—"the young woman"), but the tense of the verb used is taken to refer to a sign contemporary with the prophet.

The Hebrew word nesher is rendered "the griffon-vulture" (Deut. 14:12), the "vulture" (Deut. 28:49), and "the eagle" (Deut. 32:11; Isa. 40:31). One meets "Jesus Bar-Abbas" and "Bar-Abbas" twice each in Matthew, but the same name is "Barabbas" in Mark, Luke, and John. While no one would insist on an awkward uniformity in the rendering of words in different contexts, the degree of variety encountered creates problems for the NEB reader. *Grammateus* ("scribe"; KJV) is rendered six ways: "lawyers" (29 times), "doctors of the law" (26 times), "teachers" (4 times), "teachers of the law" (twice), "town clerk" (once), and "man of learning" (once). It is hard to imagine why one term should be both "brothers" (Rom. 1:13; 10:1; 11:25; 12:1) and "friends" (Rom. 7:1, 4; 8:12; 15:14; and 16:17). Why should heaven be "open" (Matt. 3:16; Luke 3:21) or "wide open" (John 1:51) in the Gospels but be "a rift in the sky" in Acts (7:56; 10:11)? Why should the Greek word *echō* be "have" (John 3:16), "possess" (John 3:15), and "has hold" (John 3:36) when speaking of having eternal life; or why should *peripatein* be both "live up to" (Eph. 4:1) and "manner of life" (Col. 1:10)? *Mē genoito* (paraphrased "God forbid" in KJV) occurs fourteen times in Greek but is represented by nine different renderings in the NEB, running from "Certainly not" to "Never." The word rendered "gentiles" in the KJV is "gentiles," "heathen," "foreign power," "the nations," and "the world" in the NEB. *Menō* ("abide"; ASV) occurs eight times in I John 2:17-28. Four times it is rendered "dwell"; twice it is "stay"; once, "stand"; and in the remaining instances is "keep." The use of ten words for *menō* in the Gospel of John obscures a significant line of thought. Marked variety is to be seen in the rendering of *dikaiosunē* ("righteousness"; KJV) which becomes in the NEB "way of righting wrong" (Rom. 1:17), "justice" (Rom. 3:21; cf. 3:5, 25, 26), and "righteousness" (Rom. 4:3). Of twenty-seven other occurrences in Romans, twenty-three are "righteousness"; but "the goodness of God himself" is used in another letter (II Cor. 5:21). The Greek phrase from which is derived "Your concern, mother, is not mine" (John 2:4) becomes "What do you want with me?" (Mark 5:7; cf. Luke 4:34). In the rendering of *basileia* ("kingdom"; KJV), "kingdom" is definitely avoided (cf. Luke 19:11-27); and at least in one case, "the sovereignty of the world" (Rev. 11:15) is chosen. "Whore" is used in the Book of Revelation, but "prostitute" or "harlot" is used elsewhere for the same word.

"Messiah" is at times used to translate *ho christos* when the office is spoken of (Matt. 2:4; Acts 2:36), but "Christ" is used when the term is a part of a name (e.g., Acts 10:48). The Greek New Testament has "Messiah" only at John 1:41 and 4:25. While it may be claimed that the use of "Messiah" preserves the idea that *ho christos* was a title, not just a name, nevertheless, the practice of the NEB would seem a loss, for it does not prepare the reader of the New Testament for the disciples later to be called "Christians" (cf. Acts 11:26). Furthermore, the policy is not strictly adhered to. "Christ" is used for *ho christos* at Matthew 11:2 and John 20:31, but at Luke 9:20 and at Luke 23:35 the term is "God's Messiah" and at Hebrews 11:26 is "God's Anointed." One encounters "The Christ" (I John 2:22; 5:1; II John 9) where he expects "the Messiah" which was used in Romans 9:5 — the only place in the epistles where "Messiah" is used in the NEB. He then meets "Christianity" (Heb. 6:1) and "Christian" (Rom. 9:1; 16:7; I Cor. 4:10; 7:22; II Cor. 12:2, 19; I Thess. 4:10; I Peter 3:16).

Ecclesia, rendered "congregation" when referring to the local churches — with the exceptions of the church in Jerusalem and those in Asia Minor (Rev. 1 and 2) — is "the community" in I Corinthians 12:28; 14:4; but elsewhere it is "assembly" and "meeting." "Church" is also used where there is no reference to geography. A lack of a consistently applied policy seems obvious here. The NEB has created distinctions that are not inherent in the New Testament usage of *ecclesia*.[28]

The term "saints" is used twice (Matt. 13:17; 23:29) for *dikaioi*, literally "righteous ones," but *dikaios* also has many other renderings in the NEB. *Hagioi* (sixty occurrences; "saints," KJV) are usually "God's people" (forty-two times) or "dedicated people" (Rom. 1:7); however, many other expressions are also used for the seventeen other occurrences of *hagioi*. One can further see the variety in the NEB renderings if one examines those in Mark 12:41-44 where *ballein* ("cast") occurs six times and *gazophyla-keion* ("treasure") occurs three times. "Stomach" (occurring in Matt. 15:17; Mark 7:19; Rev. 10:9, 10) is inserted in John 6:60 where it does not occur in Greek, but is made "digestion" in I Timothy 5:23, where it does occur.

Skandalidzō and its cognates ("offense," "stumble"; KJV) are rendered in sixteen different ways, such as "so they fell foul of him" (Matt. 13:57), "tonight you will all fall away from your faith on my account" (Matt. 26:31; cf. 33), "a rock to stumble against" (I Peter 2:8), and "to guard you against the breakdown of your faith" (John 16:1). *Pisteuō* ("believe"; KJV) is translated as "gave their allegiance to him" in John 2:23 and as "puts his faith in him," "unbeliever," and "not given his allegiance to" in John 3:18. *Parthenos* (traditionally "virgin") is "virgin" in Matthew 1:23 and in I Corinthians 7:28, but in verse 36 is "partner in celibacy" and in verse 37

[28]Bratcher, "The New English Bible," pp. 104-5; Danker, "The New English Bible," p. 342.

is "partner in her virginity." *Parthenos* is "girl" in Matthew 25:1 and Luke 1:27.

The NEB's treatment of the "Woe Oracles" deserves notice. At Amos 6:1 the oracle begins "Shame on you" (cf. Isa. 5:8, 11, 18, 20, 21, 22); the relevant word is passed over as though superfluous in Amos 5:18 and Isaiah 17:12; in Nahum 3:1 it is "Ah," in Isaiah 28:1 it is "Oh," but in Isaiah 6:5 it is "Woe" and at Habakkuk 2:6 "Woe betide." "Shame on you" seems hardly adequate as a rendering for *oi* ("woe"; RSV). Within the New Testament, "alas" is used in twenty-seven passages, but one verse has both "alas" and "woe betide" (Matt. 18:7). In I Corinthians 9:16 "misery" is used; and in Revelation 8:13; 9:12; 11:14; 12:12 "woe" is encountered, although "alas, alas" (Rev. 18:10, 16, 17, 19) is found elsewhere in the book.

The NEB at times translates different Greek words into the same English word, thus ignoring certain distinctions in the Greek. *Grammateus* ("scribe") and *nomikos* ("lawyer") are both "lawyer." In some instances *Messias* and *Christos* are both translated "Messiah." Mark 5:16 and Luke 8:36, though unlike in Greek, are identical in the NEB. The same is true of the phrase "tell them what the Lord ... has done for you" in Mark 5:19 and Luke 5:39. What should be "taxgatherers and sinners" in Matthew 9:10 and Mark 2:15 is rendered "taxgatherers and others," as though the Greek phrase were identical to that in the parallel passage in Luke 5:29. The NEB (as the KJV) does not make a distinction between *diabolos* and *daimonion*; it renders both as "devil." The NEB also translates "Satan" as "devil" (I Tim. 5:15); however, in the Greek New Testament there is one *diabolos* but there are many *daimonioi*, and the distinction is kept clear. In the NEB both *episkopos* (I Peter 2:25) and *epitropos* (Gal. 4:2) are "guardian."

The reader cannot trust the NEB to indicate the degree of likeness or difference in parallel passages. The same Greek words occurring in Matthew 5:25-26 and in Luke 12:55ff. are translated differently. The same is true of Matthew 8:10 and Luke 7:9; Matthew 18:6, Mark 9:42, and Luke 17:2; and of Matthew 5:29 and 18:9. We have "Place of a skull" (Matt. 27:33) and "Place of the Skull" (John 19:17). "A cock crew" occurs in two Gospels, but "the cock crew" is used in the others for the same phrase. *Paraskeuē* is "Friday" (Matt. 27:62; Luke 23:54), "Preparation-day" (Mark 15:42), and "eve" of Passover (John 19:14). Because of the variety in the rendering of terms and the failure to make distinctions, the student who does not know Greek cannot do word studies comparing different texts in the NEB. For this type of study he will still need the older versions.

The NEB seems definitely to have run aground in its effort to decide when to use "thee," and "thou," of old English, and when to use "you." Though Hebrew, Greek, and Latin have only one second-person pronoun which is used to address both God and man, in the NEB Adam addresses God as "you" (Gen. 3:1-12); but after Cain says "thou" (Gen. 4:14), all individuals except Satan (Job 1–2) address God in that form. The practice of using the old forms in the Psalms, in the language of prayer, or where divinity is addressed (for example, in Job 30:20-23; 42:1-5; John 17:3ff.; Rev. 11:17-18) forces the reader to learn the use of "thee" and "thou" and the corresponding old English verbal forms. Furthermore, the policy puts the translator in the awkward position of making a value judgment on the intent of the speaker. Psalm 2:7 uses "you" because the Psalm is thought to apply to a human king, and "you" is also used when this verse is quoted at Acts 13:33; but one encounters "Thou art my Son" at Hebrews 1:5. Psalm 45:6 uses "you," but when the same Psalm is quoted in Hebrews 1:8, "Thou" is used. Jesus is never addressed as "thou" or "thee" in the Gospels except by God (cf. Mark 1:11; Luke 3:22)—not even in citation of prophetic passages (Matt. 11:10; etc.). The subtlety which requires "thou" and "thee" at Mark 1:11 but allows "you" in Matthew 25:37-45 is likely to escape the reader. In Matthew 16:16 Peter uses "you" in addressing Jesus, though he confesses that Jesus is "Son of the Living God." Even at Acts 1:6 "you" is used. Paul says "you" at his conversion (Acts 9:5), but at the end of his missionary journeys he has learned to say "thee" (Acts 22:19). The only real solution to the "thee" and "thou" problem is to use "you" throughout. "You" has the disadvantage of making no distinction between singular and plural, a distinction made by both Hebrew and Greek. But this disadvantage is as acute when addressing human figures as when addressing God; so why retain "you" for the former and not the latter?

It seems clear that the degree of variety exercised by the NEB in its renderings—a variety greater than the KJV had—is excessive and is a hindrance to accurate communication.

Paraphrase

The NEB is a free translation, tending to paraphrase and, in some instances, to wordiness. In Job 9:34 eight words in Hebrew become twenty in English. The tendency to make unnecessary additions as a concession to contemporary usage is encountered in both the Old Testament and the New Testament. Rebecca says, "Yes, I will go," where the Hebrew merely has "I will go" (Gen. 24:59). Words occurring only once in the Hebrew text are repeated for effect, as "Fallen, fallen are the men of war" (II Sam. 1:27) and "No, no" (Ruth 1:13). There is also repetition where Greek has only one interjection; for example, "Alas, alas" (Matt. 23:13; Luke 11:44); "enough, enough" (Luke 22:38); "look, look" (Luke 13:35); and "Repent ... repent" (Acts 2:38). Additions are sometimes interpretative, such as "an army" (Jer. 10:22) and Nineveh as a three days' journey "across" (Jonah 3:3). Sometimes an explanation is given after a name; e.g., "my Ariel indeed, my fiery altar" (Isa. 29:2) and "But I am a dog, a mere nobody, how can I do this great thing?" (II Kings 8:13). "True" is added (also RSV: "true"; "real") to fortify the meaning of "Jew" (Rom. 2:28, 29). "The tiptoe of expectation" (Luke 3:15) and "taking to their heels" (Luke 8:34; for *ephugon*: "they fled") key up the meaning of the passages.

Another example of paraphrase is found in Proverbs 13:9—"The lamp of the righteous burns brightly; the embers of the wicked will be put out," in which the metaphor of the lamp in the second half of the proverb is replaced with that of the hearth. "I swear a solemn oath before the Lord" (Ruth 1:17) paraphrases the Semitic idiom which literally is "The Lord do so to me and more also." "Bless, O Lord, the tents of Shem" (Gen. 9:26) is accompanied by the more literal rendering given in a footnote: "Blessed is the Lord the God of Shem." "How long will you sit on the fence?" (I Kings 18:21), "For crime after crime" (Amos 1:3; etc.), "merchantman" (I Kings 22:48; used for "Ships of Tarshish"), and "The Lady Stupidity is a flighty creature" (Prov. 9:13)—these are all examples of paraphrase. The passage "Though I wash myself with soap" (Job 9:30) is a paraphrase resulting from the reasoning that "snow water" (the literal meaning) has no cleansing power.

There are also cases of omissions in the Old Testament, as when the interjection "O man" is dropped in Micah 6:8. Certain Greek phrases in the New Testament also seem untranslated though they are carried in Tasker's text; for example, *hupakoēn* ("obedience"; ASV; I Peter 1:2) and *dedoxamenē* ("full of glory"; ASV; I Peter 1:8).

Numerous explanatory words such as "God's" and "Adam's" (Rom. 5:15) are inserted to clarify certain points. "I am" is repeated three times in John 14:6, where the Greek requires only one occurrence; but the definite article before "life" is omitted in the same verse. "Baptism" is repeated in

Colossians 2:12; "by disobeying a direct command" (Rom. 5:14) expands *parabasis*, which could be one word—"transgression." Other additions are "Saviour" (Matt. 1:21), "the Rock" (Matt. 16:18), "again from Scripture" (Rom. 3:20), "Come, O Lord" (I Cor. 16:22), "Do not think" (II Cor. 1:24), "born and bred" (Gal. 2:14), "of flesh and blood" (Eph. 2:14). *Hupage* ("Go") is elaborated to "go home content" (Mark 7:29), and "as Scripture says" is added at Mark 4:12 and I Corinthians 10:20; 15:27; II Corinthians 3:16; Ephesians 5:31. We encounter "all good things" and "all the bad" where neither "all" is in Greek (Luke 16:25). There is the explanatory phrase "that concerns religion" (Acts 17:22).

In other cases the translators seem to assume the role of commentator. One can compile a long list of instances where explanatory additions are made to the text. "Our leader ... or bishop" (I Tim. 3:2) and "a testament, or covenant" (Gal. 3:17) are double renderings of phrases. "One dot or stroke" (Luke 16:17) is too full a rendering for *mia keraion*. The word "God" is frequently added (Gal. 2:2, 8; 3:5; 4:23, 28; 5:4, 8, 10; 6:14). Revelation 1:3 has the additions "this" and "of fulfilment," 1:4 has "the province," 1:6 has "life's" and "to serve," 1:7 has "among them" and "in remorse." The word "Passover" is added to "hymn" (Matt. 26:30; Mark 14:26), and the word "these" in Galatians 6:2 is unnecessary. *Kosmos* is made "godless world" (I John 2:15), "sleep" is "sleep in death" (I Thess. 4:13), to "body of flesh" is added "and blood" (Col. 1:22) and to "body" is added "human" (Rom. 12:4), "slave" becomes "willing slave" (Mark 10:44), "crying" becomes "crying aloud" (Mark 1:3), "tradition" is "old-established tradition" (Mark 7:3), "before Abraham was" becomes "was born" (John 8:58), and " 'Circumcision' I will not call it" (Phil. 3:2) is inserted. The rendering, "The number represents a man's name, and the numerical value of its letters" (Rev. 13:18) is a comment, not a translation.

The paraphrasing tendency is further seen when "bags of gold" is used for "talents" (Matt. 25:14ff.) when the metal might be silver, "twenty pounds" for "two hundred denarii," "miles" for "stadia," and "a day's wage" for "a denarius." "Twin brothers" are identified with "Castor and Pollux" (Acts 28:11). The name "Christian" occurs three times in the Greek New Testament and only as a noun (Acts 11:26; Acts 26:28; I Peter 4:16), but it is used in the NEB sixty-four times, often as an adjective. "The desert was strewn with their corpses" (I Cor. 10:5) paraphrases "overthrown in the wilderness." We meet "Prince Herod" (Matt. 14:1; Luke 3:1; 3:19; 9:7; Acts 13:1) and "merchant princes" (Rev. 18:23) in the NEB.

155

Still other cases of free renderings include "to those who have yielded him their allegiance" (John 1:12) for the literal "to those who have believed in his name," "How blest are those who know their need of God" (Matt. 5:3; cf. Luke 6:20) for "Blessed are the poor in spirit," and the watering down of "made themselves eunuchs" to the phrase "renounced marriage" (Matt. 19:12). One is then shocked when "eunuch" is introduced into Galatians 5:12 where it is not in the original. "Sat on them" is vaguely rendered as "Jesus mounted" (Matt. 21:7). "A man dressed in silks and satins" (Matt. 11:8; Luke 7:25), "There is a popular saying" (I Tim. 3:1), and "who have sweated the whole day long in the blazing sun" (Matt. 20:12) are all paraphrases. "Men" becomes "men of the congregation" (I Tim. 2:8). The word *raca*, whose meaning is unknown, is rendered "If he sneers at him" (Matt. 5:22), which is doubtless better than the earlier practice of transliterating the word; but it is still paraphrase. The NEB gives a general impression of what the Bible says, but it cannot be relied upon by those who are concerned about exactness in exegesis or doctrine.

Style

The style of the NEB has been widely discussed, and the reviews run from the extreme which declared that two consecutive well-written pages could not be found in it,[29] to that which insists that it is more readable for the ordinary Christian than either the KJV or the RSV.[30] Complicated Greek sentences are broken down into shorter English sentences; for example, Ephesians 1:3-14, which is a single sentence in Greek, appears in the NEB as two paragraphs and eight sentences. Colossians 1:9-17 is one sentence in the KJV, but is eight in the NEB. "Forgive us the wrong we have done" (Matt. 6:12; cf. 14, 15) is clearer than the use of either "debts" or "trespasses," neither of which is now commonly used in this sense. The phrases "has no staying-power" (Matt. 13:21) and "the false glamour of wealth" (Matt. 13:22) have been praised by some as well-turned phrases. One must admit that evaluation of style is subjective; but the NEB reads easily, and one will often wonder why the passage had not been rendered that way before. Most of the Elizabethan archaisms have been avoided.

[29]I. Robertson, *The Survival of English* (Cambridge: Cambridge University Press, 1973), p. 28.
[30]Ray Summers, review of *The New English Bible: New Testament* in *Review and Expositor* 58 (November 1961): 235; Raymond E. Brown, review of *The New English Bible: New Testament* in *Catholic Biblical Quarterly* 23 (1971): 324.

Though he was at the time discussing the question of tongues and not English versions, Paul insisted that even those outside the initiated community should be able to understand what was being said (I Cor. 14:16, 23). The NEB is a move in that direction as it strives for contemporary English. Semitisms are worked out; for example, "Blessing I will bless" (Heb. 6:14; cf. Gen. 22:17; KJV; ASV) becomes "I will bless you abundantly." "Behold" is generally avoided. The pronoun "I," which Greek puts in first position, is transposed to the end of lists of people (cf. John 10:30; I Cor. 4:6; 9:6; Gal. 2:9) as current English demands. "Slave and free" (Rev. 13:16), "year and month," and "day and hour" (Rev. 9:15) are obtained by reversal of the order of words.

Examples of use of current expressions are extensive. "Mother-in-law" replaces "wife's mother" (Mark 1:30); "listen" is used instead of "hearken." Clarity is gained by using more commonly-known terms: "sulphur" (Luke 17:29; Rev. 9:17, 18; 20:10) takes the place of "brimstone" (KJV; ASV; RSV), "power" goes out of Jesus instead of "virtue" (Mark 5:30), "mammon" has become "money" (Matt. 6:24; Luke 16:13), and "Joshua" is used for the name of the Old Testament character in Acts 7:45 and Hebrews 4:8. Many other renderings make for easy comprehension. The "sixth" and "ninth" hours have been explained as "midday" and "three in the afternoon" (Matt. 20:5); "temple-tax" (Matt. 17:24) makes clear that the tax is a religious one. "Friday" (Matt. 27:62) sets forth the traditional date of the crucifixion; and the "ABC of God's oracles" (Heb. 5:12), though paraphrastic, sets forth the general meaning.

In the NEB numerals are given in their current form—"seventy" and "eighty" (Ps. 90:10), and not as "three-score and ten" and "fourscore." The problem of official titles is solved by an attempt to supply modern administrative titles. We meet the "commander in chief," the "adjutant general," the "secretary of state," the "comptroller," the "lieutenant," the "chief officer," the "viceroy" (Isa. 41:25), the "regent" (Dan. 2:48), the "constable" (Dan. 3:2), and the "foreman" (Exod. 5:14).

"Scoundrel" is used for the Semitic epithet "son of Belial" (I Kings 21:10; etc.), and "do not think me so degraded" replaces "daughter of Belial" (I Sam. 1:16). The phrases "group of prophets" or "company of prophets" are used for the literal "sons of the prophets" (II Kings 4:38; 5:22) except in Amos 7:14, where the Semitism is retained. In general, current words and phrases are used for sex matters: "he slept with her," "intercourse," "pregnant," "rape," "impotent man and barren woman,"

157

"genitals," "semen," "menstruation," "prostitute," "whore," and "male prostitute" are all used. On the other hand, "lay with" (Gen. 4:1) is not really
current usage for the sex act, nor is "with child" (Isa. 7:14; Matt. 1:18) for
pregnancy. In the NEB "mother's son" is used for the male instead of the
graphic but embarrassing descriptive phrase used by the KJV (I Kings
16:11; etc.). "Urine" is used in some passages (II Kings 18:27; Ezek. 7:17;
21:7); however, "piss" (Job 18:11) is still embarrassing in public reading.
The suggestion that Jews offered a goat to the demon Azazel on the day
of atonement is avoided by the phrase "for the Precipice" (Lev. 16:8), with
the alternate "Azazel" as a footnote.

British English

Problems arise in the NEB Old Testament because of differences between American and British speech. Some vocabulary an American would
understand but would not use; other expressions are as foreign to him as
some KJV phrases have become. British spelling is used for words like
"odour," "labour," "labourers," "armourers," "honour," "splendour," "ru-
mours," "vigour," "centre," "hauliers," and "judgement." "Corn" (Exod.
22:6; cf. Matt. 12:1; etc.) is used in its British sense for cereal grains. Ruth
gleans "barley" in "cornfields" (Ruth 2:2; cf. Luke 6:1) after some "corn"
was dropped for her (Ruth 2:16, 17).

Most Americans would understand, but not regularly use, "Hark!" (Gen.
4:10), "Give me leave" (Gen. 24:54, 56), "folding the sheep" (Gen. 29:7),
"betimes" (Job 8:5), "blackguard" (Job 34:18), "doublet" (Job 41:13), "share
out" (Ps. 22:18), "mantle" (Ezra 9:3), "hitch up your cloak" (II Kings 4:29),
"linen drawers" (which the priest wears; Lev. 6:10), "flagon of wine" (II Sam.
16:1), "churl" (I Sam. 25:25), and "churlish." The most frequently used
word of this sort is "patrimony" (Jer. 3:18; etc.) which occurs many times.
Americans would say "heritage" or "inheritance." "He has made my way
refractory and lamed me" (Lam. 3:11) sounds strange. "Shall sanctimonious
calumny call thee partner?" (Ps. 94:20) can hardly be intended for the man
in the street. "Thou, Lord, art my felicity" (Ps. 16:2), "distrain on all his
goods" (Ps. 109:11), and "give heart to the orphan and widow" (Ps. 146:9)
would all seem foreign to most American readers.

Even less clear to an American would be "daub" (with its footnote
"mud") and "redaub" (Lev. 14:41, 43) where he would say "plaster" and
"replaster." In the NEB Jerusalem will become a "heath" (Mic. 3:12; cf.

Isa. 32:14) and other areas are "heathland" (Jer. 21:14). "A hind" (Ps. 42:1) would be more easily recognized were it a "doe," and a "cairn" (Gen. 31:46) were it a "heap." There is "to foregather" (Job 1:4), "striker" (Amos 3:5), and "batten on their iniquity" (Hos. 4:8). A wife calls her husband "lord" (Amos 4:1), and men "forswear" themselves (Hos. 2:2). "Usury" (Ps. 15:5) is sometimes used for the word that was "interest" in the Pentateuch (e.g., Lev. 25:36), and "travail" (Ps. 29:8) for that which is "labour" elsewhere. "Torrent of Egypt" (II Kings 24:7; etc.) does not seem the most apt description of the Wadi el 'Arish ("River of Egypt"; RSV).

To Americans, fig trees do not "burgeon" (Hab. 3:17), Chaldeans do not make burnt offerings to their "trawls" (Hab. 1:16), nor is "a rod in pickle" (Prov. 19:29). In the NEB Amaziah's wife will become a "city strumpet" (Amos 7:17), foreign clothes are "outlandish fashions" (Zeph. 1:8), a woman is dressed in "lawn" (Ezek. 16:10), and there are the "dhows of Arabia" (Isa. 2:16). One also encounters "festoons" (I Kings 7:17) and "trolleys" (I Kings 7:34) as furnishings of the temple. He finds "shed grain" and "self-sown" (II Kings 19:29), "swathes" (Ruth 2:7), "stooks" (Judg. 15:5), "a wanton" (Hos. 1:2), "wastrel" (Deut. 21:20), "wench" (Judg. 5:30), "fuller's soap" (Mal. 3:4), "traducers" (Ps. 71:13), "mother's bane" (Prov. 10:1), and "sheep to the shambles" (Jer. 12:3). Then there are "panniers" (Job 5:5), "fabric fund" (Ezra 2:69; Neh. 7:71; RSV: "treasury of the work"), "roisterers" (Jer. 15:17), "marjoram" (Exod. 12:22), and "temple-servitors" (Neh. 10:28).

The NEB often uses verbs which are not generally used in America today. Most frequent is "fetched," but there is also "execrate" (Gen. 12:3) and "reconnoitre" (Josh. 2:1). Micah says, "How shall I stoop before God on high?" (Mic. 6:6). No American ever used "stooped" for prostration in the presence of God. Americans "take up a matter," not "open it" (Ruth 4:4). In the NEB one reads "they . . . savage me" (Job 30:10), "I reck nothing" (Job 9:21), "be rapt like a prophet" (I Sam. 10:6), "had fallen into bad odour" (II Sam. 10:6), "to condole with" (I Chron. 19:2), "I shall think better" (Jer. 18:10; RSV: "repent"), and "resort to me" (Amos 5:5, 6) for the phrase which is "seek" in verse 14 of the same chapter. One encounters "bandy" (Job 15:3), "glutted his rage" (Lam. 4:11), "keening" (Jer. 9:17), "to beggar us" (Judg. 14:15), "the whole camp leapt up" (Judg. 7:21), and "bade" (Mal. 4:4). Ahab's chariot was "swilled out" at the pool of Samaria (I Kings 22:38), and the harlot who came before Solomon "overlaid her child," where Americans would say she "lay on it" (I Kings 3:19). Baal "must be woken up" by his prophets (I Kings 18:27).

In addition to unfamiliar verbs, the NEB uses "perfidious" (Prov. 27:6), "perquisite" (Lev. 7:33), and "palanquin" (Song of Sol. 3:9). "Blood-bridegroom by circumcision" (Exod. 4:26) is not intelligible to most readers; neither are the transliterations "Goyim" (Gen. 14:1) and "Leummim" (Isa. 43:4).

The New Testament also offers examples of words unfamiliar to the American reader. There is "saltness" (Matt. 5:13), "truckle to no one" (Mark 12:14), "meal-tub" (Mark 4:21; Matt. 5:14), "assize" (Acts 19:38; I Peter 2:12), "making away with" (Mark 11:18), "every fruiting branch he cleans" (John 15:2), "farthing" (Matt. 5:26; Mark 12:42; which coin even the British government has now terminated), "pounds" (Matt. 18:28; Mark 6:37; 14:5; John 12:5; etc.), "furlongs" (Matt. 14:24), "hundred-weight" (Matt. 13:33; Luke 13:21), "two a penny" (Matt. 10:29), "twopence" (Luke 12:6), and "fortnight" (Gal. 1:18). There is "catch me out" (Matt. 22:18; Mark 12:15), "condole with" (John 11:19, 31), "done to death" (Acts 5:30), "towns round" (Acts 5:16), "running its course" (Acts 2:1), "gibbit" (Acts 5:30), "servitor" (Heb. 3:5), "widow's weeds" (Rev. 18:7; cf. Gen. 38:14), "the Controller" of the temple (Acts 5:26), "laid an information against" (Acts 24:1), "remanded" (Acts 25:21), "impeached" (Acts 26:7), "stand in the dock" (Acts 26:6; cf. I Cor. 9:3; Phil. 1:7), "batten on her flesh" (Rev. 17:16), "bore us company" (Acts 1:21), "rising" for "uprising" (Mark 15:7), "thrown on the stove" (Matt. 6:30), "tale" (Col. 1:24), "strolling ... exorcists" (Acts 19:13), "as the days mounted up" (Acts 9:23), and "spate" (Rev. 12:15). The Pharisees "strain off a midge" (Matt. 23:24), the Corinthians are to have nothing to do with "loose livers" (I Cor. 5:9), and the people of Nazareth "fell foul" of Jesus (Mark 6:3). The Galatians are warned against fighting "tooth and nail" (Gal. 5:15). People "hail the bridegroom" (John 2:9), whereas Americans would say they "called to him." In America the living do not "forestall those who have died" (I Thess. 4:15). The deacon is not to engage in "money-grubbing" (I Tim. 3:8). The phrases "ever they were" (Rom. 8:29; cf. Phil. 2:23) and "humble folk" (Rom. 12:16) are Scotticisms. A favorite expression of the NEB is "incorporate in Christ" (Rom. 6:5; Phil. 1:1; 3:9; Eph. 1:1; Col. 1:2; etc.). It may be that the problem created by the difference between British and American expressions can only be solved by issuing an American edition which uses Americanisms.

The "Now" Language

Evidently not all the translating committee shared Dodd's desire for "timeless English." The NEB is at times crudely colloquial: "They hasten hot-foot into crime" (Prov. 1:16), "got wind of" (I Sam. 23:25; Acts 14:6), "Stop at the cross-roads" (Jer. 6:16), "make for the hill-country" (Deut. 1:7), "brushed me aside" (Deut. 3:26), "bad luck" (Jonah 1:7), "sit on the fence" (I Kings 18:21), "to have and to hold" (Hos. 2:20), "the worker earns his keep" (Matt. 10:10), "go the whole way" (Matt. 19:21; Gal. 5:12), "the whole city went wild with excitement" (Matt. 21:10), "sweated the whole day" (Matt. 20:12), "with the devil in charge made off" (Luke 8:29), "after running through your money with his women" (Luke 15:30), "to get on" (Luke 10:40), "tell her to come and lend a hand" (Luke 10:40), "to feel the pinch" (Luke 15:14), "it seemed too good to be true" (Luke 24:41)—these are all examples. Other colloquialisms are: "This is more than we can stomach" (John 6:60), "let us toss for it" (John 19:24), "Come and have breakfast" (John 21:12), "You are crazy" (Acts 12:15), "hold their own" (Acts 6:10), "this touched them on the raw" (Acts 7:54), "high standard of living" (Acts 19:25), "come ... at the double" (Acts 21:32), "hubbub" (Acts 21:34), "perfect pest" (Acts 24:5), "courtesy visit" (Acts 25:13), "in full state" (Acts 25:23), "hole-and-corner business" (Acts 26:26), "have laid themselves out to serve God's people" (I Cor. 16:15), "cheer me up" (II Cor. 2:2), "ran short" (II Cor. 11:9), "I sponged on no one" (II Cor. 11:9; cf. 12:13, 14), "sham-Christians" (Gal. 2:4), "you can take it from me" (Gal. 5:3), "ups and downs" (Phil. 4:12), "made our weight felt" (I Thess. 2:6), "hanker after marriage" (I Tim. 5:11), "have taken the wrong turning and gone to the devil" (I Tim. 5:15), and "panders to the appetites" (I John 2:16).

It seems clear that the British have not been consistent in applying the aims and principles that they announced. Despite the NEB's many examples of current speech, the goal of attaining modernity in language is only partly accomplished. There are cases where the British found it expedient to retain old phrases: "without form and void" (Gen. 1:1), "Red Sea" (Exod. 10:19; etc.), "in the twinkling of an eye" (I Cor. 15:51), "life and immortality to light through the Gospel" (II Tim. 1:10), "risked their necks" (Rom. 16:4), "hundredfold" (Matt. 13:8; etc.), "the cock crew" (Matt. 26:74; Mark 14:72), "betrothed" (Luke 2:5), "to lodge" (Luke 2:7), and "tutor" (I Cor. 4:15; Gal. 3:24, 25). The sentence "if you ask the Father for anything in my name, he will give it you" (John 16:23) continues the awkward structure of the KJV and RV/ASV. The RSV reads, "give it to you." The suitability of some of these retained phrases might be challenged, but the British could have retained other phrases with profit.

The choices of the NEB do not always improve upon what English readers already had. For example, in the twenty-third Psalm the Semitism "waters of peace" is poorer than "still waters," as is "crook" than "staff," and "whole life long" than "forever." "Of whom then should I go in dread?" (Ps. 27:1) is not better than "Of whom shall I be afraid?" (KJV). "Invited no one but myself" (Esther 5:12) is grammatically weak, though it is also found in KJV, ASV, and RSV. When read aloud the phrase "attired Mordecai" (Esther 6:11) may carry the impression of fatigue instead of dress; "resort to me" is not preferable to "seek me" (Amos 5:5, 6). The reversal of order in Isaiah 11:9, "for as the waters fill the sea, so shall the land be filled with the knowledge of the Lord," is without justification.

Other efforts at improvement are unsuccessful. "Salt to the world" does not improve "salt of the earth" (Matt. 5:13), nor does "light for all the world" improve "light of the world" (Matt. 5:14). "Thy name be hallowed" (Matt. 6:9) is no better than "Hallowed be thy name," nor is "How blest" better than "Blessed are." "What was the spectacle that drew you to the wilderness?" (Matt. 11:7) does not improve "What went ye out for to see?" "A drinker" (Matt. 11:19; Luke 7:34) is no more current than "drunkard." Stylists note that some sentences awkwardly end in "from" (Matt. 13:54, 56), "for" (Mark 6:24), "for" in a different sense (John 6:21), and "with" (Luke 13:20). "A robber's cave" (Matt. 21:13) is no improvement over "a den of thieves." "I am life" (John 14:6) is less accurate than "I am the life," since the Greek has the definite article.

Though most of its vocabulary is current, the NEB does include scattered instances in the New Testament where it is more obscure than the KJV, even for the British. "Machinations of the Jews" (Acts 20:19), "interlopers" (Gal. 2:4), "parricides and matricides" (I Tim. 1:10), and "bedizened with gold" (Rev. 17:4) would fall into this category. "Shoot the net to starboard" (John 21:6) and "leaving it to port" (Acts 21:3) are phrases known only to seafarers. "Died ... without issue" (Matt. 22:25) is legal terminology but not common speech. "Darnel" (Matt. 13:25) likely is not generally known as a plant in England. "Muster" would be preferable to "parade" (Acts 23:23). "Base-born" (John 8:41), "true born" (I Tim. 1:2), "ministrant" (Heb. 1:14), and "eternal felicity" (I Tim. 1:11) hardly qualify for current speech. Scattered here and there are archaisms not in the KJV, like "alas for you" (Matt. 23:13; etc.), "hark" (Mark 15:35), "fatted beasts" (Matt. 22:4), "half a hundredweight" (Matt. 13:33; Luke 13:21; John 19:39), and "woe betide" (Luke 17:1).

Conclusion

It is not the intention of this review to imply that everything the British have done is bad. Quite the contrary! The problematic words cited above, numerous as they appear, actually constitute a very small part of the text, and are almost inconsequential when compared with the archaisms in either the KJV or the ASV. We owe a debt to the British scholars for all the light they have cast on dark passages of Scripture and for the stimulation to study that their effort brings. There is no valid reason for an antithesis in Bible translation between the use of modern speech and loyalty to the text.

The readability of the NEB, with minor exceptions, is indisputable; the evaluation of its literary qualities must be left to the experts in that area. This discussion has been directed toward its loyalty to the text of the Hebrew and Greek Bible, toward the adequacy of its renderings of that text, and toward its interpretations. But it is precisely these areas that the average preacher and the man in the pew cannot evaluate. Though the basic duties toward God and man are clearly set forth in the NEB, the freedoms it exercises and the paraphrases it contains will likely make it unacceptable for widespread use among evangelicals. For the student, it leaves a great deal to be desired.

7

The New American Standard Bible

 T he New Testament of the New American Standard Bible, prepared by fifty-eight anonymous scholars under the sponsorship of the Lockman Foundation of La Habra, California, first appeared in 1963. The complete Bible (Old Testament and New Testament) was issued on July 31, 1970. Like the ASV, the NASB does not include the Apocrypha. More than sixteen million copies of the Bible have been distributed. The Foundation claims that it is the fastest-selling Bible in America today;[1] however, in September, 1977, the Christian Booksellers ranked it second to the Living Bible Paraphrased in sales for that month.[2] It is distributed by A. J. Holman, Moody Press, Foundation Publications, Collins-World, and Thomas Nelson.

[1]*"New American Standard Bible*: Translation and Format Facts" (La Habra, Calif.: The Lockman Foundation, n.d.), pp. 3-4.
[2]*Christian Bookseller Magazine* 23 (September 1977): 10.

From sources other than the Lockman Foundation, it is known that Dr. Reuben Olson served as chairman of the editorial board[3] and that the various translators were paid for their "continuous, intensive" work stretching over ten years. It is said that twenty-five thousand hours of research were expended on the New Testament alone. The work of the preparing committees was reviewed by critical consultants who offered suggestions that were later considered by the committees.

The stated goals of the Lockman Foundation (which also issues the Amplified translations)—that their publications be true to the original Hebrew and Greek, be grammatically correct, and be understandable to the masses—are common to the producers of all recent versions. Distinctive are the goals of "giving the Lord Jesus His proper place, the place which the Word gives Him," and that "no work will ever be personalized." The Foundation wants the translation to stand on its own merits and not to depend merely on the reputation of the translators who produced it. The Foundation states that the majority of the translators held doctoral degrees in biblical literature and languages. They represent Presbyterian, Methodist, Southern Baptist, Church of Christ, Nazarene, American Baptist, Fundamentalist, Conservative Baptist, Free Methodist, Congregational, Disciples of Christ, Evangelical Free, Independent Baptist, Independent Mennonite, Assembly of God, North American Baptist, and other religious groups.[4]

An exhaustive concordance with Hebrew and Greek equivalents of English words has been prepared for the NASB with a format similar to that of Strong's *Concordance*. It has a dictionary of the Greek Bible and a dictionary of the Hebrew Bible.[5] Other study helps for the NASB are in the process of being compiled.

The producers state their conviction that the Scriptures as originally penned in Hebrew and Greek were inspired of God. The NASB is intended to be appropriate for use in public worship as well as in private study. It has been advertised with the extravagant claims that it is "the literary masterpiece of this generation," "the major contribution of our generation

---

[3]W. L. Lane, "The *New American Standard Bible—New Testament*," *Gordon Review* 9 (Spring 1966): 156.

[4]"*New American Standard Bible*: Translation and Format Facts" (La Habra, Calif.: The Lockman Foundation, n.d.), p. 7.

[5]Ibid., p. 3.

to Biblical literature," and "destined to surpass all other translations of Holy Scripture."[6]

After praising the ASV as "the Rock of Biblical Honesty," the producers state that their motivation for producing the NASB is their regret that the ASV of 1901 is disappearing from the scene and their conviction that interest in it should be renewed and increased. However, the reader should not react to its aims or its title by thinking, "The ASV was a good translation, and the New American Standard is bound to be better." It is as legitimate for the Lockman Foundation to prepare a translation as it is for any organization; in a free society the Foundation can name the translation what it pleases; but in actuality, the gulf separating the ASV and the NASB is such that the NASB must be evaluated as a new translation. One cannot assume that it is what its title seems to imply — an update of the ASV.

New American Standard?

Rather than claiming to be a revised ASV, the NASB actually claims only "to follow the principles used in the ASV." In view of both the title and the praise given the ASV in the preface to the 1963 NASB, the observable differences between the ASV and the NASB assume more significance.

The typographical makeup of the two translations is different. One of the merits of the ASV (and of all other modern versions) was its printing of the text as paragraphs. The Geneva Bible (1560), followed by the KJV (1611), printed each verse as a separate unit. The NASB reverts to this practice. Unlike the KJV, which capitalized the beginning of each verse, the NASB starts verses with lower-case letters when they are not the beginning of sentences. Those verses which begin a paragraph are numbered in boldface type; if a paragraph begins within a verse, the first letter of the first word is in boldface type. This indicator can easily be overlooked. I Corinthians 12:31 and the middle of Isaiah 59:15 are the beginnings of paragraphs and therefore begin with a boldface letter. The first word of each chapter is printed with all capitals. So the first word of Isaiah 4:1 is in capitals, even though Isaiah 3:16 — 4:1 is treated as one paragraph. The paragraph that should begin in the middle of II Kings 24:20 is not indi-

---

[6]*Christianity Today* 9 (October 1964): 104, back cover.

cated. The first word of Isaiah 4:1; Matthew 10:1; and I Corinthians 13:1 is capitalized even though the thought of the section is broken by this traditional chapter division. Some later editions use conventional indentation to indicate paragraphs.

The ASV used no quotation marks; in the NASB, however, an elaborate system of quotation marks has been adopted. Quotations within quotations become more and more complicated, to the point that Isaiah 36:10 has four sets of marks; other sections (II Kings 19:7; II Chron. 34:28; Hag. 1:2) have three. The RSV closed the quotations of John 3 at verses 15 and 30, with a note that another division was possible. The editorial board of the NASB objected to this treatment of the passage. Therefore the NASB continued the first quotation without notation to verse 21 and the second quotation to verse 36, the end of the chapter. Some inconsistency is encountered in the NASB in its use of quotation marks. In Colossians 2:21 "Do not handle" is enclosed, but in I Corinthians 6:12 "All things are lawful" is not.[7]

An effort is made to print Old Testament poetic material in poetic form. More material is recognized as poetry than was true in the ASV, particularly in the prophetic books. Old Testament quotations in the New Testament are printed in small capital letters throughout. The margin gives the source of the quotation and the parallels if the section is quoted elsewhere. There seems to be an oversight in the capitalization and the marginal system when the allusion to Isaiah 53:12, found in Mark 10:45, is neither capitalized nor identified in the margin. The phrase "IN THE LAST DAYS" (Acts 2:17) should not be capitalized since it is not a part of Joel 2:28, which is being quoted.

Textual Base

The basic text of the NASB is aligned with that of the ASV and with those other translations which come after it, following a critical text rather than the *Textus Receptus*. In the Old Testament the third edition of the Kittel Bible—with resulting differences from the ASV—is used. It might be pointed out to the credit of the NASB that the sequence of the text has not been rearranged as was done in the NEB. The Dead Sea Scrolls

---

[7]F. W. Danker, "Another Parallel-Column Bible," *Concordia Theological Monthly* 39 (April 1968): 274.

(not available for the ASV) are followed, according to the marginal notes, in the Book of Isaiah in thirteen readings, including that of "dreamers" instead of "ravers" (Isa. 56:10). Other such readings are in Isaiah 18:7; 23:2; 34:16; 37:20, 27; 40:26; 49:17, 24; 56:5, 12; 64:7. Marginal readings from the Scrolls not accepted in the text are given at Isaiah 38:15 and 40:12.

In general, both the ASV and the NASB make less use of versional readings than does the RSV. For example, in the Book of Genesis, according to the marginal material, the RSV followed the versions rather than the Masoretic text in nineteen passages. The NASB (as does the ASV) accepts only one of these—the reading "storehouses" (Gen. 41:56), but neither the ASV nor the NASB indicates that it is following the versions. The ASV had given the versional reading in the margin of Genesis 25:22; 47:21; and 49:10. The NASB does so only at 49:10. Not included in the NASB are the supplements to the text from the versions found in the RSV: "Let us go out to the field" (Gen. 4:8), "Why have you stolen my silver cup?" (Gen. 44:4), "give Urim; but if this guilt is in thy people Israel" (I Sam. 14:41), and "So let it be, O Lord" (Jer. 15:11). Cases where the RSV indicates that it follows a versional reading and the NASB accepts that reading without indicating that it is a versional reading include "he maintained his fury forever" (Amos 1:11) and "That you may devote" (Mic. 4:13), where the Hebrew has "I will devote."

A further sampling reveals that the ASV and the NASB in certain other cases agree in following the ancient versions instead of the Masoretic text. These include the readings "stone" (I Sam. 6:18), "tribe" (9:21), "no" (10:19), "God sees not as man sees" (16:7), "Ish-bosheth" (II Sam. 3:7, 4:1), "I" (3:18), "spoke" (14:4), "But you are worth ten thousand of us" (18:3), "Protect for me" (18:12), "leaves" (I Kings 6:34), "stationed" (10:26), omission of the negative (Isa. 9:3), "will die" (Jer. 38:9) rather than "had died," "an expert warrior" (Jer. 50:9), and "another" (Ezek. 17:7) rather than "one." The ASV placed the versional reading in italics without a note at I Samuel 10:19; 16:7; II Samuel 3:7; and 4:1, but in the other instances (II Sam. 3:18; 14:4; I Kings 6:34; 10:26; Ezek. 17:7) it did not call attention to the fact that a versional reading was being followed. The RSV has also made all these same choices in readings except in II Samuel 14:4; however, only in II Samuel 18:3 does it call the reader's attention to the fact that it is following the versions.

In certain cases a reading cited in the ASV margin is moved by the NASB into the text: "many" (Jer. 50:29) with "archers" in the margin, and "when they die" (Ezek. 43:7) with "in their high places" in the margin. The RSV, citing no marginal readings, agrees in text with the ASV on Jeremiah 50:26, but drops the relevant phrase entirely in Ezekiel 43:7.

In II Samuel 19:18 (19), the NASB accepts without notation Wellhausen's textual conjecture: "Then they kept crossing the ford." Amos 6:5 reads in the ASV, as in all current English Bibles, "invent for themselves instruments of music, like David"; but the NASB has "composed songs for themselves" and then has "invented musical instruments" as a marginal reading. The translation follows the unsupported conjecture of the notes of the Kittel Bible that *kale* ("instruments") is a gloss in the text.

In many cases the NASB follows the versions and other manuscripts where the ASV followed the Masoretic text. A lengthy supplement from the Septuagint is given in brackets at Judges 16:13a-14b, with a marginal note. Versional readings are found in the reading "Me" (II Sam. 7:16) instead of "thee," "Merab" (II Sam. 21:8) instead of "Michal," "thirty" (II Sam. 23:19) instead of "three," "lowest" (I Kings 6:8) instead of "middle," and "My" (Isa. 33:11) instead of "your." Still others are "their" (Jer. 17:1), "have stumbled" (Jer. 18:15), "Let not him" (Jer. 51:3), "In the midst" (Ezek. 1:13), "beings" (Ezek. 1:20, 21), "them" (Ezek. 11:19), "have enraged" (Ezek. 16:43), "so now" (Ezek. 16:57), "Edom" (16:57), "choice men" (Ezek. 17:21), "destroyed" their fortified towers (Ezek. 19:7; Targum) instead of "knew his windows," "they" (Ezek. 32:25) instead of "he," "he" (Ezek. 43:3) instead of "I," and "Him" (Zech. 14:5) instead of "Thee." The RSV rendered the Masoretic text at Ezekiel 29:7 but had preceded the NASB in making these other choices, though carrying no note at II Samuel 7:16; Jeremiah 17:1; 51:3; Ezekiel 1:21; 11:19; 16:43; 32:25; and 43:3.

In some instances where the ASV followed the Hebrew text, the NASB gives the versional correction but carries the reading from the Hebrew text in the margin: "His" is changed to "their" (Job 27:15), "my" is used instead of "their" (Isa. 26:19), "Marduk" is used for "Merodach" (Jer. 50:2), "the spirit to go" is omitted (Ezek. 1:20), "will return ... state" is omitted after "Sodom" (Ezek. 16:55), "wound" is used for "wounds" (Mic. 1:9), and "Milcom" is used for "Malcom" (Zeph. 1:5). Of these verses, the RSV follows the Masoretic text in Jeremiah 50:2 and in Ezekiel 16:55 but precedes the NASB in its omission in Ezekiel 1:20, and the correction in number of Micah 1:9 and of spelling in Zephaniah 1:5.

Where manuscripts vary, the NASB concurs in some choices made by the ASV: "servants" (I Kings 1:27) instead of "servant," "like a threshing heifer" (Jer. 50:11) instead of "in the grass," "when I shall punish you" (Jer. 50:31) instead of "your punishment," and "drought" (Jer. 50:38) instead of "sword." Of these, the RSV differs at Jeremiah 50:11.

In certain cases the KJV, ASV, RSV, and NASB all make the same choice in the text, but the ASV and the NASB cite a versional difference in the margin: "winnow" (Jer. 51:2) instead of "foreigners," "desolate" (Ezek. 6:6), and "I saw" (Ezek. 16:50).

Versional readings given in the margin where the ASV had none include "and they spread a bed for Saul on the roof and he slept" (I Sam. 9:25), "came" (II Sam. 14:4), "he will set" (Jer. 43:12), "call the name of Pharaoh a big noise" (Jer. 46:17), "let them go forth" (Jer. 50:8), "a vision" (Ezek. 1:1), and "you" (Ezek. 5:15). Haggai 2:17 carries a note concerning the obscurity of the text, whereas the ASV had no such note.

In some cases the NASB accepts without notation a reading the RSV lists as a textual correction: cf. II Samuel 13:16; 19:18, "removed from" (II Kings 16:18), "living" (Neh. 3:26), "restrains" (Job 30:13), and "arouse" (Ps. 7:6). Though usually indicating that the translation is paraphrastic, the term "Lit." in the margin may also indicate that a versional reading is being followed: "stirring up" (Judg. 9:31), "sent them" (Jer. 27:3), "rest" (Job 14:6), and "escape" (Job 15:30). The same is true of the note introduced by "Or." It may introduce an emended text: "while he is eating"— "Or, as his food" (Job 20:23), "songs of deliverance"—"Or, shouts" (Ps. 32:7), "a swallow"—"Or, stagger" (Obad. 16).

There are, finally, those cases where there are wide differences between the ASV and the NASB. In the NASB reading "all wrists" (literally, "all joints of the hand"), the Masoretic text reads "of my hands" (Ezek. 13:18); here the NASB without a note follows the RSV. The ASV has "elbows," plus a marginal notation. Daniel 2:5, "The command from me is firm," follows the RSV, with a marginal notation, "Another reading is, 'The word has gone from me.'" The NASB paraphrases Habakkuk 2:16 as, "expose your *own* nakedness," giving the literal reading in the margin: "show yourself uncircumcised" (as in the ASV). It also cites from the Dead Sea Scrolls and ancient versions another reading, "Or stagger," which the RSV followed.

In general, it may be said that the NASB Old Testament has called the reader's attention to the existence of textual problems more frequently than did the ASV.

On examining the textual question in the New Testament, one observes that the ASV by marginal notes refers to textual variants in sixty-two instances in the Gospel of Matthew. The NASB notes only twenty of these variants in the margins. In twelve instances the Greek text of the marginal variant is chosen by the NASB over the text followed by the ASV: omission of "unto him" (Matt. 3:16), omission of "deliver thee" (5:25), "with no man in Israel have I found so great faith" (8:10), "but what went ye out to see? a prophet?" (11:9), "they ate" (12:4), "was many furlongs distant from land" (14:24), "and came" (14:29), add to text: "or his mother" (15:6), "Jesus Christ" (16:21), "were gathering themselves together" (17:22), "created" (19:4), "of this blood, see ye, etc." (27:24), and "where he lay" (28:6). Of these cases, only in 8:10; 15:6; and 27:24 is the reader's attention called to the existence of a variant. The NASB had been preceded in these textual choices by the RSV in 3:16; 5:25; 14:24; 17:22; 27:24; and 28:6, but the RSV carried marginal notes to 3:16; 8:10; 11:9; 14:24; 17:22; 27:24; and 28:6. The NASB has followed the Nestle text in all of these readings except in 11:9, where the Nestle has, "Why did you go out? To see a prophet?" The United Bible Societies' text in this case prefers the alternative followed by the NASB.

Approaching the text question from the opposite side, in the Gospel of Matthew the NASB notes textual variants in only two instances where the ASV (and RSV) did not: omission of "of the blind" (15:14) and the alternation of the order of the answers (21:29, 30) in the parable of the two sons. In the first of these the NASB prefers a variant given a "C" value by the UBS text over that followed by the ASV and RSV. In the second, its sequence is the reverse from these translations, as is also true with the Nestle and the UBS texts.

The NASB is nearer in text to the RSV than it is to the ASV. In using it, the reader has the advantage of a more current textual view than he does with the ASV; however, the reader of either the ASV or the RSV is made more aware of the existence of textual variation than is the reader of the NASB. The ASV had marginal notes to variants in the New Testament in at least 170 instances where the NASB carries none. One such case is at Mark 1:2 where the NASB reads "Isaiah the prophet," which is the more difficult reading. The preparers of the NASB state that they have followed the twenty-third edition of the Nestle text for the New Testament, but they differ from it, from the United Bible Societies' text, and from the text underlying the ASV. Nestle, the Bible Societies' text, and the ASV agree in relegating sixteen whole verses of the New Testament carried in the *Textus Receptus* to the margin. Most of these verses are also relegated to the margin in the NASB. Current printings (copyright 1977) print Mark 7:16; 9:44, 46; 11:26; 15:28 in the text enclosed in brackets. For an unexplained reason, however, Matthew 12:47 (bracketed in the Nestle text and relegated to the margin in the RSV) is restored to the NASB text without brackets or note. Matthew 18:11 and 23:14 are restored to the text but placed in brackets. The same treatment is given the doxology of Matthew 6:13. Luke 24:12 is carried in the text in brackets. The ASV carried it in the text with a marginal note, but it is found in the margin of the Nestle and the Bible Societies' texts. There seems no adequate justification for these textual reversions of the NASB.

Textual problems with the ending of Mark (Mark 16:9-20) and with the section of the adulteress (John 7:53—8:11) are indicated by brackets with a marginal note. The ASV set them off by a space in the text. Both versions omit the *Comma Johanneum* (I John 5:7-8); but the NASB carries it in a note. Unlike the ASV, the NASB prints the so-called "shorter ending of Mark." The treatment of this "short ending of Mark" is strange in a translation that claims to hold the view of Scripture the NASB does. It is printed in italics (which shows that the editorial board does not consider it as genuine) as an "Addition" following the "long ending" (Mark 16:9-20). The short ending occurs in four Greek uncials: L. Psi, 099, 042; and in the cursive 579 following verse 8. It is in each case followed by the long ending. The short ending is also found in the margin of Ms. 274 and of the Harclean Syriac, in the margin of two Mss. of the Bohairic version, and in several Mss. of the Ethiopic version between verses 8 and 9. One old Latin manuscript, Ms. k, has only the short ending; but no known manuscript has it after the long ending.[8]

The NASB abandons the textual choices underlying the ASV in numerous cases and reverts to the readings underlying the KJV. The following are some illustrative cases: "or his mother" (Matt. 15:6; ASV omits), "of the blind" (15:14; ASV omits), "God" (Mark 10:6; ASV, "he"), "when they rise again" (12:23; ASV omits), "nothing will be impossible with God" (Luke 1:37; ASV, "No word from God shall be void of power"), "expecting

---

[8]W. L. Lane, "The *New American Standard Bible*," p. 157.

nothing in return" (6:35; ASV, "never despairing"), "until the time comes" (13:35; ASV, "until"), "said" (John 4:17; ASV, "said unto him"), "Never did a man speak the way this man speaks" (7:46; ASV, "Never man so spake"), "Let her alone" (12:7; ASV, "suffer her to keep it"; margin as NASB text), "if God is glorified in Him" (13:32; ASV omits), "the Great Power of God" (Acts 8:10; ASV, "That power of God which is called Great"), "in a vision" (9:12; ASV omits), "without misgiving" (11:12; ASV, "making no distinction), "they were" (23:20; ASV, "thou wouldest"), "why does one also hope" (Rom. 8:24; ASV, "who hopeth"), "was raised" (8:34; ASV, " was raised from the dead"), "us" (15:7; ASV, "you"), "in his time" (II Thess. 2:6; ASV, "in his own season"), "will send" (2:11; ASV, "sendeth"), "In these last days" (Heb. 1:2; ASV, "at the end of these days"), "in these last times" (I Peter 1:20; ASV, "at the end of the times"), "when he appears" (I John 2:28; ASV, "if he shall be manifested"), "dipped in blood" (Rev. 19:13; ASV, "sprinkled with blood"), and "with all" (22:21; ASV, "with the saints"). Later editions of the NASB drop "then" (Heb. 9:9) to read "a symbol of the present time." The NASB has not been consistent in calling attention to its departures in text from the ASV. Many of these reversions, differing from both the twenty-third edition of the Nestle text and also from the United Bible Societies' text, cannot claim the support of the majority opinion in textual criticism.

In some cases the NASB differs from the KJV, the ASV, and the Nestle text; for example, at John 15:8 the marginal reading of the ASV, paraphrastically rendered "that you bear much fruit, and so prove to be my disciples," is followed against a variant preferred in the Nestle text. The word order in "Christ Jesus" (Phil. 2:21) and in "Jesus Christ" (Col. 4:12) is also against all the above mentioned authorities as well as against the United Bible Societies' text.

In some cases the ASV differs in text from the KJV, and the NASB disagrees with both of them. For example, Mark 1:4, "John the Baptist appeared" (KJV, "John did baptize"; ASV, "John came, who baptized"), "*began* devoting himself completely to the word" (Acts 18:5; KJV, "pressed in the spirit"; ASV, "was constrained by the word"), "they ... we" (Acts 28:1; KJV, "they ... they"; ASV, "we ... we").

In other cases the NASB differs from both the KJV and the ASV text, but adopts the ASV marginal reading: "Titius Justus" (Acts 18:7; KJV, "Justus"; ASV, "Titus Justus"), and "power of the Spirit" (Rom. 15:19; KJV, "power of the Spirit of God"; ASV, "power of the Holy Spirit").

The NASB has textual omissions in which it follows the margin rather than the text of the ASV: "on me" (Mark 9:42), "and cleave to his wife" (Mark 10:7), "them who trust in riches" (Mark 10:24), "and saith unto them, Peace *be* unto you" (Luke 24:36), the whole of Luke 24:40 with a marginal note, "who is in heaven" (John 3:13), and "upon the sons of disobedience" (Col. 3:6). A section of Acts 13:18, which appears in the text of the ASV with a marginal note, is relegated to the margin of the NASB; and the marginal reading is transferred to the text.

Variant readings are chosen which differ from those followed by the ASV: "Son of Man" is favored over "Son of God" (John 9:35) and "for forgiveness" (Luke 24:47) over "and remission." John 8:39 is rendered as an imperative: "Do the deeds of Abraham" where the ASV had a future, "ye would do the works of Abraham." In Acts 15:32 "with a lengthy message" is chosen over "with many words."

The insertion of the phrase "of the word" in the NASB (as KJV but not as ASV) arises from a different interpretation of *to logikon*. However, in this verse both versions inprove on the KJV by the addition, "unto salvation" (ASV) or "in respect to salvation" accompanied by a marginal note, "or unto salvation" (NASB). Both have "tree of life" (Rev, 22:19) where the KJV has "book of life."

In Hebrews 4:2, a textual variant is cited in the margin as though it were a translation variant: "Or, they were ... faith with those who heard."

These various phenomena leave room for debate over whether or not the NASB has attained its goal of representing the best available text.

Changing Editions

In keeping with the Lockman Foundation's promise—"The text of the Bible will be updated when appropriate, so that new discoveries as well as English language changes may be incorporated"[9]—current printings of the NASB show corrections of defects in earlier printings that were pointed out by reviewers. In 1961 the editorial board felt it would be unwise to render the historic present tenses into past tenses in English; but by 1963 they felt it would be better to do so, and marked them with an asterisk. "Says" has become "*said" (Mark 5:39; 14:63; John 8:39; Acts 8:36), "en-

---

[9]"*New American Standard Bible*: Translation and Format Facts" (La Habra, Calif.: The Lockman Foundation, n.d.), p. 7.

ters" has become "*entered" (Mark 5:40), and "takes" has become "*took" (Mark 5:40).

The word "Us" (Gen. 1:26) is now capitalized. The printing of "BRANCH" (Zech. 3:8; 6:12) has been dropped. "Sons of man" has become "sons of men" (Ps. 53:2; 58:1; 66:5), "Other masters than Thou have ruled over us" (Isa. 26:13) becomes "ruled us," the heading "Onan" (I Chron. 21) has been corrected to "Ornan," "Mago-massabib" (Jer. 20:3) is corrected to "Magor-missabib," and "Jaconiah" (Jer. 24:1) to "Jeconiah."

The prosaic, "Well then let us go straight to Bethlehem" (Luke 2:15) has become, "Let us go straight to Bethlehem then." Early in the history of the NASB, corrections were made in John 1:43; 5:14; 6:19; 13:31; and 20:26.[10] "*Begun* to be amazed" (Acts 2:7) has become "were amazed." "If he shall appear" (I John 3:2) has become "when He appears." Some printings (by Collins and A. J. Holman) now omit "The Millenium" [*sic*] as a heading to Revelation 20. This heading was "The Millenial Reign" in the 1963 printing of the New Testament by the Broadman Press.

However, there remain errors needing correction, such as "continued in amazement" (Acts 2:12) and "*began* to give them his attention" (Acts 3:5), particularly when the same idiom is elsewhere handled correctly. "Above him" (Mark 2:4), which should be as the margin, "where he was," remains unchanged.

Lexical Material

In many instances the preparers of the NASB were sensitive to archaeological discoveries resulting in vocabulary updating. One such case is where the *teraphim* are "household idols" (Gen. 31:19; I Sam. 19:13, 16), with *teraphim* relegated to the margin. "Pallet" rather than "bed" is used (Mark 2:4), "lampstand" (Rev. 1:12; etc.) instead of "candlestick." However, one wonders why the NASB did not make more of vocabulary discoveries than it has. The serpent is not considered a "beast" (Gen. 3:1, 14) in current zoology. Though the language is "Aramaic" (II Kings 18:26; Isa. 36:11; Ezra 4:7), and Jacob is a "wandering Aramean" (Deut. 26:5), for the same term Laban (Gen. 25:20; 28:5; 31:20, 24) and Naaman (II Kings 5:20; cf. Luke 4:27) are "Syrians." The people in the general Damascus area are

[10]Robert G. Bratcher, review of *New American Standard Gospel of John* in *The Bible Translator* 13 (October 1962): 234-36.

"Syrians" (II Sam. 8:5, 6, 13; 10:6ff.) and the area is "Syria" (II Sam. 8:12), though the margin carries "Aram."

The NASB continues the use of "Red Sea" and only gives "Sea of Reeds" as a marginal reading (Exod. 15:4). "Amaw" (Num. 22:5) is rejected in favor of "land of the sons of his people." The NASB also rejected "glaze" (Prov. 26:23), "upsurgings of the deep" (II Sam. 1:21), "pim" (I Sam. 13:21), "against" (II Kings 23:29), and "liver" (Ps. 16:9). "Beyond the River" continues as a direction rather than as a provincial title (Ezra 6:6, 13; etc.). "Tartan," "Rabshakeh," and "Rabsaris" (II Kings 18:17, 19, 26; Isa. 36:2, 4, 13, 22; 37:4, 8) are incorrectly treated as proper names; but "Tartan" (Isa. 20:1) and "Rabsaris" and "Rabmag" (Jer. 39:3, 13) are correctly recognized as titles.

In New Testament vocabulary, "scroll" (Luke 4:17, 20; Rev. 5:1) is given only as a marginal reading. "Idle" (as opposed to "unruly"; I Thess. 5:14; II Thess. 3:6, 7, 11), "delight in riches" (Matt. 13:22; Mark 4:19), and "after the Sabbath" (Matt. 28:1) are all rejected. "Tutor" for *paedagōgus* (I Cor. 4:15; Gal. 3:24) is retained despite the fact that a papyrus letter makes clear that the role of the *paedagōgus* and the *didaskalos* ("teacher") are different functions.

Translation Peculiarities

One of the distinctive features of the NASB is its treatment of questions which expect a negative answer, expressed with *mē* in the Greek sentence.[11] Where the ASV had "Can this man be the Son of David?" the NASB has "This *man* cannot be the Son of David, can he?" (Matt. 12:23); where there was "Would you go away?" (John 6:67; cf. 7:35, 41, 47, 52), the NASB has "You do not want to go away also, do you?"[12] Other cases include: "their unbelief will not nullify the faithfulness of God, will it?" (Rom. 3:3), "The God who inflicts wrath is not unrighteous, is He?" (Rom. 3:5), "There is no injustice with God, is there?" (Rom. 9:14), "God has not rejected His people, has He?" (Rom. 11:1), and "Surely not I, Lord?" (Matt. 26:22). Dana and Mantey list this sort of rendering as suitable for the construction;[13] however, the NASB has not been completely consistent in

---

[11]Preface to the *New American Standard Bible*, p. ix.

[12]Robert G. Bratcher, "Old Wine in New Bottles," *Christianity Today* 16 (October 8, 1971): 17.

[13]H. E. Dana and Julius R. Mantey, *A Manual Grammar of the Greek New Testament* (New York: Macmillan, 1927), p. 265, par. 241 (2).

its style. In Matthew 7:9 the text has "What man ... will give him a stone?" and the margin carries as literal "he will not give him a stone, will he?" Verse 10 of the same chapter, however, has the new form in the text and uses the more traditional question form in the margin. The policy runs into problems when the feature is followed by Paul's *mē genoito*, "by no means!" (Rom. 3:5-6), for it has weakened that expression.

Another very distinctive feature of the NASB is the use of *began* for the Greek imperfect tense when it is considered to be inceptive. *Began* is italicized to distinguish it from the translation of the Greek word ordinarily meaning "begin." This feature creates its own problems. It is not accurate to say that the man "*began* to give them his attention" (Acts 3:5), for he had done that when he began asking for alms (v. 3). One should say, "He gave them his attention." "*Began* to withdraw" (Gal. 2:12) should be "withdrew."[14] There are other instances where the effort to describe the commencement of an act (ingressive aorist) with *began* or *became* fails. These include "*has begun* to live" (Luke 15:32) and "about to go up" (Matt. 20:17). The latter case suggests that he had not started at all. The ASV had "as Jesus was going," which fits his movement that began at 19:1. "*Began* saying, 'I do believe' " (Mark 9:24) can only mean that he said it again. In addition to envisioning the imperfect as inceptive and using *began* (Matt. 16:7) or *started* (Luke 7:6), the NASB at other times conceives the imperfect as tendential; for example, "They tried to give Him wine" (Mark 15:23). Greek experts would call this "overtranslation."

The NASB ordinarily uses the past tense, e.g., "he did," for the aorist; however, some are rendered as perfects, "he has done," and others as past perfects, "he had done." The past progressive, "he was doing," is used for the imperfect, or if it is conceived as inceptive, "he began to do"; if conceived as customary past, "he used to do."[15] The translators, in this way, had to express a value judgment derived from the context in each instance. When a Greek historical present tense has been translated into an English past, the word is marked with an asterisk; for example, "says" has become "*said" (Acts 8:36), as we have noted earlier.

The NASB uses "Lord" for the divine name where the ASV used "Jehovah," except when the name occurs in close proximity to *Adonai*, in which case "God" (Amos 7:1; 8:1; etc.) is used to avoid confusion.

[14]W. L. Lane, "The *New American Standard Bible*," p. 161.
[15]Preface to *New American Standard Bible*, p. viii.

Theological Stance

The conservative theological stance of the NASB is to be seen in its consistent retention of traditional theological words. *Semeion* occurs forty-eight times in the Greek New Testament and is consistently translated "sign." The KJV translated twenty-two of these as "miracle," thereby obscuring a feature of the vocabulary of the Gospel of John. *Haima* is consistently translated "blood." In John 2:2 and 4:10 the use of "propitiation" for *hilasmos* is continued, once with a marginal reading "Or, satisfaction" and once without. "Propitiation" is also retained for *hiliaskomai* in Hebrews 2:17. Some form of the word "reconciliation" is used in thirteen instances for *allassein* (cf. II Cor. 5:19). "Saint" is retained for *hagioi* (Eph. 1:1; Phil. 1:1; etc.), though the need of a marginal explanation is recognized. "Brethren" is used (though inconsistently, as we have set forth in another section of this chapter) for the religious relationship.

The NASB makes a clear but not consistent effort in the Old Testament to drop the archaic term "seed" (Gen. 22:17, 18; Ps. 105:6) as the translation for *zera'* in connection with Abraham, usually substituting "descendant" (Gen. 12:7; 15:18; 17:8; etc.). In the New Testament the NASB wavers between "descendant" (Rom. 4:13, 18; 9:7; 11:1; II Cor. 11:22) and "offspring" (Luke 1:55; John 8:33, 37; Acts 7:5, 6; Gal. 3:29), but then continues the traditional "seed" (Acts 3:25; Gal. 3:16, 19; Heb. 2:16) in theologically crucial passages.

All pronouns referring to divinity are capitalized: "He" (Gen. 1:27), "Thee" (Gen. 3:10), "Us" (Gen. 1:26; 3:22), and "Our" (Gen. 1:26). The second person pronoun "You" when addressed to God, Christ, or the Holy Spirit, even when used by those intending Jesus no honor, is capitalized (Matt. 21:23; 22:16, 17; 26:68). The third-person pronoun referring to Jesus is usually, but not always, capitalized in the Gospels (Matt. 12:23). New Testament quotations of Old Testament material are printed in all capital letters, but the titles and pronouns begin with larger capitals. Nevertheless, "Son of Man" (Heb. 2:6) begins in regular capitals. By some sort of error, "man" is not capitalized in the first inquiry of Peter (John 18:17), while the pronouns of the second and third challenges are (John 18:25, 26).

"Spirit" (Gen. 1:2) is capitalized where interpreted to be the Holy Spirit. "Holy Spirit" and titles referring to him (John 14:16, 17; 15:26; 16:7, 8, 13, 15; Rom. 8:16) are capitalized even if supplied in italics (Acts 11:15).

179

In the Old Testament, all epithets and pronouns thought to refer to the Messiah are capitalized: "Anointed," "Son," and "King" (Ps. 2:2, 6, 12); "Holy One" (Ps. 16:10); "Shepherd" (Zech. 13:7); "One" (Mic. 5:2, 5); "Associate" (Zech. 13:7); "Son of Man" (Dan. 7:13; but not in Ps. 8:4); and "Redeemer" (Job 19:25). Also capitalized are most of the pronouns accompanying these terms. With this policy, one wonders why "him" of Genesis 3:15 and of Genesis 49:10, "star" and "scepter" of Numbers 24:17, "prophet" and "him" of Deuteronomy 18:15, and the pronouns of Psalm 22 are not capitalized. If it is said that the Psalm first applies to a human king, the same should hold true of some pronouns (for example in Ps. 45) that are capitalized. "Servant" (Isa. 42:1) and relevant pronouns are capitalized but in the other "Servant Songs" in Isaiah capitals are not used. In Isaiah 52:13 "servant" is not capitalized, but it is capitalized at 53:11. The pronouns referring to the servant throughout the section are capitalized. "Branch," though not capitalized in Isaiah 11:1, is capitalized in Isaiah 4:2, in Jeremiah 23:5; 33:15 (however, the pronouns referring to him are not), and in Zechariah 3:8; 6:12, along with the pronouns. The capitalization policy (doubtlessly thought by the translators as giving Jesus Christ the honor due him) forced the translators to indicate what passages in the Old Testament they felt had messianic import. Many evangelicals welcome such a policy but Jewish readers consider it a begging of the question. The snares of the capitalization policy could have been avoided by allowing the reader to make up his own mind.

Both in its translations and in its notes, the NASB reflects a premillennial preference. The translators chose "as" in the phrase "the mountain of the house of the Lord will be established as the chief of the mountains" (Isa. 2:2; Mic. 4:1), even though the margin acknowledges that "on" is literal. The rendering, "And those who will walk by this rule, peace and mercy *be* upon them, and upon the Israel of God" (Gal. 6:16) makes it more likely that the *kai* will be taken as coordinate rather than as explanatory. In the marginal notes, "generation" regularly carries the alternate "race" (Mark 13:30; Luke 21:32). "He is near," though with a marginal note "it" (Mark 13:29), turns the thought of the passage to the second coming. In Revelation 5:10, the Greek present tense is rendered "will reign" where the ASV had "they reign." Revelation 20:4 has "they came to life and reigned with Christ for a thousand years," which supports the contrast the premillennialist likes to make in the verse. The ASV had "they lived," which is a more literal rendering for the Greek aorist, *ezēsan*. The follow-

180

ing verse (v. 5) in the NASB has "did not come to life" for the negative of the same expression. The KJV has "lived not again" for verse 5, but has "they lived" for verse 4. The Greek, except for the negative, is the same in each verse. As previously noticed, the NASB carries a page heading "The Millenium" [sic] for the section.

Printing "I AM" (John 8:58) in capitals reflects the theory that Jesus is intending to make a claim connected with the wording given in Exodus 3:14. Full deity is attributed to Jesus Christ in the NASB. The variants "the only begotten God" (ASV: "son") in John 1:14 and "the Church of God" (ASV: "the Lord") in Acts 20:28—in keeping with current textual views—are chosen. Romans 9:5 reads, "from whom is the Christ according to the flesh, who is over all, God blessed forever," with no marginal alternate given. The punctuation in the ASV and the NIV gives the text the same translation as the NASB, but the marginal note in the ASV reads, "he who is over all, God, be blessed forever," and the NIV marginal alternates with variations in wording suggest the same interpretation. The RSV has the opposite text and margin; the NEB text has a reading similar to the RSV, but has no marginal alternate. But perhaps too great a theological zeal lies behind the interpretative note in the NASB to the word "one" in John 10:30; "Lit. (neuter) a unity, or, one essence." It is entirely possible that other types of oneness were in the mind of the writer of the Gospel. By the supplying, without italics, of a definite article not in the Greek, the centurion is made to say, "the Son of God" (Matt. 27:54; Mark 15:39). Alternatives are noted in the margin.

The added phrases in Acts 7:59 (comparable to those of the ASV) avoid having Stephen address prayer to Jesus. By the addition of the word "daughter" at several places (I Cor. 7:36ff.), the NASB perpetuates the interpretation given by the ASV of a difficult passage. The rendering "spiritual *thoughts* with spiritual *words*" (I Cor. 2:13) gets the nod over the alternate of the margin. Preference is given to the rendering "All Scripture is inspired by God and profitable" (II Tim. 3:16; as KJV); and the ASV rendering "Every Scripture inspired by [ASV: of] God is also profitable" in the margin is listed only as "possible."

Additional choices congenial to fundamentalist theology include the rendering of *monogenēs* as "only begotten" when it refers to Jesus (John 1:14; 3:16; etc.) and to Isaac (Heb. 11:17); though "only" is used for the afflicted child, Jairus' daughter, and the widow's son (Luke 7:12; 8:42; 9:38). *'Almah* is "virgin" in Isaiah 7:14 but elsewhere is "maiden" (Gen.

24:43), "girl" (Exod. 2:8), "maidens" (Ps. 68:25 [26]; Song of Sol. 1:3; 6:8), and "maid" (Prov. 30:19). "Virgin" is used in thirteen out of fourteen occurrences for *parthenos*. At Revelation 14:4, "celibates" is in the text with a note, "Or, chaste men; lit. virgins." "Virgin" is also used as a paraphrase (Matt. 1:25; Luke 1:34) for a longer phrase in which the word *parthenos* does not occur.

Fidelity to the Text

Though the Lockman Foundation's publicity material makes glowing claims for the fidelity of the NASB, claiming that it is "unequalled in its faithfulness to the Greek and Hebrew texts,"[16] an inconsistency seems apparent in the way the NASB translators perceived their task. The introductory material states that they retained conjunctions occurring in the original text even though they are superfluous in English, because the Holy Spirit led men to write that way. But did not the same Holy Spirit lead men to write many idioms which the NASB converts to English idioms? For example, in one instance, where the figure of speech known as *litotes* is converted into a declarative statement, "not a little" (Acts 14:28) becomes "a long time," but elsewhere "not a little" becomes "greatly" (Acts 20:12). Did not the Holy Spirit give many word orders which the NASB has changed, many phrases without the article where the NASB supplied the article, and many articles where pronouns have been substituted? Has it not supplied conjunctions where the original had none ("and" in Gal. 4:6; etc.)? Are there not places where modifying words such as "alone" (Gen. 7:1), "simply" (John 4:48), "only" (II Thess. 1:3; I Tim. 3:12), "carefully" (I Thess. 5:21), and "ever" (II Thess. 1:3) are added? Even though the added words are italicized, the reader will still read them and will understand the passage in the light of their implication. In at least one case (Acts 4:25), in addition to the italics, there is the note, "This word is missing in the Greek."

The NASB is relatively—though not entirely—free from paraphrasing tendencies. "And by the seventh day God completed His work" (Gen. 2:2) is paraphrased to avoid the idea of action on the seventh day. "Seared ... as with a branding iron" (I Tim. 4:2) enlarges the text without use of

---

[16]"*New American Standard Bible*: Translation and Format Facts" (La Habra, Calif.: The Lockman Foundation, n.d.), p. 5.

italics. "Poured out as a drink offering" (II Tim. 4:6) supplies the para-phrasis "as a drink offering." "Keep house" (I Tim. 5:14) would be more literal as "manage their households."[17]

Improvements over the ASV

In view of the stated aims of the NASB, those places where it is a definite improvement over the ASV become important. "The sound (*ol*) of the Lord God walking" (Gen. 3:8; also RSV) is better than "the voice of God walking." The word that was "burden" in the ASV, accompanied by the margin "oracle," becomes the reverse in the NASB as in the RSV (Nah. 1:1; Mal. 1:1). What was "bread" becomes "food," with "bread" relegated to the margin (Mal. 1:7). The attempt to be exact can be seen where the lamp is put under a "peck-measure" (Matt. 5:15; Mark 4:21) instead of the traditional "bushel." The NASB statement about Acts 8:37, "Late mss. insert verse 37," is a more accurate statement about the evi-dence than that of the ASV and RSV: "some [RSV: "other"] ancient au-thorities add all or most of verse 37." In the rendering of *akouein* in its various forms as "hear" in the narratives of Paul's conversion, the ASV retains a contradiction. The NASB solves this problem by using "under-stand" in Acts 22:9 to reflect the different Greek idiom.[18] In John 1:3, the NASB reads, "all things came into being" where the ASV and RSV had "all things were made." The NASB drops the supplied "our" of Hebrews 12:2 which the KJV, ASV, RSV, and NIV all retain. There are cases where the NASB has a more accurate rendering of tense than the ASV: "they will reign upon the earth" (Rev. 5:10; RSV, NEB, NIV) renders a future tense *basileusousin* which the ASV rendered as a present, "they reign." The rendering "Diana" in KJV and ASV has correctly become "Artemis" (Acts 19:27).

Retrogression from the ASV

Cases where the NASB abandoned the revision of the ASV and returned to the KJV include reinstatement of the "caperberry" (Eccles. 12:5) and

---

[17]W. L. Lane, "The *New American Standard Bible*," p. 164.

[18]E. E. Calverley, "The *New American Standard Bible*: New Testament," *The Muslim World* 55 (October 1965): 396-97.

having God "deceive" Jeremiah (Jer. 20:7). "Covenant" is used for *diathēkē* at Hebrews 9:16, 17 despite the general scholarly opinion that "will" is proper. One of the most marked ways in which the ASV differed from the KJV was in the interpretation given to Acts 26:28: "With but little persuasion thou wouldest fain make me a Christian." The NASB comes close to the interpretation of the KJV: "In a short time you will persuade me to become a Christian." Whether or not the translators intended the statement to be ironic, it is fairly certain that the unlettered reader will not see the irony. "From house to house" (Acts 2:46; for *kat' oikon*) compares with the ASV's "at home" or with "in their homes" or "in private homes" of other current versions. The neuter pronoun "it" (Mark 13:14) is used for the Abomination of Desolation, where the ASV used a masculine pronoun.

In isolated cases archaisms are used where the ASV had a current term; for example, "manchild" (Gen. 4:1) where the ASV had "son." The rendering "the sun being obscured" (Luke 23:45) is poorer than either that of the KJV ("the sun was darkened") or the ASV ("the sun's light was failing"). The NASB's rendering requires no more than a cloudy day to obscure the sun. "This is your god, O Israel" (Exod. 32:4) is less literal than either the KJV or the ASV, "these are thy gods."

The NASB has changed the interpretation of some passages which were not obscure in the ASV. Second Samuel 24:1, by the use of the pronoun "it," has the anger of the Lord incite David, whereas the ASV had "Jehovah" do it. The rendering "You only have Me among all the families of the earth" (Amos 3:2) is definitely inferior to "You only have I known" (ASV). In Matthew 3:16 and Mark 1:20, the ASV, in harmony with the Greek, suggests that Jesus saw the heavens opened; however, the NASB, by dropping the pronoun "he" (Matt. 3:16) to lower case, makes John the Baptist its antecedent; but then in a note it gives the alternate, "Or He." An effort to justify the change in interpretation is made by a reference to John 1:32 where John does see the Spirit descending. In Matthew 16:19 and 18:18 the ASV's "shall be bound ... shall be loosed" is changed in the NASB to "shall have been bound ... shall have been loosed." In John 20:23, the ASV's "they are forgiven ... they are retained" becomes in the NASB, "have been forgiven ... have been retained."

In the NASB, the one who believes "has received [KJV; ASV: "shall receive"] forgiveness of sins" (Acts 10:43; *aphesin harmartion labein*). The last rendering lends itself to the idea that salvation is at the point of belief. Yet other changes affecting interpretation include "grace and truth were realized [ASV, "came"] through Jesus Christ" (John 1:17), "And He made a scourge of cords, and drove *them* [ASV, "cast them"] all out of the temple" (John 2:15), and "You say *correctly* that I am a king" (John 18:37).

In yet other cases the NASB abandons the ASV and reverts not to the KJV, but to choices made in the RV. Examples include the phrase "the way of the treacherous" (Prov. 13:15) and use of the term "guilt offering" (Lev. 19:22; etc.).

Problems Continued

Some of the problem renderings of the ASV remain unchanged in the NASB. "For they said, 'He is a leper' " (II Chron. 26:23) leaves the reader wondering where they would have buried Uzziah had he not been a leper. Furthermore, as expressed in the NASB, each member of the Corinthian church is a member of each of the four parties (I Cor. 1:12).

Italics

The NASB italicizes words in at least 2,029 instances in the New Testament. Some of these cases are words that were supplied but left unitalicized in the ASV; for example, "shall come" (Num. 24:24). A preference for inserting "some" is observable: "*some* tax-gatherers" (Luke 3:12), "*some* soldiers" (Luke 3:14), "*some* Pharisees" (Luke 5:17), "*some* grain fields" (Luke 6:1), and "*some* bread" (Luke 22:19). Use of italics left the translators free to encroach on the domain of the commentator in their supplements to the text. Frequently an idea is sharpened or restricted by an added word when no addition was actually necessary: "you *alone* (Gen. 7:1), "*single* cubit" (Matt. 6:27; Luke 12:25), "that *very* hour" (Matt. 8:13), "shall *more* be given" (Matt. 13:12), "*firm* root" (Matt. 13:21; Mark 4:17; Luke 8:13), "*only* One" (Matt. 19:17), "*proper* seasons" (Matt. 21:41), "*right* at the door" (Matt. 24:33; Mark 13:29), "*any* one prisoner" (Matt. 27:15), "*only* temporary" (Mark 4:17), "*all* about" (Mark 5:16), "last *of all*" (Mark 12:6), "*merely* the beginning" (Mark 13:8), "the Father *alone*" (Mark 13:32), "*appointed* time" (Mark 13:33), "go *as a forerunner* before Him" (Luke 1:17), "How shall I know this *for certain?*" (Luke 1:18), "*properly* clothe yourself" (Luke 17:8), "*real* cause" (Acts 19:40), "accursed, *separated* from Christ" (Rom. 9:3), "you stand *only* by your faith" (Rom. 11:20), "*refreshing* rest" (Rom. 15:32), "*mere* men" (I Cor. 3:4), "*first* went forth" (I Cor. 14:36), "*only* a man's covenant" (Gal. 3:15), "God is *only* one" (Gal. 3:20), "the need *of the moment*" (Eph. 4:29), "do not *merely* look out (Phil. 2:4), "*true* circumcision" (Phil. 3:3), "a *mere* shadow" (Col. 2:17), "we *really* live" (I Thess. 3:8), "examine everything *carefully*" (I Thess. 5:21), "*only* fitting" (II Thess. 1:3), "*ever* greater" (II Thess. 1:3), "*only* just" (I Thess. 1:6), "*only* one wife" (I Tim. 3:12), "*constantly* nourished" (I Tim. 4:6), "*dependent* widow" (I Tim. 5:16), "*too* hastily" (I Tim. 5:22), "godliness *actually* is a means of great gain" (I Tim. 6:6), "*still* called 'Today' " (Heb. 3:13), "*only* of milk" (Heb. 5:13), "*only* when men are dead" (Heb. 9:17), "a *mere* copy" (Heb. 9:24), "*only* a shadow" (Heb. 10:1), "*any* offering" (Heb. 10:18), "sprinkled *clean*" (Heb. 10:22), "*only* one Lawgiver" (James 4:12), "the *very* world of iniquity" (James 3:6), "*just* a vapor" (James 4:14), and "external *only*" (I Peter 3:3). The insertion of the word "*including*" (Acts 6:9) excludes the exegetical possibility that "Freedmen" (*Libertinōn*) could be a geographical term along with the other geographical terms of the verse.

In some instances, side comments have been inserted in italics: "*He added*" (Mark 6:9), "*with the saliva*" (Mark 7:33), and "*the passage about the burning bush*" (Mark 12:26; Luke 20:37). The statement "the old is good *enough*" (Luke 5:39) has a different implication from "the old is good." Other cases include "*Roman* cohort" (John 18:3), "you say *correctly* that I am a king" (John 18:37), "Hellenistic *Jews* ... *native* Hebrews" (Acts 6:1), "*human* hands" (Acts 7:48), "translated *in Greek*" (Acts 9:36), "no *longer* consider" (Acts 10:15), "*divinely* directed" (Acts 10:22), "*just* a man" (Acts 10:26), "the days of *the Feast of* Unleavened Bread" (Acts 12:3), "led away *to execution*" (Acts 12:19), "*all of which took* about four hundred and fifty years" (Acts 13:19), "*the meeting of* the synagogue" (Acts 13:43), "the dust of their feet *in protest*" (Acts 13:51), "speaking boldly *with reliance* upon the Lord" (Acts 14:3), "the God-fearing *Gentiles*" (Acts 17:17), "*that is coming*" (Col. 4:16), "from one *Father*" (Heb. 2:11), "tempted in all things *as we are, yet* without sin" (Heb. 4:15), "spirits *now* in prison" (I Peter 3:19), "*the will of* God" (I Peter 4:6), a *special* gift" (I Peter 4:10), "*Christian* love" (II Peter 1:7), "*earthly* dwelling" (I Peter 1:14), "*really* of us" (I John 2:19), and "a *good* testimony" (III John 12).

In many cases a possessive pronoun has been substituted in italics for the definite article, or supplied where there is no article in the original: "*his* child" (Matt. 10:21), "*their* journey" (Mark 6:8), "*His* name" (Acts 5:41), "*His* resurrection" (Acts 26:23), "*my* offering" (Rom. 15:16), "*our*

brother" (II Cor. 1:1), *"their* parents . . . *their* children" (II Cor. 12:14), *"our*
faithful and beloved brother" (Col. 4:9), *"my* true child" (I Tim. 1:2), *"our*
doctrine" (I Tim. 6:1; but 6:3 has "the doctrine"), *"His* Son" (Heb. 1:2),
"their body" (James 2:16), *"our* life" (James 3:6), *"your* faith" (I Peter 5:9),
"their greed" (II Peter 2:3), *"their* lawless deeds" (II Peter 2:8), *"its* corrupt
desires" (II Peter 2:10), and *"their* mocking" (II Peter 3:3).

When two words are required in English where there was one in Greek
or Hebrew, as "fiery *serpent*" (Num. 21:8), or "corner *stone*" (Ps. 118:22;
Eph. 2:20; I Peter 2:6) for *rosh pinah / akrogōniaios*, the second word is
italicized. These italics are superfluous. "Stone" is as justified in the translation as "corner" is. Inconsistently, the word was spelled "cornerstone" in
Job 38:6 and Isaiah 28:16. The verb supplied in a sentence translating the
Hebrew nominal sentence is sometimes italicized despite the fact that it
is impossible to make an English sentence without the verb: "Now the
Canaanite *was* then in the land" (Gen. 12:6); but the verb is not italicized
at Amos 7:14 and Zechariah 13:5: "I am not a prophet."

Though italics are freely used, they cannot be depended upon to inform
the reader whether a word in the text has been supplied or was in the
original. If a literal rendering is given in the margin, the translators felt no
need to use italics in the text, but elsewhere also there are supplied words
without italics. "Own" in the phrase "his own sons" (Deut. 33:9), "in" in
the phrase "in your ways" (Deut. 28:29), "may" (Ruth 1:11), "influences"
(Isa. 2:6), "same" (Amos 2:7), "am" (Amos 7:14), "in the sight of" (Acts
7:20), "day" (Mark 16:2, 9; Acts 20:7; I Cor. 16:2), and "actually" (Acts
22:28) are all supplied. "False" is not italicized in the phrase "false circumcision" (*katatomē*; Phil. 3:2) though "true" in the phrase *"true* circumcision" (*peritomē*; Phil. 3:3) is. None of the words of "spiritual service
of worship" for *logikēn latreian* are italicized. "Long" in the phrase "all
day long" (Matt. 20:6) has no italics, but "hour" in "eleventh *hour*" does.
"Prove" in the phrase "prove to be My disciples" (John 15:8), "still" in
"still more excellent way" (I Cor. 12:31), and the words "just as" for *kathōs*
(I John 3:2, 3, 7, 23) are not italicized. "Seared in their own conscience as
with a branding iron" (I Tim. 4:2) carries none.[19] The definite article is
supplied without italics in many instances, beginning with the first words
of Genesis: "In the beginning." The reader can never be certain whether
the original had the definite article or not.

[19]W. L. Lane, "The *New American Standard Bible*," p. 163.

Italics may be used where a textual variant has been followed, though the reader is not so informed. The ASV used "Jesus" in Matthew 4:23, calling attention to the variant "he" in the margin. The NASB italicizes "Jesus" with no marginal note. Other cases of italicizing a versional reading include the supplied numerals in I Samuel 13:1. "Like" is inserted at Isaiah 21:8: *"like* a lion" for the Hebrew "a lion"; and "as" at Psalm 11:1; *"as* a bird," for a vocative, without a note that a version instead of the Masoretic text is being followed.

Marginal Notes

Though the NASB is a comparatively literal translation, even to the point of being called "severely literalistic,"[20] it supplies in the margins even more literal renderings for many verses (159 verses in Matthew, 114 in Mark, 207 in Luke, 61 in John, and 231 in Acts), each one introduced by the abbreviation "Lit." An almost equally great number of alternate renderings (affecting 203 verses in Matt., 112 in Mark, 154 in Luke, 70 in John, and 204 in Acts) are introduced by "Or." While many of these are helpful, it is not of much value to be told that "Jewish elders" are more literally "elders of the Jews" (Luke 7:3), that "sinful flesh" is "flesh of sin" (Rom. 8:3), that "fatter" is "fat of flesh" (Dan. 1:15), that a "wall" is a "fence" (Mark 12:1), that "his wife" is more literally "his own wife" (Acts 24:24), that "a great storm in the sea" (Matt. 8:24) is "a great shaking," that an alternate "of the dead" is "of corpses" (Mark 12:27), that "pretended" is "feigned themselves" (Luke 20:20), or that "is staying" is "is lodging" (Acts 10:6). "Harshly" (Mark 15:3) can hardly be called an alternate rendering of *pollu*, which has been "of many things" in all English translations since that of Tyndale and which is acknowledged as literal in the margin of the NASB.

Some lack of consistency is observable. The NASB translates *psuchē* as "life" in Mark 8:35 but as "soul" in the next two verses, giving "Gr. soul-life" in the margin; but then uses "life" for *psuchē* in Matthew 20:28; Mark 10:45; and John 12:25 with only "Or soul" in the margin. What is carried in one place in the margin as a literal rendering is in other texts introduced by the abbreviation "Gr."; for example, "Gr., *soul-life*" (Mark 8:35, 36, 37). When in one instance "congregation" carries a marginal note "Or, multitude" (Acts 6:2) and then three verses further (6:5) a second

[20]Bruce M. Metzger, "Trials of the Translator," *Theology Today* 33 (April 1976): 97.

occurrence has "Lit., multitude," one wonders what principle has been followed in determining whether to use "Or" or "Lit."

In certain cases the reading given in the margin would have been preferable to that given in the text. If "brimstone" means "sulfur" (Luke 17:29; cf. Gen. 19:24; Rev. 9:17), why would not "sulfur" be preferable in the text? Occurrences of "brimstone" in the Old Testament and at Revelation 14:10; 19:20; 20:10 have no marginal note. At Matthew 28:19, "baptized into the name" for *eis* would be preferable. The rendering that Haran died "during the lifetime of his father" (Gen. 11:28) seems preferable to "in the presence of." Is the text actually saying that his father was present at his death? "A child conductor" (Gal. 3:24), though not the best rendering, is more accurate than "tutor"; however, the same word at I Corinthians 4:15 has no marginal reading. "Laundryman" (Mal. 3:2) is clearer than "fuller," and "first fruits" (Nah. 3:12) is a slightly different image from "ripe fruit." "Birth pangs" (Mark 13:8), as a term for the end times, needs an explanatory note for the reader. The rendering "vessel" in I Thessalonians 4:4 is literal but obscure; "body" or "wife," noted in the margin, would clarify the meaning.

The marginal notes are not totally reliable; for example, "covenant" (Gal. 3:15) carries a marginal "Or, will, or testament." New Testament scholars are emphatic that except for Hebrews 9:16, 17, these terms are not the import of *diathekē* in the New Testament. "Bull of the herd" in the text and "Or, bull of the herd" in the margin (Lev. 4:14) seems an error.

The annotators did not refrain from commentary. "His name" (Acts 5:41) carries the margin "Lit., the name (par excellence)." It is not accurate to translate *baptisōntai* as "cleanse" (Mark 7:4) with a marginal reading "Or, sprinkle," and then to translate the noun of the same root in the same verse as "washing" with a marginal reading "Lit., baptizing." The rendering "For by grace you have been saved through faith; and that not of yourselves, it is the gift of God" carries a marginal note "I.e., that salvation." The phrase "have been forgiven" (John 20:23) has the marginal reading "I.e., have previously been forgiven." "In sanctification" has the note "I.e., in a state or sphere of." In each of these cases there are other possibilities in interpretation, and it is not the task of a translator to urge a single interpretation through marginal glosses.[21]

[21]W. L. Lane, "The *New American Standard Bible*," pp. 164-65.

Consistency in Rendering

The verb *mlk*, which is "wring off its head" in Leviticus 1:15, is "nip its head at the front of its neck" in Leviticus 5:8. The NASB rendered *doulos* four ways; in English Bibles since Tyndale it had been "servant" (except that the KJV used "bondservant" once and the ASV used "bondservant" in thirteen passages). "Slave" is invariably used where the actual institution of slavery is spoken of (Philem. 16; Rev. 6:15). However, Jesus in the incarnation takes the form of a "bond-servant" (Phil. 2:7), and when the relationship of the Christian to Christ is spoken of, "bond-servant" is ordinarily used (Luke 2:29; Rom. 1:1; Phil. 1:1; James 1:1; II Peter 1:1; Jude 1; Rev. 1:1; 7:3; 11:18; 15:3; 22:3, 6). Even for this relationship "bondslave" is twice used (Col. 4:7, 12), which seems hardly justified when *diakonos* in the same context is rendered "servant." "Servant" is also used for *doulos* (Rev. 19:10; 22:9). In one case one chapter uses "servants the prophets" (Rev. 10:7) and the next chapter has "bond-servants the prophets" (Rev. 11:18) for the same Greek phrase. The reluctance to use "slave" consistently for *doulos* is not understandable. In the final judgment the Lord calls the faithful a "slave" (Matt. 25:21). Jesus spoke of "slave of sin" (John 8:34), and Paul makes the contrast between "slaves" to sin and "slaves" to righteousness (Rom. 6:16-19). Peter speaks of "slaves of corruption" (II Peter 2:19). Christians are "Christ's slaves" (I Cor. 7:22; Eph. 6:6). Why should a version have "fellow bond-servant" (Col. 1:7) and "fellow-bondslave" (Col. 4:7) for the same term (*sundoulos*), describing the same relationship, in the same epistle? In Revelation 19:2 "bond-servant" is used as Old Testament phraseology, and the reference given is to Deuteronomy 32:43; but in that passage "servant" was used. The same is seen in Revelation 19:5 as compared with Psalm 134:1. Elsewhere, "fellowslave" (Matt. 18:28, 31, 33; 24:49) and "fellow servant" (Rev. 6:11; 19:10; 22:9) are used. By such variety the connection between all these statements is obscured for the reader.

More consistency in rendering Old Testament passages and their quotations in the New Testament (in cases where there is no textual difference) would add to clarity. "Your countrymen" (Deut. 18:15) becomes "your brethren" (Acts 3:22; 7:37) when quoted in the New Testament, though carrying a marginal note "Lit., *brothers*." "Scepter of uprightness" (Ps. 45:6) becomes "the righteous scepter" (Heb. 1:8), "has anointed" (Ps. 45:7) becomes "hath anointed" (Heb. 1:9), "oil of joy" (Ps. 45:7) becomes "oil of gladness" (Heb. 1:9), and "fellows" becomes "companions." Micah 5:2, "*Too* little to be among the clans of Judah," is hardly recognizable when quoted in Matthew 2:6 as "are by no means least among the leaders of Judah."

Apoluein is translated "put away" with a margin "divorce" (Matt. 1:19), and in another place is "send *her* away" with a margin "divorce" (Mark 10:4). Elsewhere it is "divorce" with a margin "send away" (Matt. 5:31). It also is "divorce" with no margin at all (Matt. 5:32; 19:3-9; Mark 10:2, 11; Luke 16:18).

At times *ho poneros* is rendered "evil" with "the evil one" (used by the ASV) given in the margin (Matt. 5:37; 6:13); at other times "the evil *one*" is retained in the text with "evil" in the margin (Eph. 6:16; II Thess. 3:3). Elsewhere "the evil one" is used (I John 5:18, 19) with neither italics nor marginal reading.

In Genesis 2:7 man is called a "living being" (margin: "soul"); but for the same term, animals are called "living creatures" (Gen. 1:24; 9:10, 12, 15, 16) with no marginal note. In Exodus 16 both the page heading and the text (v. 13) have the plural "quails," but in Numbers 11 both the heading and the text (vv. 31, 32) have "quail."

"Free gift" with no italics is continued in Romans 5:15, 16 and 6:23 as in the ASV, whereas other occurrences of *charis* are rendered as "gift." John has a "leather belt" (Matt. 3:4; Mark 1:6); but Elijah, his predecessor, had a "leather girdle" (II Kings 1:8).

The word *teleios* is translated "mature man" (Eph. 4:13), "mature" (I Cor. 2:6; 14:20; Heb. 5:14), "perfect" (Phil. 3:15; Col. 4:12; James 3:2), and "complete" (Col. 1:28). *Katartizen* is "equip you in every good thing" (Heb. 13:21), but elsewhere is "perfect" (I Peter 5:10). *Apaggellō* is once rendered "ran to report" (Matt. 28:8), but elsewhere is merely "reported" (Luke 24:9). *Adelphotēs* is "brotherhood" (I Peter 2:17), but in the second occurrence is "brethren" (I Peter 5:9) with a margin "Lit., brotherhood."

A different sort of consistency problem is encountered when a Greek term is used in two different meanings by a New Testament writer. The NASB makes no effort to distinguish in translation between those cases where *sarx* means the physical body (Rom. 3:20; 4:1) and those cases in Paul's letters where it designates the seat of sin (Rom. 8:4ff.; *kata sarka*). Both are translated "flesh."

There is also the problem of rendering two Greek words by one English word. An unfortunate choice of words gives the NASB the anomaly (which some have pointed out in several of the versions [NEB; NIV]) of having Jesus claim he came not "to abolish" the Law (Matt. 5:17), but then of having Paul say that he "abolished" it (Eph. 2:15). Since different Greek words occur in these passages, the English Bible should reflect the fact.

The policy of inclusion or exclusion of the definite article deserves attention. *Ho speiron* is "the sower" (Mark 4:3), but *ho luchnos* is "a lamp" (Mark 4:21). Actually, both cases are generic and "a" would be suitable.

The degree of variety exercised in the NASB creates confusion instead of clarity for the reader.

Communication

The advertising for the NASB claims, "The language is grammatically correct, contemporary English";[22] and most would agree that the NASB is a step forward in communication of God's Word when compared with the English of either the KJV or the ASV. When one checks the NASB against the list of archaisms and other stylistic problems previously listed for the ASV, he finds that most of the cases have been modified. The long Greek sentence of Ephesians 1:3-14 is broken into five sentences, and Colossians 1:9-17 is broken into five sentences. Second Corinthians 3:10 is rendered in clear English: "For indeed what had glory, in this case has no glory on account of the glory that surpasses *it*."

Much clarity is gained in the NASB by using current vocabulary. Improvement is seen when "travail" becomes "hardship" (Exod. 18:8), "blains" are "boils" (Exod. 9:11), and "murrain" is "severe pestilence" (Exod. 9:3). "Victuals" become "provisions" (Josh. 1:11), "passed clean over" is "finished crossing" (Josh. 3:17; 4:11), "compass" (Josh. 6:3, 7, 11, 14, 15) is "encircling" or "march around," "discomfited" is "overwhelmed" or "routed" (Exod. 17:13; I Sam. 7:10), "host" becomes "army" (II Sam. 17:25), "honorable estate" becomes "prominent" (Acts 13:50; 17:12), "give me leave" is "allow me" (Acts 21:39), "on this wise" is "was as follows" (Matt. 1:18), "privily" is "secretly" (Matt. 1:19), "parts of Galilee" is "regions of Galilee" (Matt. 2:22), "raiment" is "garment" (Matt. 3:4), "garner" is "barn" (Matt. 3:12), "suffer" is "permit" (Matt. 3:15), "straightway" is "immediately" (Matt. 4:20), "holden with divers diseases" is "taken with various diseases"

[22]Advertisement, back cover of *Christianity Today* 9 (October 23, 1964): 104.

(Matt. 4:24), "lose its savor" is "become tasteless" (Matt. 5:13), "foreswear" is "make false vows" (Matt. 5:33), "mote" and "beam" are "speck" and "log" (Matt. 7:3), "palsy" is "paralyzed" (Matt. 8:6), "nigh unto" is "near" (Acts 9:38), "thrice" is "three times" (Acts 10:16), "quarternions" is "four squads" (Acts 12:4), "provoked her sore" is "would provoke her bitterly" (I Sam. 1:6), "manchild" is "son" (I Sam. 1:11), "marked her mouth" is "was watching her mouth" (I Sam. 1:12), "countenance" is "face" (I Sam. 1:18), "morsel of bread" is "piece of bread" (I Sam. 2:36), "save he that is of God" is "except the One who is from God" (John 6:46). Paul is not "opening and alleging" that Jesus is the Christ but "explaining and giving evidence" (Acts 17:3), "Be ready against the third day" is "Be ready for the third day" (Exod. 19:15), "determinate counsel" is "predetermined plan" (Acts 2:23), "lame of his feet" is "crippled in both feet" (II Sam. 9:3), "gat him upon his mule" is "each mounted his mule" (II Sam. 13:29), "fourscore" gives way to "eighty" (Exod. 7:7; etc.), "If there falleth out any war" is "in the event of war" (Exod. 1:10), "upbraided" is "reproached" (Matt. 11:20), "undressed cloth" is "unshrunk cloth" (Matt. 9:16), "suffer" is "let" (Matt. 19:14), and "shambles" is "meat market" (I Cor. 10:25). The list could be greatly extended.

Nevertheless, one wonders if the various aims stated by the producers of the NASB are actually compatible with each other. While stating that "the attempt has been made to render the grammar and terminology of the ASV into contemporary English,"[23] it also states that the NASB kept the original word order whenever possible, believing that this was a means the writer used to accent and emphasize what he deemed most important. It is further stated:

> Words are faithfully rendered in the New American Standard Bible even to conjunctions such as "and" in the belief that these, too, helped mirror the writer's style and manner of expression. These are often ignored in free translation.[24]

These conflicting aims resulted in the NASB's failure to attain current English style and vocabulary in many instances. Its language is not contemporary and its English is not idiomatic. We see examples of this in its

[23]"*New American Standard Bible*: Translation and Format Facts" (La Habra, Calif.: The Lockman Foundation, n.d.), p. 4.
[24]Ibid., p. 6.

continuation of reversed word orders like "wicked exceedingly" (Gen. 13:13) and the use of the dangling clause: "one who shall come forth from your own body, he shall ..." (Gen. 15:4), "as for Hannah, she was speaking in her heart" (I Sam. 1:13), "the Lord, He is God" (I Kings 18:39), "Whoever swears ... he is obligated" (Matt. 23:18), and "the Holy Spirit ... He will teach you" (John 14:26). The superfluous inclusion of the pronoun in "this land to possess it" (Gen. 15:7), mars the style. Pronouns are at times retained in non-English order: "I and the Father" (John 10:30), "Me and My Father" (John 15:24), and "me and Barnabas" (Gal. 2:9). However, "you and me" (Gen. 31:49; Josh. 14:6; Matt. 17:27) is also used though the pronouns in Hebrew are in the opposite order. "Both" is used for more than two (Acts 19:16), and "the Less" is used for the superlative (Mark 15:40). In biblical quotations, "did" is retained in the past tense: "didst hide" (Matt. 11:25) and "didst send" (John 17:8). Even with these archaisms, occasional colloquialisms like "See *here*" (Matt. 9:30) and "put up with" (Acts 13:18) are encountered. There is an annoying preference for using the demonstrative pronoun "this" (Luke 18:22; 19:13). The expression "By whom was born" should be "of whom" (Matt. 1:16; ASV).

While the NASB eliminated many Semitisms, there are still some that remain. Consequently, English words are at times written in Hebrew word order: "they seek my life, to take it away" (I Kings 19:14), or "they killed each his man" (I Kings 20:20). These phrases are all Semitisms: "sound of Thee in the Garden" (Gen. 3:10), "pleased of heart" (Esther 5:9), "sons of pride" (Job 41:34), "son of wickedness" (Ps. 89:22), "sons of men" (Ps. 53:2; 58:1; 66:5), "sons of the east" (Ezek. 25:4), "fire of God" (Job 1:16), "full of days" (Job 42:17), "scribes of the people" (Matt. 2:4), "freedom of the glory" (Rom. 8:21; KJV, "glorious freedom"), "sons of this age" (Luke 16:8), "sons of light" (John 12:36), "sons of disobedience" (Eph. 2:2), "children of wrath" (Eph. 2:3), "son of the devil" (Acts 13:10), "children of light" (Eph. 5:8), "horn of my salvation" (Ps. 18:2), "horn of His anointed" (I Sam. 2:10), "horn of salvation" (Luke 1:69), and "oil of gladness" (Heb. 1:9). "Lovely in the sight of God" (Acts 7:20) is less satisfactory for dealing with a Semitism than is the "exceeding fair" of the ASV. "The Holy Spirit of promise" (Eph. 1:13) should be "the promised Holy Spirit." The excessive use of the conjunction "and" is an imitation of Hebrew style. Luke 19:1-9 has twelve instances. "Preaching, and saying" (Mark 1:7) is a Semitism. "Beautiful in appearance" (I Sam. 25:3; II Sam. 11:2) and "of beautiful appearance" (II Sam. 14:27)—both Semitisms—are used for related expressions.

There are poorly constructed sentences: "The next day *He* purposed to go forth into Galilee, and He found Philip, and Jesus said to him ..." (John 1:43), and "And the one on whom seed was sown on the rocky places, this is the man ..." (Matt. 13:20). The sentence, "and they spoke, saying to Him, 'Tell us by what authority You are doing these things, or who is the one who gave You this authority?' " (Luke 20:2) is woodenly literal.

The expressions "envisioned in visions" (Amos 1:1) and "every first-born, the first offspring of every womb" (Exod. 13:2) are redundant. The words of the marginal note "concerning saw" (Amos 1:1) seem reversed. Elsewhere the phrase is "saw ... concerning" (Isa. 2:1; Mic. 1:1). "About a hundred pounds *weight*" (John 19:39) could have been made current English if the translators had used "weighing about a hundred pounds." "Begone" (Matt. 8:32) and "Take courage" (I Sam. 4:9; Matt. 9:2, 22) are understandable but are not current. "Lord" (Gen. 18:12) meaning "husband," "manchild" (Gen. 4:1) for male child, and "seed" meaning "descendant" are also not current. The NASB often used "descendant" or "offspring" for "seed." Are the images "engraved images" (Deut. 12:3), or are they carved or hewn? The NASB used "graven" (Deut. 7:25; Isa. 10:10; 30:22; 42:8; Jer. 8:19; etc.). A slip in grammar is encountered in the phrase "she had born" (II Sam. 21:8) for "had borne."

There are some words in the NASB whose meaning is different from that of current usage. The NASB continues the use of "perfected" (Gal. 3:3) meaning "ended," "usury" (Neh. 5:7, 10) meaning "interest," and "simplicity" (II Cor. 11:3) meaning "singlemindedness." "City" (Luke 7:11) is used for a village, "answered" (Acts 15:13) for "spoke up," "slumber nor sleep" (Ps. 121:4) for "drowsy nor sleepy," "sell" (Judg. 4:9) for "deliver," "providence" (Acts 24:2) for "provision," and "visit" (James 1:27) for "look after the needs of." "Garner" is sometimes retained (Ps. 144:13) where "barn" would be better known. The words "extolled" (Ps. 66:17), "entreated" (Matt. 8:34; Mark 8:22), and "fishers" (Matt. 4:19) are used. People are "taken with various diseases" (Matt. 4:24). "Raca" (Matt. 5:22), "mammon" (Matt. 6:24), and "Maranatha" (I Cor. 16:22) are merely transliterated. Why should *anathema* in the verse deserve translating as "accursed" but "Maranatha" merit only transliteration? "Brimstone" (Gen. 19:24) would be clearer as "sulfur," "side-growth of your heads" (Lev. 19:27) could be "sideburns."

Prior to Jesus' resurrection, relatives (Matt. 12:48; Acts 7:13) and those related spiritually (Matt. 12:49; 23:8) are both "brothers"; but afterward, relatives are "brothers" (Acts 1:14) and those related spiritually are "brethren" (Matt. 28:10; John 20:17; 21:23; Acts 1:15; 3:22). However, there is a slip when Joseph's "brothers" (Acts 7:13) and his "brethren" (Acts 7:23, 25) are both encountered in the same context.

Coins, weights, and measures are always problems in translation. In certain cases an effort is made in the NASB to give current values for Greek money (Matt. 10:29; etc.). The term "cent" (Matt. 5:26; Mark 12:42) is frequently encountered; but elsewhere, by transliteration, "denarius" (Matt. 20:2, 9), "stater" (Matt. 17:27), and "mina" (Luke 19:16) are used. Other transliterations are "kors" (I Kings 4:22), "ephahs," "homers," and "baths." Some distances are given in miles (e.g., "seven miles" [Luke 24:13]), but elsewhere the measure "cubit" (Matt. 6:27) is retained. "Gallons" are used for liquid measure (John 2:6); however, "bushel" and "shekel" (Amos 8:5) inconsistently occur in the same verse.

The NASB displays a hybrid mixture of old English pronouns and current English verbs; for example, in Psalm 45:7 "has" occurs, but in the citation of the same Psalm in Hebrews 1:9, "hath" is found. The NASB runs aground in its effort to determine when to retain the traditional "Thou," "Thine," and "Thee" with appropriate old English verbal forms. The old forms are retained in the Psalms, in address to divinity, and in the language of prayer (e.g., Acts 4:25). Saul (Acts 9:5; 22:8, 19, 20; 26:15), Ananias (Acts 9:13), and people in heaven in the Book of Revelation (Rev. 4:11; 5:9, 10) use the old forms. But in the Gospels, people are represented at the judgment as saying "you" to the final judge (Matt. 7:22; 25:37, 44). The quotation from Malachi (Matt. 11:10; Mark 1:2; Luke 7:27) only merits a "you": "your face ... your way." During his earthly career and after his resurrection, Jesus is addressed as "You" by his disciples (Matt. 14:28, 33; Mark 2:18; Acts 1:6), his brothers (John 7:3, 4), the Pharisees (Matt. 22:16), the high priest (Matt. 26:62), and Pilate (Matt. 27:13). "You" and "Your" are capitalized in these statements though not capitalized elsewhere when referring to man. Why should "Thou" be used in the confession at the baptism (Mark 1:11) and in the confession of Peter at Caesarea Philippi (Matt. 16:16; Mark 8:29), and "You" be used in the equally confessional statements in John 1:38 and 6:68, 69? The whole problem could have been avoided by using "you" throughout.

Yet another case of the failure of the NASB to use current English idiom is its proclivity for using the expression "at table" in combinations with the verb "reclining," even supplying "at table" in italics (Matt. 26:20; Mark 2:15; Luke 5:29; 11:37; 22:14; John 13:12). But at times "at the table," the current idiom, is also supplied (Matt. 9:10; John 12:2). The hold of tradition is seen when the woman of Isaiah 7:14, Mary (Matt. 1:18), and the woman of Revelation 12:2 are "with child," but Bathsheba can say, "I am pregnant" (II Sam. 11:5) and Elizabeth can become "pregnant" (Luke 1:24). The NASB shows a consciousness of the need to speak of "heads of grain" (Lev. 2:14; Deut. 23:25; Job. 24:24; Matt. 12:1; Mark 2:23; Luke 6:1). If it were a thorough revision, it would not retain "ears" (Gen. 41:5ff.; Ruth 2:2; II Kings 4:42; Isa. 17:5) in other cases. There is also the expression "barley was in the ear" (Exod. 9:31).

Conclusion

This sampling of some of the strengths and weaknesses of the NASB shows that, although at many places it represents a step forward in the communication of God's Word and although it supplies many insights into obscure passages, the NASB falls short of what is most desired in an English translation. Some of its renderings are admirable, but the reader is reminded that a favorable disposition toward the ASV should not lead to a blind acceptance of the NASB. There is inconsistency in the NASB's aim of retaining Greek and Hebrew structure while straining for current English, resulting in a wooden style. The announced translation procedures were not consistently followed.

Time and usage, rather than publishers and critics, actually determine whether or not a version commends itself to believers in such a way as to become a "standard" version. In all probability, this version will not be markedly more successful in becoming the Bible of Christendom than were its predecessors, the RV and the ASV. There are several reasons: first, the sponsoring organization is not in a position to give it the needed circulation; second, the goal of a readable English style has been only partly achieved; and third, the theological peculiarities it manifests are not likely to commend themselves to the Christian world in general.

8

The Jerusalem Bible

T he Jerusalem Bible was edited by Alexander Jones of Christ's College, Liverpool, England, with the assistance of twenty-seven collaborators. It is one of several evidences of the rebirth of interest in biblical studies among Roman Catholics. Its appearance constituted a milestone in Catholic English Bible publication. For the first time, a translation of the complete Bible was made largely from the original languages rather than from the Latin Vulgate, and it received approbation from church authorities. No longer need the Catholic depend on the outdated, poorly translated, and badly annotated Challoner edition of the Rheims-Douay Version (1749); upon R. Knox's Version (1945); upon the Catholic edition of the RSV (1966); or even upon the Oxford Annotated RSV Bible (1965).[1] The JB offered him a translation in contemporary, readable English with an annotation system to help him understand it. The first edition, issued in 1966, had over two thousand pages, weighed five pounds, and cost more

[1]Approved for Catholic use by the imprimatur of Richard Cardinal Cushing, Bishop of Boston, May, 1966.

than sixteen dollars. A paperback edition with abridged notes was made available in 1971.

The publisher's claim that the JB was "an entirely new version from original sources" was, to an extent, misleading. The École Biblique in Jerusalem in 1948 began publishing, under the editorship of Roland de Vaux, fascicles of an extensive commentary with introductions to books and copious annotations. These fascicles, which represent the work of about forty scholars, are being continuously revised. But in 1961 the fascicles as they then existed were collected, abbreviated, and compressed into *La Bible de Jerusalem*.[2] Those scholars who prepared the French work are unfortunately not listed in the English edition. They have been taken to task by Ugaritic scholar M. Dahood for too often taking refuge in the Septuagint and other ancient versions and for altering the Hebrew consonants to make them conform to such readings.[3] The same type of criticism has also been made of the English edition.[4]

The JB presents to the English reader a translation of the introductions and annotations of the French work, with attention given to the decisions and general implications of the Second Vatican Council. However, for the text of the Bible itself, drafts of most books—made from Hebrew, Aramaic, and Greek, as the case may be—were then compared with the French text of *La Bible de Jerusalem* so that the text and interpretation of the French scholars could be preserved. But in some books the reverse process was true: the draft was from the French and then word-for-word comparisons with the original were made.[5] Certain stylistic features of the translation bear this out. Such a case is "Leave off! ... That will do!" (Luke 22:51), which continues French style with English words.[6]

The Notes

The most distinctive features of the JB are its introductions to each book, its notes, and its other study aids. No other one-volume Bible on

---

[2]Bruce Vawter, review of *La Sainte Bible*, traduite en Français sous la direction de l'Ecole Biblique de Jerusalem (Paris: Editions du Cerf, 1956), in *CBQ* 18 (1956): 315-17.

[3]Cited by Ignatius Hunt, "*The Jerusalem Bible* in English," *Herder Correspondence* (November 1966): 328D.

[4]Richard C. Oudersluys, review of *The Jerusalem Bible*, in *The Reformed Review* 21 (December 1967): 22-27.

[5]*The Jerusalem Bible*, p. v.

[6]I. Hunt, "*The Jerusalem Bible* in English," p. 328D.

the market has so extensive a system of annotations. These notes contain a great deal of helpful archaeological, geographical, theological, and linguistic information.

In recent years theological differences between Catholic and liberal Protestant scholars have largely vanished, and the notes of the JB reflect this change. In such an ecumenical atmosphere, the JB represents the theological stance of liberal literary and historical criticism. According to the editor, biblical inerrancy is not so much in the facts and precise circumstances in which facts occurred, but rather is in the spiritual meaning conveyed by those facts.[7] Within the introductions and notes, the Pentateuch is said to be made up of J, E, D, and P sources modified by oral tradition and cult recitations; a prophetic book is a compilation of the sayings of the prophet made by his disciples after varying lapses of time. The Book of Isaiah has eighth-century material supplemented by at least two sections, some of which is postexilic in date. The Book of Daniel was written between 167 and 164 B.C. The Book of Jonah is postexilic and is not to be interpreted as history. In the introductions, the treatment of New Testament questions may reflect more conservative positions than that given Old Testament questions. Arguments are given for the literary priority of an Aramaic Matthew. The Pauline authorship of all the letters traditionally ascribed to Paul (including the Pastorals) is accepted. However, facing the difficulties of maintaining the Pauline authorship of the pastoral Epistles and Ephesians, the translators suggest that a disciple and secretary of Paul had been given unprecedented freedom. Revelation was not written by the apostle John, though it came from his immediate circle. Many of these positions were condemned earlier in this century by the Papal Biblical Commission, but new winds have been blowing in the Catholic church since 1943.

Extensive attention is given in the notes to theological motifs and themes, representing the careful scholarship that is the trademark of the École Biblique. An index enables the student to trace any theme treated. Old Testament notes draw attention to the messianic significance of certain passages and point out relevant New Testament passages. The annotations are considerably more comprehensive and competent than those of the Oxford Annotated Bible. Over half the textual notes in the New Testament

[7]*The Jerusalem Bible*, New Testament, p. 10.

(342/618) indicate that a Vulgate reading has been displaced.[8] However, the notes do not explain why one reading has been chosen over another in the text. Most of the notes are not distinctively confessional in nature and do not carry on the Catholic-Protestant quarrel in the tradition of the Rheims-Douay Bible. In this area, that which is not annotated is almost as important in creating the tone of the Bible as that which is. Matthew 10:2; 23:8-11; Mark 3:11; 6:3 (but cf. Matt. 12:46); Luke 8:21; 23:43; and Acts 11:30—all of which had tendentious notes in the *Confraternity New Testament* (1941)—are without such notes.

Despite the ecumenical spirit of most of the notes of the JB, isolated cases of Catholic dogmatic teaching can still be found. The Gospels are titled "Saint Matthew," "Saint Mark," "Saint Luke," and "Saint John." The note to Matthew 1:25 asserts that the Gospels elsewhere suppose Mary's "perpetual virginity." The commentator thinks that Mary's reply, "I am a virgin," "perhaps expresses also her intention to remain so" (Luke 1:34). "Virginity is a higher calling than marriage, and spiritually more profitable" (note to I Cor. 7; cf. note to Matt. 19:10-12). The note to Matthew 12:46 asserts that Jesus' brothers were "Not Mary's children but near relations, cousins perhaps, which both Hebr. and Aramaic style 'brothers,' cf. Gn. 13:8; 14:16; 29:15; Lv. 10:4; I Ch. 23:22f."

While the JB straightforwardly translates Matthew 16:18, "You are Peter" (without a gloss comparable to that of Phillips, NEB, and TEV: "You are Peter the Rock"), the note on Matthew 16:19, after expounding ideas on "the keys," continues:

> Catholic exegetes maintain that these enduring promises hold good not only for Peter himself but also for Peter's successors. This inference, not explicitly drawn in the text, is considered legitimate because Jesus plainly intends to provide for his Church's future by establishing a regime that will not collapse with Peter's death. The two other texts, Lk 22:31f and Jn 21:15f, on Peter's primacy emphasize that its operation is to be in the domain of faith; they also indicate that this makes him head not only of the Church after the death of Christ but of the apostolic group then and there.

The note to James 5:14 reads: "The tradition that these prayers and this anointing with oil in the name of the Lord, and for the purpose of helping

---

[8]Erroll F. Rhodes, "Text of N.T. in *Jerusalem* and *New English Bible*," *CBQ* 32 (January 1970): 49.

the sick and forgiving their sins, are the origin of the Church's 'sacrament of the sick' (or Holy Unction), was endorsed by the Council of Trent." A note granting that the meaning is disputed identifies Romans 5:12 with the doctrine of original sin. The note to I Timothy 3:1 remarks: "The word 'episcopos' ('overseer,' 'supervisor' or 'president') has not yet acquired the same meaning as 'bishop,' cf. Tt 1:5f." That to I Timothy 3:11 notes, "This instruction is probably intended for the deaconesses, cf. Rm 16:1, rather than for the wives of deacons."

Significant admissions are made in the notes in certain texts which have in the past been used by Catholic apologists as proof texts. The note to Matthew 1:25 concedes that the verse taken by itself does not assert Mary's perpetual virginity; and the note to I Corinthians 3:15 comments, "This is not a direct reference to purgatory but several Doctors of the Church have taken it as a basis for that doctrine." Another is the note to I Corinthians 9:5: "Lit. 'a sister, a woman (wife?).' To look after the apostle's needs." The note to James 5:16 says, "Nothing special ... may be deduced about sacramental confession." The note to Romans 6:4 interprets the apostle's figure of a burial to refer to immersion.

In certain other cases attention is called to traditional exegesis without either affirming or denying its validity; for example, the note to Matthew 6:11, after an alternate comment, says, "The Fathers applied this text to the bread of the Holy Eucharist."

Textual Questions

In its approach to passages with textual problems, the JB generally follows the path widely accepted both in Catholic and non-Catholic circles. Some passages are printed in the text but are noted as problems in the notes. Such are Mark 16:9-20, whose Marcan authorship is declared to be open to question, and the *pericope adulterae* (John 7:53—8:11) which is recognized as not original because of its absence in the oldest witnesses, its occurrence in different locations in others, and its similarities in style to Synoptic material rather than to that of the Gospel of John. The absence of John 5:3b-4 in the best witnesses is noted. Other passages such as Mark 9:44 and 46 are omitted in the text, but their verse numbers are also omitted to preserve the traditional verse numbering. The reader must consult other translations to find out what the verse so treated was. First John 5:7b-8 is only commented on in the notes, and its witness to the

203

Trinity is declared to be a gloss. Still other passages like Matthew 23:14 have the traditional text given in the note with the verse declared an ancient gloss. Acts 8:37 is declared "a very ancient gloss preserved in the Western Text and suggested by the baptismal liturgy." Romans 16:24 is omitted without notation. The JB scholars have freely cited "Western" variants. They reflect a more charitable evaluation of the "Western Text" than is dominant in Protestant circles by accepting Western readings in fifteen cases in the Book of Acts.[9] In certain other cases the JB differs from commonly accepted scholarship in the treatment of a verse. Such is John 1:13 where the singular number ("who was") is accepted to make the fourth Gospel testify to the virgin birth of Christ. This Bible follows the *Textus Receptus* in having Paul stop at Trogyllium (Acts 20:15). One is not always certain that the JB has followed the best text.[10] The distinction it makes in the notes between what is authentic in a book (that is, written by the author and not by a later hand) and what is canonical Scripture (that is, accepted by the church) raises afresh the question of how canonical Scripture is determined.

Textual Emendation

The JB manifests some rearrangement within the text to give what the translators felt is a better sequence. In these cases the verse numbers given in the margin will alert the reader to the original position of the phrases; for example, Isaiah 7:8a is placed before 9a, and 8b follows 9a. Yet other examples may be found in the verse sequence of Job 24 and of Zechariah 2. An abundance of other cases can be cited.

The JB corrects what seems to be a defect in the Masoretic text, as does the RSV, by supplying from the Septuagint the alternative in the lots drawn by Saul (I Sam. 14:41).

The right to introduce numerous conjectural corrections into the biblical text has been exercised. There are seven of these in the rendering of Isaiah 53. Isaiah 53:8 changes "the faults of my people" to "our faults." First Samuel 30:17 is corrected by adding "putting them under the ban."

---

[9]Charles H. H. Scobie, "Two Recent New Testament Texts and Translations," *Canadian Journal of Theology* 14 (January 1968): 58.

[10]Gordon D. Fee, "The Text of John in the *Jerusalem Bible*: A Critique of the Use of Patristic Citations in New Testament Textual Criticism," *JBL* 90 (June 1971): 163ff., has subjected its dependence on patristic citation in the Gospel of John to a searching criticism.

In Judges 19:2, "She played the harlot against him" of the Hebrew text is turned into "In a fit of anger" with appeal to the versions. "Yahweh" of the Greek Version is preferred for "Lord Yahweh" of the Hebrew (Amos 1:8). "Assyria" from Greek is used where Hebrew has "Ashdod" (Amos 3:9), and "Harmon" is conjectured to be "Hermon" (Amos 4:3). "Many [or Great] houses" becomes "Ebony houses" (Amos 3:15) by conjecture. "He showed me" becomes "the Lord Yahweh showed me" (Amos 7:7). "One quarter-kab of wild onions" sounds more palatable than "a quarter kab of dove's dung" (II Kings 6:25), but that it is more accurate is not certain. "Telassar" becomes "Tel Basar" (II Kings 19:12; Isa. 37:12). The notes alert the reader to other conjectures that have been made, but despite the extensiveness of the note system, the reasons for the conjectures are not given, and the student must consult the more extensive commentaries for the rationale. Amos 5:7 is turned into a doom oracle by supplying "Trouble for." "Reed Sea" is omitted from Psalm 136:15. One reviewer has pointed out that the translators have not followed a scientific criticism but have allowed subjective considerations to have free rein, substituting words for the Masoretic text that have no support in the manuscripts or ancient versions. They may or may not be footnoted as "corrections," leaving the reader at the mercy of the translator (cf. Dan. 1:2).[11] A New Testament example is "into one body" (I Cor. 12:13), which is omitted without explanation. "Will" (I Cor. 1:1) is omitted and "send greetings" unnecessarily added. "Grace" has become "graces" and "of God" is omitted in I Corinthians 1:4; "in him" was deleted in I Corinthians 1:5.

The Translation

The JB belongs to that group of Bibles formed on the principle which Eugene Nida calls Dynamic Equivalence—that is, it aims more at conveying the thought of the original than at reproducing the grammatical structure. One reviewer claims it strikes a happy balance between the literalism of the ASV and the paraphrases of J. B. Phillips, being more interpretative than the RSV, but less so than Phillips and the NEB.[12]

---

[11]Gleason L. Archer, review of *The Jerusalem Bible* in *WThJ* 33 (May 1971): 191; other cases are cited in Frederick W. Danker, review of *The Jerusalem Bible* in *Concordia Theological Monthly* 38 (March 1976): 176.

[12]George M. Landes, review of *The Jerusalem Bible* in *Union Seminary Quarterly Review* 22 (March 1967): 281; G. L. Archer, review of *The Jerusalem Bible*, p. 191; and Oudersluys, review of *The Jerusalem Bible*, p. 24.

Another characterized it as a paraphrase with semantic precision.[13] It makes language training on the part of the serious Bible student all the more imperative so that he can evaluate its interpretative renderings.

The translators have chosen sides in certain linguistic disputes that are familiar to technical scholars. Solomon's horses come from "Cilicia" (I Kings 10:28). Joseph's coat is one of "long sleeves" (Gen. 37:3; cf. II Sam. 13:18). "Tares" are "darnel" (Matt. 13:25). That which was "cubit" is "span of life" (Matt. 6:27). The Persian province is "Transeuphrates" (Ezra 4:10). The rationale for some renderings remains unclear, however. Why should *luah* (Isa. 8:1) be "a seal"? What the war horse should say in the face of battle has been a thorn to all English translators since John Wyclif; here he shouts, "Hurrah!" (Job 39:25).

The paraphrasing nature of the JB is seen when it says there was "no sparkle in Leah's eyes" (Gen. 29:17), when it speaks of the "limbo of the womb" (Ps. 139:15), and when the virgins of the parable are called "brides-maids" (Matt. 25:1). The priest says to Jesus, "I put you on oath" (Matt. 26:63), and the perplexing word *raca* is rendered "renegade" (Matt. 5:22). Mary says to the angel, "I am a virgin" (Luke 1:34). Jesus uses "wine" in instituting the Lord's Supper—a phrase more restrictive than the literal "fruit of the vine" (Luke 22:18). Nicodemus is merely "a leading Jew" (John 3:1), Lazarus is "resting" (John 11:11), and the people of Athens call Paul "parrot" (Acts 17:18). Paul would like "to see the knife slip" (Gal. 5:12) where the RSV has "mutilate themselves." "Seasoned with salt" is "flavour of wit" (Col. 4:5). "Their god is the belly" (RSV) is "they make foods into their god" (Phil. 3:19). "Having preached to others" is "having been an announcer" (I Cor. 9:27).

Certain renderings reflect choices in theological issues. The phrase that is traditionally "sons of the prophets" is "brotherhood of the prophets" (I Kings 20:35). That "his virgin" of I Corinthians 7:36 is made "his daughter" is to take one specific side of the controversy on that passage. Use is made of the solecism "helpmate" (Gen. 2:18, 20) in describing Eve.

While the editor claims to have rejected any attempt to preserve "biblical English" and to have aimed at producing a completely new rendering on the basis of contemporary usage and vocabulary, he has only partly succeeded. The English of his product is less modern than that of the

---

[13]D. R. Glenn, review of *The Jerusalem Bible* in *Bibliotheca Sacra* 127 (October-December 1970): 354.

NEB[14] and is a strange combination of innovation and tradition. "Give me leave to speak" (Gen. 18:30), "Vanity of vanities" (Eccles. 1:1), "daughter of Zion" (Isa. 1:8), and "man-child" (I Sam. 1:11) are retained. "You shall not kill" (Exod. 20:13; Deut. 5:17; Matt. 5:21; Rom. 13:9; James 2:11) is retained where "not murder" would be preferable. "The Widow's Mite" is preserved in a heading (Mark 12:41-44) though "mite" occurs neither in the translation nor in the notes.

But along with the traditional features there are also innovations in the JB which give it distinctiveness. Those apocryphal books which were declared canonical by the Council of Trent in 1546 are included, scattered at traditional places among the other books. Poetry is printed as poetry to a greater extent than is true in the RSV; sections of the Gospel of John are recognized as rhythmical. The spelling of proper names in the Protestant tradition, rather than in the Latin derivations, removes one point of difference between Catholics and Protestants. In those places where the translators have despaired of translating, there is a blank in the text with dots to indicate the omission, for example, at Ezekiel 7:11; 21:15; and Zephaniah 2:1, 14.

The reader will be impressed with the fact that "Good News" is used instead of "Gospel." Abandoning "Lord" (of the KJV, RSV, and NEB) and "Jehovah" (of the ASV), the JB uses "Yahweh"—a form widely known among scholars for the divine name, but one whose suitableness is disputed.[15] The Old English usage of "thee," "thou," and "thine" is abandoned, and the second-person pronoun "you" is used even when addressing divinity (cf. Matt. 6:9ff.; Mark 1:11; Heb. 1:8ff.). "Gesture of offering" is used where "wave offering" is in the RSV (Exod. 29:24; Lev. 23:20), and "loaves of offering" for "shewbread" (Matt. 12:4). "Brothers" (Gal. 6:18; etc.) replaces "brethren." "I tell you solemnly" replaces "Verily, verily" in the Gospel of John (cf. 3:3; 21:18). The Beatitudes (Matt. 5:1ff.) begin with "Happy are." Jesus is addressed as "Sir" by outsiders but as "Lord" by his disciples, leaving the translators to pass a value judgment on the speaker's intent in each case.

Another innovative feature is that contractions like "haven't" and "wouldn't" are occasionally used. Instead of "Ten Commandments" the JB has "Ten Sayings" (Deut. 10:4), a person may be a "tittle-tattler" (Prov.

---

[14]G. L. Archer, review of *The Jerusalem Bible*, p. 191.
[15]F. W. Danker, review of *The Jerusalem Bible*, p. 176.

11:13), and *selah* is "a pause" (Ps. 9:16, 20; etc.). "Hades" is "the under-world" (Matt. 16:18; Rev. 1:18). That which was "the garden of Gethsem-ane" is "the small estate called Gethsemane" (Matt. 26:36; Mark 14:32). Paul is let over the wall in "a hamper" (II Cor. 11:33). There is the "day of Acclamations" (Num. 29:1) instead of a "day for you to blow the trum-pets" (RSV).

Preferences for certain words are obvious. In the JB one always "recon-noiters" and never "spies" (Num. 13:21, 32; 14:6, 7, 34, 38; 21:32; Deut. 1:25; Josh. 2:3). An evildoer is a "wastrel" (Deut. 21:20; Ps. 26:4).

The JB is not always consistent in its renderings. "Prostitute" (Lev. 19:29; 21:7, 9; Deut. 23:18) is often used, but there is some use of "whore" (Isa. 57:3; Ezek. 16:29) and "harlot" (Josh. 2:1). This version prefers "slept with" (Gen. 30:15, 17; 35:22; 38:16; Exod. 22:15; Deut. 22:13, 27:20ff.; II Sam. 11:4, 11) for the man-woman relationship, though sometimes "had intercourse with" is used (Gen. 4:1, 17, 25; 38:26; Exod. 22:18; Judg. 19:25; I Sam. 1:19).

In John 19:24 we read how the soldiers at the cross "throw dice," but the other Gospels refer to this act as casting "lots" (Matt. 27:35; Mark 15:24). "Lots" are also cast when Matthias is chosen (Acts 1:26). The Old Testament constantly refers to drawing "lots" (e.g., Prov. 16:33; 18:18). The prodigal wears "sandals" (Luke 15:22), but the Israelites wear "shoes" (Exod. 3:5; Acts 7:33), despite the fact that elsewhere the original word is more correctly rendered "sandals" (Deut. 29:5). The word which is ren-dered "dove" (Matt. 3:16; 10:16) is rendered "pigeon" in the cleansing-of-the-temple scene (Matt. 21:12). There is no consistency in the rendering of *doulos*; hence "slave" (Col. 3:11) and "servant" (Col. 4:12), though quite different in import, are both used. Failure to harmonize renderings of identical phrases is seen where the clause "except for the case of forni-cation" (Matt. 5:32) becomes "I am not speaking of fornication" (Matt. 19:9). Children are borne in "pain" (Gen. 3:16), but man gets his food "in suffering" (Gen. 3:17) — both are renderings of the same word. There is the "Sea of Reeds" (Exod. 10:19; 13:18; Josh. 2:10), but elsewhere the "Sea of Suph" (Num. 14:25; Deut. 1:40; 2:1) — a transliteration — and also "Red Sea" which is literal for the Greek term (Acts 7:36; Heb. 11:29). The Greek word *hadēs* is "hell" (Matt. 11:23; Luke 10:15) and "the underworld" (Matt. 16:18; Rev. 1:18), but is "hades" in other occurrences (e.g., Luke 16:23; Acts 2:27, 31; Rev. 6:8; 20:13, 14).

A woman is sometimes "with child" (II Sam. 11:4; Eccles. 11:5; Isa. 26:17; Matt. 1:18; 24:19; Luke 2:5) but elsewhere is said to "have conceived" (Gen. 16:11; I Sam. 1:20) or become "pregnant" (Gen. 19:36; 38:24, 25; Exod. 21:22; II Kings 8:12; Hos. 14:1; Amos 1:13; I Thess. 5:3; Rev. 12:2). "Woe" becomes "Trouble for" (Amos 5:18) in some cases, but "Woe" is retained in others (Amos 6:1).

The JB falls short of being a version intelligible to the common English reader in all its features. Its preparers allowed their scholarly orientation to come through in the use of technical terms that may be semantically precise but which leave the ordinary reader in darkness. The Ishmaelites and the Israelite traders carry "tragacanth" to Egypt (Gen. 37:25; 43:11). "Wadi" (Gen. 15:18; Num. 21:12, 13; Deut. 2:13, 14, 24, 37) will have meaning only to those who have had contact with the Arab world. The nature of the "caper bush" (Eccles. 12:5) is not known to the average reader.

Other perplexities will arise from the transliterated words, among which are the names of animals whose species is uncertain (Lev. 11:22, 30) and the phrases spoken by the drunkards of Ephraim (Isa. 28:10, 13). Divine names are also often transliterated: *Elyon* (Ps. 91:1), *Shaddai* (Job. 5:17; 8:3; Isa. 13:6; Joel 1:15), and *Mot* (Isa. 28:15). Place names are at times transliterated: "Leb-kamai" (Jer. 51:1), and "Doberus" (Acts 20:4). Parts of the temple are the "*Debir* (I Kings 6:20; II Chron. 3:16; 4:20; Ezek. 41:22), "*Hekal*" (I Kings 7:50; II Chron. 3:17; Ezek. 41:1), and "*Ulam*" (Ezek. 40:48). "Gallon" is sometimes used (John 2:6); but in general transliterated terms like "talent" (Matt. 18:24), "shekel," "gerah" (Ezek. 45:12-14), and "denarius" are used. "Denarius" which is "a day's wages" in Revelation 6:6 is elsewhere transliterated, but *kodrantes* is "penny" in Mark 12:42. The sixth, ninth, and eleventh hours of the day (Matt. 20:1-16; John 19:14) are translated but, like the transliterated terms, will most likely be meaningless to the American reader. There is some effort in the notes to explain these terms.

Some vocabulary is Latin and Catholic in origin. The JB uses "chrism" where the non-Catholic reader is familiar with "anointing" (Exod. 25:6; 29:7; 30:31), "pectoral" for "breastplate" (Exod. 25:8; 28:4, 22, 24), "immolate" (Lev. 4:4; Deut. 27:7) for "sacrifice," "holocaust" (Exod. 29:42) for "burnt offering," and "altar of holocaust" for "altar of burnt offering" (Lev. 4:18). "Levirate" and "levir" are used (Deut. 25:7). There is "percipience" (Dan. 5:11), "muniment rooms" (Ezra 5:17; 6:1), "quarters of the oblates"

(Neh. 3:30; 7:46; 10:29; 11:3); the "minions" of Rahab (Job 9:13; cf. Isa. 37:6, 24); and the "tents of the venal" (Job 15:34). Many of these are poorer choices than were made for the same verses in the Rheims-Douay Version.

Then there are those words which are not commonly used in America by the man of limited education: "assayer" (Jer. 6:27), "obsequiously" (Matt. 23:7; Luke 11:43; 20:46), "compatriots" (Luke 19:14), "starboard" (John 21:6), and "port" (Acts 21:3). Simon claims that he is someone "momentous" (Acts 8:9).

Though the JB avoids many Briticisms, the American reader still encounters colloquial words and phrases that are typically British: "Get my supper laid; make yourself tidy" (Luke 17:8) and "lurking unseen like a lion in his hide" (Ps. 10:9). Men "sally out" to battle (Judg. 9:38; 20:21). That in which grain is carried is sometimes a "pannier" (Gen. 42:25; Deut. 28:5), but at other times is a "sack" (Gen. 44:1, 2). There is the "gaol" (Gen. 39:20, 21) and the chief "gaoler" (Gen. 39:21, 22, 23; Acts 16:23). An animal is "savaged by beasts" (Lev. 7:24; 17:15; 22:8; Deut. 33:20; II Kings 2:24). Blood was poured on the "surrounds of the altar" (Exod. 29:20). In all of these cases the NEB and the JB differ in choice of words, but in other cases there is agreement. The lamp is put "under a tub or under the bed" ([NEB: "meal-tub"]; Mark 4:21). The barley was "in the ear" (Exod. 9:31) where an American would say "was headed out." There is "the keep" of a palace (I Kings 16:18). The harlot "overlays" a child (I Kings 3:19). "Corn" (Gen. 41:22, 49; Ruth 2:2, 16; Neh. 5:2; Isa. 17:5) is the standard British word for "wheat" but is used for "Indian maize" in America. The JB has "ears of corn" (Gen. 41:22), and the grain grows in a "cornfield" (Matt. 12:1).

There are words that sound strange; either the NEB or RSV choice (given in the brackets) is a preferable rendering: "byre" (a cowbarn [RSV: "at home"; NEB: "stall"]; I Sam. 6:10), "phial of oil" ([RSV: "vial"; NEB: "flask"]; I Sam. 10:1), "disposed the army" ([RSV: "put"; NEB: "drew up"]; I Sam. 11:11), a woman has monthly "courses" ([RSV: "uncleanness"; NEB: "periods"]; II Sam. 11:4) but elsewhere has "monthly periods" (Gen. 18:11), "barbican" ([RSV; NEB: "wall"]; II Sam. 22:30), "equeries" ([RSV: "captains"; NEB: "lieutenant"]; I Kings 9:22; II Kings 7:2, 17, 19; 15:25), "chargers" ([RSV; NEB: "horsemen"]; II Kings 2:12; 13:14), "festoons" ([RSV: "chains"; NEB: "chain-work"]; II Chron. 3:5, 16), "denizens" ([RSV: "inhabitants"; NEB: "all that live in them"]; Job 26:5), "scurrility" ([RSV: "scoffing"; NEB: "irreverent"]; Job 34:7), "caparisoned" ([RSV; NEB: "made ready"]; Prov. 21:31), and "caparisons" ([RSV: "rich carpets"; NEB: "saddle cloths"]; Judg. 5:10). There is "pennon" ([RSV: "tackle"; NEB: "rigging"]; Isa. 33:23a), "haversack" ([RSV: "bag"; NEB: "pack"]; Mark 6:8; Luke 9:3), "plinth" ([RSV: "base"; NEB: "place prepared"]; Zech. 5:11), "burgle" ([RSV: "enter"; NEB: "break into"]; Matt. 12:29), "brigands" ([RSV; NEB: "robbers" or "thief"]; Luke 10:30; John 10:1, 8), "assizes" ([RSV: "regular assembly"; NEB: "statutory assembly"]; Acts 19:39), and "bands of stuff" ([RSV: "bandages"; NEB: "linen bands"]; John 11:44). There are "outlandish gods" ([RSV: "foreign divinities"; NEB: "foreign deities"]; Acts 17:18) and "viziers of earth" ([RSV: "counselors"; NEB: "ministers"]; Job 3:14). Job "tore his gown" ([RSV: "rent his robe"; NEB: "cloak"]; Job 1:20). There is the man "whom God baulks on every side" ([RSV; NEB: "hedge in"]; Job 3:23). On the seventh day God "rested and drew breath" ([RSV: "was refreshed"; NEB: "refreshed himself"]; Exod. 31:17). Clusters of grapes are "envenomed" ([RSV: "of poison"; NEB: "poisonous"]; Deut. 32:32). The "tutelary shadow" had gone from Canaan ([RSV: "their protection"; NEB: "the protection that they had"]; Num. 14:9).

Style

Isolated examples of awkward sentences can be found: "Whatever kind of man is this?" (Matt. 8:27) and "For then there will be great distress such as, until now, since the world began, there never has been, nor ever will be again" (Matt. 24:21). Someone who hears a speech read may be confused because of the practice of starting a speech without informing the audience who the speaker is (see Mark 9:15-26). A. Gregory Murray finds the Catholic edition of the RSV more readable; he also thinks that the JB is not well suited to reading in public.[16] Reviewers have been particularly critical of the style of the Psalms. Robert Murray caustically said, "This version of the Psalms shows a sort of homing instinct for bathos, exceeding even that of the Confraternity edition."[17] There are also those cases where the chattiness of the style has drawn criticism: "go away, and don't sin any more" (John 8:11) seems too colloquial.[18]

[16]A. Gregory Murray, review of *The Jerusalem Bible* in *Downside Review* 85 (January 1967): 90-93.

[17]Robert Murray, "The Jerusalem Bible," *Clergy Review* 51 (1966): 927.

[18]F. C. Grant, review of *The Jerusalem Bible* in *Journal of Biblical Literature* 86 (March 1967): 93.

Problem Renderings

More serious than the vocabulary and stylistic problems are those renderings that affect doctrinal issues. "Integrity" is chosen for the rendering of *ṣedeq*, which makes Yahweh our "integrity" (Jer. 33:16; cf. Isa. 5:16) where "righteousness" has been used by other versions. The Hebrew word refers to outward conduct measured by an objective standard (cf. Job 22:3). In Isaiah 46:13 "salvation" is used for *ṣedaqah*. Then in the New Testament, "justice" is used for the corresponding Greek word *dikaiosunē* to give "justice of God" (Rom. 1:17), but this rendering is not really adequate for the term involved.

There seem to be inconsistencies involving theological questions as well as those of vocabulary and style. The translators vacillated on the question of which gender to use with the Holy Spirit; in the end, they used "which" (John 7:39; Rom. 5:5) and sometimes "whom" (John 14:26). *Ekklesia* gave the translators problems; it ended up being rendered as "assembly" (Acts 7:38), "church" (Matt 16:18; Acts 11:22, 26; I Cor. 12:28), and "community" (Matt. 18:17; I Cor. 14:4, 12) where there is actually little variation in meaning. There is little justification for capitalizing "church" in Matthew 16:18, I Corinthians 12:28, and Hebrews 12:23 and not capitalizing it in other passages.

The note which accompanies Ezekiel 21:25 refers to Genesis 49:10, but in the translation the allusion is to the prince of Israel who is a "vile criminal," that is, to Zedekiah. The rendering "put the child on her shoulder" (Gen. 21:14; ASV: "and gave her the child") creates serious problems concerning the child's age.

Celibate attitudes toward sex come through in the rendering "Sex is always a danger" (I Cor. 7:1). The rendering of I Corinthians 9:5 shows a reluctance to admit that Peter was married—a misplaced reluctance since Mark 1:30 shows clearly that he was.

Belief in original sin likely influenced the rendering of Psalm 51:5: "You know I was born guilty, a sinner from the moment of conception." Ideas of church order make Phoebe a "deaconess" of the church in Cenchreae (Rom. 16:1).

It would be hard to justify taking *houtōs* (Rom. 11:26) as a temporal adverb in the rendering: "And then after this the rest of Israel will be saved as well," when *houtōs* is an adverb of manner. Exception has been taken to the rendering "work for your salvation" (Phil. 2:12).[19]

The choice made by the JB to render *ethnē* by "pagans" (e.g., Acts 13:46) instead of "gentiles" is an unfortunate one. "Pagan" refers only to a religion; the opposite of "Jew," which is both a religious and a national designation, is "gentile."

This version does not reflect the distinction between "demon" and "devil" which is maintained in the Greek text of the New Testament; hence the victims are "demoniacs" (Matt. 8:28; 9:32) but are possessed by "devils" (Matt. 8:31; 9:33, 34), and sacrifices are to "demons" (I Cor. 10:20ff.). There is also the rendering "crimes" (Gal. 3:19), which to an American carries an idea quite contrary to "transgressions"—with "crime" as primarily an offense against the state and "transgression" a sin against God.

Noteworthy Renderings

A reviewer is tempted to devote his attention more to weaknesses than to strengths. No complete list of the latter for the JB is possible, but there are many. Its straightforward rendering of *kiseka 'elohim* by "Your throne, God" in Psalm 45:6; cf. Hebrews 1:8, where the RSV stumbled to give "divine throne," is one case. The troublesome *monogenes* is "only Son" of the Father (John 1:14 and all other occurrences). Jacob makes "soup" (NAB: "stew"; NEB: "broth"; ASV: "pottage"; Gen. 25:29). The *'asherah* is the "sacred post" (Judg. 6:25). "Yeast" is used where "leaven" has traditionally been used (Matt. 16:6; etc.). Solomon's splendor left the queen of Sheba "breathless" (I Kings 10:5). The tongues of Pentecost are straightforwardly "foreign languages" in some passages (Acts 2:4; cf. 10:46), but unfortunately the translators reverted to "tongues" in I Corinthians 14; cf. Acts 19:6.

Printing Problems

Though the JB is very impressive in appearance, a lack of care on the part of the typesetter and the proofreader marred the product in both the notes and the text of the 1966 edition. Adding to the long list of ludicrous

[19]F. W. Danker, review of *The Jerusalem Bible*, p. 175.

creations by Bible printers is "Pay" for "Pray for peace in Jerusalem" (Ps. 122:6) and "prisoners in the goal" for "gaol" (Gen. 39:22). Reviewers drew up extensive lists of other errors.[20] Most of these errors have been corrected in a later reprint; however, "for wife" (Gen. 28:9) is uncorrected, and "Jericho" becomes "ericho" (I Chron. 19:5) in the reprint.

It is unfortunate that the notes of the JB are printed in painfully small print, almost guaranteeing that they will not be widely read.

Conclusion

The JB marks a long step forward in Roman Catholic English Bible production. Its contribution toward a common religious terminology is beyond estimate. Most likely, the goal of a common Bible is an unattainable dream except in those circles where ecumenism makes men willing to close their eyes to basic doctrinal differences. The JB, though a gesture of ecumenism, remains considerably short of the goal of being a common Bible and is distinctly Catholic in some of its features, as this study has shown. It is chiefly valuable for furnishing an orientation on positions held by a segment of Roman Catholic biblical scholars. It is in a more modern idiom than the RSV, but it also represents a more liberal modern scholarship than the RSV does. The freedoms it has taken in dealing with the text leave it unreliable for doctrinal study or for biblical exposition.

[20]Alexander A. DiLella, review of *The Jerusalem Bible* in *CBQ* 29 (January 1967): 150-51; R. L. Child, review of *The Jerusalem Bible* in *Baptist Quarterly* 22 (July 1967): 188; Arthur S. Herbert, review of *The Jerusalem Bible* in *The Bible Translator* 18 (1967): 95; Larry L. Walker, review of *The Jerusalem Bible* in *Southwestern Journal of Theology* 11 (Fall 1968): 120.

9

The New American Bible

The New American Bible of 1970 is an outgrowth of the encyclical *Divino afflante Spiritu* issued on September 30, 1943, by Pius XII. This encyclical declared that Catholics ought to explain the original text of the Bible, which was written by the inspired author and which has more authority than any translation ancient or modern. The earlier Catholic English versions—the Rheims-Douay Version (1582-1609/10) and its revision by Bishop Challoner (1750)—had been based on the Latin Vulgate. The version of Ronald Knox. (1944-1949) had also been from the Vulgate.

The effort to produce a new translation for American Catholics began to take shape in 1936 and was well underway before 1943.[1] The outcome of this effort was the Confraternity New Testament, published in 1941. It had also used the Vulgate as its text. With the way opened by the new encyclical, the Committee of the Confraternity of Christian Doctrine in

[1]Gerard S. Sloyan, "The *New American Bible*," *Living Light* 7 (Fall 1970): 87-104; Edward P. Arbez, "The New Catholic Translation of the Old Testament," *Catholic Biblical Quarterly* 14 (July 1952): 237-54; Claude J. Peifer, "The *New American Bible*," *Worship* 45 (February 1971): 102-13.

215

1944 requested members of the Catholic Biblical Association to translate sacred Scriptures from the original languages, or from the earliest extant form of the text, and to present the sense of the text in as correct a form as possible. The translators then abandoned the revision from the Vulgate which they had begun, started over, and finally presented their new work to the public. The NAB rightly claims to be the first American Roman Catholic translation made from the original languages. The NAB appeared the same year that the NEB appeared, but received much less publicity than the NEB did and was overshadowed by it.

The completed NAB is a compilation and a reworking of the several sections of the Bible which appeared under the name of the Confraternity of Christian Doctrine: *Genesis to Ruth*, 1952; *Job to Sirach*, 1955; *Isaiah to Malachi*, 1961; and *Samuel to Maccabees*, 1969. The NAB should be thought of as a successive edition to the Confraternity Version. In the completed work, Genesis is a retranslation by D. N. Freedman with new expanded notes. New strophe divisions are made in Job and Psalms. The New Testament is a retranslation begun in 1956 to replace the earlier revision based on the Vulgate; it did not appear as a separate volume prior to the publication of the whole Bible, but portions were used in the Mass lectionaries after the introduction of the vernacular into the liturgy in 1964.

The NAB is the outcome of twenty-five years of work by fifty scholars, most of them Catholics.[2] The individual contributions of the various Catholic scholars are not revealed. After the Second Vatican Council directed that "translations be produced in cooperation with separated brothers" so that "all Christians may be able to use them," Frank Cross (on I-II Samuel), David Noel Freedman (on Genesis), James A. Sanders (on II Kings), and John Knox (on the pastoral Epistles) were invited as non-Catholics to the staff of translators, making the publication a gesture toward ecumenism. None of the translators received compensation for his work. Sixteen of the translating group died before the work was brought to completion. The NAB has been issued in printings by St. Anthony Guild Press, Paterson, New Jersey; by P. J. Kenedy and Sons, New York; and in a paperbound edition by World Publishing Company, in addition to printings by numerous other publishers. The format and the supplementary materials are not

---

[2]The list is to be found in the St. Anthony Guild edition at pp. 452-53.

entirely the same in the various printings. Pope Paul congratulated the producers with the words, "For the faithful in all English-speaking countries the publication of the New American Bible represents a notable achievement."[3]

The Text

The NAB (composed of its various segments mentioned above) is a completely new translation made from the oldest available Hebrew, Aramaic, and Greek texts of the sacred books. The Masoretic text of Samuel has been corrected in the light of Cave 4 materials of Qumran and of the Septuagint. In this one book there are 251 notes citing the Qumran scrolls, the Septuagint, and combinations of the two. The RSV has 58 notes and the NEB 104; hence it can be seen that the NAB departs from the Masoretic text in this one book much more frequently than do the others.[4] The text followed in the Psalms is that underlying the Latin Psalter of the church (*The Liber Psalmorum*, 1944, 1945), rather than the Masoretic text. An extensive supplement of 123 pages of critical notes on the Old Testament informs the scholar of places where emendation of the text has been thought justified. In this list a transliteration is given of the reading followed—a procedure more enlightening than that used by the RSV which merely gave brief footnotes stating that a conjecture or correction had been made.

In certain books where the translators thought that there was dislocation of material, lines have been rearranged; but the current versification of the Hebrew Bible is maintained, alerting the reader to the rearrangement. Exceptional dislocations are noted in the footnotes. For example, after Proverbs 5:19, verse 22 from Proverbs 6 is inserted. Even more problems are seen in Job. In chapter 28, verse 3 follows verse 24, and verses 7 and 8 follow verse 21. Verses 9, 10, and 11 follow the relocated verse 3 before continuing with verse 25. Such rearrangement is an excellent example of the translators' rewriting of Job. It is impossible to conceive that accidental transposition of the text by scribes could account for the number of displacements offered by the translators.

[3]Cited by L. Sabourin, review of *The New American Bible*, in *Biblical Theology Bulletin* 2 (July 1972): 206-8.

[4]Keith R. Crim, review of *The New American Bible*, in *Interpretation* 26 (January 1972): 77-80.

Some confusion may be experienced by the English reader in the versification of the Psalms. In the Hebrew Bible the headings of the individual psalms are included in the versification resulting in a one-verse difference from the Greek, Latin, and English Bibles. The NAB in some instances also differs from the Protestant translations by one verse. For the books of the Apocrypha where the Hebrew text is lost, the Greek text has been used. A striking innovation is seen in the printing in small type of the phrases with which rabbinic reading of Malachi ended to avoid closing the book with a curse.

In the New Testament the twenty-fifth edition of the Nestle-Aland *Novum Testamentum Graece* has been followed and sometimes supplemented by the Greek New Testament edited by Aland *et al.* for the United Bible Societies, 1966. Some departures from these were made where the editors thought necessary. Doubtful readings are bracketed so that the reader may skip them if he wishes. Poorly attested readings are not included in the text. In certain instances (Matt. 23:14; Mark 9:44, 46; Luke 17:36; 23:17) the unfortunate policy has been followed of merely informing the reader that a verse has been omitted in many manuscripts. The reader is forced to consult other Bibles to find out the content of these omitted verses. Acts 8:36-38 has been renumbered to cover omission of verse 37, and I John 5:7-8 renumbered to cover that omission. No note accompanies either passage. For Mark, the longer ending, the shorter ending, and the *Freer Logion* are all printed with marginal notations. In numerous cases brackets designate sections as glosses where there is no supporting textual evidence for the opinion.

The NAB, as all other Catholic translations, includes the apocryphal books, found in various Greek and Latin manuscripts, which the Council of Trent declared to be canonical. Protestants call these books apocryphal and usually publish them as a separate anthology. Catholics call them deuterocanonical and disperse them at various places in the Old Testament.

Introductions

The NAB is briefer in introductions than is the JB. The introductory material represents the advanced higher-critical positions popular in Protestant theological circles that have recently come to be widely accepted in Catholic circles. These positions are in marked conflict with the traditional positions maintained by the Papal Biblical Commission at the beginning of this century, and they reflect some of the current conflict in the Catholic church. The reader of the NAB is informed that the Pentateuch is the outgrowth of the sources usually abbreviated as J, E, D, and P; that Moses, while perhaps responsible for some of the material, was not the author of the books in the modern sense of the term. The story of the flood is designated a composite narrative based on two separate sources interwoven into an intricate patchwork. There are two Isaiahs. The Book of Isaiah is an anthology of poems composed chiefly by the great prophet, but also by disciples, some of whom came many years after Isaiah. The Book of Daniel was composed during the persecutions of Antiochus Epiphanes; Joel was written about 400 B.C. Mark is the first of the Gospels and originally ended at 16:8. John may not have written the fourth Gospel. Paul is probably not the author of Ephesians in the same sense that he is of such epistles as Romans, Galatians, and I and II Corinthians. Second Peter is pseudonymous and dates between A.D. 100 and 125. The identity of the author of the Epistle to the Hebrews "is a matter of pure speculation. Among those considered, Apollos seems more likely than Luke or Barnabas."

Annotations

It is also to be expected that in keeping with canon law a Catholic translation would have annotations. The annotative material, like the introductions, represents the stance of the higher critical approach. Various sections of books are assigned to alleged sources. Sections like the genealogical lists (Gen. 46:9-27) are attributed to the redactor or to later editors (cf. Lev. 6:12-16; Mic. 2:12). The annotations are not such as to inspire confidence on the part of the reader in the integrity of the text.

A surprisingly small amount of the material is distinctively Catholic. In the Ten Commandments the traditional Catholic division of the commandments is followed (Exod. 20:1-17). Elsewhere, attention is called to passages used in the Catholic liturgy (Isa. 60:1-6; Ps. 95; 116:13, 15; Wisd. of Sol. 1:7; Jth. 15:9). The note on Isaiah 7:14 alludes to the doctrine of the perpetual virginity of Mary. A note affirms that the doctrine of guardian angels is common in the Old Testament (Ps. 91:11). Another note affirms that the church has always included the additions to Daniel in the inspired writings. Psalm 51:7 is declared to expound the doctrine of original sin. On the other hand, a crucial passage for the Catholic teaching of intercession of saints such as II Maccabees 15:14 merely carries the notation: "Who ... prays for his people: a clear belief in the intercession of the saints." That on Judges 17:3 states, "The Mosaic law forbade the making of an image even of the true God."

The notes contain an abundance of archaeological, geographical, traditional, and conjectural information relevant to the text. For example, the mark on Cain is said to have probably been a tattoo (Gen. 4:15). Camels in the patriarchal stories are designated an anachronism (Gen. 12:16). To call Laban an Aramean is said to be an anachronism (Gen. 31:20). Whereas the text has "Red Sea," the annotation takes notice of the opinion that "Reed Sea" is more literal and proposes identification with a shallow body of water north of the body presently called "Red Sea." The four empires in Daniel are identified as the Babylonian, the Median, the Persian, and the Hellenistic (Dan. 2:36), thereby affirming that the vision goes only to the Maccabean period.

The approach to the Old Testament is christological throughout. Attention is called to those passages specifically cited in the New Testament (e.g., Isa. 53; Jer. 31:31; Dan. 7:13), to those not cited which traditionally have been thought to be of messianic import, to those thought to have typological significance (e.g., the Paschal lamb is a type of Christ [Exod. 12:46]; manna is a type of the Eucharist [Exod. 16:4]), as well as to those used christologically by the Fathers but not thought to be so by the present translators. Attention is also called to passages that parallel Christian religious and ethical teaching.

Each reviewer can compile his own list of commendable and objectionable notes on the New Testament. Only a selected list is attempted here. *Anawim* (the poor) used in a note is left unexplained (Matt. 5:3-12) and will mean nothing to the uninitiated reader. The annotator plays with the solecism "helpmate" (I Tim. 2:9-13) despite the fact that the Old Testament translation used "suitable partner" (Gen. 2:18). He expounds the traditional position on the Antichrist which amalgamates a series of passages that may or may not be related (I John 2:18). On the translation "mad" he comments: "literally, 'You have a demon.' The insane were thought to possess or to be possessed by a demoniacal spirit. One has to determine from the context whether the charge in our terms is one of insanity or of possession" (John 7:20). After noting the weakness of the manuscript evidence for John 7:53ff., it is observed, "The Catholic Church accepts it as inspired Scripture." The languages used on Pentecost are explained as "ecstatic prayer in praise of God" (Acts 2:4). It is asserted that at the time of the letters to Timothy, the relation of presbyter to bishop is obscure and that these offices reflect a transitional stage that developed into the monarchial episcopate of the second century (I Tim. 5:17-25).

In general, the notes do not carry on the Catholic-Protestant quarrel characteristic of the notes of earlier Bibles. Notes of a distinctively confessional nature are limited to a few key passages, and controversial topics are definitely toned down from those in either the Rheims-Douay or the Confraternity versions. The doctrine of the perpetual virginity of Mary evokes the following notes: "Her firstborn son: a reference to the preferential status of the oldest son rather than an implication of subsequent offspring" (Luke 2:7). "He does not concern himself here with the period that followed the birth of Jesus, but merely wishes to show that Joseph fully respected the legal character of the paternity imposed on him by divine will. Moreover the New Testament makes no mention anywhere of children of Joseph and Mary" (Matt. 1:25). "The question about the brothers of Jesus and his sisters (v. 3) cannot easily be decided on linguistic grounds. Greek-speaking Semites used the terms *adelphos* and *adelphē*, not only in the ordinary sense of blood brother and sister, but also for nephew, niece, half-brother, half-sister, and cousin. The question of meaning here would not have arisen but for the faith of the church in Mary's perpetual virginity" (Mark 6:1-6).

The doctrine of the primacy of Peter calls forth these comments: "Matthew adds the doctrine of the divinity of Christ, together with Jesus' prophecy that he will successfully build a new Israel, i.e., the church upon Peter. ... For Matthew, Jesus' building of the new people of God upon Peter is a continuing reality for the Christian community of his time" (Matt. 16:16-20). " 'Rock' is here conferred on Simon as a personal name to indicate his role as the firm foundation on which Jesus builds his church" (Matt. 16:18). "The exact nature of the extraordinary power here conferred becomes clear through the historical development of the Christian community in terms of the primacy of Peter, i.e., his supreme authority in teaching, governing and sanctifying the people of God" (Matt. 16:19). The note on Acts 12:17 surprisingly says: "He ... left them to go off to another place: the conjecture that Peter left for Rome at this time has nothing to recommend it."

Less explicit are the remarks on using titles: "Typical hyperbolic speech of the time. It does not reject authority in principle, but authoritarianism;

221

not the use of titles, but the failure to acknowledge that authority exists to serve God, his anointed One, and one's neighbor" (Matt. 23:8ff.). And then there is the note on anointing the sick: "The Council of Trent (Sess. 14) declared the Anointing of the Sick to be a sacrament 'instituted by Christ our Lord and promulgated by blessed James the apostle'" (James 5:15).

Despite the ecumenical gesture that the NAB represents, the Catholic scholars could hardly expect that these notes would be palatable to non-Catholics.

The Translation

The NAB is more faithful to the original texts than is either the JB or the NEB. Furthermore, while it is a modern speech version, it maintains the traditional Bible format. It is bound in traditional black and has two columns to the page. Paragraphing is used with the verse numbers inserted at appropriate places in the text rather than each verse being a separate paragraph as it was in the Rheims-Douay Version. Asterisks call attention to annotations which are printed in uncomfortably small print as footnotes below lists of parallel passages. Supplied subject headings direct the reader to thought units. Poetic sections are printed in the form of poetry.

The translators aim at a translation rather than at a paraphrase. Consequently, sentences and constructions that would be considered overloaded in contemporary Western writing have been retained because they are a part of Greek or Hebrew style. However, long sentences (i.e., Eph. 1:3-15) are broken up into smaller units in an effort to achieve contemporary language. The translators are seeking a translation suitable for private reading, liturgical use, and scholarly study. One reviewer credits the NAB with "striking the finest balance between readability and literalness of any of the modern translations available."[5] In the completed edition the proper names of biblical characters follow the KJV and RSV forms. This achieving of uniformity of spelling is one of the most important contributions of the NAB toward ecumenism. Catholics need no longer talk of Abdias, Osee, and Isaias (forms derived from the Latin Vulgate) while their Protestant contemporaries use Obadiah, Hosea, and Isaiah (derived from Hebrew). Nevertheless, while striving to be current, the NAB

[5]Robert L. Alden, review of *The New American Bible*, in *Westminster Theological Journal* 34 (May 1972): 217.

retains a great deal that is traditional, especially in vocabulary. "Lord" is used to render the divine name, as was the case with the KJV and the RSV.

The translators used a richer vocabulary than did either Phillips or the producer of Today's English Version; yet the vocabulary is not as rich as that of the New English Bible.[6] Clarity is sought over resonance. The old English pronouns "thee" and "thou" and the accompanying verb forms have been dropped, making no distinction between speech addressed to God and to man. "Brothers" is used instead of the traditional "brethren" (Gal. 4:1). Modern place names are used to identify locations: Paul's ship is driven in the Ionian Sea (Greek: Adria), and he is shipwrecked at Malta. Considerable variety is seen in the effort to be current in describing the human reproductive process. A man "is intimate with" (Gen. 19:5), "has relations with" (Gen. 4:1, 17; Deut. 22:13ff.; II Sam. 11:4; 13:14; Matt. 1:25), or "has intercourse with" (Gen. 16:2; Lev. 18:6ff.) a woman—using the current idioms—rather than the more literal Hebrew expressions: "He knew her" or "he went in unto her." A woman becomes "pregnant" (Gen. 16:4, 11; Exod. 21:22), or at times is still said "to be with child" (Gen. 38:24; II Sam. 11:5; Matt. 1:18, 23; Luke 2:5).

The NAB has some innovative renderings of interest. The structure previously known to English readers as "the tabernacle" is the "dwelling" (Exod. 25:8ff.; 38:31; I Chron. 16:39; 23:26); however, "tent" (Pss. 15:1; 61:5) and "tabernacle" (Ps. 78:60; Heb. 9:2, 11, 21; 13:10) are used elsewhere. The offering known as the "burnt offering" is the "holocaust"; "the mercy seat" is a "propitiatory" (Exod. 25:17); and the abode of the dead, whether translating *sheol* or *hades*, is designated as "the nether world" (Gen. 37:35; 42:38; Acts 2:31; Rev. 1:18) or "the abode of the dead" (Luke 16:23). "The fiery serpent" is a "seraph serpent" (Num. 21:6, 8) with the adjective only transliterated. The governmental district previously literally rendered "Beyond the River" is "West-of-Euphrates" (Ezra 5:6). "Wild onion" (II Kings 6:25) sounds more palatable than "dove's dung," but the linguistic evidence for the choice is unclear. "Scribes" are "experts in the law" (Mark 7:1). The letters to the churches in the Book of Revelation are addressed "To the presiding spirit" (Rev. 2:1; etc.). The innovations in the New Testament most likely to raise discussion include the use of "reform" (Matt. 3:8, 11; 12:41; Mark 1:15; Luke 11:32; Acts 2:38) where the reader

---

[6]"New Bible for Catholics: *New American Bible*," *Time* 96 (October 12, 1970): 58.

is accustomed to "repent." However, "repentance" is sometimes retained (Mark 1:4; Acts 11:18), and "penance" also is found (Luke 24:47). "Trust" is used where one expects "believe." People are cured by "trust" (Matt. 8:13). However, "faith" is not avoided in Hebrews 11 or in James 2.

Some other distinctive renderings show the flavor of the NAB. "Not the smallest letter of the law, not the smallest part of a letter" is used for "jot" or "tittle" (Matt. 5:18). "Speck" and "plank" are used where the KJV had "mote" and "beam" (Luke 6:42). The Baptizer's food was "grasshoppers" (Matt. 3:4). Instead of "saints" there are "holy people" (Acts 9:13; I Cor. 1:2) or "holy ones" (Phil. 1:1; Col. 1:2); however, the verb "sanctified" is not avoided (Heb. 10:29). Instead of "shewbread" there is "holy bread" (Matt. 12:4); instead of "raca" there is "holds . . . in contempt" (Matt. 5:22). The functions which are attributed to the heart in Hebrew psychology are here attributed to the mind (Matt. 12:34; 15:18). In certain cases *psuchē* (KJV: "soul") is rendered "self": "What profit does a man show who gains the whole world and destroys himself in the process?" (Mark 8:36).

Specific hours of the day are omitted in the parable in favor of "early morning," "mid-morning," "noon," "afternoon," and "late afternoon" (Matt. 20:5ff.). Instead of "talents" there are "silver pieces" (Matt. 25:15). At times, sums of money are designated "coins" (Luke 7:41) without an indication of their value. Measures of length and of content are merely transliterated; hence we still read of "omers" (Exod. 16:22), "ephahs" (Exod. 16:36; I Sam. 1:24), "cubits" (I Kings 7:16), "shekels," and "seahs." While the decision is regrettable, most translation groups have finally concluded that it is impossible to use current measures in the Bible.

Many examples of good choices can be cited. Rather than "worship," men pay "homage" (Matt. 2:2, 8) or "reverence" (Matt. 9:18) to human superiors. "Decapolis" is rendered "the Ten Cities" (Matt. 4:25; Mark 5:20). "The lure of money chokes out the word" (Matt. 13:22). John is designated "the Baptizer" (Matt. 14:1ff.). "May you and your money rot" (Acts 8:20) is less profane than Phillips' "To hell with you and your money."

The NAB occasionally fails to use contemporary idiom. Less sophisticated wording would have been more easily understood. A note was required for "caper berry" (Eccles. 12:5) to explain that it was considered a stimulant of appetite. "Succor" (Deut. 23:5) is not current, nor are "octaves" (Isa. 1:13) or "benumbed" (Hab. 1:4). An unfortunate choice is seen in "for fear of disedifying them [the kings of the world]" (Matt. 17:27). "We shall be quit of the oath" (Josh. 2:20) is awkward. Those crucified with Jesus

224

are "insurgents" (Matt. 27:38; Mark 15:27)—a perfectly good English word but not the best choice here. The phrase "swaddling clothes" (Luke 2:7) retains an archaism. That "a father be split against son" (Luke 12:53) is no improvement over "divided" (RSV; NEB). "Leaven" and "leavened" (Gen. 19:3; Exod. 12:34; Lev. 23:6) are retained where "yeast" and "risen" would be more current. "Rent" (II Sam. 1:11; 15:32) should be "tore" (as II Kings 6:30; Job 1:20; Acts 14:14). "Mourned her lord" (II Sam. 11:26) would be better "mourned her husband." "Minions" (Rev. 12:9) would be clearer if it were "host," and "genuflected" (Mark 15:19) if it were "bowed."

"Do not . . . take umbrage" (I Sam. 29:10) could have been "Do not take offense." "Wadi" (Gen. 15:18; 26:17; Num. 13:23; 21:14, 15; 32:9; Deut. 1:24; 2:13, 24; 9:21; 10:7; 21:4; Judg. 5:21) is familiar to the person who has knowledge of Arabic culture, but to translate Hebrew into Arabic terms for the English reader is not really a gain. "Valley Gate" is better understood and is retained in Nehemiah 2:13. "Byssus" (Esther 1:6) is not a currently known cloth, nor is "torque" known as an ornament (Prov. 1:9). "After-growth" (Isa. 37:30) is not satisfactory for that which grows without cultivation. "Mien" (Job 22:29) would be clearer if it were "countenance," "in a trice" (I Kings 18:45) if it were "in a moment," and "cursed me balefully" (I Kings 2:8), if it were "curse me harshly."

In certain cases, striving for technical accuracy has given words not likely to be known to the American reader: "buckthorn" (Judg. 9:14), "weaver's heddle-bar" (I Sam. 17:7; II Sam. 21:19; I Chron. 11:23; 20:5), and "greensward" (II Sam. 23:4). "Steppe" (Job 24:5; Isa. 35:1; 42:11; RSV: "wilderness") is beyond question a good technical geographical word but one which is not used by less educated Americans. Neither is "must" (Joel 1:10; RSV: "wine") and "tillage" (Ps. 104:23; RSV: "labor"). "Major-domo" (I Kings 4:6) is better known, but is no real improvement over "in charge of the palace." "Do not descry for us what is right" (Isa. 30:10) is less understandable than "Do not prophesy to us what is right" (RSV). "Gith" (Isa. 28:25, 27) is not listed as a plant in Webster's *Third New International Dictionary*.

There are renderings whose accuracy can be questioned. "Ears of grain" (Gen. 41:6) is more accurately "heads of grain" when cereal grains are meant; Americans use "ears" for corn. "Cylinder-seal" (Isa. 8:1) for *lauch* (RSV: "tablet") is unjustified, the inhabitants of waste places may be "wild goats" instead of the mythical "satyrs" (Lev. 17:17; Isa. 13:21; 34:11, 14), and an allusion to the "sand" (KJV; RSV) is preferable to an allusion to the mythical "phoenix" (Job 29:18).

The translators subscribe to the idea that the groups of prophets were "guild prophets" (I Kings 20:35; II Kings 2:5; 5:22; 9:1). The problem over Jeremiah's having gone to the Euphrates with his loincloth is solved by transliterating the location by "Parath" (Jer. 13:5) with an accompanying note which states that the location may be near Anathoth.

The translation procedures that were followed created difficulties which could have been avoided if other choices had been an option. For example, Hagar is said to have put Ishmael on her back (Gen. 21:14). Now according to the data given in the translation, Abraham was eighty-six when Ishmael was born (Gen. 16:16) and was a hundred when Isaac was born (Gen. 21:5); hence the emendation which is followed has the absurdity of Hagar's carrying a fourteen-year-old boy on her back. The note which claims that the text is corrupt cannot alleviate this absurdity. In another instance it is quite one thing to call attention in a note to the parallels between the proverbs of Amen-em-ope and those of Proverbs 22ff., but it is quite another to insert in the text, "I make known to you the words of Amen-em-ope" (Prov. 22:19).

An occasional explanatory gloss has been inserted in the text: "Candace (a name meaning queen)" (Acts 8:27) and "At that time the Nephilim appeared on earth (as well as later)" (Gen. 6:4).

The NAB shows the disadvantage of a project stretched over almost three decades without a final revision to bring all of its parts into a unified plan. This problem surfaces in the treatment of such a common word as *metanoieō* which is "reform" in the Gospels (Matt. 3:8, 11; 12:41; Mark 1:15; Luke 11:32; Acts 2:38; 3:19)—a questionable rendering—but which is "repent" in the Epistle to the Hebrews (6:1; 6:6) and in the Book of Revelation (2:5; 9:20). Another example is the treatment of the commandment "You shall not kill" (Exod. 20:13; Deut. 5:17; Matt. 19:18; Luke 18:20; James 2:11) which more correctly reads "You shall not murder" (Matt. 5:21; Rom. 13:9). In the synoptic Gospels no effort is made to render repeated words or phrases identically, but this policy results in an undue variety in rendering such a common phrase as *tou basilea tou theou* as "kingdom of God," "God's kingdom," "kingdom of heaven," and "reign of God." This variety is seen even in adjacent verses (see Luke 18:16, 17, 25, 29). The phrase *hē basilea tōn ouranōn* ("kingdom of heaven") may be either "reign of God" (Matt. 3:2; 5:3, 10; 10:7; 13:11, 24, 31, 33, 44, 52;

18:23; 19:12; 20:1; 22:2; 25:1), "kingdom of God" (Matt. 5:19, 20; 7:21; 8:11; 11:11, 12; 18:1, 3; 19:14, 23; 23:13), or "kingdom of heaven" (Matt. 4:17; 13:45; 16:19) in the same context. *Makarios* is rendered "blest" in the beatitudes of Matthew but is "happy" in the Book of Revelation (Rev. 14:13). *Su legeis* is "as you say" (Matt. 27:11), "You are the one who is saying it" (Mark 15:2), and "That is your term" (Luke 23:3). The phrase in other translations rendered as "Woe" is here "It will go ill with you" (Matt. 11:21), "What terrible things will come on the world" (Matt. 18:7), "woe" (Matt. 23:13, 15, 23, 25, 27, 29; 26:24; Luke 6:24, 25, 26; Rev. 8:13; 9:12; 11:14; 12:12), "It is an evil day for you" (Matt. 23:16), "It will be hard on . . ." (Matt. 24:19), "I am ruined if I do not . . ." (I Cor. 9:16), "So much the worse for them" (Jude 11), and "Alas" (Rev. 18:10, 16, 19).

The exegesis revealed in rendering certain passages is questionable: "And then all Israel will be saved" (Rom. 11:26) here treats *houtōs* as a temporal adverb when in reality it is an adverb of manner. "Whatever you declare bound" (Matt. 18:18) perhaps reflects a Catholic concept of legislative authority. "I have come to call, not the self-righteous, but sinners" (Matt. 9:13) is a paraphrase. "Jesus, the so-called Messiah" (Matt. 27:22) is a case of overtranslation. So also is "All Hail" (Matt. 27:29) for *chaire*. "That very moment her daughter got better" (Matt. 15:28) suggests a slow convalescence which is alien to the passage. "You are Rock" (Matt. 16:18) lays a basis for understanding the church to be built on Peter, but is hardly suitable unless Peter's name is also translated in its other occurrences. "They came to life again" (Rev. 20:4, for *ezēsan*) weights the scales in favor of a particular understanding of this section of Scripture. "Yet time will prove where wisdom lies" (Matt. 11:19) is a free paraphrase of a saying which more literally is "Wisdom is justified by her deeds."

The translators despaired of translating numerous passages of Job and in these cases left blanks in the text, sometimes with a note discussing the problem (Job 24:19-21; 28:4; 36:16-20).

The literary merits of the NAB must be left to those who are experts in such matters. One reviewer has characterized it as stylistically inferior to the NEB.[7] Even to the nonexpert it is obvious that the literary charms which endear the KJV to the reading public have not been equalled in the NAB. Readers of the KJV will doubtless prefer "He makes me lie down

[7]L. Sabourin, review of *New American Bible*, in *Biblical Theology Bulletin* 2 (July 1972): 206-8.

in green pastures" to "In verdant pastures he gives me repose" (Ps. 23:2); "I shall dwell in the house of the Lord forever" to "And I shall dwell in the house of the Lord for years to come" (Ps. 23:6); "I once was young and now I am old, yet I have not seen the righteous forsaken nor his seed begging bread" to "Neither in my youth, nor now that I am old, have I seen a just man forsaken nor his descendant begging bread" (Ps. 37:25); and "The wicked flee when no man pursues but the righteous are as bold as a lion" to "The wicked man flees although no one pursues him; but the just man, like a lion, feels sure of himself" (Prov. 28:1). Occasional passages in the NAB will sound strange when read orally: "If you cannot be trusted with elusive wealth, who will trust you with lasting?" (Luke 16:11); "Every worthwhile gift, every genuine benefit comes from above, descending from the Father of the heavenly luminaries, who cannot change and who is never shadowed over" (James 1:17); and "The Lord's are the earth and its fullness" (Ps. 24:1).[8]

Conclusion

The NAB is likely the most readable translation into English that Catholic scholars have yet produced. Nevertheless, the various strictures mentioned above make it obvious that despite its ecumenical gesture, the NAB is not likely to become the Bible of English-reading Christendom. It does move the English-reading Catholic in one stage from that which is archaic and difficult reading into a readable, usable English Bible of comparable scholarship and literary merit to those available to the non-Catholic public. Its impact upon popular American Catholic thought will be immeasurable. With the NAB, Bible reading for Catholics now becomes a viable option. Herein lies its significance.

[8]Bruce M. Metzger, review of *The New American Bible, 1970*, in *The Princeton Seminary Bulletin* 64 (March 1971): 90-99; Frederick W. Danker, review of *The New American Bible*, in *Catholic Biblical Quarterly* 33 (July 1971): 405-9; anonymous review of *The New American Bible*, in *Christianity Today* 15 (October 23, 1970); 29; John Reumann, review of *The New American Bible*, in *Journal of Biblical Literature* 92 (July 1973): 275-78; Frank Stagg, review of *The New American Bible*, in *Review and Expositor* 68 (Summer 1971): 400-2.

10

The New World Translation of the Holy Scriptures

The New World Translation, prepared and circulated by the Watchtower Bible and Tract Society, has been prepared by a group of scholars who "wish to remain anonymous even after death." These scholars worked from the Westcott-Hort text, but many other sources were utilized. The translation was designed for the use of Jehovah's Witnesses, who previously had used the King James Version, the American Standard Version, and the Emphatic Diaglott. The New Testament section of this work was issued in 1950; later the Old Testament came out periodically in five sections; a completed Bible was ready in 1961, a second revision in 1970, and a third in 1971. The third edition has a complex system of notes and references. An extensive appendix attempts to justify the distinctive features of this translation in sixteen key verses.

[1]H. H. Rowley, "How Not to Translate the Bible," *Expository Times* 65 (November 1953): 41-42.

The NWT received a review by H. H. Rowley in the *Expository Times* entitled "How Not to Translate the Bible."[1] It falls in the category scholars designate "tendentious translations" because it fosters the distinctive views of a particular sect, as those familiar with Jehovah's Witnesses' teachings will recognize. The manifestation of this trait begins with the names given to the two divisions of the Bible. "The Hebrew-Aramaic Scriptures" and "The Christian Greek Scriptures" are used to avoid the use of the words "Old Covenant" and "New Covenant," for Jehovah's Witnesses deny that these Bible portions are rightly designated "covenant." There is a polemic in the preface of the work against the commonly used terminology. This peculiarity does not preclude the use of "covenant" in other settings: "new covenant" (Jer. 31:31), "blood of the covenant" (Matt. 26:28), "reading of the old covenant" (II Cor. 3:14), "new covenant," "former covenant" (Heb. 9:15), and "mediator of a new covenant" (Heb. 12:24).

While admitting that "Jehovah" is a mispronunciation of the Tetragrammaton,[2] the New World translators insist that it should be used. After all, the sect's name comes from this mispronunciation! While questionable enough in the Old Testament, the use of "Jehovah" is entirely without justification in the New Testament. Yet the name "Jehovah" has been introduced 237 times in the New Testament despite the fact that the Greek had *Kurios* (Lord) in each instance. The translators attempt to justify their choice on the evidence of nineteen Hebrew translations of Scripture from the fourteenth century onward and from the practice of thirty-eight different modern missionary translations — all of which are irrelevant to the question. The notes insist that the Scriptures have been tampered with on the matter of the divine name.[3] Evidence is against the Witnesses on this. Jesus, when citing "The Lord said unto my Lord" (Ps. 110), used *Kurios* and not "Jehovah." Paul used *Kurios* repeatedly (Rom. 9:29; 15:11; II Cor. 6:17). It is used in Jude 14, and it is used in the Greek text of the Book of Enoch, which antedates the Christian period.

The cross is a "torture stake" (Matt. 10:38; 27:32); and Jesus was "impaled" (Luke 23:21), instead of crucified, on his stake. A long note attempts to justify these renderings. Jehovah's Witnesses believe Jesus was nailed to the cross, but argue that it was an upright pole and that the position

[2]*New World Translation of the Christian Greek Scriptures*, rev. ed. (Brooklyn, N.Y.: Watchtower Bible and Tract Society, Inc., 1951), p. 25.

[3]Ibid., p. 18.

of the victim was different from that ordinarily accepted. "Impale" is the thrusting of the stake through the vitals. The English dictionary does not give nailing as a meaning for "impale." The position Witnesses contend for ignores the fact that classical sources speak of the slave about to be crucified carrying the crossbar to his own crucifixion, and that the *Epistle of Barnabas* 10:8 compares the cross to the Greek letter *tau*. See also Irenaeus's *Against Heresies* 2.24.4. Their position also ignores the evidence from the remains of the crucified man discovered in a tomb near Jerusalem in 1968.

"Holy Spirit" is not capitalized (Matt. 28:19; Acts 1:8; II Cor. 13:14) because of opposition to trinitarian ideas. "End of the World" (or "end of the age") is "conclusion of the system of things" (Matt. 13:39, 49; 24:3; 28:20). The wicked go away into "everlasting cutting off," but the righteous into "everlasting life" (Matt. 25:46). "Gehenna," "Hades," and "Tartarus" are used instead of the "hell" of the KJV. The practice is not objectionable, but "Gehenna" is explained in the notes to mean the incinerator for refuse outside of Jerusalem.

Luke 23:43 is punctuated to read: "Truly I tell you today, You will be with me in Paradise." Here the Jehovah's Witnesses' bias clearly comes through. The antithesis between the thief's indefinite "When you come in your kingdom" and Jesus' "Today you shall be ..." is destroyed. Furthermore, the formula "Truly I say unto you" in other New Testament settings (Matt. 5:26; John 1:51; 3:3; etc.) is so used that what follows is always a part of the statement and not part of the formula. The Witnesses can claim the Curetonian Syriac and the church father Theophylact on their side of the issue, but the whole affair was perhaps best characterized by Henry Alford as "something worse than silly."[4]

In the effort to manipulate John 1:1 against Greek usage of the article, the NWT reads "The word was a god," and the footnote reads " 'A god' in contrast with 'the God.' " There is no way to understand this rendering except to understand it as teaching polytheism. A lengthy note in the appendix (pp. 1362-63) attempts unsuccessfully to justify the rendering, explaining that the rendering is a reaction to Goodspeed's and Moffatt's rendering, "the word was divine." However, the example the Witnesses cite

---

[4]Henry Alford, *The Greek Testament*, rev. by E. F. Harrison, vol. 1 (Chicago: Moody Press, 1958), p. 661.

from Xenophon, if actually parallel to John 1:1, would justify the rendering "A God was a word," which they admit is possible, rather than their choice. They say, "The word or Logos is not God or *the* God, but is the Son of God, and hence, a god. That is why, at John 1:1, 2 the apostle refers to God as the God and to the Word, or Logos, as a god to show the difference between the two."

Out of the long list of unarthrous predicate nominatives in the Gospel of John, which the Witnesses cite in justification of their choice, only one, *huios tou theou* (John 10:36), is a definite predicate nominative which precedes the verb, paralleling the grammatical structure of John 1:1. One certainly would not translate John 10:36 "A Son of God." Nor do the New World people so translate it. They render it, "I am God's Son." Their claim that Acts 28:6 exactly parallels John 1:1 is false, for in Acts 28:6 *theos* follows the verb rather than precedes it.

E. C. Colwell ("A Definite Rule for the Use of the Article in Greek New Testament," *Journal of Biblical Literature* 52 [1933]: 12-21) demonstrated that definite predicate nouns which precede verbs are regularly unarthrous in Greek. In the case of John 1:1, "and the Word was God" is correct. Another reflection of the Witnesses' views of the Father and Son is seen in John 10:30 which states, "I and the Father are one," but the footnote explains "are at unity." A lengthy appendix argues the case for these and other tendentious choices.

While insisting that other modern versions reflect religious and higher critical bias, the NWT has not hesitated to reflect its own bias and to engage in criticism of its own. *'Adonai* is rendered "Jehovah" in Genesis 18:3, against the Hebrew text, when the story actually turns on Abraham's ignorance of the identity of the guests. "Sir" would have been a better choice. While claiming that it has not paraphrased, it has in fact done so, as one can see by examining Matthew 26:26 ("This means"), 26:64 ("That was for you to say"—the translation is changed in the 1961 edition to "You yourself said [it]"), 28:19 ("make disciples of people of all the nations"), and others. "Other" has been added four times with no support in Greek in Colossians 1:16-17 to make Paul say that Jesus Christ is one among "other" created things. Thus Paul's statement is falsified to make it state exactly what Paul is refuting. The Greek New Testament does not use "created" to describe the relation of the Son to the Father. The denial of the divinity of Jesus Christ by the Jehovah's Witnesses comes out in the rendering of Titus 2:13 and II Peter 1:1 as "Our God and [the] Saviour Jesus Christ," which properly should be, "Our God and Saviour Jesus Christ."

The NWT is described by its promoters as designed "not merely for good enjoyable reading, but more particularly for use of searching students of God's Word who do not have ready access to Greek dictionaries and exhaustive Bible Concordances."[5] Thus an effort is made to justify fine distinctions in verb forms and the distinction made in the singular and plural of the second person pronoun. The plural pronoun is printed in all capitals ("YOU"). While fine distinctions are admirable, the method used in this case is disastrous, for the ordinary reader will need to realize that "YOU" is not capitalized for emphasis.

By the use of certain auxiliary words, the translators have attempted to strengthen the expression shown by the verb. However, when the same verbal construction is "began" in Exodus 14:10 but "continue" in Numbers 14:1, we have arbitrariness that is misleading. The translators in such cases are rewriting the Bible.

An effort is made to render each major biblical word by the same English word without regard to the requirements of context. The outcome is a specious show of faithfulness resulting in a woodenly awkward English style. For example, *psuche* is rendered "soul" in each of its 102 occurrences; but when it designates animal life and bodily appetites (Matt. 2:20; 6:25; 10:39; 20:28; Luke 12:19; 14:26; John 10:11; I Cor. 15:45), perhaps "self" would be a better rendering. Long ago, Jerome said that he had resolved not to translate words but the sense. The New World's uniformity of rendering does not extend to *pneuma* ("spirit"). "Her breath" returns to Jairus' daughter (Luke 8:55), and "the body without breath is dead" (James 2:26); but Daniel says, "my spirit was distressed within" (Dan. 7:15) and Jesus and Stephen yield "up their spirit" (Matt. 27:50—the earlier edition had "ceased to breathe" with a footnote "yielded up his breath"— Acts 7:59; cf. I Thess. 5:23; I Peter 3:18, 19).

The NWT is printed in paragraphs rather than in individual verses. It abandons archaic language, even in the prayers. "You" is used even when addressing God. The expression previously rendered "behold" is "look"

[5]"How Bible Translators Work," *Christian Century* 68 (May 9, 1951): 587.

(Matt. 1:23; 7:4; 21:5; etc.) in this version, not always with fortunate results. While claiming to use modern idiom, it is not a modern speech version. The English style is very faulty. Each reader can come up with his own examples (e.g., Gen. 4:7; 6:3; 15:5-6; 18:20; 19:22; 24:66). We read, "How long will you behave drunk?" (I Sam. 1:14) and "the matter devolves upon you" (Ezra 10:4).

Other translation traits are seen in that *le'olam* (traditionally "forever") is uniformly "to time indefinite," even when Jehovah is being described (Ps. 102:12; 146:10; etc.). *Le'olam wa'ed* (traditionally "forever and ever") is "to time indefinite, even forever" (Exod. 15:18; Ps. 45:6). However, in the New Testament, the translators do not seem to avoid "forever" (Luke 1:33) or "forever and ever" (Rev. 11:15). This creates the anomaly that God's Word is for "indefinite time" in the Old Testament (Isa. 40:8), but is "forever" in the New Testament (I Peter 1:25). The land of Palestine is "from long ago and to a long time to come" (Jer. 25:5). It is promised to Abraham until "time indefinite" (Gen. 13:15; 17:8; 48:4; Isa. 60:21; Jer. 7:7), but the promise to Abraham is "forever" in the New Testament (Luke 1:55). David's throne is "to time indefinite" (Ps. 89:4), but is "forever" in the New Testament application to the reign of the Christ (Luke 1:33).

In the New Testament we have "They came to life" and "the rest of the dead did not come to life" (for *ezēsan*; Rev. 20:4, 5) which supports the contrast the premillennialists like to make on these verses. "They lived" would be a better choice. A main fault of the NWT is overtranslation. Occasionally "means" is supplied for "is" (Matt. 26:28; Luke 22:19, 20) which is commentary, not translation.

This review has concentrated on the faults of the NWT, and in this respect the reviewer may be accused of being unfair. In commendation it may be said that the NWT follows the practice now fairly standard both in Greek texts and in English translations of indicating passages in which there are textual problems. Some of these are printed in smaller type (e.g., Mark 16:9-20; John 7:53—8:11), others have a space in the text after the verse number (e.g., Acts 8:37) with an explanatory footnote, still others have only an explanatory footnote (e.g., I John 5:7, 8). The NWT is one of the rare translations into any language which has rendered *'almah* consistently in all of its seven occurrences (Gen. 24:43; Exod. 2:8; Prov. 30:19; Isa. 7:14; Ps. 68:25; Song of Sol. 1:3; 6:8). It has used "maiden," which is a good opposite of "lad" used for its masculine form *'elem* (I Sam. 17:56; 20:22). Isaiah 9:6 is rendered to have four titles, which is correct.

This study is by no means a comprehensive review of all the merits or faults of the NWT. These examples are adequate, however, to show that it is unsuited for the use of people who want to know what the Bible really teaches.[6]

---

[6]Other available sources are: Steven Byington, "A Review of the New World Translation," *Christian Century* 57 (November 1, 1950): 1295; "Jehovah's Witnesses' Version of O.T.," *Christian Century* 70 (October 7, 1953): 1134; S. S. Haas, "New World Translation of the Hebrew Scriptures," *Journal of Biblical Literature* 74 (March 1955): 282-83; J. F. Mattingly, "New World Translation of the Hebrew Scriptures," *Catholic Biblical Quarterly* 13 (October 1951): 439-43; B. M. Metzger, "Jehovah's Witnesses and Jesus Christ," *Theology Today* 10 (April 1953-54): 76ff.; "New World Translation of the Christian Greek Scriptures," *Bible Translator* 15 (July 1964): 150-52; H. H. Rowley, "Jehovah's Witness' Translation of the Bible," *Expository Times* 67 (January 1956): 107-8; R. H. Countess, "*The New World Translation*: A Critical Analysis" (Ph.D. Thesis, Bob Jones University, 1966).

11

The Living Bible Paraphrased

T he Living Bible Paraphrased by Kenneth N. Taylor is the outcome of sixteen years of work which began in 1954 when Taylor started paraphrasing Scripture for use with his children in family devotions. Much of the work was done at night, on weekends, during vacations, and as Taylor commuted to and from his job at Moody Press. Taylor's work was first shared with the public in 1962 when two thousand copies of the segment The Living Letters were printed at Taylor's own expense. Then installments appeared—Living Prophecies (1964), The Living Gospels (1966), The Living New Testament (1967), Living Psalms and Proverbs (1967), Living Lessons of Life and Love (1968), Living Books of Moses (1969), and Living History of Israel (1970). The completed work was issued in July 1971 by the Tyndale House in Wheaton, Illinois, and by the Coverdale House in London.[1] The edition was designated a tentative edition which would likely be changed in future printings in response to criticisms

---

[1]"A Plowman's Bible?" *Time* 100 (July 24, 1972): 73; D. Michel, "Miracle of the *Living Bible*," *Saturday Evening Post* 247 (April 1975): 58-59.

that were received. Taylor announced some time ago that he was spending the next three years in revision work which all agree is needed, but, though each printing differs in some respects from the preceding one, the revised edition has not yet been offered to the public.[2]

Taylor's work has appeared in a number of different forms. A printing of the New Testament is called the Reach Out Version (1969); a printing of the whole Bible is called The Way (1972); a printing for Catholics, The Way: Catholic Edition (1973); and a printing for blacks is called Soul Food. There are also other forms.[3] Though moving slowly at first, once Taylor's material had received the endorsement of Billy Graham in 1963 and was offered on Graham's television program, its sales became fantastic. Over nine million copies of Living Letters were sold.[4] The LB was the best-selling book in the United States in 1972, and the royalties for the year amounted to four million dollars. Royalties for 1973 were eight million dollars. By 1974 it accounted for 46 percent of the sales of Bibles in the United States, and the paraphrase had produced royalties in excess of twenty million dollars.[5] For the month of September 1977 the *Christian Bookseller's Magazine* 13 (September 1977):10 listed it as leading all other Bibles in sales. The profits support the Tyndale House Foundation, which sponsors translators working in forty-two countries.[6] Through Living Bibles, International, paraphrases of this kind are being prepared in 110 languages. Some time ago the Gideon Society announced that it was placing copies of The Reach Out New Testament in motel rooms. A contribution of one dollar is requested, but not demanded, of the guest who takes one. More than twenty-three million copies of Taylor's paraphrase have been circulated.

The Aims of Paraphrase

Though often erroneously called a translation, the LB must first be evaluated in the light of what a paraphrase aims at doing. A *translation*

---

[2]Kenneth N. Taylor, "A Response: Dear Brother Editor," *Brethren Life and Thought* 18 (Summer 1973): 143.

[3]A schedule of publication is carried in "The Story of the *Living Bible*," *Eternity* 23 (April 1973): 65.

[4]Russell T. Hitt, review of *The Living Bible Paraphrased*, in *Eternity* 22 (December 1971): 48-49.

[5]William F. Kerr, "*The Living Bible* — Not Just Another Version," *Christianity Today* 19 (May 23, 1975): 29; Jonathan R. Laing, "*The Living Bible* Lives and Sells and Makes Kenneth Taylor Happy," *Wall Street Journal*, 1 March 1974, pp. 1, 21.

[6]E. E. Plowman, "The Living Bible: A Record," *Christianity Today* 15 (September 10, 1971): 42.

aims at making the same impression upon the reader of the new language that the original made upon the readers in the original language by reproducing in the second language the nearest equivalent of the author's words. Since no two languages have the same idioms and grammar, some paraphrase is inevitable in all translation work, and the degree allowable is a debatable point among translators; but a good translation seeks to hold paraphrasing to a minimum. A *paraphrase*, on the other hand, aims at restating in simplified but related ways the ideas conveyed in the original language. The paraphraser states in different language what he understands to be the author's meaning. The paraphrase expands or abbreviates where it seems advantageous in order to make the meaning clear to the modern reader. In this way it has the nature of a brief commentary on Scripture. If one wants to study the specific words given by the original writers or their nearest equivalents in the new language, then one should not go to a paraphrase. The producer of the LB acknowledges these features of his work in his preface:

> To paraphrase is to say something in different words than the author used. It is a restatement of the author's thoughts, using different words than he did. Its purpose is to say exactly as possible what the writers of the Scriptures meant, and to say it simply, expanding where necessary for a clear understanding for the modern reader.[7]

The idea of paraphrase is not new in the history of the English Bible. The earliest extant Scripture rendered into the English tongue — the paraphrases of Genesis, Exodus, and Daniel by Caedmon (A.D. 690) and those of the Pentateuch, Joshua, and Judges by Aelfric (c. 1000) — are paraphrases rather than translations. The *Ormulum* by Orm (twelfth century) was a metrical paraphrase of the Gospels. Paraphrases from the Gospels by Nicholas Love were approved for reading in 1410 by Archbishop Arundel, who had called Wyclif's work that of the Antichrist and had in 1408 prohibited translation and reading without approval of the bishop.[8] The sixteenth century saw the issuing of numerous books which contained some Scripture in paraphrase.[9] J. Campensis did a Latin paraphrase of

---

[7]Preface, *The Living Bible Paraphrased* (Wheaton, Ill.: Tyndale House, 1971).

[8]Margaret Deanesly, *The Lollard Bible* (Cambridge: University Press, 1920; reprinted 1966), pp. 321-26.

[9]A. W. Pollard and G. R. Redgrave, *A Short Title Catalogue of Books Printed in England, Scotland, & Ireland and of English Books Printed Abroad, 1475-1640* (London: The Bibliographical Society, 1926), nos. 1978, 10902, 23876.

Psalms which was translated into English in 1535.[10] Edward VI ordered in 1547 that a copy of Erasmus' *Paraphrase on the New Testament* should be in every church within a year, and in 1549 Erasmus' book was issued in English.[11] In 1653 Henry Hammond published *A Paraphrase and Annotations upon All the Books of the New Testament*[12] containing the KJV text and the paraphrase side by side. It went through eight editions, the last printed in 1845. There was a paraphrase by three Oxford scholars in 1675, and Richard Baxter published one of the New Testament in 1685. Others appeared in the eighteenth, nineteenth, and twentieth centuries.

One of the major problems in widespread use of a paraphrase lies not in the idea of paraphrase itself but in men's failure to realize its purpose. They then mistakenly treat it as if it were a translation, which it is not intended to be. The glamorous advertising campaign that has accompanied the LB in which it is hailed as one of the most significant translations of our age has not decreased this problem. It has been promoted on television, displayed in supermarkets, and offered free in subscription campaigns.

Another danger—that of theological distortion—is well-stated in the preface to the LB:

> For whenever the author's exact words are not translated from the original languages, there is a possibility that the translator, however honest, may be giving the English reader something that the original writer did not mean to say. This is because a paraphrase is guided not only by the translator's skill in simplifying but also by the clarity of his understanding of what the author meant and by his theology. For when the Greek or Hebrew is not clear, then the theology of the translator is his guide, along with his sense of logic, unless perchance the translation is allowed to stand without any clear meaning at all. The theological lodestar in this book has been the rigid evangelical position.[13]

Is there a place for a paraphrase of the Bible among people who believe in the inspiration of the Bible? Some doubtless will answer this question

---

[10]T. H. Darlow and H. F. Moule, *Historical Catalogue of Printed Editions of the English Bible, 1525-1961*, revised and expanded by A. S. Herbert (London: The British and Foreign Bible Society, 1969), no. 14.

[11]Ibid., nos. 72, 73.

[12]Ibid., no. 640.

[13]Preface, *The Living Bible Paraphrased.*

with an emphatic No. It seems, however, that it is the same kind of question as, "Do we need commentaries on Scripture?" Commentaries are to be used to simplify and clarify Scripture but are not to be confused with it. A speaker may elaborate upon a verse in the light of what he has read in a commentary. Very likely most of the ideas he has on the verse came from commentaries he has read or from comments he has heard, but the impression should not be given that the elaboration is what Scripture actually says. In the same way a paraphrase may suggest clearly the substance of a passage, but it should never be confused with the wording of the passage. A skillfully done paraphrase may be helpful in communicating, but it would be regrettable if a paraphrase were adopted without explanation for the public reading of Scripture.

The Qualities of the Living Bible Paraphrased

The Textual Basis

In evaluating the reliability of a paraphrase, one must know which text is the source of the paraphrase. Taylor, acknowledging that his training in Hebrew and Greek is inadequate for him to work reliably from these languages, has usually chosen to paraphrase the English text of the 1901 (ASV) revision.[14] He states that his work was reviewed by Hebrew and Greek scholars and that the suggestions of his consultants were usually followed.[15] He does not name these scholars.

Had Taylor been content to paraphrase the text of the ASV, he might have blamed any textual shortcomings on those scholars and on what has happened since their day; but he has not consistently followed the ASV in textual questions. Having launched into the sea of textual criticism, he must account to the experts for the choices he has made. His paraphrase has omissions where there is no textual problem involved. For example, names in Numbers 27:1 are omitted. The list of musical instruments (Dan. 3:5, 10) is dropped in favor of "when the band strikes up." The cry "A sword for the Lord" becomes "For the Lord" (Judg. 7:20). There are additions to the text with no manuscript or versional support. For example, "Arabs" is added to a list (Jer. 9:25). Taylor's footnotes to the Old Testament seldom suggest that versions are being followed instead of the Maso-

---

[14]Taylor, interview in "The Story of 'The Living Bible,'" *Eternity* 23 (April 1973): 74.
[15]Preface, *The Living Bible Paraphrased*.

retic text; nevertheless, readings from the versions which were not accepted in the ASV but which now are in vogue among scholars have been introduced into the text. For example, we read "Let's go out into the fields" (Gen. 4:8), "Thus all the people of Egypt became Pharaoh's serfs" (Gen. 47:21); and "Where did you make your raid today?" (I Sam. 27:10). At I Samuel 13:1, a problem text, the LB abandons the conjectural "thirty" of the ASV and reverts to the incorrect suggestion of the KJV—"reigned for one year." A conjectural reading (not in the ASV), "blessings of the grain and flowers" (Gen. 49:26), is accepted without a marginal note. In another case—"sticks his finger in Jehovah's eye" (Zech. 2:8)—the text is corrected, without a note; Jewish tradition held that ancient scribes had modified the text to safeguard God's majesty.

It is not to be concluded that Taylor has consistently upgraded the text of the ASV in keeping with current textual views. He has not followed all the versional variants ordinarily accepted in modern translations. For example, the marginal alternate "pomegranates" (I Kings 7:18), accepted by the RSV over "pillars" of the ASV text, is rejected by the LB. The reading "Zedekiah" (Jer. 27:1; RSV; NEB) is rejected for "Jehoiakim" despite the fact that the context favors "Zedekiah." An occasional reading from the versions not in vogue with scholars is accepted; for example, "Isaac says nothing" (Gen. 27:38). The reading "the eleventh year" is chosen where most other English versions choose "twelfth year" (Ezek. 33:21). Taylor accepts "captains," a marginal reading from the ASV, at I Chronicles 12:18, but rejects the same alternate at I Chronicles 11:11.

In the New Testament Taylor has called attention in the footnotes to many textual variants, but has neither consistently followed the ASV in textual questions nor consistently reverted to the *Textus Receptus*. Taylor's views do not represent the consensus of opinion of modern textual students of either the conservative or the liberal persuasion. There are omissions with no textual support for the omission, such as "first" (Luke 12:1) and "that all might believe through him" (John 1:7). "Churches of Christ" (Rom. 16:16) becomes "all the churches here." Like the ASV, Taylor relegates many verses and phrases found in the *Textus Receptus* to the margin. Agreeing with the ASV and with current textual opinion, he relegates to the notes the close of the Model Prayer (Matt. 6:13), the phrase "and the man who marries a divorced woman commits adultery" (Matt. 19:9), the verse "If any man has ears to hear, let him hear" (Mark 7:16), phrases of Luke 9:55, 56; 23:17; and phrases of Acts 9:5, 6. The LB joins the ASV and other modern texts in omitting, without notation, some material found in the *Textus Receptus*. Examples include the allusion to a prophet (Matt. 27:35), allusion to Sodom and Gomorrah (Mark 6:11), reference to Daniel (Mark 13:14), the phrase "because I go to the Father" (John 16:16), the phrase "of our Lord Jesus Christ" (Eph. 3:14), "and the Lord Jesus Christ" (Col. 1:2), and the heavenly witness passage (I John 5:7-8). In other cases, such as "without cause" (Matt. 5:22) and Acts 15:34, the ASV noted the omission but Taylor did not.

At times, unlike the ASV, Taylor follows a current textual opinion in choosing between variants. His paraphrase "You go on, and I'll come later" (John 7:8) is based on the inclusion from some manuscripts of the word *oupō* ("yet"). He notes that some manuscripts add the reading "many of the wives of the leading men" (Acts 17:4). The reading "God's Son, holds him securely" chooses *auton* as opposed to *heauton* (I John 5:18) and takes "the one begotten" to be Jesus. Following current opinion, Taylor changes "his wrath" to "their anger" (Rev. 6:17).

But then, against the consensus of current textual opinion, Taylor restores to the text verses and phrases that were relegated to the notes by the ASV and the translations made since 1901. He restores Matthew 17:21; 18:11; 23:14; Mark 15:28; John 5:3b-5; and Acts 8:37 to the text with footnotes calling attention to the contrary opinion. Luke 17:36; Acts 24:6b-8a; and Romans 16:24 are restored to the text without a notation of the problem. Contrary to the ASV and current textual opinion, Taylor includes "wife" (Matt. 19:29), "new" (Matt. 26:28; Mark 14:24), "for those who trust in riches" (Mark 10:24), "a rooster crowed" (Mark 14:68), "Joseph" (Luke 2:33), "I must ... be at Jerusalem for the holiday" (Acts 18:21), and "with his blood" (Col. 1:14).

Some words which were included in the ASV have been dropped by Taylor; for example, "oft" (Matt. 9:14), "disciples" (Matt. 26:20), "and drinketh" (Mark 2:16), and "and pray" (Mark 13:33). There are cases where readings cited in the margin of the ASV have been moved into the text: "children" (Matt. 11:19; in the note as the literal rendering), "good" (Matt. 19:16), "Why callest thou me good? None is good ..." (Matt. 19:17), "sprinkle themselves" (Mark 7:4), "they" (Mark 11:19), "don't believe and obey" (John 3:36). In John 3:15 the form of the critical text (ASV margin; RSV text) has been followed, but the change from "in him" to "in me" is without manuscript support.

In textual questions where the evidence between variants is balanced, the LB chooses one alternative without always noting the other. For example, in II Corinthians 8:7, "your . . . love for us" is chosen over "our love for you." There are also cases where the paraphrase has no resemblance to the underlying text. Such a case is I Corinthians 1:15 where the text reads "so no one can say that you were baptized into my name," but the paraphrase is "For now no one can think that I have been trying to start something new, beginning a 'Church of Paul.'"

These samplings, by no means exhaustive, justify the opinion that the LB has not applied sound principles of textual criticism consistently.

Communication

The LB is an imaginative effort to communicate the message of the Bible in the language of today. Its sales success shows that people think they understand what it is saying. The Bible is recast into colloquial speech. Current United States money values are generally used with their British equivalents given in the footnotes (e.g., Acts 19:19). A "denarius" becomes $20.00 (Matt. 20:9). Measures are sometimes made current, but in Ezekiel 45:10ff. we still encounter homer, shekel, bath, ephah, and maneh. Modern time designations are used, such as "nine A.M." where the original text has "third hour" (Acts 2:15) and "December" where the text has "the ninth month" (Jer. 36:9). Place names have usually been modernized, despite the anachronism involved. Thus one reads of "Troas, Turkey" (Acts 20:6) and of "the Turkish province of Ausia" [sic] (Acts 19:10); however, places like Galatia and Phrygia are not so identified.

In Taylor's work the language has been keyed up for impact. Abraham promises the servants that he would "come right back" (Gen. 22:5), and "fire" becomes "the flint for striking a fire" (Gen. 22:6, 7). Job is said to be the "richest cattleman in that entire area" (Job 1:3). "Holy One of God" becomes "holy Son of God" (John 6:69). Exclamation points are abundant. Though graphic, Taylor's work can claim no real literary merit. Quotation of Scripture is sometimes given indirectly (e.g., Matt. 4:4) with no gain in clarity. Rather than reflecting the variety of style of the biblical writers, all Scripture is reduced to Taylor's style of writing. There is an abundant use of "O" in direct address (Mic. 6:3, 5; Ezek. 37:4), which is now used only in religious settings or in conscious archaism. Also, "lest"

244

has passed out of current use.[16] Unlike the translations (KJV; ASV; NASB) where italics are used for items supplied by the translator to complete the sense, Taylor uses italics for emphasis: "*living* water" (John 4:10), "*eternal life*" (I John 2:25), "and we really *are*" (I John 3:1), and "*born again*" (I John 3:9). However, in certain instances italics are also used to indicate phrases that Taylor has supplied, as "*to love one another*" (I John 2:8) and "*for he says we have sinned*" (I John 1:10). No notes are given to guide the reader in interpreting the italics.

Taylor has made no effort to render the Psalms as poetry though elsewhere in his paraphrase some passages, such as the oracles of Balaam (Num. 23–24), are made poetry. This failure is a reversion from current practice and is a definite loss. Psalm 19:7-9 is quite prosaic in the paraphrase when compared with its usual translation. The Song of Solomon is divided up among speakers as though it were drama, a questionable interpretation.

Taylor has at times used the language of the street. One case which has drawn much fire from critics is Saul's epithet for Jonathan, "You son of a bitch!" (I Sam. 20:30). Other examples are, "You illegitimate bastard" (John 9:34) and the statement, "Come to bed with me, my darling" (II Sam. 13:11), which has been labeled "crude."

Other renderings are chatty and unsuited to the material: "kicked me out" (Gen. 26:27), "Hey, who's that girl over there?" (Ruth 2:5), "some drunken bum" (I Sam. 1:16), "The Reluctant Dragon" (Isa. 30:7), "talk is cheap" (Luke 5:23), "Martha was the jittery type" (Luke 10:40), "all mankind scratches for its daily bread" (Luke 12:30), "why pick on me?" (John 7:19), "Barny the Preacher" (Acts 4:36), "Having started the ball rolling" (II Cor. 8:11), "how harsh and rough I can be" (II Cor. 10:2), "phonies" (II Cor. 11:13), "a sneaky fellow" (II Cor. 12:16), and "sweet talk" (Gal. 1:10). To say the least, the page title, "Additives to faith" (II Peter 1), lacks the dignity demanded by the Christian graces.

Taylor has only partly achieved his goal of communication as far as the American reader is concerned. "Corn" is used in its British sense for cereal grains (as KJV; Hos. 2:9), whereas Americans limit the term to Indian maize. One must wonder why Taylor uses "You whitewashed pigpen" (Acts

[16]Keith Crim, review of *The Living Bible Paraphrased*, in *The Bible Translator* 23 (July 1972): 343.

23:3). "Whitewashed wall" evokes a mental image, but most people are not familiar with a "whitewashed pigpen."

Accuracy of the Paraphrase

While Taylor has affirmed that his intention is to be accurate in paraphrasing,[17] and while his work has drawn endorsements of religious leaders like Billy Graham and W. A. Criswell, scholarly notices of his paraphrase have almost without exception been unfavorable.[18] Despite the favorable things that might be said about the LB, reviewers have amply demonstrated that Taylor has not given us "as exactly as possible" what the writers meant; in some details he has not come close to it. Each reviewer has his own list of examples. The task of compiling them suggests the comment made by Thomas More about finding errors in Tyndale's work: "He that should study for that, should study where to find water in the sea."[19]

One may begin with anachronisms. Og's bedstead is kept in a "museum" at Rabbah (Deut. 3:11). To call the Old Testament people "Israelis" (Exod. 9:4; 12:34; 14:20; 19:1; Judg. 7:14; I Sam. 14:21) and their army "the Israeli army" (I Sam. 4:1) is to suppose that there is a connection with the people of the modern state of Israel, a connection which does not exist. The problem becomes more acute in prophecy that could have implications about territorial rights: "But the Lord will have mercy on the Israelis; they are still his special ones. He will bring them back to settle once again in the land of Israel" (Isa. 14:1). Such a paraphrase locks and bars the book from the Arab world. The paraphrase speaks of "young prophets of Bethel seminary" (II Kings 2:3) and of a "summit conference" (Ps. 2:2). For Jonah to call himself "a Jew" (Jonah 1:9; cf. Jer. 33:26; 34:9) anticipates by centuries the use of that term. Another anachronism is "Your words are a flashlight to light the path" (Ps. 119:105). In some settings, instead of "Assyria" and "Assyrian" Taylor speaks of "Iraq" (Isa. 19:23, 25) and "Iraqi" (Isa. 19:23). He also uses "make horoscopes" (Jer. 10:2). Taylor admits in

[17]Taylor, "A Response: Dear Brother Editor," pp. 143-44.

[18]An exception is: William F. Kerr, "*The Living Bible* — Not Just Another Version," *Christianity Today* 19 (May 23, 1975): 29-40; the article has been reprinted and circulated as advertising by the Tyndale House.

[19]Thomas More, *Dialogue* 3.8, reprinted in A. W. Pollard, *Records of the English Bible* (London: Oxford University Press, 1911), p. 127.

a note that his rendering of Matthew 13:52 — "double treasures — from the Old Testament as well as from the New" — is "highly anachronistic." Other examples include "July" for the "fifth month" (Jer. 1:3), "give their support money to the church instead" (Matt. 15:6) for "given to God," "Lord's Day" (I Cor. 16:2) and "Sunday" (Acts 20:7) for the "first day of the week," "the whole Bible" (II Tim. 3:16) for "all scripture" or "every scripture," and "the rabbi of the local synagogue" for "the ruler of the synagogue" (Matt. 9:18; cf. 9:23). Taylor also uses the phrase "eating non-kosher food" (Matt. 15:11, 15) for foods that defile.

Next, one may turn to lapses in historical information. Grain was not threshed with "iron rods" (Amos 1:3). A "tetrarch" was a person of different rank from "a king" (Matt. 14:1). Modern students are in agreement that the Gospels are not "biographies"; yet Luke 1:1 is paraphrased, "Several biographies of Christ have already been written." A person in Palestine would more likely be on a "roof" than on a "porch" (Matt. 24:17). Taylor identifies a quotation which is possibly from a noncanonical source as "God says in the Scriptures" (Eph. 5:14). The addition "with my own eyes I saw Christ dying on the cross" (I Peter 5:1) is in conflict with the Gospels where all the disciples flee (Mark 14:50) and only the beloved disciple was present (John 19:26). "Draw straws" (Jonah 1:7; Acts 1:26), "throwing dice" (Esther 3:7; Matt. 27:35; Mark 15:24), or "tossing the coin" (Prov. 16:33; 18:18) are not particularly good choices when "cast lots" (Lev. 16:8) is elsewhere retained.

Lack of geographical information is evident in the paraphrase "Rabbah and its beautiful harbor are ours" (II Sam. 12:27). Rabbath Ammon is the location of modern Amman, capital of Jordan, and is miles inland from any sea or lake. Nahor's village is placed in Iraq (Gen. 24:10) when actually Haran is in southern Turkey.

Lack of Hebrew knowledge is reflected when the paraphrase informs us that *Samuel* means "asked of God" (I Sam. 1:20) — the name really means "God heard"; that *Seth* means "granted" — it means "put" or "placed"; that *Noah* means "relief" — it means "rest"; that *Edom* means "red stuff" — it merely means "red"; and that *Reuben* means "God noticed my trouble" — it means "Look, a son!" Taylor does not hesitate to have Isaac be "half-blind" (Gen. 27:1). He changes "These are your gods who brought you out of the land of Egypt" to "This is the god" (Exod. 32:4, 8), and then reverts in verse 31 of the chapter to "gods." "Six things — yea, seven," a literary device in Hebrew (Prov. 6:18; cf. 30:15ff.) is missed by Taylor and turned into a statement of absent-mindedness: "There are six things the Lord hates—no, seven!"[20]

A linguistic lapse, perpetuating an error of the KJV and ASV, is encountered in the paraphrase "teacher and guide" for *paedagōgus* (Gal. 3:24; cf. I Cor. 4:15). A papyrus letter demonstrates that the *paedagōgus* and the *didaskalos* (teacher) are two different individuals. "Custodian" would have been a better choice. It is not accurate to make "the Law" to be "the Ten Commandments" (Gal. 3:17); that the term elsewhere becomes "the laws" (Gal. 3:19, 21, 25) is no less misleading. Elizabeth is called Mary's "aunt," but the Greek word merely means "relative" (Luke 1:36), as Taylor's note admits. The margin to "shameful idols" (Exod. 34:13) gives as literal, " 'Asherim.' These were carved statues of male and female genital organs." The explanation is of questionable validity. "Leviathan" becomes "the sea-god" (Ps. 74:14), "a fast" is "to attend the services at the Temple" (Jer. 36:9), and either "illustration" or "hard-to-understand illustration" (Matt. 13:10) is ordinarily used for "parable" (but cf. Matt. 13:35) with resulting impoverishment of the idea.

A great deal of what Taylor has supplied is commentary pure and simple, with no original text to back it. In the effort to attain a contemporary atmosphere, some of Paul's letters are paraphrased to open with "Dear friends" and to close with "Sincerely, Paul." The letters of James and John end similarly. Exceptions to this manner of closing are seen in Philemon which ends with just "Paul" and in Peter's letters which end abruptly with "Peter." The Philippian letter even has a "P.S." composed of the last three verses. The Second Epistle of John is addressed to "Cyria" (II John 1) which is a possible, but not a certain, interpretation of the Greek term *kuria*. The addresses "From: John, The old Elder" (II John 1) and "From: John, the Elder" (III John 1)—both for *presbuteros*—are definitely interpretation. In Greek the name is not given. Taylor has made the Fourth Gospel to be by the "beloved disciple" by inserting the first-person pronoun as the paraphrase for that term (John 13:23-26; 19:26, 27, 35; 20:2-10; 21:2-25). The footnote at John 13:23, "All commentators believe him to be John, the writer of this book," is a false statement.

The additions to the text are inserted in the paraphrase in an inconsistent manner. Sometimes they are bracketed with a footnote (e.g., Rom. 5:13; 7:6; 9:6; II Cor. 7:11; Gal. 2:12). Some carry no notation at all; for

[20]Crim, review of *The Living Bible Paraphrased*, pp. 341-42.

example, the phrase "to find enjoyment" is elaborated, "Well, one thing, at least, is good: it is for a man to eat well, drink a good glass of wine, accept his position in life" (Eccles. 5:18). The phrase "wine, women, and song" (Hos. 4:11) adds "song" from a current saying. "O little town of Bethlehem" (Matt. 2:6) is from the Christmas song. Elaboration gives, "How can a student know more than his teacher? But if he works hard, he may learn as much" (Luke 6:40). Yet another addition without notation that is far from the original writing is: "Don't ever forget the wonderful fact that Jesus Christ was a Man, born into King David's family; and that He was God, as shown by the fact that He rose again from the dead" (II Tim. 2:8). Side comments are thrown in: "only a few would welcome and receive him" (John 1:11) and "For none of us is perfect!" (Gal. 6:5). The comment on the law which speaks of "its rigid demands and merciless justice" (John 1:17) is foreign to the context and to Scripture as a whole. Apollos' sermon is elaborated, " 'The Messiah is coming! Get ready to receive him!' ... and it was a powerful sermon" (Acts 18:26). We are informed that it is fifty miles from the Galilee area to Tyre (Matt. 15:21),[21] that "in the book of Amos' prophecies the Lord God asks ..." (Acts 7:42), and that Apollos had heard about John the Baptist while he was in Egypt (Acts 18:25). A lengthy homiletical expansion is inserted at I Corinthians 7:14:

> For perhaps the husband who isn't a Christian may become a Christian with the help of his Christian wife. And the wife who isn't a Christian may become a Christian with the help of her Christian husband. Otherwise, if the family separates, the children might never come to know the Lord; whereas a united family may, in God's plan, result in the children's salvation.

Still other examples of the many explanatory glosses in the paraphrase include the one where prophets prophesying in the name of Jehovah are called "heathen prophets" (I Kings 22:6). Where the text has "wanderers," Taylor elaborates from the children's song to give "wandering Jews" (Hos. 9:17). "I know him" (*egnōka auton*) is expanded to "I am a Christian; I am on my way to heaven; I belong to Christ" (I John 2:4). "He said to them" becomes "Then, teaching them more about prayer, he used this illustration" (Luke 11:5). "Fishermen" becomes "commercial fishermen"

---

[21]Taylor, "A Response: Dear Brother Editor," p. 143, states that such items will be removed in the next printing.

(Matt. 4:18), and "David" becomes "King David" (Heb. 4:7). "Don't count your chickens before they hatch!" (I Kings 20:11) substitutes a modern proverb for the easily understood "Let not him that girds on his armor boast himself as he that puts it off."

A third group of additions carries a note. Taylor has interpreted his task as a paraphraser to mean that he is free to insert information not given in the text so long as he indicates that it is implied. "Implied" may mean that an item has been inserted in its setting because it occurs somewhere else in Scripture, that it is derived from the history of the period, or that it has been logically deduced. "Implied" may also mean that something has been changed, as when "My father is working still" (John 5:17) becomes "My Father constantly does good." Taylor inserts implied statements in other ways to cover three levels of additions. One group is inserted in brackets in the text. These may be pure comment: "For these promises are only to those who are truly Jews" (Rom. 9:6) or "Don't take the law into your own hands" (Rom. 12:19). A second group is in the text with an accompanying note as when "Samaritan" becomes "despised Samaritan" (Luke 17:15) (but the same addition is also made at John 4:9 without notation). "Mother-in-law" becomes "honored mother-in-law" (Luke 12:53). A third group of implied items is in the text but is accompanied by the literal rendering in the notes. The alleged implied phrase "shown us a different way to heaven" (Rom. 3:21) has literally "a righteousness of God has been manifested." That Jesus "walked the fifty miles to Tyre and Sidon" is said to be implied from the literal "withdrew into the parts of Tyre and Sidon" (Matt. 15:21). Some things said to be implied are not implied at all, such as, "God announced that he would send his Son to earth" (Mark 1:2). The statement is implied neither in Isaiah nor in the context in Mark where it occurs. The alleged implied paraphrase of Hebrews 5:7—that Christ prayed to be saved from a premature death—is not really implied in the passage. Neither was the sprinkling of blood done as a proof of Christ's death (Heb. 9:18). The word "unnecessary" in the phrase "unnecessary work" (Jer. 17:21) is said to be implied, but Taylor does not make the same deduction at Exodus 20:10 or at Deuteronomy 5:14 where his phrase is "work of any kind." The addition "only" cannot be thought implied in Proverbs 10:15—"The rich man's wealth is his only strength."

Taylor has also interpreted his task as one that allows him the greatest liberties as long as he gives the literal rendering in the margin. In many instances these literal renderings are as readable as his paraphrases and are preferable to them. "Nose-ring" (Gen. 24:22) need not become "ear-ring," "two encampments" (Gen. 32:2) become "God's territory," "the sev-enty years" become "these years of slavery" (Jer. 25:12),[22] "said" become "sang" (Luke 2:14), or "I heard the altar cry" become "I heard the angel of the altar say" (Rev. 16:7). In the paraphrase, the literal "to God" becomes "to the church" (Matt. 15:5), the literal phrase "when he sees the children the work of my hands in his midst" becomes the sonorous "when they see the surging birth rate and the expanding economy" (Isa. 29:23), and "eat, drink, and be merry" (Luke 12:19) becomes "wine, women, and song." The literal "Not many (of you) should become masters (teachers)" (James 3:1) becomes, "Don't be too eager to tell others their faults." "Having a form of godliness" (II Tim. 3:5) is "they will go to church." "The Pharisees sit on Moses' seat" becomes "You would think . . . these Pharisees were Moses, the way they keep on making up so many laws!" (Matt. 23:2). "The stars shall fall" becomes "seem to fall" (Matt. 24:29). Figures of speech like "bridegroom" (Matt. 9:15) or "king" (Matt. 25:34) that may refer to the Christ are paraphrased to the first-person pronoun, "I." The "strong man" (Matt. 12:29) becomes "Satan"; and the statement "produces a crop many times greater than the amount planted—thirty, sixty, or even a hundred times as much" (Matt. 13:23) becomes "goes out and brings thirty, sixty, or even a hundred others into the Kingdom." "This is the law and the prophets" becomes "This is the teaching of the laws of Moses in a nutshell" (Matt. 7:12). "Moses and the prophets" becomes "the Scriptures" (Luke 16:29), but is unchanged in Luke 16:31. "Your right eye" becomes "your best eye" (Matt. 5:29). "Blessed is he who comes in the name of the Lord" becomes "God's Man is here" (Matt. 21:9), and "I know you not" becomes "It is too late" (Matt. 25:12). Encountering either the marginal note "im-plied" or "literal" should put the reader of the LB on the alert that liberties have been taken with the text.

Questionable Interpretation

The list of passages in which Taylor has missed the proper interpretation is long indeed. Taylor tends to make corrections in the text to alleviate problems. For example, "Zedekiah" (Jer. 27:3) is omitted without a note, likely because its presence creates problems with "Jehoiakim" which oc-

---

[22]In a note to Daniel 9:2, Taylor refers the reader to this verse as the place where Jeremiah had spoken of seventy years, but actually, he has paraphrased the "seventy" away.

curs in verse one. In II Samuel 21:19, Elhanan is said to kill the "brother of Goliath," in order to harmonize the passage with I Chronicles 20:5 and probably to relieve possible tension with the story of David and Goliath. Second Samuel 24:1 is softened by omitting the phrase "he incited" because of tension with I Chronicles 21:1. Where the Hebrew (and the ASV) has a difficult "forty years" (II Sam. 15:7), Taylor follows the Lucianic Septuagint, Syriac, and Josephus in reading "four years," but has no footnote to the verse. The details of Sisera's death are omitted (Judg. 5:27), likely because of problems with statements of Judges 4:21. "He restores my failing health" (Ps. 23:3) is hardly satisfactory as a paraphrase for "he restores my soul." That our "altar" is "the cross where Jesus was sacrificed" (Heb. 13:10) is questionable. The problem of interpretation of I Corinthians 7:36ff. —whether daughter or fiancée is being spoken of—is solved by omitting altogether the perplexing word *parthenos* ("virgin"). The passage is then made a general permission to marry.

Other changes are notable. "One of his father's wives" (Deut. 27:20) introduces an idea of polygamy that is not in the text; "bread, peas, and stew" (Gen. 25:34) would have been accurate were it "bread and pea stew." Taylor inserts the correction that the Sabbath is "a holy day to be used to worship Jehovah" (Exod. 35:2). He changes the disciples' request, "teach us to pray," to "teach us a prayer to recite" (Luke 11:1). By recasting a statement from singular to plural, Taylor makes Jeremiah 22:10 speak of the captives in general instead of Jehoahaz in particular.

It is not possible to explain how one can arrive at "My Spirit must not forever be disgraced in man" from the Hebrew word *yadhon* (Gen. 6:3). Isaiah 14 has the page heading "Lucifer—fallen from heaven," and the text then perpetuates the translation "Lucifer" for *Helel ben-shachar* (v. 12), inviting the reader to suppose the chapter involves the fall of the devil when it really discusses the descent of the King of Babylon to Sheol. For Isaiah to describe himself as "a foul-mouthed sinner" (Isa. 6:5) conveys a different idea from that implied in "a man of unclean lips."

Taylor has introduced changes in import where no paraphrase was needed: "in all that land" (Matt. 9:31) becomes "all over the town"; "kissed" (Matt. 26:49) becomes "embraced him in friendly fashion."

In the Old Testament, christological interpretation is reflected in all traditional places: "the Sun of Righteousness" will rise with healing in his wings (Mal. 4:2), "the Desire of All Nations" shall come to this Temple (Hag. 2:7), and "the future splendor of this Temple will be greater than the splendor of the first one!" (Hag. 2:8). A footnote explains that this comes through Christ's visiting the temple. Isaiah 9:6 has the traditional five names where the linguistic parallel demands that each name be of two elements; hence, the first must be "Wonderful Counselor," not "Wonderful, Counselor."

In those cases where more than one interpretation of a passage is possible, the paraphrase has given only one and the reader would not be aware of the other. For example, "like Adam" (Hos. 6:7; KJV; ASV) is possible; but many scholars prefer identification with a place rather than a person, and thus render the passage "at Adam." "She shall be saved in childbearing" (I Tim. 2:15) becomes "he will save their souls." "Can two walk together unless they be agreed?" (Amos 3:3) becomes "For how can we walk together with your sins between us?"

Variety in Paraphrase

Taylor has used speaker identifications in some sections, as for example, in Genesis 27 which deals with Isaac's blessing of Jacob; but he does not use them in a narrative like that of the Book of Ruth or in most of the exchanges in the Old Testament. The preface of the LB lists a group of words, including the word "saint," which it claims are particularly in need of paraphrasing. "Saint" is most frequently rendered "God's people"; almost as often it is rendered "Christians." Sometimes it is "believers." One is then shocked to encounter "saints" in a number of other passages (Zech. 14:5; Acts 26:10; II Thess. 1:10; Rev. 14:12; 18:24). To have Paul persecute "saints" in Acts 26:10, but persecute "believers" in the parallel account of Acts 9:13, 32, 41 baffles the reader. If "saint" needs paraphrasing, then what about the passages in which it is allowed to stand?

Equally capricious is the treatment of the phrase which the KJV readers knows as "sons of Belial." The paraphrase has "worthless rabble" (Deut. 13:13), "sex perverts" (Judg. 19:22), "evil men" (Judg. 20:13), "drunken bum" (I Sam. 1:16) for "daughter of Belial," "stubborn lout" (I Sam. 25:17), "bad-tempered boor" (I Sam. 25:25), "ruffians" (I Sam. 30:22), "scoundrel" (II Sam. 16:7; cf. I Kings 21:10), "hot-head" (II Sam. 20:1), "godless" (II Sam. 23:6), "men who had no conscience" (I Kings 21:13), and "worthless rebels" (II Chron. 13:7). This epithet occurring sixteen times in the Old Testament is paraphrased twelve different ways.

The kiss of the sinful woman (Luke 7:45) and of Judas (Luke 22:48) need no paraphrase, but the "holy kiss" becomes "shake hands warmly." Though foot washing is alluded to in the Old Testament (Gen. 24:32;

253

43:24), though Jesus alludes to the washing of feet in his rebuke of Simon (Luke 7:44) and washes the feet of his disciples (John 13:5), the LB completely omits the washing of the saints' feet as a qualification of a needy widow (I Tim. 5:10).

The LB does not always attempt to harmonize the paraphrase of identical phrases that occur in more than one setting. It renders one of the commandments "You must not murder" in Exodus 20:13 and Deuteronomy 5:17. The same commandment reads "Don't kill" in the New Testament (Matt. 19:18; Mark 10:19), which could be an entirely different idea. In James 2:11 it reverts to "murder." "We ask that your kingdom will come now" (Matt. 6:10) and "send your Kingdom soon" (Luke 11:2) are from identical Greek phrases. "Boils" (I Sam. 5:6) and "tumors" (I Sam. 6:5) are alternates of the same word in similar settings. "Son, your sins are forgiven" (Mark 2:5) and "son! . . . I have forgiven your sins" (Matt. 9:2; cf. Luke 5:20) are also identical Greek phrases.

In successive verses God makes an "everlasting covenant" (Gen. 17:13) with Abraham, but those who do not keep it have broken a "contract" (Gen. 17:14). In Exodus we again read of a "covenant" (Ex. 24:7). In the New Testament "Scripture" (II Cor. 3:14), "agreement" (Heb. 9:1, 18, 20; 10:16), "ark of the covenant" (Heb. 9:4), "old system" (Heb. 9:15), and "will" (Heb. 9:16, 17) are used. "Will" is satisfactory in these last verses, for here *diathēkē* is used differently. The reader finds "new contract" in Jeremiah 31:31; but when the same passage is cited in Hebrews 8:8, it is "new agreement."

In Amos 9:11 one reads, "Then, at that time, I will rebuild the City of David, which is now lying in ruins, and return it to its former glory." The Hebrew text says nothing about the City of David; it is referring to the dynasty of David. When the passage is cited in the New Testament, it is "Afterwards [says the Lord], I will return and renew the broken contract with David" (Acts 15:16). The same sort of difference in wording is seen in Psalm 2 and its citation in Acts 4:25, 26 and Hebrews 1:5, so that no one could see the connection between the two. There is no resemblance between Psalm 16 and Peter's citation of it in Acts 2:25-28, and there is little resemblance between Joel 2:28-32 and Peter's citation on Pentecost in Acts 2:17-21.

The familiar statement about "salt of the earth" (Matt. 5:13) is "You are the world's seasoning," but in Mark 9:50 (cf. Luke 14:34) it is "Good salt is worthless if it loses its saltiness."

"Pastor" is used in some places for *presbuteros* (I Tim. 3:1; 5:17, 19); but I Peter 5:1 has "elder," and Titus 1:5, though using "pastor," has the footnote: "More literally 'elders.'" When *poimēn* ("pastor" or "shepherd") actually occurs in Greek (Eph. 4:11), Taylor paraphrases it "shepherd." In Exodus 14:3 we have "Israelites," but 14:5 has "Israelis," and at 14:26 we are back to "Israelites." Beelzebub is paraphrased as "Satan" (Matt. 12:24, 27), but then in the same context "Satan" from *satanas* is also retained. The phrase "You have heard it was said" becomes "the laws of Moses said" (Matt. 5:27), "the law of Moses says" (Matt. 5:33, 38), and "there is a saying" (Matt. 5:43).

Acts 20:7 reads, "On Sunday we gathered for a communion service," but the footnote explains: "'on Saturday night.' Literally, 'the first day of the week,' by Jewish reckoning, from sundown to sundown." However, I Corinthians 16:2 is "on every Lord's Day." Elsewhere the Greek phrase *mia tōn sabbatōn* is "Sunday" (Matt. 28:1; Luke 24:1; John 20:1), except that it is dropped completely in Mark 16:2 and John 20:19. Perhaps the practice will be judged by some as less objectionable than that of the NEB which puts "Saturday night" in the text of Acts 20:7. Is "Sunday" really clearer than "the first day of the week"? Why do we need the variety "Lord's Day" and "Sunday" for the same phrase?

There is no relationship between the number of times a word or expression occurs in the Greek or Hebrew texts and the number of times that Taylor uses it. For example, the word "Christian" appears three times in the New Testament, but is used many times (Gal. 1:1, 13, 22; 2:4; 3:3; I John 2:4, 5, 6; Jude 1; etc.) in Taylor's paraphrase. "Your church" and "our churches" are not in the New Testament at all, but are often used by Taylor. The Law becomes "the Ten Commandments" (Gal. 3:17) or "the laws" (Gal. 3:19). No distinction is made in the paraphrase between "hades," the state of the dead (cf. Luke 16:23; Acts 2:27), and "hell," the final place of punishment for the wicked; in the KJV both are "hell." The page heading for Luke 16 is "The rich man in Hell," and the text has "[the rich man's] soul went into hell" (Luke 16:22). Jesus' soul is not left in "hell" (Acts 2:27).

A key phrase like "son of man" becomes in the Old Testament "a Man— or so he seemed to be" (Dan. 7:13), "mere puny man" (Ps. 8:4), and "son of dust" (Ezek. 4:1; 5:1; 15:1; 16:1; etc.). In the New Testament the phrase is used solely by Jesus except for Acts 7:56 and occurrences in the Book of Revelation. It is paraphrased thirteen ways, including: "Son of mankind,"

"I, the Son of Mankind," "Messiah," "I," "Me," "My," "Mine," "He," and "Him." "Son of Man" is retained only at John 5:27, Revelation 1:13, and Revelation 14:14; elsewhere the literal phrase is relegated to the footnotes. While the meaning of the phrase "Son of Man" as used by Jesus is disputed, scholars generally agree that its intent was to conceal Jesus' messiahship rather than openly to reveal it. The LB has missed the interpretation of this phrase in its tendency to strengthen claims of Jesus' divinity beyond those actually made in the Greek text. Additional evidences of this tendency are "his Son" inserted at Mark 1:2, "Son of God" at Mark 1:24, and the choice of "When you call me good . . ." at Matthew 19:17. The variant "Why do you ask me about the good?" is not noted in the LB, but textual scholars favor it as the proper reading. Taylor justifies his use of "Messiah" for "Son of Man" by contending that in the first century they were synonymous terms.[23] Even if this is granted, confusion results when *messias* (John 1:41) is also paraphrased as "messiah." Had the two terms been synonymous, the Holy Spirit need not have inspired use of both of them. Actually, in the Greek New Testament direct claims of messiahship on the part of Jesus are few. In the LB they are abundant. These examples, which are not at all exhaustive of the problem, suffice to show that Taylor has done his work capriciously rather than carefully.

Theological Questions

Taylor acknowledges the dangers of theological distortion in a paraphrase, but insists that it was not his intent to advance a particular theological position.[24] Nevertheless, one must insist that whether intentionally or unintentionally, consciously or unconsciously, Taylor has fallen into theological traps. One may be willing to grant that Taylor thinks the biblical writers intended to expound the ideas he expounds, but one must assert that his interpretations are often incorrect.

The notes are not entirely reliable. The comment that "man" (*'adam*) is literally "men" (Gen. 1:26) is not true. God did not create men; he created one man.

The paraphrase tends to heighten the miraculous.[25] The word "miracle," not in the original, is inserted at John 10:32. Jesus is said to "read their

---

[23]Taylor, "A Response: Dear Brother Editor," p. 143.
[24]Ibid.
[25]Robert C. Bowman, "*The Living Bible* — A Critique," *Brethren Life and Thought* 18 (Summer 1973): 139.

minds" (Mark 2:8) and to supply missing arms and legs (Matt. 15:31). Neither English nor Greek supports this interpretation. Unsound members were healed; new ones were not created. The angel Gabriel "appeared" and "disappeared" (Luke 1:28, 38). Jesus is to be judged by his miracles (John 10:37), whereas the expression "works of my Father" need not be so limited.

The LB clearly expounds the doctrine of original sin: "When Adam sinned, sin entered the entire human nature. His sin spread death throughout all the world, so everything began to grow old and die, for all sinned" (Rom. 5:12). Psalm 51:5 reads, "But I was born a sinner, yes, from the moment my mother conceived me." Ephesians 2:3 reads, "We started out bad, being born with evil natures, and were under God's anger just like everyone else."

There are also problems concerning the time of regeneration. Colossians 3:1 reads, "Since you became alive again, so to speak, when Christ arose from the dead, now set your sights on the rich treasures and joys of heaven where he sits beside God in the place of honor and power." Romans 6:4-5 states, "Your old sin-loving nature was buried with him by baptism when he died, and when God the Father, with glorious power, brought him back to life again, you were given his wonderful new life to enjoy. For you have become a part of him, and so you died with him, so to speak, when he died [note: Literally, 'united with him in the likeness of his death']; and now you share his new life, and shall rise as he did."

One detects a note of antilegalism when "freedom" is expanded by the phrase in brackets "from trying to be saved by keeping the laws of God" (II Cor. 3:17) which the paraphrase insists the text implies. Can one be saved without keeping the laws of God? Can the laws be kept without trying to keep them? Further evidence turns up in the phrase "for it was through reading the Scripture that I came to realize that I could never find God's favor by trying—and failing—to obey the laws. I came to realize that acceptance with God comes by believing in Christ" (Gal. 2:19). Taylor avoids occurrences of *nomos* and uses "Jewish laws" (Acts 18:15; 21:24; 25:8), "Jewish customs and ceremonies" (Acts 15:5), "Jewish traditions and customs" (Acts 21:20), "Jewish beliefs" (Acts 23:29), and "the laws of Moses" (Acts 6:13). "Law" is omitted in the series of Matthew 23:23; the paraphrase does not have Jesus mention it in Luke 24:44; and at Acts 28:23 "law" becomes "the five books of Moses." Taylor declares that "Moses gave us only the Law" (John 1:17). "The curse of the law" becomes "the doom of that impossible system" (Gal. 3:13). Instead of "legal demands" (Col. 2:14) we read "this list of sins"; instead of "the law of the Spirit of life" (Rom. 8:2) we read, "the power of the life-giving Spirit." "Born under the law" becomes "born as a Jew" (Gal. 4:4).

The paraphrase eliminates the name "Cephas" and uses only "Peter" for this disciple (John 1:42; I Cor. 1:12; 3:22; 9:5; Gal. 2:9). An unnecessary gloss is inserted on Peter's name: "You are Peter, a stone; and upon this rock I will build my church" (Matt. 16:18). Though "stone" is different from "rock," what uninstructed reader will notice it? Had Taylor said in John 1:42, "Peter (which means rock)" he would have avoided a possible misunderstanding.

Though it is said that Taylor is a premillennialist, not a dispensationalist,[26] support for both of these positions is given by his capitalizations in the phrase "the Great Tribulation" (Rev. 7:14). Further encouragement can be found in the paraphrase of II Timothy 4:1: "who will some day judge the living and the dead when he appears to set up his kingdom." This rendering conflicts with I Corinthians 15:24ff. where Jesus renders up the kingdom to God at his coming. Elsewhere, the paraphrase does speak of the redeemed "brought into the kingdom of his dear Son" (Col. 1:13). "In the last days Jerusalem and the Temple of the Lord will become the world's greatest attraction" (Isa. 2:2) is a distortion, as is "For in those days the whole world will be ruled by the Lord from Jerusalem. He will issue his laws and announce his decrees from there" (Mic. 4:2; cf. 5:3). The rendering of Ezekiel 37:28 is slanted in the same direction. It is suggested that Hebrew is the pure speech with which the returning people will serve the Lord (Zech. 3:8). The paraphrase "then all Israel will be saved" (Rom. 11:26) makes a temporal statement out of what is really a statement of manner, "in this way all Israel will be saved." Further eschatological difficulty is encountered when "this generation shall not pass away until all these things be accomplished" (Mark 13:30; cf. Matt. 24:14) becomes "Yes, these are the events that will signal the end of the age."

The LB expounds the idea that God had to be turned from his wrath in order to save sinners: "God sent Christ Jesus ... to end all God's anger against us" (Rom. 3:25). Several passages set forth the idea of a direct communication of the Holy Spirit. Romans 8:16 says, "For his Holy Spirit speaks to us deep in our hearts, and tells us that we really are God's

---

[26]Kerr, *"The Living Bible*—Not Just Another Version," p. 32.

children." Galatians 5:16 states, "I advise you to obey only the Holy Spirit's instructions. He will tell you where to go and what to do, and then you won't always be doing the wrong things your evil nature wants you to." First John 5:7-8 speaks of "the voice of the Holy Spirit in our hearts." And in I Corinthians 2:14 we read, "Only those who have the Holy Spirit within them can understand what the Holy Spirit means." In the paraphrase the Spirit is made to operate mysteriously: "We do not know on whom he will next bestow this life from heaven" (John 3:8).

The teaching of "faith only" is stated: "for Abraham found favor with God by faith alone, *before he was circumcised*" (Rom. 4:12). That statement cannot be harmonized with James 2:21-24. "That a man is justified by faith apart from the works of the law" (Rom. 3:28) becomes "So it is that we are saved by faith in Christ and not by the good things we do." The statement "to those who received him, who believed in his name, he gave power to become children of God" becomes "But to all who received him, he gave the right to become children of God. All they needed to do was to trust him to save them. All those who believe this are reborn ..." (John 1:12, 13).

The LB reflects belief in salvation before baptism. John's baptism is "a public announcement of their decision to turn their backs on sin" (Mark 1:4; cf. Luke 3:3)—hardly equivalent to "for the remission of sins." "In baptism we show that we have been saved from death and doom by the resurrection of Christ" (I Peter 3:21); the more literal rendering "baptism ... saves you" has been relegated to a footnote. A note explains that in the phrase "born of water and the Spirit" (John 3:5), "born of water" means the normal process observed during every human birth.

Wives are exhorted "Fit in with your husbands' plans" (I Peter 3:1), which may be pleasing to the women's liberation movement but is far from what Peter actually said.

In these various cases Taylor has given the paraphrase a turn which makes it say something different from that which the original writers meant. The authors are right; Taylor is wrong.

Conclusion

The remarkable popularity of the LB loudly proclaims a message that those who love the cause of the Lord but champion the exclusive use of the KJV and/or the ASV should be hearing. The masses of people not conditioned by a lifetime of study to the archaisms of these versions have a deep hunger for a translation they can easily read and understand—a hunger so urgent that they, the blind led by the blind, grasp at broken reeds like the LB.

A review which focuses on problems tends to overlook the hundreds of passages in the LB where familiar phrases remain unchanged in meaning and many other passages where the paraphrasing is excellent. Lengthy, complex sentences are broken into simple ones. Most of the vocabulary is contemporary. The material in general is presented in an exciting style. Gripping phrases are used, such as "rotting stench" (Joel 2:20) for "stench and ill savor." Prophets are accused of being "windbags full of words with no divine authority" (Jer. 5:13), man at creation became "a living person" (Gen. 2:7), "worthless food" becomes "insipid manna" (Num. 21:5). "It is what you *say* and *think* that makes you unclean" (Matt. 15:11) is an exact, clear statement. Despite its omission of some items in the original, the paraphrase "For you tithe down to the last mint leaf in your garden, but ignore the important things" (Matt. 23:23) is close to the general thought of the passage.

Though the LB is easy reading and provides the general outline of the biblical story, it is not sufficiently reliable to be useful for serious study by any person who is concerned over details of what the Word of God says either in historical matters or in doctrinal matters. One might take Taylor's advice: "For study purposes, a paraphrase should be checked against a rigid translation."[27] The person who is unable to make detailed comparison of the paraphrases with the original Hebrew, Aramaic, and Greek statements can never be certain that he is not being misled.

[27]Taylor, quoted in S. Kubo and W. Specht, *So Many Versions?* (Grand Rapids: Zondervan, 1975), p. 190; Frederick A. Rusch, "Living with *The Living Bible*," *Currents in Theology and Mission* 2 (1975): 280-81.

12

The Good News Bible
(Today's English Version)

The New Testament of The Good News Bible, under the name Good News for Modern Man, prepared in two and a half years' work by Robert G. Bratcher with the aid of the Translations Department and members of the Translations Committee of the American Bible Society, was issued September 15, 1966. It was the first translation of the New Testament into English prepared by that Society.[1] The impetus for Today's English Version arose out of the success of the Version Popular, the Spanish translation, which, though prepared for the Indians of Latin America, proved more popular among those living in the cities than it did among the Indians.

The innovative cover decoration of the paperbound TEV uses the mastheads of leading newspapers throughout the world to call attention to the fact that it is as easy to read as the newspaper. At first a copy sold for

---

[1]Robert G. Bratcher, "Good News for Modern Man," *The Bible Translator* 17 (1966): 159-72; 18 (1967): 127-28; "The Nature and Purpose of the New Testament in *Today's English Version,*" *The Bible Translator* 22 (July 1971): 105-7.

twenty-five cents. Later, the price was raised to sixty cents (the printing costs), but even then it remained a book bargain. In the first three years, twelve million copies were sold, surpassing all records for paperback book sales.[2] By 1976 more than fifty-two million copies had been sold.[3] Catholic authorities granted imprimaturs for it, opening the way for its use by Catholics.[4]

In the light of the early success of the New Testament, a committee composed of seven men was formed to prepare the Old Testament. Their work began in September 1967. The committee was comprised of Robert G. Bratcher, chairman; Roger A. Bullard; Keith R. Crim; Herbert G. Grether; Barclay M. Newman; Heber F. Peacock; and John A. Thompson. All held doctorates and all except one had foreign missionary experience. From R. Kittel's *Biblia Hebraica*, 3rd ed., in consultation with the ancient versions, one scholar would draft a translation of a book for which he was responsible. He also supplied explanatory notes setting forth reasons for particular choices. Other members of the committee made their comments on the translator's draft, and these comments were weighed by the translator. The committee then met for face-to-face consideration of each line, verse, and punctuation mark. Finally the copy was read aloud to evaluate the impression it made on the listener. The draft was then sent to over two hundred translators and consultants throughout the world for their suggestions. Later, with consideration given to suggestions received, the copy went through another review comparable to the first. The text was next submitted to eight Bible specialists representing seven different religious groups. It was then reviewed for English style. Finally it was reviewed by the Translations Committee of the American Bible Society.[5]

As the work progressed, some trial books of the Old Testament (Psalms, Job, Proverbs, Ecclesiastes, Jonah, Hosea, Amos, and Micah) were released at intervals after 1970. The completed Bible, with the fourth edition of the New Testament included, was issued in 1976, nine years after the beginning of the project. William Collins Sons & Co., Ltd., a British

[2]Carroll Stuhlmueller, "Probings into the Mystery of the Text," *The Bible Today* 58 (February 1972): 657.

[3]G. E. Jones, "Another 'Readable' Bible, But Is It Any Better?" *U.S. News & World Report* 81 (December 20, 1976): 54; Eugene A. Nida, *Good News for Everyone* (Waco, Texas: Word Books, 1977), p. 115.

[4]Stuhlmueller, "Probings into the Mystery of the Text," p. 657.

[5] Herbert G. May, "Good News for All People Everywhere," *Interpretation* 32 (April 1978): 187-88.

publisher, sponsored the translation of the Apocrypha.[6] The Bible Society included these books in a complete Bible in 1979.

Not a revision of previous English translations, the GNB attempts to set forth the biblical content and message in standard, everyday English just as the New Testament was originally written in Koine Greek, the language of the first-century common man. With the non-Christian reader in mind, the GNB is pitched at the elementary school reading level.[7] It is aimed at all who use English as a means of communication, whether as an acquired language or as a native language in which they have little formal education.[8] The GNB strives to give the reader a maximum understanding of the contents of the original texts, trusting that he may find a saving hope through its message. Though no artificial limit was set on the range of vocabulary—to make what is understood as "a simplified translation"[9]—words have been avoided that are not in common use. With "clarity of meaning" placed above "literary form," the GNB uses clear, simple, unambiguous language in a style natural to English. A British edition seeks to remove features natural to Americans but strange to the British. Insisting that the aim of translation is not to teach the reader Hebrew or Greek but to communicate with him, the translators have made no effort to maintain the sentence structure, parts of speech, order of words, and grammatical devices of the original language.[10] The GNB is to be classified as a common-language, Dynamic Equivalence translation, less paraphrastic than the work of J. B. Phillips but more paraphrastic than any of the productions included in this study with the exception of the LB. Since its aim is not primarily for advanced study by the serious student of the Bible, the GNB regularly needs checking with more technical translations in the light of the original texts.

Format

The GNB supplies the reader with a brief introduction and outline to each of the biblical books. These notes are descriptive in nature, generally

[6]R. C. Fuller, "Today's Bible," *Scripture Bulletin* 7 (Winter 1976-77): 28.

[7]Ibid., pp. 27-28.

[8]Edward B. Fiske, "New Testament Is Made Simpler," *The Bible Society Record* 111 (October 1966): 145.

[9]Ibid.; Bratcher, "Good News for Modern Man," pp. 159ff.; Bratcher, "Nature and Purpose," pp. 97-107.

[10]Euan Fry, "The Good News Bible Translation Principles," *The Bible Translator* 28 (October 1977): 410; Bratcher, "Good News for Modern Man," pp. 159-60.

avoiding critical and theological speculation on matters of authorship, date, and unity of the books. However, the introduction to the Song of Songs, though calling the book "love poems," recognizes that both Jews and Christians have at times interpreted these poems allegorically. A three-fold division of material in the Book of Isaiah is recognized, and chapters 40-55 are said to be exilic. Dates are suggested for the Minor Prophets. Joel is assigned to the fifth or fourth century. The Book of Zechariah is divided into two sections.

Notes refer the reader to a "Word List" at the end of the Bible, which supplies definitions of a selected list of words used. Additional helps are a "Chronology of the Bible," a series of maps with an "Index" to them, and a "Subject Index" for the Bible (using pages rather than chapters and verses), aiding in the location of important subjects.

Titles are supplied for the books; unfortunately, that of the last book is "The Revelation to John" rather than "of John." The text of the GNB is printed in double columns with the material paragraphed into thought units. Verses are indicated by elevated Arabic numerals within the line. Factual subject headings in boldface type have been supplied throughout. Parallel passages may be noted beneath these headings. Various Psalms have headings, but the traditional headings handed down in the Hebrew manuscripts are relegated to the footnotes (e.g., Ps. 60, 62, 63, etc.). The musical notation "Selah" has been omitted throughout. Speaker identifications, "The Man" and "The Woman," are supplied in the Song of Songs. By conjecture, speakers are suggested at Job 24:18; 26:5; 27:13-23, but Job 28 is left without a speaker. The accompanying note would be more accurate if it had "sometimes assigned" to the speaker rather than "usually assigned." Unfortunately, the heading at Romans 1:18 removes the force of *gar* ("for") in the text, and that of Romans 5:12 obscures rather than clarifies the argument being made in the book. These headings are the same as those in the UBS Greek text.[11] Lists of material and of persons are printed in tabular form (e.g., I Kings 4:1ff; Ezra 2:3ff; Neh. 7:8ff.). Quotation marks are used to indicate direct address. Italics, not used in the traditional way to indicate words supplied by the translators to complete the sense, are used for emphasis (I Kings 20:11; I Cor. 15:27; 16:21; Philem. 19), to indicate titles of source materials (e.g., II Kings 8:23; etc.),

[11]Frederick W. Danker, review of *Good News for Modern Man: The New Testament in Today's English Version*, trans. R. G. Bratcher in *CBQ* 29 (April 1967): 258.

and to transliterate Aramaic words (Mark 5:41; 15:34). Poetic material is printed in poetic lines, as are certain New Testament passages (Luke 1:46ff., 68ff., 2:29ff.; Phil. 2:6ff.; I Tim. 3:16; II Tim. 2:11ff.; etc.) that have a poetic quality.

The Bible Society's policy of publishing Scripture without note or comment was changed in 1967.[12] The notes accompanying the text of the GNB supply cultural (Josh. 14:2; Lev. 19:29) and historical (Acts 12:1) information to help the reader understand the text (cf. Exod. 4:25), call attention to departures from Masoretic text whether the recourse is to one of the ancient versions (indicated by "One/Some ancient translation") or to conjectural emendation (indicated by "Probable text"; e.g., Gen. 49:26), give alternate renderings (e.g., Gen. 28:14; Deut. 7:20; Rom. 3:9a), or give references to passages where identical or similar material is to be found. This last group includes cross-references to echoes of Old Testament material within the New Testament and New Testament references back to the Old Testament. Notes like that commenting on "Red Sea" (Exod. 13:18) and that on "ephod" (Exod. 25:7) should help the reader. Notes explain terms like "mandrakes" (Gen. 30:14), "Freedmen" (Acts 6:9), and "usual way" (Rom. 9:8) which the reader would not know; explain a paraphrase of a term whose literal meaning the reader would not grasp (e.g., Ezek. 18:17); and explain customs (e.g., Gen. 24:2; Exod. 29:37).

Unlike most translations, which use no illustrations, the GNB contains five hundred line drawings by a Swiss-born artist, Mlle. Annie Vallotton, illustrating various biblical motifs.[13] The illustrations are intended to draw the reader to the texts. When such drawings first appeared in the New Testament, they provoked both vigorous disapproval and enthusiastic approbation. One might be reminded that the KJV had illustrations in the 1611 edition, and its mythological illustrations such as that of Neptune taming the sea horses, found at the beginning of the Gospel of Matthew, could under no circumstances be called appropriate for a Bible. The illustrations of the GNB cannot be said to be unsuitable in this way; rather, they communicate the essence of the episode to the reader whatever his level of culture may be. Maps dispersed through the text should further aid the reader.

[12]C. E. B. Cranfield, "Are Annotated Bibles Desirable?" *The Churchman* 82 (Winter 1968): 290-96; Cranfield, "A Reply to Mr. Bradnock," *The Churchman* 83 (Spring 1969): 28-30; W. J. Bradnock, "Mr. Cranfield and Annotated Bibles," *The Churchman* 83 (Spring 1969): 21-27.

[13]"Annie Vallotton," *Bible Society Record* 113 (July-August 1968): 86.

The Text

The Old Testament of the GNB is rendered basically from the third edition and notes of R. Kittel's *Biblia Hebraica*;[14] however, now that the *Biblia Hebraica Stuttgartensia* has been published, future editions of the GNB will likely show modifications in its light. In the GNB, the Hebrew words have been divided differently at times from the Masoretic text. Also at times vowels other than those of the Masoretic text have been followed. Variants supported by one or more Hebrew manuscripts may have been followed. Septuagintal or other versional readings have been chosen where they are deemed superior to the Masoretic text, and in some difficult cases conjectural readings are followed. Notes usually call attention to such cases. For example, Psalm 2:12 offers a conjectural "bow down to him" and relegates "kiss the Son" to the notes. The above mentioned procedures are standard in translation; however, the individual cases where they are applied are open to debate. In the GNB I Samuel 13:1, a defective verse in the Masoretic text, is dropped to the notes. Emendations are frequent, some (Ps. 87:4; 92:11) occurring without warning in the notes. The numeral "thirty" (Prov. 22:20) is supplied without notation. Rearrangement of the text is less frequent than in the NEB. In a few cases where the RSV emended the text, the GNB stays with the Masoretic text. Such a case is the reading "Ashdod" (Amos 3:9). One reviewer, generally critical of the GNB, points out that in the Psalms the GNB follows the Masoretic text more closely than the RSV does.[15]

An examination of the notes reveals that readings from the versions are frequently preferred to those of the Masoretic text, but the particular version followed is not identified in the various cases. Neither has Dead Sea Scroll evidence been identified. Conjectural correction of the Masoretic text has been frequent. There are more places in the GNB where the Hebrew text is said to be unclear than in most English translations.

In its New Testament text, except for a few passages, most of which Bratcher has been kind enough to list and to defend,[16] the GNB followed the second edition of the United Bible Societies' Greek text modified in

---

[14]Fry, "*The Good News Bible* Translation Principles," pp. 408-12.

[15]J. Judd Jackson, review of *Psalms for Modern Man*, in *Interpretation* 26 (January 1972): 95-96.

[16]Robert G. Bratcher, "The T.E.V. New Testament and the Greek Text," *The Bible Translator* 18 (October 1967): 167-74.

the light of the third edition of that text. Differences from the UBS text result in the renderings: "the daughter of Herodias" (Mark 6:22), "already" (Mark 15:44), "the God of Jacob" (Acts 7:46), "three" (Acts 10:19), "from Jerusalem" (Acts 12:25), "in all things God works" (Rom. 8:28), "to be burned" (I Cor. 13:3), "your love for us" (II Cor. 8:7), "accept it" (Heb. 4:2), "will vanish" (II Pet. 3:10), "the Lord" (Jude 5), *hos* ("as it were") omitted (Rev. 14:3), and "people" (Rev. 21:3). The UBS text changed its opinion between the second and third edition on "he was disturbed" (Mark 6:20) and now agrees with the GNB text.

According to Bratcher, differences in punctuation from the UBS text were followed at Mark 1:27; 2:15-16; 9:16; 14:1, 60; John 1:3-4; 4:35-36; 7:28; 8:25, 54; II Corinthians 12:6-7; Ephesians 1:4-5; I Thessalonians 1:2-3; Titus 3:8; and James 4:2. To these may be added Romans 9:5 where the punctuation chosen is also different from that chosen in the UBS text. As rendered, the verse does not ascribe divinity to Christ.

The UBS Greek text is a critically reconstructed one with marked differences from the *Textus Receptus*. Sixteen passages of the *Textus Receptus* containing as much as a whole verse (Matt. 17:21; 18:11; 23:14; Mark 7:16; 9:44, 46; 11:26; 15:28; Luke 17:36; 23:17; John 5:3b-4; Acts 8:37; 15:34; 24:6b-8a; 28:29; Rom. 16:24) are relegated to the apparatus in the UBS text as secondary (also carried in the margin by the ASV, RSV, NEB, etc.). These verses were carried in single brackets within the text of the first edition of the TEV and finally were relegated to the margin in the completed Bible. Luke 22:43-44, in keeping with current textual opinion, is restored to the text with the marginal note: "Some manuscripts do not have verses 43-44."

Phrases in the *Textus Receptus* (and the KJV) of less than a whole verse are dropped as secondary: "firstborn" (Matt. 1:25), the doxology of the Model Prayer (Matt. 6:13), "wife" (Luke 2:5), "by Jesus Christ" (Eph. 3:9), "and the Lord Jesus Christ" (Col. 1:2), "through his blood" (Col. 1:14), "from God our father, and the Lord Jesus Christ" (I Thess. 1:1), and "I am the Alpha and the Omega, the first and the last" (Rev. 1:11). Modern textual scholars consider these phrases to be scribal additions and not a part of the authentic New Testament text. John 7:53—8:11 is bracketed with an explanatory note, and I John 5:7 (the *Comma Johanneum*) is omitted without notation. Both the longer and the shorter endings of Mark have been printed in brackets, preceded by the headings "An Old Ending of the Gospel" and "Another Old Ending." For these endings, an explanatory footnote is given.

There are also a few passages where modern scholars think the *Textus Receptus* (and the KJV) has lost words that can be restored to the text by textual study. First Peter 2:2 had lost the concluding words "and be saved."

In cases where textual evidence supporting a variant is inconclusive, the GNB carries one choice in the text and the other in the notes. In agreement with the *Textus Receptus* is the preference for "pity" over "anger" (Mark 1:41), and "your love for us" (II Cor. 8:7) over "our love for you." Differing from the *Textus Receptus* are the choices of "child's father" (Luke 2:33), "His parents" (Luke 2:43), "nor the Son" (Matt. 24:36), "the Son of Man" (John 9:35), "seventy-two" as opposed to "seventy" (Luke 10:1, 17), "I am not going to this festival" as opposed to "I am not yet going" (John 7:8), and "Lord" as opposed to "Christ" (I Cor. 10:9).

In other cases the text followed is in agreement with the reading of *Textus Receptus* rather than that followed by some other modern versions, thus the inclusion of the phrase "in the Lord" (rendered "Christian"; Eph. 6:1) and the choice of the variant "God" as opposed to "Lord" (Acts 20:28). Less defensible is the choice without notation of the variant "Jesus Barabbas" (Matt. 27:16, 17; as Moffatt and NEB), not in the *Textus Receptus*, which is carried as a bracketed variant in the UBS text.

These cases are only examples. Because textual criticism is a continuous process, it is inevitable that scholars will differ in judgment about the weight of evidence on some points; but in general, defensible choices—choices that are accepted by a portion of scholars—have been made in the GNB.

Changing Editions

The New Testament of the GNB, now appearing in its fourth edition, has been modified in text, translation, and illustration from edition to edition as the producers have shown themselves sensitive to changing scholarly opinion and to criticisms received from reviewers. The second edition of the GNB had between 700 and 800 changes.[17]

[17]H. K. Moulton, review of *The New Testament in Today's English Version*, 2nd ed., *The Bible Translator* 19 (October 1968): 184-87.

The first edition was based chiefly on the second edition of the United Bible Societies' Greek text. With the appearance of the third edition of that text, changes made from the second edition have been incorporated into the GNB. Luke 22:19-20 carries a note that some manuscripts lack its phrases. Sixteen verses that were bracketed are relegated to the notes; however, the GNB continues to carry "Lord" at I Corinthians 10:9 where the UBS text has shifted to "Christ."

In the translation itself, some modifications toward the traditional can be seen. Whereas the 1966 edition used "meeting house" (Luke 4:15, 38), the 1976 edition reverts to "synagogue." "Imposter" (Matt. 7:5) gives way to "hypocrite," "talking against God" (Matt. 9:3) to "speaking blasphemy," and "cuts deeper" to "sharper" (Heb. 4:12). "All Greece" (II Cor. 1:1) reverts to "Achaia."

The New Testament illustrations in the fourth edition are considerably different from those of the first. For the Gospel of Matthew only four pictures are the same; four others use the same theme but have been redrawn; sixteen have been omitted; and only four new illustrations have been added. In Mark, eleven illustrations are omitted; nine are redrawn; one is the same; and one new one has been added.

The impact of the women's liberation movement on English speech was taken into account when the preliminary publications of the Old Testament books were revised,[18] but no attempt was made to remove the writer's prejudices in favor of the male. The GNB uses "person," "people," "someone," "anyone," or "mankind" instead of "man" or "men" where the male is not specified. When the reference is to people in general, a shift is made from the singular to the plural; for example, "Happy are those" (Ps. 1:1). "Blind men" is corrected to "blind people" (John 10:21). Additional attention to this problem of gender-oriented language is still in order. In Psalm 37 where there are three occurrences of "man" in Hebrew, the GNB has seventeen; and in Psalm 10 where there are two, it has ten.[19]

Certain flaws of the 1966 edition have been corrected. For example, "God is your Father, and he already knows" (Matt. 6:8) is replaced with "Your Father already knows"; "crowds" become "crowd" (John 7:12); and the "and" (*kai*), previously neglected in Matthew 21:5, has been inserted. *Paroikos*, first rendered "only man living in" (Luke 24:18), is corrected to

[18]Roger Bullard, "Sex-Oriented Language in TEV Proverbs," *The Bible Translator* 28 (April 1977): 243-45.

[19]May, "Good News for All People Everywhere," p. 190.

"only visitor in." "Forever and ever" (Rom. 16:27) becomes "forever," and "God" becomes "my God" (I Cor. 1:4). "All men take part in his death" (II Cor. 5:14) becomes "they all share in his death." "Instructor" for *paidagōgos* has given way to "was in charge of us" (Gal. 3:24), and "teacher" (I Cor. 4:15) to "guardian." "Enoch, the sixth direct descendant" (Jude 14) now replaces "seventh direct descendant." The prior statement was in conflict with the list given in Genesis. In the Greek text of Jude, the idiom is inclusive, saying that Enoch is "the seventh" from Adam. "All men" (II Cor. 5:14) becomes "they all." "Punishes ... whips" (Heb. 12:6) becomes "corrects ... punishes." Critics can no longer speak of "the whipping God." "Preached" for the activity of Philip's daughters (Acts 21:9) is changed to "proclaimed." "Given" is omitted in I Corinthians 11:24, "I am a Pharisee" is changed to "I was" (Phil. 3:5), and the error "forever" becomes "forever and ever" (Rev. 19:3). "Live with it" (Luke 11:26) gives way to "live there," "that the Lord had said" (Acts 9:27) to "that the Lord had spoken," and "damage" (Acts 27:10) to "great damage." The first clause of Luke 17:17 is made a declaration where it had been a question.

In other notable improvements, the GNB moves from "to give them real meaning" (Matt. 5:17) to "to make their teachings come true." "It is through faith alone, from beginning to end" (Rom. 1:17) becomes "it is through faith from beginning to end"; however, the inserted "only" remains at Romans 3:28. "On this rock I will build my church" (Matt. 16:18) becomes "on this rock foundation." "But now you obey" (Rom. 6:17) becomes "you have obeyed." "Hideout for thieves" (Matt. 21:13) replaces "robbers' den." "Glorious creatures" (Heb. 9:5) becomes "winged animals." "Change your ways" (Matt. 3:2) becomes "Turn away from your sins." "Speak with strange sounds" (I Cor. 14:2, 26) becomes "speaks in strange tongues." The italics for emphasis are dropped at Mark 9:23 and "yourself" is added. The modern figure—"flickering lamp"—which replaced an ancient one (Matt. 12:20) has been dropped entirely. The impression that the servant suffered from nostalgia is avoided by changing "home sick in bed" (Matt. 8:6) "to sick in bed at home." "Thrown down hard" (Rev. 18:21) becomes "violently thrown down."

An interesting change is encountered in Luke 1:27 where "virgin" was used for *parthenos* in 1966 but now has become "girl."[20] "Virgin" has been used in verse 34 where *parthenos* does not occur in Greek as an

[20]See Bratcher's defense, "The Nature and Purpose," pp. 103-4.

equivalent of "I know not a man." Though the GNB prefers the rendering "girl" for *parthenos* where the doctrine of the virgin birth is not under consideration (Matt. 25:1, 7, 11; I Cor. 7:36, 37), the translators cannot justly be charged with prejudice against the word "virgin" or against the belief in the virgin birth in the light of their use of the term in Matthew 1:23; I Corinthians 7:34; and II Corinthians 11:2. The first edition had "they were unmarried" in Revelation 14:4, but the fourth has "they are virgins."

The English Understood by All

The shifting from traditional theological language to language as common as that used in the newspaper — in many cases with a gain in accuracy in communication — is everywhere evident in the GNB. Old English pronominal and accompanying verbal forms are everywhere shunned in favor of you, your, etc. As is true in Hebrew and Greek, God is addressed with the same pronouns used for man. Contractions are freely used, even in address to God (Deut. 9:26) and in angelic speech (Num. 22:33; Luke 1:13, 30). Weights ["twenty-five pounds" (Ruth 2:17); "fifty pounds" (Ruth 3:15)], measures, currency, and hours are given in their modern counterparts; the measurements of the Tabernacle and the Temple are not exceptions. Rather than saying that the Mount of Olives is a "Sabbath day's journey" from Jerusalem, it is said to be "half a mile away" (Acts 1:12). The coin found in the fish's mouth was of enough value to pay the tax for two persons (Matt. 17:24-27).

A long list of examples can be compiled where simplicity is gained in the GNB without change of meaning by using a word, even more common than that used in the RSV. Should the vocabulary be compared with the KJV, the list would be even longer. For example, *evangellion* (traditionally "gospel") becomes "Good News"; "discomfited" (Judg. 4:15) becomes "threw into confusion." "Usury" (Deut. 23:19) becomes "interest." "Piece of broken pottery" (Job 2:8) replaces "potsherd," "waist" (II Chron. 10:10) replaces "loins," and "dome" replaces "firmament" (Gen. 1:6; Ezek. 1:22, 26; 10:1). "Adamant" is replaced by "diamond" (Ezek. 3:9) or by "rock" (Zech. 7:12). "Sulfur" replaces "brimstone" (Ps. 11:6; Isa. 34:9), "ditch" is used for "conduit" (Isa. 36:2), "burning stick" (Amos 4:11; cf. Isa. 7:4) or "stick snatched from the fire" (Zech. 3:2) for "brand," "valley" for "glen" (Zech. 1:8), and "weeds" for "cockle" (Job 31:40). "Cavalry" is used for "horsemen" (Isa. 36:9), "succeeded him" for "reigned in his stead" (Isa. 37:38), "deer" (Ps.

18:33) for "hind," "basket" (Zech. 5:6) for "ephod," "the shield for the battering ram" (Nah. 2:5) for the "mantelet," and "live for a while" (Ruth 1:2) for "sojourn." Other examples of improvement are "crying" (II Sam. 13:36; I Sam. 11:5) for "He began weeping," "fortuneteller" (I Sam. 28:3) for "soothsayer," "loot" (I Sam. 30:26) for "booty," "chasing" (II Sam. 2:26) for "pursue," "boy" for "lad" (II Sam. 17:18), "snake" for "serpent" (Gen. 3:1; I Kings 1:9; Ezek. 8:10; Amos 5:19), "Let us be allies" for "let there be a league" (I Kings 15:19), and "jar" for "cruse" (I Kings 17:12, 16). "Making fun of" (I Kings 18:27 is used instead of "mocked," "hit" instead of "smite" (I Kings 20:35), "slapped" him (I Kings 22:24) instead of "struck him," "dedicate" instead of "sanctify" (Lev. 27:14), and "bedroom" instead of "bedchamber" (Exod. 8:3). The queen of Sheba was said to be "left ... breathless and amazed" rather than that "there was no more spirit in her" (I Kings 10:5).

The effort to express family relationships in modern terms results in simplicity; hence, 'ab may be "father," "grandfather" (Gen. 32:9), or "great-grandfather" (I Kings 15:3); and 'em at times may be "grandmother" (I Kings 15:13). "Ancestors" (Deut. 11:21) is preferred to "fathers" for 'aboth when carrying the meaning "predecessors." Terms like "daughters-in-law" (Ezek. 22:11), "half-sisters" (Ezek. 22:11; cf. Lev. 18:9ff.), "aunt" (II Kings 11:2), and "nephews" (II Chron. 22:8) are used for Hebrew circumlocutions.

New designations are found for many items. The "Golden Calf" becomes a "gold bull" (Exod. 32:4). Moses is put on the river in a "basket" (Exod. 2:3) which was waterproofed with "tar" (Exod. 2:3; cf. Gen. 6:14). Jacob was cooking "bean soup" (Gen. 25:29) rather than "pottage." "Unleavened bread" becomes "bread made without yeast" (Josh. 5:11); however, the term "Festival of Unleavened Bread" is retained (Exod. 34:18). What has been called "leprosy" is "a dreaded skin disease" (Lev. 13:1ff.; Num. 12:10; Deut. 24:8; II Kings 5:1; cf. Luke 17:12), but is "mildew" when in houses (Lev. 14:35) and in clothing (Lev. 13:47ff.). "Provender" becomes "fodder" (Gen. 24:25, 32). He who was "the preacher" becomes "the Philosopher" (Eccles. 1:1). "Hideout for thieves" (Luke 19:46) replaces "den of thieves." The "abomination of desolation" (Dan. 9:27; 11:31; 12:11; Matt. 24:15; Mark 13:14) becomes "The Awful Horror"; and the "man of lawlessness" (II Thess. 2:3) is "the Wicked One."

In keeping with the frankness of current speech regarding sex, men "had intercourse with" (Gen. 4:1; Deut. 22:22-24), "sleep with" (Gen. 16:2), "made love to" (II Sam. 11:4), or "have sex with" (Gen. 19:5) women. The women (even Mary) become "pregnant" (Gen. 4:1; Isa. 7:14; Matt. 1:23; Luke 1:24), are "going to have a baby" (Matt. 1:18), or are "soon to give birth" (Rev. 12:2). They "went into labor" (I Sam 4:19). What has traditionally been "seed" is "semen" (Gen. 38:9); and words like "rape" (Deut. 22:25), "castrated" (Deut. 23:1; Isa. 56:3; Gal. 5:12), "penis" (Lev. 15:1; Deut. 23:1), "wet dream" (Deut. 23:10), and "genitals" (Deut. 25:11) are used. "Tokens of virginity" becomes "blood-stained wedding sheet" (Deut. 22:15).

The effort to communicate with the reader is further seen when some place names, traditionally transliterated, are translated; for example, "Graves of Craving" (Num. 11:34), "Trouble Valley" (Josh. 7:24, 26; Hos. 2:15), "Oak of Weeping" (Gen. 35:8), "tower of Eder" (Gen. 35:21), "Harosheth-of-the-Gentiles" (Judg. 4:13), "Baal-of-the-Covenant" (Judg. 9:4, 46), "Camp of Dan" (Judg. 18:12), "Field of Swords" (II Sam 2:16), "Acacia" (Josh. 2:1; Mic. 6:5); "Acacia Valley" (Joel 3:18), "Valley of Gog's Army" (Ezek. 39:11, 15), and "Shepherds' Camp" (II Kings 10:12). In a few cases the opposite is true; what was traditionally translated is transliterated to create terms like "Sela" (II Chron. 25:12) and "Miphkad Gate" (Neh. 3:31).

Other words that traditionally have been transliterated or anglicized from Hebrew and Greek are translated. For example, "Sheol" is "the world of the dead" (Job 26:6; Ezek. 32:30); "Abaddon" is "the place of destruction" (Ps. 88:11); "flaming creatures" (Isa. 6:2) replaces "seraphim"; "living creatures" replaces "cherubim" when supernatural beings are spoken of (Gen. 3:24; Ezek. 1; cf. Rev. 4), but "winged creatures" (Exod. 25:18; Num. 7:89; cf. "animals" Heb. 9:5) is used in graphic representation. The "cherub" is "terrifying angel" (Ezek. 28:14). "Teraphim" are "household gods/idols" (Gen. 31:19, 34; I Sam. 19:13), "ephod" is "sacred linen apron" (I Sam. 2:18), the "magi" become "men who studied the stars" (Matt. 2:1). "Raca" becomes "You good-for-nothing" (Matt. 5:22). "Rabbi" at times becomes "teacher" (Matt. 23:7, 8; John 1:49), "Hosanna" (Matt. 21:9) becomes "Praise to David's Son," and "mammon" (Matt. 6:24) becomes "money" or "wealth" (Luke 16:11). "Dispersion" becomes "people scattered over the whole world" (James 1:1). The wife-names in Isaiah are translated as "Forsaken," "The Deserted Wife," "God Is Pleased with Her," and "Happily Married" (Isa. 62:4). However, inconsistency with the policy occurs when Isaiah's second son is "Quick-Loot-Fast-Plunder" (Isa. 8:1, 3) but the name of the first is retained in transliteration, "Shear Jashub" (Isa. 7:3), when it could be "A Few Will Return."

Some personal names which traditionally have been transliterated are translated. "Ahasuerus" becomes "Xerxes" (Esther 1:1) and "Osnapper" is "Ashurbanipal" (Ezra 4:10). "Jesus called Justus" becomes "Joshua, also called Justus" (Col. 4:11) in order to retain the name "Jesus" solely for the Savior.[21] The quasi-proper name "Antichrist" (I John 2:18, 22; 4:3; II John 7) becomes "Enemy of Christ," though the gain is doubtful.

Personal names that occur in more than one form are all reduced to their most familiar spelling. For example, "Jechoniah" (Jer. 24:1; 27:20) and "Coniah" (Jer. 22:24, 28; 37:1) become "Jehoiachin," "Joash" becomes "Jehoash" (Amos 1:1), and "Cephus" becomes "Peter" (I Cor. 1:12; 9:5; 15:5; Gal. 2:9).

Geographical names occurring in multiple forms are also given one familiar form. Hence, "Horeb" becomes "Sinai" (Exod. 3:1; 17:6; Ps. 106:19; etc); "Senir" becomes "Mount Hermon" (Ps. 29:6; Ezek. 27:5); "Ephrathah" becomes "Bethlehem" (Ps. 132:6); "the sea" (Isa. 9:1), "the great sea" (Ezek. 47:10, 15), and the "Western Sea" (Josh. 1:4; Joel 2:20) become "the Mediterranean"; the "salt sea" (Gen. 14:3; Num. 34:12) or the "eastern sea" (Ezek. 47:18; Joel 2:20) becomes "the Dead Sea"; and "the Arabah" (Deut. 11:30; Ezek. 47:8) becomes "the Jordan Valley"; however, "Brook of the Arabah" (Amos 6:14) remains.

In a few instances the language of the GNB is racy; for example, "You bastard" (I Sam 20:30), "that damned woman" (II Kings 9:34), "May you and your money go to hell" (Acts 8:20),[22] and "For God's sake, I beg you, don't punish me" (Mark 5:7).

Vocabulary Innovations

The reader familiar with the traditional translations will find in the GNB both the traditional and the innovative in vocabulary. Words like "Sabbath" (Matt. 12:1), "Passover" (Mark 14:12), "Unleavened Bread" (Mark 14:12), "Pentecost" (Acts 2:1), "Pharisees" (Matt. 23:1ff.), "Sadducees" (Matt. 3:7), "elders" (Acts 6:12), "prophet" (Matt. 1:22), "apostle" (Matt. 10:2), and "parable" (Matt. 13:3) are used with definitions supplied in the Word List. "Rabbi" (John 1:38; 3:2) is sometimes used, but at other times (Matt. 23:7; John 1:49; 3:26; 6:25) it is translated "teacher." "Hades" (Luke

[21]Bratcher, "The T.E.V. New Testament and the Greek Text," p. 168.
[22]A defense is offered by Nida, *Good News for Everyone*, p. 68.

16:23) is at times retained, but "world of the dead" (Acts 2:27) may be used.

There are many innovations. Though the divine name is retained as "Lord" (as in KJV; RSV; NEB; and NAB), the term previously rendered "Lord Jehovah" is "Sovereign LORD" (Gen. 15:2, 8; Amos 3:7, 13; 4:2, 4; etc). That which was "Lord of hosts" becomes "LORD Almighty" (I Sam. 4:4) or the "triumphant LORD" (Ps. 24:10), but is retained as "LORD of Armies" (Isa. 13:4) where armies are mentioned in the context. One also encounters "the Sovereign LORD Almighty" where terms are combined (Isa. 10:23, 24; Amos 6:8, 9:5).

There are some innovations in religious terminology. Noah's ark is a "boat" (Gen. 6:14), but the ark of the covenant becomes the "Covenant Box" (Exod. 25:10; 37:1ff.; Josh. 4:5; I Sam. 3:3; 4:4). What has been "the mercy seat" becomes either the "lid" (Exod. 25:17) or "the place where sins were forgiven" (I Chron. 28:11; Heb. 9:5). The tabernacle becomes "the tent" (Deut. 31:14) or "the sacred Tent" (Exod. 25:8; 26:1; 36:1), and the "tent of meeting" is "the Tent" (Deut. 31:14) or "the tent of the LORD's presence" (Exod. 30:16; Josh. 18:1; I Sam. 2:22). Instead of "cereal offering" there is "offering of grain" (Lev. 2:1), instead of "peace offering" there is "fellowship offering" (Lev. 3:1), and instead of "guilt offering" there is "repayment offering" (Lev. 5:15). "Harvest Festival" (Deut. 16:10; Exod. 34:22) is used instead of "Feast of Weeks," "Festival of Shelters" (Deut. 16:13; Lev. 23:33ff.) instead of "Feast of Tabernacles," and "religious festivals" instead of "solemn assemblies" (Amos 5:21). The "Year of Restoration" (Lev. 25:15) was previously called "the Jubilee."

"Corners of the altar" (I Kings 1:51) is used for "horns of the altar"; the term "high place" (*bamah*) is at times retained (Ezek. 20:29); at other times it becomes "place of worship" (I Sam. 9:19, 25), "holy place" (I Sam. 11:15), "pagan places" (II Kings 12:3; 16:4), "pagan hill shrines" (Isa. 65:7), or "hilltop shrines" (Hos. 10:8). What was "the host of heaven" becomes "the stars" (Deut. 17:3); "leaders" and "leading" are at times used instead of "judges" and "judging"; however, in the New Testament these figures are called "judges" (Acts 13:20). The "Pit" is "the grave" (Ps. 103:4) or "the world of the dead" (Job 17:16). "Woe" becomes "Doomed is" (Jer. 22:14). "Council" (as KJV; Acts 4:15; etc.) is used instead of "sanhedrin." Instead of "propitiation" (Rom. 3:25; I John 2:2; 4:10), "the means by which ... sins are forgiven" is used; and for "justify," "declares ... innocent" (Rom. 4:5) or "declares ... not guilty" (Rom. 8:33) is used. Rather than "redemption," the GNB uses "set free" (Eph. 1:7; Heb. 9:15) or "bought" (Rev. 5:9); and rather than "reconcile," "making friends" is used (II Cor. 5:18-20). Rather than "anointed," "the king he chose" (cf. Pss. 2:2; 84:9) or "the one who will rule" (Isa. 44:28) is preferred.

"Red Sea" (Exod. 14:1; Josh. 2:10) is usually retained for *yam suph*, though Sea of Reeds (Neh. 9:9) can be found for the body of water the Israelites crossed. An effort is made to distinguish segments of the sea. "The tongue of the sea of Egypt" becomes "the Gulf of Suez" (Exod. 10:19; Isa. 11:15), and the sea which the Israelites visited after their stay at Kadesh is the "Gulf of Aqaba" (Num. 14:25; Judg. 11:16; Jer. 49:21). In certain cases a geographical name obtained by transliteration is translated. Thus, rather than "Lebo Hamath," which has become popular in technical circles for the north border of Palestine, "the Hamath Pass" (Judg. 3:3; Amos 6:14) is used. "Foothills" (Josh. 9:1) is preferred over "Shephelah." "The Ten Towns" (Matt. 4:25; Mark 5:20; 7:31) is used rather than "the Decapolis."

Current or known geographical names are supplied for ancient ones. "Cush" (KJV; ASV; RSV: "Ethiopia") becomes "Sudan" (Amos 9:7; Nah. 3:9; Zeph. 2:12), and "Cushite" is "Sudanese" (II Sam. 18:21; II Chron. 14:9). "Caphtor" is "Crete" (Amos 9:7); "Sheba" is "Arabia" and "Seba" is "Ethiopia" (Ps. 72:10); "Syene" is "Aswan" (Isa. 49:12; Ezek. 29:10; 30:6); and "Tarshish" is "Spain" (Gen. 10:4; Jonah 1:3; 4:2; Jer. 10:9; Ezek. 27:12). "Dodanim" is "Rhodes" (Gen. 10:4), "Gebal" is "Byblos" (Ezek. 27:9), "Lud" is "Lydia," and "Put" is "Libya" (Ezek. 27:10). "Tadmor" is the "city of Palmyra" (II Chron. 8:4), and "Aram" is "Syria" (II Kings 6:8ff.); but the language there spoken is "Aramaic" (II Kings 18:26; Isa. 36:11). "Greece" is used for "Yavan" (Isa. 66:19).

Geographical references are made clear by using more definite terms. Thus "sea to sea" (Amos 8:12) becomes "Dead Sea to the Mediterranean." "By the sea" becomes "along the Mediterranean Sea" (Josh. 5:1). "The Sea Coast" is "the Philistine Plain" (Ezek. 25:16), and "*Aram Naharim*" (KJV: "Mesopotamia; Gen. 24:10) becomes "northern Mesopotamia." "Beyond the River" is "Mesopotamia" (Josh. 24:15), and "West-of-Euphrates Province" (Ezra 4:10) stands for "Beyond the River."

Climatic allusions are also clarified. The "former rain" (Joel 2:23) is the "autumn rain," and the "latter rain" is the "spring rain" (Hos. 6:3).

"The king" or "the king of Egypt" replaces the term "Pharaoh" (Gen. 12:15; 41:1; Exod. 2:15; etc.). The rulers of Assyria (cf. II Kings 17:24) and of Persia (cf. Ezra 4:3) are "emperors," but in other cases *melek* has the traditional rendering of "king" (cf. II Kings 17:2, 4). "Scribe" (*sopher*) is "scholar of the Law" (Neh. 8:1).

The Greek use of the passive for divine action is recognized;[23] hence, the beatitude is actively rendered "God will comfort them" (Matt. 5:4). The expectation of the Moses-like Prophet is recognized and indicated by the capitalization of "Prophet" (John 1:21, 25; 6:14; 7:40). The GNB attempts to avoid phrases that could be misunderstood. "He cried out" could be taken to mean "he wept" by a new reader; hence in some cases "screamed" (Matt. 8:29; 14:26) or "shouted" (Matt. 20:30; Mark 15:13) is used.

Style

The preparers of the GNB, placing communication with the reader above the pursuit of English literary style, have avoided rhetorical elaboration. Those who love the rhythms of the KJV will find the GNB deficient in literary merits. No effort has been made to reproduce stylistic differences between the various biblical writers, which results in a flatness of style. One can only feel that the poetic style of the Bible is impoverished when rendered. "There are four things that are too mysterious for me to understand" (Prov. 30:18) and "Love is as powerful as death; passion is as strong as death itself" (Song of Sol. 8:6). "The lines have fallen to me in pleasant places/Yea, I have a goodly heritage" has a beauty not found in "How wonderful are your gifts to me/how good they are" (Ps. 16:6). A statement such as "I am an old man now; I have lived a long time, but I have never seen a good man abandoned by the Lord or his children begging for food" (Ps. 37:25), though understandable enough, is pedestrian. One reviewer classifies the style of the Psalms as "deliberately prosaic."[24]

On a more positive note, the GNB has made a diligent effort to convert semitisms into natural English phrases. Gone are the "and it came to pass" introductions to sentences, the "beholds," and the "sons of" and "daughters of" in expressions giving qualities. "Israelite," "Moabite," and the like replace "sons of Israel/Moab"; and "sons of prophets" are "prophets" (II Kings 2:7). "Sons of the resurrection" (Luke 20:36) becomes "they have

---

[23]Friedrich Wilhelm Blass and Albert Debrunner, *A Greek Grammar of the New Testament and Other Early Christian Literature*, trans. and rev. Robert W. Funk (Chicago: University of Chicago Press, 1961), Par. 130 (1).

[24]Jackson, review of *Psalms for Modern Man*, p. 95.

risen from death." "Daughter of Zion" becomes "city of Jerusalem" or "city of Zion" (II Kings 19:21; Matt. 21:5), and "daughter of Egypt" becomes "people of Egypt" (Jer. 46:11). "Daughter of a strange god" becomes "women who worship foreign gods" (Mal. 2:11). "A son of gods" is "a god" (Dan. 3:25), and "a son of peace" is "a peace-loving man" (Luke 10:6). "Sons of the bridechamber" (Mark 2:19) are "guests at a wedding party." This quest for English idiom is carried through even genitive forms like "Hill of Moreh" and "Rock of Rimmon" which become "Moreh Hill" (Judg. 7:1) and "Rimmon Rock" (Judg. 20:45). "Old and advanced in years" (Josh. 13:1) becomes "very old." "Old and full of days" (Job 42:17) becomes "at a very great age." Joshua is admonished to "be determined and confident" (Josh. 1:6, 9) instead of to "be strong and of a good courage."

In addition to striving for an English idiom, the GNB has divided long sentences into shorter ones. Ephesians 1:3-14, which is one sentence in Greek, has become fifteen; Colossians 1:9-17 is eleven; Romans 1:1-7 is six; I Peter 1:3-5 is five; Hebrews 2:2-4 is four; and Acts 8:14-16 and Galatians 1:15-17 are three each. Noun antecedents are supplied for pronouns where the context in English would be unclear without them; for example, "the enemy" (Jer. 4:13), "Judah" (Jer. 4:18), and "Jesus" (Luke 6:1).

By avoiding slang and jargon, the GNB escapes the accusation of being crassly colloquial. It has, nevertheless, made frequent use of colloquialisms throughout: "Make way" (Gen. 41:43), "Let's get out of here" (Exod. 14:25), "until it comes out of your ears" (Num. 11:20), "Where is all your big talk now?" (Judg. 9:38), "she nagged him" (Judg. 14:17), "He got so sick and tired" (Judg. 16:16), "You smart aleck, you" (I Sam. 17:28), "good-for-nothing" (I Sam. 25:25), "lift a finger" (II Sam. 18:12), "How could I ever hold up my head in public again?" (II Sam. 13:13). "Who asked your opinion?" (II Sam. 19:22), "ranting and raving" (I Kings 18:29), "a real soldier does his bragging *after* a battle, not before it" (I Kings 20:11), "smashed ... to bits" (II Kings 23:12), "lost face" (Neh. 6:16), "attacks me head-on" (Job 30:12), "What do you have to show for it?" (Eccl. 1:3), "I had all the women a man could want" (Eccl. 2:8), "a fool talks on and on" (Eccl. 10:14), "too stupid to find his way home" (Eccl. 10:15), "minding their own business" (Prov. 9:15), "The Harmless Dragon" (Isa. 30:7), "That was an awful thing to do" (Jonah 1:10), and "owed him millions of dollars" (Matt. 18:24).

Though the colloquialisms of the above list are only a minor element in the GNB, they do somewhat set the flavor of its style. The reader finds this Bible speaking as he speaks.

There are a few places in which a current English idiom could have been used. An American might say "Be brave!" but he would not say "Courage" (Mark 6:50); he might say "ten thousands" (I Sam. 18:7; 21:11; 29:5), but not "tens of thousands" unless he were imitating the traditional biblical language. He would likely say "proud, evil men" rather than "they are proud and evil men" (Job 35:12).

Dynamic Equivalence

Eugene Nida[25] distinguishes between *Formal Equivalence translation*, in which the grammatical structure of the original is reproduced as much as possible in the receiving language; *paraphrase*, in which the ideas of the original are restated in different language; and *Dynamic Equivalence*, which attempts to make the same impression on the current reader that the original did on its readers. The basic question of a Dynamic Equivalence translation is "How would an English-speaking person normally say that?" The passage should read so that the reader gets the same impression from it that he would have received had it been written in English originally. Like all translations, the Dynamic Equivalence translation seeks to be faithful to the text, but seeks that faithfulness at the semantic level—that is, at what the reader understands—rather than at the level of reproducing words, phrases, and grammatical forms. Where both form and content cannot be preserved in the translation, form is sacrificed in the interest of meaning.[26]

In application of the Dynamic-Equivalence principle, the GNB prefers coordination of clauses to subordination. Some rhetorical questions are converted into declarative statements; for example, "Are the trees your enemy?" (Deut. 20:19) becomes "the trees are not your enemies." "Do not even the tax collectors do that?" (Matt. 5:46) becomes "Even the tax collectors do that!" "For what can a man give in return for his life?" (Mark 8:37) is rendered "There is nothing he can give to regain his life." "For to what angel did God ever say?" (Heb. 1:5) becomes "For God never said to any of his angels."

[25]Eugene Nida, *The Theory and Practice of Translation* (Leiden: E. J. Brill, 1969), p. 175.
[26]Batcher, "Good News for Modern Man," p. 173.

Other rhetorical devices are changed into plain English. The conditional clause "If you being evil" (Luke 11:13) becomes "bad as you are." The double negative "a prophet is not without honor" (Mark 6:4) becomes "A prophet is respected everywhere except." The litotes "not a few" becomes "as many ... as you can" (II Kings 4:3); "no mean city" (Acts 21:39) becomes "an important city." "I am not ashamed of the Gospel" (Rom. 1:16) becomes "I have complete confidence in the Gospel." "I am not ashamed" becomes "I am still full of confidence" (II Tim. 1:12). The chiasmus "Do not give dogs what is holy; and do not throw pearls before swine, lest they trample them under foot and turn to attack you" becomes "Do not give what is holy to dogs—they will only turn and attack you. Do not throw your pearls in front of pigs—they will only trample them underfoot" (Matt. 7:6).

Metaphors may be changed to similes, resulting in, for example, "women of Samaria, who grow fat like the well-fed cows of Bashan" (Amos 4:1). Metaphors are also often changed to nonmetaphors. "A land of milk and honey" becomes "a rich and fertile land" (Exod. 33:3; Num. 13:27), but "streams that flow with milk and honey" (Job 20:17) is retained. "Tabernacle of David" (Amos 9:11) becomes "kingdom of David." The epithet "a dog's head" (II Sam. 3:8) is omitted entirely, "a dog" becomes "a nobody" (II Kings 8:13), "horsemen of Israel and its chariots" becomes "mighty defender of Israel" (II Kings 2:12; 13:14), "He poured water on the hands of Elijah" (II Kings 3:11) becomes "He was Elijah's assistant," "windows of heaven" becomes "if the LORD himself were to send grain at once" (II Kings 7:2, 19), "ears will tingle" becomes "will be stunned" (II Kings 21:12), and "dust and ashes" becomes "no better than dirt" (Job 30:19). "A bag with holes" becomes "the working man cannot earn enough to live on" (Hag. 1:6). A double figure like "cleanness of teeth ... lack of bread" (Amos 4:6) becomes simply "famine." "Apple of the eye" becomes "what is most precious to me" (Zech. 2:8; cf. Deut. 32:10; Ps. 17:8; Prov. 7:2; Lam. 2:18). "Bring down my gray hairs with sorrow to Sheol" (Gen. 42:38) becomes "would kill me." In Matthew 12:20 the double figure is dropped entirely in favor of "He will be gentle to those who are weak and kind to those who are helpless." "Their feet are swift to shed blood" (Rom. 3:15) becomes "They are quick to hurt and kill." "He does not bear the sword in vain" (Rom. 13:4) becomes "his power to punish is real." "A wide door" (I Cor. 16:9) becomes "a real opportunity." *Adelphēn gunaika* (I Cor. 9:5; KJV: "a sister, a wife") becomes "a Christian wife." "Threshing with in-

struments of iron" (Amos 1:3) becomes "treated . . . with savage cruelty."
"Risked their necks" (Rom. 16:4) becomes "risked their lives."

Customs or expressions not likely to be common in English culture are
expressed in paraphrased terms. "Anointed my head with oil" (Ps. 23:5)
becomes "welcomed me as an honored guest." "I will throw my sandal on
Edom" (Ps. 60:8) becomes " . . . on Edom, as a sign that I own it." "Let
not your left hand know what your right hand does" (Matt. 6:3) becomes
"that your closest friend will not know." "Fell on his neck" becomes "threw
his arms around" (Gen. 33:4; Luke 15:20) or "hugged" (Acts 20:37). "When
there were yet three months to the harvest" (Amos 4:7) becomes "when
your crops needed it most."

The GNB is less meticulous than the Formal Equivalence translations
about technical distinctions. For example, ignoring the distinction between
a well and a cistern, *bor* is at times rendered "well" (Gen. 37:22; II Kings
18:31; Isa. 36:16; Jer. 38:6; 41:7) and at others "cistern" (Jer. 2:13). "The
brook of Egypt" becomes merely "the Egyptian Border" (II Chron. 7:8; Isa.
27:12; Ezek. 47:19). How Joshua (Josh. 11:9) and David (I Chron. 18:4)
"crippled the horses" is left unexpressed. "All the streams of Egypt" (II Kings
19:24) becomes "the Nile River." The "hornet" of the conquest (Exod.
23:28; Deut. 7:20; Josh. 24:12) becomes "I will throw . . . into panic."
"These uncircumcised" becomes "godless Philistines" (I Sam. 31:4) or
"pagans" (II Sam. 1:20). "Go down to the pit" is "about to die" (Ps. 88:4).
"The Lord's anointed" is "the LORD's chosen king" (II Sam. 1:14); "five
hundred yoke of oxen" becomes "one thousand head of cattle" (Job 1:3)
despite the fact that "two oxen" (I Sam. 11:7) or "a team of oxen" (I Kings
19:19, 21) are used in plowing contexts. "The barley was ripe" (Exod. 9:31)
replaces "the barley was headed"; actually the one stage can follow the
other. "Purge me with hyssop" (Ps. 51:7) becomes merely "Remove my
sin." Rather than attempting the four terms for "locust," the GNB has
"swarm after swarm of locust" (Joel 1:4). "Tread olives" (Mic. 6:15) and
"tread grapes" (Job 24:11) becomes "press" olives and grapes. "The national temple" for Bethel (Amos 7:13) raises the question whether or not
there was actually a temple there. "Something to write with" (Ezek. 9:2)
is less inclusive than "writing kit." What was "gopher wood" becomes
"good timber" (Gen. 6:14). That which was "the adder" becomes "a poisonous snake" (Isa. 11:8; cf. Rom. 3:13). "Spirit of divination" (Acts 16:16)
becomes "evil spirit." *Kephalen gonias* (traditionally "head of the corner";
cf. Isa. 28:16) becomes "the most important of all" (Ps. 118:22; Mark 12:10;

Acts 4:11; I Peter 2:7). "Fuller's soap" (Mal 3:2) is "strong soap," "water with your feet" (Deut. 11:10) is "work hard to irrigate," and "washed the saints' feet" (I Tim. 5:10) becomes "performed humble duties for fellow Christians."

In a few cases the GNB is more specific than the original was; for example, where Amos speaks of "musical instruments" (Amos 6:5), the GNB uses "harps."

The KJV identified the emotions with "the reins" (the kidneys); later translations used "heart" (ASV; RSV; NIV). The GNB uses "conscience." Hence, "my reins instruct me in the night" becomes "in the night my conscience warns me" (Ps. 16:7). "Abraham's bosom" becomes "beside Abraham at the feast in heaven" (Luke 16:22).

However, of questionable validity are the several cases where a colorful Semitic idiom is replaced by an English one. "Stubborn as mules" (Hos. 4:16), substituted for "a stubborn heifer," seems no gain, since plowing with a cow is spoken of later in the same book in which the figure occurs ("Israel was once like a well-trained cow"; cf. Hos. 10:11; Judg. 14:18; Deut. 22:10; I Sam. 14:14). Other cases are: "It takes a man to do a man's job" (Judg. 8:21), "You are breaking my heart" for "You have brought me very low" (Judg. 11:35), "You'll feel better" for "strengthen your heart" (Judg. 19:5), "please marry me" for "spread your skirt over your handmaid" (Ruth 3:9), "Evil is done only by evil men" for "out of the wicked comes forth wickedness" (I Sam. 24:13), "stop chasing me" for "turn aside to your right hand as to your left" (II Sam. 2:21), and "rubbing salt in a wound" for "vinegar on a wound" (Prov. 25:20).

Whereas the formal equivalence translations deal with that which is explicit in the original text, the Dynamic Equivalence translation makes use of implicit information—that which was known to the ancient reader but which likely is not known to the modern reader. What has previously been left to the commentary is introduced into the text and is sometimes elaborated in the notes (e.g., Job 18:15). It may be specified that a name is that of a town, place, country, or river. For example, "Zoan" and "Hanes" are "Egyptian cities" (Isa. 30:4). There is " 'the province of' Asia" (Acts 16:6) and " 'the province of' Bithynia" (Acts 16:7). "My holy Mount" becomes " 'Zion,' my sacred hill" (Isa. 65:25). Still other additions include: "you women of Samaria" (Amos 4:1), "its capital city" (Isa. 7:8, 9), "as a signal" (Isa. 7:18), " 'ruling' prince" (Ezek. 45:7), " 'guardian' angel" (Dan. 10:21), " 'to take offerings of' raisins 'to idols' " (Hos. 3:1), " 'the holy place at' Shechem" (Hos. 6:9), "like pagans" (Hos. 7:14), "a thousand 'soldiers' " (Amos 5:3), " 'burning' bush" (Deut. 33:16), " 'religious' festivals" (Amos 5:21), " 'Temple' columns" (Amos 9:1), " 'olive' oil" (I Sam. 16:1, 13; Ezra 3:7; Mic. 6:7; Ezek. 16:9), " 'ritually' clean" (Gen. 7:2; Deut. 12:15), " 'ritually' unclean" (II Chron. 29:16), "took a small jar of olive oil" (II Kings 4:5), "to the god of Moab" (II Kings 3:27), "Law 'of Moses' " (Rom. 2:12), " 'true' circumcision" (Phil. 3:3), " 'Roman' Emperor" (Acts 25:8), and " 'church' elders" (Acts 21:18).

Qualifying words are supplied to avoid misunderstanding: "King of Babylon" (Isa. 14:12), "where the gods assemble" (Isa. 14:13), "in the proverb" (Isa. 28:20), "their brothers, 'the Israelites' " (Amos 1:11), "kissing my hand 'in reverence' " (Job 31:27), and "weak 'in the faith' " (I Cor. 8:9).

Other phrases have the appearance of commentary even more than those already cited. "One of my own kind" (Gen. 2:23) explains "this is bone of my bones." God's hand is stretched out "to punish" (Isa. 9:12, 17). Jonah sets out "in the opposite direction" (Jonah 1:3). Other cases are: "But he was not buried in the royal tombs" (II Chron. 26:23), "that is, they had not washed them in the way the Pharisees said people should" (Mark 7:2), "food 'that is ritually unclean because it has been' offered to idols" (Acts 15:20, and "the ceremony of circumcision 'as a sign of the covenant' " (Acts 7:8). "Worshipped Baal and Asherah" becomes "worshipped the idols of Baal and Asherah" (Judg. 3:7); "Asherah" becomes the "symbols of the goddess Asherah" (Deut. 7:5; Judg. 6:25). The coin in the fish's mouth was "worth enough for my temple tax and yours" (Matt. 17:27). "By the finger of God" becomes "By means of God's power" (Luke 11:20). "Do not weep for King Josiah . . . weep . . . for Joahaz, his son" (Jer. 22:10) substitutes the names for cryptic allusions. "Maiden" becomes "slave girl" (Amos 2:7); "wine mixed with a drug called myrrh" (Mark 15:23) comes from a Greek phrase not alluding to myrrh as a drug. "God's gift, the Holy Spirit" (Acts 2:38) supplies "God" to the text. "You are Peter" (Matt. 16:18) becomes "Peter: you are a rock." "Tithe" becomes "sacred tithe" (Deut. 26:13), and "Appear before the Lord" becomes "go to the one place of worship" (Deut. 19:17). Sulfur is sprinkled "to disinfect" (Job 18:15). To the phrase "I will throw my sandals on Edom" is added "as a sign that I own it" (Ps. 60:8). The incompleted oath may be paraphrased "May the LORD's worst punishment come upon me . . . " (Ruth 1:17); but is most frequently completed as "May the LORD strike me dead if . . . " (I Sam. 14:44; 20:13; 25:22; II Sam. 3:10, 35; I Kings 2:23).

When one statement suffices for the meaning in English, words or phrases repeated in Hebrew are compressed in the GNB. For example, the repetition of "firstborn" is dropped in Exodus 11:4-6. "King" is not repeated with each town in Joshua 10:23, and "says the Lord" is not repeated (Amos 4:5ff.) since it is declared at the beginning of the section that the Lord is speaking. A literal rendering of Genesis 1:12 is redundant; hence it is reduced to "the earth produced all kinds of plants." Parallel statements are telescoped if the reader might otherwise conclude that two statements are being made. The phrase "hates and lies in wait" describing the murderer (Deut. 19:11) becomes "deliberately . . . in cold blood." Information judged superfluous is dropped; for example, "on her mound" (Jer. 30:18). The harshness of rendering *gunai* as "woman" (John 2:4) is avoided by leaving the term unrendered.

Because it searches for contextual consistency rather than literalness, a variety in rendering of terms is to be expected in an equivalence translation.[27] In the GNB there is a variety that works to the reader's disadvantage. He finds "tree that gives life" (Gen. 2:9), "tree of life" (Gen. 3:22, 24), and "tree that gives knowledge of what is good and what is bad" (Gen. 2:9, 17), all for the same sort of genitival construction.

Bene 'adam, traditionally "son of man," becomes "mortal man" (Ezek. 7:1), "like a human being" (Dan. 7:13; Rev. 1:13), and "mere man" (Ps. 8:4; Heb. 2:6); but then "Son of Man" is retained in Gospel sayings (Matt. 16:13; etc.; cf. Acts 7:56). *'Almah* is "young woman" (Gen. 24:43; Isa. 7:14; and Song of Sol. 6:8), "girl" (Exod. 2:8; Ps. 68:25), and "woman" (Prov. 30:19; Song of Sol. 1:3). In an extensive note the translators explain why Matthew used *parthenos* as the translation in quoting Isaiah 7:14. *Parthenos* is rendered "virgin" (Matt. 1:23; II Cor. 11:2), "unmarried" (Acts 21:9), or "girl" (Matt. 25:1, 7, 11); and the phrase "from her virginity" (Luke 2:36) is unrendered.

'Ebed is alternately "slave" (Gen. 12:5; 15:4; 32:5) or "servant" (Gen. 24:2; 32:4, 16; 39:4; 43:28) in the Old Testament; and *doulos* in the New Testament, though at times "slave" (Rom. 6:16, 18, 19; Philem. 16; I Peter 2:16), is also "servant." The point of the parable is dulled when the plowman is a "servant" (Luke 17:7); the degree of Jesus' lowliness (Phil. 2:7) and of Paul's humility is obscured when *doulos* is rendered "servant"

[27]Bratcher, "The Nature and Purpose," p. 98.

(II Cor. 4:5; Gal. 1:10; Phil. 1:1). "Hired workers" should contrast with "slaves" (Luke 15:17, 22) where *misthios* and *doulos* are opposite each other.

Midhbar may be rendered either "desert" (Deut. 1:19; Josh. 5:6) or "wilderness" (Num. 14:2), and *eremos* may be "lonely places" (Luke 5:16) or "desert" (Luke 1:80; 4:1). The qualification for the elder is "have only one wife" (I Tim. 3:2), but the widow must be "married only once" (I Tim. 5:9).

The act of "casting lots" gets a multiple treatment. It is "throwing dice" (Joel 3:3; Matt. 27:35; John 19:24), "gamble" (Ps. 22:18; John 19:24), "draw lots" (Lev. 16:8; Josh. 18:10; I Chron. 24:5; Jonah 1:7), "decide" (I Sam. 14:42), and "divided among themselves" (Isa. 34:17; Obad. 11; Nah. 3:10). A note to the effect that drawing lots was usually done by using specially marked stones to determine God's will is at Joshua 14:2. It would seem that clarity would be gained if one term were used throughout for an act of this sort.

Metanoiein can be either "turn away from your sins" (Matt. 3:2; Acts 2:38) or the traditional "repent" (Luke 15:7, 10; Acts 3:19; Rev. 2:22). Both *gehenna* (Matt. 5:22, 29, 30) and *hades* (Matt. 11:23; Luke 10:15) are rendered "hell." Also *apōleia* (traditionally "destruction"; Matt. 7:13; Acts 8:20; Phil. 3:19; II Thess. 2:3) is rendered "hell."

The term "uncircumcised" in an epithet tends to be paraphrased "heathen Philistine" (Judg. 14:3; 15:18; I Sam. 14:6; 17:26, 36), "godless Philistines" (I Sam. 31:4; I Chron. 10:4), "heathen" (Isa. 52:1), "ungodly" (Ezek. 31:18), or "dog" (Ezek. 28:10). However, "uncircumcised" may be retained as an adjective (Exod. 12:48; Acts 11:3).

The treatment of the word for prophesy is interesting. At times it is "shouting" ("shout like prophets," Num. 11:26ff.; cf. I Sam. 19:20, 21, 23, 24); when describing the literary prophets, it is "prophesy" (Amos 7:13) or "preaching" (Amos 7:12). Amos is made to say, "I am not the kind of prophet who prophesies for pay" (Amos 7:14). There were "prophets" in the church at Antioch (Acts 13:1), but Philip's daughters "proclaimed God's message" (Acts 21:9).

The term *blasphēmein* is at times transliterated to give the term "blasphemy" (Matt. 26:65; Mark 2:7; John 10:33; I Tim. 1:20). Often it is rendered by other terms as "This man is talking against God" (Matt. 12:31; Luke 22:65; Acts 6:11; Rom. 2:24; I Tim. 1:13; Rev. 2:9; 13:1, 6), "deny their faith" (Acts 26:11); "insults" (Col. 3:8), or "slander" (II Tim. 3:3).

285

Accuracy

Since there are no perfect translations, opinions will always differ over whether or not a translation is accurate enough to be usable. In comparing the accuracy of the GNB with that of the other translations, the reader should be reminded that the GNB is made from the best Hebrew and Greek critical texts now available.

The accuracy of a translation is also related to the clarity of understanding it affords the reader.[28] It is at this accuracy that the GNB is aimed. One is likely to take personally the warning "I will get rid of anyone who whispers evil things about someone else" (Ps. 101:5); the traditional formulation of the statement, "Him who slanders his neighbor secretly I will destroy," seems impersonal. "Hands that kill innocent people" (Prov. 6:18) is more direct in thrust than "Hands that shed innocent blood." "The sin which holds onto us so tightly" (Heb. 12:1) can be compared with "the sin that doth so easily beset us," and "Christ himself is the means by which sins are forgiven" (I John 2:2) with "He is the propitiation for our sins."

Understanding is also enhanced when words are used in their current meanings. "A capable wife" (Prov. 31:10) avoids possible moral implications that could be attached to "virtuous woman." "Nothing green is left" (Isa. 15:6) will be understood; "the verdure is no more" likely will not. "He makes me surefooted as a deer" (II Sam. 22:34) cannot be misunderstood; "He made my feet like hinds' feet" may be. "Beautiful, beautiful" (Zech. 4:7) is a more likely cry than "Grace, grace to it!"

Though unmercifully castigated by M. Dahood for failure to accept his views on Ugaritic matters,[29] the preparers of the GNB have been alert to the archaeological advances discussed in previous chapters. The cities of Palestine stood on "mounds" (Josh. 11:13). *Mitzraim* is in some passages conjecturally identified with *Musri* (II Chron. 9:28), thought to be in the Syrian area. Solomon's horses are from there and from Cilicia (II Chron. 1:16), the Israelites pay the Philistines money for sharpening tools (I Sam. 13:21), "Pul" is the same figure as "Tiglath Pileser" (I Chron. 5:26), the Assyrian official titles are recognized (Jer. 39:3), Necho goes to help the king of Assyria (II Kings 23:29), God rides on the clouds (Ps. 68:4 [5]),

---

[28]Fry, *"The Good News Bible* Translation Principles," p. 410, comments, "Accuracy ... is measured by the degree to which the reader of the translation understands the meaning of the text in the same way as the reader of the original text did."

[29]Mitchell Dahood, review of *The Psalms from Modern Man*, in *CBQ* 34 (April 1972): 240-42.

and "Danel," the figure alluded to in the book of Ezekiel (14:14; 28:3), may not be the biblical Daniel. There are "lamps" and not "candles" (Matt. 5:15; etc); the "Asherah" is encountered rather than "groves" (KJV; Judg. 3:7; etc.). That which has been rendered the mythical "satyr" becomes "the wild goat" (Isa. 13:21). Liquid is kept in "wineskins" (Matt. 9:17) rather than "bottles." *Oikoumenē* is "throughout the Roman Empire" (Luke 2:1).

Many individual verses are more accurately rendered than they were in some earlier translations. A "nose ring" (Gen. 24:22, 30, 47) is more accurate than "earring" or "a jewel on thy forehead" (Ezek. 16:12; KJV). In the GNB the Israelites "ask" items from the Egyptians (Exod. 11:2) rather than "borrow" them. Rather than "panting for the streams" (an action not suggested in the Hebrew verb), the deer "longs for the streams" (Ps. 42:1). For the heavens, "No speech or words are used, no sound is heard" (Ps. 19:3). "Doze or sleep" (Ps. 121:4) avoids the anomaly that "slumber" and "sleep" are now synonymous. The four titles (not five) of Isaiah 9:6 are correctly recognized by the punctuation used. It is made clear that Isaiah is dealing with the king of Babylon and not with the devil, as the term "Lucifer" (Isa. 14:12) suggested. The commandment is correctly given as "Do not commit murder" (Exod. 20:13). In those cases where the GNB uses "desert" (Exod. 14:3; Deut. 1:19; Josh. 5:6; Isa. 35:1; Matt. 3:1; 4:1) it more correctly describes the area concerned than does "wilderness," used in other translations. "Wilderness" connotes a wooded area to most readers.

The gain in New Testament vocabulary from papyrus finds is also recognized. We read, "One of the occupation troops forces you" (Matt. 5:41). *Apechein* is "paid in full" (Matt. 6:2), and the Spirit is the "guarantee" (Eph. 1:14). Matthew 28 begins "After the Sabbath"; Jonah is swallowed by a "big fish," not a "whale" (Matt. 12:40); "them all" rather than "both" (Acts 19:16) is used; Paul says of Onesimus, "I am sending him back" (Philem. 12) rather than "have sent." One is "to take care of orphans and widows (James 1:27), not "visit" them. The act of repentance is recognized to be an active act, not a passive one—"change and become like children" (Matt. 18:3), or "repent" (Acts 3:19). "Be converted" is rejected.

Beyond these undeniable gains, there are other choices to evaluate. In cases like Romans 9:5 and Philippians 2:6b where there is an unresolved difference of opinion among scholars about the proper interpretation, the GNB gives one choice in the text and the other in the margin. In II Peter 1:1, "Our God and Savior Jesus Christ" contrasts in interpretation with the KJV: "God and our Saviour Jesus Christ."

Just this item of curiosity: All English translators have puzzled over what to have the horse say when he is confronting the noise and danger of battle (Job 39:25). One early translator had him say, "Fi!"; the KJV has him say, "Ha, ha"; the ASV, RSV, and the NEB have him say, "Aha!"; but the GNB has him "snort"!

A reader of the GNB must ask if the expression "created the universe" (Gen. 1:1) is the same as "created the heavens and the earth," if "as he has promised" (Ps. 23:3) is the same as "for his name's sake," and if "I have everything I need" (Ps. 23:1) is the same as "I shall not want." Does not "God was pleased with what he saw" (Gen. 1:12, 31) suggest less to the reader than the literal "it was very good"? Is "have sinned again and again" (Amos 1:3; etc.) equivalent to "for three transgressions, yea for four"?[30]

The rendering of Song of Songs 1:9 seems to be more sensuous than the literal rendering which compared the beloved to a mare of Pharaoh's chariot. The GNB reads, "You, my love, excite men as a mare excites stallions of Pharaoh's chariots." "We won't have to kill any of our animals" (I Kings 18:5) suggests violence where the danger may only be starvation. Where some scholars have thought the relative pronoun could have "Kish" as its antecedent, the GNB is explicit that it is Mordecai who was carried off by Nebuchadnezzar (Esther 2:6); and the GNB calls Haman a descendant of Agag (Esther 3:1), passing by the possibility that "Agagite" might designate his region of origin.

Items in the GNB which have particularly stirred the ire of reviewers include the classifying of "snake" as an "animal" (Gen. 3:1), which it is not in modern zoology. "Creature" would have been a better choice. There is also the interpretation of "water" as "baptism" (I John 5:6), and the use of "death of Christ" or "sacrifice of Christ" instead of the traditional and literal "blood of Christ" in some passages (Acts 20:28; Rom. 3:25; 5:9; Eph. 1:7; 2:13; Col. 1:20; Heb. 10:19; 13:20; I Peter 1:19; Rev. 1:5; 5:9). "Blood" is retained in other passages (Luke 22:20; John 6:53; I Cor. 10:16; 11:27; Heb. 9:22). The translator reasons that "blood" was often a synonym for "death" in ancient days (Matt. 27:4, 25) but that it is not so used in English now; hence, he contends that "death" is the proper rendering in the above passages.[31] The GNB also prefers the term "set free" (Rom. 3:24; Eph. 1:7; Heb. 9:15) to the traditional theological term "redemption."

---

[30]The question is discussed in H. G. Grether, "Some Problems in Equivalence in Amos 1:3," *The Bible Translator* 22 (July 1971): 116.

[31]See Bratcher's defense in "The Nature and Purpose," p. 104.

Mia tōn sabbatōn in the GNB is rendered "Saturday evening" (Acts 20:7), with "Sunday" given as an alternate in the margin when used for the meeting at Troas; but the term is "Sunday" in its other occurrences (I Cor. 16:2; John 20:1).

The GNB takes sides in disputed passages. *Ruach 'elohim* (Gen. 1:2) is "power of God" with alternatives given in the margin. In Acts 2:1, 4, *pantes*, the subject of the verb, is interpreted to be "all believers"; however, other interpreters consider this to be "the apostles." Since the Greek text itself is not conclusive, the GNB could have given the alternate in a note, as has been done in some other disputed cases. For example, *harpagmos* (Phil. 2:6) is rendered "by force he should try to become equal with God" with the margin reading "become; *or* remain." Romans 9:5 gives alternatives where there is a question of whether it is God or Christ who is being referred to.

In some instances the GNB has renderings which one could only characterize as Free Paraphrase — and a paraphrase which differs in meaning from the original — not as Dynamic Equivalence. Such a case is "Long ago, in the days before Israel had a king" (Ruth 1:1), replacing the literal "When the judges judged" — or if one wants to use the vocabulary of the GNB, "When the leaders led." "Break the engagement" (Matt. 1:19) for *apoluein* (traditionally "divorce") represents a cultural shift. "Heaping coals of fire on his head" (Prov. 25:22; Rom. 12:20) becomes "make him burn with shame." "Dust will be the serpent's food" (Isa. 65:25) becomes "snakes will no longer be dangerous." "Syria was in league with Egypt" (Isa. 7:2) becomes "the armies of Syria were already in the territory of Israel." "A razor" (Isa. 7:20) becomes "a barber." "Wipes her mouth" (Prov. 30:20) becomes "takes a bath." Equally questionable would be "Invest your money in foreign trade, and one of these days you will make a profit" (Eccles. 11:1) and "come and destroy your country" (Mal. 4:6) when the latter stands for "smite the land/earth with a curse."

The GNB has not been meticulous in using words only in the way in which they are used in the original texts. For example, the word "Christian" occurs in the Greek New Testament only three times as a noun (Acts 11:26; 26:28; I Peter 4:16) and does not occur as an adjective at all. In the GNB it is also used as a noun at Acts 16:1; Romans 12:13; I Thessalonians 4:6; and Hebrews 6:10, and is freely used as an adjective (I Cor. 7:12-16; 9:5; Gal. 6:6; Eph. 6:1; Heb. 3:1; 6:1; 13:1).

Other than in the use of modern geographical names, there are not many anachronisms in the GNB, but it does speak of coins (I Sam. 13:21) before there was coinage of money. Though Moses (Acts 7:33) and most others wear "sandals," the prodigal gets "shoes" (Luke 15:22).

In some few cases, words of unknown meaning (some of which were transliterated in the other translations) are left unrendered in the GNB; and a note calls attention to the fact. *Harmon* (Amos 4:3) is such a case. Other examples are at I Kings 9:25; 14:14; II Kings 15:25; Isaiah 28:25; Jeremiah 25:34; Ezekiel 19:10; 40:19; and Daniel 7:15. When one tries to explain the ASV treatment of one of these passages (I Kings 14:14) "...that day: but what? even now," he has a new appreciation of the difficulty offered by these unknown words.

Conclusion

Reviewers' opinions of the GNB run the gamut from "excellent" through "one of the modern translations which do not take seriously the verbal inspiration of the Bible"[32] to "the worst I have yet seen." Those not persuaded of the validity of the Dynamic-Equivalence principle of translation will continue to denounce the freedoms and paraphrases of the GNB. The GNB forces the reader to confront the question of whether there is a religious jargon that must be preserved or whether other words are preferable. The GNB seriously reckons with the fact that out of the billion people who speak English, only a small number are able to fully understand the traditional translations. One might be reminded that it is estimated that seven out of eight Christians do not own a New Testament. The GNB comes very close to its goal of being a version that anyone who reads English can read and understand.[33] Those who realize that there must be different translations to meet the needs of varying levels of readers will find it fills an important niche.

As a first step in Bible reading, the GNB may convey the general message of the Bible to people for whom it has been a closed book. A translation using a limited vocabulary and simplified structures as the GNB

[32]Zane C. Hodges, review of *Good News for Modern Man: The New Testament in Today's English Version*, in *Bibliotheca Sacra* 126 (January-March 1969): 86-87.

[33]One reviewer (William E. Hull, review of *Good News for Modern Man*, in *The Review and Expositor* 64 [Fall 1967]: 535) said, "Nothing but sheer traditionalism can commend the K.J.V. over the T.E.V. for educational purposes where comprehension is the crucial factor."

must lose certain shades of meaning found in the original Hebrew, Aramaic, and Greek texts.[34] Vivid idioms and figurative language have to be avoided; nevertheless, the basic beliefs and the basic duties to God and man are clearly set forth. From the knowledge gained from reading the GNB, some may move into a deeper study of God's truths. Those who ordinarily read the more literary translations may find that the GNB helps them understand difficult passages. Though each reviewer can present his list of preferences, the reader will see that, despite its limitations, most of the GNB says just what he has always understood the Bible to say. Readers who want to know more precisely what the biblical writers said and how they said it will have to look elsewhere.

[34]Bratcher, "Good News for Modern Man," pp. 171-72.

13

The New
International Version

T he New International Version, the latest addition to the multiplicity of translations prepared for the English reading public, arose out of evangelicals' dissatisfaction with the existing translations.[1] In 1965 the Committee on Bible Translation, composed of fifteen scholars from many religious groups, was formed to plan the project; and in 1968 the New York Bible Society International agreed to sponsor and finance the translation. Edwin H. Palmer was selected as executive secretary. Printing was entrusted to Zondervan of Grand Rapids, Michigan. The New Testament was issued in 1973, with the name changed from the earlier projected name of A Contemporary Translation to The New International Version. A paperback edition was issued by the Bible Society under the name The

---

[1]See Stanley E. Hardwick and R. Laird Harris, "Do Evangelicals Need a New Translation?" *Christianity Today* 12 (September 27, 1968): 10-15; Stephen Paine, "Why We Need Another Translation," *United Evangelical Action* 26 (October 1967): 21-24; Carolyn J. Youngblood, "The *New International Version* Translation Project: Its Conception and Implementation," *Journal of the Evangelical Theological Society* 21 (September 1978): 239-41.

Great News.[2] In 1974 an anglicized edition was published for the British Commonwealth by Hodder and Stoughton.[3]

Meanwhile, work had gone forward on the Old Testament. Isaiah and Daniel were issued in trial volumes in 1976, and Proverbs and Ecclesiastes in 1977. The completed Bible, the preparation of which is reputed to have cost $2,500,000, appeared on October 27, 1978. By that time, advance sales of the translation had reached 1,200,000 copies. Its first printing was the largest ever done for an English Bible.

The more than 110 scholars participating in the project represent evangelical scholarship of the United States, Canada, Great Britain, Ireland, Australia, and New Zealand. They also unofficially represent thirty-four different religious groups. An hourly stipend, in addition to travel expenses, was paid to the translators for the time they spent. They were divided into twenty teams with a translator, co-translator, two consultants, and an English stylist assigned to each team. The teams prepared trial translations of their respective biblical books. These translations were screened and edited by two editorial committees, and then were finally examined and approved by the Committee on Bible Translation before being made available to the public.

The book design of the NIV was done by Ernst Reichl. The text (including footnotes, special symbols, and format conventions essential to reading the NIV) was keyboarded and stored on computer tape to permit the setting of many forms of the NIV without the rekeyboarding of any text.[4]

Format

The NIV, designed for both young and old, for private study and public reading, provides ease in reading and comprehension. Direct quotations are enclosed in quotation marks; the discourse of Jesus in John 3 is continued to verse 21 instead of verse 15, and Paul's rebuke in Galatians 2 concludes with verse 21 instead of verse 14 — both the converse of the RSV. The words of each speaker in a conversation are printed as separate

[2]"NIV New Testament Is Here," *Bible World* (Anniversary Issue 1973): 1.

[3]B. R. Doyle, review of "The Holy Bible: *New International Version*: The New Testament," in *The Australian Biblical Review* 23 (October 1975): 37-38.

[4]Paul Doebler, "New Bible Translation Computerized for Automatic Setting of Editions," *Publisher's Weekly* 204 (October 1973): 56-62.

paragraphs, as in current literature; this makes it much easier to follow the conversation.

Parentheses are used for matter the translators deemed parenthetical (cf. II Sam. 4:4; 9:10; 11:4; Rev. 20:5; etc.). Lists are printed in tabular form (e.g., Ezra 1:9-10; 2:3ff.; 8:2ff.; Neh. 7:7ff.). Other material has been broken into paragraphs, which are more numerous than in other English translations. Small elevated Arabic numerals in the text mark the beginning of verses, enabling the reader to know exactly where a verse begins and ends. The verse designations are usually the traditional ones; however, a verse traditionally at the end of one chapter may be included in verse one of the following chapter if it introduces the subject matter of that chapter (e.g., Hos. 7:1; Rev. 13:1). The notes on the Old Testament do not inform the reader of those cases where the Hebrew text begins or ends a chapter at a different verse from that used in English (e.g., Exod. 8:5; Deut. 12:32; 22:30; I Sam. 20:42; 23:29; Zech. 1:18; etc.). The New Testament adheres to the chapter division of the Greek critical text but indicates by the paragraphs or supplied headings that some material belongs with the preceding or following chapter. John 7:53 is put with John 8, Acts 8:1a with Acts 7, Acts 22:30 with Acts 23, I Corinthians 11:1 with I Corinthians 10, I Corinthians 12:31b with I Corinthians 13, Philippians 4:1 with Philippians 3, and Revelation 13:1a with Revelation 12. These divisions agree with the UBS text divisions, but that text connects Luke 23:56b with Luke 24 and Galatians 5:1 with Galatians 4, which the NIV does not. There are other instances where a chapter begins with a paragraph that continues a theme rather than introducing a new subject: Luke 23:1; John 16:1; Acts 22:1; 26:1; Romans 10:1; 15:1; I Corinthians 2:1; II Corinthians 2:1; 3:1; 6:1; 7:1; 9:1; Galatians 4:1; Ephesians 5:1; Colossians 2:1; 4:1; I Thessalonians 3:1; 5:1; I Timothy 6:1; II Timothy 2:1; 4:1; Hebrews 5:1; 6:1; I Peter 2:1; I John 2:1; 3:1; Revelation 9:1. Subject headings in italics (not a part of the original text and not intended for oral reading) have been supplied for the guidance of the reader.

More obvious words or phrases, not represented in the original text but supplied by the translators for clarification, are enclosed in half brackets (e.g., Lev. 11:26; Judg. 2:3; I Sam. 13:1; II Sam. 1:21; 21:2, 16; 22:15; 23:9; I Kings 10:16; 11:24; 20:34; Neh. 6:9; 10:37; 12:36; Dan. 8:12; 9:27; Eccles. 5:6; 7:18, 28; Pss. 45:13; 49:19; 57:2; 58:9; 68:17; 78:61; 137:5; 141:7; 144:6; Isa. 27:7; 37:9; 41:22; Ezek. 20:24; 24:17; 48:28; Nah. 1:8, 11, 12, 14; 2:1, 7; John 1:14, 18; Gal. 2:4; 4:17). The brackets indicate that there may be uncertainty about the addition. The brackets are not numerous; but their presence should not lead to a false confidence, for there are some supplied words without brackets [e.g., "your" (Matt. 13:32); "for a while" (John 1:14); "truly" (John 21:15, 16); "spiritual" (I Cor. 1:7); "setting our hearts" (I Cor. 10:6); "group" (Gal. 2:12); "party" (Gal. 3:20); "to which he has called" (Eph. 1:18); "kingdom" (Col. 1:12); "shed" (Col. 1:20); "produced," "prompted," "inspired" (I Thess. 1:3); "really" (I Thess. 3:8); "suffer" (I Thess. 5:9); "evil" (James 1:14); and "the truth" (I John 2:20)]. No English translation has been successful in indicating all supplied words. It is a misconception to suppose that translation can be done that way, and the Dynamic Equivalence translation feels no need to indicate every word not represented in the original.

In Genesis 1 the account of each day of creation is given as a separate paragraph. Rhythmical material throughout the Bible has been printed in poetic style (e.g., II Sam. 1:19-27; 3:33, 34; Rev. 5:12, 13). Psalm 136 is printed with the responses in italics, suggesting responsive reading. Psalm 119 is divided into sections headed by letters that are both in Hebrew and in transliterated form. The headings of the various Psalms are retained and are retranslated where possible. From the gender of the pronouns, speakers are suggested in the Song of Solomon; however, the introduction admits the divisions and captions are debatable. Correspondence within the biblical text is set off in letter form (e.g., Acts 15:23-29; 23:26-30). Notes to the translation are numbered on the relevant page by the letters *a, b, c,* etc., followed by the verse number, for ease in locating the relevant passage.

English plural forms, e.g., "Baals," "Asherahs," "Ashtoreths" (I Sam. 7:4; 12:10; Judg. 3:7), and "seraphs" (Isa. 6:2) are ordinarily used for transliterated words rather than the transliterated plural forms ("Baalim," "Ashtoroth," etc.); why then is "cherubim" regularly retained (e.g., Exod. 25:19; 26:1; 37:7, 9; I Sam. 4:4; Ezek. 10:1ff.) as the plural of "cherub"?

The capitalization policy followed in the NIV has resulted in the generous use of capitals, making proper names of what had been common nouns. One encounters "Desert of Sin" (Exod. 16:1), "Desert of Shur" (Exod. 15:22), "Desert of Sinai" (Exod. 19:1, 2), "Sabbath" (Exod. 16:25, 26, 29; 31:14ff.), "Year of Jubilee" (Lev. 25:13), "the Testimony" (Exod. 16:34), "City of David" (I Kings 3:1; 14:31; 15:8; Isa. 22:9), "Kidron Valley" (I Kings 15:13), "Kishon Valley" (I Kings 18:40), "Valley of Vision" (Isa. 22:5), "Palace of the Forest" (Isa. 22:8), "Lower Pool" (Isa. 22:9), "Old

Pool" (Isa. 22:11), "Valley of Achor" (Isa. 65:10), "Ravine of the Poplars" (Isa. 15:7), "Valley of Rephaim" (Isa. 17:5), "Ulai Canal" (Dan. 8:2), "Ahava Canal" (Ezra 8:21, 31), "Beautiful Land" (Dan. 8:9), and "Three" and "Thirty" (I Chron. 11:25).

Many additional expressions have been interpreted as titles: "Book of the Covenant" (Exod. 24:7), "Tent of Meeting" (Exod. 27:21), "Do-Nothing" (Isa. 30:7), "Repairer of Broken Walls" (Isa. 58:12), "The City of Right-eousness," "The Faithful City" (Isa. 1:26), "Salvation" (Isa. 60:18), "Re-storer of Streets with Dwellings" (Isa. 58:12), "Praise" (Isa. 60:18), "The City of Truth" (Zech. 8:3), and "The Holy Mountain" (Zech. 8:3).

All terms (but not the pronouns) referring to divinity, to the Spirit, and to the Messiah are capitalized: "Name" (Exod. 23:21; I Kings 9:7; 11:36; Neh. 1:9; Isa. 30:27; Jer. 7:11), "Presence" (Exod. 33:14; Deut. 4:37), "Shep-herd" (Gen. 48:15), "Ancient of Days" (Dan. 7:9, 13, 22), "Maker" (Isa. 17:7; 45:9; 54:5), "Creator" (Deut. 32:6; Isa. 27:11; 43:15), "Angel" (Gen. 48:16), "Angel of the Lord" (Zech. 12:8), "Branch" (Isa. 11:1), "One" (Job 31:15; Ps. 2:4; Isa. 22:11; 26:7), "Anointed One" (Ps. 2:2; Dan. 9:25, 26), "Right-eous One" (Isa. 24:16), "Holy One" (Ps. 16:10), "Son" (Ps. 2:12), "Rock" (Deut. 32:15; Ps. 28:1; 42:9; Isa. 17:10), "Rock of Israel" (Isa. 30:29), "Sav-ior" (Isa. 43:3; 49:26), "Redeemer" (Isa. 44:24), "Father" (Mal. 2:10, with a note), "Glory" (Jer. 2:11), "Portion of Jacob" (Jer. 10:16; 51:19), "King" (Ps. 2:6), "Spirit" (Isa. 34:16; 44:3; Zech. 12:10), "Holy Spirit" (Isa. 63:10, 11), and "Spirit of God" (I Sam. 10:10; 19:20, 23). When there is doubt whether "spirit" is God's Spirit or man's (Zech. 12:10), whether "Lord" (Josh. 5:14) or "one holy" (I Sam. 2:2) is divine or human, whether "god" (Gen. 41:37; Deut. 4:33) is the God of Israel or a pagan one, a note gives the alternate capitalized or lower case form.

The NIV is not entirely consistent in capitalizing terms that are mes-sianic items in the New Testament. The terms "prophet" (Deut. 18:15, 18, 19; cf. Acts 3:22-23; 7:37), "priest" (Ps. 110:4; cf. Heb. 5:6), "servant" (Isa. 52:13), and "king" (Zech. 9:9) are uncapitalized. Capitalization alternates are suggested for "son" (Ps. 2:7, 12) and "Anointed One" (Dan. 9:26). It would probably have been better not to capitalize messianic terms in the Old Testament. Furthermore, the treatment given the phrase "An Oracle" followed by "The word of the Lord," though identical in Hebrew in its occurrences, is given three treatments (Zech. 9:1; 12:1; and Mal. 1:1).

Notes

The notes printed with the NIV text, less extensive than those of the NASB but more so than those of the RSV, call attention to alternate textual variants from manuscripts and ancient versions without attempting to evaluate the balance of evidence. These notes include allusions to versional readings not accepted into the text (e.g., Exod. 14:25). They may call attention to rabbinic scribal tradition which gives a different interpretation to that followed (Gen. 18:22; I Sam. 3:13; Jer. 2:11; Hos. 4:7 [but not at Ezek. 8:17]). The reader should not interpret too literally the prefatory statement: "Where there is uncertainty about the wording of the original text or its precise meaning, footnotes call attention to this." There are many verses with textual variants which the NIV does not indicate in the notes, and also there are verses which are not indicated where the Hebrew is deemed obscure by some scholars. The GNB notes many more textual variants than does the NIV.

The notes explain the meaning of personal names (e.g., Exod. 2:10, 22; 18:3, 4) and place names (e.g., Exod. 15:23; 17:7; Num. 13:23), especially when there is a play on them in the text. Places are identified: "Sirion" is "Mt. Hermon" (Ps. 29:6), "Cush" is the "upper Nile region" (Ps. 68:31), "the River" is the "Euphrates" (Ps. 72:8), "Shihor" is a branch of the Nile (Jer. 2:18), and "The Arabah" is the "Jordan Valley" (Jer. 39:4). Weights, measures, sums of money, and the like are explained in American and in metric equivalents. Scripture cross-references are given to other events or statements (II Kings 9:36; 15:12; Zeph. 1:9), but the NIV lacks the helpful references in the Old Testament to New Testament allusions for those events which the RSV and some other translations carried. New Testament notes do give the location of Old Testament Scriptures that are cited.

In many cases, reflecting the divergent views represented in the translating committees, the notes record the minority opinion, showing an interest in conciliation and in making place for opposing viewpoints. For example, *hayyah* ("was") could be "became" (Gen. 1:2), *shabhath* ("rested") could be "ceased" (Gen. 2:3), and *zera'* ("offspring") could be "seed" (Gen. 3:15; 21:12; 24:7). In Exodus, where in each instance with *'elohim* the accompanying verb is plural in form (Exod. 32:1, 4, 8, 23, 31), the NIV, though translating the term "gods," gave the singular "god" as a marginal alternate. The phrase "of God" has a note "of a god" (Deut. 4:33); "tabernacle" (I Sam. 1:9; 3:3) is an alternate for "temple." "Hell" is given as a marginal alternate to "Hades" (Matt. 16:18), and "race" is an alternate to "generation" (Matt. 24:34; Mark 13:30; Luke 21:32). The omission of I John 5:7b-8a is noted though this text occurs in no early Greek manuscript. The question of whether the flood was twenty feet over the mountains or was twenty feet deep and covered the mountains (Gen. 7:20) is noted. At issue is whether the present configuration of the earth was already in the writer's view. "Wonderful Counselor" (Isa. 9:6) carries a note giving a different punctuation—"Wonderful, Counselor." "A voice of one calling: 'In the desert . . . ' " (Isa. 40:3) has a note "Or a voice of one calling in the desert . . . and," "so will he sprinkle many nations" (Isa. 52:15) has a note "Hebrew; Septuagint 'so will many nations marvel at him.' "

Certain words are explained more prominently than others. For example, a word like *herem*, however translated, regularly carries the note: "The Hebrew term refers to the irrevocable giving over of things or persons to the Lord, often by totally destroying them" (Exod. 22:20; Num. 21:2; Deut. 2:34; 3:6; 7:2; 13:15, 17; 20:17; Josh. 2:10; 6:17, 18, 21; 7:1; 8:26; 10:1; 11:11; 22:20; Judg. 1:17; I Kings 9:21; 20:42; I Chron. 4:41; Isa. 34:2; 43:28). A term like "horn" has a note at some of its occurrences (I Sam. 2:1, 10; Ps. 92:10; Luke 1:69) stating that it means "strength"; but at other occurrences has no note (cf. Ps. 75:10).

The notes may give more literal renderings than are in the text; for example, "now bring Jacob back from captivity" (Ezek. 39:25) has the note "now restore the fortunes of Jacob." Various renderings of *sheol* always carry the transliterated term in the notes (Num. 16:30, 33); and "Red Sea" always has "*Yam Suph*, that is, 'Sea of Reeds' " (Exod. 13:18; 23:31; Num. 14:25; Deut. 2:1; I Kings 9:26; Neh. 9:9; etc.). That such a note is suitable in the New Testament for the Greek term *eruthros thalassa* (Acts 7:36; Heb. 11:29) is debatable. The phrase "sacrifices his son or daughter" (Deut. 18:10) has the note "Or who makes his son or daughter pass through." "Give glory to the Lord" (Josh. 7:19) is "a solemn charge to tell the truth." "Give him the praise" (Josh. 7:19) has the alternate, "Or and confess to him"; and "advisers" (II Sam. 8:18) are "priests." Where a term could be taken either of two ways, the note gives the alternate. For example, "angel" could be "messenger" (Rev. 1:20; 2:8, 12, 18); however, that possibility is not noted at Acts 12:15. In a few cases a note calls attention to the fact that a second-person pronoun is plural in Hebrew (I Sam. 2:29; I Kings 9:6; Ps. 118:26) and at other times to the fact that it is singular (Jer. 9:6).

At times the notes take on the role of commentary. Persons are identified; for example, "Pul" is "Tiglath-Pileser" (II Kings 15:19), "So" is possibly "Osorkon" (II Kings 17:4), "Evil-Merodach" is "Amel-Marduk" (II Kings 25:27), and "Uzziah" is "Azariah" (II Kings 14:21). A family relationship may be clarified; for example, "daughter" may be "granddaughter" (II Chron. 13:1), and where the Hebrew text has "daughter" the rendering may be "sister" (Gen. 34:17); "queen mother" is an alternate for "queen" (Dan. 5:10); "ancestor" or "predecessor" are alternates for "father" (Gen. 5:6-26; 11:11-25; Dan. 5:2, 11, 13, 18); "Father" may be "civic leader" or "military leader" (I Chron. 9:35); "descendant" or "successor" are alternates for "son" (Gen. 10:2; Dan. 5:22); and "brother" is "ally" or "relative" (Gen. 14:13). Ancient place names are at times identified with modern geographical terms; for example, "Caphtor" is "Crete" (Deut. 2:23; Jer. 47:4), "Cush" is said to be the "upper Nile region" (Esther 1:1; 8:9), "Sinim" is "Aswan" (Isa. 49:12), "Kittim" is "Cyprus" (Jer. 2:10). Plants may be identified. The "rose of Sharon" is "Possibly a member of the crocus family" (Song of Sol. 2:1).

In other notes, concepts are elaborated. "Unclean food" means "ceremonially unclean" (Hos. 9:3), "no interest" may mean "excessive interest" (Exod. 22:25; Lev. 25:36), "sin" (II Cor. 5:21) may be "sin offering," "foolish" denotes "moral deficiency" (Job 2:10), and Rahab as a "harlot" is "possibly an innkeeper" (Josh. 2:1; 6:17, 22, 25); but no note is at Hebrews 11:31 and James 2:25. "Prostitution" is "spiritual adultery" (Ezek. 43:7, 9); "Sheshach is a cryptogram for Babylon" (Jer. 25:26; 51:41). "Sapphire" may be "lapis lazuli" (Song of Sol. 5:14; Lam. 4:7; Ezek. 1:26). "Horn" symbolizes "strength" (Pss. 18:2; 89:17, 24; 92:10), "dignity" (Ps. 112:9), or "a king" (Pss. 132:17; 148:14).

Though many notes are helpful, it seems superfluous to inform the reader in a note that "Hittites" are literally "sons of Heth" (Gen. 23:3, 5, 7, 10, 16, 18, 20; 25:10; 49:32) when so many "sons of" (e.g., I Chron. 19:2) are rendered with no note, and when *bene yisrael* are regularly "Israelites" (cf. Exod. 2:25). The note "Or his" (Gen. 24:36) seems to have no textual support. Furthermore, one wonders what is meant by "Darius, that is, the reign of Cyrus" (Dan. 6:28).

Text

According to the introduction to the NIV, "In the Old Testament, the Masoretic text as published in the latest edition of the *Biblia Hebraica* has generally been followed except where the Dead Sea Scrolls, the Septuagint and other versions, variant manuscript readings and internal evidence have led to corrections in the Masoretic text." In such cases where a variant Hebrew reading from the margin of the *Biblia Hebraica* has been followed, no note to that effect was deemed necessary. When the consonantal text is divided differently from the Masoretic text (e.g., Num. 24:23), the case is noted. Cases in which the versions other than Hebrew have been followed are usually noted. Where different vowels from those used by the Masoretes are followed, the cases are usually not noted.

According to the notes of the NIV, the Dead Sea Scrolls, supported by some Masoretic manuscripts and some ancient versions, are deemed to have preserved a better text than the majority of Masoretic manuscripts in I Samuel 1:24; II Samuel 22:33; Psalms 119:37; 144:2; 145:5, 13; Isaiah 14:4; 21:8; 33:8; 37:20, 25, 27; 45:2; 49:24; 51:19; 52:5; 53:11. When a New Testament quotation of Old Testament material agrees with a Dead Sea Scroll reading rather than with the Masoretic text, the fact is noted (Heb. 1:6). Of the ten Scroll readings in Isaiah accepted in the text, versional support is also claimed for all except for "witness" in Isaiah 33:8 where the Scroll reading alone is cited. The RSV, though following some Scroll readings, usually lists them as "one ancient manuscript" rather than as "Dead Sea Scrolls." The RSV (citing the evidence of the versions) had previously made most of the choices followed in the NIV in these verses; however, the NIV differs from the RSV in Isaiah 37:20, 25; 52:5; 53:11. Dead Sea Scroll variants from the Masoretic text that are not accepted in the text of the NIV are cited at Exodus 1:5; Deuteronomy 32:43; I Samuel 1:23; Isaiah 7:14; 15:9; 19:18; 23:2, 3, 10; Habakkuk 2:16. Of these, the RSV carried "Dibon" in the text and "Dimon" in the margin (Isa. 15:9), preferred "City of the Sun" to "City of Destruction" (Isa. 19:18), and "Sidon" to "Nile" (Isa. 23:2, 4).

In certain instances, the NIV has retained in the text Masoretic phrases which the RSV relegated to the margin; e.g., "of his mother Sarah" (Gen. 24:67).

A check of the RSV notes against those of the NIV leaves one with the impression that the NIV was less willing to supplement the Masoretic text from the versions than was the RSV. Some cases where the NIV followed the Masoretic text but the RSV supplemented it from the versions include Genesis 10:5; 21:9; 31:49; 44:4; Exodus 1:22; I Samuel 9:16; 14:41; 19:23; 20:12. Conjectures or variants from the versions are chosen in the RSV at

Joshua 12:4, 23; Ruth 4:5; I Samuel 2:27, 33; 3:4, 13; 7:12; 9:4, 25; 12:15; 14:33, 41; 18:28; 19:10; 20:16, 41; 23:25; 26:20; 31:9. However, the numeral "seventy" for the sons of Joseph (from the Masoretic text) is preferred to the "seventy-five" of the versions (Exod. 1:5) by both the RSV and NIV.

An examination of the notes to the Book of Isaiah (one book in which some evangelicals protested the RSV's treatment of the text) reveals that in general the NIV followed the Masoretic text more closely than did the RSV. They agree in following a versional reading rather than the Masoretic text in certain verses (Isa. 5:17; 14:4; 22:3; 26:19; 34:9; 41:25; 48:10, 11; 29:24; 52:14; 53:10; 66:19).

In some cases where the RSV followed the versions or made a conjecture, the NIV rendered the Masoretic text, often not literally, and cites no versional option: Isaiah 2:12, "and they will be humbled"; 3:13, "the people"; 8:6, "rejoices over"; 9:11, "Rezin's foes"; 9:20, "offspring"; 10:34, "before the Mighty One"; 14:30, "I will"; 16:10, "I have put"; 17:2, "the cities of Aroer"; 17:9, "thickets and underbrush"; 32:19, "though hail flattens the forest"; 35:7, "jackals once lay"; 42:10, "you who go down to the sea"; 42:20, "you have seen"; 44:4, "grass in a meadow"; 44:7, "since I established my ancient people, and what is yet to come—"; 44:24, "by myself"; 45:9, "potsherds"; 45:11, "concerning things to come"; 47:13, "from what"; 50:11, "provide yourselves with flaming torches"; 51:16, "set the heavens in place"; 56:12, "let me"; 65:7, "your"; 66:2, "came into being." The NIV does not insert "by night" (Isa. 60:19) and "know" (66:18) which the RSV did on evidence of the versions.

In other cases the versional option preferred by the RSV is cited in the notes of the NIV, but the text follows the Masoretic text: Isaiah 10:27, "broken from your shoulders." In other cases the RSV and NIV agree on text, but the RSV cites a variant while the NIV does not: Isaiah 63:9, "he did not afflict."

In yet other cases where a version or a conjecture is being followed, the RSV so indicates in a note; the NIV does not: Isaiah 2:6, "diviners/divination"; 3:24, "shame/branding"; 15:2, "Dibon"; 41:27, "I was the first to tell"; 44:12, "a tool" (Heb. "axe"); 45:8, "let salvation spring up"; 48:1, "line"; 48:11, "myself be defamed"; 56:8, "those already gathered"; 64:5, "be saved."

Both versions note some obscurities in the text (Isa. 25:11; 26:16); however, the RSV carries a note that the Hebrew is obscure in eight cases; the NIV does not reflect the same consciousness of the obscurity: Isaiah

2:16; 22:6; 23:13; 33:7; 38:8; 43:14; 57:8; 64:5. On the other hand, the NIV cites an alternate versional reading where the RSV does not in at least six cases: Isaiah 6:9, 10; 11:6; 19:18; 23:10; 29:13.

In a few cases the NIV and the RSV choose the opposite variant but cite the alternative in the notes: Isaiah 15:9; 23:2; 53:10.

The procedure of rearranging verses and transposing phrases from one setting to another in the RSV, NEB, and NAB has not been followed in the NIV. In Exodus 18:10b the phrase "who rescued the people from the hand of the Egyptians"[5] is not transferred to verse 11; and Exodus 22:3-4 is not transposed to follow Exodus 22:1 as the RSV did.

There has not, however, been an unbending allegiance to the Masoretic text. Omitted without notes are the Masoretic negative at Isaiah 9:3; the phrase "these are the years of the life of Sarah" (Gen. 23:1), rejected by current scholars; and the second occurrence of "I" (Hos. 5:14). At I Samuel 13:5 the NIV chose the versional reading "three thousand" where the RSV retained the Masoretic text reading "thirty thousand"; and "Zimri" (Josh. 7:1, 17, 18) is preferred to the Masoretic text (and RSV) "Zabdi."

Numerous other versional readings (especially Septuagint readings) have been preferred to the Masoretic text where they appear to have preserved a better text. Hence, the NIV inserts "Let's go out into the field" (Gen. 4:8), "not so" (Gen. 4:15), "Joseph reduced the people to servitude" (Gen. 47:21), "to whom it belongs" (Gen. 49:10), "fourth" (Judg. 14:15), "fabric ... tightened it with the pin" (Judg. 16:13-14), and "the stone" (I Sam. 20:41). "Gibeon" is preferred to "Geba" (II Sam. 5:25; supported by I Chron. 14:16). The RSV preferred "Geba." Both the NIV and RSV followed a corrected text in the versions at I Samuel 6:19; 8:16; 12:11; 13:20; 17:52 20:25, 41; 25:22. The NIV notes a variant at Ruth 4:20; I Samuel 1:23; and 6:18 where the RSV carried no note. "Zedekiah" is inserted at Jeremiah 27:1 as in the minority of Hebrew manuscripts and the Syriac version. "Rhodes" at Ezekiel 27:15 is from the Septuagint. However, at I Samuel 14:41 (contrary to the RSV and NEB) the Septuagint addition is carried in the notes only. Septuagint additions inserted by the RSV are also rejected at Deuteronomy 30:16; I Sam. 10:1, 21; 12:3, 6, 8, 9. The NIV (and RSV) follows ancient scribal tradition, some Septuagint manuscripts, and the Vulgate in reading "Moses" (Judg. 18:30) where the Masoretic text has

[5]See the United Bible Societies, *Preliminary and Interim Report on the Hebrew Old Testament Text Project: The Pentateuch* (London, United Bible Societies, [1973]), p. 111.

"Manasseh." A Targum reading "He broke down" is followed at Ezekiel 19:7.

In a number of cases the NIV has registered versional readings in the margin that have not ordinarily been registered in English translations; for example, "all the wild animals of" (Gen. 1:26) is from Syriac.

The NIV supplies the age of Saul from a few late Septuagint manuscripts and supplies the length of his reign from Acts 13:21 (I Sam. 13:1).

The NIV reader has not been invariably informed when a versional or conjectural reading is being followed. For example, "the rest of it" (Exod. 29:12) for "all the blood," and "beside him" (I Kings 1:2) which in the Masoretic text is "in your bosom" are from paraphrased readings. The NIV follows the Septuagint in reading "crown" rather than the Masoretic text "crowns," but gives no note (Zech. 6:11). The accompanying verb of verse 14 is singular. In other passages where the RSV accepts a versional reading and notes that it does, the NIV, though following the same reading, has no notation (I Sam. 2:14, 29; 17:12; 22:3 [conflation], 14; 24:10 [11]; 30:2).

In the New Testament, the NIV allies with translations of the twentieth century in following a critically reconstructed text rather than the *Textus Receptus*. The result is that verses and phrases carried in the *Textus Receptus* (and thereby found in the KJV), but not supported by the older evidence, are relegated to the margin in forty-five cases. The RSV and NIV are in agreement over the omission of all of these except one; the RSV includes the phrase "and Sidon" (Mark 7:24) in its text with a note concerning its absence in some manuscripts. In twelve of the cases (Matt. 5:44; 15:14; 27:35; Mark 12:23; Luke 11:2, 4; Rom. 8:1b; 11:6b; I Cor. 10:28b; Col. 1:2, 14; I John 5:7, 8), both omit the same material, but the RSV carries no note of the omission. The NIV notes the omission of I John 5:7b-8a despite the fact that the passage occurs in no ancient Greek manuscript—only in late ones.

Of the eighteen passages carried in the text of the NIV with a note concerning the omission of phrases in some manuscripts, the NIV differs from the RSV in only six. The RSV relegates the material to the margin at Matthew 12:47; 21:44; Mark 3:14; and Ephesians 1:1. The RSV carries the phrases "against you" (Matt. 18:15) and "If God is glorified in him" (John 13:32) in the text without noting that they are omitted in some manuscripts. All of these phrases, though bracketed in the UBS text, are given a "C" rating of authenticity.

The long passages of Mark 16:9-20 and John 7:53—8:11 are set off from the rest of the text in the NIV, with a note that they are absent in "the two most reliable early manuscripts." Although the first printings of the RSV relegated these passages to the footnotes, current printings treat them in the same manner as the NIV.

Forty-eight cases of variant readings in the New Testament are cited by the NIV. In fourteen of these (Luke 11:2; John 14:7; Acts 7:46; 10:19; 15:18; I Cor. 14:38; II Cor. 1:11; 8:7; Col. 2:3; Heb. 8:8; 10:38; James 2:20; I Peter 1:22; II Peter 2:4) the NIV and the RSV are agreed on the variant accepted into the text; but the NIV calls attention to the variant while the RSV does not. The UBS text is in agreement with these judgments except in four cases where it favors "house" (Acts 7:46) over "God," "your love for us" (II Cor. 8:7) over "our love for you," "from a pure heart" (I Peter 1:22) over "heart," and "chains" (II Peter 2:4) over "dungeons" or "pits." In thirteen cases (Luke 3:32, 33; 10:1, 17; 14:5; John 1:18; 5:2; 7:8; Acts 20:28; Col. 1:12; I Thess. 3:2; I John 2:20; Jude 5) the NIV and RSV select different variants. At II Peter 3:10 different variants are also chosen, but the RSV does not note a variant. Of these variants, the UBS text agrees with the judgment of the RSV at Luke 3:32, 33; John 5:2; 7:8; and I John 2:20, but agrees with the NIV against the RSV at Luke 10:1, 17; 14:5; Acts 20:28; Colossians 1:12; I Thessalonians 3:2; II Peter 3:10; and Jude 5. The UBS differs from both in its preference for "only God," John 1:18. In the remaining twenty-one cases the NIV and the RSV are in agreement on the text and the note.

There are fewer textual notes in the NIV than in the RSV, NEB, or NASB. Galatians, Philippians, II Timothy, and Titus have none; Ephesians (1:1), I Thessalonians (3:2), I Timothy (3:16) and Revelation (13:1) have only one each. Colossians has seven (1:2, 7, 12, 14; 2:2; 3:4, 6), and II Thessalonians has two (2:3, 13).

The NIV sometimes makes a choice between variants without a notation. "King of the ages" (Rev. 15:3) agrees with the RSV, but is against the UBS text, which gives "King of the nations" a "C" probability. The *Textus Receptus* reads "King of saints." The reading "The grace of the Lord Jesus be with God's people. Amen" (Rev. 22:21) is also at variance with the UBS text which prefers "The grace of the Lord Jesus be with all" and omits the "Amen." Luke 22:19b-20, which the UBS text gives a "C" probability, and the phrases "and was taken up into heaven" (Luke 24:51) and "worshipped him and" (Luke 24:52) are included without notation. The inclusion gets a "D" rating with the UBS text. The RSV carries notes on them.

Although the NIV and the NASB are both in general agreement with the Nestle critical text, they differ from each other in some details on textual choices. The NIV includes in its text certain verses and phrases which are bracketed in the UBS text and which are given a "D" probability. The NASB carried them only in its marginal notes. Luke 24:12, bracketed in the text of the NASB, is included in the NIV without notation. The phrases "Peace be with you" (Luke 24:36), "When he had said this, he showed them his hands and feet" (Luke 24:40), "was taken up into heaven" (Luke 24:51), and "worshipped him" (Luke 24:52) are included. The variants "their children" (Acts 13:33) as opposed to "your children," and "God" (Gal. 1:15) as opposed to "he" are chosen. Still other variants — "believe in me" (Mark 9:42) as compared with "believes," "the Father" (John 8:16) as compared with "He," and "If you were" (John 8:39) as compared with "If you are" — which are included in the NIV, are given a "C" probability in the UBS text. In these cases the NIV represents a more current view of textual questions than the NASB does; however, at Luke 24:6, the NIV differs from the NASB in the insertion of "with you," which seems unsupported in either the UBS or the Nestle texts.

It is inevitable that different textual scholars will give different weight to the manuscript evidence supporting textual variants. The United Bible Societies' Greek Text and Commentary differ from both the RSV and NIV at II Thessalonians 2:13. The NIV accepts a text at variance with most current textual critics at Revelation 15:3 and 22:21 without a notation.

Changing Editions

The Committee on Bible Translation has maintained an open invitation to suggestions from readers. The Gospel of John in the first edition of the New Testament benefited in numerous instances from suggestions readers made on its preliminary publication.[6] In the completed NIV, alternate translations, not given in the preliminary publications of Proverbs, Ecclesiastes, Isaiah, and Daniel, are carried at Proverbs 3:6; Isaiah 24:22; 28:15; 33:9; 54:11; 60:9; 65:20. One new note (Isa. 54:11) calls attention to uncertainty about the meaning of a word. In new notes of an explanatory

[6]"ACT: A Contemporary Translation," *The Bible in New York* 16 (October 1969): 3.

nature, "conies" are "the hyrax or rock badger" (Prov. 30:26) and "Asherah poles" are "symbols of the goddess Asherah" (Isa. 17:8; 27:9).

A few note changes concern the underlying text. That to Ecclesiastes 12:6, reading: "Septuagint, Vulgate, and Syriac; Hebrew 'is removed,'" is dropped. Isaiah 38:11 adds a note: "A few Hebrew manuscripts; most Hebrew manuscripts 'in the place of cessation.'" Isaiah 66:18 reverses the authority cited and identifies the marginal reading with the Septuagint rather than with the Hebrew as in the earlier edition.

Removing "Syria" and moving "Aram" into the text accounts for the dropping of some notes (Isa. 7:1, 2, 4, 5, 8; 9:12; 17:3). "The Babylonians" is moved into the text and "the Chaldeans" into the margin (Isa. 13:19; 23:13; 47:1, 5; 48:14, 20). The notes to "Cush" shift its identification from "ancient Ethiopia" to "the upper Nile region" (Isa. 11:11; 18:1; 20:3, 5; 37:9; 43:3; 45:14). "Release" (Isa. 61:1) is moved into the text and "recovery of sight" into the margin, thereby correcting the mixed figure "recovery of sight to the prisoners." Metric equivalents are added to notes on measures (e.g., Dan. 3:1).

The NIV New Testament, appearing in its second edition, has made changes in text, notes, and translation from the first edition. At least one hundred five new notes have been added in the New Testament. Textual variants not listed in the first edition are listed at Matthew 18:15; 27:46; John 3:13; 14:17; Romans 11:31; Colossians 2:13; 3:4; 4:8; I Thessalonians 1:1. Many of the new notes deal with renderings differing from those in the text. The use of "capstone" carries an alternate "cornerstone" (Matt. 21:42; Mark 12:10; Luke 20:17; Acts 4:11; I Peter 2:7). "Hades" has the alternate "hell" (Matt. 16:18); the spelling "Eloi" (Matt. 27:46), harmonized with Mark 15:34, in place of "Eli" has a note. It is suggested that "Aramaic" is "possibly Hebrew" (Acts 21:2, 40). The rendering "sinful nature" for *sarx* drew fire from critics of the NIV; now it regularly carries the alternate "Or flesh" (Rom. 7:5, 18, 25; 8:3, 4, 5, 9, 12, 13; 13:14; I Cor. 5:5; Gal. 5:13, 16, 17, 19, 24; 6:8; Eph. 2:3; Col. 2:11, 13; II Peter 2:10). "To lead us to Christ" (Gal. 3:24) carries the alternate "until Christ came." "With" or "by" in baptismal settings carries the alternate "in" (Mark 1:8; Acts 1:5; 11:16; I Cor. 12:13). Other notes with conciliatory alternate renderings include "after" (Acts 19:2) and "is from faith to faith" (Rom. 1:17). "Sonship" carries the alternate "adoption" (Rom. 8:15), "martyr" that of "witness" (Acts 22:20), and "one" that of "something" (Luke 11:31, 32). Where American sums of money, measures of content, and measures of length have been used, the Greek terms are usually given in transliteration with metric equivalents supplied (Matt. 5:26; 14:24; Mark 12:42; Luke 12:6, 59; 16:6, 7; 21:2; 24:13). Attention is called to some cases in which Greek has a plural (Luke 5:4; 22:31; John 1:51) and to others in which it has a singular (Acts 13:47).

Scripture cross-references have been added at Ephesians 4:26; Hebrews 12:13; II Peter 1:17; Revelation 19:15; more cross-references were added to those previously cited at Matthew 15:4; Mark 7:10; Romans 15:9; Galatians 3:16. A second reference is dropped at Romans 11:34; Hebrews 1:6.

A very few notes carried in the first edition are dropped from the second. The rendering "Why do you involve me?" (John 2:4; cf. 19:26) with the note "Greek 'involve me, woman' (a polite form of address)" is dropped, and "Dear woman" is now in the text. A cross-reference is omitted at II Corinthians 3:16. The alternate translations "Or sanctuaries" (Matt. 17:4; Mark 9:5; Luke 9:33) and "Or High Council" (John 11:47) are absent, as is "Or Originator" (Heb. 2:10; 12:2).

Explanations that occurred in close proximity are combined to make fewer notes than were in the first edition (e.g., Matt. 21:9, 15; Mark 1:23, 26, 27). The note regularly accompanying "leprosy" in the text has been modified to read "The Greek word was used for various diseases affecting the skin—not necessarily leprosy" (cf. Luke 5:12). Changes within the text have brought about modifications in the notes at Matthew 9:18, John 2:23, and Acts 23:23. The verse number missing in the first edition at Hebrews 5:5 is inserted. Some notes modify the American equivalents given to distances (e.g., "200 miles" becomes "about 180" [Rev. 14:20] and "1500" becomes "about 1400" [Rev. 21:16]). "Day's wage" becomes "day's wages" (Luke 7:41).

The translation, "My daughter has just died" (Matt. 9:18) replaces "is at the point of death"; "believed in his name" (John 2:23) replaces "trusted in his name." "If it were not so, I would have told you" (John 14:2) replaces "otherwise . . . ," "the one doomed to destruction" replaces "child of hell" (John 17:12), "gave up his spirit" (John 19:30) replaces "gave up his life" in order to harmonize with Matthew 27:50 and Luke 23:46, "who believed" (Acts 11:17) replaces "when we believed," "spirit of sonship" (Rom. 8:15) replaces "Spirit who makes you sons," "God's people" used for *hagioi* reverts to the traditional "saints" (I Cor. 6:2), "to will and to act" (Phil. 2:13) replaces "to will and to do," "in the order of Melchizedek" (Heb. 6:20) replaces "just like Melchizedek," and "ark of the covenant" (Heb. 9:4) replaces "chest of the covenant." The adjective "spiritual" (I Peter 4:10) is dropped.

These are only samplings of the changes that have been made. Further consideration will be given to suggestions from readers at five-year intervals. As has become standard in translations, the NIV will be progressively improved.

Features of the Translation

The Traditional

Not seeking variety for novelty's sake, the NIV is a combination of traditional renderings, renderings that have previously appeared in other modern translations, and innovative renderings. The language does not startle or shock; striking, novel, and racy language has been avoided. The NIV uses the traditional "son of a perverse and rebellious woman" (I Sam. 20:30) and "May your money perish with you" (Acts 8:20) rather than the coarser renderings of some other versions.

Those who already know the English Bible will find enough of the traditional forms to make them feel at home. Sonorous phrases like "gorging on meat and guzzling wine," proposed for Isaiah 22:13, were rejected as too flamboyant. "Eating of meat and drinking of wine" was chosen. "Amen" is retained as an affirmative both in secular (I Kings 1:36) and religious (Neh. 5:13; 8:6; Rev. 3:14) settings. "Long live King Adonijah [Solomon]" (I Kings 1:25, 34, 39) is retained. "Shadow of death" (Job 38:17; Ps. 23:4) is retained with the alternates "Or 'deep shadows' " and "Or 'through the darkest valley' "; but the same term is also "darkness" at Jeremiah 2:6. The woman of Isaiah 7:14 and Mary (Matt. 1:18; Luke 1:31) are "with child," but all other expectant women are "pregnant" (Gen. 29:32; II Kings 4:17). The reader will find "Hallowed be your name," "debtors," and "debts" (in the prayer of Matt. 6:9ff.); "fishers of men" (Mark 1:17); "a great company of the heavenly host" (Luke 2:13), and "have not love" (I Cor. 13:1, 2, 3).

Some traditional religious terminology is retained. For example, "tithe" is used in Numbers 18:25ff., and Deuteronomy 12:17, though outside the Pentateuch "tenth" is used. Also, theological words like "justification" (Rom. 4:25; 5:16, 18), "saint" (I Cor. 6:2), "sanctifying" (II Thess. 2:13; I Peter 1:2), and "blood" (I Peter 1:19; Rev. 12:11) are retained. The term "speaking in tongues" (with "languages" in the margin; Acts 2:4, 10:46; 19:6; I Cor. 14:1) is retained, making no distinction between the phenomenon of Acts 2 and of I Corinthians 14.

In certain cases RSV innovations are rejected in favor of a return to a KJV phrase. Ishmael is "mocking" (Gen. 21:9) rather than "playing." There is a reversion to the spelling "Beelzebub" (Mark 3:22) with "Beezeboul" or "Beelzeboul" carried only as a footnote. Psalm 42:1 reads "As the deer pants for (RSV "longs for") streams of water" despite the fact that the act of panting is not explicit in the original verb.

Innovative Renderings

The NIV has a long list of what may be called "experimental renderings" — renderings which must wait the evaluation of time.

Divine name

Like most English translations, "Lord" has been chosen to render *Yahweh*. *'Adon Yahweh* (Exod. 23:17) and the *Qere* form, *'Adonai 'elohim*, both become "Sovereign Lord" (Judg. 6:22; II Sam. 7:22, 28, 29; Isa. 7:7; Jer. 1:6; cf. Rev. 6:10) as in the GNB; but the same term with *'elohim* actually written in the text is "Lord God" (II Sam. 7:25; Dan. 9:3), also following the pattern set by the GNB. *'Adonai ṣeba'oth* is "Lord Almighty" (I Sam. 4:4; 15:2; II Sam. 6:2, 18; Isa. 1:24; Nah. 3:5; Hab. 2:13; Hag. 1:2, 5, 7, 9); and *'Elohim ṣeba'oth* is "God almighty" (Ps. 80:7 [8], 14 [15]). "Lord Almighty" is then adopted in the New Testament for *kuriou Sabaōth* (James 5:4). The introduction to the NIV claims that these terms convey the sense that God is sovereign over all the "hosts" (armies) of Israel, admits that a confusion is created in that *Shaddai* is also rendered "Almighty" (Exod. 6:3; Isa. 13:6; Joel 1:15), but claims that the footnotes resolve the confusion. However, one must feel that there is a loss of clarity where the text plays on *ṣeba'* in a statement like "Lord Almighty, the God of the armies of Israel" (I Sam. 17:45). Furthermore, the rendering "the Lord, the Lord Almighty" for *'Adonai Yahweh Ṣeba'oth* (Isa. 10:16, 23, 24, 33) is rather awkward.

Religious Institutions

When one looks at the religious institutions in the NIV he finds some new terms. That which he knew as the "peace offering" (RSV) has now become a "fellowship offering" (Exod. 20:24, 32:6; Lev. 3:1; Judg. 21:4), and the "cereal offering" has become a "grain offering" (Lev. 2:1). The tabernacle is covered with "hides of sea cows" (Num. 4:12) where the RSV had "goatskins." The *'aron 'es* is at times "a wooden chest" (Exod. 25:10; Deut. 10:1) with a note that it is "an ark"; however, ordinarily "ark" is used. The "teraphim" become "household gods" (Gen. 31:19, 34) or "idols" (Judg. 18:18; I Sam. 19:13, 16), and the *pesel* (Judg. 18:30 is also an "idol."

Personal names

Most proper names in the NIV are spelled as they are in the KJV, though without the variety in spelling exercised by the KJV. The effort to reflect the divergent spelling of names in Hebrew and Greek is abandoned in favor of a common spelling; for example, *Hizkiah* is "Hezekiah" (Zeph. 1:1). "Hiram" is "Huram" (I Kings 7:13, 40, 45). Notes may at times indicate that a name has been spelled two or more ways in the original. At times, slight interpretive shifts are made. Where the Hebrew text and the RSV have "Milcom" or "Malcom," the NIV renders the name "Molech" (Zeph. 1:5). The spelling "Toi" is abandoned in favor of "Tou" (II Sam. 8:9, 10; I Chron. 18:9, 10).

Perhaps most innovative is the relegation of the transliterated name "Ahasuerus" to the footnote while using "Xerxes" in the text as the GNB did, informing the reader that it is a variant of "Ahasuerus" (Ezra 4:6; Dan. 9:1). A differently worded note is encountered at Esther 1:1, and then no note at all is given at Esther 1:10, 15, 16, 17; 8:10, 12; 9:2; 10:1, 3. "Ashurbanipal" in the text (Ezra 4:10) carries a note that he is to be identified with the traditional name "Osnapper." "Jechoniah" (Jer. 27:20; 28:4; 29:2) and "Coniah" (Jer. 22:24, 28) are rendered "Jehoiachin." "Gashmu" is "Geshem" (Neh. 6:6) and "Bigthan" is "Bigthana" (Esther 2:21).

Geographical terms

There are some innovations in geographical terminology. *Nahal*, mostly rendered "valley" (I Kings 2:37), may be "gorge" (Deut. 3:12; Josh. 13:9, 16), "river" (Josh. 12:2; Judg. 4:7, 13; 5:21), "ravine" (Josh. 16:8; 17:9; I Sam. 30:9, 10; Isa. 15:7), or "brook" (I Kings 17:6, 7; Prov. 18:4). Earlier translations used "brook," "river," and "valley" for *nahal*. In the NIV one encounters "Wadi of Egypt" for the southern boundary of Palestine (I Kings 8:65; Isa. 27:12; Ezek. 48:28) and the "Arnon Gorge" (Josh. 13:9, 16) for the stream in Trans-Jordan. In some cases "rivers" have become "canals," as the "Ahava Canal" (Ezra 8:15, 21, 31). The term *Negev* is at some points transliterated (I Sam. 30:1; Isa. 30:6) but at others is "southland" (Isa. 21:1). The district previously known by the transliterated term "Shephelah" becomes "the foothills" (II Chron. 1:15). "Wells of the Jaakanites" (Deut. 10:6) replaces "Beeroth Bene-jaakan." "Stone quarries" (Josh. 7:5) replaces "Shebarim."

"Shinar" becomes "Babylonia" (Isa. 11:11; Dan. 1:2; Zech. 5:11); "Chaldea" is "Babylonia" (Jer. 51:24), and "Chaldeans" are "Babylonians" in some settings (Jer. 51:24; Dan. 1:4; 5:30), accompanied by a note (Isa. 13:19; Jer. 24:5; 25:12). At other times "Chaldeans" are "astrologers" (Dan. 2:4). "Pathros" becomes "Upper Egypt" (Isa. 11:11; Jer. 43:1), and "Egypt and Pathros" becomes "Upper and Lower Egypt" (Jer. 44:15). "Noph" is "Memphis" (Jer. 2:16), and "temple of the sun" replaces "Heliopolis" (Jer. 44:13). The territory to the northeast of Israel, previously called "Syria," is "Aram" (II Kings 6:8ff.; Hos. 12:12; Ezek. 27:16); the people from there are "Arameans" (I Kings 20:20; 22:11, II Sam. 8:6; 10:13ff.), and their language is "Aramaic" (Ezra 4:7; Isa. 36:11). The area "Yaudi" (II Kings 14:28) has a note "Or Judah."

The phrase which the RSV translated "entrance of Hamath" is transliterated "Lebo Hamath" (Num. 13:21; Judg. 3:3) as has become common in current scholarship. The NIV also gives a transliteration "Leb Kamai" (Jer. 51:1) where the RSV has "Chaldea." In some other terms the NIV has followed the RSV in transliterating geographical terms which were translated in the KJV: "Beth Haggan" (II Kings 9:27), "Beth Eked of the Shepherds" (II Kings 10:12), and "Havvoth Jair" (Deut. 3:14).

There is continued acceptance of certain geographical identifications already made in the RSV. "Kittim" is Cyprus (Isa. 23:1, 12; Ezek. 27:6), but is only so in a note at Jeremiah 2:10; it is "western coastlands" at Daniel 11:30. "The River" is the "Euphrates River" (Isa. 11:15), and the Persian province is that of "Trans-Euphrates" (Ezra 4:10).

The NIV makes some geographical identifications not made in the RSV; for example, "Canaan" becomes "Phoenicia" (Isa. 23:11). The place where Jeremiah hid his clothes (Jer. 13:4), which previously was "Euphrates," becomes "Perath," with "Euphrates" in the margin. The valley at Jerusalem, previously that of the "son of Hinnom," becomes "of Ben Hinnom" (II Chron. 28:3; Jer. 32:35).

Other terms are identified in the notes in keeping with current views: "Caphtor" with "Crete" (Deut. 2:23; Amos 9:7), "Sea of Kinnereth" with the "Sea of Galilee" (Num. 34:1; Josh 12:3; 13:27), "the Salt Sea" (Deut. 3:17; Josh. 3:16) and the "Sea of the Arabah" (II Kings 14:25) with the "Dead Sea," the "Western Sea" (Deut. 11:24) and the "Great Sea" (Josh. 9:1; Ezek. 47:10) with the "Mediterranean," and "Cush" with "the upper Nile region" (Amos 9:7). However, "the Sea of the Philistines" (Exod. 23:31) carries no identification.

Miscellaneous words

The "winter rain" and the "spring rain" (Hos. 6:3), though paraphrastic, clarify weather terms in keeping with the climate of Palestine. The "milo" of Jerusalem is identified with "terraces" (I Kings 9:15, 24). *'Elon* which has traditionally been "oak" or "terebinth" of Moreh or of Mamre (KJV, "plain") becomes "great trees" (Gen. 12:6; 13:18; 14:13; 18:1; Deut. 11:30); however, "oaks of Bashan" is retained (Isa. 2:13; Ezek. 27:6; Zech. 11:2). The term "oak" (for *'allon*) has been used in some cases (Gen. 35:8; Isa. 6:13; 44:14; Hos. 4:13; Amos 2:9).

A distinctive vocabulary change has Noah's ark to be made of "cypress wood" (Gen. 6:14) with a note that the meaning of the Hebrew word is uncertain. *Sopher*, traditionally "scribe," is "teacher" (Ezra 7:6) and "secretary" (Isa. 36:22; 37:2). What was traditionally "gird your loins" is "tuck your cloak into your belt" (II Kings 9:1; etc.). *Ṣara'at*, which has traditionally been translated "leprosy," becomes "an infectious skin disease" (accompanied by a note to the traditional rendering) when a disease of mankind (Lev. 13:1ff.); however, when actual persons are victims, "leprosy" is retained (Num. 12:10; II Kings 5:1ff.; 7:3; II Chron. 26:19, 20, 21, 23; cf. Mark 1:40; Luke 5:12), and the alternate term is given in a note. It was discovered that the term "leper" was considered derogatory; hence, "but he had leprosy" is used (II Kings 5:1). When the disease affects "clothing" (Lev. 13:47ff.) or houses (Lev. 14:33-34), it is called "mildew."

Another innovative rendering is that of the incompleted-oath formula: traditionally, "May the Lord do so and may he add to it ... " which becomes "May the Lord deal ... be it ever so severely" (I Sam. 20:13; 25:22; II Sam. 3:9, 35; 19:13; I Kings 2:23; 19:2; II Kings 6:31). That which was "Books of the Chronicles of the Kings" becomes at times "annals of the Kings" (I Kings 15:7; etc.); however, "chronicles" is retained in some passages (Esther 6:1) and in the titles of the canonical books. Distinctive to the NIV is the rendering "love ... always protects" (I Cor. 13:7).

313

Of the translations that have theological import, perhaps the choice of "grave" regularly accompanied by a note (Gen. 37:35; 42:38; 44:29, 31; Num. 16:30, 33; I Sam. 2:6; I Kings 2:6, 9; Job 7:9; Pss. 6:5; 9:17; Prov. 1:12; 7:27; 9:18; 30:16; Isa. 14:9, 11, 15; 28:15, 18; 38:18; 57:9) for the rendering of *sheol* will provoke much discussion. Though the KJV had used "grave" in about half of the occurrences of *sheol*, the ASV and the RSV consistently transliterated the term. The NIV also reverts to using "grave" for *hades* (Acts 2:27, 31) when an Old Testament passage is being quoted, though in the other occurrences it uses "Hades" (Matt. 16:18; Rev. 1:18; 6:8; 20:13, 14) and "depths" (Matt. 11:23; Luke 10:15). *Hades* is once rendered "hell" (Luke 16:23), and the participle *tartaroun* is also once "hell" (II Peter 2:4). "Pit" carries a note "grave" (Job 33:22, 24, 28, 30; but not at Pss. 28:1; 30:3, 9; etc.).

Accuracy

The question of technical accuracy must be faced in regard to some choices. "Nitre" (KJV) and "lye" (RSV) in Proverbs 25:20 and Jeremiah 2:22 become "soda"; in Job 9:30 "snow" becomes "soap." The *Kethib* reading *hare yonim* with the *Qere* reading *dibyonim* becomes "seed pods" (II Kings 6:25) which, though conjectural, certainly sounds more palatable than "dove's dung." A pen with a "flint point" (Jer. 17:1) replaces "diamond point." The *Bene nebi'im* ("sons of the prophets") are a "company of prophets" (II Kings 6:1; 9:1).

Those figures who have traditionally been called "judges" (cf. Judg. 2:16, 17-19; Ruth 1:1) are "leaders" (I Sam. 7:6; II Sam. 7:11; I Chron. 17:6, 10) who are said to have "led" (not "judged") Israel (Judg. 4:4; 10:2; 12:7; 15:20; I Sam. 4:18; 8:5, 6, 20); yet the term "judges" is retained for them in the New Testament (Acts 13:20).

Qoheleth becomes "the Teacher," and he complains "Meaningless! Meaningless! ... Utterly meaningless! Everything is meaningless!" (Eccles. 1:1). The animals Solomon acquired by trade are "baboons" (I Kings 10:22; the RSV has "peacocks," giving "baboons" as a marginal alternate). The coats of Joseph and of Tamar are "ornamented" robes (Gen. 37:3, 23, 32; II Sam. 13:18, 19).

Modern Speech

While striving for accuracy, dignity, and clarity, the NIV has moved beyond the RSV, the NEB, and the NASB in attaining a contemporary style for the English reader. The Psalms and the liturgical passages have been completely retranslated. "You" and "your" with appropriate current verb forms have been used throughout when addressing either God or man. "Brother" has been used throughout rather than the traditional "brethren." Contractions (cf. Exod. 5:17; Judg. 11:7; I Kings 3:26) are used in human conversation (including that of Jesus), but are not used when God is addressed or when God speaks.

The NIV aims at an English untainted by either Briticisms or Americanisms. Though "cubits" is retained for the measurements of the tabernacle (Exod. 27) and the temples of Solomon (I Kings 6:10, 16ff.) and Ezekiel (Ezek. 42:3; 45:3; 48:8, 9), the notes carry equivalents in yards, feet, and inches, and sometimes give metrical equivalents. However, the ark of Noah (Gen. 6:15), the great image of Nebuchadnezzar (Dan. 3:1), Zerubbabel's temple (Ezra 6:4), Haman's gallows (Esther 5:14), and some other objects (Josh. 3:4; Zech. 5:2) are measured in feet and inches, with the cubits and the metric equivalents in the notes. The New Testament uses "miles" (Luke 24:13; John 6:19; 11:18) in some cases, but retains "stadia" (Rev. 14:20; 21:16) in others. "Acre" (I Sam. 14:14; Isa. 5:10) is used where the Hebrew had "yoke." A note explains that "yoke" is the area a pair of oxen could plow in a day (I Sam. 14:14).

Transliterated names of wet and dry measures are retained in the Old Testament with an effort made in the notes to give current equivalents; however, the *ephah* is in one case "a measuring basket" (Zech. 5:6; cf. 7-11). The New Testament is more bold and uses "gallons" and "bushels" (Luke 16:6, 7; John 2:6) in the text for measures. There is a table of weights and measures at the end of the volume.

Money sums are given in transliterated terms such as "shekel" (Gen. 23:15; Exod. 21:32), "drachma," and "mina" (Ezra 2:69). Where the value is unknown, "pieces of silver" (Gen. 33:19; Josh. 24:32), accompanied by a note, may be used. The New Testament uses "talents" or "talents of money" (Matt. 18:23-25; 25:14-30) and "denarius" (Matt. 18:28; Mark 12:15; Luke 20:24); but for "mina" it may use "eight months' wages" (John 6:7), and for "300 denarii," "a year's wages" (John 12:5). The transliteration "mina" (Luke 19:13) replaces the traditional "pound" derived from British coinage in Jesus' parable.

Time is sometimes given in modern terms—"three in the afternoon" (Acts 10:3), "about noon" (Acts 10:9)—but elsewhere is retained in the traditional "sixth hour" and "ninth hour" (Luke 23:44). "On the third day" is "the day after tomorrow" (I Sam. 20:19). The Troas meeting is "on the first day of the week" (Acts 20:7) with no note to a contrary view.

Some terms which traditionally have been transliterated in English versions have been translated. "Abaddon" becomes "Destruction" (Job 26:6; 28:22; 31:12), but must be retained with "Apollyon" in the New Testament (Rev. 9:11) because of the explanation there given. "Lemuel, king of Massa" becomes "King Lemuel—an oracle," with a note to the other possibility (Prov. 31:1). "Muth-labben" in the Psalm title (9:1) becomes "The Death of the Son," "mammon" becomes "money" (Matt. 6:24; Luke 16:13), but "Raca" is still "Raca" (Matt. 5:22). *"Ephod"* as an item of clothing (Judg. 18:17; I Sam. 2:18, 28; 14:3; 22:18; 23:9; 30:7) remains unexplained. Where the RSV translated "Hephzibah" as "My delight is in her" and "Beulah" as "Married" (Isa. 62:4), the NIV reverts to transliteration; and the reversion seems unjustified when the other two female names of the passage, "Deserted" and "Desolate," are translated.

In the NIV, lesser-known English terms are replaced by more familiar ones. For example, "glen" gives way to "ravine" (Zech. 1:8), "brand" to "burning stick" (Amos 4:11; Zech. 3:2), "lees" to "dregs" (Zeph. 1:12), and "mantelet" (Nah. 2:5) to "protective shield." A "hind" is a "doe" (Gen. 49:21; Jer. 14:5). "Mad" gives way to "insane" (I Sam. 21:14); however, in the same context "madman" (I Sam. 21:13, 15; II Kings 2:11, 12; Jer. 29:26) and "madness" (Deut. 28:28; Eccles. 1:17; 2:12; 7:25; 9:3; 10:13; Zech. 12:4; II Peter 2:16) are retained where "insanity" and "insane man" would appear to have been better choices. "Anointed with oil" becomes "rubbed with oil" (II Sam. 1:21), "hinds' feet" become "feet of a deer" (II Sam. 22:34), and "the sycamore" becomes "sycamore-fig" (I Kings 10:27; Amos 7:14; Luke 19:4). All the "asses" have become "donkeys." "Ascent of" becomes "up the road to" (II Kings 9:27).

"The verdure is no more" (Isa. 15:6) becomes "nothing green is left." "Pottage" becomes "stew" (Gen. 25:29; Hag. 2:12), "kinsman" becomes "relative" (Gen. 31:37), and "sojourn" becomes "stayed" (Gen. 37:1). "Wilderness" as a rendering for *midhbar* has been replaced by "desert" (Deut. 1:19; 32:51) or "wasteland" (II Sam. 2:24), calling to mind a more accurate image of the areas concerned; but *'arabah* remains as "wilderness" (Isa. 40:3). "Yeast" is used where one read "leaven" before (Deut. 16:3, 4), but "unleavened" (Exod. 12:39; 13:7; Deut. 16:8) and "Feast of Unleavened Bread" (Lev. 23:6) have at times been retained. "Interest" is an improvement over "usury" (Deut. 23:19), though "usury" still occurs in some settings (Neh. 5:10; Ezek. 18:17). "Jug" (I Kings 17:12) replaces "cruse," and "dynasty" (I Kings 11:38) replaces "sure house." "Dog" is "male prostitute" (Deut. 23:18), but not at Revelation 22:15. "Abomination" is "detestable god" (I King 11:5) or "detestable" (Deut. 18:12), but "abomination that causes desolation" (Dan. 11:31; Matt. 24:15; Mark 13:14) is retained.

Family relations are more detailed than is traditional; hence, 'aboth becomes "forefathers" (Zech. 1:4; etc.) in some settings, but may alternate with "fathers" in others (Jer. 34:13, 14). "Brother" becomes "uncle" where the context shows such a relation (II Chron. 36:10). *Progonoi*, traditionally "parents," is elaborated to "parents and grandparents" (I Tim. 5:4). "Son's son" is "grandchildren" (Exod. 10:2), "children" at times become "grandchildren" (Gen. 31:28, 55), and "uncle's daughter" is "cousin" (Esther 2:7). "Brother" may be "relative" (Gen. 24:27); then "brother, mother's own son" (Deut. 13:7 [6]) is "very own brother." There is also "brother-in-law" (in the note, "father-in-law") in Judges 4:11.

"Washerman's Field" (II Kings 18:17; Isa. 7:3; 36:2) replaces "Fuller's field," and "launderer" replaces "fuller" (Mal. 3:2). "Cupbearer" replaces "butler" (Gen. 40:2ff.), "slave drivers" (Exod. 5:6) replaces "taskmasters," and "gentle whisper" (I Kings 19:12) replaces "still small voice." "Look after orphans and widows in their distress" (James 1:27) replaces "visit orphans and widows in their affliction."

A diligent effort is made to use idioms native to English. The Queen of Sheba is "overwhelmed" (I Kings 10:5); earlier translations read, "there was no more spirit in her." "The king would then have my head" (Dan. 1:10) is used for "so you would endanger my head with the king." "Inflicted a hundred thousand casualties" (I Kings 20:29) is used for "smote a hundred thousand foot soldiers." "In high spirits" (Esther 5:9) replaces the Semitism "happy of heart." "Wicked men" (Judg. 20:13) and "scoundrels" (I Kings 21:10) replace "sons of Belial." "Not one of them survived" replaces "none remained" (Exod. 14:28), and "He left no survivors" (Josh. 10:28, etc.) replaces "left none remaining." "The sweat of your brow" (Gen. 3:19) replaces "sweat of your face"; "don't reduce the quota" (Exod. 5:8, 14, 18) is used where early translations read, "the number of bricks which they made heretofore you shall lay on them." "As security" (Deut. 24:6) replaces "in pledge."

The NIV marks a step forward in eliminating Semitisms that through biblical influence have become an accepted part of English style. The redundant "stone him with stones" is reduced to "Stone him" (Deut. 13:10).

The sentences beginning "And it came to pass" are begun in a variety of ways. "The liberty of the glory" (ASV, Rom. 8:21) becomes "the glorious freedom." At the same time, the NIV could have gone further in translating Semitisms into English phrases. For example, "old and full of years" (Gen. 25:8; I Chron. 23:1) and "old and well advanced in years" (Josh. 23:1, 2) are raw Semitisms that may be compared with "He died at a good old age" (I Chron. 29:28). "Daughter of Zion" (Isa. 1:8) for "Jerusalem"; "Daughter of Babylon" (Zech. 2:7) for "Babylon"; and "daughter of a foreign god" (Mal. 2:11) for "a worshipper of a foreign god" are retained. "A man ... his neighbor" (Jer. 31:34) could be "one another." "Each by the sword of his brother" (Hag. 2:22) could be "each other's swords." "Man of peace" (Luke 10:6) could have been "peaceable man," and "Son of Encouragement" (Acts 4:36) could have been "an encouraging man."

The same movement toward current speech is evident in the New Testament. There is "lazy servant" for "slothful servant" (Matt. 25:26), "also heaped insults on him" (Matt. 27:44; KJV, "cast the same in his teeth"), and "Leave him alone" (Matt. 27:49; KJV, "Let be"). There is "leather belt" (Mark 1:6) for "leathern girdle," "whom I love" (Mark 1:11) for "beloved," "everyone is looking for you" (Mark 1:37) instead of "all men seek for thee." We find "pledged to be married" (Luke 2:5) for "his betrothed," "strips of cloth" (Luke 2:7) for "swaddling clothes" (KJV, ASV) or "swaddling cloths" (RSV), "piece of bread" (John 13:26) for "morsel of bread," and "physical body" (Col. 1:22) for "body of flesh."

Colloquialisms have not been avoided; for example, "Where is your big talk now ... ?" (Judg. 9:38). One reads "holds a grudge" (Gen. 50:15) and "nursed a grudge" (Mark 6:19). "Your clothes and your food" (Judg. 17:10) contrasts with "a suit of apparel, and your living." "But we had to celebrate" (Luke 15:32) is used for "it was fitting to make merry." "You're out of your mind" (Acts 12:15) replaces "you are mad." Paul "talked on and on" (Acts 20:9). We read, "those who sit in judgment on me" (I Cor. 9:3); the RSV had "those who would examine me." "They are not busy; they are busy-bodies" (II Thess. 3:11) is well expressed.

Despite its striving for current speech, the NIV retains a few words and idioms that need revision. What place has "she-camel" (Jer. 2:23) in a translation that elsewhere freely speaks of "male" and "female" animals (Gen. 31:12; 32:15; Lev. 5:6; 9:3; etc.)? Why "menservants" and "maidservants" (Deut. 15:17; I Sam. 8:16) instead of "male slaves" and "female slaves"? Would not "barren" be more accurate than "sterile" for Manoah's wife (Judg. 13:2, 3)? Idioms could also have replaced "Pressed hard after Saul" (I Sam. 31:2) and "journeyed" (I Sam. 31:12).

English style requires that the word order used in the original be transposed in the following phrases: "I and the boy" (Gen. 22:5), "I and the Father" (John 10:30), "I and Barnabas" (I Cor. 9:6), "me and Barnabas" (Gal. 2:9), "small and great" (Rev. 11:18), and "cold nor hot" (Rev. 3:15).

More consistency in capitalization is needed: "City of David" is ordinarily capitalized, but not so at I Kings 11:27, 43; 22:50; II Chronicles 9:31. "Name" is used twice in Jeremiah 34:15-16, but is only capitalized once. A shift from "dung" to "offal" (Exod. 29:14; Lev. 4:11; 16:27; Num. 19:5; Mal. 2:3) is not an improvement. How is "myriads" (Deut. 33:2) an improvement over "thousands," and how is "calamus" (Isa. 43:24; Jer. 6:20) better than "cane"? "Faced each other" might be better if it were "confronted each other" (II Chron. 25:21). "Take courage" (Ezra 10:4; Matt. 14:27; Mark 6:50; Acts 23:11) and "Take heart" (Matt. 9:2, 22) for *tharseite* are both understandable enough, but neither is a current American expression; elsewhere (Mark 10:49) "cheer up" is used. "You led captives in your train" (Ps. 68:18; cf. Eph. 4:8) uses an archaic term. "Satraps" (Dan. 6:1) might have been clarified as "provinces," especially since *medina* is elsewhere translated "provinces" (Esther 1:1).

Judgments on style are subjective with each reviewer expressing his own taste.[7] "The army melting away in all directions" (I Sam.14:16) seems hardly the best choice of idiom (the RSV had "was surging hither and thither"); would not "scattering in all directions" be better? Would not "I have reared and brought up children" (Isa. 1:2) be preferable to "I reared children and brought them up"? "Then he looked for a crop of good grapes, but it yielded only bad ones" (Isa. 5:2) seems smoother than the NIV reading "but it yielded only bad fruit." Would not "Return to him whom you have so greatly revolted against" be preferable to "Return to him you have so greatly revolted against" (Isa. 31:6)? And would it not be more natural to speak of "subordinates" than of "underlings" (Isa. 37:6)? Also cumbersome is "It will remain in his house and destroy it, both its timbers and its stones" (Zech. 5:4). "The city streets will be filled with boys and girls playing there" (Zech. 8:5) is less literal and less desirable than "playing in its streets" (RSV). "They spread the word concerning what had been

[7]Leland Ryken, "The Literary Merit of the *New International Version*," *Christianity Today* 23 (October 20, 1978): 76-77, finds the RSV "a much better literary achievement and more worthy of acceptance as the standard media Bible."

told them about this child" (Luke 2:17) could be made less cumbersome. "Have not love" (I Cor. 13:1, 3) could have been modernized as "do not have love." "Rode off . . . and fled" (I Sam. 30:17) is redundant.

Degree of Literalness

The NIV has attempted to steer a middle course between the excessive literalness of the NASB on the one hand and the excessive paraphrases of Phillips, the NEB, and Taylor on the other. Loyalty to the text has been defined in terms of a compromise between the Dynamic Equivalence principle and literalness, rather than in terms of Lightfoot's translation rule which stated, "the same English words to represent the same Greek words" and "as far as possible in the same order."[8]

In the NIV nouns have been supplied for pronouns to gain clarity in the English sentence; for example, by supplying "his brothers" for "they," the NIV makes it explicit who pulled Joseph out of the pit (Gen. 37:28; cf. Acts 7:9). Other nouns for pronouns are "Jethro" (Exod. 18:6), "the Lord" (Exod. 24:16), "the table" (Exod. 25:26), "God" (Exod. 3:12; Heb. 8:11), "Moses and Eleazer" (Num. 31:52), "people" (Heb. 8:8), and "the dragon" (Rev. 13:1). Third-person-singular pronouns of the original are often interpreted as collectives (Exod. 22:22, 23; Num. 24:8; Deut. 4:37). Other pronoun adjustments are made in Exodus 38:2, 7, 8. Fluctuations in the use of singular and plural in the original are adjusted in English (Exod. 39:7). Voice is sometimes changed from passive to active where English style requires it, and the genders of inanimate objects have been adjusted in keeping with English usage.

Where Greek phrases recur in the New Testament they are rendered alike. Old Testament quotations repeated in different places in the New Testament are harmonized with each other (Matt. 13:13; Acts 28:26) and are rendered as in the Old Testament if the Greek will allow it. At the same time there is a simplification of language.

The NIV has attempted to avoid anachronism; hence it uses "cloaks" instead of "coats," "sandals" instead of "shoes," and "mat" instead of "bed." "Telescoping" is considered objectionable. "Go to the prophets of your father and the prophets of your mother" (II Kings 3:13) is not shortened to

---

[8]Cited in Willis P. DeBoer, review of "The *New International Version* of the New Testament," in *Calvin Theological Journal* (April 1975): 67; also see J. B. Lightfoot, *On a Fresh Revision of the New Testament* (London: Macmillan, 1972), pp. x, 33ff.

"Go to the prophets of your father and mother." Though the latter has the same meaning as the former, it lacks the flavor appropriate to its time.

Some tendency to explanatory expansion is seen. Hence, "unclean" becomes "ceremonially unclean" (Lev. 13:3; Deut. 12:15; I Sam. 20:26; Ezek. 22:10). Samson's statement about the Philistines is paraphrased, "I have made donkeys of them" (Judg. 15:16). The *massebhah* is a "sacred stone" (Exod. 34:13; Deut. 12:3; II Kings 23:14) and *'asherim* are "Asherah poles" (Exod. 35:13; Deut. 12:3; I Kings 16:33). "Peaceably" becomes "Yes, peacefully" (I Kings 2:13). The "shewbread" becomes "consecrated bread" (I Chron. 28:16; II Chron. 2:4; 29:18; Matt. 12:4; Mark 2:26; Luke 6:4; Heb. 9:2). "Look upon" becomes "look lustfully at" (Job 31:1). "Interest" becomes "excessive interest" (Ezek. 18:8, 13, 17; 22:12); one wonders why "You shall not take interest of any kind" (Lev. 25:36) calls forth the note "Or take exorbitant interest." "Wicked fools" (Isa. 35:8) will not go on the holy way. The note gives "Or the simple will not stray from it" as the alternate. *Megedh shamayim mittal* becomes "precious dew from heaven above" (Deut. 33:13), a translation of a corrected text. "Kinsman-redeemer" is given for *go'el* (Ruth 2:20; 3:9, 12; 4:1, 3, 6), *kedheshah* is "shrine prostitute" (Gen. 38:21, 22), "know" becomes "If you really knew me" (John 14:7), and "wash" becomes "ceremonial washing" (Mark 7:3). "Lights" become "heavenly lights" (James 1:17) and "signs" become "miraculous signs" (John 20:30). "Pagan revelry" (I Cor. 10:7) is used for *paizen*; "For now we really live" (I Thess. 3:8) for *nun zōmen*.

There are many examples of Dynamic-Equivalence renderings. "Amen, Amen" (Num. 5:22) becomes "So be it." The American euphemism "sleep with" (Gen. 26:10; 35:22; 39:14; Exod. 22:16; Num. 5:19; 31:18, 35; II Sam. 11:4) or "come to bed with" (Gen. 39:10; II Sam. 13:11) usually (but not always; Gen. 34:7) replaces the Hebrew one—"lay with"—to describe the sex act. "Sleep with" (Gen. 19:8; 38:26), "lay with" (Gen. 4:1, 17, 25; I Sam. 1:19), "have sex with" (Gen. 19:5), or "had intimate relations with" (I Kings 1:4) replaces the euphemism "knew." "Sleep with" is also used for "Go in unto" (Gen. 16:2, 4; 19:8, 38:16; II Sam. 3:7); and for "bow down upon" (Job 31:10). "I'm having my period" (Gen. 31:35) is used for "the manner of women is upon me."

"Go, and I wish you well" (Exod. 4:18) is substituted for "go in peace," "I'm convinced" (Gen. 45:28) for "it is enough," "obey me fully" (Exod. 19:5) for "obey my voice." "Not loved" (Gen. 29:33), "unloved" Deut. 21:17), or "dislike" (Deut. 22:13; 24:3; cf. Luke 14:26) is sometimes used for "hated," but in other cases "hated" is retained (Mal. 1:3; Rom. 9:13). "Flesh and blood" (Gen. 29:14; Judg. 9:2) is used where the Hebrew had "bone and flesh." "Drop in a bucket" (Isa. 40:15) replaces "drop from a bucket" (RSV). The cry at the completion of Zerubbabel's temple is "God bless it" (Zech. 4:7; RSV: "Grace, Grace to it."). Habakkuk 2:2 becomes "So that a herald may run with it," but "herald" has the note "so that whoever reads it." "Empty stomachs" (Amos 4:6) replaces "cleanness of teeth," "faltering lips" (Exod. 6:30) replaces "uncircumcised lips," "forbidden" (Lev. 19:23) is used for "uncircumcised" fruit, and "Jews" (Rom. 15:8) is used instead of "circumcision." When referring to ears, "uncircumcised" becomes "closed" (Jer. 6:10).

The phrase "blessed be" becomes "Praise be to" (Exod. 18:10; I Kings 1:48; 10:9). "Your cloak tucked into your belt" (Exod. 12:11) replaces "your loins girded." Moses puts "his hand into his cloak" (Exod. 4:6) instead of "into his bosom." *Paracletos* is "one who speaks to the Father in our defense" (I John 2:1), but is "Counselor" in the Gospel of John (14:16; 16:7). "The islanders" (Acts 28:2) is used where the RSV had "natives" and the ASV "barbarians."

Words are expanded in order to express an idea in English. In I Corinthians 4:9 the Greek has twenty words, but there are forty-four in the NIV. In other cases words are compressed when the Hebrew is redundant. Where the RSV has the literal Hebrew rendering "he seized her and lay with her and humbled her," the NIV compresses the phrase to "he took her and violated her" (Gen. 34:2).

Implicit information is used in the rendering "Wine was served in goblets of gold" (Esther 1:7) where the literal rendering would be "The drinks were . . . ." The noun "wine" is derived from the second half of the sentence. "It is beyond understanding" (Judg. 13:18) has the note "is wonderful," which is a more literal rendering.

Variety of Rendering

Because the NIV does not always render a Hebrew or Greek word by the same English word, it shows a great variety in interpretation; this promises to make the forming of a concordance a complicated task. One has to recognize that words do have varieties of meaning, and the only question is whether or not the variety used is excessive. The variety may be seen in the words "articles," "accessories," and "utensils," all renderings of one term, *kelim* (Exod. 31:8-9). The treatment of *naham* is also illustrative. When describing God, the traditional "repent" is avoided. God "relents" (Jer. 18:8; 26:3, 13, 19; Amos 7:3, 6; Joel 2:13; Jonah 3:9; 4:2), "turns back" (Jer. 4:28), "changed his mind" (I Sam. 15:29), is "grieved" (Gen. 6:6; I Sam. 15:11, 35; II Sam. 24:16; I Chron. 21:15; Jer. 42:10), has "compassion" (Ps. 90:13; Isa. 49:13; 51:3; Jer. 15:6; Jonah 3:10), has "pity" (Joel 2:14, 18; Zech. 8:14), "gets relief from" (Isa. 1:24), and "comforts" (Zech. 1:17). When applied to man, the same root may signify "repent" (Job. 42:6; Jer. 8:6), "grieved" (Judg. 21:6; Joel 2:11), "consoled" (II Sam. 13:38), "comforted" (Gen. 24:67; Ruth 2:13; Ps. 77:2 [3]; 86:17; Jer. 31:13, 15), and "recovered from his grief" (Gen. 38:12).

Zera', dealing with the promise to Abraham, is "offspring" (Gen. 12:7; 13:16; 24:7) with "seed" as the marginal option, or "descendant" (Neh. 9:8); the same options (without the margin) are true of the promise to David, with "offspring" (II Sam. 7:12) and "descendants" (II Sam. 22:51; Ps. 18:50) used; but in the New Testament *sperma* is "family" (John 7:42), "descendant" (Luke 1:55; John 8:33, 37; Acts 7:5, 6; 13:23; Rom. 1:3; 9:7; 11:1; II Cor. 11:22; II Tim. 2:8; Heb. 2:16), and "offspring" (Acts 3:25; Rom. 4:13, 16, 18; 9:7, 8; Heb. 11:18). "Seed" is retained from tradition only in the technical argument of Galatians 3:16, 29. The wording of the Old Testament as rendered makes no preparation for Paul's argument.

Shekar (KJV and RSV: "strong drink") is "beer" (I Sam. 1:15; Prov. 31:4, 6; Isa. 24:9; 28:7; 29:9; 56:12; Mic. 2:11), "other fermented drink" (Lev. 10:9; Num. 6:3; Deut. 14:26; 29:6; Judg. 13:4, 7, 14; Luke 1:15), and "drinks" (Isa. 5:11, 22). The same Hebrew expression *he'amin* is at times "believed" (Gen. 15:6; cf. Isa. 43:10; Jonah 3:5; Rom. 4:3; Gal. 3:6; James 2:23). At other times it is "put their trust in" (Exod. 14:31; 19:9), "trusted" (I Sam. 27:12; Dan. 6:23), be "confident" (Ps. 27:13), or "have faith in" (II Chron. 20:20). One word, *shuf*, is "crush" and "strike" in the same setting (Gen. 3:15). *'Ebed* is "slave" (Exod. 21:32), "servant" (II Sam. 3:18), and "official" (Exod. 8:3, 29). *Hōra* is "hour" at John 12:23, 27, but is "time" at John 2:4, 7:30; 8:20. *Arsenokoitēs* is both "homosexual offender" (I Cor. 6:9) and "pervert" (I Tim. 1:10). *Ergon* (James 2:14, 17; Rom. 3:27) is "deeds," "actions," and "observing."

Biblical characters, where known by two names, may be called by their more familiar name with the literal rendering relegated to the notes. While Cephas is carried in the text at John 1:42; I Corinthians 1:12; 3:22; and 9:5, "Peter" is carried in the text and "Cephas" assigned to the notes at I Corinthians 15:5 and Galatians 1:18; 2:9, 11, 14. Although one might justify translating all the occurrences as "Peter," a half-and-half policy seems arbitrary. Is it not to be revealed to the reader that the Greek of Galatians 2:7 uses *Petros* and that the later verses of the chapter use "Cephas"?

The NIV retains "ships of Tarshish" (Ps. 48:7; Isa. 23:1, 14; 60:9; Ezek. 27:25) where trade on the Mediterranean can be thought of, but has elsewhere accepted the suggestion of some scholars that Solomon's "ships of Tarshish" are "trading ships" (I Kings 10:22; 22:48; II Chron. 9:21; 20:36; Isa. 2:16). However, it finds itself in a bind on these ships not going to "Tarshish" (II Chron. 20:37) and renders the expression "were not able to set sail to trade."

"Kittim" is at times retained in the text with a note that it is "Cyprus" (Jer. 2:10; Ezek. 27:6), but elsewhere it is rendered as "Cyprus" (Isa. 23:1, 12) or "western coastlands" (Dan. 11:30) with "Kittim" in the margin. The phrase *baruch 'Adonai*, usually rendered "Praise be to the Lord" (Gen. 24:27; Exod. 18:10; etc.), is sometimes retained in the traditional "Blessed be the Lord" (Gen. 9:26), but may also be "Praise the Lord" (Zech. 11:5).

The fact that *psuchē* can mean either "life" or "soul" allows the translators to shift from the first term to the second within one saying (Matt. 16:25, 26) even though there is no shift in subject matter.

In connection with baptism, *eis* is rendered "in" at Matthew 28:19 with "into" in the margin, but in other cases the opposite practice is followed (Acts 8:16; 19:5; Rom. 6:3; I Cor. 1:13; 10:2; Gal. 3:27).

These are only scattered samplings of the variety in renderings found in the NIV. More attention should have been given to uniformity of rendering where no difference in import is intended.

Theological Stance

The NIV reflects without apology the messianic interpretation of the Old Testament. It does not go to the extremes seen in some translations in which every appearance of the angel of the Lord is said in a note to be that of the Messiah. The messianic interpretation is seen in the capitalization of epithets traditionally interpreted messianically, such as "Anointed One" (Ps. 2:2; Dan. 9:25, 26), "Son" (Ps. 2:12), "King" (Ps. 2:6), "Holy One" (Ps. 16:10), and "Branch" (Isa. 11:1). "The Anointed One" (Dan. 9:25, 26) is preferred over "an Anointed one." The christological interpretation is further revealed in the supplying of the future tense "will be" (as KJV and

ASV; but in contrast to ASV margin; RSV; and NEB) in rendering the nominal sentence (Mal. 1:11) which in Hebrew has no expressed verb.

The Christian understanding of the Holy Spirit is reflected in the capitalization of "Spirit" (Isa. 44:3; 61:1): "Spirit of God" (Gen. 1:2; I Sam. 10:6; 19:20, 23), "Spirit of the Lord" (I Sam. 10:6; Isa. 63:14), "Holy Spirit" (Isa. 63:10, 11), and the rendering "a spirit of grace and supplication" in the text with "the Spirit" as alternate in the margin (Zech. 12:10). In contrast to these, "spirit" in "an evil spirit from God" (I Sam. 18:10; 19:9) is not capitalized; neither is the human spirit. Where there may be doubt whether or not the Holy Spirit is being spoken of, the uncapitalized or the capitalized form is given in the notes.

An understanding of Scripture congenial to evangelical thought is reflected. If one takes R. Laird Harris's article criticizing the RSV as a point of departure,[9] one discovers that in each item of criticism the NIV has adopted positions congenial to Harris's contentions. The NIV does not abandon the Masoretic text in favor of a versional or conjectural reading as frequently as the RSV did. In Psalm 2:11, 12, the NIV, reflecting a messianic interpretation of the verses and rejecting the RSV textual emendation which gave "kiss his feet," translates, "kiss the Son." The RSV carried a note that the text was unclear. Harris denied that it is. In Leviticus 16:8, 10, 26, the NIV reverts to the rendering "scapegoat" with a note: "That is, the goat of removal: Hebrew, *azazel*." The RSV had used "Azazel" without a note. It is assumed that the wilderness demon was intended. In the NIV the orientation of *'ebher hayyarden* (Deut. 1:1; 4:46) is given as "east of the Jordan" and that of Joshua 9:1 as "west of the Jordan," avoiding critical implications about the viewpoint of the author. In Psalm 29:1, rejecting alleged Ugaritic parallels and the understanding of Genesis 6:2 which embodied mixed marriages, and taking Psalm 96:7-8 as a point of departure, the NIV renders *bene 'elohim* as "O mighty ones." Elsewhere, however, the same phrase is translated "sons of God" (Gen. 6:2) or "angels" (Job 1:6; 2:1).

Harris, arguing that Psalm 49:12 should be understood as an exhortation to wisdom rather than as a denial of immortality, insisted that the Septuagint likely should be followed in reading *bin* (understand) in verse 12 where the present text has *lin* (abide). The difference is one Hebrew letter;

---

[9]R. Laird Harris, "Do Evangelicals Need a New Bible Translation? Yes," *Christianity Today* 12 (September 27, 1968): 1242, 1244-46.

but the RSV had emended *bin* to *lin* in verse 20, harmonizing the two verses. The NIV renders verse 12 as "does not endure," but carries a note that the Septuagint and Syriac read, "But a man who has riches without understanding / is." It then renders verse 20 as "without understanding" where the RSV had emended the text, getting the translation "cannot abide."

Harris charged that the RSV reflected a prejudice against the messianic prophecy. The NIV in Psalm 45:6 reverts to the rendering previously used in the KJV, "Your throne, O God," which it also carries at the quotation of the Psalm in Hebrews 1:8. The RSV had carried "Your divine throne" in the text of Psalm 45:6 with alternates in the notes: "your throne is a throne of God, or your throne, O God," but then had "Thy throne, O God" in Hebrews 1:8. Psalm 16:10 is cast in the future tense in the NIV: "will not abandon" and "nor will you let your Holy One see decay," with a note "Or your faithful one." The rendering agrees with the use of the word "decay" in Acts 2:29-31; 13:35-37. Harris had argued that the future is proper and that the noun is from *shachath* ("to go to ruin"), as the Septuagint took it to be, and not from *shuach* which the RSV considered it to be. It is to be noted, however, that in the NIV, the phrase which follows "You have made known ... ," in verse 11 is cast in the pluperfect (from the Septuagint and harmonized with Acts 2:28) and that the future (of the Masoretic text) is given as an alternate only in the footnote.

With the furor some evangelicals raised over the RSV's treatment of Isaiah 7:14, it was inevitable that *'almah* should there be rendered "virgin"; and perhaps it is not surprising that a marginal note to the contrary opinion is absent, though the ASV, RSV, NASB, and NAB each carried one. Elsewhere in the NIV, *'almah* is "maiden" (Gen. 24:43; Ps. 68:25; Prov. 30:19; Song of Sol. 1:3), "girl" (Exod. 2:8), and "virgin" (Song of Sol. 6:8)—all without notation. It was also inevitable that the quotation of John 3 be terminated at verse 21 rather than at verse 15, and that of Galatians 2 at verse 21 rather than at verse 14, though in each of these cases a contrary opinion is acknowledged in the notes.

The rendering "expressing spiritual truths in spiritual words" is preferred over the margin's "spiritual truths to spiritual men" (I Cor. 2:13). The translation and marginal reading followed by the RSV is reversed at Romans 9:5 to give "Christ, who is God over all, forever praised," in the text. "Our great God and Savior, Jesus Christ" (Titus 2:13) is chosen without notation over the textual variant "of the great God and our Savior."

On many other questions, the NIV notes theological alternatives; for example, Isaiah 52:15 reads "sprinkle many nations" but notes in the margin that the Septuagint has "so will many nations marvel at him." "Generation" carries the alternate "race" in a note (Matt. 24:34; Mark 13:30; Luke 21:32). "Servant" (Rom. 16:1) and "wives" (I Tim. 3:11) carry the alternates "deacon" and "deaconesses."

Why?

A reviewer inevitably finds in every translation some renderings about which he would like to talk with his colleagues of the translation groups and ask "Why?" The NIV is no exception. Why is there no note to Deuteronomy 33:17 stating that the versions are being followed? Why prefer the supplied adverb in "where their voice is not heard" (Ps. 19:3) over the marginal options? Why "sinner" in "I have been a sinner from birth" (Ps. 51:5) as opposed to the traditional "I was born in sin"?

Though Hebrew scholars recognize that the words of Isaiah 28:10, 13 are, as the margin suggests, possibly unintelligible words, how were the words in the text chosen? What is their relation to the Hebrew words of the passage? Is not the literal "third day" of the margin (Amos 4:4) preferable to the "three years" of the text despite any possible harmonization of the latter with the tithing law of the Pentateuch? Is not the marginal reading "faithfulness" actually preferable at Habakkuk 2:4 over the "faith" of the text? *'Emunah* is elsewhere rendered "faithfulness" (Isa. 11:5; Hos. 2:20 [22]), "steady" (Exod. 17:12), "faithfully" (II Kings 22:7), "truth" (Jer. 5:1; 7:28), and "truthful" (Prov. 12:17). Is not the literal margin "brothers" also preferable to "believers" (Acts 1:15)? How is "evil spirit" preferable to "unclean spirit" (Matt. 12:43; Mark 5:2, 8, 13; Luke 6:18; Acts 5:16; Rev. 18:2; etc.)? Is not "until Christ came" (Gal. 3:24) preferable to "to lead us to Christ"?

Could not *kataluein* ("abolish"; Matt. 5:17) and *katargein* (also rendered "abolishing"; Eph. 2:15) be distinguished to avoid anyone's supposing that there is tension between the two verses? Why supply the indefinite article at I John 5:16: "a sin"?

Conclusion

The King James scholars expected to be "tossed up on tongues." The

NIV translators are now in the throes of that process. A harsh reviewer speaks of its being "tinctured throughout with the erroneous doctrines of original sin, hereditary depravity, restoration of national Israel, premillennialism, and predestination."[10] Another says, "At times it is so close to the RSV that one wonders why all this energy and money should have been spent on another version."[11]

More friendly reviews note that "one finds less to quarrel with in it than in the RSV and NEB."[12] Another says, "The first impression of the NIV is highly favorable."[13]

Those who have worked on the NIV would be the last to claim infallibility or any sort of finality for what they have produced. As the King James scholars said, "Nothing is begun and perfected at the same time." Only time will reveal whether its readers will find in the NIV that which speaks to them. Likely the goal "To do for our time what the King James Version did for its day" (publisher's release) is too ambitious. The NIV does mark one more step in the direction of supplying God's Word in current and understandable English. Perhaps it can achieve the more modest goal of casting light upon the way for some who otherwise would have been in darkness.

[10]Foy E. Wallace, Jr., "Some Important Corrections." *Gospel Advocate* 67 (April 10, 1975): 235.

[11]D. Evert, "New Translation Enters Crowded Field," *Mennonite Brethren Herald* (December 14, 1973): 22.

[12]Reginald Fuller, "New Testament Version," *The Review of Books and Religion* 4 (April 1975): 14.

[13]F. F. Bruce, "The *New International Version*: Is It Living? Is It Today's English? Is It Revised? Will It Become the New American Standard?" *Eternity* 30 (January 1976): 46-47.

14

The New King James Version

The New King James Version (NKJV) developed out of a revision project set in motion in 1975 by Thomas Nelson Publishers, Nashville, Tennessee, which styles itself the "World's Leading Bible Publisher." Advertising material claims that the NKJV is the fifth major revision of the KJV and the first since 1769. (There were revisions in 1629, 1638, 1762 [by Thomas Paris], and in 1769 [by Benjamin Blayney].) The publisher considers hundreds of other efforts at revising the KJV to be minor; the RV (1881-85), ASV (1901), and RSV (1952) are also ignored. The NKJV is advertised as the "first major revision of the classic Bible in more than 200 years." The N.T. of the NKJV appeared in 1979 (a printing of 250,000 copies), and the complete Bible was issued in 1982 with some modifications in the N.T. Production cost for the whole reached 4.5 million dollars.

The N.T. of the NKJV was hailed extravagantly in advertising as "the most important event in Bible publishing since the original King James was released in 1611." Nelson has advertised the NKJV as "the Accurate One," has attempted with limited success to convince churches to accept it as the translation to use, and, according to the Memphis *Commercial Appeal* (May 26, 1984), spent 1.6 million in 1984 on that campaign.

While advertising material claims "the entire text of the original King James Version is included in the New King James," the Apocrypha (which was a part of the original KJV) is not included. Since the early nineteenth century, it has not been the custom to print the Apocrypha between the O.T. and N.T. of Protestant Bibles.

The NKJV is published in numerous shapes and sizes. The text has been issued for children ages five to eight in the NKJV Little Hands Bible, which contains colorful illustrations. For very young children there is the NKJV Precious Moments™ Baby Bible. Nelson has also issued the Open Bible Expanded Edition with either the KJV or NKJV text, an NKJV Scofield Reference Bible, the Ryrie Study Bible, and the Businessman's and the Businesswoman's NKJV Bibles. These last two have center reference columns, introductions to the books, concordances, and explanatory notes. NKJV Slimline New Testaments contain cross-references, explanatory notes, and a discussion of the plan of salvation. In addition, a complete concordance, published by Nelson in 1983, is quite essential for study since the vocabulary change is extensive.

More than 130 evangelical scholars worked over a seven-year period in making the revision.[1] The executive committee was composed of six persons. The executive editor of the N.T. group was Arthur Farstad. The O.T. executive editor was initially William White but later was James D. Price. Books were assigned to various scholars across the English-speaking world. They worked privately to make proposed revisions; the outcome of their work was then submitted to the executive editor of the N.T. or the O.T., who reviewed the revised material word for word, line by line, making recommendations for any further changes. Each book was submitted to William H. McDowell, the English editor, to be checked for grammatical accuracy, literary beauty, and effective communication. Advisors who served on the British and the North American Overview Committees regularly reviewed the work as it was edited. The material was then read by a separate executive review committee for each Testament. Changes were made by majority vote. The system of italicizing was worked out by the executive editors, and the subject headings were developed jointly by the executive editors and the English editor.

All participants signed "a document of subscription to the plenary and verbal inspiration of the original autographs of the Bible." The statement affirmed that those autographs were "free from error." Taking their cue from a statement made in the preface of the 1611 KJV, the preparers of the NKJV describe their effort as "a continuation of the labors of the earlier translators, thus unlocking for today's readers the treasures found especially in the Authorized Version of the Holy Scriptures." The transla-

---

[1]A list is to be found in the advertisement in *Christianity Today* 26 (September 3, 1982):60-61.

tors claim to have sought Complete Equivalence to the original (as contrasted with Dynamic Equivalence) where a new translation has been necessary.[2] They "have sought to maintain that lyrical quality which is so highly regarded in the Authorized Version."

The preparers of the NKJV recognize that the English language has changed since 1611 and that alterations have been made in the KJV in the intervening years. They see their product as a further step to keep abreast: "Where obsolescence and other reading difficulties exist, present-day vocabulary, punctuation, and grammar have been carefully integrated." While granting that punctuation rules differ considerably from those in 1611, NKJV editors note that the NKJV "has been updated only in those specific instances where clarity would definitely be enhanced through more modern punctuation and grammar." Advertising material states that the NKJV "restores and protects the originally intended beauty, authority and meaning of every verse" and "makes the King James even better." It is claimed that the congregation can follow without difficulty in the NKJV while the KJV is being read. Why the KJV should be read while listeners have the NKJV is not explained.

The KJV format is maintained throughout with a double column page, the verses in numbered paragraphs, and the words of Jesus printed in red. This last feature has appeared in KJV printings only since 1899. "Lord" spelled in capital and small capital letters is retained for the name of the God of Israel. Unlike the KJV, paragraph divisions are indicated by printing the relevant verse numbers in bold print. This practice is continued throughout the N.T. despite the fact that paragraph indicators in 1611 ended at Acts 22. Letters to individuals and royal decrees are set off by indentation (Ezra 4:9-10, 11-16, 17-22; 6:3-12). The NKJV abandons the practice of printing the first word of a chapter in all capital letters (the 1611 edition had a block initial letter and then capitalized only the second letter of such a word).

Other obvious differences from the 1611 KJV include the use of quotation marks indicating both direct address and quotation of O.T. Scriptures. The first quotation of John 3 is continued to verse 21 and the second to verse 36 despite the uncertainty about where either quotation ends and the writer's comments begin. Since each verse is a paragraph, each successive verse is indicated as a quotation. "Who" is used instead of "which" and "that" when referring to persons. "Its" is used instead of "his" for the possessive of inanimate objects. Current forms of pronouns have been substituted for "thee," "thou," "mine" and "thine," and cur-

---

[2]See James D. Price, *Complete Equivalence in Bible Translation* (Nashville: Nelson, 1985).

rent verb forms have been substituted for "eth" and "est." One reads, "Your rod and Your staff, they comfort me" (Ps. 23:4) and "Your kingdom come. Your will be done . . ." (Matt. 6:10).

In place of the archaic pronouns, the NKJV capitalizes pronouns to show reverence and to distinguish between human and divine persons. Also capitalized are all titles and terms interpreted as applying to any member of the Trinity: "Seed" (Gen. 3:15), "Him" (Gen. 49:10), "Star" and "Scepter" (Num. 24:17), "Redeemer" (Job 19:25), "Son" (Isa. 7:14; 9:6), "Child" (Isa. 9:6), "Rod" and "Branch" (Isa. 11:1), "Root" (Isa. 11:10), "Servant" (Isa. 52:13), "the Son of God" (Dan. 3:25), "Angel" (margin: or "angel" [Dan. 3:28]), "Son of Man" (Dan. 7:13), "Desire of all Nations" (Hag. 2:7), and "Sun of Righteousness" (Mal. 4:2). The capitalization of "I AM" (John 8:58) reflects a theological viewpoint which contends that Jesus is identifying himself with the figure revealed at the burning bush (Exod. 3:14).

Poetry is structured as contemporary verse in poetic books, prophetic books, and in Luke 1:46-55 but not in Philippians 2:6-11. The KJV of 1611 had only rhythmical prose. Italic type in the N.T. indicates an O.T. quotation while the footnotes indicate the O.T. source. Subject headings (all reworked) have been added in the text, not carried at the top of the page as in the KJV. Speaker identifications are supplied in the Song of Solomon.

Footnotes indicate variant readings but supply no means of evaluating them. The KJV in 1611 cited only about fifteen variants in the N.T. and these notes are not now commonly printed. Ussher's chronology is omitted as well as the Christological headings to some of the Psalms, to chapters in the Song of Solomon, and to some chapters in Isaiah. "Saint" is gone from Gospel titles, and The Revelation of St. John the Divine becomes The Revelation of Jesus Christ. Postscripts to certain N.T. epistles in the KJV are dropped.

Text

For the O.T., the 1966/1977 edition of the Stuttgart Bible was used with comparison to the earlier Rabbinic Bible of 1516. The Greek, Latin, and other versions, as well as the Dead Sea Scrolls, were consulted. Significant variations from the text followed in the KJV are referenced in the footnotes. It becomes obvious that the preparers of the NKJV were more satisfied with the current O.T. text criticism than with N.T. text criticism.

The text followed in the N.T. showcases the most distinctive and inno-

traditionalism's dying struggle to maintain itself. Though there have been many efforts to reverse history, in general, people have never been able to turn processes backward. Only those willing to take the step backward will find the NKJV desirable.

The preparers of the NKJV take for granted that the reader, informed by the notes, can mark out or discount those verses or phrases which he considers not well founded. This position, however, assumes a knowledge of textual processes which the ordinary reader lacks. It is more in keeping with human nature for the uninformed reader to take the text as authoritative and ignore the notes. Many readers believe that because a phrase was in the KJV it is Scripture; however, this opinion is fallacious. If he is convinced that a word, phrase, or a verse was a part of the original text, no reviser would leave it out. Neither would he insert words were he not convinced that scribes dropped them out. The basic question is not what was or was not in the KJV but what the original writers wrote. Those phrases added by Erasmus from the Latin text which have no known Greek support as well as some other scribal insertions cannot claim such validity.

Updating

The updated spelling in the NKJV is so extensive that one can do no more than mention it. "Shewbread" becomes "showbread" (Exod. 25:30; etc.). English plurals are dropped from the transliterated Hebrew plurals: "cherubim" (Gen. 3:24; Heb. 9:5; etc.), "Anakim" (Deut. 2:10; etc.), "seraphim" (Isa. 6:2; etc.), and "Nethinim" (I Chron. 9:2; etc.). However, the NKJV has both "stiff-necked" (Exod. 32:9; 33:3, 5; 34:9; Deut. 9:6, 13; 10:16) and "stiffnecked" (II Chron. 30:8; Acts 7:51).

The list of doctrinal problems noted in the KJV review in this book[5] reveals much modification in the NKJV. "Borrow" becomes "ask" (Exod. 3:22; 11:2); "Thou shalt not kill" becomes "You shall not murder" (Exod. 20:13; etc.). "Fold . . . one fold" becomes "fold . . . one flock" (John 10:16). "Drink ye all of it" becomes "Drink from it, all of you" (Matt. 26:27). "For we offend all" becomes "For we all stumble in many things" (James 3:2). Giving "with simplicity" becomes giving "with liberality" (Rom. 12:8). "Easter" (Acts 12:4) rightly has become "Passover," and the phrase "and drinks" (I Cor. 11:27) becomes "or drinks." A distinction is made between "devil" and "demon" (Matt. 11:18; John 8:48) which the KJV neglected in rendering *daimonion* as "devil." "Food" is used instead

---

[5]Jack P. Lewis, *The English Bible from KJV to NIV*, 1st ed. (Grand Rapids: Baker, 1982), 35-68.

of "meat" when flesh is not in view (John 4:34; etc.). An example of a contemporary word with a different meaning from that of 1611 would be "rioting," for which the NKJV uses "revelry" (Rom. 13:13), and "riotous" becomes "prodigal" (Luke 15:13), "gluttonous" (Prov. 23:20), and "gluttons" (Prov. 28:7). However, despite the updating, "tithes of all that I possess" (Luke 18:12) remains unchanged though tithing did not apply to capital holdings.

The vocabulary modification in the NKJV is extensive. The NKJV makes use of many words known in the twentieth century which either were not around in 1611 or were not used. In the examples cited, the KJV word is given in the parenthesis following the Scripture location: "routed" (Josh. 10:10; Judg. 4:15; 8:12; "discomfited"), "refugee" (Lam. 2:22; "none escaped"), "stragglers" (Deut. 25:18; "hindmost of them"), "Regiment" (Acts 10:1; 27:1; "band"), "was remorseful" (Matt. 27:3; "repented himself"), "sullen" (I Kings 20:43; "heavy"), "strata" (Amos 9:6; "troop"), "shifts" (I Kings 5:14; "courses"), "in shambles" (Joel 1:17; "laid desolate"), "waterfalls" (Ps. 42:7; "waterspouts"), vegetation "wilts" (Nah. 1:4; "languishes"; Ezek. 31:15; "fainted"), "saturated" (Isa. 34:7; "made fat"; Job 37:11; "wearieth"), and "savage wolves" (Acts 20:29; "grievous wolves"). The list is not exhaustive.

One can see on every page the effort to update the language of the KJV. Modern pronouns are used throughout. One reads "In the day of my trouble I will call upon You, For you will answer me" (Ps. 86:7), and "Your rod and Your staff, they comfort me" (Ps. 23:4). "Holy Spirit" replaces "Holy Ghost" (Matt. 1:20; etc.), and "Himself" replaces "itself" for the Spirit (Rom. 8:26). "Tax collectors" replaces "publicans" (Matt. 9:10; etc.), and "Rejoice" (Matt. 28:9) displaces "All hail." The head of John the Baptist is on a "platter" (Mark 6:28) rather than on a "charger," and "launderer" displaces "fuller" (Mark 9:3), but "Fuller's" is retained at some points (Isa. 7:3; etc.). "Fetched a compass" (II Sam. 5:23; Acts 28:13) becomes "circle around," and "letteth" becomes "restrains" (II Thess. 2:7). Jacob "cooked a stew"; the KJV had him "sod pottage" (Gen. 25:29). "How shall we order the child?" (Judg. 13:12) becomes "What will be the boy's rule of life?" "Kine" becomes "cows" (Gen. 41:3), "murrain" becomes "severe pestilence" (Exod. 9:3), and "ass" has become "donkey" (Gen. 22:3; Isa. 1:3; etc.). "Mean man" becomes "people" (Isa. 2:9; 5:15) or "unknown men" (Prov. 22:29), and "basest of men" becomes "lowest of men" (Dan. 4:17). "Grain-fields" and "heads of grain" replaces "corn" and "ears of corn" (Matt. 12:1). "Cauls" becomes "scarves" and "round tires like the moon" becomes "crescents" (Isa. 3:18). "Ouches" becomes "settings" (Exod. 28:25). Solomon loved "foreign women" instead of "strange women" (I Kings 11:1), and there are "pagan women" instead of "strange women" and "outlandish women" (Neh. 13:26). "Naughty figs" becomes "very bad figs" (Jer. 24:2). The mythical "unicorn" has become the "wild ox" (Deut. 33:17; Ps. 22:21; Isa. 37:4), the "satyr" is a "wild goat" (Isa. 13:21; 34:14), the "cockatrice" is a "viper" (Isa. 11:8; 14:29; Jer. 8:17), and the "dragon" is a "serpent" (Ps. 91:13) or a "jackal" (Job 30:29; Ps. 44:19). The margin of the 1611 KJV containing "arrow-snake" is no longer printed; hence, the NKJV did not have to bother with that note. However, "arrow-snake" is inserted at Isaiah 34:15 where the KJV had "great owl." "Severely" (I Sam. 1:6; etc.) replaces "sore" as an adverb. "Speck" and "plank" replace "mote" and "beam" (Matt. 7:3). "Sick people" replaces "impotent folk" (John 5:3). "Do not worry" replaces "Take no thought" (Matt. 6:25). "Conversation" has been replaced by "conduct" (Phil. 1:27; I Tim. 4:12; Heb. 13:5, 7; I Pet. 2:12; etc.) or by "citizenship" (Phil. 3:20), and "honest" by "honorable" (I Pet. 2:12). "Prevent" is displaced by "come to meet me" (Ps. 59:10), "come speedily to meet us" (Ps. 79:8), "comes before You" (Ps. 88:13), "overtake us" (Amos 9:10), or "precede" (I Thess. 4:15). "Overflow of wickedness" (James 1:21) replaces "superfluity of naughtiness," and "make known to you" (II Cor. 8:1) replaces "do you to wit." The prodigal would have eaten "pods" (Luke 15:16), not "husks." "After the Sabbath" (Matt. 28:1) displaces "in the end of the Sabbath." "Each of you says, 'I am of Paul,' or . . ." displaces "and" (I Cor. 1:12), which could be read that each one in Corinth claimed membership in more than one party. The word "fear" in human relations is modified. One is to "revere" his mother and his father (Lev. 19:3; "fear"), and the wife is to "respect" her husband (Eph. 5:33; "reverence").

The long-standing printing errors of the KJV are corrected. "Strain out a gnat" (Matt. 23:24) replaces "strain at a gnat," and "propriety" (I Tim. 2:9) replaces "shamefacedness."

The KJV was apparently unwilling to use the same verb for God and Satan and has God "move" David (II Sam. 24:1) but has Satan "provoke" him (I Chron. 21:1). The Hebrew is the same, and the NKJV uses "moved" in both cases. Passages dealing with practices of the human male which were formerly embarrassing for public reading (e.g., I Sam. 25:22, 34; I Kings 14:10; 16:11; 21:21; II Kings 18:27; Isa. 36:12) have been made more readable.

Some transliterated words of the KJV are translated. The NKJV records "accursed" and "O Lord, Come!" (I Cor. 16:22), and "*Shittim*" becomes "Acacias" (Joel 3:18; Mic. 6:5). Some titles of the Lord are translated, for example, "You-Are-the-God-Who-Sees" (Gen. 16:13), "The-Lord-Will-Provide" (Gen. 22:14), and "The Lord-Is-My-Banner" (Exod.

17:15); however, "The-Lord-Shalom" (Judg. 6:24; "Jehovah-shalom") is retained. "My Husband" and "my Master" (Hos. 2:16) are translations. The occurrence of "teraphim" (Judg. 17:5; 18:14, 20; Hos. 3:4) has been replaced in all but one verse (Hos. 3:4) by the use of "household idols." The KJV used "images" (Gen. 31:19, 34, 35). As in the KJV, "Sabaoth" is used only in Romans 9:29 and James 5:4. The corresponding Hebrew term is rendered "hosts" (I Sam. 1:3; etc.) in the O.T. But "Raca" (Matt. 5:22), "Hosanna" (Matt. 21:9; etc.), "mammon" (Matt. 6:24; Luke 16:9, 11, 13), "Bar-Jonah" (Matt. 16:17), and "Didymus" (John 11:16; 20:24; 21:2) are retained.

The preparers of the NKJV make use of modern archaeological scholarship in reading "hovering" (Gen. 1:2) instead of "moved upon," "their mounds" (Josh. 11:13) instead of "their strength," "pim" (I Sam. 13:21) instead of "file," "Keveh" (I Kings 10:28) instead of "linen yarn," and in identifying "Pul, that is [KJV: "and"], Tiglath-Pileser" (I Chron. 5:26) as the same person. "Syrian" as a language has rightly become "Aramaic" (Ezra 4:7; Dan. 2:4; "Syriack"), but "Syrian" (Gen. 25:20; Deut. 26:5; etc.) is retained for the identification of nationality. One wonders why "a mist went up" (Gen. 2:6) is used for water which must have come from underground sources (NIV: "streams"; NEB: "flood"), why "Lucifer" (Isa. 14:12) is kept (along with a heading titled "The Fall of Lucifer") when the section deals with the king of Babylon, and why "Diana" (Acts 19:24, 27, 28) is preferred over "Artemis," which is recorded in the Greek, as the note system recognizes.

"Tabernacle" (I Sam. 3:3) is used for *hekhal* instead of "temple." "Voice of the turtledove" (Song of Sol. 2:12) replaces "voice of the turtle" and "plant" (Jonah 4:6) replaces "gourd." "Grain offering" (Lev. 2:1; Joel 1:13) replaces "meat offering." The NKJV, however, retains "disorderly" (II Thess. 3:6, 7, 11) where the meaning should be "idle." "Helper" (as in the NASV) is chosen for *paracletos* (John 14:16, 26; 15:26; 16:7), but "Advocate," now capitalized, is retained for *paracletos* in I John 2:1, thus obscuring a connection which probably should be retained.

The NKJV also contains examples of what might be called Dynamic Equivalence with the 1611 KJV. "God save the King" becomes "Long live the King" (I Sam. 10:24; II Sam. 16:16; II Kings 11:12; II Chron. 23:11), which itself is not strictly literal. "God forbid!" becomes "Certainly not!" (I Sam. 14:45; Luke 20:16; Rom. 3:4, 6; 7:7, 13; 9:14; 11:1, 11; I Cor. 6:15; Gal. 2:17; 3:21). "Would God" becomes "Oh, that" (Exod. 16:3; Deut. 28:67; Josh. 7:7; II Cor. 11:1), "If only" (Num. 14:2; Judg. 9:29; 2 Sam. 18:33; II Kings 5:3), and "I could wish" (I Cor. 4:8). "God forbid that" becomes "Far be it from" (Gen. 44:7, 17; Josh. 22:29; 24:16; I Sam. 12:23; Job 27:5) and "By no means" (I Sam. 20:2). However, Galatians 6:14 is retained as "God forbid" with no italics.

The NKJV makes some passages more understandable for readers who have stumbled with the KJV. The NKJV records "fill the earth" (Gen. 1:28; 9:1) where the KJV has "replenish," a word that is understood by some who claim support for the gap theory to mean "do over again." "Living being" (Gen. 2:7) replaces "living soul," but the NKJV retains an unnecessary variety in the rendering of *nephesh chayah* (Gen. 1:20, 21, 24; 2:7). "Helper comparable to him" replaces "help meet for him" (Gen. 2:18), so removing the basis for the English solecism "helpmate." "Beautiful" replaces "fair" (Gen. 6:2) and robs racists of this proof text. The adverb "unworthily" becomes "in an unworthy manner" (I Cor. 11:27). This change removes the possibility of less-informed people thinking that they are charged not to take communion if they are unworthy. I Peter 3:21 becomes "There is also an antitype" (KJV: "the like figure where unto").

Some of the passages formerly accused of having been unduly influenced by Calvinism have been modified. "Were being saved" (Acts 2:47) replaces "should be saved." "As many as had been appointed to eternal life believed" (Acts 13:48) replaces "were ordained to." However, the passive "be converted" for an active Greek form, though changed in John 12:40 and Acts 28:27, remains in Acts 3:19.

Shortcomings

The rules for the definite article in Hebrew and English do not correspond. The NKJV did not solve the KJV's problem of when to insert and when to omit the definite article. That which in Hebrew is "the raven" becomes "a raven" and "the dove" becomes "a dove" (Gen. 8:7, 8) in both versions. "Tartan" (Isa. 20:1) and "the Tartan" (II Kings 18:17) occur for the same term. The supplied definite article is not italicized in 2 Kings 18:17 for "the Rabshakeh" but is in the parallel in Isaiah ("*the* Rabshakeh"; Isa. 36:2, 4, 11, 12, 13, 22).

One must ask while noting the undeniable improvements of the NKJV over the KJV, "Why stop here with a new old English? Why not come to current English?" One cannot put gingerbread on a Gothic structure and still have the original. Why create something which is unlike the way English-speaking people ever expressed themselves?

The process of modernization has been inconsistently carried out. In O.T. promises "descendants" (Gen. 12:7; 13:15; 24:7) is used, but in the N.T. citations of these promises "seed," which is not twentieth-century usage, is retained (Acts 13:23; Gal. 3:16, 19, 29), as is also done in Genesis 3:15. In other settings "offspring" (Gen. 15:3; Mark 12:19, 20; etc.) is also used.

The reverence for the KJV limited the revisers and caused them to ignore in many cases the contribution of the papyri discoveries at the beginning of this century. The outcome is what Soderlund designated "a curious mixture of Elizabethan style with glosses of twentieth century vocabulary and grammar."[6] Peacock wrote that "the voice is Jacob's voice, but the hands are the hands of Esau."[7] One still reads of "Hew down trees" (Jer. 6:6), "the wind was boisterous" (Matt. 14:30), "purge His threshing floor" (Matt. 3:12), "exceedingly great joy" (Matt. 2:10; "exceeding"), "exceedingly angry" (Matt. 2:16; "exceeding wroth"), "exceedingly high mountain" (Matt. 4:8; "exceeding"), "exceedingly glad" (Matt. 5:12; "exceeding"), "exceedingly sorrowful" (Matt. 17:23; "exceeding sorry"; 26:22; "exceeding sorrowful"), a hand "restored as whole" (Mark 3:5), "leaven" (Matt. 13:33), and "brethren" (Rom. 1:13). The change of "ships" to "sloops" (Isa. 2:16) and "company of horses" to "filly" (Song of Sol. 1:9) contributes little to clarity.

The NKJV policy has been to keep much that is perhaps still understood but is not the current manner of speech. An impressive list can be compiled: "day of his espousals" (Song of Sol. 3:11), "eventide" (Isa. 17:14; "eveningtide"), "high degree" or "low degree" for status (I Chron. 17:17; Ps. 62:9), "dandled" (Isa. 66:12), "carriages" (Isa. 46:1) for that which is carried, "befall" for happen (Gen. 42:4, 38; etc.), "befitting" (meaning "suitable") for "meet" (Acts 26:20), "beget" for fathering (Gen. 17:20; etc.), but God is the one "who fathered you" (Deut. 32:18; "formed thee"). There is "fatling" (Isa. 11:6; etc.) and "fatted calf" (I Sam. 28:24; "fat calf"; Luke 15:23, 27, 30), "fatter in flesh" (Dan. 1:15), "feigned" for pretended (I Sam. 21:13), "frontlets" (Exod. 13:16; Deut. 6:8; 11:18), "manifold" (Neh. 9:19; Ps. 104:24; Amos 5:12; Eph. 3:10; I Pet. 4:10), "mansions" (John 14:2), "manslayer" (Num. 35:6; etc.), "mete out the waters by measure" (Job 28:25), "the matrix of My mother" (Isa. 49:1; "bowels of my mother"), "offscouring" (Lam. 3:45; I Cor. 4:13), "onward" (Exod. 40:36; Num. 15:23; "hence forward"; Isa. 18:2, 7), "outward" (Num. 35:4), "outgoings of the morning" (Ps. 65:8), "paramours" (Ezek. 23:20), and "pinions" (Job 39:13; Ezek. 17:3; "feathers").

Other examples include "monthly prognosticators" (Isa. 47:13),

---

[6]Sven K. Soderlund, review of *The New King James Bible: New Testament,* in *Crux* 16 (June 1980):31-32.

[7]Heber F. Peacock, review of *The New King James Bible New Testament,* in *The Bible Translator* 31 (July 1980):338-39.

"upbraid" (Matt. 11:20), which elsewhere becomes "ridiculed" (Judg. 8:15), "rebuked" (Mark 16:14), and "without reproach" (James 1:5). There is a "vehement flame" (Song of Sol. 8:6), a "vehement east wind" (Jonah 4:8), and "the stream beat vehemently" (Luke 6:48, 49). "Wayfaring man" is made "traveler" (Judg. 19:17) and "whoever walks the road" (Isa. 35:8), but then "wayfaring man" is retained in other texts (II Sam. 12:4; Isa. 33:8; Jer. 9:2; 14:8). "Wayside" is retained (I Sam. 4:13; Ps. 140:5; Matt. 13:4, 19; Mark 4:4, 15; Luke 8:5, 12) but is then added (Ps. 110:7) where the KJV has "in the way." Still other examples are "winebibber" (Prov. 23:20; Matt. 11:19; Luke 7:34), "fuller" (II Kings 18:17; Isa. 7:3; 36:2; Mal. 3:2), "tidings" (Exod. 33:4; etc.), and "firmament" (Gen. 1:6).

The NKJV includes vocabulary which many readers do not use and likely will not know: "offal" (Exod. 29:14; Lev. 4:11; 8:17; 16:27; Num. 19:5). Some words, while technologically correct, are less known than the KJV renderings. "Selvedge" (Exod. 26:4; 36:11; "edge") is one such example.

The NKJV is a mixture of the old and the new, retaining archaic words but also supplying current terms. "Lay with" and "know" are retained as euphemisms for sexual intercourse (Gen. 4:1, 17, 25), but "know" is combined with a modern expression: "know a man intimately" (Num. 31:17, 18, 35; Judg. 21:11, 12). "With child" (Gen. 16:11; 19:36; 38:24; II Sam. 11:5; Hos. 13:16; Matt. 1:23; Rev. 12:2) is used for pregnancy; however "pregnancy" (Hos. 9:11) and "pregnant" (Matt. 24:19; Mark 13:17; Luke 21:23; I Thess. 5:3) are used in other contexts. Men "violate" women (Gen. 34:2; Ezek. 22:10, 11). There are "genitals" (Deut. 25:11) and "semen" (Lev. 15:16, 17, 18, 32; 22:4; "seed"). The KJV used "conceive" and its use is continued in the NKJV (Gen. 4:1; Luke 1:24, 36). A woman may give birth prematurely (Exod. 21:22). There are "illegitimate birth" (Deut. 23:2 [cf. Heb. 12:8]) and the "placenta" (Deut. 28:57). A woman is in "labor" (Mic. 4:9; 5:3; "travail") and "gives birth" (Mic. 5:3; "bring forth"). There is the "stillborn child" (Job 3:16; Ps. 58:8; Eccl. 6:3; "untimely birth"). *Porneia* may be either "fornication" (John 8:41; Gal. 5:19; Eph. 5:3) or "sexual immorality" (I Cor. 5:9, 10; Rev. 21:8; 22:15). "Dog" is retained for the male prostitute (Deut. 23:18; Rev. 22:15) but "prostitute" (Lev. 19:29; 20:5, 6) is preferred to "whore." "Harlot" may be "ritual harlot" (Hos. 4:14). People are forbidden to "mate with a beast" (Lev. 18:23; 20:15, 16) but an animal has a time for "mating" (Jer. 2:24). "Nurse," "nursing," and "infant" are used for the feeding of the child where the KJV used "suck/suckling" (Deut. 32:25; Ps. 8:2; Jer. 44:7). "Sucklings" (Ps. 8:2) becomes "infants," but are "nursing infants" (Matt. 21:16) when the Psalm is cited in the N.T. "Babe" is retained, most noticeably in the birth narratives of the Gospels (Luke 1:41, 44; 2:12, 16; Heb. 5:13). The "sucking lamb" (I Sam. 7:9) becomes a "suckling lamb."

One must wonder why the preparers of the NKJV felt obliged to retain archaisms like those just listed. The N.T., which was written in Koine Greek, the language of the common man, gives strong witness to the idea that current Englich is suitable to communicate the message of Scripture.

The NKJV retains the KJV punctuation of Isaiah 9:6 ("Wonderful, Counselor") for *pele' yo'ets* instead of considering the two words as one name ("Wonderful Counselor") to match the other three titles in the verse.

Isolated cases can be found where the NKJV is a step backward even from the KJV; for example, "children of God" (Matt. 5:9) becomes "sons of God." "Old men" (Joel 1:2) becomes "elders." There are "rivulets" (Ezek. 31:4; "little rivers"), "sloops" (Isa. 2:16; "pictures"), "waifs" (Lam. 5:3; "fatherless"), and "savor" (Amos 5:21; "smell").

Translation Presuppositions

Translation presuppositions also must be evaluated. It is now standard practice for new translations to deny (as the NKJV does) that they are paraphrases. As do all other English translations, the NKJV uses Dynamic Equivalence. This is noticeable in verses such as "Curse God and die" (Job 2:9), "Hold your tongue" (Amos 6:10), "do not spout against the house of Isaac" (Amos 7:16), and when "reins" becomes "heart" (Job 16:13) or mind (Ps. 7:9). The NKJV also paraphrases passages dealing with the functions of the body.

The NKJV claims to have followed the literal approach to translation except where the original language cannot be translated directly into English. Preparers of the NKJV contend that they have followed the principle of Complete Equivalence, and they give "only begotten Son" (John 3:16; etc.) as the example. The example, however, brings into question the veracity of such a claim. When "only begotten" is not used of the widow's son (Luke 7:12), Jairus's daughter (Luke 8:42), and the epileptic child (Luke 9:38)—even though the same term is used in Greek—one wonders if theological concerns and loyalty to tradition have not been more important than Complete Equivalence. Actually, Jerome's Latin *unigenitus,* rather than the Greek *monogenes,* is being rendered. The retention of "behold," where statements are interpreted as distinctive, is another cited example. While admitting that the Hebrew word *hinneh* can be translated variously, special merit is claimed for retention of "Behold" in Isaiah 7:14. Here again, following theological motivation rather than linguistic data becomes evident.

It is claimed that "some words in the King James Version are so critical to basic Christian doctrines that to change them is unthinkable" and "to protect these basic Christian truths, all theological terms have been kept unchanged." Here we have Thomas More redivivus. More denounced William Tyndale's use of "congregation," "love," and "elder," instead of the then established ecclesiastical words. In the NKJV the KJV theological words are retained: "propitiation," "justification," and "sanctification." In fact, the NKJV has added "propitiation" (Heb. 2:17) in a text where the KJV had "reconciliation." It is claimed that these terms are generally familiar to speakers of English, but it would probably be more accurate to say to English-speaking churchmen. To these could be added "baptize/baptism," "saint," "brethren," "bishop," "deacon," and perhaps others. Every activity has its own vocabulary. The current religious jargon was developed when all education included the study of Latin. Now that very few study Latin, the ordinary person may hear familiar sounds but have little clear comprehension of their meaning. For others even the sounds are not familiar. Is the contention that sinners should learn the church's vocabulary in order to have salvation valid, or is it mere servitude to tradition?

Despite their lip service to the 1611 revisers, the NKJV preparers hold different presuppositions which come to light in their work. Although the erroneous Christological headings of the KJV in the Song of Solomon, some Psalms, and some chapters of Isaiah have been dropped, the Christological interpretation of the O.T. is more obvious in the NKJV than in the KJV. Witness the capitalization of pronouns thought by the revisers to refer to the Christ (Gen. 3:15; 49:10; Isa. 52:13-53:12; Mal. 3:1), the continued capitalization of supposed titles (Deut. 18:18; Isa. 9:6), and capitalization of epithets (Isa. 7:14; 52:13; Dan. 3:25; Zech. 13:7). Of this last group, only "Son of God" (Dan. 3:25) is capitalized in the KJV. In Genesis 3:15 both "Seed" and "He" are capitalized. The KJV had only "seed" and "it." Supplying the definite article (as the KJV does) also contributes to the Christological interpretation (cf. Dan. 3:25). These translation practices write the interpretation for the reader.

While the N.T. of the NKJV was at first issued without italics, italics were inserted in the complete Bible. That special merit is to be found in italicizing words not in the original but thought required in English is certainly debatable.[8] In English translation the practice goes back to the

[8]See Jack P. Lewis, "Italics in English Bible Translation," in *The Living and Active Word of God: Studies in Honor of Samuel J. Schultz,* ed. Morris Inch and Ronald Youngblood (Winona Lake, Ind.: Eisenbrauns, 1983), 255-70.

Geneva Bible (1560), which had predecessors in other languages. The NKJV has been no more successful in italicizing all words it has supplied than was the KJV; the number of italicized words was never constant through various printings of the KJV. Examples of words supplied without italics in the NKJV include "God" (Gal. 6:14) and the definite article of "the Tartan" (II Kings 18:17). "Good" (Amos 5:18) without italics is supplied, but *"is"* which follows is italicized. "Is" is necessary for the English sentence, "good" is not. The uninformed reader needs to be on guard lest he be lured into a false sense of security. He might mistakenly assume that because a word is not italicized it must be in the original.

The nominal sentence in Hebrew may be taken as a point for consideration. In Hebrew such a sentence has no expressed verb, but one is required in English. A few examples are: "Where *are* you?" (Gen. 3:9); "What *is* this you have done?" (Gen. 3:13); "I *am* with child" (II Sam. 11:5); "I *was* no prophet, Nor *was* I a son of a prophet, But I *was* a herdsman" (Amos 7:14). Or one might take a Hebrew expression which requires two English words like "dry *land*" (Gen. 1:10; Jonah 2:10). The italics are superfluous, for the word does not mean "dry" but "dry land." *Tamidh* in the setting does not solely mean "daily"; hence, to italicize "sacrifices" in "daily *sacrifices*" (Dan. 8:11, 12, 13) is unnecessary. "*Ritually* clean" (Ezra 6:20) gets italics, but the numerous cases of "sexual immorality" (two words for one) get none. In addition to these problems, the use of italics can invite confusion. The uninitiated reader might wrongly emphasize italicized words since that is the most widely known use of italics in current English.

The NKJV is not the first translation in which an effort has been made to revise the use of italics.[9] There are cases of improvement; for example, the addition "unto him" of John 3:34 is dropped. This leaves the statement correctly "God does not give the Spirit by measure." "*Unknown*" in the phrase "*unknown* tongue" is dropped in I Corinthians 14:2. However, "*Where* their voice is not heard" (Ps. 19:3) remains unchanged, modifying the meaning of the statement. In John 20:5, the KJV italicized "*and looking in*"; the NKJV has these same words without italics. The definite article "the" with "living creature" has been inserted in Genesis 1:24 by the KJV and continued in the NKJV with italics in neither. The NKJV's use of italics has been seen as an attempt to justify insertion of interpretative comments not in the KJV: "*rightly* judged by no one" (I Cor. 2:15), "like *mere* men" (I Cor. 3:3), and Nineveh is a city of three days' journey "*in extent*" (Jonah 3:3). One can read "Long live the king" (I Sam. 10:24; II

[9]Ibid.

344

Kings 11:12) and *"Long* live the king" (II Sam. 16:16; 2 Chron. 23:11) for the same phrase *Yehe hammelekh* and "God forbid" (Gal. 6:14) for *me genoito* with no italics. Therefore, what reliance can be put on italics?

English Style

The Hebrew *waw* consecutive begins many sentences but it receives a different treatment in the NKJV from the KJV, which monotonously used "and." The conjunction may be passed over entirely (II Kings 9:10), translated "So" (II Kings 9:9) or "Then" (II Kings 9:11; "then"), or treated in other ways.

The dangling clause is a natural feature of Hebrew style but in English is used only by the uneducated. An obvious case like "Now Hannah, she spoke" (I Sam. 1:13) is corrected to "Now Hannah spoke"; but other cases are retained in the NKJV: "The elder and honorable, he *is* the head; the prophet who teaches lies, he *is* the tail" (Isa. 9:15). One still reads, "The Lord, He *is* God!" (I Kings 18:39) as though special emphasis should be put on "He." Another case is "Your rod and Your staff, they comfort me" (Ps. 23:4).

Supplied headings in the text do give some suggestion of thought groups. But the capitalization of the first word of every verse and of every line of poetry will contribute to fragmentation of material rather than to flow of thought. This can cause the reader to disregard what should be kept together.

While the NKJV changes "dumb" to "mute" (Exod. 4:11; Matt. 9:32; Luke 11:14; etc.) in some cases, in others "dumb" is retained (Isa. 35:6; 56:10; Mark 9:25; I Cor. 12:2; II Pet. 2:16). No attention has been paid to some of the issues which have concerned modern translators. For example, people suffering from Hansen's disease do not like to be called "lepers" (Matt. 8:2; etc.).

Some attention has been given to male-oriented language. Psalm 143:2 no longer reads, "No man living is righteous before me" (where Hebrew does not have the word "man"), but "no one living." One reads, "If anyone desires to come after me" (Matt. 16:24) and "If anyone has ears to hear" (Mark 4:23; 7:16). But only little ground has been yielded to the drive for nonsexist language. One reads, "If a man acts with premeditation" (Exod. 21:14), "If a man steals" (Exod. 22:1), "Blessed *is* the man" (Ps. 1:1), "Take heed that you do not do your charitable deeds before men" (Matt. 6:1), "trampled under foot by men" (Matt. 5:13), and other examples.

Despite the effort to revise, the NKJV still maintains examples of inverted English style: "But all their works they do" (Matt. 23:5). And

345

there are cases of redundancy, such as "return again to him anymore" (Gen. 8:12).

Theological Bias

In a translation where alternate renderings are given in the footnotes for many terms, only theological bias can determine that "almah" be rendered "virgin" in Isaiah 7:14 without even the note (such as that carried in the ASV) giving the alternate "maiden." The KJV, though using "virgin" (Gen. 24:43; Song of Sol. 1:3; 6:8), had "maid" in Exodus 2:8 and Proverbs 30:19 and had "damsels" in Psalm 68:(26)25 for the same term. The NKJV has "maiden" in Exodus 2:8 and Psalm 68:(26)25.

Reverence for the deity is presumably shown in capitalization of pronouns used for the Father, Son, and Holy Spirit (a policy earlier used in the NASV but not in the KJV). However, this is likely as temporary a tradition as the contention that the use of old English pronouns showed special reverence. Capitalization of pronouns in the Psalms may obscure the fact that certain Psalms (e.g. Pss. 2, 45) had a first reference to an earthly king and then a secondary reference to the Messiah. The earthly aspect of these Psalms is swallowed up by capitalization. Neither Hebrew nor Greek supports a policy of capitalizing pronouns referring to deity. The outcome is that even those who did not intend to imply divinity do so. The woman of Samaria says, "Sir, I perceive that You are a prophet" (John 4:19). The Jews say, "For a good work we do not stone You, but for blasphemy, and because You, being a Man, make Yourself God" (John 10:33). In the trials of Jesus the tormenters said, "Who is the one who struck You?" (Matt. 26:68), and Pilate says, "Do You not hear how many things they testify against You?" (Matt. 27:13). The mob at the cross says, "Save Yourself!" (Matt. 27:40).

A distinction is made by capitalization between "Antichrist" (I John 2:18; 4:3) and "antichrist" (I John 2:22; II John 7). In I John 2:18 the definite article "the" is supplied (which the KJV did not have) on the basis of a textual variant. A marginal note points out that the NU-Text omits it.

"Dispensation" (Eph. 1:10; 3:2) is preserved. This term has taken on theological implications in modern discussion. "Plan" or "stewardship" would be better.

An interpretive method which prefers the personification of evil is responsible for "Deliver us from the evil one" (ho poneros; Matt. 6:13; cf. Matt. 5:37) where the KJV had "from evil." There is no linguistic way to know which is the more correct choice. Interpretation is also responsible for "induced that prophet" (Ezek. 14:9) where the KJV had "deceived." Christ becomes "Overseer" in 1 Peter 2:25 and the elders of Ephesus are

346

"overseers" (Acts 20:28), but "bishop" is retained for *episkopos* in church organization (Phil. 1:1; I Tim. 3:1, 2; Tit. 1:7). However, "bishopric" (Acts 1:20) is displaced by "office." A "distressing spirit" from the Lord troubles Saul (I Sam. 16:14; "evil spirit"). The capitalization in "only He who now restrains *will do so*" in replacing "only he who now letteth will let" (II Thess. 2:7) lends encouragement to the dispensational interpretation of this passage and will for them confirm the dispensationalist's supposition that the Holy Spirit is being mentioned.

Summary

In the second half of the twentieth century, every major religious group—Jewish, Catholic, Jehovah's Witnesses, British Protestants, and evangelicals of various persuasions—has offered a new translation. Bible publication is big business and these efforts have an equal right to compete in the marketplace. The NKJV is no exception.

The NKJV has yet to prove itself a viable alternative to the KJV. After seven years, sales statistics from *Publisher's Weekly* (1990) rank the NIV and KJV one and two in sales with the NKJV (despite its impressive sales record) never more than third. The appearance of the REB and NRSV, both of which are current speech translations, will make the survival of archaic English language Bibles more difficult.

One can learn his duty towards God and man out of the NKJV if he studies it diligently. The bottom line is whether the drive to persuade the public that the *Textus Receptus* and the Majority Text are superior to the Critical Text will succeed. If it fails, the NKJV will be a passing phenomenon.

15

The Revised English Bible

The Revised English Bible (REB) was jointly published by the Oxford and Cambridge university presses on September 28, 1989. The first printing produced 150,000 copies and $200,000 was spent in advertising and publicity. (As part of the sales campaign, the publishers of the REB contributed fifty cents for each copy purchased in the United States before January 1990 to one of six selected charities.) The REB is a radical revision of the New English Bible (NEB) which was earlier prepared under the directorships of C. H. Dodd, G. R. Driver, and W. S. McHardy.

The NEB N.T. appeared in 1961 and enjoyed six months on the *New York Times* best-seller list. The complete Bible including the O.T., the Apocrypha, and a slight revision of the N.T. appeared in 1970. In two years nearly two million copies were sold; 750,000 of them were sold in the United States before the end of 1970. A 1972 edition had slight corrections.

The progress of biblical studies since 1970 prompted the REB, which is issued with or without the Apocrypha. Though the inclusion seems strange to non-Catholic readers, English Bibles (except the Douay, which had the books scattered through the O.T.) from the time of Coverdale (1535) through the KJV (1611) had the Apocrypha assembled as an anthology between the O.T. and N.T. Early in the nineteenth century the Apocrypha generally ceased to be included in this position. In the copies of the REB containing the Apocrypha, it appears between the O.T. and the N.T.

Modern marketing techniques have accustomed readers to such claims as "The Revised English Bible is the most accurate—and readable—translation of the Bible available in English today. . . It brings to the world the most comprehensive and precise English translation of the Bible ever made," and it is "the Bible for the English-speaking world on the threshold of a new century." The REB also declares it remains scrupulously faithful to the full intent of the original texts and is unencumbered by doctrinal bias. It is purported that the REB "has avoided technical language, removed archaic words and sentence structure, and provided the world with a Bible that reads as if it were written in modern English by the original authors."

The REB is advertised as "the Bible that speaks your language" and as being "easily understood by people wherever in the world English is read or spoken." Yet again, "The Revised English Bible is designed to meet two essential needs: a Bible for the church that has dignity, fluency, and power; at the same time a text for private reading, study, and devotion. The REB is clear and direct in expression, has elegance of style, remains free of doctrinal bias, and avoids both technicality and over-simplification." Selected reviewers have been lavish in their praise.

In 1973 the Joint Committee of the British Churches decided to carry through a major revision of the NEB. W. D. McHardy was appointed the director of revision to head a multi-denominational committee. The committee, whose chairman is Donald Coggan, is composed of representatives of the Baptist Union of Great Britain and Ireland, the Church of England, the Church of Scotland, the Congregational Church of England and Wales, the Council of Churches for Wales, the Irish Council of Churches, the London Yearly Meeting of the Society of Friends, the Methodist Church of Great Britain, the United Reformed Church (Presbyterian and Congregational), the British and Foreign Bible Society, the National Bible Society of Scotland, the Salvation Army, and the Moravian Church in Great Britain and Ireland. Roman Catholic representatives of England and Wales first attended as observers and later entered in full membership.

The revisers undertook a verse-by-verse comparison of the original texts, incorporating current scholarship. Comments from people worldwide who use the New English Bible were considered. The desire was to provide a Bible that is as accurate as possible but yet is full of the richness of the English language. The REB uses a wider vocabulary than that found in the TEV and NIV. The REB was examined by writers and poets who made comments; readability was a primary concern. It is claimed that the colloquial has been avoided.

Meetings of the joint committee, held once or twice a year in the Jerusalem Chamber of the Westminster Abbey, allowed members to receive progress reports about the revision and to inspect drafts as each book neared completion. Committee members often made comments and criticisms.

The revisers strove for an appropriately dignified style and one with a level of intelligibility suited for worshipers of a wide range of ages and backgrounds. The "thou" forms of pronouns and corresponding forms of verbs in the prayers of the NEB have been abandoned.

The older English translations introduced gender-specific language where such is not required by the Hebrew and Greek. The REB revisers have attempted to be sensitive to the problem of more inclusive language, as contrasted to male-oriented language, without compromising "scholarly integrity or English style." The language which in the original text refers to Deity in masculine terms remains unchanged, but "person," "mankind," "mortals," "human beings," or "one" may be used where "man" occurs in the KJV. Specific examples of this change will be considered later in this chapter.

Yet another marked difference from the NEB is the inclusion of the headings found in the Hebrew manuscripts in the Psalms. A wider use of other subject headings printed in italics has been used for convenience. These headings are not intended to be considered a part of the biblical text. The word *selah*, which the NEB omitted, has been included in various Psalms and in Habakkuk 3.

Unlike the NEB, the REB has a two-column page. Chapter and verse numbers are no longer on the outer margin. The REB has integrated them into the text, making it easy to know specifically where each verse begins, and for ease of reference the verse numbers of the KJV have been followed. Where verses of the KJV are not supported by the manuscripts followed in the REB, the verse number is skipped and the verse is printed in a footnote. Marginal notes are listed by chapter and verse, so they are easier to connect with the text than those in the NEB or NRSV. A table of weights, measures, and values has been supplied with approximate metric equivalents. (Precise modern equivalents cannot be given.) Subject headings are at the top of the page and footnotes indicate where the text is uncertain or unclear as well as where ancient versions differ. Subheadings have been inserted in the text wherever there is a major change in theme. Speaker identifications have been supplied in the Song of Solomon.

Treatment of the Text

The *Biblia Hebraica Stuttgartensia* 1967/77 has been followed in the O.T. with consideration of ancient versions and patristic quotations. The contribution of archaeological studies and studies of cognate Semitic languages, including discoveries at Ras Shamra in Syria, has been considered. Conjectural emendations, where judged necessary, are marked in the footnotes as *prob. rdg.* Technical terms like *Sheol* are transliterated and the terms for sacrifice have been revised. Nouns have been substituted for pronouns where clarity requires. Expansion has been employed where it seemed necessary, and some abbreviation has been done where the Hebrew text seemed unduly repetitious.

A case of abbreviation to avoid redundancy is seen in Genesis 30:32. Rather than repeating "every spotted and brindled sheep" which immediately follows, as the Hebrew and NEB do, the REB has "from them."

The REB has continued the NEB transposition of verses to give what the revisers consider a better sequence of text. The reader is alerted to transpositions by a footnote and the sections also carry the traditional verse numbers. Genesis 26:18 is placed after 26:15. Deuteronomy 15:18 is placed between verses 14 and 15. I Samuel 9:9 and 10 are transposed. I Samuel 24:4-7 is rearranged in the sequence 4a, 6, 7a, 4b, 5, 7b. I Kings 11:25 follows verse 22. Job 3:16 is transposed to follow verse 12. A phrase of Job 4:21 is transposed to follow Job 5:4. A section of Job 14:14 is transposed into verse 12. Job 20:10 and 11 are reversed. Job 24:2-10 has the order 2, 6, 3, 9, 4, 5, 7, 8, 10. Job 29:21-25 is placed between verses 10 and 11. Job 31:1 follows 31:5; Job 31:35 has a line from verse 34 (with the NEB note to the fact omitted). Job 31:38-40, except for the last line, is inserted between 31:28 and 31:29. Job 34:25 follows verse 22. Verses 20 and 21 of Job 36 are transposed, and verse 31 follows verse 28. A portion of Job 39:30 and 41:1-6 follows 39:30. A portion of Ecclesiastes 2:12 is transposed to follow verse 18. Song of Solomon 4:12 follows 4:14. Isaiah 9:20 has a statement transposed from verse 19, and 10:16 had one from verse 18. Isaiah 38:6 is followed by verses 21 and 22. Isaiah 41:1 has a phrase from verse 5. Isaiah 41:6, 7 follow Isaiah 40:20. A phrase of Jeremiah 6:28 is transposed to the end of verse 29. Ezekiel 1:14 and 40:30 are relegated to the notes. Ezekiel 41:10 and 11 are transposed. Amos 5:7 follows 5:9. Zechariah 4:1-3 is transposed to follow 4:10 and words from verse 10 to 4:3.

Other rearrangements found in the NEB are abandoned. The placing of Job 12:22 after verse 25 is rejected. The reversal of Job 14:21, 22 is rejected, and the NEB marginal rendering is preferred to the text. The transposition of Isaiah 5:24, 25 to follow Isaiah 10:4 of the NEB is rejected. Isaiah 9:15 is restored to the text with space before and after but is enclosed in parentheses. The placing of portions of Jeremiah 12:14, 15 into verse 17 is rejected, as is the dropping of Jeremiah 15:13-14 from the text into the footnotes. Hosea 1:7 is restored to the text. The transposition of Hosea 2:11 and 12 is rejected. Zechariah 3:1-10 and 13:7-9 are retained in their traditional position. The notes list no transpositions of text in the New Testament.

In many cases the translators have preferred the text of the versions to the Masoretic text. The Samaritan Pentateuch has been followed in Genesis in the readings "Let us go out into the country" (Gen. 4:8), "the God Bethel" given as an alternate to "the God of Bethel" (Gen. 31:13, where the NEB had followed the Greek "the God who appeared to you at Bethel"), "son" (Gen. 36:2, following the Samaritan Pentateuch where the Hebrew has "daughter"), "son of Zibeon" (Gen. 36:14), "the one" (Gen. 43:14), "Paddan-aram" (Gen. 48:7), and "gelded" (Gen. 49:14). The Septuagint has been followed in reading "sixth" (Gen. 2:2), "for his father" (Gen. 27:5), "from them" (Gen. 30:32), "between us" (Gen. 31:53), "his father and" (Gen. 37:9), "and she was" (Gen. 38:5), "the granaries" (Gen. 41:56), "food" (Gen. 42:33), "Why have you stolen the silver goblet?" (Gen. 44:5), and "and the sons of Bela" (Gen. 46:21). Syriac has been followed in reading "of Seir" (Gen. 36:6). Additional examples could be compiled from other books.

As is true with the NEB, numerous phrases in the Hebrew text are dropped to the footnotes in favor of probable readings. This category is too extensive to do more than sample. Probable readings are followed in Genesis 9:7, 26; 16:13; Exodus 5:5; Leviticus 6:20; 21:4; Numbers 4:49; 8:8; 12:6; 18:29; Deuteronomy 31:23; and other places. Scattered examples include "the king of Egypt at So" (II Kings 17:4; NRSV: "King So of Egypt"), "to the sharks" (Ps. 74:14; NRSV: "for the creatures . . ."), "prop and stay" (Isa. 3:1), "Judah" (Isa. 7:17), and "Euphrates" (Isa. 7:20).

The REB differs considerably, however, from the NEB on the matter of probable readings. Numerous conjectural readings of the NEB are rejected: "how can they raise themselves?" (Isa. 2:9), "a sacred pole thrown out from its place in a hill-shrine" (Isa. 6:13), "and buffaloes" (Isa. 34:7) are only a few examples.

In certain cases the REB carries over these readings listed as probable in the NEB and notes that they are only probable: "tent," omitting "Sarah his mother" (Gen. 24:67); "Horite," where Hebrew has "Hivite" (Gen. 36:2); "Sodom" (Isa. 1:7); "pilgrim's way" (Isa. 35:8); and others.

The REB includes "and in the fear of the Lord will be his delight" (Isa. 11:3) from the Hebrew text, which the NEB rejected.

The REB further indicates as conjectural readings which were not so noted in the NEB: "dance over" (Isa. 11:8), "defence" (Isa. 12:2), "carrion" (Isa. 14:19), and others.

The REB has its own conjectural readings to offer. Where the NEB supplied "he," the REB has "they" (Isa. 16:7). Other probable readings include "I bring near" (Isa. 51:5), "striding" (Isa. 63:1 ["stooping"]), and "her babes" (Isa. 66:12). The list is not comprehensive.

Brackets indicating what the NEB translators thought were late additions to the text are dropped from Job 11:6; 26:14c; and Isaiah 6:13.

The 26th edition (1979) of *Novum Testamentum Graece* has been the point of reference in the N.T. Both the NEB and REB reflect the differences in this text from the *Textus Receptus,* relegating the close of the Lord's Prayer (Matt. 6:13); Matthew 16:3; 23:14; John 5:4; and Acts 8:37 to the notes. Mark 16:9-20 is set off with accompanying explanatory notes. John 7:53-8:11 is printed at the end of the Gospel of John. The *Comma Johanneum* (I John 5:7) goes unnoticed. Notes call attention to readings which were followed in the NEB but which now seem less probable than those followed in this revision.

While it is quite possible that the REB will be issued with fuller notes than the printing which is now available, the extent of the revision in the N.T. is to be seen in the different evaluations of the witnesses for establishing the text. The REB had access to the Bodmer materials, which were not available when the NEB was being prepared. The citation in the notes of textual variants is considerably less in the N.T. of the REB; the following verses were cited a variant in the NEB but not in the REB: Matthew 1:16; 4:17; 5:44; 7:14; 14:24; 16:15; Mark 10:8; 15:34; Luke 1:78; 2:14; 4:44; 7:11; 11:13, 42; 12:14, 27. Again, the list is not exhaustive.

Hereafter where attention is given to the REB differences from the NEB, the NEB rendering is given in brackets following the Scripture citation. Sample cases where the REB evaluated the textual evidence differently from the NEB include "Thaddaeus" (Matt. 10:3 ["Lebbaeus"]). The REB omits "Isaiah" (Matt. 13:35), inserts "and laid waste" (Matt. 23:38), "of me and my words" (Luke 9:26 ["of me and mine"]), "son" (Luke 14:5 ["donkey"]), "will be in you" (John 14:17 ["is in you"]), "hyssop" (John 19:29 ["javelin"]), "John" (Acts 4:6 ["Jonathan"]), inserts "weak as it is" (I Cor. 8:12), and "this perishable body has been clothed with the imperishable" (I Cor. 15:54), "Here is a saying you may trust" (I Tim. 3:1 ["There is a popular saying"], "suffered" (I Pet. 3:18 ["died"]), and "Bosor" (II Pet. 2:15 ["Beor"]). The NEB followed those manuscripts

354

which read "faithful man or woman" (I Tim. 5:16), the REB (as do the NIV and NRSV) those which read "faithful woman," which carries a "C" probability rating in the Bible Societies text. Another revising group would doubtless evaluate some of these, and others, differently.

Translation Choices

The advertising material points out that an effort has been made to use consistently the idiom of contemporary English with its natural vocabulary, constructions, and rhythms. Archaisms, technical terms, and pretentious language have been avoided as much as possible. The translators felt no obligation to attempt always to render the same Greek term by the same English one. As translators of the KJV had done, they used a variety of terms.

Innovative translation choices already made in the NEB are continued in the REB. Significant differences from the NRSV (and tradition) are reflected in both the NEB and REB. The woman's descendants are interpreted as "they" (Gen. 3:15) rather than "he" (which has been significant in messianic interpretation). The REB uses "Ancient in Years" (Dan. 7:13, 22) and says Og's "sarcophagus was of basalt" (Deut. 3:11 [margin: "iron"]). A price of "a quarter of a kab of locust-beans" is given (II Kings 6:25), and "mother's son" is a paraphrase for the male (I Kings 16:11; etc.). *Barukh* in the O.T. and *makarios* in the N.T. are both translated as "happy" rather than the traditional "blessed." *Hagioi* are "God's people" (Rom. 16:15; Eph. 1:1; Phil. 1:1; Col. 1:2; NRSV: "saints"). "Inspired utterance" (Rom. 12:6) is for prophecy.

An impressive list of cases can be cited where the REB abandoned the innovative renderings of the NEB, moved its marginal options into the text, and either relegated its rendering to the margin or left it unnoticed. Some examples (with the NEB rendering in the brackets) include "be like God himself" (Gen. 3:5; ["be like gods"]), "you hold your head up" (Gen. 4:7 ["you are accepted"]), "I am going to bring the whole human race to an end" (Gen. 6:13 ["The loathsomeness of all mankind has become plain to me"]), "planted a tamarisk" (Gen. 21:33 ["a strip of ground"]), and the goat is for "Azazel" (Lev. 16:8 ["for the Precipice" with a footnote "for Azazel"]).

In other changes, "Round Tower" of the NEB becomes "guardhouse" (Gen. 39:20); "Wench" becomes "damsel" (Judg. 5:30); "stooks" (Judg. 15:5) becomes "sheaves"; and "had fallen into a bad odour" is replaced by "had given offence to David" (II Sam. 10:6). "Overlaid it" (I Kings 3:19) becomes "lay on it." "Shed-grain" becomes "leavings of the grain"

(II Kings 19:29); "traducers" becomes "accusers" (Ps. 71:13); "mother's bane" becomes "a sorrow to his mother" (Prov. 10:1), "dhows of Arabia" (Isa. 2:16) becomes "stately vessels"; and "does not burgeon" becomes "has no buds" (Hab. 3:17); and "ape outlandish fashions" (Zeph. 1:8) becomes "appear in foreign apparel." "They fell foul of" is improved to "they turned against" (Mark 6:3), and "loose livers" (I Cor. 5:9) is improved to "those who are sexually immoral."

In some cases these choices represent a return to traditional renderings: "In the beginning God created the heavens and the earth" (Gen. 1:1 ["in the beginning of creation"]), "the spirit of God hovered" (Gen. 1:2 ["a mighty wind that swept"]), "put on fresh clothes" (Gen. 35:2 ["see that your clothes are mended"]), "was at Kezib" (Gen. 38:5 ["ceased to bear children"]), "God" (Gen. 41:39 ["god"]), "counsellor" (Gen. 45:8 ["father"]), "may bless them" (Gen. 48:9 ["take them on my knees"]), "hills" (Gen. 49:26 ["pools"]), "fist" (Exod. 21:18 ["spade"]), "cistern" (Exod. 21:33 ["well"]), "Testimony" (Exod. 25:16 ["Covenant"]), "Tent of Meeting" (Exod. 27:21 ["of the Presence"]), and "Ten Commandments" (Exod. 34:28 ["Ten Words"]).

Other reversions to tradition, some of which were in the NEB margin, include "nor the staff from between his feet" (Gen. 49:10 ["from his descendants"]) and, in the same verse, "until he receives what is his due" ("so long as tribute is brought to him") with the option "Shiloh comes." The NEB cited no option. Still other examples are "so that it [the tent-peg] went down into the ground" (Judg. 4:21 ["his brains oozed out . . . , his limbs twitched"]), "garrison" (I Sam. 13:3 ["governor"]), "If only you yourself will seek God" (Job 8:5 ["will seek God betimes"]), "May you always be in good heart!" (Ps. 22:(25)26 ["those . . . be in good heart forever"]), "Bashan" (Ps. 68:22 ["Dragon"]), "the prize of a life" (Prov. 6:26 ["out for bigger game"]), and "Who will go for us?" (Isa. 6:8 [". . . go for me?"]).

The rendering of Psalm 19:14 returns to the traditional: "May the words of my mouth and the thoughts of my mind (KJV: "heart") be acceptable to you." In Job, "Adversary" is moved from the margin to the text (Job 1:9, 12; 2:1, 2, 4). Job 1:6 has the explanatory gloss "the Adversary, Satan," but Zechariah 3:1-2 drops "Adversary" for "Satan" in all cases, as do the NEB and RSV for I Chronicles 21:1. The NEB has "Satan" in the Lord's address (Zech. 3:2). "Danel" becomes "Daniel" (Ezek. 14:14), which corresponds to the Masoretic spelling. Other reversions include "Let her put an end" (Hos. 2:2 ["Plead with her to forswear"]), "ripped open the pregnant women in Gilead" (Amos 1:13 ["invaded the ploughlands of Gilead"]), "I was no prophet" (Amos 7:14

356

["am"]) with the present tense alternative given in the footnote, and "until she who is pregnant has given birth" (Mic. 5:3 ["only so long as a woman is in labour"]). Whereas one "stooped before God," now he "bows before God on high" (Mic. 6:6). Other reversions to traditional wording and interpretation include "having a meal" for "at table" (Matt. 9:10) and "intruders" in place of "interlopers" (Gal. 2:4).

The REB also prefers a more traditional rendering of the following verses: "bowed in worship by the head of his bed" (Gen. 47:31 ["sank down over the end of the bed"], "fled from his presence" (Exod. 2:15 ["made good his escape"], "walk humbly with your God" (Mic. 6:8 ["walk wisely before God"]), "mountain" (Matt. 5:1; 8:1 ["hill"]), "scribe" (Matt. 8:19 ["doctor of the law"]), "an official" (Matt. 9:18 ["a president of the synagogue"]), "no room for them at the inn" (Luke 2:7 ["in the house"]), and "the kingdom of God come with power" (Mark 9:1 ["already come in power"]), However, "is upon you" (Matt. 3:2; 4:17; 10:7) for *eggiken* and "among you" for *entos humon* (Luke 17:21) with marginal options are retained. "Life" replaces "true self" (Matt. 16:26).

Inserted from the notes of the NEB into the text of the REB are "least among" (Matt. 2:6 ["far from least in the eyes of"]), "Decapolis" (Matt. 4:25; Mark 5:20 ["Ten Towns"]), "a single day to your life" (Matt. 6:27 ["a foot to his height"], "You have said it" (Matt. 26:25 ["the words are yours"]), "bystanders" (Mark 14:47 ["party"]), and "Praetorium" (Mark 15:16 ["Governor's headquarters"]). The rendering for the kingdom "has come upon you" (Luke 10:9) gives the NEB "has come close to you" as a marginal option.

Numerous optional renderings suggested in the NEB notes have been dropped, for example, "incensed" (Gen. 27:33), "executioner" (Gen. 37:36), "stolen" (Gen. 40:15), "lioness" (Gen. 49:9), and "Oholiab" (Exod. 31:6). In the N.T., there is "Am I to come and cure him?" (Matt. 8:7), "the gates of death shall never close upon it" (Matt. 16:18), "Look, your home is desolate" (Matt. 23:38), "agreed to pay him" (Matt. 26:15), "Friend, what are you here for?" (Matt. 26:50), "it was so obscure to them that they could not" (Luke 9:45), and "and he will have no way at all to harm you" (Luke 10:19). The listing is only partial.

In the REB, notes giving alternates not in the NEB have been added as "make compartments in it" (Gen. 6:14), an alternate to "cover it with reeds" (which both the NEB and REB have). Other translations have "gopher wood" for the phrase. A note states that the Samaritan Pentateuch gives 145 for the age of Terah (Gen. 11:32). Other alternates include "will be blessed because of you" (Gen. 12:3), "wonderful garden" (Gen. 13:10), and "Salt Sea" (Gen. 14:3). At Genesis 18:22 it is suggested

357

that the original reading was probably "the Lord remained standing before Abraham." Other cases of notes not in the NEB include "son" (Gen. 29:5; where the texts of both the NEB and REB have "grandson"), "an ornamental robe" (Gen. 37:3 ["long, sleeved robe"]), "tested" where the text has "tempted" (Matt. 4:1), "gates of Hades" where the text has "powers of death" (Matt. 16:18), and others.

The material in explanatory notes has undergone modification. The text has "bishops and deacons" (Phil. 1:1), a note gives the option "overseers and assistants," and the NEB had no note.

Archaeology

The REB continues the insights into vocabulary from archaeology which were already reflected in the NEB. Examples include "Moisture used to well up out of the earth" (Gen. 2:6 ["a flood" or "mist"]), "Kue" (I Kings 10:28) as the place where Solomon obtained horses, "bull-gods" (Hos. 12:11), "Aram" (Hos. 12:12), "Aramean" (Deut. 26:5); "Aramaic" (II Kings 18:26; Ezra 4:7), "calf-images" (Hos. 13:2), and "temple girls" (Amos 2:7 ["same girl"]). Archaeological insights are reflected in the choice of "ruined mounds" (Josh. 11:13), "two-thirds of a shekel" as the charge for sharpening the axes (I Sam. 13:21), and in the identification of Pul with Tiglath-pileser (I Chron. 5:26). The list is not exhaustive.

Style Changes

Some changes reflect only stylistic matters. The capitalization policy has been modified. Uncapitalized are "baalim and the ashtaroth" (I Sam. 7:4; 12:10) and "controller of the temple" (Acts 4:1). Another such word is "vale" (Josh. 7:26). "Prophet" in the N.T. when of messianic import is capitalized (John 6:14; 7:40, 52 ["prophets"]). Hyphenation is dropped in many spellings such as "stillborn" (Ps. 58:8 ["still-born"]), "hothead" (Prov. 29:22 ["hot-head"]), and "sea monster" (Matt. 12:40 ["sea-monster"]), but in others hyphenation is added, as when "idol king" becomes "idol-king" (Amos 5:26).

Unlike the American practice, in both the NEB and REB quotations are enclosed in single quotation marks. Double quotation marks are reserved for quotations within a quotation as in Acts 17:23, 28; 20:35.

The REB has also removed some redundant passages. "Hesitant of speech" becomes "hesitant" (Exod. 4:10).

Changes in wording with no essential change in interpretation have been made: "my child for the sin I have committed" (Mic. 6:7 ["my children for my own sin"]), "to call the virtuous" (Matt. 9:13 ["virtuous people"]), "sold an estate which he owned" (Acts 4:37 ["owned an estate, which he sold"]), "'knowledge' so-called" (I Tim. 6:20 ["so-called 'knowledge'"]), and "No widow's weeds for me, no mourning!" (Rev. 18:7 ["No mourning for me, no widow's weeds!"]).

Cases where passives are rendered as actives in both the NEB and REB include "we despised him" (Isa. 53:3; NRSV: "he was despised").

Statements from the O.T. which are quoted in the N.T. are made to differ in the NEB when there is no issue at stake. One reads "her sons" (Jer. 31:15) and "her children" (Matt. 2:18); but both are inclusive terms. "Every word that comes from the mouth of the Lord" (Deut. 8:3) becomes "every word God utters" (Matt. 4:4). The one is literal, the other a paraphrase. The REB renders these alike.

As do many other current translations, the NEB and REB supply noun antecedents where pronouns would be obscure. For example, "my people" (Isa. 52:14) is in apposition to "you."

Corrections

Some of the obvious shortcomings in communication of the NEB have been corrected in the REB. "There was a time when" (Gen. 11:1) replaces "once upon a time." "Linen drawers" (Lev. 6:10) has become "linen shorts." In some instances where the NEB rendered *daimonios* as "devil," the REB has chosen "demon" (Matt. 8:16, 28, 31), thereby making a correct distinction between "devil" and "demon." However, this improvement is only partially carried through; Matthew 12:24-28 should have "demon." In the Gospel of John, Jesus says to the Jews, "Your father is the devil" (John 8:44; *diabolos*). When being accused, Jesus is merely said to be "possessed" (John 8:48, 52).

The name "Jehovah" has been dropped in favor of "the Lord" where it stands alone (Exod. 3:15; 6:3; 33:19) and where it is an element of a name (Gen. 22:14; Exod. 17:15; Judg. 6:24; Ezek. 48:35).

Translation Policies

The REB is not designed to be the sort of translation in which the reader can reconstruct the Hebrew, Aramaic, or Greek statement of the source language. An equivalent impact is attempted by using English phrases of similar import rather than aiming at word-for-word, grammar-for-grammar correspondence. There is always room for debate about whether an actual equivalence has been attained. A current rather than a literal expression may be supplied. *Halilah lannu/li* is rendered

"Heaven forbid" (Gen. 44:7, 17 ["God forbid"]), "God forbid" (Josh. 22:29; 24:16; I Sam. 12:23; 14:45; 20:2), and "the Lord forbid" (I Kings 21:3) but is also "Far be it from me" (Job 27:5 ["God forbid"]). A literal "flesh and blood" becomes "any human being" (Matt. 16:17 ["mortal man"]).

The word "Christian," which occurs in the Greek New Testament three times (Acts 11:26; 26:28; I Pet. 4:16), and never occurs as an adjective, occurs sixty-three times in the NEB. At least seven of these (Acts 22:5; 24:22; Rom. 14:14; Gal. 1:2; Eph. 6:4; I Tim. 3:7; II Tim. 3:12) are dropped in the REB; at least one new case (Rom. 14:15 ["brother"]) is created. "Christian" is used in the REB as in the NEB as a substitute for *adelphos/ adelphe* in "fellow-Christians" (Acts 11:29; 16:40; Rom. 16:1; Phil. 1:14; Heb. 13:1), but the REB differs from the NEB in using "fellow-Christian" (Philemon 20 ["Christian"]; I Thess. 4:6 ["brother"]), and "Christians" (Col. 4:15 ["brothers"]. Both versions use "sham Christians" (Gal. 2:4) and "Jewish Christians" (Col. 4:11). "Christian" is used frequently as an adjective in phrases such as "Christian greetings" (Rom. 16:22), "Christian congregations" (Gal. 1:22 ["Christ's congregations"]), "Christian duty" (Col. 3:18), "Christian way" (Col. 3:20), and "Christian dead" (I Thess. 4:16). One finds "Christianity" (Heb. 6:1) in both translations.

The REB is likewise not the sort of translation where one can study how many times a term occurs in the original text. *Nesher* remains "griffon-vulture" (Deut. 14:12), "vulture" (Deut. 28:49), and "eagle" (Exod. 19:4; Deut. 32:11; Isa. 40:31). Though the specific identity of the bird may be in doubt, the variety is only confusing to the reader. Since the revisers did not search for consistency in rendering, the variety gives "everlasting life . . . eternal abhorrence" (Dan. 12:2) for the same adjective. John's baptism is "for the forgiveness of sins" (Mark 1:4; Luke 3:3; translating *eis aphesin hamartion*) and Jesus' shed blood is "for the forgiveness of sins" (Matt. 26:28), but the same phrase in Acts 2:38, which in the NEB was also "for the forgiveness of your sins," has become "then your sins will be forgiven."

One might, for further consideration, take *glossais*, which is at different times "tongues" (Acts 2:4; I Cor. 12:10 ["ecstatic utterance"], 14:2, 4 ["language of ecstasy"], 13, 39 ["ecstatic utterance"]), "language" (I Cor. 14:10, 11 ["sound"]), "ecstatic utterance" (I Cor. 14:26), "language of ecstasy" (I Cor. 14:19), and "tongues of ecstasy" (Acts 10:46; 19:6; I Cor. 12:30). The NEB had used the same terms with similar slight variations which also suggested interpretation.

The confusion created by the variety of renderings may be seen in the treatment of *sarx* in Romans, where the word occurs with different connotations. *Sarx* becomes in the REB a "human being" (Rom. 3:20; 6:19) and a mark "in the flesh" (Rom. 2:28). When dealing with descent, it becomes "human level" (Rom. 1:3), "natural descent" (Rom. 4:1 ["natural line"], 9:3 ["natural kinsfolk"], 5, 8 ["in the course of nature"]), and "my race" (Rom. 11:14). But in the distinctive Pauline use of *sarx,* the REB uses even more variety than the NEB. In this related context *sarx* becomes "mere human nature" (Rom. 7:5 ["lower nature"]), "unspiritual self" (Rom. 7:18 ["unspiritual nature"]), "unspiritual nature" (Rom. 7:25; 8:7 ["lower nature"], cf. 13:14 ["bodily appetites"]), "human weakness" (Rom. 8:3 "nature"]), and "old nature" (Rom. 8:4, 5, 12 ["lower nature"]). The scholarly sophistication needed to detect these varieties of meaning in the context will be far beyond the common reader, and the additional variety that could be compiled from the rest of the Pauline correspondence has not been listed.

Other numerous examples serve to show that no effort has been made to render a phrase the same way in all of its occurrences. "Scoundrels" (I Sam. 2:12) and "unprincipled rogues" (I Kings 21:10 ["scoundrels"]; etc.) are used for the semitism "sons of Belial," but "so devoid of shame" ("Do not think me so degraded") is used for "daughter of Belial" (I Sam. 1:16). "A group of prophets" (II Kings 4:38) and "the company of prophets" (II Kings 5:22) are for "sons of the prophets," but "a prophet's son" (Amos 7:14) also is used. "Sons of disobedience" (RSV) in Ephesians 5:6 becomes "God's rebel subjects." "Fabric fund" (Ezra 2:69) becomes "treasure for the fabric," but the term remains "fabric fund" in Nehemiah 7:71. The term "wilderness" is retained (Exod. 3:1; etc.), but also "assembly ["assembled there"] in the desert" is in Acts 7:38.

There are yet additional examples of variety. Torah is both "law" (Neh. 8:2) and "teaching" (Isa. 42:4). Genesis 49:17 uses "snake." Moses' rod becomes a "snake" in Exodus 4:3, a "serpent" in Exodus 7:9, 12, but is again a "snake" in Exodus 7:15. Snakes bite the people, but Moses lifts up the "serpent" in the wilderness (Num. 21:6-8), and the N.T. allusion to the same event is to a "serpent" (John 3:14). "Serpent" occurs in Genesis 3:1, 4, 13, 14; II Corinthians 11:3; and Revelation 20:2 where the devil is mentioned.

The REB (as does the NEB) has "vale of Achor" (Josh. 7:26) and "valley of Achor" (Isa. 65:10 ["Vale"]; Hos. 2:15 ["Vale of Trouble"]) for the same location. The REB translates the semitism *ben 'adham* "O Man" in Ezekiel (Ezek. 2:3; 5:1; etc.) and "a human being" in the Psalms (Ps. 8:4 ["mortal man"]). The Aramaic *bar 'enosh* is "a human being" (Dan. 7:13 ["a man"]) and *huios tou anthropou* is "a man" ("son of man") when Psalm 8:4 is quoted in Hebrews 2:6. It is elsewhere "like a man" (Rev.

1:13 ["a son of man"]) but is "Son of Man" when on the lips of Jesus or spoken about Jesus (Matt. 24:39; Mark 14:62; Acts 7:56).

The word *'almah,* which has provoked much discussion in translations, is also variously rendered—as it was in the NEB: "young woman" (Gen. 24:43; Song of Sol. 6:8; Isa. 7:14), "she" (Exod. 2:8 ["the girl"]), "girls" (Ps. 68:(26)25; Prov. 30:19), and "maiden" (Song of Sol. 1:3). The same word in its masculine form *'elim* is "stripling" (I Sam. 17:56 ["lad"]) and "him" (I Sam. 20:22 ["lad"]).

There is variety in measures. The ark of Noah (Gen. 6:15), the tabernacle and its furniture (Exod. 25:8ff.), and the temple (I Kings 6:2ff.) are in cubits, but Goliath is over nine feet tall (I Sam. 17:4), and Haman's gallows is seventy-five feet high (Esther 7:9). There are cases where measures are determined by the "bushel" (Amos 8:5), "quart" (Rev. 6:6), and in "gallons" (John 2:6); however, "a thousand gallons" in the NEB becomes "a hundred jars" (Luke 16:6) in the REB. As in the NEB, the quantity "a homer of barley" (Hos. 3:2) has dropped *lethekh,* which is a portion of a homer. While some distances are in cubits (Num. 35:4-5), some are in furlongs (Rev. 21:16), and some in miles (Luke 24:13; John 6:19; 11:18; Rev. 14:20). References to time are adjusted to current usage: "between three and six in the morning" (Matt. 14:25), "three in the afternoon" (Matt. 27:45), "nine in the morning" (Mark 15:25; Acts 2:15), "midday" (Mark 15:33; Luke 23:44), and "one o'clock" (John 4:52 ["one in the afternoon"]), but "second or third watch" is paraphrased to "middle of the night or before dawn" (Luke 12:38). In sums of money, one encounters the British "twopence" (Luke 12:6) and in quantity a "hundredweight" (John 19:39; Rev. 16:21). However, the half a hundredweight of Matthew 13:33, and Luke 13:21 in the REB becomes "three measures."

Modern Vocabulary

Numerous examples can be cited where the NEB translators sought modern terms and the REB has continued to use them. The REB uses "vault" for the expanse of the sky instead of "firmament" (Gen. 1:6, 8). It uses "close kinsmen" instead of "brothers" (Gen. 13:8) and "forefathers" instead of "fathers" (Acts 7:44), "massacred" (I Sam. 11:11), "not even know the way to town" (Eccl. 10:15), "mirage" (Isa. 35:7), "make a feint at" (Dan. 11:40 ["make feints at"]), "litigation" (Hos. 10:4), "grant them no reprieve" (Amos 1:3; etc.), "hurricane" (Jonah 1:4), and "goodbye" (Acts 21:6 ["good-bye"]).

In matters of human sexuality, the REB combines the archaic and the modern, with little change from the NEB. One reads "played the whore" (Isa. 1:21; Ezek. 23:3), "male prostitute" (Ezek. 23:20), "perverts" (I Tim. 1:10), "bastards" (Hos. 5:7), "when she is asked in marriage" (Song of Sol. 8:8), "menstruation" (Lev. 12:5; KJV: "her separation"), "intercourse" (Gen. 6:4; 19:5; I Sam. 1:19; Rom. 1:26), and "sleeping together and making love" (Isa. 57:8 ["sleeping together"]). Four Hebrew expressions for the sex act are translated "lie with," though that term is not current terminology: *yada'* ("know"; Gen. 4:1, 17), *shakhabh* ("lie with"; Gen. 19:32, 34; I Sam. 2:22), *bo'* ("go in unto"; Gen. 16:4), and *qarabh* ("approach"; Isa. 8:3). While a man is forbidden "intercourse" with an animal (Lev. 20:15), a woman is forbidden to "mate with" one (Lev. 20:16 ["have intercourse with"]). Although frequently using "beget" (Gen. 5:12, 15, 25, 32), the REB varies its translation by using "had other sons and daughters" (Gen. 5:4, 7). The N.T. has "was the father of" (Matt. 1:2-16).

"Pregnant" (Gen. 16:4, 5; I Sam. 4:19; Hos. 13:16 ["with child"], "becomes pregnant" (Lev. 12:2 ["conceives"]), "going to have a child" (Matt. 1:18 ["with child"]), and "about to bear a child" (Rev. 12:2 ["pregnant"]) are all used, but when an angel speaks, the term is "with child" (Gen. 16:11). "With/in labour" (Gen. 3:16; Song of Sol. 8:5; Mic. 4:9; Rev. 12:2), "go/went into labour" (Exod. 1:19 ["in labour"]; I Sam. 4:19 ["her labour suddenly began"]), "like a woman in labour" (Isa. 42:14), and "give birth" (Hos. 9:16) are all encountered, but there is also "writhe in travail" (Ps. 29:8 ["writhe"]). The NEB and REB have rendered *'itstsabhon* as "labour" when describing both woman (Gen. 3:16) and man (Gen. 3:17), a choice which should be welcome to advocates of natural childbirth. Other translations use "pain" in the one case and "labour" in the other. There is "childbirth" (Exod. 1:16; Hos. 9:11) and "stillborn child" (Eccl. 6:3 ["still-born child"]).

"Nursed" is used for the feeding of a child (Exod. 2:9 ["suckle"]; I Sam. 1:23), but there is also "sucking infant" (Lam. 4:4), "be suckled" (Isa. 60:16), and "suck" (Isa. 60:16; 66:11). For whales there is "the teat" (Lam. 4:3). The term "wet-nurse" occurs in Exodus 2:7.

Readers encounter the REB's effort at a more modern lexicon in the terms "unchaste woman" (Hos. 1:2 ["a wanton"]), "promiscuous" (Hos. 5:3; 6:10 ["played the wanton"]), "prostitute" (Amos 7:17 ["city strumpet"]), "prostitution" (Mic. 1:7 ["harlotry"]), "sexual pervert" (I Cor. 6:9 ["homosexual perversion"]), "raped" and "ravished" (Lam. 5:11 ["raped . . . raped"]), and "betrothed" (Joel 1:8 ["bridegroom"]). "Betrothed" is used in both versions at Matthew 1:18.

Gender-Oriented Language

The REB has made an attempt to avoid gender-oriented language. Readers will find that "man" is now "human beings" (Gen. 1:26 ["man"])", "the human race" (Gen. 6:1 ["mankind"]), or "mortals" (Mic. 6:8 [not translated in NEB]). It will take some time for this reviewer to become accustomed to reading the Psalm as "Turn back you children of mortals" (Ps. 90:3). The application of the policy has God make "human beings" in Genesis 1:26 but make "a human being" in Genesis 2:7, although 'adham is being rendered in both places. There is "start a child" (Prov. 22:6 ["boy"]), and "if you forgive anyone's sins" (John 20:23 ["any man's"]), but then there is "I may speak in tongues of men or of angels" (I Cor. 13:1), which may be an oversight.

In cases where Paul addresses churches, the REB translates *adelphoi* as "brothers and sisters" (Rom. 1:13 ["my brothers"]), "my friends" (Gal. 1:11; I Thess. 2:1 ["brothers"]), or "dear friends" (Phil. 4:1; I Thess. 1:4 ["friends"]). Paul refers to his associates as "colleagues" (Phil. 4:21; Col. 1:1 ["brothers"]). The REB also strives for gender-neutral language in "Now God has his dwelling with mankind!" (Rev. 21:3), "I am coming soon, and bringing with me my recompense to repay everyone according to what he has done!" (Rev. 22:12), and "If anyone takes away from the words in this book . . . take away from him his share . . ." (Rev. 22:19). In the last two examples, the third-person masculine singular pronoun is not avoided.

Some of the difficulty in moving from gender-oriented language may be seen in the treatment of the term "brotherhood." The NEB used "brotherhood" in eleven passages. The REB retains the term in five (Acts 1:15; 15:1; 21:7; I Thess. 4:9; I Tim. 4:6) but modifies other uses of the term to "congregation" (Acts 18:18, 27; 21:17), "Christian community" (Rom. 12:10), "community" (Eph. 6:23), and "them all" (I Thess. 5:27). However, the REB also retains "brothers" (Heb. 3:1), "brotherly affection" (I Pet. 3:8), and "family of brothers" (Rom. 8:29). The REB uses "Happy is the man" for *ho teron* (Rev. 22:7). The same sort of structure, but a plural, is found in Revelation 22:14 and is rendered as "Happy are those who. . . ." "Mankind" (I Thess. 4:13) is treated as unobjectionable as a substitute for "men," but it is likely to attract much scrutiny. Since there is no inclusive third-person singular pronoun, the REB has retained "him" and "himself" (II Thess. 3:14). "She" and "herself" would not be acceptable as inclusive, and "he/she" is pedantic. Further sensitivity for inclusive language would make the REB a more consistent revision. The NRSV carries this issue further than the REB.

Colloquial Phrases

Despite advertising assertions that colloquialisms have been avoided, many colloquialisms are carried over from the NEB to the REB. A part of the question may be definition. One reads: "drown ourselves in pleasure" (Prov. 7:18), "double-dealer" (Prov. 14:2), "eyes are bloodshot" (Prov. 23:29), "have duped me" (Jer. 20:7), "a mere puppet" (Jer. 22:28), "King Bombast" (Jer. 46:17), "took to their heels" (Matt. 8:33), "made for the town" (Matt. 8:33), "talk of the whole district" (Matt. 9:26 ["of all the country round"]), "touched them on the raw" (Acts 5:33; 7:54), "hold their own" (Acts 6:10), "a man of action" (Acts 7:22), "took him in hand" (Acts 18:26), "hubbub" (Acts 21:34), "at their heels" (Acts 21:36), "put him in irons" (Acts 22:29), "finding myself out of my depth" (Acts 25:20), "remanded in custody" (Acts 25:21), "hole-and-corner business" (Acts 26:26), "no one has a good word to say for it" (Acts 28:22), "square with the truth" (Gal. 2:14), "a Jew born and bred" (Gal. 2:14), "fighting one another, tooth and nail" (Gal. 5:15), "curry favour" (I Thess. 2:4), "made our weight felt" (I Thess. 2:7), and "left me in the lurch" (II Tim. 4:16).

Beyond those colloquial expressions carried over from the NEB, there are new ones in the REB: "fume at" (Ps. 80:4 ["resist"]), "be abashed" (Ps. 86:17 ["to their shame"]), "tight-fisted" (Prov. 11:24 ["sparing"]), "play the grandee" (Prov. 12:9 ["be conceited"]), "fritter them away" (Prov. 21:20 ["is a mere spendthrift"]), "I am paying off an old score" (Prov. 24:29 ["I will requite him"]), "turned tail" (Ps. 78:9 ["turned and ran"]; Jer. 46:21 ["turned and fled"]), "smuggle us out by stealth" (Acts 16:37 ["smuggle us out privately"]), "bypass Ephesus" (Acts 20:16 ["pass by"]), and "spiked themselves on many a painful thorn" (I Tim. 6:10 ["many thorny griefs"]).

At the same time, the REB has refrained from some of the colloquial renderings of the NEB: "temple police" (John 19:6 ["their henchmen"]), "addressed the populace" (Acts 12:21 ["harangued them"]), "I am accused, . . . and accused . . ." (Acts 26:7 ["I am impeached, and impeached . . ."]), "extortioners" (I Cor. 5:10; 6:10 ["grabbers"]), "give all" (I Cor. 13:3 ["dole out all"]), "We are not adulterating" (II Cor. 2:17 ["go hawking the word of God about"]), "will want to" (I Tim. 5:11 ["hanker after"]), "smashing them to pieces" (Rev. 2:27 ["to bits"]), and "devour" (Rev. 17:16 ["batten on"]).

Sophisticated Vocabulary

Each translating group has to decide the reading comprehension level of the audience for which it is translating. Should a translation use a vocabulary easy for all to understand or should it teach vocabulary by the words it uses? The REB in some cases has revised the NEB in the direction of less sophisticated speech. Examples include "cancelled" (Matt. 18:27 ["remitted"]), "restrain" (Luke 19:39 ["reprimand"]), "illegitimate" (John 8:41 ["base-born"]), "strenuously" (Acts 18:28 ["indefatigable"; corrected in 1970 edition]), "intrigues" (Acts 20:19 ["machinations"]), "calling on his name" (Acts 22:16 ["invocation of his name"]), "to envy" (Rom. 11:11 ["to emulation"]), "those in darkness" (Rom. 2:19 ["the benighted"]), "show itself in mutual affection" (Rom. 12:10 ["breed a warmth"]), "long hair" (I Cor. 11:14 ["flowing locks"]), "with special respect" (I Cor. 12:23 ["more than ordinary seemliness"]), "two weeks" (Gal. 1:18 ["fortnight"]), "their minds are closed" (Eph. 4:18 ["their wits are beclouded"]), "by the law's standard of righteousness" (Phil. 3:6, 9 ["in legal rectitude"]), "consideration of others" (Phil. 4:5 ["magnanimity"]), "grow strong" (Col. 2:7 ["be consolidated"]), "have no advantage over" (I Thess. 4:15 ["not forestall"]), "insist on abstinence" (I Tim. 4:3 ["inculcate abstinence"]), "those who opposed him" (II Tim. 2:25 ["refractory"]), "servant" (Heb. 3:5 ["servitor"]), "ineffective" (Heb. 7:18 ["impotent"]), "an evil thing" (James 3:8 ["intractable evil"]), "malicious talk of any kind" (I Pet. 2:1 ["recrimination"]), "comes in judgement" (I Pet. 2:12 ["to hold assize"]), "carousal" (I Pet. 4:3 ["tippling"]), "start abusing" (I Pet. 4:4 ["vilify"]), "crown" (I Pet. 5:4 ["garland"; but REB retains "garland" in II Tim. 4:8]), "renounce" (Rev. 2:22 ["forswear"]), "nobles" (Rev. 6:15 ["magnates"]), "completed" (Rev. 15:1 ["consummated"]), "decked out" (Rev. 17:4; 18:16 ["bedizened"]), "pomp and luxury" (Rev. 18:7 ["voluptuous pomp"]).

The phrases that follow (continued from the NEB), however, show that the REB presupposes a certain sophistication from its readership: "calyxes" (Exod. 25:31), "pustule" (Lev. 13:2), "minions" (II Kings 19:6; Isa. 37:6 ["lackeys"]), "emulate" (Prov. 3:31), "perfidious" (Prov. 27:6), "palanquin" (Song of Sol. 3:9), "paragon" (Song of Sol. 5:10), "palm-fronds" (Song of Sol. 5:11; 7:8), "assayer/assay" (Jer. 6:27), "keening" (Jer. 9:17), "perennial pastures" (Jer. 50:44; NRSV: "strong sheepfold"), "pinions" (Ezek. 17:3), "peremptory" (Dan. 2:15 ["peremptory"]; 3:22 ["was urgent"]), "vintagers" (Obad. 5; NRSV: "grape gatherers"), "resplendent day" (Acts 2:20), "without demur" (Acts 10:29), "retinue" (Acts 13:7), "obdurate" (Acts 19:9), "interminable myths" (I Tim. 1:4), "pompous ignoramus" (I Tim. 6:4), and "charge of . . . indiscipline" (Tit. 1:6 ["are not out of control"]).

The REB has its colorful phrases as "Do not be dilatory in paying" (Eccl. 5:4 ["be not slow"]) and "so does the number of parasites living off them" (Eccl. 5:11 ["so do those who live off them"]). Phrases of pagan background include "womb of mother earth" (Eccl. 5:15), "goddesses of the field" (Song of Sol. 2:7), and "dragon" (Isa. 51:9).

Other scattered examples suggest that the REB is a revision of the NEB that aspires to additional sophistication rather than simplification: "vitiligo" (Lev. 13:39 ["dull-white leprosy"]), "reconnoitred" (Judg. 1:23 ["sent spies to"]), "connivance" (Prov. 6:35; Acts 5:2 ["full knowledge"]; 14:5), "the perfidious" (Prov. 2:22; 21:18; ["traitor"]; 11:3 ["rogues"]; 13:2 ["treacherous"], II Tim. 3:4 ["strangers to all goodness"]), "penury" (Prov. 10:4 ["make a man poor"]), "invidious" (Prov. 24:23; 28:21 ["not good"]), "canker in his bones" (Prov. 12:4 ["rot"]), "perfidy" (Prov. 13:15 ["treachery"]), "son is a wastrel" (Prov. 17:2 ["a disappointing son"]), "recompense" (Prov. 19:17 ["repay him"]), "given privily" (Prov. 21:14 ["in secret"]), "onerous" (Prov. 25:27 ["burdensome"]), "untrammelled liberty" (Ps. 18:19 ["into an open place"]), "discomfited" (Ps. 22:5; 35:26; 40:14 ["put to shame," "disgraced"]), "pleasant converse" (Ps. 55:14 ["pleasant company"]), "scimitar" (Jer. 6:23; 50:42 ["sabre"]), "steppeland" (Jer. 17:6 ["desert"]), "decanted" (Jer. 48:11 ["emptied"]), "statutes that were malign" (Ezek. 20:25 ["not good statutes"]), "strategems" (Eph. 6:11 ["devices"]), "unimpeachable character" (I Tim. 3:10 ["no mark against them"]; Tit. 1:7): "subordinate to" (Heb. 2:7 ["lower than"]), "immutable" (Heb. 6:17 ["unchanging"]): "intimidated by" (Heb. 11:23 ["afraid of"]), "impeded" (I Pet. 3:7 ["hindered"]), and "cleverly concocted" (II Pet. 1:16 ["artfully spun"]).

The vocabulary, as in the NEB, will be in some instances familiar to seafarers: "To the harbor they were making for" (Ps. 107:30 ["they desired"]), "the sea was running higher and higher" (Jonah 1:13), "trawls" (Hab. 1:16), "leaving it to port" (Acts 21:3), "making very heavy weather" (Acts 27:18), "jettisoned" (Acts 27:19), and "slipped the anchors" (Acts 27:40).

Some modern Semitic geographical terms have come to be widely enough used that the reader is assumed to know them. Where the NEB used "gorge," "valley," or "ravine," the REB has "wadi" (Josh. 17:9; I Kings 15:13; II Chron. 15:16; 20:16; Isa. 7:19; Jer. 31:40; Joel 3:18; Amos 6:14). "Torrent of Egypt" becomes "wadi of Egypt" (II Kings 24:7). As the NEB, the REB has "Negeb" (Gen. 12:9; 13:1) and "Arabah" (Jer. 39:4).

Yielding to popularly accepted but ungrammatical speech, the REB has "to such a halting speaker as me" (Exod. 6:12) where the NEB stayed with "as I am." Also one finds "accepted Barnabas and myself" (Gal. 2:9) where there is no reflexive situation. The order of mention in pronouns

367

is kept as in Hebrew "me and you" (Gen. 23:15 ["you and me"]) but in other cases is reversed to give a polite English form (Gen. 31:44). A dangling clause is used in poetry: "Zion, delightful and lovely, her end is near" (Jer. 6:2).

Use of Paraphrase

The REB claims to be a translation rather than a paraphrase. It attempts faithfulness to the meaning without reproducing the grammatical structure or translating word for word. Nevertheless, the paraphrasing tendency of the NEB is continued in numerous instances: "sang her praises" (Gen. 12:15 ["praised her"]), "when she is asked in marriage" (Song of Sol. 8:8; KJV: "when she shall be spoken for"), "abandon me to death" (Acts 2:27 ["abandon my soul . . ."]), "no one's fate can be laid at my door" (Acts 20:26 ["man's fate"]), and church of the Lord which he "won for himself by his own blood" (Acts 20:28).

The use of paraphrase produces "the dearest thing you have" (Ezek. 24:16) where the NRSV has the more literal "delight of your eyes"; however, the reader is left without means of connecting this phrase with "delight of your/their eyes" which follows in Ezekiel 24:21, 25. "Israel" (Luke 1:33) is preferred to "house of Jacob."

In its effort at communication, the NEB supplied modern proverbs for Semitic ones. An example is, "The lame must not think himself a match for the nimble," an expression which is not used in America. The REB chose "The time for boasting is after the battle."

Interpretative modifiers already inserted in the NEB are retained: "sanctuary at Shechem" (Gen. 12:6), "a rejected bride" (Exod. 11:1), "follow at your heels" (Exod. 11:8), "the Adversary, Satan" (Job 1:6 ["Satan"]), "a chariot-horse" (Song of Sol. 1:9 ["chariot-horses"; sex and number are both given in Hebrew; NRSV: "mare"]), "beds inlaid with ivory" (Amos 6:4), and "sacred way to Beersheba" (Amos 8:14). Abner's comparison to a "baboon" (NEB) becomes one to "a Judahite dog" (II Sam. 3:8); the Masoretic Text has "dog's head." "Crime after crime" replaces "three or four" (Amos 1:3, 6, 9, 11, 13; 2:1, 4, 6); however, the Book of Proverbs retains the idiom "three things . . . four things" (Prov. 30:15-31). "The powers of death" (Matt. 16:18) stands for "gates of Hades." "A full day's wage" and "the usual day's wage" (Matt. 20:2, 9, 13) are used for "a denarius." "His own Father" (John 5:18), "the great Jewish festival" (John 6:4), "new way" (Acts 24:14), "eyes for nothing but loose women" (II Pet. 2:14 ["women"], and "physically weaker" (I Pet. 3:7 ["weaker"]) are encountered.

A variant paraphrase to that used in the NEB is "of God" (Mark 14:62; margin: "of the Power") which becomes in the REB "of the Almighty."

Paraphrase renderings are sometimes chosen where the NEB was the more literal: "Give me your solemn oath" (Gen. 24:2; 47:29 ["put your hand under my thigh"]), "chief counselor" (Gen. 45:8 ["father"]), "tickle his fancy" (II Tim. 4:3 ["tickle their ears"]), and "they had reached the depths of despair" (Exod. 6:9 ["they had become impatient"]). What once was a list of qualifications for elders in the NEB (Tit. 1:6) is recast into questions in the REB, as "Is each the husband of one wife?"

Improvements

An impressive list of improvements made over renderings in the NEB can be compiled. The NEB interpretation of Judges 1:14, "she broke wind," has been eliminated. The revised text says Achsah "dismounted from her donkey," and a footnote "or made a noise" is inserted. A problem passage in Job 18:11 read in the KJV "Terrors shall make him afraid on every side, and shall drive him to his feet." The second clause became in the NEB "and make him piss over his feet," but now the REB renders the phrase "so that he cannot hold back his urine."

There are other divergent choices in the REB. The Lord "brought to an end all the work" (Gen. 2:2 ["ceased"]) instead of "resting" as in the KJV, which could suggest fatigue. "A time to discard" (Eccl. 3:6 ["throw away"]), "irrelevant" (Hos. 8:12 ["invalid"]), "brotherly alliance" (Amos 1:9 ["ties of kinship"]), and "divans" (Amos 3:12 ["couch"]) all reflect change.

The name of Adam's and Eve's clothing made out of fig leaves is an issue of long standing. Tyndale had "apurns," the Geneva Bible had "breeches," the KJV had "aprons," but the NEB and REB chose "loincloths" (Gen. 3:7). Where the NEB had the Lord make "tunics," the REB has "coverings" (Gen. 3:21).

The revisers favor the word "flay" which produces "My father whipped you, but I shall flay you" (I Kings 12:14 ["use the lash"]). The revisers continue "gibbet" (Acts 5:30; 10:39; 13:29; I Pet. 2:24) as a preference to "tree" for the means of crucifixion. They prefer "Messiah" to "Christ" when Jewish people are speaking or being spoken to, even where the Greek has *Christos* (Mark 14:61; John 3:28; 4:29; 7:26, 27, 31, 41; Acts 17:3). However, where the Greek text explains the meaning of *messias* as being Christos, "Christ" (John 1:41; 4:25) is retained.

Spelling

Someone has said that the British and the Americans are two people separated by a common language, and in the spellings in the REB that difference comes to light. Words spelled with the "our" form, correct in Britain but not used in America, are numerous such as "tumour" (I Sam. 5:9, 12), "vigour" (Prov. 5:9 ["dignity"]; Isa. 40:29), "coloured" (Prov. 7:16), "neighbour" (Prov. 25:9), "splendour" (Isa. 35:2), "rumour" (Isa. 37:7), "armoury" (Isa. 39:2), "remould" (Jer. 18:4 ["mould"]), "dishonour" (Hos. 4:7, 18), "behaviour" (Hos. 6:9 ["deeds"]), "honour" (Hos. 9:11; Acts 12:23; I Thess. 2:6), "saviour" (Hos. 13:4; Acts 5:31; 13:23), "labour" (Mic. 4:9; 6:14; etc.), "labourers" (Matt. 9:38), "colour" (Nah. 2:10), "harbour" (Matt. 9:4), "harboured" (Acts 17:7), "fervour" (Acts 18:25), and "splendour" (II Thess. 1:9; 2:14). One also encounters "Harran" (Gen. 11:31; Acts 7:4), "centre" (Num. 35:4), "milch" (I Sam. 6:7), "ploughmen/plough" (Ps. 129:3; 141:7), "jewellery" (Ezek. 16:11), "judgement" (Hab. 1:7), and "haemorrhages" (Matt. 9:20). Other occurrences of these words and other examples can be collected. These spelling differences are not significant enough to create any real communication problem for the American reader.

British Vocabulary

The vocabulary of the REB is familiar to most English readers, but sizeable list can be made of NEB renderings strange to American ears: "daub" and redaub" (Lev. 14:41, 43), "to beggar us" (Judg. 14:15), "must be woken up" (I Kings 18:27), "the chariot was swilled out" (I Kings 22:38), "mantle" (Ezra 9:3), "bandy" (Job 15:3), "blackguard" (Job 34:18), "doublet of hide" (Job 41:13), "creditor distrain on" (Ps. 109:11 ["moneylender distrain on"]), "glutted his rage" (Lam. 4:11), and "money-grubbing" (I Tim. 3:8; Tit. 1:7).

Though understood in America, "fetched" (I Sam. 10:23; Jer. 26:23; etc.) is more common in the REB than in its use in America. Other vocabulary choices, probably suitable in Britain but not commonly used in America, include "cairn" (Gen. 31:46), "ground down their Israelite slaves" (Exod. 1:13 ["treated . . . with ruthless severity"]), "bone lazy" (Exod. 5:17 ["lazy"]), "make over to" (Exod. 13:12 ["surrender to"]; I Sam. 1:28 ["lend"]; 2:20 ["for which you asked"]), "caught in . . . toils" (Exod. 10:7), "wastrel" (Deut. 21:20), "was rapt like the prophets" (I Sam. 10:11), "festoons of chain-work" (I Kings 7:17), "trolley" (I Kings 7:27; Jer. 27:19), "self-sown" (II Kings 19:29), "to condole with" (I Chron.

19:2), "temple servitors" (Neh. 10:28 ["temple-servitors"]), "panniers" (Job 5:5), "the miscreant" (Job 29:17), "they . . . savage me" (Job 30:11), and "shambles" (Jer. 12:3).

Other words, unusual in America, include the prophetic woe as "Woe betide" where the NEB used variety (Isa. 5:8; Mic. 2:1; Amos 6:1 ["Shame on you!"]; Amos 5:18 ["Fools"]; Nah. 3:1 ["Ah!"]; Hab. 2:6, 9, 12, 15, 19; Luke 7:2 ["Woe betide"]; Matt. 18:7 ["Alas for"]). Also unusual are "moorland" (Mic. 3:12 ["heath"]) and "moor" (Mic. 7:14 ["heath"]). While in the first case, "heath" was changed to "moorland," "heath" has been retained in Isaiah 32:14 and "heathland" in Jeremiah 21:14. One is no more common in America than the other. "Madman" (Prov. 26:18 ["madman"]; Hos. 9:7; Matt. 8:33), "madness" (Eccl. 2:2, 12; 9:3), and "mad" (Eccl. 10:13; Acts 26:24) are used for insanity. Nevertheless, "crazy" (Acts 12:15) is also used. The REB also includes these examples: "poverty will come on you like a footpad" (Prov. 6:11; 24:34 ["robber"]), "knave" (Prov. 6:12 ["mischievous man"]), "setting his clothes alight" (Prov. 6:27 ["burning his clothes"]), "contumely" (Prov. 6:33; Isa. 37:3 ["contempt"]), "betimes" (Jer. 21:12), "short bushel" (Mic. 6:10), "venal judge" (Mic. 7:3 ["the judge who gives judgment for reward"]), "squadrons of horse" (Nah. 2:3), "bestir" (Hab. 2:19), "meal-tub" (Matt. 5:15), and "take heart" (Matt. 9:22).

Additional vocabulary examples not commonly used in America include "hatch their futile plots" (Ps. 2:1; Acts 4:25 ["lay their plots in vain"]), "runnels of water" (Prov. 5:16; 21:1), "a boorish son" (Prov. 17:21), "there is a rod in pickle for the arrogant" (Prov. 19:29), "besmirch the name" (Prov. 30:9 ["blacken the name"]), and "sally forth in formation" (Prov. 30:27 ["in detachments"]). There is "go circumspectly" (Eccl. 5:1 ["go carefully"]), "close-locked" (Song of Sol. 4:12), and "mulled wine" (Song of Sol. 8:2).

"Grain" (Deut. 33:28; Judg. 15:5; Isa. 36:17) is substituted for "corn" in some cases, but "corn" is retained in others as "corn" (Joel 2:19; Amos 7:1) and "seed-corn" (Lev. 27:16) for grain. "Cornfields" (Matt. 12:1) is for grainfields. The REB records "corn" three times in the N.T., a reduction from eight (Matt. 13:26; Mark 4:7; Luke 17:35). Barley is said to be "in the ear" (Exod. 9:31) where the American agricultural term would be "headed."

Also more familiar to British readers are "abominate" (Amos 5:10 ["loathe"]), "follow hard on" (Amos 9:13), "the crop is heavy" (Matt. 9:37), "warders" (Acts 5:23), "made for the house of" (Acts 12:12), "sued for peace" (Acts 12:20), "ruffians" (Acts 17:5 ["low fellows"]), "with all speed" (Acts 17:15), and "battered and naked" (Acts 19:16 ["stripped and battered"]). There are "dignitaries of the province" (Acts 19:31), "assizes" (Acts 19:38), "folded Paul in their arms" (Acts 20:37), "true-born Jew" (Acts 22:3), and "true-born son" (Tit. 1:4).

"Fuller's Field" (II Kings 18:17; Isa. 36:2) and "fuller's soap" (Mal. 3:2) occur in the O.T., but the term becomes "no bleacher" in the N.T. (Mark 9:3). There are "a deed of divorce" (Isa. 50:1), "swill it down" (Isa. 56:12 ["drain it down"]), "spawn of an adulterer" (Isa. 57:3), and "a sheep-walk" (Ezek. 25:5). Pharisees "strain off a midge" (Matt. 23:24); Paul "rounded on the spirit" (Acts 16:18 ["rounding . . ."]); and women are not to be "scandalmongers" (I Tim. 3:11 ["talk scandal"]; II Tim. 3:3; Tit. 2:3).

The British are unconcerned about any confusion the meaning of "dumb" might create; hence, they continue to write that the mute are "dumb" (Exod. 4:11; Matt. 9:32; Luke 1:22). The "dumb heathen gods" (I Cor. 12:2) are silent ones, and a "dumb beast" (II Pet. 2:16) is a mute one. The leprous are "lepers" (II Kings 7:3; Matt. 8:2; Luke 4:27; etc.) in the REB despite the resentment held by victims of Hansen's disease to the term "lepers." Naaman is a leper (II Kings 5:1) with the marginal option "or his skin was diseased." Gehazi ends up (as in the NEB) with his skin diseased (II Kings 5:27). That which was a "malignant skin disease" has become a "virulent skin disease" (Lev. 13:2; Deut. 24:8). The "wild ass" (Hos. 8:9; etc.) is retained but the domestic animal becomes "donkey" (Gen. 22:3; Exod. 4:20; 13:13; 22:10; 23:12; I Sam. 8:16; 9:3).

"The restraining power" (II Thess. 2:6) gives less encouragement to a particular eschatological view than "the "Restrainer" did. "Whitsuntide" correctly becomes "Pentecost" (I Cor. 16:8). "Friday" is dropped for "day of preparation" (Matt. 27:62; Luke 23:54). The adjective "guardian" is dropped from "angels" (Matt. 18:10). "Peter, the Rock" (Matt. 16:18; John 1:42), which explains the name but which invites the thought that the church rests on Peter, and "Passover meal" (John 18:28) are retained.

At the same time, the revision has been extensive. Some official titles used in the NEB have been abandoned: "regent" becomes "gave him authority over" (Dan. 2:48), "chief prefect" becomes "put him in charge" (Dan. 2:48), and "chief constables" becomes "magistrates" (Dan. 3:2). Many other cases of continuing titles used in the NEB can be cited: "comptroller of the household" (Isa. 36:3), "adjutant-general" (Isa. 36:3), "secretary of state" (Isa. 36:3), "an officer in the royal service" (John 4:46), "controller of the temple" (Acts 4:1), "a military orderly" (Acts 10:7), "commandant" (Acts 22:26, 27), and "commanding officer" (Acts 24:22).

In treating the question of divine repentance, the REB has the Lord "bitterly regret" (Gen. 6:6 ["was sorry"]), "I shall think again" (Jer. 18:10

["think . . . better"]), or "relent" (Jer. 26:19; Joel 2:14; Jonah 3:10; ["repent"]). The NEB used "relent" in Amos 7:3.

All current translations have the problem of identifying biblical animal, bird, and plant species. Where the NEB and REB have "bull and bison" (Isa. 34:7), the NRSV has "young steers with mighty bulls." The "jackal" of the NRSV is "wolf," and the "eagle" (Mic. 1:16) at times is a "vulture" in the REB. There is "dugong-hide" (Ezek. 16:10 ["stout hide"]) and the bird "wryneck" (Jer. 8:7) where the NRSV has "crane" with a note. There is the tree named "ilex" (Isa. 44:14). The ordinary reader cannot be expected to know these technical terms (no matter how scientifically accurate they may be) but must consult his dictionary if he wants a definition.

Transliteration

As with the NEB, place names in Genesis are transliterated, and the explanation is given in the notes (Gen. 32:2; 33:17, 20; etc.). The view that the place of the hiding of Jeremiah's undergarment was near at hand is reflected in the transliteration *Perath* (Jer. 13:5, 6). Other transliterations include *Magor-missabib* (Jer. 20:3), *baalim* (Hos. 2:13, 17; 11:2 [*Baalim*]), *Baal* (Hos. 2:16), *teraphim* (Hos. 3:4 ["household gods"], but *teraphim* is "household gods" in Genesis 31:35 and I Samuel 19:13. The word often transliterated *Sakkuth* becomes "idol-king," and *Kaiwan* becomes "pedestals" (Amos 5:26). The place names *Shittim* and *Gilgal* (Mic. 6:5) are transliterated in a traditional manner. In some instances the REB chose the transliterated *bamah* over "hill-shrine" (Ezek. 20:29).

The Article

The inclusion or exclusion of the definite article continues to be a problem. *En synagoge* is "in the synagogue" (John 6:59 ["in synagogue"]) and "in synagogues" (John 18:20 ["in synagogue"]). Cases of inclusion of the definite article where it is present in Greek but was omitted in the NEB include "Jesus and the Resurrection" (Acts 17:18) and "to the synagogue" (Mark 1:21; Luke 4:16), but "to synagogue" continues in Acts 13:14 for the same structure. English translations in general insert the definite article with "Holy Spirit" (Matt. 3:11), and the REB is no exception. A case where the Greek has no definite article but where traditionally (since William Tyndale) "the" has been inserted is "water and the Spirit" (John 3:5). The NEB, REB, and

NRSV do not insert the article, and the NEB and REB drop the capitalization of "spirit."

Additional Evaluation

If one looks at those topics which have become shibboleths in discussions of current translations, the NEB and REB use "Peter, the Rock" (Matt. 16:18; earlier considered in this study). "Only Son" for *monogenes huios* (John 1:18; 3:16, 18; etc.) and "unspiritual nature" Galatians 5:19 ("lower nature") with the variety earlier illustrated for *sarx* are used. Psalm 51:5 reads, "From my birth I have been evil, sinful from the time my mother conceived me" ("In iniquity I was brought to birth and my mother conceived me in sin"). Jonah's "great fish" (Jonah 1:17 ["great fish"]) is a "sea monster" (Matt. 12:40). The REB, as the NEB, uses "abolish" in Jesus' statement about the law and his purpose in coming (Matt. 5:17) but then uses "annulled" (Eph. 2:15) and "cancelled" (Col. 2:14 [as do the NIV and NRSV]) in Paul's statements. The RSV, NIV, and NRSV used "abolished" also in Ephesians 2:15, which appears to have Jesus do what he said he did not come to do.

Reflecting ecclesiastical thinking, the REB continues the "laymen" of Acts 4:13 but reduces the "laying on hands in ordination" to "laying on of hands" (I Tim. 5:22).

Among items the reviewer sees in need of further attention would be the cases where "only" is inserted in the text. The inserted "only" of the NEB has been dropped in Mark 5:40 and Romans 8:24, but "only done our duty" (Luke 17:10; already inserted by Goodspeed in his translation) and "only through faith" (Gal. 2:16) are continued. Critics will point out that, as rendered, Galatians 2:16 can be interpreted as a "faith only" teaching.

Much of the sacrificial terminology chosen by the NEB is continued in the REB: "shared-offering" (Lev. 3:1; Num. 7:17), "food-offering" (Lev. 1:17; Num. 28:2), "grain-offering" (Num. 28:8; Isa. 43:23 ["offering"]), "whole-offering" (Lev. 1:3, 9), "thank-offering" (Lev. 7:16), "freewill-offering" (Lev. 7:12); "holy-gifts" (Lev. 22:16), and "votive offering" (Lev. 7:16). Then there are modified terms: "purification-offering" (Lev. 4:3, 14 ["sin-offering"]), "reparation-offering" (Lev. 5:15), and "reparation victim" (Lev. 7:2 ["guilt-offering"]), "a dedicated portion" (Lev. 7:30; 8:29 ["special gift"]), and "ordination-offering" (Lev. 7:37 ["installation-offering"]) with "ordination-basket" (Lev. 8:31 ["installation-basket"]).

The REB returned to the traditional vocabulary associated with the cult; some examples include "Tent of Meeting" (Lev. 3:8; 6:30; Josh. 18:1

["of the Presence"]), "censers" (Lev. 10:1 ["firepans"]), "the pilgrim-feast of Booths" (Lev. 23:34 ["of Tabernacles"]), "Ark of the Testimony" (Josh. 4:16 ["of the Tokens"]), and "solemn abstinence from work" (Lev. 23:3 ["a sabbath of sacred rest"]). As in the NEB, the priests "fling" blood (II Chron. 30:16). There is "leavened bread" (Lev. 7:13), "unleavened cake" (Lev. 2:5; 6:16), "Bread of the Presence" (Exod. 25:30), and "sacred bread" (Matt. 12:4).

Revisions reflecting significant differences in interpretation of passages include "will wish to be blessed" (Gen. 12:3 ["will pray"]; cf. 18:18), "sons-in-law" (Gen. 19:14 ["intended sons-in-law"]), "hot springs" (Gen. 36:24 ["mules"]), "threshing-sledges spiked with basalt" (Amos 1:3 ["iron"]), and "infringe my law" (Amos 4:4 ["rebel"]). Where the NEB used "grave" (Gen. 37:35), the REB transliterates *Sheol* with the marginal option "the underworld," but retains "grave" in Genesis 42:38. "Hyssop" (John 19:29 ["javelin"]) and "corner-stone" (Acts 4:11 ["keystone"]) are used.

No doubt "Send your grain across the seas" (Eccl. 11:1) of the NEB and REB is better than "Lay your bread on wet faces" of the 1568 Bishops' Bible. It contrasts with the NRSV's "Send out your bread upon the waters."

The NEB and REB differ from the traditional translations in rendering *'adham* in Genesis which in some passages designates humanity and in others is the name of the first man. The NEB translate only Genesis 3:21; 4:25; and 5:1, 3 as "Adam;" the rest are "the man." The REB has "Adam" only at 4:25 and 5:1, 3. The RSV had "Adam" at Genesis 3:17, 21; 4:1, 25; 5:1, 3, 4, 5. The NRSV begins to use "Adam" only at Genesis 4:25.

Despite Jesus' warning against calling another a fool (*more*; Matt. 5:22), the REB has N.T. writers do so (James 2:20 ["quibbler"]) where the Greek has *kene* rather than *moros*.

The REB after having described Cain as one who "worked the land" (Gen. 4:2 ["a tiller of the soil"]) then names Noah "the first tiller of the soil" (Gen. 9:20 ["a man of the soil"]). Still another item is the rendering of *houtōs* (Rom. 11:26), an adverb of manner, with a temporal one: "once that has happened" (NEB: "when that has happened"). This item has eschatological significance.

The REB reads that the meeting at Troas was "on the Saturday night" (Acts 20:7), but the same phrase in other occurrences is rendered "first day of the week" (Matt. 28:1; Mark 16:2; Luke 24:1; John 20:1) or "Sunday" (I Cor. 16:2). The occurrence of "Sunday" (used by the NEB in each of these passages) has been reduced to only one reference (I Cor. 16:2).

The REB has Phoebe to be "a minister in the church at Cenchreae" (Rom. 16:1) as contrasted to NEB's "holds office in the congregation." In I Timothy 3:11, discussing qualifications of deacons, the Greek merely has *gynaikas,* while the REB has "Women in this office" ("their wives, equally" with marginal option "Deaconesses"), ruling out the possibility that these women are the wives of the deacons. "Their wives" is given as a marginal option.

New translations often challenge thought, and the NEB/REB have their examples. Renderings like "no fool will trespass on it" (Isa. 35:8) and "I shall make prosperity flow over her like a river, and the wealth of nations like a river in spate" (Isa. 66:12; cf. 45:18) will avoid the pitfalls into which some of the uninformed have fallen when dealing with these sayings. "The law was put in charge of us until Christ should come" (Gal. 3:24 ["a kind of tutor"]) is an improvement. "When I was a stranger, you took me into your home" (Matt. 25:35) challenges in a way which "you took me in" (KJV) did not.

The sponsorship of this revision plus the standing of the issuing presses guarantee that the REB will have a wide circulation. It conveys the general message of the Bible. Duties to God and man are plainly laid out. The reviewer believes, however, that it is not likely to become the translation chiefly used by those who want to know in the nearest English equivalent the specific details of exactly what the original texts say.

16

The New Revised Standard Version

Realizing the need for ongoing revision of the English Bible, the Division of Education and Ministry of the National Council of Churches, through its Policies Committee of the Revised Standard Version, in 1973 set in motion a project to revise the RSV (1952). At that time the entire RSV had been in circulation for twenty years and its N.T. (1946) for almost three decades. A second edition of the RSV N.T. had been issued in 1971. Since 1946, substantial archaeological discoveries had been made in the Dead Sea Scrolls (in addition to Isaiah and Habakkuk), in the Nag Hammadi manuscripts, in the Bodmer, and in other papyrus materials. Significant strides had been made in the study of comparative Semitics, Greek, and other relevant areas of scholarship. Furthermore, the English language is continually changing; words go out of style, meanings are modified, and new words come into use. This last feature alone would justify a revision. Since 1952 there have been twenty-seven other renderings of the Scriptures into English and twenty-six additional renderings of the New Testament alone.[1]

Unlike the NEB, TEV, NIV, and NAB, which attempt completely new translations, the NRSV is an effort at further revision of that line of Bibles which began with William Tyndale (1525) and continued through

[1]B. M. Metzger, "The Processes and Struggles Involved in Making a New Translation of the Bible," *Religious Education* 85 (Spring 1990):174-84.

377

the KJV (1611), the RV/ASV (1881-1885/1901), and the RSV (1952). The O.T., N.T., and Apocrypha are all included, although copies will be available either with or without the Apocrypha. Eventually a common Bible suitable for Protestants, Roman Catholics, and Eastern Orthodox will be issued. The revision, which was issued officially on September 30, 1990, but which was available for purchase after May 1, 1990, can be thought of as an authorized version for those associated with the National Council of Churches. That organization's governing board met in Louisville, Kentucky, May 19, 1989, and passed a resolution which "authorized and endorsed the New Revised Standard Version for use in worship, study, and personal use, commending it to the churches for their use."

The translation group (the Revised Standard Bible Committee), composed of about thirty members, meets twice each year and has been at work for fifteen years. Bruce M. Metzger of Princeton Theological Seminary chairs the group. The committee, which receives no personal financial compensation for its services, is made up of both men and women representative of Protestant, Roman Catholic, Eastern Orthodox, and Jewish groups. For a time there were members from Canada and England.[2] After the committee completed its work in 1988, smaller editorial committees for the O.T. and N.T. attempted to give the rendering a still greater degree of homogeneity. This editorial work was done on the O.T. by Robert Denton, Walter Harrelson, and Bruce M. Metzger over a total of seventy-six days. The work on the N.T., which took thirty-three days, was done by Paul Minear, Lucetta Mowry, and Bruce M. Metzger.[3]

Translations have been produced in this century by secular businesses aiming at a specific market, by teams of translators representing one segment of the church community, and by individual translators. The producers of the NRSV claim that no other translation has been produced by such a broadly representative group. The academic qualifications of the translators are impeccable. The producers hope for an unbiased text.

The NRSV Bible is published in the United States by seven publishers: The American Bible Society, Cambridge University Press (represented by Baker Book House), Holman Bible Publishers, Thomas Nelson Publishers, Oxford University Press, World Bible Publishers, and Zondervan Corporation. William Collins and Sons will publish the NRSV

---

[2]Lists of names of the committee members are to be found in Bruce M. Metzger, "The Revised Standard Version," in *The Word of God,* ed. Lloyd R. Bailey (Atlanta: John Knox, 1982):42-44, and in Metzger, "The Processes."

[3]Metzger, "The Processes."

in the United Kingdom. The old RSV will remain in publication for at least five more years.

The translation team claims to have worked under the maxim "as literal as possible, as free as necessary." The group realized that there is a place for the different types of translations which have appeared in the last few decades. Thus they sought to produce a standard Bible text which is an absolutely trustworthy rendering of the ancient manuscripts into modern, understandable English. It is designed for use in worship, education, and private meditation.

The team recognizes that no language can be translated line for line and word for word into another language and remain completely understandable. The NRSV is therefore a free translation wherever freedom is necessary in order to guarantee that the meaning in English is the same as it was in the ancient languages. Paraphrastic renderings have been adopted only sparingly and then chiefly to compensate for deficiencies in the English language. (For example, Hebrew has no neuter gender. Neither Hebrew nor English has a common gender third person singular pronoun, and there are also other difficulties.) It is claimed in the advertising that "the language of the New RSV Bible is more understandable and more accurate than any other translation."

The authorization under which the revision was made issued four mandates requiring change:

> (1) in paragraph structure and punctuation; (2) in elimination of archaisms while retaining the flavor of the Tyndale—King James Bible tradition; (3) in attaining greater accuracy, clarity, and/or euphony; and (4) in eliminating masculine-oriented language, so far as this could be done without distorting passages that reflect the historical situation of ancient patriarchal culture and society.[4]

While special attention has been given to the problem of non-sexist language, "the pronouns for God and Christ are consistently rendered masculine, the same way they are in the ancient manuscripts." Where common gender is intended, the original used the masculine and the RSV used "men" (John 12:32), but the revision uses "all people." Masculine pronouns are replaced where both men and women are clearly intended. Other applications of the policy will be considered later in this chapter.

In the revision, archaic forms have been removed. The RSV retained old English forms in liturgical passages and in prayers addressed to God.

[4]Ibid.

However "thee," "thou," "thine," and the verb forms "eth" and "est" have been dropped in the NRSV in the Psalms, in prayers addressed to God, and in material about God and Christ. In the ancient Hebrew and Greek texts, God is addressed in the same forms used to address people, and this is the policy followed by the NRSV. Pronouns referring to the Father, Son, and Holy Spirit are uncapitalized, a practice also in keeping with the usage of the ancient languages as well as the KJV.

Text of the O.T.

For the O.T., use was made of the 1977 consonantal text of the *Biblia Hebraica Stuttgartensia* with revisions of 1983. Where different vowels from those of the Masoretes were followed, no notation is made. When an alternate reading given by the Masoretes is translated, it is noted by "Another reading is." Most corrections are based on one or more of the ancient versions which are older than Masoretic activity, and a footnote specifies the version followed. Corrections of ancient Hebrew scribes are noted by "Ancient Heb. tradition." Where the Hebrew text is thought to be corrupt, a correction is made accompanied by a note.

The apocryphal/deuterocanonical books of the O.T. are translated from a number of texts which include Rahlfs' Septuagint, the Göttingen Septuagint, Theodotion's Daniel, Hebrew fragments, and others. Third and Fourth Maccabees and Psalm 151 are included in the Apocrypha.

The NRSV revisers used the Masoretic text as the basis of their revision. But like most modern versions, the NRSV does not hesitate, as the notes make clear, to follow the Greek and other versions where they are judged to preserve better readings. The readings "Let us go out to the field" (Gen. 4:8), "she" rather than "he" (Gen. 38:5), "twenty" (Ezek. 48:13), and others were already followed in the RSV. This dependence on the versions, however, is more extensive in the NRSV than in the RSV.

Any two groups of scholars will evaluate textual evidence differently. For example, the NEB chose the Greek reading "sixth" (Gen. 2:2) where the NRSV follows "seventh" of the Hebrew text. As can be seen by a check of the footnotes (which could be more easily done had the NRSV identified the notes by their relevant verses), the NRSV identifies readings taken from the versions which the RSV followed but whose source it did not identify: "how" (Jonah 2:4).

The revision assigns to the footnotes certain phrases from the Hebrew text which were included in the RSV: "to the house of Israel" (Amos 5:3), "my heights" (Hab. 3:19), and others.

380

Phrases are restored from the Hebrew text which the RSV had in the margin: "his mother Sarah's" (Gen. 24:67). There are cases where the RSV followed the Greek or other versions and the NRSV follows the Hebrew (Lam. 1:21; Ezek. 45:12; Zech. 10:12; etc.). There are also cases where the NRSV followed the Greek or other versions while the RSV remained with the Hebrew: "he began to weaken" (Judg. 16:19), "Now Saul committed a very rash act" (I Sam. 14:24), "Ishbaal" (II Sam. 2:8), and "man of God proclaimed" (II Kings 23:16).

In the material that follows, the RSV words are given in brackets after the Scripture citation. In a few cases both versions (RSV and NRSV) depart from the Hebrew text but in different ways: "my people" (Mic. 3:3 ["from them"]) and "downfall" (Mic. 7:10 ["gloat over her"]). Where the Hebrew has "sells," the RSV had "betrays," and the NRSV has "enslaves" (Nah. 3:4). The Hebrew text has "him," which the RSV rendered "them," but the NRSV conjectures "us" (Mic. 7:15). Rabbinic tradition is followed in reading "you" (Hab. 1:12 ["We"]) and in "my eye" (Zech. 2:8 ["his eye"]); however, "my eye" is not identified as such a reading. The tradition is cited in the notes in Genesis 18:22. The listings given are not comprehensive.

The RSV had already adopted certain Qumran scroll readings in Isaiah; among them are "insolence" (Isa. 14:4 ["insolent fury"]), "I" (Isa. 14:30), "Dibon" (Isa. 15:9), and "from" (Isa. 18:7), the last of which is not indicated as a scroll reading in the RSV. Others are "the mountains" (Isa. 45:2), "salvation may spring up" (Isa. 45:8), "Syene" (Isa. 49:12), "a tyrant" (Isa. 49:24), "comfort you" (Isa. 51:19), and "us" (Isa. 56:12).

The Qumran manuscripts (often supported by versions) have been followed in certain other readings in the NRSV. Four sentences were added from the scrolls to I Samuel 10:27. Other scroll readings include "nazirite" (I Sam. 1:22), "three-year-old bull" (I Sam. 1:24), "have it attested" (Isa. 8:2 ["I got reliable witnesses"]), "did not have pity on" (Isa. 9:17 ["rejoice over"]), "watcher" (Isa. 21:8), "crossed over the sea" (Isa. 23:2), "oaths" (Isa. 33:8 ["witnesses"]), "your rising up" (Isa. 37:28), "his tomb" (Isa. 53:9 ["in his death"]), and "light" (Isa. 53:11).

There are revisions which bring the English text more into harmony with the Hebrew text, such as the dropping of the modifier "of God" (Hab. 1:1). The phrase was not in Greek or Latin, or in either the KJV or ASV.

Many of the conjectural readings of the RSV are continued. Some conjectural readings in the RSV but not noted as such are followed: "after his glory" (Zech. 2:8). Then other conjectural renderings in the

NRSV give statements quite different from those of the RSV: "a ruler who oppresses" (Prov. 28:3 ["a poor man who . . ."]), "like the forests of Lebanon" (Hos. 14:5 ["like the poplar"]), and "those who ate" (Obad. 7 ["your trusted friends"]). Conjectures where the RSV followed Hebrew include "devise wickedness and evil deeds" (Mic. 2:1 ["work evil"]) and "pervert justice" (Mic. 7:3 ["weave it"]). Similarly, places which are noted as obscure in Hebrew may reflect different choices: "that which does not profit" (Hos. 7:16 ["to Baal"]), "It is decreed" (Nah. 2:7 ["its mistress"]), "faces pressing forward" (Hab. 1:9 ["terror of them"]; "capital" ["cities"]), "Azal" (Zech. 14:5 ["stopped up"]), and "Did not one God make her? Both flesh and spirit are his" (Mal. 2:15 ["Has not one God made and sustained for us the spirit of life?"]). Unlike the RSV, the NRSV points out that the Hebrew is uncertain in some passages: "grievous destruction" (Mic. 2:10), "shatterer" (Nah. 2:1), and "healthy" (Zech. 11:16 ["sound"]). The illustrations of these categories are not comprehensive.

Text of the N.T.

The third edition of the United Bible Societies Greek New Testament was followed with consultation of material being prepared for the fourth edition. Double brackets are used to enclose material thought to be additions to the text. In rare instances, there are departures from the text where the translators thought another alternative superior. Metzger lists "become" (*genesthai;* Acts 26:28), "gentle" (*epioi;* I Thess. 2:7), and "with all the saints. Amen." (Rev. 22:21) as cases where different variants were followed from those chosen by the editors of the United Bible Societies Greek text.[5] It is not indicated in the notes of the NRSV that a textual variant has been chosen in Acts 26:28.

The NRSV represents the Critical Text. This contrasts with the NKJV, which champions the reliability of the *Textus Receptus.*

The NRSV notes more textual variants in the N.T. than the RSV did: "we" (John 9:4 ["I"]) and "no one takes" (John 10:18 ["has taken"]) are only two cases.

In an impressive number of cases, textual variants were judged differently from the choice of the preparers of the RSV, resulting in different translations. Examples include "What . . . to see? A prophet?" (Matt. 11:9). Additionally, the NRSV omits "to hear" (Matt. 11:15), includes "crowds" (Matt. 12:15), "strong wind" (Matt. 14:30 ["the wind"]), "of the

[5]Bruce M. Metzger, "Some comments on the New RSV Bible," in *Scribes and Scripture: New Testament Essays in Honor of J. Harold Greenlee,* ed. David Alan Black (Winona Lake: Eisenbrauns, 1991).

blind" (Matt. 15:14), "seventy-seven times" (Matt. 18:22 ["seventy times seven"]), omits "and of the plate" (Matt. 23:23), includes "Jesus" (Matt. 27:16), "they" (Mark 1:29 ["he"]), "whom he also named apostles" (Mark 3:14), "and sisters" (Mark 3:32), omits "to do" (Luke 6:2), includes "and had spent all she had on physicians" (Luke 8:43), "or under the bushel basket" (Luke 11:33), adds "He is not here, but has risen" (Luke 24:5), includes Luke 24:12, "and said to them, Peace be with you" (Luke 24:36), and "worshipped him, and" (Luke 24:52). These examples are only a sampling.

The NRSV at times made the opposite text choice from that of the RSV, exchanging footnote and text: "Hellenists" (Acts 11:20 ["Greeks"]), "say was gained by" (Rom. 4:1 ["say about"]), "my God" (I Cor. 1:4 ["God"]), "mystery" (I Cor. 2:1 ["testimony"]), "that I may boast" (I Cor. 13:3 ["body to be burned"]), includes "in Ephesus and are faithful" (Eph. 1:1), "your" (Col. 1:7 ["our"]), "you" (Col. 1:12 ["us"]), includes "on those who are disobedient" (Col. 3:6), "first fruits" (II Thess. 2:13 ["from the beginning"]), "I have entrusted to him" (II Tim. 1:12 ["he . . . to me"]), "us" (Heb. 13:21 ["you"]), "suffered" (I Pet. 3:18 ["died"]), includes "exercising the oversight" (I Pet. 5:2), includes "as God would have you do" (I Pet. 5:2), "by" (II Pet. 1:3 ["to"]), "chains" (II Pet. 2:4 ["pits"]), and "an example of what is coming to the ungodly" (II Pet. 2:6 ["an example to those who were to be ungodly"]).

The NRSV reverts to the textual variant followed in English Bibles from Wycliffe through the ASV: "all things work together for good" (Rom. 8:28). The RSV had predecessors in the Twentieth Century New Testament and in Moffatt in choosing "in everything God works for good." At other times variants not noted in the RSV are chosen: the NRSV inserts "in a vision" (Acts 9:12) and "Even" (Heb. 7:4).

The debate over the ending of Mark (Mark 16:9-20) is indicated by the use of double brackets. The short ending is printed, then the long ending, and finally the Freer Logion is given in a footnote. Double brackets are used for Luke 22:43-44, 23:34, and for John 7:53-8:11. Both the RSV and the NRSV relegate the doxology of the Lord's Prayer (Matt. 6:13; 18:11; 23:14; Mark 7:16; 9:44, 46; Luke 17:36; John 5:4; and Acts 8:37) to the footnotes. The *Comma Johanneum* (I John 5:7, 8), unlisted in the RSV, is given in a footnote.

Marginal Notes

The marginal notes alert the reader to certain supplements to the Greek text such as "she bought it" (John 12:7). Some RSV choices are dropped to the footnotes as options: "Saviors" (Obad. 21) and "beam" (Hab. 2:11). In other cases the NRSV ignores certain marginal options offered in the RSV: "one of the sons of the prophets" (Amos 7:14) and "marshalls" (Nah. 3:17). The NRSV duplicates many marginal options offered in the RSV, but the NRSV also supplies marginal options of its own: "sanctify war" (Joel 3:9), "Does one plow them with oxen?" (Amos 6:12), "was" (Amos 7:14), and "Nubians" (Amos 9:7). In other cases the NRSV adopts RSV marginal options into the text: "Be silent" (Amos 8:3) and for some verses the NRSV moves the text to the margin: "locust" (Mal. 3:11 ["devourer"]) and "born from above" (John 3:3, 7 ["anew"]). The margin alerts the reader to some words' uncertain meanings in cases where the RSV did not: "covenant to the people" (Isa. 49:8).

Vocabulary

The NRSV replaces those English words which though understandable are not the common idiom outside of religious circles. "Live" (Gen. 13:6, 7; 34:23; 36:7; 37:1; Isa. 33:14; Jer. 2:6; 4:29; Amos 8:8; 9:5; Nah. 1:5; Hag. 1:4; Rev. 14:6) or "settle" (Gen. 35:1; Ps. 139:9; Isa. 65:9) are chosen instead of "dwell"; however, "dwell" is at times retained (Rev. 21:3). "Abide" replaces "inhabit" (Prov. 2:21), but "abide" is retained in Isaiah 32:16. "Reside" (Gen. 20:1; 21:34; 26:3; 47:4; Lev. 19:33; 20:2; Num. 15:16; Deut. 12:12; Isa. 52:4) is used instead of "sojourn." "Alien" displaces "sojourner" (Zech. 7:10; Mal. 3:5). "Live as an alien" (Gen. 28:4; 32:4; cf. Ps. 120:5) replaces "land of sojournings" but there is "earthly sojourn" (Gen. 47:9 ["sojournings"]). "Strike" (Amos 4:9; Mic. 6:13 ["smite"]), "killed" (Amos 4:10; 9:1 ["slay"]), "snatched" (Amos 4:11 ["plucked"]), "fire" (Amos 4:11 ["burning"]), and "snake" (Exod. 4:3; 7:9, 10, 12; Deut. 8:15; Amos 5:19; Matt. 23:33; Luke 10:19 ["serpent"]) are modernizations, but "serpent" is retained in other contexts (Gen. 3:14; Num. 21:6; John 3:14).

Other word changes include "festivals" (Amos 5:21 ["feasts"]), "beg" (Amos 7:2, 5 ["beseech"]), "news" (Jonah 3:6 ["tidings"]), and "report" (Obad. 1 ["tidings"]). "Bad news" replaces "evil tidings" (Jer. 49:23), but the parallel to Obadiah in Jeremiah 49:14 retains "tidings," as does Nahum 1:15. "Stew" (Gen. 25:29, 34; II Kings 4:39; Hag. 2:12 ["pottage"]) and "pot" (Ezek. 11:3, 7 ["caldron"]) are modernizations, but "caldron" is retained in I Samuel 2:14 and Micah 3:3. "Soldiers" (Joel 3:9 ["men of war"]) is used, but "warriors" (Jer. 5:16; Zech. 10:5) replaces "men of war" and is also used for "mighty men" (Joel 3:9; Obad. 9). "Test" (Luke 4:12, 13) is preferred over "tempt," and "mute" (Ps. 38:13;

Matt. 15:30), "silent" (Ps. 39:9; Isa. 53:7), and "speechless" (Dan. 10:15) replace "dumb," which has now come to mean "stupid." "Dumb dogs" becomes "silent dogs" (Isa. 56:10) and "dumb ass" a "speechless donkey" (II Pet. 2:16). "Leper" (Matt. 8:2; etc.) is retained but regularly carries an explanatory note. "Manager" (Luke 16:1) replaces "steward." "Staff" (Exod. 4:2; Num. 17:2; 20:9) is preferred over "rod" or "club" (Isa. 10:5), but is retained at Isaiah 10:15.

The NRSV replaces archaic forms, for example, "there" (Isa. 55:10 ["thither"]), "from there" (Isa. 52:11; Amos 6:2 ["from thence"]), "where" (Isa. 49:21; Jonah 1:8; Nah. 3:7 ["whence"]), "pay attention" (Isa. 49:1 ["hearken"]), "listen" (Isa. 46:3, 12; 51:1, 7; 55:2; Zech. 11:3 ["hearken" or "hark"]), "dug" (Isa. 5:2 ["were digged"]), and "lean on" (Isa. 48:2 ["stay themselves on"]).

The striving for current idiom is obvious: "pleasant company" (Ps. 55:14 ["sweet converse"]), "holy splendor" (Ps. 96:9 ["holy array"]), "Braggart who missed his chance" (Jer. 46:17 ["noisy one who lets the hour go by"]), "skilled in intrigue" (Dan. 8:23 ["understands riddles"]), and "clothing" (Dan. 7:9 ["raiment"]). "Lazybones" (Prov. 6:6, 9) and "lazy person" (Prov. 19:24; 20:4; 22:13; 26:14) replace "sluggard." In family relationships, "fathers nor his fathers' fathers" becomes "predecessors" (Dan. 11:24). "Ancestor" replaces "forefather" (Rom. 4:1) and "father" (Gen. 47:30; 49:29; Mic. 7:20; Zech. 1:2; Mal. 2:10; 3:7; Rom. 4:12) when speaking of a distant relative. "Kinsfolk" (Gen. 31:37) and "relatives" replace "kinsmen" (Rom. 16:7, 11, 21) and "kindred" (Acts 7:3). "Grandchildren" (Exod. 10:2) replaces "son's son." "Nephew" (Gen. 14:16) is used instead of "kinsman" where the relation can be determined, and "infants" replaces "babes" (Matt. 11:25; I Cor. 3:1), but not entirely (Isa. 3:4; Lam. 2:11).

"Yeast" is experimented with (Matt. 13:33; Luke 13:21; I Cor. 5:6; Gal. 5:9), but there are ample cases of "leaven" (Exod. 12:15, 19; 13:7; 34:25; Lev. 2:11), "leavened" (Hos. 7:4; Amos 4:5; Matt. 13:33; Luke 13:21), and "unleavened" (Gen. 19:3; Exod. 12:39; Lev. 2:4, 5; 7:12; 8:26; Num. 6:19; Josh. 5:11; Judg. 6:19, 20, 21). "Farmers" replaces "tillers of the soil" (Joel 1:11), and "sheep merchants" (Zech. 11:7) replaces "those who trafficked in the sheep." "First installment" (II Cor. 1:22 ["a guarantee"]), "goodwill" (Acts 2:47 ["favor"]), "coats" (Acts 7:58 ["garments"]), "share" (Acts 8:21 ["lot"]), and "countryside" (Acts 8:1 ["region"]) are changes, but "region" is inserted elsewhere (Acts 8:40 ["passing on"]).

Substitutes for "behold" include "look" (Acts 7:56), "At this moment he is praying" (Acts 9:11 ["behold, he is praying"]), and "listen" (Acts 13:11). "Hired workers" (Mal. 3:5) or "hired hand" (John 10:12

["hireling"]), "increased in numbers" (Acts 9:31 ["was multiplied"]), and "dazzling clothes" (Acts 10:30 ["bright apparel"] are used, but this effort for current idiom was not carried far enough to put "cry" in place of "weep" (Gen. 43:30; 45:2; 46:29; 50:1; Judg. 2:4; I Sam. 30:4; John 20:11, 13, 15; Acts 9:39; etc.). Already in the RSV (Exod. 2:6; KJV: "wept") the infant Moses was crying.

Other contemporary phrases include "quickly and decisively" (Rom. 9:28 ["rigor and dispatch"]), "lag" (Rom. 12:11 ["flag"]), "vinegrower" (John 15:1 ["vinedresser"], "worship" (John 16:2 ["service"]), "persecution" (John 16:33 ["tribulation"]), "crippled" (Luke 14:13, 21 ["maimed"]), "sanctify" (John 17:19 ["consecrate"]), and "temple robbers" (Acts 19:37 ["sacrilegious"]).

Yet other examples of modern expressions include "Let us be on our way" (Gen. 43:8, 13 ["we will rise up and go"]), "lord it over us" (Num. 16:13 ["make yourself a prince over us"]), "we detest this miserable food" (Num. 21:5 ["loathe this worthless food"]), "made a fool of me" (Num. 22:29 ["made sport of me"]), "when we had headed out" (Deut. 2:8 ["so we went on"]), "we headed up the road" (Deut. 3:1 ["went up the way"]), "they do not even know the way to town" (Eccl. 10:15 ["to the city"]), "was customary" (Dan. 3:19 ["was wont to be"]), "working like a slave for you" (Luke 15:29 ["served you"]), "put up with" (II Cor. 11:19, 20 ["bear with"]), "as rubbish" (Phil. 3:8 ["refuse"]), and "making money" (James 4:13 ["get gain"]).

In describing animal life, where the RSV had "cattle" the NRSV uses "livestock" (Gen. 13:2; 31:18; 36:6; Exod. 9:21; Lev. 1:2; Deut. 5:14; etc.) when more than cows are intended. "Animals" (Jonah 4:11; Hag. 1:11; Zech. 2:4) is sometimes used where the RSV had "cattle." "Animal" usually replaces "beast" (Lev. 26:6; Dan. 2:38; 4:32; Joel 1:18; 2:22; Zeph. 1:3; 2:15; Zech. 8:10; 14:15; Luke 10:34). However, "beast" is retained in Daniel's vision and in the Apocalypse (Dan. 7:3; 8:4; Rev. 13:1; 20:10). The NRSV uses "donkey" (Gen. 22:3), no doubt because of the other meaning of "ass," but, as in the REB, a distinction is made between "ass" and "wild ass" (Job 6:5; 24:5; 39:5; Jer. 2:24; Hos. 8:9), with the latter retained. Ishmael is a "wild ass of a man" (Gen. 16:12)

Time is stated in modern terms: "nine o'clock" (Acts 2:15 ["third hour"]), "noon" (Mark 15:33; John 4:6; 19:14; Acts 10:9 ["sixth hour"]), "three o'clock in the afternoon" (Mark 15:34; Luke 23:44; Acts 3:1; 10:30 ["ninth hour"]), and "four o'clock in the afternoon" (John 1:39 ["tenth hour"]). Night hours are "nine o'clock" (Acts 23:23 ["third hour of the night"]), "middle of the night" (Luke 12:38 ["second watch"]), and "near dawn" (Luke 12:38 ["third watch"]). Numbers are modernized: "seventy" (Ps. 90:10 ["threescore and ten"]), "eighty" (Ps. 90:10 ["fourscore"]), and "200 million" (Rev. 9:16 ["twice ten thousand times ten thousand"]). Some measurements are in yards (John 21:8) and in miles (Luke 24:13; Rev. 14:20), but others are retained in cubits (Num. 35:5; Ezek. 41:1).

Semitic idioms are translated into English equivalents: "called his name" becomes "named him" (Gen. 16:15; 29:32, 33, 35; etc.); "lay hands on" becomes "assassinate" (Esther 2:21); "legs of a man" (Ps. 147:10) becomes "speed of a runner"; "in our watching, we watched" becomes "watching eagerly" (Lam. 4:17); "in your ears" (Isa. 49:20) becomes "in your hearing"; "wine on the lees well refined" becomes "well-aged wines" (Isa. 25:6); "keeps his hand from" becomes "refrains from" (Isa. 56:2); "daughter of my people" becomes "my poor people" (Jer. 9:1); and "turn his face to" becomes "turn to" (Dan. 11:18). "Given the hand to" becomes "made a pact" (Lam. 5:6). "Lift up your eyes" or "I lifted my eyes" becomes "looked up" (Jer. 3:2; Dan. 10:5); "Ancient One" (Dan. 7:13, 22) replaces "Ancient of Days"; "confusion of face" (Dan. 9:7, 8) becomes "open shame"; and "hast made thee a name" becomes "made your name renowned" (Dan. 9:15). However, this effort does not go far enough to modify the redundant Hebrew idiom "burn it with fire" (Jer. 34:2, 22; 37:10; 38:23; 51:32).

One of the problems in remodeling is that the product still has signs of the original structure when one finishes. A revision carries vestigial remains of its former editions which would not have been used if a completely new translation were attempted. This complication has led various groups to abandon the revision of previous English Bibles and to start afresh. The NRSV is by intent an extensive revision, but it retains forms of its predecessors. Only a few examples will be listed: "ceased to be . . . after the manner of women" (Gen. 18:11), "he took courage" (II Chron. 15:8), and "described a circle" (Job 26:10). "Dead bodies" (Jer. 33:5) could be "corpses"; "Thus says the great king" (II Kings 18:19) could be "the great king says"; "noontide" (Isa. 38:10) could be "noontime"; and "habitations" (Isa. 54:2) could be "residences"; however, "homestead" is used in Acts 1:20 ("habitation"). Neither "Ho" (Isa. 55:1) nor "lo" (Zech. 6:8) is a current expression. "And behold" (Isa. 59:9) becomes "and lo," but "for lo" becomes "for now" (Zech. 11:16). Other cases of retained phrases include "stay his hand" (Dan. 4:35), "Darius, son of Ahasuerus, by birth a Mede" (Dan. 9:1), and "He shall work his will" (Dan. 11:28).

387

The NRSV fails to capture modern idiom in examples such as "upbraided him" (Judg. 8:1), "wayfarer" (Judg. 19:17), "Goliath by name" (I Sam. 17:23), "disdained him" (I Sam. 17:42), "morsel of bread" (I Sam. 28:22), and "man-child" (Job 3:3). "Fatlings" (Isa. 5:17; Ezek. 34:3), "fatted fowl" (I Kings 4:23), "fatted cattle" (I Kings 1:25), "fatted animals" (Amos 5:22; cf. Prov. 15:17), and "fatted calf" (I Sam. 28:24; Luke 15:23, 27, 30) could be "fattened animals," "fowl," and "calf." Other cases include "winebibbers" (Prov. 23:20), "ceased from its raging" (Jonah 1:15), "swallow up" (Jonah 1:17), and "had not got into the boat" (John 6:22 ["had not entered"]).

Other expressions are retained and are understandable enough. However, one senses that these phrases would have been expressed differently were translation or revision not being practiced. Examples include "God rested" (Gen. 2:2, 3) when the term means "ceased activity." "They were fair" (Gen. 6:2) would be "they were beautiful" (this is what "fair" becomes in other contexts [Dan. 4:21; Amos 8:13]). "Savory food" (Gen. 27:14, 17, 31) would be "delicious food," and "journeyed" (Gen. 35:5) would be "traveled." There is "entreat for me" (Gen. 23:8), "upbraided" (Gen. 31:36), "farewell" (Gen. 31:28), and "grievous" (Gen. 41:31; 50:11) when "severe" (Gen. 43:1) is used elsewhere. "Ears of grain" (Gen. 41:6, 22, 27; II Kings 4:42; Isa. 17:5) should be "heads of grain," and "the barley was in the ear" should be "was headed" (Exod. 9:31) in American farming vocabulary. As long as the text had "corn," Americans found "ears" acceptable. "Silage winnowed with shovel and fork" is hardly American usage, but whether "silage" (Isa. 30:24) is technically a proper term or is an anachronism, it is an improvement over "salted provender." "Provender" (*mispo'*) elsewhere becomes "fodder" (Gen. 24:25, 32; 42:27; 43:24; Judg. 19:19), but it is doubtful that Joseph's brothers had gone to Egypt for sacks of "fodder."

There are some continuations and some vocabulary choices which seem to be aiming at the sophisticated reader: "dishevel your hair" (Lev. 10:6; 13:45; 21:10; cf. Num. 5:18 ["let the hair of your heads hang loose"]), "lacerate" (Deut. 14:1 ["cut"], "fledglings" (Deut. 22:6 ["young ones"]), "manacles" (II Chron. 33:11) ["hooks"]), "gossamer" (Job 8:14 ["breaks in sunder"]), "covert of the cliff" (Song of Sol. 2:14; NIV: "hiding places"), "like loathsome carrion" (Isa. 14:19 ["a loathed untimely birth"]), "verdure" (Isa. 15:6), "raucous" (Ezek. 23:42 ["carefree"]), "fiancée" (I Cor. 7:36-38 ["betrothed"]), "malign" (I Pet. 2:12 ["speak against"]), and "maligned" (I Pet. 3:16 ["abused"], 2:12 ["reviled"]). "Sentinel" displacing "watchman" (Isa. 21:11, 12; 56:10; 62:6; Jer. 6:17; Ezek. 3:17; 33:2, 3) is another case.

Description of Sex Activities

In regard to the descriptions of sexual activity in contemporary vocabulary, the NRSV is inconsistent. Reproductive parts are given modern names: "penis" (Deut. 23:1 ["male member"]) and "uterus" (Num. 5:21, 27 ["thigh fall away"]). "Semen" (Gen. 38:9; Lev. 15:16) is used as in the RSV. There is "sterility nor barrenness" (Deut. 7:14 ["male or female barren"]), "intermarry" (Deut. 7:3 ["make marriages"]), "he married" (Gen. 26:34 ["took to wife"]), and "married woman" (Gen. 20:3) ["a man's wife"]). The Semitic idioms "know" (Gen. 4:1; 17, 25; 19:5, 8) and "lie with" (Gen. 19:32, 34, 35; 26:10; 30:15, 16; Deut. 22:22) are retained in the O.T. The NRSV also uses "sleeping with" (Num. 31:17, 18, 35; Prov. 6:29 ["lying with" or "go in to"]), "have sexual relations with" (Lev. 18:23; 19:20; Num. 25:1 ["lie with" or "play the harlot with"]), "had marital relations with" (Matt. 1:25 ["knew"]); "lived together" (Matt. 1:18 ["came together"]), and "had intercourse with" (Num. 5:13 ["lie with carnally"]; Rom. 1:26 ["relations"]). Oholah "bestowed her favors upon them" (Ezek. 23:7 [". . .her harlotries upon"]).

However, as in the RSV, "became the father of" (Gen. 5:3) and "was the father of" (Matt. 1:3-16) replace the "begets" of the KJV. Instead of "rape" one reads "he lay with her by force" (Gen. 34:2 ["lay with her"]), but "rape" is also used (Lam. 5:11; Zech. 14:2 ["ravished"]), and "violate women" (Ezek. 22:10) replaces "humble women."

On the other hand, women "become pregnant" (Gen. 19:36; 38:25; Amos 1:13; Matt. 24:19; Mark 13:17; Rev. 12:2 ["with child"]) or are "expecting a child" (Luke 2:5 ["with child"]); however, "with child" is retained in Isaiah 26:17, 18; and Jeremiah 31:8. Women are "in labor" (Song of Sol. 8:5; Isa. 13:8; 21:3; 42:14; Mic. 4:10; 5:3; John 16:21; Rom. 8:22 ["in travail"]). There is also the "stillborn" (Num. 12:12; Eccl. 6:3 ["one dead" or "untimely birth"]).

Women "nurse children" (Gen. 21:7; cf. Mark 13:17) instead of "suckle children," but "sucking child" (Num. 11:12), "breasts for me to suck" (Job 3:12), "infants at the breast" (Joel 2:16 ["nursing infants"]), and "breasts that nursed you" (Luke 11:27 ["that you sucked"]) are also used. "Infant" replaces "nursling" (Lam. 4:4).

"Whore" (Gen. 34:31; 38:24; Isa. 57:3; Jer. 3:1, 3, 6, 8; Ezek. 16:15, 30; 23:3; Rev. 17:1) is used where the RSV had "harlot," but there is also "prostitute" (Gen. 38:15; Prov. 6:26; 7:10; Jer. 5:7; Amos 7:17; Nah. 3:4), which the NRSV usually prefers over "harlot." "Whoredom" is chosen over "harlotry" (Jer. 3:9). There is "temple prostitute" (Gen. 38:21 ["harlot"]), "male prostitutes," and "sodomites" (I Cor. 6:9 ["sexual perverts"]);

389

I Tim. 1:10 ["sodomites"]). "Immorality" (I Cor. 7:2) is clarified as "sexual immorality."

One is somewhat perplexed to find in the NRSV the statement "every male among the men of Abraham's house" (Gen. 17:23)—a rendering which is literal enough for the Hebrew *kol zakhar be'anshe betho* but which sounds rather ridiculous in English. One wonders whether there are any among the men that are not males. Tyndale rendered the phrase "menchildren" and the Geneva had "man childe." But "males" began in the English Bible with the Douay (1609), was used in the KJV, and then continued in its successors. The NIV and REB have "every male in his household." If one wants to make a distinction from children, then "every male among the adults" might be suggested.

One finds "male goats" (Gen. 31:10; Jer. 50:8; Ezek. 43:22; 45:23; Dan. 8:5) and "female goats" (Gen. 15:9; 31:38) instead of "he-goats" and "she-goats" and the same is true of donkeys (Gen. 12:16). However, the NRSV includes "he-goat" (Prov. 30:31) and "she-bear" (Prov. 17:12). There is "deer" (Ps. 42:1; Isa. 35:6 ["hart"]), "doe" (Jer. 14:5 ["hind"]), "stag" (Song of Sol. 2:9; Lam. 1:6 ["harts"]), and "fawn" (Jer. 14:5 ["calf"]). There are "stallions" (Ezek. 23:20 ["horses"]) and a "rooster" (Prov. 30:31 ["cock"]). As in the RSV, animals "were breeding" (Gen. 30:41), but there is "mother sheep" (Isa. 40:11 ["those that are with young"]) and animals "are nursing" their young (Gen. 33:13 ["giving suck"]).

Innovations

Certain innovations which the reader will find striking include "a wind from God" (Gen. 1:2 ["Spirit of God"]) which swept over the water at creation. Hebrew *ruach* can mean either "wind" or "spirit," and *'elohim* can be adjectival; however, the rendering is likely to draw fire from those who want the Trinity already revealed at creation. In contrast to the NRSV, the REB dropped "wind" (from the NEB) and reverted to "spirit."

Other innovations are the "dome" (Gen. 1:6; Ezek. 1:22; 10:1) which God made and "the sky" (Dan. 12:3) for "firmament"; however, "firmament" is retained in Psalm 150:1. "Sky" (Gen. 1:8) is used instead of "heaven." Instead of a "mist" going up, "a stream would rise from the ground and water the earth" (Gen. 2:6); woman is "a helper as his partner" (Gen. 2:18, 20 ["helper fit for"]); the serpent is a "wild animal" (Gen. 3:1 ["wild creature"; REB: "creature"]); "loincloths" (Gen. 3:7 ["aprons"]) are made from fig leaves; and the ark is made of "cypress wood" (Gen. 6:14 ["gopher"]). All of these passages attract notice.

Throughout the NRSV *christos* is translated "Messiah"; Christ is given as the literal rendering in the notes (Matt. 16:16; John 1:20, 25; Acts

2:31, 36; 3:18, 20; 8:5 ["Christ"]), doubtless on the argument that the Greek is itself a translation. This practice overlooks the fact that *messias* also occurs in the Greek text (John 1:41; 4:25). Someone should explain why *christos* should be revised to "Anointed" in John 1:41 but retained as "Christ" in John 4:25 when in both places the name is explaining *messias*. The RSV has "Christ" in both places.

"Good news" is preferred to "gospel" (Matt. 4:23; 24:14; 26:13; Mark 1:1, 14; Luke 4:18; Acts 14:7; 16:10; Rom. 15:19, 20; etc.). Rather than the transliteration "mammon," the NRSV translation is "wealth" (Matt. 6:24; Luke 16:9, 11, 13)—certainly a gain. The rough breathing accent mark of Greek is followed to produce "Harmagedon" (Rev. 16:16) instead of "Armageddon." At times the word "mad" has been abandoned as a designation of insanity; "out of your mind" (I Cor. 14:23) may be used. But there are exceptions, as when "mad" (Eccl. 2:2), "madness" (Eccl. 2:12; 7:25; 9:3; 10:13; Zech. 12:4; II Pet. 2:16), and "madman" (II Kings 9:11; Jer. 29:26) are carried over from the RSV. Paul describes his behavior as that of "a madman" (II Cor. 11:23). "Insane, "insanity," and "insane person" for these terms would be more in keeping with current usage.

Among the considerable variety of renderings of *paracletos* in various English translations, the NRSV uses "Advocate" (John 14:16, 26; 15:26; 16:7 ["Counselor"]), which was used earlier by John Broadus in a translation. The marginal option is "Helper." The NRSV is innovative in rendering *paracletos* alike in the Gospel of John and in I John 2:1. *Paidagogos* becomes "guardian" (I Cor. 4:15 ["guides"]) but in other settings is "disciplinarian" (Gal. 3:24, 25 ["custodian"]).

The statement of Agrippa is interpreted as a question: "Are you so quickly persuading me to become a Christian?" (Acts 26:28 ["In a short time you think to make me a Christian!"]). The Greek variant *ginesthai* ("become") is followed rather than *poiesai* ("make"), which the RSV and REB favored. A note tells the reader that *poiesai* in this case could mean "play."

A striking vocabulary revision concerns the word "fear." It becomes "respect" when used with masters (Mal. 1:6) but is "reverence" or "revere" when dealing with a person's attitude toward God (Mal. 1:14; 2:5; 3:16; 4:2). *'Ashre*, which was "blessed" in the RSV, becomes "happy" (Ps. 1:1; Mal. 3:12, 15), but *makarios* in the N.T. remains "blessed" (Matt. 5:3-11). *Shalom* ("peace") becomes "prosperity" (Dan. 4:1), "well-being" (Mal. 2:5), and "integrity" (Mal. 2:6). "Prosperity . . . like a river" (Isa. 48:18 ["peace"]) is used and then four verses later (Isa. 48:22) *shalom* is "peace." "Teacher" is preferred over "Preacher" for *qoheleth* (Eccl. 1:1, 2, 12; 7:27; 12:8, 9, 10).

Corrections

In keeping with the mandate of the Council of Churches, the NRSV seeks to correct the few inaccuracies and errors of the RSV. One case is "Noah, a man of the soil, was the first to plant a vineyard" (Gen. 9:20). The RSV had "Noah was the first tiller of the soil" despite the fact that earlier Cain was "a tiller of the ground" (Gen. 4:2). "Mowed down Amalek" (Exod. 17:13) becomes "defeated." "Sea monster" (Matt. 12:40) replaces "whale." However, "three days walk across" (Jonah 3:3) is interpretative and no more certain than the addition "in breadth" of the RSV.

The NRSV has David "improvise on" instruments of music (Amos 6:5 ["invent"]), which suggests playing rather than making the instruments (the Hebrew verb is *chashabh*). There were instruments before David's time (cf. Gen. 4:21). The NRSV makes clear that the whip of cords was used on the animals (John 2:15), not on the moneychangers. God did not "withhold his own Son" (Rom. 8:32 ["spare"]). It was Moses and not Pharaoh who was in hot anger (Exod. 11:8). It is the first wife who is not to be neglected (Exod. 21:10), and "everyone's right eye" is put out (I Sam. 11:2), not "all your right eyes."

Rather major revision has made clear some statements which were obscure before: "If you do not stand firm in faith, you shall not stand at all" (Isa. 7:9 ["If you will not believe, surely you shall not be established"]).

One may wonder if "of your very own issue" (Gen. 15:4) is any improvement over "your own son," "fill of fatness" (Jer. 31:14) over "with abundance," "the pivots on the thresholds" (Isa. 6:4) over "foundations," and "cleft mountain" (Song of Sol. 2:17) over "rugged mountain." And one might also wonder how "even if Noah, Daniel, and Job, these three, were in it, they . . ." is an improvement over "even if these three men, Noah, Daniel, and Job, were in it, they . . ." (Ezek. 14:14).

Style

The NRSV preparers were also authorized to make changes in paragraph structure and punctuation. The classic distinction between "shall" and "will" is retained in the O.T. but is abandoned in the N.T. as being unsuitable for the colloquial nature of Koine Greek used by most of the authors. The revision has attempted to avoid language reflecting current moods and has sought simple, enduring words and expressions worthy of the tradition of the King James Bible.

An effort has been made to clarify Scripture for oral reading. Rewording has been done where the listener would have difficulty in making distinctions, as between "their" and "there": "because it was there that God revealed himself" (Gen. 35:7 [". . . there God . . ."]). Changes have been made simply because they sound better: "those that were sent departed" (Luke 19:32 ["those who were sent went away"]). The infelicitous "I will accept no bull from your house" (Ps. 50:9) becomes "I will not accept a bull." "You who hew a tomb" (Isa. 22:16) becomes "cutting a tomb." The revisers also changed "once I was stoned" (II Cor. 11:25) to "once I received a stoning." "The salvation we share" (Jude 3) avoids a misconception of the meaning of "common."

Awkward word order has been corrected. The ambiguous "Joshua was standing before the angel, clothed in filthy garments" (Zech. 3:3) is clarified to "Now Joshua was dressed with filthy clothes as he stood before the angel."

Rhythmical material is recognized and printed in poetic form (Num. 12:6-8; 14:18; Dan. 8:23-25) in the NRSV more often than was the case in the RSV. Hebrew word order which mentions the speaker first, and the NRSV reverses this syntax in numerous cases (as did the RSV) to give a polite English order (Gen. 23:14; 26:28; 31:44; 41:11). But it is not done in either the RSV or NRSV when the Lord speaks, as in Genesis 17:2, 10, 11; Ezekiel 20:12, 20 ("me and you").

There are changes in the capitalization policy. These alterations result in "nazirites" (Amos 2:11, 12), "king" (Zeph. 3:15), "Son of Man" (John 3:14 ["Son of man"]), "spirit" (Gen. 41:38; Isa. 63:10; Ezek. 3:12, 14; 11:1; 37:1, 14; Zech. 4:6; 7:12; Rev. 1:10; 4:2 ["Spirit"]), "assassins" (Acts 21:38 ["Assassins"]), "even the Fast" (Acts 27:9), "ardent in spirit" (Rom. 12:11 ["be aglow with the Spirit"]), and "shepherd and guardian" (I Pet. 2:25). Pronouns referring to God are uncapitalized. This is likewise true in Hebrew, Greek, and the KJV: "he" (Isa. 46:4).

Punctuation changes are numerous: "two-thirds" (Zech. 13:8 ["two thirds"]). Psalm 121:1 uses a dash rather than two sentences. The first quotation of John 3 is continued to verse 21, whereas the RSV stopped it at verse 15. The second ends at verse 30, as in the RSV. Other differences in use of quotation marks are to be seen in Zephaniah 3:7.

"That" in many instances has replaced "which" (Jer. 2:11; Dan. 8:26; Amos 3:1; 9:15). According to Dr. Walter Harrelson, if "which" is preceded by a comma, it is retained; otherwise it becomes "that."[6] "On" has replaced "upon" (Amos 1:4, 7; Obad. 16; Hag. 1:11); "to be" replaces "for" (Amos 2:11); and "they who" (Amos 2:7) replaces "they that." "Until" replaces "till" (Mal. 1:4; 3:3).

6Quoted in Tom Bailey, Jr, "Updated Bible Awaits Baptism; It's Less Beholden to Maleness," *Memphis Commercial Appeal*, 3 March 1990, A 7.

Redundant words have been eliminated: "around" (Joel 3:11 ["around about"]), "gather you" (Zeph. 3:20 ["gather you together"]), and "a hundred pounds" (John 19:39 ["hundred pounds' weight"]). However, the colloquial redundant use of "myself" is followed: "I myself" (Acts 9:16 ["I"]).

While shifting from "seraphim" to "seraphs" (Isa. 6:2), the NRSV continued the transliterated forms "teraphim" (Judg. 17:5; Ezek. 21:21; Zech. 10:2) and "cherubim" (Gen. 3:24; Exod. 25:18; Isa. 37:16; etc.) in numerous instances. Rather than being transliterated, *teraphim* is translated "household gods" in Genesis 31:19, as rendered in the RSV.

Hebrew style repeatedly uses the word *"hinneh,"* which is traditionally translated "behold." The NRSV generally omits this word as being redundant in English style (Isa. 50:9; Amos 4:2; 7:1, 4, 7; 8:1, 11; 9:8, 13; Nah. 3:5; Hab. 2:13; Zeph. 3:19; Mal. 2:3). In other cases "see" (Isa. 32:1; 47:14; 48:10; 52:13; Amos 6:11; 7:8; Mal. 3:1; 4:1), "indeed" (Amos 6:14), "lo" (Mic. 1:3; Mal. 4:5), "look" (Nah. 1:15; Hab. 2:4), "look at" (Nah. 3:13), "now" (Mic. 2:3), and "surely" (Obad. 2) are used.

Another feature of Hebrew style is the abundance of sentences which begin with the conjunction *waw,* traditionally rendered "and" or "but." The NRSV has eliminated the conjunction where it is not natural to English style: "In that day" (Joel 3:18 ["and in . . ."]) and "He will" (Mal. 4:6 ["And he will"]).

Gender adjustment is also made. The neuter is used for animals (Dan. 8:6), for land (Ezek. 22:24), and for cities (Zeph. 3:1). References to land and cities are feminine in the Hebrew and the RSV. Hebrew has only two genders.

An effort has been made to avoid the dangling clause normal to Hebrew but no longer used in English: "The Lord indeed is God" (I Kings 18:39 ["The Lord, he is God"]). However, the reader will find that the dangling clause "The Lord . . . , he" remains at Genesis 24:7 and "Your rod and your staff—they comfort me" at Psalm 23:4.

The Hebrew genitive construction (the construct state) does not take a definite article. The translator must decide whether English requires one. This results in differences of opinion: "a blast from the Lord" (Hos. 13:15 ["the wind of the Lord"]), "daughter Zion" (Mic. 1:13 ["the daughter of Zion"], and "An oracle" (Mal. 1:1 ["The oracle of"]).

The NRSV has dropped the definite article in other cases where it is not present in Hebrew but was supplied in the RSV: "a shatterer" (Nah. 2:1 ["the shatterer"]), "a pleasant land" (Zech. 7:14 ["the"]), "one God" (Mal. 2:15 ["the one God"]). Both versions have supplied the noun "God" for the pronoun "he" in this statement. "God" occurs later in the verse; the NRSV repeats the noun but the RSV in the second occurrence had the pronoun "he." The definite article has been dropped also in some instances where it does not occur in Greek but was continued from the KJV by the RSV: "water and spirit" (John 3:5 ["water and the Spirit"]), but the article is not dropped in this phrase in Acts 1:5; 2:4. Another instance is "a sabbath" (John 5:9 ["the sabbath"]).

As is now standard in twentieth-century translations, nouns are substituted for pronouns, adding to clarity. A few illustrative cases include "fire" (Amos 1:1["it"]), "the sailors" (Jonah 1:7 ["they"]), "the Lord" (Mic. 2:4 ["he"]), "the enemy" (Hab. 1:15 ["he"]), "the sun" (Hab. 3:10 ["it"]), "the one God" (Mal. 2:15 ["he"]), "Jesus" (John 11:3 ["him"]), "Lazarus" (John 11:6, 17 ["he"]), "Peter and John" (Acts 4:1 ["they"]), "their bodies" (Acts 7:16 ["they"]), "Philip" (Acts 8:38 ["he"]), "Paul and Barnabas" (Acts 14:1 ["they"]), "the people" (Acts 19:29 ["they"]), "Crete" (Acts 27:14 [Gk. "it"; RSV "the land"]), and "God" (Rom. 16:25 ["him"]). By supplying the pronouns, the NRSV suggests interpretations: Jonah pays "his" fare (Jonah 1:3 ["the"]), eliminating the rabbinic interpretation that he chartered the ship.

In certain instances possessive pronouns have been added: "my wife" (Gen. 12:19 ["a wife"]), "my love-song" (Isa. 5:1 ["a love song"]), and "his burning place" (Isa. 30:33 ["a . . ."]). "His burning place" is a Kittel proposal.

The euphemism "fell asleep" is paraphrased "have died" (Acts 7:60; I Cor. 15:6; II Pet. 3:4); however, "lie down" is substituted in Deuteronomy 31:16, and "sleep" for "death" is retained in Matthew 27:52 and John 11:11. "Death" (II Pet. 1:14) replaces the image formerly used: "the putting off of my body."

Invocations begin with "May your . . ." (Acts 8:20 ["Your . . ."]).

The NRSV has recast some questions to now anticipate a negative answer: "You are not also one of this man's disciples, are you?" (John 18:17 ["Are not you also one of this man's disciples?"], "I am not a Jew, am I?" (John 18:35 ["Am I a Jew?"]), and "Children, you have no fish, have you?" (John 21:5 ["Children, have you any fish?"]). Other examples are seen in John 7:41, 51, 52; 9:40. The very frequent "very truly" (John 16:20, 23 ["truly, truly"]) is used in the Gospel of John.

The litotes "not a few" (II Kings 4:3; Isa. 10:7; Jer. 30:19; Acts 17:4, 12) is retained, but in some cases a litotes is changed to a direct statement: "he gives the Spirit without measure" (John 3:34 ["it is not by measure . . ."]) and "a citizen of an important city" (Acts 21:39 ["of no mean city"]). In imitation of Greek, the NRSV has a double negative: "I do not want you to be unaware" (I Cor. 10:1 ["I want you to know"]).

In many instances the revision is merely a rearranging of word order:

"but the chief baker he hanged" (Gen. 40:22 ["but he hanged . . ."]), "A jealous and avenging God is the Lord" (Nah. 1:2 ["The Lord is a jealous God and avenging"]), "by him the rocks are broken in pieces" (Nah. 1:6 ["the rocks are broken asunder by him"]), "There the fire will devour you" (Nah. 3:15 ["There will the fire devour you"]), "Lord's house" (Hag. 1:2 ["house of the Lord"]), "Lord's temple" (Hag. 2:15 ["temple of the Lord"]), "the prophet Haggai" (Hag. 2:1 ["Haggai the prophet"]), and "the prophet Elijah" (Mal. 4:5 ["Elijah the prophet"]). The reversed word order of the RSV is often dropped: "Do not fear" (Isa. 54:4 ["fear not"]), "Do not let" (Isa. 56:3 ["let not"]), "they do not know me" (Jer. 4:22 ["they know me not"]), "do not delay" (Jer. 4:6 ["stay not"]), and "do not delay" (Dan. 9:19 ["delay not"]). This category has no end.

The revisers have left to the various publishers the matters of section headings, cross-references, and clues to pronunciation of proper names. One may expect considerable variety in these matters.

To the long list of printers' errors in English Bibles, the NRSV adds an unfortunate dittography in II Chronicles 3:17 where "the one on the right he called Jachin" is repeated in the Zondervan printing.

Additional Vocabulary Considerations

There is vocabulary change in the interest of technical accuracy: "papyrus" (Exod. 2:3 ["bullrushes"]), "handmill" (Exod. 11:5 ["mill"]), "tomb" (Isa. 53:9 ["grave"]), trees are "cut down" (Jer. 6:6; Dan. 4:14, 23 ["hew down"]), and cisterns are "dug out" (Jer. 2:13 ["hewed"]). The NRSV includes "siege ramp" (Isa. 37:33 ["siege mound"]), "stylus" (Isa. 44:13 ["pencil"]), "sandals" (Amos 2:6 ["shoes"]), and "hold of the ship" (Jonah 1:5 ["inner part"]). To describe a color, "gum resin" (Num. 11:7) replaces "bdellium," a term going back to the KJV but hardly known to modern Western people. There is "desert owl" (Zeph. 2:14 ["vulture"]), "buzzard" (Isa. 34:15 ["kite"]), "screech owl" (Zeph. 2:14 ["hedgehog"]), "hedgehog" (Isa. 34:11 ["porcupine"]), "blacksmiths" (Zech. 1:20 ["smiths"]), and "bulrush" (Isa. 58:5 ["rush"]). "Bronze" was already used in the RSV, but at least one case (Isa. 48:4) of "brass" for *nechosheth* remains unchanged in the NRSV. One can say farewell to the bagpipe! In the NRSV the *sumphonyah* becomes a "drum" (Dan. 3:5, 7, 15). It was a "dulcimer" in the KJV and ASV ("bagpipe" was a marginal option of the ASV).

There are also modified identifications for precious stones: "amber" (Ezek. 1:4, 27; 8:2 ["bronze"]), "beryl" (Ezek. 1:16; 10:9 ["chrysolite"]), "chrysolite" (Job 28:19 ["topaz"]), "moonstone" ("jasper"), "beryl" ("sapphire"), and "turquoise" (Ezek. 28:13 ["carbuncle"]). The stone may be unidentified: "jewels" (Isa. 54:12 ["carbuncles"]) and "hardest stone" (Ezek. 3:9 ["adamant"]); however, "adamant" is also retained (Zech. 7:12).

"Mountain" may replace "hill" (Dan. 9:16, 20); "town" may replace "city" (Jer. 2:28; 4:29; Ezek. 35:4; Amos 4:8); and "soil" (Hag. 1:11) may replace "ground." "Carved image" (Isa. 48:5) replaces "graven image," and "cast image" (Ps. 106:19; Isa. 48:5) replaces "molten image." "A single hour" (Matt. 6:27) replaces "cubit," and "common purse" (John 12:6; 13:29) replaces "money box." "Bands of cloth" (Luke 2:7) replaces "swaddling cloths." "Bandit" (Matt. 26:55; 27:38; Mark 14:48; John 18:40 ["robber"]), "sour wine" (John 19:29 ["vinegar"]), and "a day of great solemnity" (John 19:31 ["high day"]) are other examples of improved accuracy.

The NRSV retains the mythical "dragon" (Isa. 27:1; 51:9; Ezek. 29:3; 32:2 [KJV "whale"; ASV, NIV: "monster"]) and inserts it where the RSV had "sea monster" (Job 7:12), but chooses "goat-demon" (II Chron. 11:15; Isa. 13:21; 34:14) over "satyr." Rather than the "night hag," there is the transliterated term *Lilith* (Isa. 34:14).

Some technical terms are made more explicit. The gift of Abraham's servant is a "nose ring" (Gen. 24:22, 30 ["ring"]). Other examples include "sulphur" (Gen. 19:24; Isa. 30:33; 34:9; Ezek. 38:22; Rev. 19:20 ["brimstone"]), "ceremonially unclean" (Lev. 12:2 ["unclean"]), "temple tax" (Matt. 17:24 ["tax"]), "grain offering" (Dan. 2:46 ["offering"], "rainstorm" (Isa. 25:4 ["rain"]), "winter rainstorm" (Isa. 25:4 ["storm"]), and "gate" (John 10:7 ["door"]).

Other vocabulary modifications include "Certainly not!" (Acts 16:37 ["No!"]) and "condemned" (John 16:11 ["judged"]). *Doulos* is at times "slave" (Acts 16:17 ["servants"], but in the Epistles, after much discussion by the committee, the practice of the RSV is followed. The NRSV puts "servant" in the text and "slave" in the margin.[7] Other examples are "rooted out" (Acts 3:23 ["destroyed"]), "cornerstone" (Acts 4:11 ["head of the corner"]), "bail" (Acts 17:9 ["security"]), "conspiracy" (Acts 23:12 ["plot"]), "consistent with repentance" (Acts 26:20 ["worthy of"]), "violent wind" (Acts 27:14 ["tempestuous wind"]), "reef" (Acts 27:41 ["shoal"]), "violation" (Rom. 4:15 "transgression"]), and "entrusted" (Rom. 6:17 ["committed"]). Other revised renderings are "Do not claim to be wiser than you are" (Rom. 12:16 ["never be conceited"]), "confess" (Rom. 15:9 ["praise"]), "purpose" (I Cor. 1:10 ["judgment"]), "our proclamation" (I Cor. 1:21 ["of what we preach"]), "who are spiritual" (I Cor. 2:13 ["who possess the Spirit"]), "rubbish" (I Cor. 4:13 ["refuse"]), "dregs" (I Cor. 4:13

[7]Metzger, "The Processes."

["offscouring"]), "periods" (Acts 1:7 ["seasons"], "withhold" (Acts 10:47 ["forbid"]), "circumcised believers" (Acts 11:2 ["circumcision party"]), and "hinder God" (Acts 11:17 ["withstand God"]).

Modifiers (often identified in the notes) are added for clarification: "the day of Jerusalem's fall" (Ps. 137:7 ["day of Jerusalem"]), "taunt-songs" (Lam. 3:63 ["songs"]), "carry off . . . as spoils of war" (Dan. 11:8 ["carry off"]), "exiles of the Israelites" (Obad. 20 ["exiles"]), "temple doors" (Mal. 1:10 ["doors"]), "distribution of food" (Acts 6:1 ["distribution"]), "human hands" (Acts 7:48 ["hands"]), "the thong of the sandals" (Acts 13:25 ["the sandals"]), "holy promises" (Acts 13:34 ["holy and sure blessings"]), "experience" (Acts 13:35 ["see"]), "entertained them as guests" (Acts 17:7 ["received them"]), and "sexually immoral" (I Cor. 5:11; 10:8 ["immoral"]).

The NRSV paraphrase gives in many instances a more familiar idiom: "Is the Lord's power limited?" (Num. 11:23 ["hand shortened"]), "wages of a male prostitute" (Deut. 23:18 ["dog"; but retained in Rev. 22:14]), "my complexion grew deathly pale" (Dan. 10:8 ["my radiant appearance was fearfully changed"]), "you are safe" (Dan. 10:19 ["peace be with you"]), "since I am a virgin" (Luke 1:34 ["since I know not a man"]), "eighteen long years" (Luke 13:16 ["years"]), "very last penny" (Luke 12:59 ["very last copper"]), and "the one destined to be lost" (John 17:12 ["son of perdition"]). Some additions may eliminate other possible interpretations: "Your sister church" (I Pet. 5:13 ["she"]).

The prophetic "woe" has been rendered with variety: "Alas" (Isa. 31:1; Amos 5:18; 6:1, 4; Mic. 2:1; Hab. 2:6, 9, 12, 15, 19) and "Ah" (Isa. 29:1; 33:1; Nah. 3:1; Zeph. 2:5; 3:1), but the NRSV also retains "woe" in other verses (Isa. 6:5; Hos. 7:13; 9:12; Mic. 7:1). "Woe" is used in statements about the Pharisees (Matt. 23:13, 16, 23, 25, 27, 29) and in the series of Luke 6 and for pregnant women (Matt. 24:19).

The Lord "was sorry" (Gen. 6:6), "changes his mind" (Jer. 18:8, 10; 26:3; Jonah 3:10), or "relents" (Joel 2:13, 14; Amos 7:3, 6; Jonah 3:9; 4:2) where in the RSV he "repented."

The NRSV has used much variety in rendering terms, and the English reader may well be frustrated in searching his concordance for occurrences of terms in various contexts. *Tser'ah* (of uncertain meaning) is revised to "pestilence" in Exodus 23:28 and Deuteronomy 7:20, but the word is left "hornet" at Joshua 24:12. The same variety is seen in dealing with *nephesh:* Jonathan loves David as his "own soul" (I Sam. 18:3) or as "his own life" (I Sam. 20:17). The Semitism "son of man" is "a human being" in Daniel 7:13, is "mortal" in Psalm 8:4 and Daniel 8:17, alternates capriciously as "O Mortal" or "Mortal" in Ezekiel, but is retained as

"Son of Man" in the Gospels. "A human being" of Daniel 7:13 will not suggest to the reader the source for "Son of Man" thought.

The terms "officials" (Jer. 38:17, 22; 39:3; Amos 1:15; Mic. 7:3) and "attendants" (Jer. 49:3) are often used where the RSV had "princes," but there are cases where "prince" is retained (Ps. 107:40; 119:23; Prov. 14:28). Instead of "officers" there are "temple police" (John 7:45), and instead of "commanders" there are "deputies" (Jer. 51:23, 57). Rather than attempting to transliterate official titles, the NRSV uses "officer" (Dan. 11:5 ["prince"]), "chief executioner" (Dan. 2:14 ["captain of the king's guard"]), "royal official" (Dan. 2:15 ["captain"]), "diviners" (Dan. 2:27; 4:7; 5:7, 11 ["astrologers"]), "the ruler" (Matt. 14:1; Luke 3:1, 19; 9:7; Acts 13:1 ["tetrarch"]), and "officials" (Acts 19:31 ["Asiarchs"]) with the transliteration given in the notes. This practice produces "emperor" (John 19:12, 15; Acts 17:7; 25:10, 11, 12, 21; 26:32; 28:19 ["Caesar"]) and "imperial guard" (Phil. 1:13 ["praetorian guard"]).

A similar policy is employed with locations. The NRSV uses "headquarters" (Matt. 27:27; Mark 15:16; John 18:28, 33; Acts 23:35 ["praetorium"]). The NRSV drops the transliterated *parbar* in favor of "colonnade" (I Chron. 26:18). Some money sums also are not transliterated: "coin" (Matt. 17:27 [*shekel*]), "the usual daily wage" (Matt. 20:2 [*denarius*]), "six months' wages" (John 6:7 ["two hundred denarii"]), but denarii is kept as the price of Mary's ointment (John 12:5). "Talent" (Matt. 25:15) is retained, as is the British sum "pound" (Luke 19:13).

Cult Terminology

Cult terminology has undergone modification. The NRSV gives "the ark of the covenant" (Num. 7:89 ["ark of the testimony"]) and "tent of the covenant" (Num. 9:15 ["of the testimony"]); however, the N.T. adopts "tent of testimony" (Acts 7:44 ["of witness"]). "Laver" becomes "basin" (Exod. 30:17). There is the "grain offering" (Lev. 2:1 ["cereal offering"]), "sacrifice of well-being" (Lev. 3:1) or "offering of well-being" (Amos 5:22 ["peace offering"]), "elevation offering" (Lev. 7:30 ["wave offering"]), "the offering of ordination" (Lev. 7:37 ["of consecration"]), "regular burnt offering" (Dan. 8:11; 11:31 ["continual"]), and "thank-offering" (Amos 4:5 ["sacrifice of thanksgiving"]). "Suet" (Lev. 1:8, 12; 8:20 ["fat"]) is for the fat of sheep, but after these verses, the NRSV uses "fat." There are "rows of bread" (Neh. 10:33 ["showbread"]) and "dough" (Neh. 10:37 ["coarse meal"]). There is "festival of Booths" (John 7:2 ["feast of Tabernacles"]), "victims" (Acts 7:42 ["beast"]), "profane" (Acts

10:15, 28 ["common"]), "festivals" (Lev. 23:4 ["feasts"], "sacred donations" (Lev. 22:3; Num. 15:19; Deut. 12:26; Neh. 10:33 ["holy things" or "offering"]), "choice flour" (Lev. 2:1, 2 ["fine flour"]), and "loaves" (Lev. 24:5 ["cakes"]). Paul speaks of being "poured out as a libation" (II Tim. 4:6 ["on the point of being sacrificed"]). An earlier English translation quarrel is reopened with the rendering "idol" (Deut. 4:16 ["image" or "molten image"; Dan. 11:8]) though the same word *pesel* is "image" (II Kings 21:7; Isa. 40:20; 44:15; Nah. 1:14; Hab. 2:18) in some other settings. "Statue" is favored over "image" (Dan. 2:31; 3:1). "Temple prostitute" (Gen. 38:21; Deut. 23:17) is preferred over "harlot" or "cult prostitute."

Certain creatures are said to be "detestable" (Lev. 11:12, 13, 20 ["abomination"]), behaviors are "abhorrent" (Deut. 20:18; 22:5; 24:4 ["abomination"]), and the immoral woman committed a "disgraceful act" (Deut. 22:21 ["wrought folly"]). Sin may be done "unintentionally" (Lev. 4:2; Num. 15:24 ["unwittingly"]).

Scholarly Vocabulary

Changes in vocabulary to bring the translation into harmony with current scholarly views give the transliteration *Lebo-hamath* (Num. 13:21; Ezek. 47:15, 20; 48:1; Amos 6:14 ["entrance of Hamath"]). The RSV in a note had already adopted "Aramaic" (Dan. 2:4 [KJV:"Syriack"]; cf. Isa. 37:11), but the NRSV goes further with "Aram" (Isa. 7:1, 2; 17:3 ["Syria"]), and "Arameans" (Isa. 9:12; Amos 9:7 ["Syrians"]). "Thickets of the Jordan" (Jer. 49:19; 50:44) displaces "jungle of the Jordan." The word "wadi," adopted from Arabic, is judged to be widely enough known to be treated as a standard word: "Wadi Arabah" (Amos 6:14 ["the Brook of the Arabah"]). The occurrences of "wadi" (Num. 21:14; Deut. 2:13, 36, 37; I Kings 8:65; Job 30:6; Jer. 31:40; Ezek. 47:19; 48:28; etc.) are too frequent to try to list, and one wonders if the word is this common in English usage outside the scholarly community. One encounters "Wadi Eshcol" (Num. 13:23; 32:9) and "Valley of Eshcol" (Deut. 1:24) and "Wadi Besor" (I Sam. 30:9) and "brook Besor" (I Sam. 30:21) for the same two locations. "Zaphon" (Job 26:7) ["north"]) comes from Ugaritic studies. Transliteration gives *Ir-moab* (Num. 22:36) for what was translated "city of Moab," but the transliteration brings the term into line with other city names in the section. Other changes of geographical names are "Dragon's Spring" (Neh. 2:13 ["Jackal's Well"]), Leb-qamai (Jer. 51:1 ["Chaldea"]), Mount Samaria (Amos 4:1 ["mountain of Samaria"]), and "People's Gate" (Jer. 17:19 ["Benjamin Gate"]).

Gender-Oriented Language

The effort to avoid gender-oriented language has brought many revisions. In order to include both sexes in a reading, sometimes rephrasing is used, sometimes the NRSV supplies a noun for a pronoun, and sometimes plural forms are used though the original text used singular. For example, "Thieves must give up stealing; rather let them labor and work honestly with their own hands" (Eph. 4:28). However, in narratives and parables no effort is made to generalize sex.

"Man" or "men" is eliminated when neither is in the original text; the statements may become "someone" (Matt. 13:44), "persons/person" (Zeph. 3:4; I Cor. 5:9), "mortals" (Mic. 6:8; I Cor. 4:9), or "believer" (I Cor. 6:6 ["brother"]). Examples of change include "You of little faith" (Matt. 6:30), "Everyone serves the good wine first, and then the inferior wine after the guests have become drunk" (John 2:10), "will draw all people to myself" (John 12:32), and "they are prominent among the apostles" (Rom. 16:7). "Man" becomes "humankind" (Gen. 1:26; 5:1; Job 28:28), "human beings" (Hag. 1:11), "a person" (Rom. 3:28), "people" (Gen. 6:7; Zeph. 3:6; Mal. 2:7), and "a human" (Gen. 9:6; 32:28; Hab. 2:8, 17; Zeph. 1:3). "Man/men" is sometimes expanded to "men and women" (II Pet. 1:21 ["men"]) or a pronoun is substituted as in "to us" (Acts 5:4 ["to men"]) and "You that are Israelites" (Acts 2:22 ["men of . . ."]). The NRSV reads "the home of God is among mortals" (Rev. 21:3 ["the dwelling . . . is with men"]). "Armed man" *('ish maghen)* becomes "armed warrior" (Prov. 6:11).

There can be little dispute that the use of "humankind" sounds awkward to today's hearers: "his [God's] gaze examines humankind" (Ps. 11:4; cf. 12:1; 14:2). It will take some effort to get used to "The Sabbath was made for humankind, and not humankind for the Sabbath" (Mark 2:27). In James 3:7 "humankind" gives way to "human species."

There is the elimination of unnecessarily masculine renderings: "One does not live by bread alone" (Matt. 4:4), "the good person . . . the evil person" (Luke 6:45), "Those who are taught . . . share . . . with their teacher" (Gal. 6:6), and "Let anyone who has an ear listen" (Rev. 2:17).

The NRSV avoids the pronouns "he" and "his" and instead supplies "the one" (Prov. 18:1) and "that person's lifetime" (Rom. 7:1). The words "deacon" (Rom. 16:1 ["deaconess"]) and "prophet" (Exod. 15:20; Luke 2:36; Rev. 2:20), used for females also, seem to reflect the effort to avoid gender-oriented expression. However, "prophetess" (Judg. 4:4; II Kings 22:14; Neh. 6:14; Isa. 8:3) is not shunned in other texts. "Parents" displaces "fathers" and "a man" (Jer. 6:21; Mal. 3:17; 4:6) in some statements. "Children" (Mal. 3:6, 17) or "descendants" (Mal. 3:3) is used instead of "sons" (Prov. 19:18; Isa. 51:20; 54:13; Jer. 3:19), and "child" is used instead of "son" (Prov. 19:13) in cases that can be inclusive.

In this same effort, the plural takes the place of the singular. Recasting the singular into a plural form is very common in the Proverbs to avoid gender-oriented statements: "those who" (Prov. 13:24; 22:29 ["see a man"]) and "Train children in the right way, and when old, they will not stray" (Prov. 22:6). The same is found in other books: "our own way" (Isa. 53:6); "Here they are" (Jer. 4:16), "their lives" (Amos 2:14 ["his life"]), "those" (Amos 2:15, 16 ["he who"]), and "their" (Zech. 13:3). The statements made in singular form in the RSV but now interpreted as inclusive are numerous: "Happy are those who do not follow the advice of the wicked" (Ps. 1:1), "Those who go out weeping" (Ps. 126:6 ["He who . . ."]), "They who have my commandments" (John 14:21 ["He who . . ."]), "Servants are not greater" (John 15:20 ["A servant . . ."]), and "For it is not those who commend themselves" (II Cor. 10:18 ["the man who . . ."]) are only a few examples. Common gender phrases take the place of masculine ones: "it" and "its" are used for "he," "his," and "her" (Amos 3:4, 9). "The one who" (Amos 5:8 ["he who"]) and "the one whom they have pierced" (John 19:37 ["him whom"]) are used. The shift from "my God" to "our God" (Zech. 13:9) agrees with "their," the previous pronoun used, but may reflect a less personal confession.

Inclusive statements addressed in Hebrew or Greek to "brothers" ('ach/adelphoi) become "brothers and sisters" in cases too abundant to list (cf. Ps. 22:22; Acts 16:40; Rom. 1:13; 7:1; I Cor. 1:10; I John 2:10; etc.). In these cases a footnote gives "brothers." "Brothers and sisters" speak the word with greater boldness (Phil. 1:14). Paul has been in danger from "false brothers and sisters" (II Cor. 11:26). Many expedients are enlisted to avoid using "brothers": "friends" (Acts 1:16; Rom. 7:4), "students" (Matt. 23:8), "kindred" (Ps. 133:1; Mic. 5:3), "in a family" (Prov. 6:19 ["among brothers"]), "kinsfolk" (Prov. 17:17 ["brethren"]), "kinship" (Amos 1:9 ["brotherhood"]), and "members of my family" (Matt. 25:40) are examples. "A member of the church" (Matt. 18:15, 17, 21; I Tim. 6:2), "believer" (Acts 1:15), "a large family" (Rom. 8:29 ["many brethren]); "my own people" (Rom. 9:3 ["brethren"]), and "comrades" (Rev. 22:9) illustrate the way in which the NRSV avoids rendering adelphos/adelphoi as "brother." The notes pointing out that these are not literal renderings are perhaps the most frequently used notes in the revision.

Policies are difficult to apply consistently. "Believers" (the footnote points out that the Greek has "brothers"; Acts 10:23) go with Peter to

Cornelius's house, but when Peter tells of the affair, they are "brothers" (Acts 11:12). "Brothers" is sometimes retained where the Greek text has *"andres adelphoi"* (Acts 2:37; 7:2; 13:15, 26, 38; 15:7, 13; 22:1; 23:1, 6; 28:17 ["brethren"]), but in other cases "Fellow Israelites" (Acts 2:29) or "Friends" (Acts 1:16) is used. At a gathering where it is known that only males would be present, "brothers" (Acts 23:1, 6; 28:17) is used. "Human form" replaces "likeness of men" (Acts 14:11). "Mortal" is used sometimes when only a male is being designated (Acts 12:22). The policy forces the revisers to give a value judgment on the question of whether "brothers" includes only males (Acts 15:1, 13, 23) or is all-inclusive (Acts 15:3). How did the revisers know that only males ("brothers") welcomed Paul in Acts 21:17? When *aner* must be rendered as "representatives" (Acts 15:25 ["men"]) where males have been specifically listed by name, an anti-male bias appears to be in play. It should be noticed, however, in a context like I Timothy 2:8, where *aner* ("men") contrasts with *gune* ("women"), the NRSV has faithfully retained "men." The same is true in the O.T. in the contrast between "young man" *(na'ar)* and "woman" *('ishshah;* Prov. 7:7-10).

One reads in the NRSV "Folly is bound up in the heart of a boy" (Prov. 22:15 ["child"]). The reviewer recognizes that "boy" is a completely accurate rendering of *na'ar*. However, in the light of what has been done with other gender-oriented statements, it would seem inconsistent to shift from "child" to "boy." The very next chapter renders the same term as "children" (Prov. 23:13; cf. *ben* in Prov. 29:17). Rendering the Hebrew word *ben* as "child" (as that term is understood in popular usage) rather than as "son" addresses the advice of the first part of Proverbs to minors. Included would be warnings against murder (Prov. 1:11), the loose woman (Prov. 2:16; 5:1-14; 6:20-35) or the prostitute (Prov. 29:3), despising the Lord's discipline (Prov. 3:11), and drunkenness (Prov. 23:19-21). But there is not complete consistency. In Proverbs 5:1, *beni* is "my child," but in Proverbs 5:20 the same term is "my son."

The revising committee of the NRSV was commissioned to deal with gender-oriented language. The REB and NRSV reflect considerable difference from each other in this area, and the NRSV goes further than the REB in this effort. Only time will tell how the NRSV effort commends itself to the Bible-reading public. The success or failure of the NRSV in becoming a popular version outside those circles pushing for non-gender-oriented language will to a large extent turn on this issue.

The NRSV revisers, also seeking to be non-racist, have rendered a phrase "I am black and beautiful" (Song of Sol. 1:5 ["very dark, but comely"]) and have displaced "Arab" with "nomad" (Jer. 3:2). The NRSV retains "white" as the color of goats, teeth, manna, leprous skin and hair, garments, wool, snow, a stripped tree, and milk. It, however, drops "white" as the image for cleansing and instead has "cleansed" or "purified" (Dan. 11:35; 12:10), and has "though your sins are like scarlet, they shall be like snow" (Isa. 1:18). The Hebrew verb in this last sentence is *labhan.*

For *glossais,* the NRSV chooses "languages" ("tongues") in Acts 2:4 but retains "tongues" later in Acts and in I Corinthians (Acts 10:46; 19:6; I Cor. 12:10, 28, 30; 13:1; 14:4, 6, 9, 13, 14, 18, 22, 27).

The NRSV's practice of reverting vocabulary or interpretation to the translations before the RSV includes "Your throne, O God" (Ps. 45:6 ["Your divine throne"]), "encompasses" (Jer. 31:22 ["protects"]), and "open their mouths against" (Lam. 3:46 ["rail against"]). Where the RSV transliterated to give *Asherah,* the NRSV has translated "sacred pole" (Deut. 7:5; 16:21; Isa. 17:8; 27:9; Jer. 17:2; Mic. 5:14) and relegates *Asherah/Asherim* to the footnote.

The gain in shifting from "fight with" to "do battle against" (Dan. 11:11) is not obvious.

Items of Earlier Controversy

The NRSV did not yield ground to the opposition on those points against the RSV which in some instances led to its being burned. *'Almah* is "young woman" (Gen. 24:43; Isa. 7:14)—a footnote lists "Gk *the virgin*" as an option), "girl" (Exod. 2:8; Ps. 68:25; Prov. 30:19 ["maiden"]), or "maiden" (Song of Sol. 1:3; 6:8). The masculine form, *'elem,* is translated "stripling" (I Sam. 17:56 ["lad"]) and "young man" (I Sam. 20:22 ["lad"]). The RSV had already preferred "maidens" to "virgins" (Matt. 25:1). The NRSV, while using "maiden" in some settings (Song of Sol. 1:3; 7:1) as the RSV, extends this preference; "maiden" (Amos 5:2) or "young woman" (Amos 8:13) often replace "virgin." But "girl" (Esther 2:4, 12; Jer. 2:32; Lam. 1:4; 2:10) and "young woman" (Jer. 31:13; Lam. 1:18; 2:21; 3:51; Zech. 9:17) replace "maiden" in some cases. "Bridesmaid" is used in Matthew 25:1. This practice does not question the teaching of the virgin birth, which is plainly stated in the Gospels of Matthew and Luke.

The rendering of *monogenes* as "only" (Luke 7:12; 8:42; 9:38; John 1:14; 3:16; Heb. 11:17; etc.) was disputed when the RSV appeared but is now accepted in most translations. "Rooms" in the Father's house in place of "mansions" was also disputed, but now becomes "dwelling places" (John 14:2). The NRSV reflects less certainty about Phoebe's posi-

Epilogue

At long last, the goal toward which this study has been moving has been reached. The story of the making of an English Bible translation simple enough for the boy who drives the plow has been told. No longer is the Bible locked from the common man who has no knowledge of Hebrew, Aramaic, Greek, and Latin; no longer is it chained to the pulpits of the churches. It is openly obtainable almost everywhere, even in the supermarkets. However, complete communication of God's Word — the goal of Bible translation — has been only partly achieved in the various efforts that have been surveyed here. In the words of Joshua, "there are still very large areas of land to be taken over" (Josh. 13:1, NIV).

A translation starts to become outdated from the moment it is completed. Information from new manuscript materials, new insights into the languages in which the Bible was first written, and new data concerning biblical history need to be communicated to the reader. Changing ideas about translations and changes in the English language itself[1] all outdate

---

[1] The supplement to *The Oxford English Dictionary* contains 85,000 entries — these are words that have entered the English language since the dictionary was published (1924). There is no count available of words that dropped out of use or that changed in meaning during that same period.

a version, thus preparing the way for the process to be started all over again.

The question of when a new translation is needed is a matter of judgment. Some people will tenaciously hold on to the past, while others are ever looking to the new. Modern translations will always be harshly condemned by those who fancy themselves able to see the "motes" in the eye. There have always been those who have insisted that the time or the scholarship was not "right" for a new translation. If the work waited until these people were ready, however, it would never be accomplished.

As the author of this study, my horizons have been greatly widened in the years I have spent with the English Bible versions; it is my hope that the horizons of the reader may also be widened by the material I have collected. The one truth that stands out most clearly is that translation, in the end, is a human process; it is not a divinely inspired one. The expectation of a perfect translation is a vain hope; certainly none of the present translations even approach perfection. Yet despite the errors of man, the truths of God are to be found in God's Book in translation. Though our feeble translation efforts may at times obscure the light, yet through the shadows the light shines. If one studies the Book, it is able to make him "wise unto salvation . . . in Christ Jesus" (II Tim. 3:15).

I have been impressed with the number of times that I thought I had found an error in the work of a translation group, but additional investigation made it clear that the beam was in my own eye, not in the translator's. Careful students may still find some items in my study that were erroneously cited as errors. Some items may have been given significance that are actually only matters of taste and judgment. There are, most likely, instances in which judgments should have been more charitable. In the face of such faults, I can only ask for the charity of the experts until I am better instructed.

If one should ask if there are too many translations, the reply must be that the question is really irrelevant. The translations are here; they are not going away; and they must be dealt with. To hide one's head in the sand will not make the translations disappear; it will not bring back the so-called "good old days" when everyone read one translation. As long as there is financial gain in it, publishers will push translations, old or new. Also, the needs of different reading audiences are served by different translations. It is estimated that today there are one billion readers of English, but that only about 35 percent of the world's population are nominally

410

Christian. Rather than being looked on as a gigantic conspiracy to draw people into religious error, the translation effort should be thought of as a sincere effort to reach the unreached. With the rapid growth of world population, by the year 2000 Christians may constitute only 15 percent of the world's population. There is a continuous need to greatly increase Bible circulation.

Samuel Johnson (1709-1784) once said,

> Dictionaries are like watches;
> the worst is better than none,
> and the best cannot be expected to go quite true.[2]

The same may also be said of translations. None is perfect, but the poorest is better than none. Those critical of the translation effort might well ponder the admonition given in the preface of the translation of William Tyndale, the first of the English translators:

> And if they perceive in any places that I have not attained the very sense of the tongue, or meaning of the Scripture, or have not given the right English word, that they put to their hands to amend it, remembering that it so is their duty to do. For we have not received the gifts of God for ourselves only, or to hide them. But for to bestow them unto the honoring of God and Christ and edifying of the congregation, which is the body of Christ.[3]

One asks, "What version should I read?" Another asks, "Are there doctrinal problems in this version or that?" Asking questions like these is like asking, "What car shall I drive?" One's background, education, aims, and purposes are the determining factors. If one wants the most literal equivalent of the original language, he will be disappointed with a paraphrase. If he wants something as easy to read as the newspaper, the traditional translations cannot fill his needs. If he has studied the Bible from childhood, the traditional may be quite clear to him; but if he is reading God's Word for the first time, the older versions may seem quite obtuse.

[2]Quoted in Gerhard Friedrich, "Pre-history of the Theological Dictionary of the New Testament," in *Theological Dictionary of the New Testament*, ed. Gerhard Friedrich, trans. and ed. G. W. Bromiley (Grand Rapids: Eerdmans, 1976), 10:613.

[3]The spelling has been modernized.

While versions differ in translating specific statements, all of the available English translations present the basic duties toward God and man. By comparing one with the other, the person who has no language training can be warned against going astray because of the peculiarities of one translation. He may be challenged to new ideas by reading a new translation. The religious problems of the world are not caused by people reading different translations; the most serious problem is that many read no translation!

Augustine in his *Confessions* tells of hearing a child at play who cried, *Tolle lege! Tolle lege!* ("Take up and read; Take up and read").[4] Augustine, not able to identify the cry with any known children's game, took it as a message to him from God. He picked up one of Paul's epistles, opened it at random, and read the very words that condemned his past, opened the door of hope to him, and led to his conversion. Your own English version cries, "Take up and read! Take up and read!"

---

[4]Augustine *Confessions* 8.12.

Bibliography of Modern Versions

General Treatments

Anderson, Christopher. *The Annals of the English Bible*. Abridged and continued by S. I. Prime. New York: Robert Carter & Brothers, 1849.

Beegle, Dewey M. *God's Word into English*. New York: Harper & Brothers, 1960.

Bruce, Frederick F. *History of the Bible in English*. 3d ed. New York: Oxford University Press, 1978.

The Cambridge History of the Bible. 3 vols. Cambridge: University Press, 1963-70. Vol. 3: *The West from the Reformation to the Present Day*, edited by S. L. Greenslade.

Darlow, T. H., and Moule, H. F. *Historical Catalogue of Printed Editions of the English Bible. 1525-1961*. Revised and expanded by A. S. Herbert. London: British and Foreign Bible Society, 1968.

Dennett, Herbert. *A Guide to Modern Versions of the New Testament*. Chicago: Moody Press, 1965.

Dore, John R. *Old Bibles*. London: Eyre and Spottiswoode, 1888.

Eadie, John. *The English Bible*. 2 vols. London: Macmillan and Co., 1876.

Edgar, Andrew. *The Bibles of England*. London: Alexander Gardner, 1889.

413

Grant, Frederick C. *Translating the Bible*. Edinburgh: Thomas Nelson and Sons, 1961.

Hills, Margaret T. *The English Bible in America*. New York: American Bible Society, 1961.

_____. *A Ready Reference History of the English Bible*. New York: American Bible Society, 1971.

Kenyon, Frederic G. *Our Bible and the Ancient Manuscripts*. Revised by A. W. Adams. New York: Harper & Brothers, 1958.

Kubo, Sakae, and Specht, Walter. *So Many Versions?* Grand Rapids: Zondervan, 1975.

Lea, John W. *The Book of Books and Its Wonderful Story*. Philadelphia: John C. Winston Co., 1922.

Lewis. John. *A Complete History of the Several Translations of the Holy Bible and New Testament into English*. London: W. Baynes, 1818.

MacGregor, Geddes. *The Bible in the Making*. Philadelphia and New York: J. B. Lippincott Co., 1959.

_____. *A Literary History of the Bible*. Nashville and New York: Abingdon Press, 1968.

Margolis, Max L. *The Story of Bible Translations*. Philadelphia: The Jewish Publication Society, 1948.

May, Herbert G. *Our English Bible in the Making*. Philadelphia: The Westminster Press, 1952.

Mombert, Jacob I. *English Versions of the Bible*. London: Samuel Bagster, 1907.

Moulton, William F. *The History of the English Bible*. New rev. ed. London: Charles H. Kelley, 1911.

Muir, William. *Our Grand Old Bible*. 2d ed. London: Morgan and Scott, 1911.

Partridge, Astley C. *English Bible Translation*. London: André Deutsch, 1973.

Pollard, Alfred W., ed. *Records of the English Bible*. London: Oxford University Press, 1911.

Pope, Hugh. *English Versions of the Bible*. Revised and amplified by Sebastian Bullough. St. Louis and London: B. Herder Book Company, 1952.

Price, Ira M. *The Ancestry of Our English Bible*. 3d ed. Revised by W. A. Irwin and A. P. Wikgren. New York: Harper and Brothers, 1956.

Robertson, Edwin H. *The New Translations of the Bible*. London: SCM Press, 1959.

Robinson, H. Wheeler, ed. *The Bible and Its Ancient English Versions*. Oxford: Clarendon Press, 1940.

Schwarz, Werner. *Principles and Problems in Biblical Translation. Some Reformation Controversies and Their Background*. Cambridge: University Press, 1955.

Wallace, Foy E., Jr. *A Review of the New Versions*. Fort Worth: Foy E. Wallace, Jr., Publications, 1973; 3d printing, 1976.

414

Weigle, Luther A. *The English New Testament from Tyndale to the Revised Standard Version*. London: Thomas Nelson and Sons, 1949.

Westcott, Brooke F. *A General View of the English Bible*. 3d ed. Revised by W. A. Wright. New York: The Macmillan Company, 1927.

What Bible Can You Trust? Nashville: Broadman Press, 1974.

The King James Version

Allen, Paul E., Jr. "Shaping the Gospel According to St. Mark: A Note on the Work of King James' Translators." *The St. Luke's Journal of Theology* 17 (June 1974): 39-43.

Allen, Ward S. "Influence of Greek Rhetorical Structure on the English of the Authorized Version of the New Testament." Ph.D. dissertation, Vanderbilt University, 1963.

_____, ed. *Translating for King James: Notes Made by a Translator of King James' Bible*. Nashville: Vanderbilt University Press, 1969.

Beaton, D. "Notes on the History of the Authorized Version of The Bible in Scotland." *The Princeton Theological Review* 9 (July 1911): 415-37.

Bridges, Ronald, and Weigle, Luther A. *The Bible Word Book, Concerning Obsolete and Archaic Words in the King James Version of the Bible*. New York: Thomas Nelson & Sons, 1960.

Bromiley, Geoffrey W. "The KJV: The Genius of Its Predecessors." *Eternity* 21 (March 1970): 30.

Bruce, Frederick F. *The King James Version: The First 350 Years, 1611-1961*. New York: Oxford University Press, 1960.

Butterworth, Charles C. *The Literary Lineage of the King James Bible, 1340-1611*. Philadelphia: University of Pennsylvania Press, 1941.

Carleton, James G. *The Part of Rheims in the Making of the English Bible*. Oxford: Clarendon Press, 1902.

Carson, D. A. *The King James Version Debate*. Grand Rapids: Baker Book House, 1979.

Conger, Lesley. "Forty-seven Writers: Most Read, Least Known: King James Bible." *Writer* 84 (July 1971): 7-8.

Cook, Albert S. *The Authorized Version of the Bible and Its Influence*. New York and London: G. P. Putnam's Sons, 1910.

Craig, Clarence T. "The King James and the American Standard Versions of the New Testament." In *An Introduction to the Revised Standard Version of the New Testament*, pp. 15-21. By members of the Revision Committee. Chicago: International Council of Religious Education, 1946.

Daiches, David. *The King James Version of the English Bible*. Chicago: University of Chicago Press, 1941; reprint ed., Hamden, Conn.: Archon Books, 1968.

Davies, T. Lewis. *Bible English*. London: George Bell and Sons, 1875.

415

Douglas, J. D. "The King Behind the Version." *Christianity Today* 19 (March 28, 1975): 632-34.

Elliott, Melvin E. *The Language of the King James Bible —A Glossary Explaining Its Words and Expressions*. Garden City, New York: Doubleday, 1967.

Evans, Bergen, and Evans, Cornelia. "Biblical English." In *A Dictionary of Contemporary English Usage*, pp. 61-62. New York: Random House, 1957.

Fox, Adam. "The Influence of the Authorized Version on the Religious Life of Britain." *London Quarterly & Holborn Review* 186 (April 1961): 95-108.

Fries, Charles C. "One Stylistic Feature of the 1611 English Bible." In *The Fred Newton Scott Anniversary Papers*, pp. 175-87. Freeport, New York: Books for Libraries Press, 1929; reprinted 1968.

Fuller, David Otis. *Is the King James Version Nearest to the Original Autographs?* St. Louis: Facts for Faith, 1972.

_____. *Which Bible?* 2d ed. Grand Rapids: Grand Rapids International Publications, 1971.

Goddard, Burton L. "Crucial Issues in Bible Translation." *Christianity Today* 14 (July 3, 1970): 900.

Goodspeed, Edgar J., ed. *The Translators to the Reader: Preface to the King James Version*, 1911. Chicago: The University of Chicago Press, 1935.

Grainger, James Moses. *Studies in the Syntax of the King James Version*. Chapel Hill, North Carolina: The University Press, 1907.

Green, William M. "Which Version Shall We Use?" *Restoration Quarterly* 12 (First Quarter 1969): 26-36.

Harwell, John H. "King James's Revised Translation of the Bible." *Sewanee Review* 79 (Spring 1971): 285-87.

Hills, Edward F. *The King James Version Defended!* Des Moines: Christian Research Press, 1973.

Hodges, Zane C. "The Greek Text of the King James Version." *Bibliotheca Sacra* 125 (October-December 1968): 334-35.

Hornsby, Samuel. "Punctuation in the Authorized Version of the Bible." *The Bible Translator* 24 (January 1973): 139-41.

_____. "Style in the Bible: A Bibliography." *Style* 7 (Fall 1973): 349-74.

Isaacs, J. "The Authorized Version and After." In *The Bible in Its Ancient and English Versions*, pp. 196-234. Edited by H. Wheeler Robinson. Oxford: Clarendon Press, 1940.

_____. "The Sixteenth-Century English Versions." In *The Bible in Its Ancient and English Versions*, pp. 146-95. Edited by H. Wheeler Robinson. Oxford: Clarendon Press, 1940.

Jackson, Robert S. "The Inspired Style of the English Bible." *Journal of Bible and Religion* 29 (January 1961): 4-15.

416

Jacobs, Edward C. "A Bodleian Bishops' Bible, 1602." Ph.D. dissertation, University of Alabama, 1972.

Jewett, Paul K. "Majestic Music of King James." *Christianity Today* 1 (November 26, 1956): 13-15.

Kay, J. Alan. "The Authorized Version and the New English Bible." *London Quarterly & Holborn Review* 186 (April 1961): 79-83.

Kehl, D. G., ed. *Literary Style of the Old Bible and the New*. Indianapolis and New York: The Bobbs-Merrill Company, Inc., 1970.

Levi, Peter. *The English Bible, 1534-1859*. Grand Rapids: William B. Eerdmans Publishing Co., 1974.

Lewis, C. S. *The Literary Impact of the Authorized Version*. London: The Athlone Press, 1950; reprint ed., Philadelphia: Fortress Press, 1963.

Lightfoot, J. B. *On a Fresh Revision of the English New Testament*. 2d ed. London and New York: Macmillan and Co., 1872.

Lowes, John Livingston. "The Noblest Monument of English Prose." In *Essays in Appreciation*, pp. 3-31. Boston: Houghton Mifflin Company, 1936.

McAfee, Cleland Boyd. *The Greatest English Classic: A Study of the King James Version and Its Influence on Life and Literature*. New York and London: Harper and Brothers, 1912.

McClure, Alexander W. *The Translators Revived*. New York: Board of Publication of the Reformed Protestant Dutch Church, 1855.

MacDonald, Dwight. "The Bible in Modern Undress." *The New Yorker* 29 (November 14, 1953): 183-208.

McGill, James W. "An Experimental Study of the Effect of King James Version Archaisms upon Reading and Listening, Comprehension and Retention." Ph.D. dissertation, George Peabody College for Teachers, 1970.

Marshall, R. "Words Must Have Meaning." *War Cry* (September 7, 1974): 3.

Maveety, Stanley Roswell. "A Study of the Style of the King James and of the Rheims-Douay Translation of the Bible." Ph.D. dissertation, Stanford University, 1956.

Meyers, Robert. "Will the Real King James Version Please Stand Up?" *Restoration Review* 9 (November 1967): 161-66.

Mihelic, Joseph Ludwig. "A Study of the Literary Style of the Old Testament in the King James Version." Ph.D. dissertation, University of Chicago, 1941.

Montgomery, Frank William. "An Experimental Study of the Comparative Comprehensibility for High School Students of the King James and Revised Standard Versions of the Bible." Ph.D. dissertation, University of Pittsburgh, 1955.

Newth, Samuel. *Lectures on Bible Revision*. London: Hodder and Stoughton, 1881.

Nix, W. E. "Theological Presuppositions and Sixteenth Century English Bible Translation." *Bibliotheca Sacra* 124 (January-March 1967): 42-50; (April-June 1967): 117-24.

417

Paine, Gustavus Swift. *The Men Behind the King James Version*. Grand Rapids: Baker Book House, 1977.

Parker, Pierson. "In Praise of 1611." *Anglican Theological Review* 46 (July 1964): 251-60.

Raysor, Cecily. "A Comparison of the Style of Four Recent Translations of the New Testament with That of the King James Version." *Journal of Religion* 41 (April 1967): 73-90.

Report on the History and Recent Collation of the English Version of the Bible. New York: American Bible Society, 1852.

Scrivener, F. H. A. *The Authorized Edition of the English Bible (1611): Its Subsequent Reprints and Modern Representatives*. Cambridge: The University Press, 1884; reissued 1910.

Sheahan, Joseph F. *The English in the English Bibles: Rhemes 1582, Authorized 1611, Revised 1881; St. Matthew 1-14*. Poughkeepsie: Columbus Institute, 1928.

Skilton, John H. "The King James Version Today." In *The Law and the Prophets*, pp. 94-114. Edited by John H. Skilton. Nutley, N. J.: Presbyterian and Reformed Publishing Co., 1974.

Smith, Walter E. "The Great 'She' Bible." *The Library* ser. I, 2 (1890): 1-11, 96-102, 141-53.

Smither, Ethel L. "Which Translation of the Bible for Children?" *International Journal of Religious Education* 27 (December 1950): 8-9.

Thompson, Dorothy. "The Old Bible and the New." *Ladies' Home Journal* 70 (March 1953): 11, 14, 203-6.

Todd, Henry J. *A Vindication of our Authorized Translation and Translators of The Bible*. London: F. C. and J. Rivington, 1819.

Trench, Richard C. *On the Authorized Version of the New Testament*. London: John W. Parker and Son, 1859.

Tucker, Susie I. "The Historical and Literary Setting of the Authorized Version." *London Quarterly and Holborn Review* 186 (April 1961): 89-94.

Wedgwood, Cicely V. *Seventeenth Century English Literature*. London: Oxford University Press, 1950; 2d ed., 1970.

Weigle, Luther A., ed. *Bible Words That Have Changed in Meaning*. New York: Thomas Nelson & Sons, 1955.

Willoughby, Edwin Eliot. *The Making of the King James Bible*. Los Angeles: Printed for Dawson's Book Shop at the Plantin Press, 1956.

Wilson, P. W. "Modernizing the English of the Bible." *New York Times*, 23 March 1941, Sec. 7, pp. 10, 21.

American Standard Version

American Bible Revision Committee. *Anglo-American Bible Revision: Its Necessity and Purpose*. Rev. ed. Philadelphia: American Sunday School Union, 1879.

————. *Documentary History of the American Committee on Revision*. New York: n.p., 1885.

Burgon, John W. *The Revision Revised*. London: John Murray, 1883.

Chambers, T. W. *A Companion to the Revised Old Testament*. New York: Funk and Wagnalls, 1885.

Cox. S. "Doctrinal Effects of the Revised Version." *The Expositor*, 2d ser., 3 (1882): 434-53.

Craig, Clarence T. "The King James and the American Standard Versions of the New Testament." *The Bible Translator* 2 (January 1951): 43-48.

Dobbs, C. E. W. "The Preferences of the American Revisers." *Homiletic Review* 25 (February 1893): 180-2.

Ellicott, Charles J. *Considerations on the Revision of the English Version of the New Testament*. London: Longmans, Green, Reader, and Dyer, 1870.

Faulkner, John Alfred. "English Bible Translation." *Biblical Review* 9 (April 1924): 199-231.

Jackson, Wayne. "American Standard Version—A Recommended Translation." *The Christian Courier* 7 (September 1971): 18-19.

Langdon, William M. "Some Merits of the American Standard Bible." *Bibliotheca Sacra* 70 (July 1913): 486-97.

Lockyer, Thomas F. "The Bible in English. Some Recent Versions and Editions." *London Quarterly Review* 98 (July 1902): 119-39.

Luccock, G. N. "The New Translations." *Biblical Review* 11 (January 1926): 11-28.

McClellan, J. B. "The Revised Version of the New Testament. A Plea for Hesitation as to Its Adoption." *The Expositor*, 6th ser., 10 (1904): 187-202.

Milligan, George. "The Doctrinal Significance of the Revised Version." *The Expository Times* 7 (1895-96): 377-79, 452-54; 8 (1896-97): 171-75.

Radford, Benjamin J. "Some Unfortunate Translations." *Christian Standard* 48 (December 12, 1912): 2093.

Riddle, Matthew B. "The American Revised Bible." *Christian Standard* 53 (October 27, 1917): 101-2.

————. *The Story of the Revised New Testament, American Standard Edition*. Philadelphia: The Sunday School Times Co., 1908.

Roberts, Alexander. *Companion to the Revised Version of the New Testament*. New York: Cassell, Petter, Galpin & Co., 1881.

————. "Renderings and Readings in the Revised New Testament." *The Expository Times* 3 (1891-92): 129-30.

Schaff, David S. "Fiftieth Anniversary of the American Bible Revision." *Reformed Church Review* 2 (July 1923): 258-90.

419

Schaff, Philip. *The Revision of the English Version of the Holy Scriptures*. New York: Harper & Brothers, 1877.

Specht, Walter F. "Use of Italics in English Versions of the Bible" *Andrews University Seminary Studies* 6 (January 1968): 88-109.

VanderPloeg, John. "American Standard Version Recommended." *The Banner* 91 (October 12, 1956): 1252-53.

Votaw, Clyde W. "The American Standard Edition of the Revised Bible." *Biblical World* 18 (October 1901): 259-69.

Warfield, Benjamin B. Review of *"The Holy Bible . . . Newly Edited by the American Revision Committee, A.D. 1901."* *Presbyterian and Reformed Review* 13 (October 1902): 645-48.

Whitney, Henry M. "The Latest Translation of the Bible." *Bibliotheca Sacra* 59 (April 1902): 217-37; (July 1902): 451-75; (October 1902): 653-81; 60 (January 1903): 109-20; (April 1903): 342-57; 61 (April 1904): 248-71; 62 (January 1905): 71-89; (April 1905): 245-63.

Whiton, James M. "The American Revision of the Bible" *Outlook* 58 (February 12, 1898): 417-19.

Wilkinson, Benjamin G. *Our Authorized Bible Vindicated*. Washington, D.C.: n.p., 1930.

Wylie, David G. The American Standard Edition of the Revised Bible in Pulpit and Pew. New York: n.p., 1903.

Revised Standard Version

Allis, Oswald T. *Revised Version or Revised Bible?* Philadelphia: Presbyterian and Reformed Publishing Co., 1953.

————. *Revision or New Translation? The Revised Standard Version of 1946*. Philadelphia: The Presbyterian and Reformed Publishing Co., 1948.

————. "RSV Appraisal: Old Testament." *Christianity Today* 1 (July 8, 1957): 6-7, 21-24.

Arbez, Edward P. "Modern Translations of the Old Testament." *Catholic Biblical Quarterly* 17 (July 1955): 456-85.

Arndt, William. "The Revised Standard Version of the New Testament." *Concordia Theological Monthly* 17 (May 1946): 333-39.

Baker, Nelson B. "Revised Version in the Light of History." *Review and Expositor* 51 (January 1954): 62-73.

Barnhouse, Donald G. "I Have Read the RSV." *Eternity* 21 (April 1970): AF-6.

Beegle, Dewey M. "Evaluation of the RSV OT." *Asbury Seminarian* 7 (Spring-Summer 1953): 16-28.

Bender, Harold Stauffer, ed. *The Revised Standard Version: An Examination and Evaluation*. Scottdale, Pa.: Herald Press, 1953; reprinted 1964.

Black, Matthew. "Modern English Versions of the Scriptures." In *The New Testament in Historical and Contemporary Perspective*, pp. 83-98. Edited by Hugh Anderson and William Barclay. Oxford: Blackwell, 1965.

Blank, Sheldon H. Review of *The Holy Bible, Revised Standard Version, Containing the Old and the New Testaments*. *The Journal of Religion* 33 (April 1953): 148-49.

Bowie, Walter R. "Some Preaching Values in the Revised Standard Version of the New Testament." *Interpretation* 4 (January 1950): 51-61.

Bowman, John W. Review of *The Revised Version New Testament*. *Christendom* 11 (Summer 1946): 388-91.

Bratcher, Robert G. "Changes in the New Testament of the Revised Standard Version." *The Bible Translator* 12 (April 1961): 61-68.

Bright, John. "Commended—With Reservations." *Interpretation* 7 (July 1953): 338-44.

Burrows, Millar. *Diligently Compared*. New York: Thomas Nelson and Sons, 1964.

_____. "The Revised Standard Version of the Old Testament." In *Supplements to Vetus Testamentum*, 7: 206-21. Leiden: E. J. Brill, 1960.

Cadbury, Henry J. "The New Translation's First Year." *The Christian Century* 64 (February 5, 1947): 170-71.

Campbell, J. Y. Review of *The New Testament—RSV*. *The Journal of Theological Studies* 49 (Jan.-April, 1948): 118-24.

Carnell, Edward J. Review of *The Harper Study Bible*. *Christianity Today* 9 (February 12, 1965): 514.

Clark, Kenneth W. "Theological Relevance of Textual Variation in Current Criticism of the Greek New Testament." *Journal of Biblical Literature* 85 (March 1966): 1-16.

Cooper, Charles M. "The Revised Standard Version of Psalms." In *The Seventy-fifth Anniversary Volume of the Jewish Quarterly Review*, pp. 137-48. Edited by Abraham A. Neuman and Solomon Zeitlin. Philadelphia: The Jewish Quarterly Review, 1967.

Crabtree, A. R. "The Revised Standard Version of the Psalms." *Review and Expositor* 50 (October 1953): 443-52.

_____. "Translation of Romans 5:1 in the Revised Standard Version of the New Testament." *Review and Expositor* 43 (October 1946): 436-39.

Craig, Clarence T. "The Revised Standard Version." *Journal of Bible and Religion* 14 (February 1946): 33-36.

_____. "Word of God For Today." *International Journal of Religious Education* 22 (February 1946): 4-6.

Cross, Frank M. "Notes on the RSV Old Testament." *McCormick Speaking* 6 (November 1952): 7-10.

Drake, Charles. "Battle on the Revised Standard Version." *Christianity and Crisis* 13 (July 6, 1953): 90-92.

Enslin, Morton S. Review of *The Revised Standard Version of the New Testament.* *Crozer Quarterly* 23 (July 1946): 271-73.

Fenton, J. C. "Greek Text Behind the 'Revised Standard Version' of Mark." *Studia Evangelica* 5 (1968): 182-87.

Fergin, A. F. "A Critical Review of the RSV of the New Testament." *Concordia Theological Monthly* 24 (March 1953): 208-13.

Filson, Floyd V. "The Revised Standard New Testament." *Theology Today* 3 (July 1946): 221-34.

Foster, R. C. *The Revised Standard Version of the New Testament: An Appraisal.* Cincinnati: Standard Publishing Co., 1946.

_____. *The Revised Standard Version. A Reply to Dr. Clarence T. Craig.* Pittsburgh: The Evangelical Fellowship, Inc., 1947.

Fox, Adam. "RSVCE(NT)." *Theology* 69 (April 1966): 164-70.

Francisco, Clyde T. "Revised Standard Version of the Old Testament." *Review and Expositor* 50 (January 1953): 30-55.

Fuller, David Otis. *Which Bible?* 2d ed. Grand Rapids: International Publications, 1971.

Garrison, W. E. "A New New Testament—Coming." *The Christian Century* 63 (February 6, 1946): 171-72.

_____. "The New New Testament—Here." *The Christian Century* 63 (February 13, 1946): 202-4.

_____. Review of *The Holy Bible, Revised Standard Version. The Christian Century* 69 (October 8, 1952): 1160-61.

Gibson, George Miles. "The New Bible and Preaching." *McCormick Speaking* 6 (November 1952): 3-6.

Gilmour, S. Maclean. "A New 'Textus Receptus'?" *Christianity Today* 4 (September 26, 1960): 1026-30.

Good, Edwin M. "With All Its Faults." *Christianity Today* 5 (January 16, 1961): 306-7.

[Goodpasture, B. C.] "The Revised Standard Version." *Gospel Advocate* 114 (October 19, 1972): 658, 666; reprinted 118 (October 14, 1976): 658, 666-67.

Gossip, Arthur J. "A New Revised Version of the New Testament." *Expository Times* 57 (July 1946): 259-60.

Grant, Frederick C. "The New American Revision of the Bible." *Zeitschrift für die neutestamentliche Wissenschaft* 45 (1954): 217-29.

_____. "Only Begotten—A Footnote to the Revised Standard Version." *The Bible Translator* 17 (January 1966): 11-14.

_____. "Preaching Values in the Revised Standard Version." *Religion in Life* 20 (Winter 1950-51): 114-32.

Greenlee, J. Harold. "Revised Standard New Testament." *Asbury Seminarian* 7 (Spring-Summer 1953): 29-45.

Grobel, W. Kendrick. "The Revision of the English New Testament." *Journal of Biblical Literature* 66 (1947): 361-84.

Harrison, Everett F. Review of *New Testament. The Revised Standard Version. Bibliotheca Sacra* 103 (April-June 1946): 247-49.

Hartmann, Kurt Carl. "More About the RSV and Isaiah 7:14." *Lutheran Quarterly* 7 (November 1955): 344-47.

Heim, Ralph D. "RSV and New Possibilities For Christian Education." *Religious Education* 52 (January 1957): 28-34.

Introduction to the Revised Standard Version of the New Testament. Chicago: International Council of Religious Education, 1946.

Introduction to the Revised Standard Version of the Old Testament. New York: Thomas Nelson & Sons, 1952.

Irwin, William A. "That Troublesome 'almah and Other Matters." *Review and Expositor:* 50 (July 1953): 337-60.

James, Fleming. "The Use of the Versions in the Revised Standard Version." *Religious Education* 47 (July 1952): 248-52.

Johnson, Alan, and Goldberg, Louis. "Which Version Shall I Use?" *Moody Monthly* 67 (November 1966): 30-33.

Johnson, Sherman E. "The Revised Standard Version." *Anglican Theological Review* 30 (April 1948): 81-90.

Jones, Gwilym H. Review of *The Holy Bible Revised Standard Version.* 2d ed. *Religious Studies* 9 (September 1973): 366-68.

Katt, Arthur F. "Does the RSV Mutilate the New Testament Text?" *Concordia Theological Monthly* 26 (August 1955): 561-68.

Kline, Meredith G. Review of *The Holy Bible. Revised Standard Version, Containing Old and New Testaments. Westminster Theological Journal* 16 (November 1953): 97-103.

Knoff, Gerald E. "Catholic Edition of the RSV." *International Journal of Religious Education* 43 (March 1967): 17.

Knudsen, J. "Problem of the Two Cups." *Lutheran Quarterly* 2 (February 1950): 74-85.

Kraft, Robert A. Review of *The Holy Bible, RSV Catholic Edition and the Oxford Annotated Bible with the Apocrypha. Journal of Biblical Literature* 85 (December 1966): 486-91.

Ladd, George Eldon. "RSV Appraisal: New Testament." *Christianity Today* 1 (July 8, 1957): 7-11.

Larue, Gerald A. "Another Chapter in the History of Bible Translation." *The Journal of Bible and Religion* 31 (October 1963): 301-10.

Lightfoot, Neil R. "A Critical Examination of the Revised Standard Version of the New Testament." Ph.D dissertation, Duke University, 1958.

_____. "Textual Base of the RSV New Testament." *Restoration Quarterly* 5 (Second Quarter 1961): 62-66.

Lilly, Joseph L. Review of *The New Covenant Commonly Called The New Testament. Theological Studies* 7 (June 1946): 321-25.

Lincoln, C. F., ed. "A Critique of the Revised Standard Version." *Bibliotheca Sacra* 110 (January 1953): 50-66.

McKenzie, John L. Review of *The Holy Bible: Revised Standard Version. Catholic Biblical Quarterly* 17 (January 1955): 88-90.

Mackie, George A. "Revised New Testament to Be Published Soon." *International Journal of Religious Education* 22 (September 1945): 33.

Major, H. D. A. Review of *The American Revised Standard Version of the Bible. Modern Churchman* 44 (June 1954): 134-35.

May, Herbert G. "Revised Standard Version After Twenty Years." *McCormick Quarterly* 19 (May 1966): 301-8.

_____. "Revised Standard Version Bible." *Vetus Testamentum* 24 (April 1974): 238-40.

_____. "The Revised Standard Version in the Classroom." *Journal of Bible and Religion* 21 (July 1953): 174-79.

_____. "The RSV Bible and the RSV Bible Committee." *Perspective* 12 (Fall 1971): 217-34.

Meek, Theophile James. "The RSV of the Old Testament: An Appraisal." *Religion in Life* 23 (Winter 1953-54): 70-82.

Metzger, Bruce M. "The Revised Standard Version." *The Duke Divinity School Review* 44 (Spring 1979): 70-87.

_____. "The Revised Standard Version of the New Testament." *Princeton Seminary Bulletin* 39 (Spring 1946): 18-23.

_____. "The RSV—Ecumenical Edition." *Theology Today* 34 (October 1977): 315-17.

_____. "The Story Behind the Making of the Revised Standard Version of the Bible." *The Princeton Seminary Bulletin* n.s. 1 (1978): 189-200.

_____. "Trials of a Translator." *Theology Today* 33 (April 1976): 96-100.

Moffatt, James. "Revision Revised." *International Journal of Religious Education* 17 (February 1941): 18-19.

Montgomery, Frank William. "An Experimental Study of the Comparative Comprehensibility for High School Students of the King James and Revised Standard Versions of the Bible." Ph.D. dissertation, University of Pittsburgh, 1955.

Moody, Dale. "God's Only Son: the Translation of John 3:16 in the Revised Standard Version." *Journal of Biblical Literature* 72 (December 1953): 213-19; abridged in *The Bible Translator* 10 (October 1959): 145-47.

_____. "Isaiah 7:14 in the Revised Standard Version." *The Review and Expositor* 50 (January 1953): 61-68.

_____. Review of *The New Oxford Annotated Bible. Revised Standard Version. Review and Expositor* 70 (Fall 1973): 515-16.

Morris, Raymond P. "The Revised Standard Version of the New Testament—A First Impression." *Religion in Life* 15 (Spring 1946): 174-81.

Mueller, John Theodore. "What Bible Version Should We Adopt?" *Concordia Theological Monthly* 17 (March 1946): 223-24.

Mueller, Walter. "A Virgin Shall Conceive." *Evangelical Quarterly* 32 (October-December 1960): 203-7.

Muilenberg, James. "The Literary Values of the Revised Standard Version." *Religious Education* 47 (July-August 1952): 260.

Murch, James DeForest. "New Bible Translation." *Christian Standard* 102 (May 20, 1967): 309.

Myers, J. M. Review of *The Holy Bible: Revised Standard Version. Lutheran Quarterly* 4 (November 1952): 457-58.

Nakarai, Toyozo W. "Notes on the Revised Standard Version." *Jewish Quarterly Review* 45 (July 1954): 59-62.

Nesbitt, Charles F. Review of *The Revised Standard Version. Journal of Bible and Religion* 21 (January 1953): 33-34.

Orme, Dan. "A Second Look at the RSV." *Eternity* 18 (August 1967): 16-18.

Otey, William Wesley. *Christ or Modernism*. Austin, Texas: Firm Foundation Publishing House, 1953.

Oxtoby, Gurdon C. "An Estimate of the Revised Standard Version." *Theology Today* 10 (April 1953): 19-33.

Paschal, George W. "The Revised Standard Version of the New Testament." *Review and Expositor* 44 (April 1947): 171-85; (July 1947): 331-42.

Phelps, Dryden L. "Bible Study Is Exciting for Adults Using the New Version of the New Testament." *International Journal of Religious Education* 22 (July-August 1946): 10-11.

Polhill, John B. "The Revised Standard Version and the Oxford Annotated Bible." *Review and Expositor* 76 (Summer 1979): 315-24.

Price, P. Frank. "The 1946 Version of the New Testament—From a Reader's Point of View." *Union Seminary Review* 57 (May 1946): 202-18.

Raysor, Cecily. "A Comparison of the Style of Four Recent Translations of the New Testament with That of the King James Version." *Journal of Religion* 41 (April 1961): 73-90.

Reider, Joseph. "The Revised Standard Version." *The Jewish Quarterly Review* 43 (April 1953): 381-84.

Roels, E. Review of *The New Testament, Revised Standard Version, Catholic Edition. Calvin Theological Journal* 1 (April 1966): 112-16.

425

Ross, Roy G. "Dr. Swaim Represents Revised New Testament." *International Journal of Religious Education* 23 (January 1947): 17.

————. "Who Are These Bible Translators?" *International Journal of Religious Education* 21 (March 1945): 35.

Roy, Ralph L. " 'Modernism'—and the 'Battle of the Bible.' " In *Apostles of Discord*, pp. 203-27. Boston: Beacon Press, 1953.

Saleska, E. J. "Our English Bible." *Concordia Theological Monthly* 24 (January 1953): 13-25.

Schick, George V. "The Holy Bible, Revised Standard Version." *Concordia Theological Monthly* 24 (January 1953): 1-12.

————. "The Revised Standard Version and the Small Catechism." *Concordia Theological Monthly* 27 (March 1956): 161-83.

Scott, John A. Review of *The New Testament. Revised Standard Version. The Classical Weekly* 40 (January 6, 1947): 68-71.

Stonehouse, N. B. Review of *The New Covenant Commonly Called the New Testament of Our Lord and Savior Jesus Christ. Revised Standard Version. Westminster Theological Journal* 9 (November 1946): 128-31.

Swaim, Joseph Carter. "House of Many Rooms." *International Journal of Religious Education* 26 (May 1950): 3.

————. "It Makes Teaching Easier." *International Journal of Religious Education* 24 (January 1948): 12-13.

————. "Lands Beyond: Light on Strange Passage. From a New Translation." *International Journal of Religious Education* 26 (April 1950): 3.

————. *New Insights into Scripture: Studying the Revised Standard Version.* Philadelphia: Westminster Press, 1962.

————. "RSV and a New Decade of Religious Education." *Religious Education* 57 (July-August 1962): 283-89.

Swanton, R. Review of *The Revised Standard Version with Apocryphal/ Deuterocanonical Books.* An Ecumenical Edition, 1973. *The Reformed Theological Review* 32 (September-December 1973): 99-100.

Trever, John C. "RSV Bible Nears Completion." *International Journal of Religious Education* 28 (October 1951): 12-13, 42.

————. "Teaching with the RSV Bible." *International Journal of Religious Education* 29 (March 1953): 15-17.

Turkington, W. D. "The Revised Standard Version of the New Testament." *Asbury Seminarian* 1 (Summer 1946): 71-72.

Turner, G. A. "Viewing the Versions." *Asbury Seminarian* 7 (Spring-Summer 1953): 3-8.

Ward, James M. Review of *The New Oxford Annotated Bible with the Apocrypha. Perkins Journal* 27 (Summer 1971): 46.

Warden, Francis Marion. "God's Only Son." *The Review and Expositor* 50 (April 1953): 216-23.

Weigle, Luther A. "Bible in Living Language." *International Journal of Religious Education* 39 (February 1963): 36-37, 39.

_____. "The English of the Revised Standard Version of the New Testament." In *An Introduction to the Revised Standard Version of the New Testament*, pp. 53-58. Chicago: International Council of Religious Education, 1946.

_____. "The Making of the Revised Standard Version of the New Testament. " *Religion in Life* 15 (Spring 1946): 163-81.

_____. "New Editions of the Scriptures." *Princeton Seminary Bulletin* 60 (February 1967): 43-45.

_____. "New New Testament." *International Journal of Religious Education* 22 (March 1946): 8-9, 31.

_____. "Revised Standard Version." *Christian Scholar* 36 (December 1953): 330-35.

_____. "The Revised Standard Version of the Bible." *Catholic Biblical Quarterly* 14 (October 1952): 310-18.

_____. "RSV Translation of Isaiah 7:14." *International Journal of Religious Education* 29 (February 1953): 2.

_____. "Scholarship, Education, and the Bible." *The Journal of Bible and Religion* 22 (October 1954): 227-35.

_____. "The Standard Bible Committee." In *Translating and Understanding the Old Testament*, pp. 29-41. Edited by H. T. Frank and W. L. Reed. Nashville: Abingdon, 1970.

_____. "Use of the Revised Standard Version in Liturgy and Education." *Religious Education* 52 (January-February 1957): 22-28.

Wentz, Abdel R. "The New Testament and the Word of God." In *An Introduction to the Revised Standard Version of the New Testament*, pp. 64-70. Chicago: International Council of Religious Education, 1946.

Whitworth, J. H. "Textual Emendations Used in the *RSVOT*." *Asbury Seminarian* 7 (Spring-Summer 1953): 9-15.

Wikgren, Allen Paul. "A Critique of the Revised Standard Version of the New Testament." In *The Study of the Bible Today and Tomorrow*, pp. 383-400. Edited by H. R. Willoughby. Chicago: The University of Chicago Press, 1947.

_____. Review of *The Revised Standard New Testament. Journal of Religion* 27 (April 1947): 120-25.

Wuest, Kenneth S. Review of *The Revised Version of the New Testament. Moody Monthly* 46 (June 1946): 592, 643, 646.

The New English Bible

Abbot, W. Review of *The New English Bible. America* 104 (March 18, 1961): 790.

Allis, Oswald T. *The New English Bible*. Philadelphia: The Presbyterian and Reformed Publishing Company, 1963.

427

_____. Review of *The New English Bible with the Apocrypha*. *Westminster Theological Journal* 33 (November 1970): 81-93.

Baker, Aelred E. "The New English Bible." *New Blackfriars* 51 (May 1970): 218-22.

Barr, James. "After Five Years: A Retrospect on Two Major Translations of the Bible." *The Heythrop Journal* 15 (October 1974): 381-405.

Bartels, Robert A. Review of *The New English Bible, New Testament*. *The Lutheran Quarterly* 13 (August 1961): 269-71.

Barton, John M. T. "The New English Bible." *Clergy Review* 46 (April 1961): 217-23.

Beardslee, William A. "The New English Bible: N.T." *Chicago Theological Seminary Register* 51 (November 1961): 7-12.

Beare, Frank W. "The New English Bible: New Testament." *New Testament Studies* 8 (October 1961): 80-92.

Benoit, P. Review of *The New English Bible: New Testament*. *Revue Biblique* 69 (January 1962): 147-49.

"The Bible as Bestseller." *Time* 77 (March 24, 1961): 49-50.

Biggs, Charles R. "N.E.B.—The Minor Prophets." *Australian Biblical Review* 18 (October 1970): 21-24.

Bligh, John, "The New Testament (N.E.B.)." *The Heythrop Journal* 2 (July 1961): 199-215.

Boling, Robert G. Review of *The New English Bible with the Apocrypha*. *McCormick Quarterly* 23 (May 1970): 277-83.

Bos, A. Review of *The New English Bible*. *Cithara* 11 (May 1972): 99-102.

Bradnock, Wilfred J. "The New English Bible Reviewed." *The Bible Translator* 17 (1966): 197.

Bratcher, Robert G. Review of *The New English Bible: New Testament*. *The Bible Translator* 12 (July 1961): 97-106.

Brockington, Leonard H., ed. *The Hebrew Text of the Old Testament: The Readings Adopted by the Translators of the New English Bible*. Oxford: Oxford University Press, 1973.

Brown, Raymond E. Review of *The Greek New Testament: Being the Text Translated in the New English Bible*, by R. V. G. Tasker. *Theological Studies* 25 (December 1964): 682-83.

_____. Review of the *New English Bible: New Testament*. *The Catholic Biblical Quarterly* 23 (July 1961): 321-24.

Brown, Robert M. "The New English Bible." *Christianity and Crisis* 21 (April 17, 1961): 55-56.

Browne, S. G. " 'Leprosy' in the New English Bible." *The Bible Translator* 22 (January 1971): 45-46.

Bruce, F. F. "Editorial." *Evangelical Quarterly* 36 (October-December 1964): 193-94.

_____. "The English Bible: A History of Translation." *Anglican Theological Review* 45 (October 1963): 434.

_____. "The New English Bible." *Christianity Today* 5 (March 13, 1961): 493-96.

_____. "The New English Bible." *Christianity Today* 14 (January 30, 1970): 384-87.

_____. "The New English Bible." *Faith and Thought* 92 (Summer 1961): 47-53.

_____. "The New English Bible: New Testament." *Scottish Journal of Theology* 14 (June 1961): 194-96.

_____. "New English Bible, 1970." *Princeton Seminary Bulletin* 63 (Winter 1970): 99-104.

_____. Review of *The New English Bible: New Testament. Evangelical Quarterly* 33 (April-June 1961): 112-16.

Bullard, Roger A. "The New English Bible." *The Duke Divinity School Review* 44 (Spring 1979): 104-23.

Bullough, S. "The New English Bible: A Survey of the Critics." *Blackfriars* 42 (September 1961): 377-80.

Burrows, Millar. Review of the *New English Bible with Apocrypha. Journal of Biblical Literature* 79 (June 1970): 220-22.

Cadbury, Henry J. "The New English Bible." *Theology Today* 18 (July 1961): 188-200.

"Camels and Castor Oil; Disappearance of Familiar Words." *Tablet* 216 (August 25, 1962): 792.

"Catholic Observers for NEB." *Tablet* 220 (May 7, 1966): 545.

Cherian, C. M. "Why a New Translation of the Bible?" *Clergy Monthly* 25 (August 1961): 241-52.

Child, R. L. Review of *The New English Bible. Baptist Quarterly* 19 (April 1961): 52-58.

_____. Review of *The New English Bible. Baptist Quarterly* 23 (June 1970): 330-31.

Clements, Ronald E. Review of *The New English Bible. Church Quarterly Review* 2 (April 1970): 335-38.

Clines, D. J. A. Review of *The New English Bible. Evangelical Quarterly* 42 (July-September 1970): 168-75.

_____. Review of *The New English Bible: Old Testament. Theological Students Fellowship Bulletin* 58 (Autumn 1970): 6-9.

Colwell, Ernest C. "The English Bible." *Religion in Life* 31 (Spring 1962): 294-303.

Corbishley, T. Review of *The New English Bible. Month* 1 (April 1970): 255.

Crim, Keith R. "The New English Bible." *The Bible Translator* 21 (July 1970): 149-54.

Crotty, Robert. "N.E.B.: The Books of Samuel." *Australian Biblical Review* 18 (October 1970): 16-20.

Cruttwell, Patrick. "Fresh Skins for New Wine." *Hudson Review* 23 (Autumn 1970): 546-56.

Dahood, Mitchell. Review of *The New English Bible: Old Testament, Apocrypha. Biblica* 52 (Fas. 1, 1971): 117-23.

Daiches, David. "Translating the Bible." *Commentary* 49 (May 1970): 59-68.

Daly, R. J. Review of *The New English Bible. New Testament Abstracts* 6 (Fall 1961): 116.

Danker, Frederick W. "The New English Bible." *Concordia Theological Monthly* 32 (June 1961): 334-47.

————. Review of *The Greek New Testament. Being the Text Translated in the New English Bible*, by R. V. G. Tasker. *Concordia Theological Monthly* 37 (November 1966): 681-82.

Davidson, Robert. Review of *The New English Bible: Old Testament, Apocrypha, New Testament. Scottish Journal of Theology* 23 (May 1970): 231-36.

Davies, Paul E. "Great Britain's New Translation." *Interpretation* 15 (July 1961): 339-44.

Degabriele, Victor. Review of *The New English Bible. Cross and Crown* 23 (June 1971): 232.

Demaray, Donald E. "The New English Bible with the Apocrypha." *Asbury Seminarian* 25 (April 1971): 44.

"Designing and Producing the New English Bible." *Publisher's Weekly* 197 (March 9, 1970): 74.

Dodd, C. H. "Revision to the New Bible." *Times Literary Supplement* 69 (December 25, 1970): 1511-12.

————. "The Translation of the Bible: Some Questions of Principle." *The Bible Translator* 11 (January 1960): 4-9.

Dollen, C. Review of *The New English Bible. Priest* 26 (April 1970): 68.

Driver, G. R. "The New English Bible: The Old Testament." *Journal of Jewish Studies* 24 (Spring 1973): 1-7.

Duncan, G. S. "How the English Bible Was Made." *London Quarterly & Holborn Review* 186 (April 1961): 108-13.

Eppstein, Victor. "The New English Bible." *Midstream* 16 (October 1970): 50-66.

Evenson, George O. "'Righteousness' in the New English Bible." *The Lutheran Quarterly* 16 (November 1964): 349-53.

Filson, Floyd V. "New English Bible." *Episcopalian* 135 (April 1970): 13.

————. "The New English Bible." *Presbyterian Life* 23 (March 15, 1970): 20.

Gaebelin, Paul W., Jr. "N.E.B. 'Ifs' and 'Ands.'" *Christianity Today* 14 (May 8, 1970): 741.

Garrard, L. A. "The New English Bible: New Testament." *The Hibbert Journal* 59 (July 1961): 371-73.

Garton, C. "The New English Bible." *Durham University Journal* 55, 1 (1962): 23-31.

Gaumer, Tom. "An Examination of Some Western Textual Variants Adopted in the Greek Text of the New English Bible." *The Bible Translator* 16 (October 1965): 184-89.

Giblin, Charles H. Review of *The New English Bible with the Apocrypha*. *Thought* 45 (Winter 1970): 629.

Gibson, Arthur. "Ṣnḥ in Judges 1:14; NEB and AV Translations." *Vetus Testamentum* 26 (July 1976): 275-83.

Glenn, D. R. Review of *The New English Bible with the Apocrypha*. *Bibliotheca Sacra* 127 (October 1970): 353-54.

Goetchius, Eugene Van Ness. Review of *The Greek Testament: Being the Text Translated in the New English Bible*, by R. V. G. Tasker. *Anglican Theological Review* 47 (July 1965): 330-31.

_____. "Review Article: The New English Bible." *Anglican Theological Review* 52 (July 1970): 167-76.

Gordon, Cyrus H. "The New English Bible Old Testament." *Christianity Today* 14 (March 27, 1970): 574-76.

Gordon, Robert P. "The Citation of the Targums in Recent English Translations (RSV, JB, NEB)." *Journal of Jewish Studies* 26 (Spring, Autumn 1975): 50-60.

Grant, Frederick C. "The New English Bible: New Testament." *Journal of Biblical Literature* 80 (June 1961): 173-76.

Grant, Robert M. Review of *The New English Bible*, 1970. *The New York Times Book Review* (March 15, 1970): 8, 38.

Grayston, Kenneth. "Religious Values of the New Version." *London Quarterly & Holborn Review* 186 (April 1961): 113-18.

Gregory, T. S. "The New English Bible." *Tablet* 224 (March 21, 1970): 281.

Gundry, Robert H. "'Ecstatic Utterance' (N.E.B.)?" *Journal of Theological Studies* 17 (October 1966): 299-307.

Hale, William Harlan. "To Me, It Sounds Like Newspeak." *Horizon* 3 (March 1961): 97.

Harrington, W. Review of *The New English Bible*. *Furrow* 13 (January 1962): 40-44.

Harvey, A. E. *The New English Bible Companion to the New Testament*. Oxford: Oxford University Press and Cambridge University Press, 1970.

Hayden, E. W. "I Have Read the NEB." *Evangelical Christian* (September 1963): 12.

Hibbitts, J. B. "The New English Bible: New Testament." *Canadian Journal of Theology* 7 (October 1961): 286-90.

Higgins, A. J. B. "N.E.B. Greek Text." *Church Quarterly Review* 166 (January-March 1965): 108-9.

Hobbs, Edward C. Review of *The New English Bible: New Testament*. *Anglican Theological Review* 48 (October 1961): 413-15.

Hodges, Zane C. Review of *The New English Bible: New Testament*. *Bibliotheca Sacra* 118 (October 1961): 351-54.

Holwerda, David E. "New English Bible: A Review." *Banner* 110 (June 20, 1975): 4-5; (June 27, 1975): 4-5.

Howes, John. "The English of the New English Bible." *Frontier* 5 (Summer 1962): 429-33.

Hubbard, David A. "A Lucid and Powerful Translation." *Eternity* 21 (April 1970): 54-55.

Hughes, P. E. "Review of Current Religious Thought." *Christianity Today* 5 (May 22, 1961): 752.

Hunt, Geoffrey. *About the New English Bible*. New York: Oxford University Press and Cambridge University Press, 1970.

Hunt, G. N. S. "The NEB New Testament and Problems of Liturgy." *Studia Evangelica* 3 (1964): 236-45.

Johnston, L. Review of *The New English Bible*. *Tablet* 215 (March 18, 1961): 250.

Jones, Alex. "The New English Version of the N.T." *Scripture* 13 (July 1961): 65-74.

Kay, J. Alan. "The Authorized Version and the New English Bible." *London Quarterly & Holborn Review* 186 (April 1961): 79-83.

Kennedy, Gerald. *The Preacher and the New English Bible*. New York: Oxford University Press, 1972.

Kent, Homer A., Jr. Review of *The New English Bible: New Testament*. *Grace Journal* 2 (Spring 1961): 33-36.

Kerr, Hugh T. "Theological Table Talk: The N.E.B." *Theology Today* 18 (October 1961): 344-45.

Klijn, A. F. J. Review of *The Greek New Testament*, by R. V. G. Tasker. *New Testament Studies* 11 (January 1965): 184-85.

Kraus, C. Norman. Review of *The New English Bible*. *Mennonite Quarterly Review* 45 (October 1971): 390-91.

Krodel, G. H. "The Greek New Testament, Being the Text Translated in the New English Bible." *Lutheran Quarterly* 17 (February 1965): 85-86.

Kubo, Sakae. "Nature and Quality of the Text of the New English Bible." *Andrews University Seminary Studies* 5 (July 1967): 131-57.

Kuhn, Harold B. "The New English Bible with the Apocrypha." *The Asbury Seminarian* 24 (April 1970): 33-34.

"Language in the New Bible." *The Times Literary Supplement* 3082 (March 24, 1961): 184-85.

Lawrence, Ralph. "Reflections on the New English Bible." *English* 13 (Summer 1961): 178-80.

Lewis, Jack P. "The New English Bible." *Firm Foundation* 87 (May 19-26, 1970): 312, 313, 315, 326, 332.

————. "The New English Bible." *20th Century Christian* 34 (March 1972): 36-39.

Lloyd, G. G. "The New English Bible." *Japan Christian Quarterly* 27 (October 1961): 282-84.

Lucas, F. L. "The Greek 'Word' Was Different." *The Saturday Review of Literature* 44 (April 1, 1961): 12-14.

McCaughey, J. D. "The Epistles of Paul: Some Notes on the Translation of *dikaiosyne* and *dikaioun*." *Australian Biblical Review* 9 (November 1961): 18-23.

MacIntosh, A. A.; Stanton, Graham; and Frost, David L. "The 'New English Bible' Reviewed." *Theology* 74 (April 1971): 154-66.

McKenzie, John L. Review of *The New English Bible*. *Critic* 19 (May 1961): 59.

McNaspy, C. Review of *The New English Bible*. *America* 122 (April 27, 1970): 455.

Mann, C. S. *The New English New Testament: An Introduction*. London: The Faith Press, 1961.

Martindale, C. C. Review of *The New English Bible*. *Month* 25 (June 1961): 369.

Metzger, Bruce M. "Four English Translations of the New Testament." *Christianity Today* 8 (November 22, 1963): 168-72.

————. "How Good Is the New English Bible?" *Eternity* 12 (April 1961): 42-48.

————. "The New English Bible." *The Princeton Seminary Bulletin* 55 (September 1961): 56-63.

————. "The New English Bible, 1970." *Princeton Seminary Bulletin* 63 (March 1970): 99-104.

————Review of *The New English Bible*. *Interpretation* 24 (July 1970): 375-78.

Meyer, William F. "The New English Bible: Old Testament." *Springfielder* 34 (June 1970): 51-55.

Mickelson, Berkeley. Review of *The New English Bible: New Testament*. *United Evangelical Action* 20 (April 1961): 27.

Milner-White, E. M. "New Joint Translation of the Bible." *Church Quarterly Review* 160 (July-September 1959): 293-301.

Mitton, C. L. "The N.E.B." *The Expository Times* 72 (April 1961): 206-7.

Moir, Ian A. Review of *The Greek New Testament*, edited with introduction, textual notes, and appendix by R. V. G. Tasker. *The Bible Translator* 16 (January 1965): 49-51.

————. Review of *The Greek New Testament*, edited with introduction, textual notes, and appendix by R. V. G. Tasker. *Scottish Journal of Theology* 18 (June 1965): 242-44.

Moser, M. L., Jr. *The New English Bible: Satan's Polluted Translation*. Little Rock, Arkansas: Challenge Press, 1971.

Moss, John. "I Corinthians xiii. 13." *The Expository Times* 73 (May 1962): 253.

433

Murphy, Roland E. Review of *The New English Bible with the Apocrypha*. *Theological Studies* 31 (June 1970): 320-21.

Murray, Robert. "The N.E.B. (1970)." *Heythrop Journal* 11 (July 1970): 298-303.

"New Bible's Debut to Climax 13-Year Effort." *Christianity Today* 5 (January 30, 1961): 365-66.

"The New English Bible." *The Living Church* 160 (April 19, 1970): 15.

"The New English Bible." *Modern Churchman* 4 (April 1961): 150-52.

"The New English Bible: Back to Beginnings." *Time* 95 (March 23, 1970): 56-57.

"The New English Bible: The First Four Years." *The Times* (London) *Literary Supplement*, No. 3288, March 4, 1965, p. 182.

The New English Bible. New Testament. Evangelical Quarterly 33 (April-June 1961): 112-16.

"New English Bible: On Its Way to Best-Seller Lists." *U.S. News & World Report* 68 (April 6, 1970): 34-35.

"The New English Bible: Text and Meaning." *The Times Literary Supplement* 3082 (March 24, 1961): 177-78.

Newton, W. Review of *The New English Bible. Priest* 17 (May 1961): 400-4.

Nineham, Dennis, ed. *The New English Bible Reviewed*. London: Epworth Press, 1965.

Northcott, Cecil. "A Sharp Sword of the Lord." *Christian Century* 78 (March 15, 1961): 320-21.

"On Translating the Bible." *The Times* (London) *Literary Supplement*, Religious Books Section 3077, February 17, 1961, p. iv.

O'Neill, J. C. "Ephesians and First Timothy." *Australian Biblical Review* 9 (November 1961): 13-17.

Osborn, E. F. "The Fourth Gospel." *Australian Biblical Review* 9 (November 1961): 23-32.

Osterle, W. Review of *The New English Bible. Best Sellers* 30 (April 15, 1970): 21.

Patterson, D. "On Translating the Bible." *Jewish Heritage* 14 (Fall and Winter 1972): 46-50.

Payne, D. F. "The New English Old Testament." *The Churchman* 84 (Summer 1970): 109-14.

_____. "Review of the New English Bible Old Testament." *Biblical Theology* 20 (May 1970): 30-32.

Perry, Victor. "Two Modern Versions Compared." *Evangelical Quarterly* 49 (October-December 1977): 206-19.

Petersen, Lorman M. Review of *The New English Bible: New Testament. The Springfielder* 25 (Spring 1961): 65-67.

Petrie, C. S. Review of *The New English Bible: New Testament. Reformed Theological Review* 20 (June 1961): 57-58.

Pfeiffer, Charles F. Review of *The New English Bible: The Old Testament. Christianity Today* 14 (March 27, 1970): 581-84.

"A Readable Bible." *Newsweek* 75 (March 23, 1970): 113-14.

Reardon, Bernard M. G. "The New English Bible." *The Quarterly Review* 299 (October 1961): 422-28.

Reid, John K. S. "Concerning the New Translation of the Bible." *The Expository Times* 63 (September-October 1952): 172-76.

_____. "Concerning the New Translation of the Bible in Great Britain." *Religious Education* 48 (March 1953): 101-7.

_____. "The New English Bible." *Biblical Theology* 20 (May 1970): 25-29.

Reumann, John. Review of *The Greek New Testament*, edited with introduction, textual notes, and appendix by R. V. G. Tasker. *Journal of Biblical Literature* 84 (March 1965): 100-1.

Rexroth, Kenneth. Review of *The New English Bible: The New Testament. Nation* 92 (April 8, 1961): 307-8.

Rhodes, Erroll F. "Text of the New Testament in the Jerusalem and New English Bibles." *The Catholic Biblical Quarterly* 32 (January 1970): 42-57.

Rice, Gene. "Isaiah 28:1-22 and the New English Bible." *The Journal of Religious Thought* 30 (Fall-Winter 1973-74): 13-17.

Robb, J. D. " 'Who Is to Come'—N.E.B." *Expository Times* 73 (August 1962): 338-39.

Roberts, J. W. "The New English Bible and Acts 20:7." *Restoration Review* 17 (First Quarter 1974): 61-64.

Robertson, E. H. "The Bible of the English-Speaking World: 1949-1969." *The Expository Times* 81 (January 1970): 100-4.

_____. "N.E.B. 1970." *Expository Times* 81 (April 1970): 203-4.

Robertson, James D. "The New English Bible: New Testament." *The Asbury Seminarian* 15 (Spring-Summer 1961): 55-58.

Robinson, John A. T. "New English Bible." *Times* (London) *Educational Supplement* 2391, March 17, 1961, p. 519.

Robinson, T. H. "A New Translation of the English Bible." *The Bible Translator* 2 (October 1951): 167-68.

Rosseau, Richard W. Review of *The New English Bible. Thought* 37 (Spring 1962): 154-56.

Ryan, Dermot. "New Translations of the Bible." *Scripture Bulletin* 2 (July 1970): 77-81.

Salom, A. P. "The NEB Translation of 1 Thessalonians." *Andrews University Seminary Studies* 1 (1963): 91-104.

Sanders, J. A. "The New English Bible: A Comparison." *The Christian Century* 87 (March 1970): 326-28.

Sauer, Alfred von Rohr, and Danker, Frederick W. "A Look at the N.E.B.—OT." *Concordia Theological Monthly* 41 (September 1970): 491-507.

Shelly, M. "Reads Good as the Good Book Should." *Mennonite* (March 17, 1970): 183.

Sheriffs, R. J. A. "A Note on a Verse in the New English Bible." *Evangelical Quarterly* 34 (April-June 1962): 91-95.

Sikes, Walter W. "The Word of God in the Words of Men: Some Observations on the New English Bible." *Encounter* 22 (Autumn 1961): 473-77.

Skilton, John H. "The New English Bible: New Testament." *Westminster Theological Journal* 25 (November 1961): 70-79.

Smalley, William A. "Phillips and the New English Bible: Some Comments on Style." *The Bible Translator* 16 (October 1965): 165-70.

Smith, R. L. Review of *The New English Bible*. *Southwestern Journal of Theology* 13 (Fall 1970): 85.

Smyth, K. Review of *The New English Bible*. *Studies* 50 (Fall 1961): 343.

Stanley, D. Review of *The New English Bible*. *Catholic Messenger* 79 (June 15, 1961): 11.

Stendahl, Krister. "Distance and Proximity: Reflections on the New English Bible." *Harvard University Divinity School Bulletin* 27 (October 1962): 25-30.

Storman, E. J. "The Synoptic Gospels." *Australian Biblical Review* 9 (November 1961): 4-10.

The Story of the New English Bible. New York/Toronto: Oxford University Press and Cambridge University Press, 1970.

Stuhlmueller, Carroll. "The Bible in English." *The Bible Today* 55 (October 1971): 458-74.

Summers, Ray P. Review of *The New English Bible: New Testament*. *The Review and Expositor* 58 (April 1961): 233-37.

Swaim, J. Carter. "The Newest New Testament." *Christian Century* 78 (March 15, 1961): 322-26.

————. Review of *The New English Bible with the Apocrypha*. *Journal of Ecumenical Studies* 7 (Fall 1970): 823-24.

Tait, R. C. Review of *The New English Bible with the Apocrypha*. *The Modern Churchman* n.s. 14 (January 1971): 169-70.

Tasker, R. V. G. *The Greek New Testament: Being the Text Translated in the New English Bible, 1961*. London: Oxford University Press and Cambridge University Press, 1964.

Tate, Marvin E. "The Oxford Study Edition of the New English Bible with Apocrypha." *The Review and Expositor* 76 (Summer 1979): 325-39.

Taylor, Charles L. "The New English Bible Translation of Psalms." *Anglican Theological Review* 54 (1972): 194-205.

Terrien, Samuel. "The New English Bible with the Apocrypha." *Union Seminary Quarterly Review* 25 (Summer 1969-70): 549-55.

Thomas, R. L. "Philosophy of Translation and the New English Bible." *Bulletin of the Evangelical Theological Society* 5 (Summer 1962): 80-89.

Thorman, D. Review of *The New English Bible*. *National Catholic Reporter Supplement* 6 (April 17, 1970): 12.

Throckmorton, Burton H., Jr. "Judging on the Merits: A Criticism of J. Carter Swaim's Treatment of the New English Bible." *Christian Century* 78 (May 24, 1961): 656-57.

————. "The New English Bible." *Journal of Bible and Religion* 29 (July 1961): 193-203.

Turner, George A. Review of *The New English Bible. The New Testament*. *The Asbury Seminarian* 15 (Spring-Summer 1961): 55-58.

VandenBerge, Peter N. "After One Year—An Appraisal of the New English Bible." *Reformed Review* 15 (May 1962): 29-38.

Vawter, Bruce. Review of *The New English Bible with the Apocrypha. The Catholic Biblical Quarterly* 32 (July 1970): 426-28.

Volckaert, J. K. "The New English Bible." *Clergy Monthly* 34 (September 1970): 360-66.

Wand, J. W. C. "Editorial." *Church Quarterly Review* 162 (July-September 1961): 265-67.

Warne, Nicholas. "The Book of Revelation." *Australian Biblical Review* 9 (November 1961): 32-36.

————. "N.E.B.: The Psalms." *Australian Biblical Review* 18 (October 1970): 25-30.

Waterman, G. "The New English Bible." *Alliance-Witness* (March 18, 1970): 14.

Welby, James F. "The New English Bible: New Testament." *Dunwoodie Review* 2 (January 1962): 86-90.

Wiend, David J. "The New English Bible." *Messenger* (May 21, 1970): 10.

Wikgren, Allen. Review of *The New English Bible, New Testament. The Journal of Religion* 41 (July 1961): 226-27.

Wilcox, Max. "The Acts of the Apostles." *Australian Biblical Review* 9 (November 1961): 10-13.

Williams, Alwyn T. P. "The English of the New Translation." *London Quarterly and Holborn Review* 186 (April 1961): 118-22.

Wills, G. Review of *The New English Bible. The National Review* 10 (May 6, 1961): 284.

Wrenn, C. "The NEB: The N.T. Reconsidered." *Studia Evangelica* 3 (1964): 289-96.

Wright, E. Review of *The New English Bible. National Catholic Reporter* 6 (March 11, 1970): 4.

New American Standard Bible

Barabas, Steven. Review of *The New American Standard Bible. Christian Life* 33 (September 1971): 22, 26.

Bechtel, Paul, and Bechtel, Mary. Review of *The New American Standard Bible: New Testament. Christian Life* 25 (April 1964): 74.

Bennett, Lorraine. "Foundation Rests on the Bible." *Los Angeles Times*, 16 May 1977, sec. 5, pp. 1, 4, 5.

Bratcher, Robert G. "Old Wine in New Bottles." *Christianity Today* 16 (October 8, 1971): 16-19.

_____. Review of *New American Standard Bible New Testament. Eternity* 15 (June 1964): 43-45.

_____. Review of *New American Standard Gospel of John. The Bible Translator* 13 (October 1962): 234-36.

Calverley, Edwin E. "The New American Standard Bible: New Testament." *Muslim World* 55 (October 1965): 396-97.

Culpepper, R. Alan. "The New American Standard Bible." *Review and Expositor* 76 (Summer 1979): 351-61.

Danker, Frederick W. "Another Parallel-Column Bible." *Concordia Theological Monthly* 39 (April 1968): 273-75.

Dolak, George. Review of *The Four Translation New Testament. Springfielder* 31 (Autumn 1967): 59-61.

Epp. Theodore H. "An Excellent Translation." *Good News Broadcaster* 30 (January 1972): 2-3.

Fee, Gordon D. "Text of the New Testament and Modern Translations." *Christianity Today* 17 (June 22, 1973): 982-87.

Gerlack, Joel C. "Update on Bible Translations." *Wisconsin Lutheran Quarterly* 69 (April 1972): 80-85.

Goldberg, Louis. "The Enduring Rock of Biblical Honesty." *Moody Monthly* 72 (January 1972): 64-67.

Hodges, Zane C. Review of *The New American Standard Bible —New Testament. Bibliotheca Sacra* 121 (July-September 1964): 267-68.

Lane, William L. "The New American Standard Bible —New Testament." *New Testament Abstracts* 11 (Winter 1966): 183.

_____. Review of *The New American Standard Bible —New Testament. Gordon Review* 9 (Spring 1966): 154-70.

Lewis, Jack P. "The New American Standard Bible." In *The Inspiration and Authority of the Bible*, pp. 90-105. Edited by W. B. West, Jr., Bill Flatt, and Thomas B. Warren. Nashville: Gospel Advocate Company, 1971.

438

Lightfoot, Neil R. "Two Translations: A Study in Translation Principle." *Restoration Quarterly* 11 (2d Quarter 1968): 89-100.

New American Standard Bible: Translation and Format Facts. La Habra, Calif.: Lockman Foundation, n.d.

Panning, Armin. "The New American Standard Bible: Is This the Answer?" *Wisconsin Lutheran Quarterly* 70 (January 1973): 6-32.

Review of *The Four Translation New Testament*. *Evangelical Quarterly* 38 (July-September 1966): 184.

Smith, Wilbur M. "The Best of All the Recent Translations of the Bible." *Moody Monthly* 64 (July-August 1964): 13-15.

Stagg, Frank. "The Four Translation New Testament." *Review and Expositor* 64 (Winter 1967): 84-85.

Turner, George A. Review of *The New American Standard Bible*. *Asbury Seminarian* 28 (January 1973): 38-39.

The Jerusalem Bible

Archer, Gleason L. Review of *The Old Testament of The Jerusalem Bible*. *Westminster Theological Journal* 33 (May 1971): 191-94.

Avery, Benedict R. Review of *La Bible de Jerusalem*. *Worship* 32 (December 1957): 30-31.

Baker, John. Review of *The Jerusalem Bible*. *Heythrop Journal* 8 (October 1967): 413-16.

Barrois, Georges A. "Reflections on Two French Bibles." *Theology Today* 15 (July 1958): 211-16.

Benoit, Pierre. "The Jerusalem Bible." *Review and Expositor* 76 (Summer 1979): 341-49.

Brennan, James. "The Jerusalem Bible." *The Irish Ecclesiastical Record*, 5th ser., 107 (May 1967): 319-26.

Child, R. L. Review of *The Jerusalem Bible*. *The Baptist Quarterly* 22 (July 1967): 186-88.

"Curt, Clear, Complete: Jones's Jerusalem Bible." *Time* 88 (November 4, 1966): 53-54.

Danker, Frederick W. "The Jerusalem Bible: A Critical Examination." *Concordia Theological Monthly* 38 (March 1967): 168-80.

De Vault, Joseph J. Review of *The Jerusalem Bible*. *Review for Religious* 26 (March 1967): 364-65.

Dewitz, Ludwig R. M. Review of *The Old Testament of the Jerusalem Bible*. *Christianity Today* 14 (January 16, 1970): 350-52.

Dierickx, J. "Attitudes in Translations: Some Linguistic Features of the Jerusalem Bible." *English Studies* 50 (February 1969): 10-20.

Di Lella, Alexander A. Review of *The Jerusalem Bible*. *Catholic Biblical Quarterly* 29 (January 1967): 148-51.

Dunstan, G. R. Review of *The Jerusalem Bible*. *Theology* 69 (December 1966): 529-30.

Fee, Gordon D. "The Text of John in the Jerusalem Bible: A Critique of the Use of Patristic Citations in New Testament Textual Criticism." *Journal of Biblical Literature* 90 (June 1971): 163-73.

Fitzmyer, Joseph A. Review of *The Jerusalem Bible*. *Theological Studies* 28 (March 1967): 129-31.

Flack, Elmer E. Review of *The Jerusalem Bible*. *Lutheran Quarterly* 19 (May 1967): 202-3.

Frost, David L., and MacIntosh, A. A. Review of *The Jerusalem Bible: The Psalms for Reading and Recitation*. *Theology* 73 (January 1970): 33-36.

Glenn, D. R. Review of *The Old Testament of the Jerusalem Bible*. *Bibliotheca Sacra* 127 (October-December 1970): 354.

Gold, Victor R. Review of *The Jerusalem Bible*. *Lutheran World* 15 (1968): 354.

Gordon, Robert P. "The Citation of the Targums in Recent Bible Translations (RSV, JB, NEB)." *Journal of Jewish Studies* 26 (Spring-Autumn 1975): 50-60.

Grant, Frederick C. Review of *The Jerusalem Bible*. *Journal of Biblical Literature* 86 (March 1967): 91-93.

Harrington, W. J. Review of *La Bible de Jerusalem*. *Revue Biblique* 75 (July 1968): 450-52.

Herbert, Arthur S. Review of *The Jerusalem Bible*. *The Bible Translator* 18 (April 1967): 95-97.

Hughes, Philip E. Review of *The Jerusalem Bible*. *The Churchman* 81 (Summer 1967): 134.

Hunt, Ignatius. "The Jerusalem Bible in English." *Herder Correspondence* 3 (November 1966): 328B-328F.

Johnston, L. Review of *The Jerusalem Bible*. *Tablet* 220 (October 22, 1966): 1182.

Jones, Alexander. "The Jerusalem Bible." *Jubilee* 14 (December 1966): 34-39.

Kuyper, Lester J., and Oudersluys, Richard C. Review of *The Jerusalem Bible*. *Reformed Review* 21 (December 1967): 22-27.

Landes, George M. Review of *The Jerusalem Bible*. *Union Seminary Quarterly Review* 22 (March 1967): 280-83.

LaSor, William Sanford. Review of *The Jerusalem Bible*. *Eternity* 18 (June 1967): 41-43.

MacKenzie, R. A. F. *La Sainte Bible: Les Psaumes*. 2d ed. *Theological Studies* 17 (September 1956): 414-15.

McNamara, M. "The Jerusalem Bible." *Doctrine and Life* 16 (1966): 689-91.

McPolin, James. Review of *The Jerusalem Bible*. *Studies* 56 (1967): 310-15.

440

Metzger, Bruce M. "New Editions of Scripture: The Jerusalem Bible." *Princeton Seminary Bulletin* 60 (February 1967): 45-48.

Moriarty, Frederick L. Review of *The Jerusalem Bible. Thought* 42 (Spring 1967): 143-44.

Murray, A. Gregory. Review of *The Jerusalem Bible. Downside Review* 85 (January 1967): 90-93.

Murray, Robert. "The English 'Jerusalem Bible': Two Letters." *Heythrop Journal* 12 (January 1971): 61.

————. "The Jerusalem Bible." *The Clergy Review* 51 (December 1966): 924-31.

O'Grady, D. "The Jerusalem Bible and the Ecole Biblique." *U.S. Catholic and Jubilee* 34 (September 1968): 39-43.

Peerman, Dean. Review of *The Jerusalem Bible. Christian Century* 83 (November 2, 1966): 1343.

Peters, Paul W. "Variants of the Isaiah Scroll Adopted by the Revised Standard Version and the Jerusalem Bible." *Wisconsin Lutheran Quarterly* 71 (April 1974): 134-38; (July 1974): 209-23.

Quinn, Jerome D. Review of *The Jerusalem Bible. Worship* 40 (December 1966): 663.

Review of *The Jerusalem Bible. Month* n.s. 36 (November 1966): 231-32.

Review of *The Jerusalem Bible. Times Literary Supplement* no. 3382 (December 22, 1966): 1191.

Rhodes, Erroll F. "Text of New Testament in Jerusalem Bible and New English Bibles." *Catholic Biblical Quarterly* 32 (January 1970): 41-57.

Rhymer, Joseph, and Kilpatrick, G. D. "The Jerusalem Bible as a Translation." *Scripture Bulletin* 5 (Summer 1974): 4-6.

Rowley, H. H. "The Jerusalem Bible." *Expository Times* 66 (1954-55): 94.

Schoenberg, Martin W. Review of *The Jerusalem Bible. Homiletic and Pastoral Review* 67 (December 1966): 256-58.

Scobie, Charles H. H. "Two Recent New Testament Texts and Translations." *Canadian Journal of Theology* 14 (January 1968): 54-63.

Stamp, H. A. Review of *The Jerusalem Bible. Australian Biblical Review* 16 (October 1968): 54.

Van Buren, James G. "The Jerusalem Bible." *Christian Standard* 102 (April 1, 1967): 9-10.

Vawter, Bruce. "The Jerusalem Bible." *The Duke Divinity School Review* 44 (Spring 1979): 88-103.

Volckaert, J. Review of *The Jerusalem Bible. Eastern Churches Review* 1 (Winter 1967-68): 438-39.

Walker, Larry L. Review of *The Jerusalem Bible. Southwestern Journal of Theology* 11 (Fall 1968): 120.

Worden, T. Review of *The Jerusalem Bible. Scripture* 19 (January 1967): 1-2.

441

The New American Bible

Alden, Robert L. Review of *The New American Bible. Westminster Theological Journal* 34 (May 1972): 217-23.

Barr, James. "After Five Years: A Retrospect on Two Major Translations of the Bible." *Heythrop Journal* 15 (October 1974): 381-405.

"Catholics Replace Douay with New American Bible." *Publisher's Weekly* 198 (September 7, 1970): 37.

Clifford, Richard. "The New American Bible." *America* 123 (November 21, 1970): 435-36.

Crim, Keith R. Review of *The New American Bible. The Bible Translator* 23 (October 1972): 444-48.

_____. Review of *The New American Bible. Interpretation* 26 (January 1972): 77-80.

Danker, Frederick W. Review of *The New American Bible. Catholic Biblical Quarterly* 33 (July 1971): 405-9.

Harrelson, Walter. "The New American Bible." *The Duke Divinity School Review* 44 (Spring 1979): 124-36.

Jackman, Edward. Review of *The New American Bible. Cross and Crown* 23 (June 1971): 233-35.

Maly, E. "The New American Bible." *The Priest* 27 (March 1971): 57-59.

_____. "The New American Bible; Interview by G. Kramer." *Religion Teacher's Journal* 5 (February 1971): 3-5.

Manz, J. "The New American Bible." *Lutheran Witness* 90 (April 1971): 14.

Metzger, Bruce M. "The New American Bible, 1970." *The Princeton Seminary Bulletin* 64 (March 1971): 90-99.

"The New American Bible." *Christianity Today* 15 (October 23, 1970): 83.

"New Bible for Catholics." *Time* 96 (October 12, 1970): 58-59.

Peifer, Claude J. "The New American Bible." *Worship* 45 (February 1971): 102-13.

Reumann, John. Review of *The New American Bible. Journal of Biblical Literature* 92 (June 1973): 275-78.

Sabourin, L. Review of *The New American Bible. Biblical Theology Bulletin* 2 (July 1972): 206-8.

Shea, T. "A New American Bible; Condensed from *The National Observer*, September 28, 1970." *Catholic Digest* 35 (January 1971): 23-26.

Sloyan, Gerard S. "The New American Bible." *Living Light* 7 (Fall 1970): 87-104.

Stagg, Frank. Review of *The New American Bible. Review and Expositor* 68 (Summer 1971): 400-2.

Stuhlmueller, Carroll. "The Bible in English." *The Bible Today* 55 (October 1971): 458-74.

The New World Translation

Austin, J. S. "Question and Answer." *Scripture* 11 (April 1959): 59-61.

Barnett, Maurice. "The Jehovah's Witness Translation." *Searching the Scriptures* 10 (July 1969): 311-13; (October 1969): 356-57.

"Basis for the New World Translation." *The Watchtower* 91 (December 15, 1970): 759-62.

Byington, Steven T. "Jehovah's Witnesses' Version of O.T." *Christian Century* 70 (October 7, 1953): 1133-34.

_____. Review of *New World Translation of the Greek Scriptures. Christian Century* 67 (November 1950): 1295-96.

_____. Review of *New World Translation of the Hebrew Scriptures. Vol. II. Christian Century* 72 (October 5, 1955): 1146.

Countess, Robert H. "*The New World Translation*: A Critical Analysis." Ph.D dissertation, Bob Jones University, 1966.

_____. "The Translation of *Theos* in the New World Translation." *Bulletin of the Evangelical Theological Society* 10 (Summer 1967): 153-60.

Gruenthaner, Michael J. "Jehovah's Witnesses Translate the New Testament." *Catholic Biblical Quarterly* 13 (January 1951): 105.

Gruss, Edmond C. "The New World Translation of the Holy Scriptures." *The Bible Collector* 7 (July-December 1971): 3-8.

Haas, Samuel S. Review of *New World Translation of the Hebrew Scriptures. Journal of Biblical Literature* 74 (December 1955): 282-83.

Heydt, Henry J. *Jehovah's Witnesses: Their Translation*. New York: American Board of Missions to the Jews, n.d.

Lewis, Jack P. "The New World Translation of the Holy Scriptures." *The Spiritual Sword* 6 (October 1974): 32-36.

Light, Dennis W. "Some Observations on the New World Translation." *The Bible Collector* 7 (July-December 1971): 8-10.

McCoy, Robert M. "Jehovah's Witnesses and their New Translation." *Andover Newton Quarterly* 3 (January 1963): 15-31.

Mattingly, John F. "Jehovah's Witnesses Translate the New Testament." *Catholic Biblical Quarterly* 13 (October 1951): 439-43.

Metzger, Bruce M. "Jehovah's Witnesses and Jesus Christ." *Theology Today* 10 (April 1954): 65-85.

_____. Review of *New World Translation of the Christian Greek Scriptures. The Bible Translator* 15 (July 1964): 150-52.

_____. Review of *New World Translation of the Hebrew Scriptures. Evangelical Quarterly* 26 (January 1954): 59-60.

Rowley, H. H. "How Not to Translate the Bible." *Expository Times* 65 (November 1953): 41-42.

443

_____. "Jehovah's Witnesses' Translation of the Bible." *Expository Times* 67 (January 1956): 107-8.

Stedman, Ray C. "The New World Translation of the Christian Scriptures." *Our Hope* 50 (July 1953): 30.

Sturz, Harry A. "Observations on the New World Translation." *The Bible Collector* 7 (July-December 1971): 11-16.

Swartz, Frank. *A Close Look at the Jehovah's Witness Bible.* Little Rock, Ark.: Challenge Press, 1974.

Wright, Gerald N. *Perversions and Prejudices of the New World Translation.* Fort Worth: Star Bible and Tract Corporation, 1975.

Yankaya, Annis R. *The New World Translation: Version or Perversion?* Singapore: World Literature Publications, 1978.

The Living Bible Paraphrased

Ackroyd, Peter R. Review of *The Living Bible Paraphrased.* In *Bible Bibliography 1967-1973.* Edited by Peter R. Ackroyd (Oxford: Basil Blackwell, 1974), p. 451.

Bennett, Mabel. "The Living Bible." *Scripture Bulletin* 7 (Summer 1976): 1-2.

Bowman, Robert C. "The Living Bible—A Critique." *Brethren Life and Thought* 18 (Summer 1973): 137-42.

Boyd, James W. "The Living Bible and Today's English Version." In *The Church Today,* pp. 155-57. Edited by William Woodson. Nashville: Gospel Advocate Company, 1975.

Bratcher, Robert G. Review of *The Living New Testament Paraphrased.* *The Bible Translator* 20 (July 1969): 36-39.

Clifford, R. J. Review of *The Living Bible.* *America* 125 (November 27, 1971): 460.

Crim, Keith R. Review of *The Living Bible Paraphrased.* *The Bible Translator* 23 (July 1972): 340-44.

Douglas, J. D. "The Living Bible: For Children Only?" *Christianity Today* 23 (October 5, 1979): 1367, 1371.

Duncan, Clarence. "Growing Up with the Living Bible." *Crusader* 3 (July 1973): 14.

Ellington, John. "The Living Bible Examined." *Presbyterian Survey* 68 (October 1978): 9-11.

Garland, David E. "The Living Bible." *Review and Expositor* 76 (Summer 1979): 387-408.

Goff, Nathan W. Review of *Living Prophecies.* *Eternity* 17 (February 1966): 44.

Hitt, Russell T. Review of *The Living Bible Paraphrased.* *Eternity* 22 (December 1971): 48, 51.

Houston, Jack. "He Paraphrased the Bible." *Moody Monthly* 72 (November 1971): 28, 68, 69.

Interview With Kenneth N. Taylor. Wheaton, Illinois: Tyndale House Publishers, n.d.

444

"Ken Taylor: God's Voice in the Vernacular." An Interview by Harold Myra. *Christianity Today* 23 (October 5, 1979): 1307-11.

Kerr, William F. "*The Living Bible* — Not Just Another Version." *Christianity Today* 19 (May 23, 1975): 29-40.

Laing, Jonathan R. "*The Living Bible* Lives and Sells and Makes Kenneth Taylor Happy." *Wall Street Journal*, March 1, 1974, p. 1.

Lanier, Roy H., Sr. "The Living Bible Paraphrased." *Firm Foundation* 89 (May 30, 1972): 345.

Lewis, Jack P. Review of *The Living Bible Paraphrased*. *Christian Bible Teacher* 16 (August 1972): 328, 346, 347.

"Living Bible Paraphrased." *Banner* 107 (November 24, 1972): 6-8; (December 1, 1972): 8-9.

Merideth, J. Noel. "The Living Bible Paraphrased." *Gospel Advocate* 114 (September 14, 1972): 577, 583.

Michel, Don. "Miracle of the *Living Bible*." *Saturday Evening Post* 247 (April 1975): 58, 88, 114.

Moody, Dale. Review of *Would You Believe*, by Kenneth Taylor, Dave Grant, and Jack Weims. *Review and Expositor* 70 (Winter 1973): 103-4.

Moser, M. L. *A Critique of the Living Bible*. Little Rock, Arkansas: Challenge Press, 1973.

Mulcahy, F. "New Translations of the Bible." *Scripture Bulletin* 3 (Spring 1971): 4-5.

Nowlin, Gene. *The Paraphrase Perversion of the Bible*. Edited by W. A. Waite. Collingswood, N. J.: The Bible For Today, 1974.

Oostendorp, Elco H. "Arminianism in the Living Bible." *Banner* 109 (August 23, 1974): 16-17.

Owens, John Joseph. Review of *The Way*. *The Review and Expositor* 70 (Spring 1973): 240-41.

Plowman, Edward E. "The Living Bible: A Record." *Christianity Today* 15 (September 10, 1971): 1108.

"A Plowman's Bible?" *Time* 100 (July 24, 1972): 73.

Roth, Wolfgang. "The Living Bible — An Evangelical Paraphrase." *Explore* 2 (Fall 1976): 23-28.

Rowell, Edmon L., Jr. "What the Scripture Writers Meant." *Christian Century* 91 (November 20, 1974): 1104-6.

Rusch, Frederick A. "Living with the Living Bible." *Currents in Theology and Mission* 2 (October 1975): 277-83.

Sheridan, J. Mark. Review of *The Way: Catholic Edition*. *Catholic Biblical Quarterly* 36 (July 1974): 439-40.

445

Smalley, Stephen. "Living Letters: The Paraphrased Epistles." *The Churchman* 79 (December 1965): 298-99.

Smart, James D. "The Invented Bible." *Presbyterian Record* 100 (July-August 1976). Reprinted as "The Living Bible." *The Duke Divinity School Review* 44 (Spring 1979): 137-41.

"The Story of the Living Bible." *Eternity* 24 (April 1973): 64, 65, 74, 75.

Synodical Committee on Bible Translation. Review of *The Living Bible Paraphrased*. *Banner* 107 (November 24, 1972): 6-8; (December 1, 1972): 8-9.

Taylor, Kenneth N. "A Response: Dear Brother Editor." *Brethren Life and Thought* 18 (Summer 1973): 143-44.

"Updating the Bible: K. N. Taylor's Living Bible." *Newsweek* 78 (September 27, 1971): 102.

Waltke, Bruce K. Review of *Living Psalms and Proverbs with the Major Prophets Paraphrased*. *Bibliotheca Sacra* 125 (January 1968): 73-74.

"Which Bible Is Best for You?" *Eternity* 25 (April 1974): 27-31.

Good News Bible (Today's English Version)

"Annie Vallotton." *Bible Society Record* 113 (July-August 1968): 86.

Bankston, Benjamin A. "Goodwill Ambassador for Today's English Version." *Bible Society Record* 114 (October 1969): 150-52.

"Biggest ABS Paper Order Ever for TEV." *Bible Society Record* 112 (January 1967): 13.

Bivens, Marshall. "Today's English Version of the New Testament, Called Good News for Modern Man, Leaves Me with at Least 2 Points of Concern." *Christian Standard* 103 (February 24, 1968): 122.

Bratcher, Robert G. "Good News for Modern Man." *Bible Society Record* 111 (October 1966): 132-33.

_____. "Good News For Modern Man." *The Bible Translator* 17 (October 1966): 159-72.

_____. "Good News for Modern Man." *The Bible Translator* 18 (July 1967): 127-28.

_____. "Good News for Modern Man—Today's English Version." *Bulletin of the United Bible Societies* 70 (2d Quarter 1967): 52-54.

_____. "The Nature and Purpose of the New Testament in Today's English Version." *The Bible Translator* 22 (July 1971): 97-107.

_____. "The T.E.V. New Testament and the Greek Text." *The Bible Translator* 18 (October 1967): 167-74.

_____. "Translating the TEV New Testament." In *The New Testament Student and Bible Translation*, pp. 146-52. Edited by John H. Skilton. Phillipsburg, New Jersey: Presbyterian and Reformed Publishing Co., 1978.

Bullard, Roger A. "Sex-Oriented Language in TEV Proverbs." *The Bible Translator* 28 (April 1977): 243-45.

Butrim, C. "'Good News for Modern Man' Is Bad News for the Discerning Christian." *Baptist Bulletin* (September 1977): 10.

Coggan, F. D. Review of *Good News for Modern Man. The Church Quarterly* 1 (July 1968): 66-67.

Coogan, Michael D. Review of *Good News Bible: The Bible in Today's English Version. America* 136 (March 5, 1977): 196-97.

Dahood, Mitchell. Review of *Psalms for Modern Man. Catholic Biblical Quarterly* 34 (April 1972): 240-42.

Danker, Frederick W. Review of *Good News for Modern Man. Catholic Biblical Quarterly* 29 (April 1967): 257-58.

_____. Review of *Today's English Version of the New Testament. Concordia Theological Monthly* 39 (March 1968): 216.

Early, Tracy. "Good News from the Old Testament." *Christian Herald* 100 (February 1977): 4-6, 12, 14.

Ellingsworth, Paul. "Talking About Translations." *The Bible Translator* 23 (April 1972): 219-24.

_____. "Which Way Are We Going?" *The Bible Translator* 25 (October 1974): 426-31.

Fiske, Edward B. "New Testament Is Made Simpler." *The Bible Society Record* 111 (November 1966): 145-47.

"5,000,000 Have It! How About You?" *The Bible Society Record* 112 (October 1967): 125.

"Five Millionth TEV." *The Bible Society Record* 112 (December 1967): 149.

Fry, Euan. "The Good News Bible Translation Principles." *The Bible Translator* 28 (October 1977): 408-12.

Fueter, Paul D. "Dynamic Equivalent Interpretation." *The Bible Translator* 25 (July 1974): 344-51.

Fuller, R. C. "Today's Bible: An Assessment of the Complete Today's English Version." *Scripture Bulletin* 7 (Winter 1976-77): 26-28.

Garrison, W. "Good News for Modern Man." *Presbyterian Life* 22 (October 1, 1969): 9.

Glassman, Eugene H. "Letter to a Friend." *The Bible Translator* 28 (April 1977): 220-25.

"Good News for Indianapolis." *The Bible Society Record* 114 (September 1969): 128-30.

"Good or Bad?" *Banner* 106 (Nov. 26, 1971): 14; (Dec. 3, 1971): 14.

Graesser, Carl, Jr. Review of *The Psalms for Modern Man: Today's English Version. Concordia Theological Monthly* 42 (September 1971): 558-59.

Greenlee, J. Harold. "Good News for Moderns." Review of *Today's English Version of the New Testament. Christianity Today* 11 (December 23, 1966): 317-18.

447

Grether, Herbert G. "Some Problems of Equivalence in Amos 1:3." *The Bible Translator* 22 (July 1971): 116-17.

Hobbs, A. G. *What About "Today's English Version"?* Fort Worth, Texas: Hobbs Publications, 1968.

Hodges, Zane C. Review of *Good News For Modern Man. Bibliotheca Sacra* 126 (January-March 1969): 86-87.

Hull, William E. Review of *Good News For Modern Man. Review and Expositor* 64 (Fall 1967): 534-35.

Hutchinson, W. "The Good News Completed." *Christian Life* 38 (November 1976): 60.

Jackson, Jared Judd. Review of *The Psalms For Modern Man. Interpretation* 26 (January 1972): 95-96.

Johnson, Alan F. Review of *Good News for Modern Man: The New Testament in Today's English Version. Moody Monthly* 68 (July-August 1968): 49-50.

Jones, George E. "Another 'Readable' Bible, But Is It Any Better?" *U.S. News & World Report* 81 (December 20, 1976): 54-55.

Kinkaid, R. "Graphics Matter." *Bulletin of the United Bible Societies* 85 (First Quarter 1971): 31-32.

Legrand, L. "The Good News Bible. A Reaction from India." *The Bible Translator* 29 (July 1978): 331-36.

Lightfoot, Neil R. "Two Recent Translations: A Study in Translation Principle." *Restoration Quarterly* 11 (Second Quarter 1968): 89-100.

Lithgow, David. "Some Notes on the Use of Today's English Version as a Translation Source Text by Translators Who Speak English as a Second Language." *The Bible Translator* 27 (October 1976): 438-45.

Loke, Margarett. "Today's English Comes to the New Testament." *The Bible Society Record* 113 (March 1968): 40-41.

Loewen, Jacob A. "Why Bantu Translators Use the R.S.V. and the T.E.V. as Their Textual Base." *The Bible Translator* 25 (October 1974): 412-16.

McIntyre, J. Ainslie. Review of *The Good News Bible. Scottish Journal of Theology* 31 (1978): 190-91.

MacLennan, David A. *Preaching Values in Today's English Version*. Nashville: Abingdon Press, 1971.

McLester, Margaret W. "Why Another Translation?" *Presbyterian Journal* 37 (February 22, 1978): 7-9.

Maly, Eugene H. "Good News Bible." *The Bible Today* 89 (March 1977): 1177-82.

May, Herbert G. "Good News for All People Everywhere." *Interpretation* 32 (April 1978): 187-90.

Metzger, Bruce M. Review of *Good News For Modern Man: The New Testament in Today's English Version. Princeton Seminary Bulletin* 60 (February 1967): 67-68.

Moody, Dale. "The Good News Bible." *Review and Expositor* 76 (Summer 1979): 409-16.

Moulton, Harold K. Review of *The New Testament in Today's English Version*. 2d ed. *The Bible Translator* 19 (October 1968): 184-87.

"The Much-Quoted TEV." *American Bible Society Record* 115 (September 1970): 129.

Nettinga, James Z. "New Knowledge and the Bible." *The Link* 27 (October 1969): 26.

Nida, Eugene A. "Bible Translation in Today's World." *Bulletin of the United Bible Societies* 65 (First Quarter 1966): 22-27.

————. *Good News for Everyone*. Waco, Texas: Word Books, 1977.

Nixon, Robin E. "Good News Bible." *Churchman* 91 (January 1977): 3-4.

"1 Million TEV's in Atlanta." *The Bible Society Record* 112 (December 1967): 156.

Pack, Frank. "Today's English Version." *20th Century Christian* 34 (March 1972): 40-42.

Payne, D. F. Review of *The Good News Bible: Today's English Version*. *Evangelical Quarterly* 49 (July-September 1977): 180-83.

Perry, Victor. "Two Modern Versions Compared." *Evangelical Quarterly* 49 (October-December 1977): 206-19.

Phillips, J. B. Review of *Good News for Modern Man*. *The Bible Translator* 18 (April 1968): 99-100.

Prickett, Stephen. "What Do the Translators Think They Are Up To?" *Theology* 80 (November 1977): 403-10.

Reumann, John. Review of *Good News For Modern Man*. *Journal of Biblical Literature* 86 (June 1967): 234-36.

Rhys, Howard. Review of *The Good News Bible: Deuterocanonicals /Apocrypha*. *Saint Luke's Journal of Theology* 23 (December 1979): 76-77.

Rice, Charles L. Review of *Preaching Values in Today's English Version*. *American Bible Society Record* 117 (June-July 1972): 25.

Robertson, E. H. "The Bible of the English-Speaking World: 1949-1969." *The Expository Times* 81 (January 1970): 100-4.

Schiemann, Donald. "Another Translation: Another Disaster." *Concordia Theological Quarterly* 42 (April 1978): 167-69.

Scobie, Charles H. H. "Two Recent New Testament Texts and Translations." *Canadian Journal of Theology* 14 (January 1968): 54-63.

Skilton, John H. Review of *Today's English Version of the New Testament*. *Eternity* 18 (March 1967): 50-53.

Smalley, William A. "Translating Luke's Passion Story from the TEV." *The Bible Translator* 28 (April 1977): 231-35.

Stinespring, W. F. "Today's English Version or The Good News Bible." *The Duke Divinity School Review* 44 (Spring 1979): 142-63.

449

Stuhlmueller, Carroll. "Probings into the Mystery of the Text." *The Bible Today* 58 (February 1972): 657-61.

"Supermarket Has Bible 'Special.'" *The Bible Society Record* 113 (June 1968): 77.

Synodical Committee on Bible Translation. "The Good News Bible." *The Banner* 114 (July 20, 1979): 14-15; (July 27, 1979): 16-17.

Taber, Charles R. "Explicit and Implicit Information in Translation." *The Bible Translator* 21 (January 1970): 1-9.

"Talking Points from Books." *The Expository Times* 84 (February 1973): 130-32.

"The 10 Millionth TEV." *The Bible Society Record* 113 (July-August 1968): 87.

"TEV—Good News or Bad?" *American Bible Society Record* 118 (April 1973): 5-9.

"TEV Reactions." *The Bible Society Record* 112 (January 1967): 10-11.

"TEV Translator Honored." *The Bible Society Record* 112 (September 1967): 107.

Thomas, J. D. "Changes in the TEV." *Firm Foundation* 87 (November 3, 1970): 699.

————. "Changes in the TEV." *Gospel Advocate* 112 (November 19, 1970): 741.

————. "Meeting on the TEV." *Gospel Advocate* 111 (January 2, 1969): 7-8.

————. "Today's English Version." *Gospel Advocate* 108 (December 29, 1966): 820-21.

"Toward a Today's English Version Bible." *The Bible Society Record* 115 (March 1970): 42-43.

"Translator Bob Bratcher." *The American Bible Society Record* 116 (August-September 1971): 126-27.

Vallotton, Annie. "Bible Illustration as Interpretation." *The Bible Translator* 19 (January 1968): 28-29.

————. "An Illustrated Bible—Why and How?" *Bulletin of the United Bible Societies* 70 (2d Quarter 1967): 55-57.

VanderPloeg, J. P. M. "TEV—How Reliable Is It?" *The Banner* 105 (October 2, 1970): 8-9.

Williamson, Lamar, Jr. "Translations and Interpretation: New Testament." *Interpretation* 32 (April 1978): 158-70.

Wonderly, William L. *Bible Translations for Popular Use*. London: United Bible Societies, 1968.

————. "Some Principles of 'Common-Language' Translation." *The Bible Translator* 21 (July 1970): 126-37.

"Would You Believe? TEV Tops Lists." *The Bible Society Record* 113 (November 1968): 150.

Wright, Cecil N. "TEV and the Blood of Christ." *Gospel Advocate* 111 (May 1, 1969): 287-88.

Youngblood, Ronald F. "Good News for Modern Man: Becoming a Bible." *Christianity Today* 21 (October 8, 1976): 14-17.

The New International Version

"ACT: A Contemporary Translation." *The Bible in New York* 61 (October 1969): 3.

Baird, James O. "Unfortunate Renderings in the NIV." *Gospel Advocate* 121 (March 22, 1979): 181, 185.

Barker, Kenneth L. "An Insider Talks About the NIV." *Kindred Spirit* 2 (Fall 1978): 7-9.

Bechtel, Paul. "The New International Bible." *The Christian Bookseller* 29 (February 1974): 15, 36.

Benes, L. H. "Another New Translation." *Reformed Church* 31 (May 17, 1974): 8-9.

Blum, E. A. "The Gospel According to John—A Contemporary Translation." *Bibliotheca Sacra* 127 (October 1970): 356-57.

Blume, Frederic E. "The New International Version—First Impressions." *Wisconsin Lutheran Quarterly* 71 (April 1974): 126-33.

Board, Stephen, and Swanson, Clifford. "Will the New International Version Win the Translation Race? NIV Report: Interview with Edwin Palmer." *Eternity* 29 (October 1978): 28-30, 42-45.

Bratcher, Robert G. "The New International Version." *The Duke Divinity School Review* 44 (Spring 1979): 164-79.

————. Review of *The Holy Bible—New International Version*. *The Bible Translator* 30 (July 1979): 345-50.

Britnell, Eugene. "The New International Version." *Gospel Guardian* 27 (June 15, 1975): 2-3.

————. "More on the New International Version." *Gospel Guardian* 27 (July 15, 1975): 3.

Bruce, Frederick F. "A Contemporary Translation." *Christianity Today* 17 (September 28, 1973): 1303-7.

————. "The New International Version: Is It Living? Is It in Today's English? Is It Revised? Will It Become the New American Standard?" *Eternity* 30 (January 1979): 46-47.

Bynum, E. L. "Should We Trust the New International Version?" *The Baptist Challenge* (July 1974): 9, 11.

Carson, D. A. Review of *The Holy Bible, New International Version (NIV): The New Testament*. *Themelios* 1 (Autumn 1975): 24.

Craigie, Peter C. "The New International Version: A Review Article." *Journal of the Evangelical Theological Society* 21 (September 1978): 251-54.

DeBoer, Willis P. Review of *The New International Version of the New Testament*. *Calvin Theological Journal* 10 (April 1975): 66-78.

Demaray, Donald E. Review of *The New International Version of the New Testament*. *The Asbury Seminarian* 30 (July 1975): 45-56.

451

Dickson, Roger E. "New International Version." *The Gospel Light* 44 (September 1974): 136-37, 142.

Doebler, Paul. "New Bible Translation Computerized for Automatic Setting of Editions." *Publisher's Weekly* 204 (October 1, 1973): 56-62.

Doyle, B. R. Review of *The Holy Bible: New International Version: The New Testament. Australian Biblical Review* 23 (October 1975): 37-38.

Franzen, Jan. "The Right Bible at the Right Time." *Christian Life* 35 (October 1973): 71-72, 74.

Fuller, Reginald H. "New Testament: The New Internaional Version." *The Review of Books and Religion* 4 (April 4, 1975): 14.

Gaebelein, Frank A. "Evangelicals Draft New Version." *Eternity* 21 (April 1970): 46-49.

Goddard, Burton L. "The Crucial Issue in Bible Translation." *Christianity Today* 14 (July 3, 1970): 900-1.

Harris, R. Laird, and Hardwick, Stanley E. "Do Evangelicals Need a New Bible Translation?" *Christianity Today* 12 (September 27, 1968): 1242-47.

[Hayden, Edwin]. "Review of New International Version." *Christian Standard* 109 (March 17, 1974): 219.

Hobbs, A. G. "New International Version." *Christian Light* 1 (June 1980): 161, 176.

Holy Bible: New International Version. Grand Rapids: Zondervan Bible Publishers, n.d.

Johnson, Alan. "Not Perfect, Yet Commendable." *Moody Monthly* 74 (February 1974): 70-72.

Jones, David. "NIV Review." *Salt* 4 (December 1973): 5.

Kelley, Page H. Review of *The Book of Isaiah, 'The New International Version.' Review and Expositor* 75 (Winter 1978): 120-22.

LaSor, William Sanford. "What Kind of Version Is the New International?" *Christianity Today* 23 (October 20, 1978): 78-80.

Lewis, Jack P. "A Look at the New International Version." *The Apostolic Reflector* 1 (April 1974): 56-57.

Linton, Calvin D. "The NIV Style." *Christianity Today* 17 (September 28, 1973): 1317.

Lowe, G. Duncan. "A Close Look at the NIV." *The Presbyterian Guardian* 44 (March 1975): 52.

Ludlow, William L. "The New International Version." *Church Management* 50 (January 1974): 23-25.

Lyles, Don. "The NIV Translation." *Firm Foundation* 91 (January 22, 1974): 53.

_____. Review of *The New International Version: The New Testament. The Christian Bible Teacher* 18 (October 1974): 422.

McCord, Hugo, "Isaiah in the NIV." *Gospel Advocate* 118 (August 5, 1976): 502–3.

McKaig, C. Donald. "In the Modern Idiom." *Alliance Witness* 108 (December 5, 1973): 23.

MacRae, George W. "The Holy Bible: New International Version: The New Testament." *America* 131 (November 23, 1974): 330.

Marshall, Alfred, ed. *The New International Version. Interlinear Greek-English New Testament*. Grand Rapids: Zondervan Publishing House, 1976.

Merideth, J. Noel. "New International Version." *Gospel Advocate* 118 (February 5, 1976): 86-87.

Miller, Donald G. "Is the 'NIV' What Evangelicals Want?" *Eternity* 25 (March 1974): 46-47, 50, 53.

Miller, Edward L. "The *New International Version* on the Prologue of John." *Harvard Theological Review* 72 (July-October 1979): 307-11.

Moody, Dale. Review of *The New International Version: New Testament*. *Review and Expositor* 71 (Summer 1974): 397-98.

Murray, Iain. "Which Version? A Continuing Debate. ... " In *The New Testament Student and Bible Translation*, pp. 124-38. Edited by John H. Skilton. Phillipsburg, New Jersey: Presbyterian and Reformed Publishing Company, 1978.

Newman, Barclay. "Readability and the New International Version of the New Testament." *The Bible Translator* 31 (July 1980): 325-36.

"NIV New Testament Is Here." *The Bible World* (Anniversary Issue 1973): 1.

Paine, Stephen W. "Why We Need Another Translation." *United Evangelical Action* 26 (October 1967): 21-24.

Palmer, Edwin. "About That Review of the NIV ... Dear Duncan." *The Presbyterian Guardian* 44 (August/September 1975); photographically reproduced in *Christian News* (September 22, 1975): 11.

————. "A Contemporary Translation." *Banner* 105 (January 23, 1970): 5.

————. "New International Bible." *Banner* 107 (January 28, 1972): 15.

Partain, Terry. "Breakfast with the NIV Translators." *Vanguard* 5 (May 1979): 2-3.

Patterson, Pat. "A Careful New Translation." *Christian Standard* 109 (March 17, 1974): 227-29.

Peterson, William J. "Spelling the B-i-b-l-e via NIV." *Eternity* 29 (October 1978): 10-11.

Pressley, Johnny. "The Version for Our Time: An Interview with Dr. Lewis A. Foster." *Christian Standard* 113 (August 13, 1978): 740-42.

Richards, H. J. "The New Testament: New International Version." *The Tablet* 16 (February 1974): 156.

Rimbach, James A. Review of *The Book of Isaiah from the New International Version*. *Journal of Biblical Literature* 96 (March 1977): 122-23.

Ryken, Leland. "The Literary Merit of the New International Version." *Christianity Today* 23 (October 20, 1978): 76-77.

Scaer, David P. "The New International Version—Nothing New." *Concordia Theological Quarterly* 43 (June 1979): 242-43.

Scholer, David M. Review of *The Holy Bible: New International Version: The New Testament. Journal of Biblical Literature* 93 (December 1974): 591-94.

Skilton, John H. Review of *The Holy Bible: New International Version: The New Testament. Westminster Theological Journal* 37 (Winter 1975): 256-65.

Stagg, Frank. "The New International Version: New Testament." *Review and Expositor* 76 (Summer 1979): 377-85.

Staton, Knofel. "Good, But Not Final." *Christian Standard* 110 (March 2, 1975): 187-88; (March 9, 1975): 204; (March 16, 1975): 231-32.

Story of the New International Version. New York: New York International Bible Society, 1978.

Studer, Gerald C. Review of *The Holy Bible: New International Version: New Testament. The Bible Collector* 36 (October-December 1973): 8.

Surburg, Raymond F. Review of *The New International Version, Interlinear Greek-English New Testament. Concordia Theological Quarterly* 41 (July 1977): 94-95.

Synodical Committee On Bible Translation. "The New International Version." *The Banner* 111 (July 23, 1976): 12-13; (July 30, 1976): 14-15.

Tate, Marvin E. "The New International Version: The Old Testament." *Review and Expositor* 76 (Summer 1979): 363-75.

Taylor, Robert R., Jr. "Modern Versions and Increasing Errors." *Words of Truth* 9 (March 21, 1975): 1,4.

Thompson, Keith T. Review of *The New International Version: The New Testament. Gospel Herald* 40 (April 1974): 69.

Wallace, Foy E., Jr. *An Evaluation of the New International Version: A Supplement to "A Review of the New Versions."* Fort Worth, Texas: Foy E. Wallace, Jr., Publications, 1976.

Ward, Hilley. "Mich. Firm Publishes New Bible Translation." *Detroit Free Press*, 11 August 1973, p. 3-C.

Waterman, G. Henry. "A Contemporary Translation." *Alliance Witness* 108 (December 19, 1973): 8-10.

"Why Burton L. Goddard Calls NIV Unique." *Eternity* 25 (March 1974): 62.

Young, M. Norvel. "To Enjoy and to Trust." *20th Century Christian* 36 (March 1974): 3.

Youngblood, Carolyn Johnson. "The New International Version Translation Project: Its Conception and Implementation." *Journal of the Evangelical Theological Society* 21 (September 1978): 239-49.

The New King James Version

Bandstra, Andrew J. Review of *The Holy Bible, New King James Version. Calvin Theological Journal* 19 (November 1984):226-30.

Beegle, Dewey M. "What Does the Bible Say?" *Biblical Archaeology Review* 8 (November-December 1982):56-61.

Buls, Harold H. "The New King James Bible: New Testament." *Concordia Theological Monthly* 46 (1982):351-52.

Ehlert, Arnold D. Review of *Holy Bible: The New King James Version. The Bible Collector* 18 (July-September, 1982):7-8.

Elwell, Walter A. "The King James Even Better?" *Christianity Today* 23 (November 2, 1979):1477-83.

Evans, Owen E. "A Twentieth Century 'King James'." *The Expository Times* 91 (August 1980):343.

Farstad, Arthur L. *The New King James Version in the Great Tradition.* Nashville: Thomas Nelson Publishers, 1989.

Howard, David M., and Walter W. Wessel. "The Holy Bible, New King James Version." *Journal of the Evangelical Theological Society* 26 (September 1983):369-73.

Keylock, Leslie R. "Bible Translations: A Guide Through the Forest." *Christianity Today* 27 (April 22, 1983):10-15.

Kubo, Sakae, and Walter F. Specht. *So Many Versions?* (Grand Rapids: Zondervan, 1983):273-307.

Lewis, Jack P. "Why Stop Here?" *Christianity Today* 26 (October 8, 1982):108-10.

Moody, Dale A. Review of *The New King James Bible: New Testament. Review and Expositor* 77 (Winter 1980):110-13.

Pace, Martel. "A Brief Analysis of the New King James Version." *Words of Truth* 16 (March 1980):1.

Peacock, Heber F. Review of *The New King James Bible New Testament. The Bible Translator* 31 (July 1980):338-39.

Scanlin, Harold P. "The Majority Text Debate: Recent Developments." *The Bible Translator* 36 (January 1985):136-40.

Soderlund, Sven K. Review of *The New King James Bible: New Testament. Crux* 16 (June 1980):31-32.

Sparks, Ken, and Ken Powers II. "*Advantage* Interviews: Sam Moore." *Advantage: The Nashville Business Magazine* 1 (March 1979): 45-58.

Studer, Gerald C. "Dusting Off the KJV." *Eternity* 30 (November 1979):44-45.

Wessel, Walter W. "The New King James Bible New Testament." *Journal of the Evangelical Theological Society* 23 (December 1980):346-48.

Woudstra, Marten H. "The New King James Bible." *Banner* 120 (March 11, 1985):14-15.

The Revised English Bible

Bratcher, Robert G. "Translating for the Reader." *Theology Today* 47 (October 1990): 290-98.

Fontaine, Carole R. "The NRSV and the REB: A Feminist Critique." *Theology Today* 47 (October 1990):273-80.

Grether, Herbert G. "Translations and the Gender Gap." *Theology Today* 47 (October 1990):299-305.

Rodd, C. S. "Revised English Bible." *The Expository Times* 101 (October 1990): 12-16.

Robertson, J. W., and Graham N. Stanton. "The Revised English Bible: New Wine in Old Wineskins?" *Theology* 93 (January/February 1990):38-45.

Throckmorton, Burton H., Jr. "The NRSV and the REB: A New Testament Critique." *Theology Today* 47 (October 1990):281-89.

The New Revised Standard Version

Bratcher, Robert G. "Translating for the Reader." *Theology Today* 47 (October 1990): 290-98.

Bailey, J. Martin. "The New RSV: Another Translation Breakthrough." *Circuit Rider* 13, 5 (June 1989):8, 9.

____. "Why One More Bible?" *The Disciple* 16 (July 1989:17-19.

Bailey, Tom, Jr. "Updated Bible Awaits Baptism; It's Less Beholden to Maleness." *Memphis Commercial Appeal,* 3 March 1990, A7.

Grether, Herbert G. "Translations and the Gender Gap." *Theology Today* 47 (October 1990):299-305.

Fontaine, Carole R. "The NRSV and the REB: A Feminist Critique." *Theology Today* 47 (October 1990):273-80.

Harrelson, Walter. "Recent Discoveries and Bible Translation." *Religious Education* 85 (Spring 1990):186-200.

Metzger, Bruce M. "Handing Down the Bible Through the Ages: The Role of Scribe and Translator." *Reformed Review* 43 (Spring 1990):161-70.

____." The Processes and Struggles Involved in Making a New Translation of the Bible." *Religious Education* 85 (Spring 1990):174-84.

____. "Some Comments of the New RSV Bible." In *Scribes and Scripture: New Testament Essays in Honor of J. Harold Greenlee,* ed. David Alan Black. Winona Lake: Eisenbrauns, 1991.

Ostling, Richard N. "Farewill to Thee's and He's." *Time* (May 7, 1990):117

Stek, John H. "The New Revised Sandard Version" A Prelininary Assessment." *Reformed Review* 43 (Spring 1990):171-88.

Throckmorton, Burton H., Jr. "The NRSV and the REB: A New Testament Critique." *Theology Today* 47 (October 1990):281-89.

Van Eck, Author O. "The NRSV—Why Now?" *Religious Education* 85 (Spring 1990):163-72.

Winfield, Tom. "New RSV Bible Debuts." *Christion Retailing* 36, 4 (April 14, 1990):1, 12.

Wink, Walter. "The NRSV: The Best Translation, Haolfway There." *The Christion Century* 107 (September 19-26, 1990) :829-33.

Index of Biblical Names

457

Index of Non-Biblical Names

Index of Scripture References

467

473

8:6—145, 277, 341
8:8—363, 368

Isaiah

Book of—14, 52, 110, 134, 201, 219, 264, 294, 302, 306
1:2—319
1:3—336
1:7—353
1:8—207, 318
1:13—224
1:18—404
1:21—363
1:24—310, 323
1:26—297
1:29—110, 111
2:1—195
2:2—180, 258
2:6—187, 302
2:9—55, 99, 125, 336, 353
2:12—302
2:13—313
2:16—159, 302, 324, 340, 342, 356
3:1—134, 353
3:4—385
3:13—302
3:16ff.—167
3:18—102, 336
3:22—55
3:24—302
4:1—167, 168
4:2—180
5:1—395
5:2—319, 385
5:8—152, 371
5:10—315
5:11—152, 323
5:15—55, 99, 125, 336
5:16—212
5:17—302, 388
5:18—152
5:20–22—152
5:22—323
5:23—141
5:24—353
5:24–25—135
5:25—353
5:27—140
6:2—273, 296, 335, 394
6:4—392
6:5—152, 252, 398
6:8—134, 356

6:9–10—303
6:13—132, 144, 313, 353, 354
7:1—134, 400
7:1–2—307
7:2—289, 400
7:3—273, 317, 336, 341
7:4—271
7:4–5—307
7:7—310
7:8—307
7:8–9—204, 282
7:9—392
7:14—111, 112, 149, 158, 181, 197, 219, 234, 273, 284, 301, 309, 326, 332, 342, 343, 346, 362, 404
7:16—112
7:17—134, 353
7:18—282
7:19—367
7:20—134, 289, 353
7:23—103
8:1—206, 225, 273
8:2—381
8:3—273, 363, 401
8:4—112
8:6—302
8:18—112
9:1—274
9:3—81, 169, 303
9:6—59, 95, 234, 253, 287, 299, 332, 342, 343
9:11—302
9:12—283, 307, 400
9:15—124, 134, 345, 353
9:17—283, 381
9:19—352
9:20—302, 352
10:4—353
10:4–5—135
10:5—385
10:7—395
10:10—195
10:15—385
10:16—310, 352
10:18—352
10:20—54
10:23–24—275, 310
10:27—302
10:28—57
10:33—310
10:34—302
11:1—180, 297, 324, 332

11:3—354
11:5—327
11:6—303, 340
11:8—63, 141, 281, 337, 354
11:9—162
11:10—332
11:11—307, 312
11:15—276, 312
12:2—354
13:4—275
13:6—209, 310
13:8—389
13:15—99
13:19—307, 312
13:21—63, 225, 287, 337, 397
14—252
14:1—246
14:4—301, 302, 381
14:9—314
14:11—314
14:12—65, 252, 283, 287, 338
14:13—283
14:15—314
14:19—354, 388
14:23—102, 124
14:28—96
14:29—63, 337
14:30—110, 302, 381
15:1—96
15:2—302
15:6—286, 316, 388
15:7—297, 311
15:9—110, 301, 303, 381
16:7—354
16:10—302
17:2—302
17:3—307, 400
17:5—197, 210, 297, 388
17:7—297
17:8—307, 404
17:9—302
17:10—297
17:12—152
17:14—340
18:1—307
18:2—340
18:7—169, 340, 381
19:8—93
19:18—301, 303
19:23—246
19:25—246
20:1—96, 121, 140, 177, 339
20:3—112, 307